INTERNATIONAL
ECONOMICS

AND

INTERNATIONAL
ECONOMIC
POLICY

A READER   **FOURTH EDITION**

Contributors

Gaetano Antinolfi

Jagdish Bhagwati

Drusilla K. Brown

Abbigail J. Chiodo

Cletus C. Coughlin

Richard Cooper

Sam Cross

Dirk Dohse

David Dollar

Daniel C. Esty

Robert C. Feenstra

Martin Feldstein

Atish R. Ghosh

Edward Gresser

Mark Groombridge

Anne-Marie Gulde

Greg Hopper

Gary Clyde Hufbauer

Todd Keister

Peter B. Kenen

Philip King

Sharmila King

Aart Kraay

Christiane Krieger-Boden

Anne McGuirk

Ramon Moreno

Joanna Moss

Moisés Naím

Barbara Oegg

Jonathan D. Ostry

Michael T. Owyang

Patricia S. Pollard

William Poole

Steve Radelet

Dani Rodrik

Jeffrey Sachs

Jeffery J. Schott

Rüdiger Soltwedel

Miriam Wasserman

Kevin Watkins

Holger C. Wolf

The World Bank

Mark Wynne

INTERNATIONAL
ECONOMICS

AND

INTERNATIONAL
ECONOMIC
POLICY

A READER   FOURTH EDITION

PHILIP KING
SHARMILA KING

McGraw-Hill
Irwin

Boston   Burr Ridge, IL   Dubuque, IA   Madison, WI   New York
San Francisco   St. Louis   Bangkok   Bogotá   Caracas   Kuala Lumpur
Lisbon   London   Madrid   Mexico City   Milan   Montreal   New Delhi
Santiago   Seoul   Singapore   Sydney   Taipei   Toronto

McGraw-Hill
Irwin

INTERNATIONAL ECONOMICS AND INTERNATIONAL ECONOMIC POLICY: A READER

Published by McGraw-Hill/Irwin, a business unit of The McGraw-Hill Companies, Inc., 1221 Avenue of the Americas, New York, NY, 10020. Copyright © 2005, 2000, 1995, 1990 by The McGraw-Hill Companies, Inc. All rights reserved. No part of this publication may be reproduced or distributed in any form or by any means, or stored in a database or retrieval system, without the prior written consent of The McGraw-Hill Companies, Inc., including, but not limited to, in any network or other electronic storage or transmission, or broadcast for distance learning.

Some ancillaries, including electronic and print components, may not be available to customers outside the United States.

This book is printed on acid-free paper.

2 3 4 5 6 7 8 9 0 DOC/DOC 0 9 8 7 6 5 4

ISBN   0-07-287333-7

Publisher: *Gary Burke*
Executive sponsoring editor: *Lucille Sutton*
Editorial assistant: *Rebecca Hicks*
Marketing manager: *Martin D. Quinn*
Project manager: *Susanne Riedell*
Production supervisor: *Debra R. Sylvester*
Freelance design coordinator: *Kami Carter*
Senior digital content specialist: *Brian Nacik*
Cover designer: *Adam Hoff*
Interior design: *Sarah Jamelo*
Cover image: *© Getty Images*
Typeface: *9/11 Sabon*
Compositor: *GTS—York, PA Campus*
Printer: *R. R. Donnelley*

Library of Congress Control Number: 2004101381

www.mhhe.com

Table of Contents

Preface

When I first proposed a reader to McGraw-Hill in 1988, I had no idea that the book would be as successful as it has become, or that it would continue into the next millennium. At that time, international economics was still one of the lesser fields in economics, though its importance grew in the 1980s. Today the field is of increasing importance and the topic of globalization, financial crises, and related issues have lead to a great deal of activism on our campuses. This edition adds a co-author, my wife, Sharmila, who teaches international finance and macroeconomics. It is perhaps no coincidence that the finance section of this edition is more comprehensive than it ever has been before.

As in past editions, this reader is virtually all new, with over 80% of the articles from the last edition replaced. One deletion will be missed. Paul Krugman's classic "Is Free Trade Passé?" has been dropped from this edition since most of the content of the article, including the widely used Boeing-Airbus example, has now found its way into most trade texts. In addition, the article is widely available on the web through JSTOR. Krugman's article was the last remnant of the first edition.

In talking with a number of professors who use our text, we have made a few changes, some of which hark back to the first edition. We have chosen more short articles as well as articles which are slightly easier to read than in the second and third editions and we have selected a few more specific case studies, which a number of people asked for. As in past editions, the focus here is to provide students with a deeper appreciation of the policy debates and institutional structure surrounding international trade and finance than is possible in a standard textbook. We have tried to choose articles that would be topical for a number of years, though clearly new issues will surface (e.g., the devaluation of the dollar and revaluation of the Chinese yuan is likely to be a big issue in the next few years, but debate is only beginning to surface in 2003). Also, as in previous editions, we have tried to present a wide variety of views, but we did not want to be constrained by a Pro-Con approach which oversimplifies many debates.

If there is a theme to this edition, it is the unfinished business for the Doha round in trade and the increasingly complex exchange rate institutions now available to all countries. Our coverage of globalization has been expanded significantly as the topic has become even more important. We also have devoted more space to trade and labor issues as well as to immigration issues.

As in past editions, many people have been helpful in putting this book together. Sarah Jamelo was responsible for the desktop publishing of this book. Luther Scott did an excellent job proofreading. Lucille Sutton was once again my editor and assisted in many ways. Becca Hicks at McGraw-Hill was also helpful at numerous stages.

We both encourage feedback on this edition and plan on a fifth in a few years. Feel free to contact us at pgking@sfsu.edu or sking1@pacific.edu.

Issues in Trade and Protectionism

I

The vast majority of economists generally favor free trade and this section focuses on the costs of protectionism, which are sometimes hidden. The first article, "How Costly is Protectionism," carries over from the last edition and attempts to quantify the welfare losses (those triangles and rectangles every trade student studies) from restricting trade. Feenstra enumerates welfare loss estimates for particular industries, which generally range from several billion dollars to tens of billions. Unlike many texts, he examines not only the small domestic (triangle) loss, but the loss from quota rents and losses to foreign countries as well. While these losses are quite large in absolute terms they are extremely small in relationship to US or foreign GDP, generally much less than 1%. Feenstra points out that these losses should be taken as a lower bound, since they do not include a number of other losses such as the costs of lobbying for protectionism by domestic industries (i.e., Posner-Tullock losses).

In "Toughest on the Poor: America's Flawed Tariff System," Gresser points out that while the overall effective tariff in the US is quite small (roughly 1.6%), this estimate masks the fact that our tariffs for what he refers to as "low-tech consumer goods" such as handbags, cutlery and bicycles have "an average rate of 10.5%" while the rest of US imports average only 0.8% tariffs. Gresser argues that the political economy of tariffs explains the reason for this disparity. Domestic producers of inexpensive goods like apparel, cutlery, and plastic items have low margins and face tough competition from foreign producers with lower labor costs. As a result, these producers lobby heavily for protection, since without it they would likely go out of business. In contrast, producers of higher tech, higher value added goods or goods with well-established brand names face less competition and have a reduced incentive to lobby for protectionism. The unintended consequence of this policy is that poor countries, such as Bangladesh, face a much tougher tariff system than do countries such as France, which exports much higher value added goods. Indeed, Gresser points out that the US collects more tariff revenue form the $2 billion in trade from Bangladesh than it does from the $30 billion in trade from France. Given the US position that developing countries should grow through free trade, its policy of restricting exports from poor countries is hypocritical. Reforming these policies is one key issue in the Doha round of WTO negotiations and this theme will be developed later in this reader.

In the first two years of the Bush administration, its policy towards the steel industry came under careful scrutiny from economists who pointed out that the industry suffered from inefficiency and excess capacity; these critics argued that protectionism was precisely the wrong medicine for the US steel industry. In "Steel Policy: The Good, the Bad, and the Ugly," two economists from the Institute for

International Economics examine the steel industry and steel tariffs in detail. They point out that smaller so-called mini-mill companies, like NuCor, have thrived in the market by producing steel efficiently while older firms such as US Steel have continued to languish. One public policy area that does need to be addressed, however, is the issue of legacy costs—the costs that US Steel and other older companies must bear in pension and health care obligations as their workers retire. While this issue needs to be addressed, protecting the steel industry is not an efficient way to do so.

The article entitled "America's Bittersweet Sugar Policy" examines a key US industry which enjoys both protectionism and heavy US subsidies. The article points out that the US produces 88% of domestic sugar consumption, despite the fact that the US clearly lacks a comparative advantage in this industry. Further, giving up sugar would not lead to a huge loss in jobs but it would allow poor countries, which could produce sugar at much lower costs without any subsidy, to increase exports to the US

The final article, "Using Sanctions to Fight Terrorism," examines the impact of sanctions imposed over the past twenty years on countries supporting terrorism and other policies antithetical to the US. The article examines a number of specific case studies. It concludes that these policies have not been effective in reducing state-sponsored terrorism.

How Costly Is Protectionism?

ROBERT C. **FEENSTRA**

When economists attempt to measure the gains from trade and costs of protection for industrial countries, the resulting estimates often look small. As Krugman (1990, p. 104) recently wrote:

> Just how expensive is protectionism? The answer is a little embarrassing, because standard estimates of the cost of protection are actually very low. America is a case in point. While much US trade takes place with few obstacles, we have several major protectionist measures, restricting imports of autos, steel, and textiles in particular. The combined costs of these major restrictions to the US economy, however, are usually estimated at less than three-quarters of 1 percent of US national income. Most of this loss, furthermore, comes from the fact that the import restrictions, in effect, form foreign producers into cartels that charge higher prices to US consumers. So most of the US losses are matched by higher foreign profits. From the point of view of the world as a whole, the negative effects of US import restrictions on efficiency are therefore much smaller – around one-quarter of 1 percent of US GNP.

Are the efficiency costs of protection really so small? While the estimate cited by Krugman for the US costs of its own protectionism is a plausible lower bound, I will argue that the rents arising from import quotas should not be thought of as simple, nondistortionary transfers to trading partners. On the contrary, the evidence is that US quotas impose a loss on our trading partners, and that in some cases this loss is comparable in magnitude to the transfer of rents. This means that even when foreign firms earn quota rents through higher selling prices in the US, the foreign countries gain by less due to the efficiency losses, and in some cases do not gain at all. It follows that the world efficiency losses from US protection are as large as the US costs.

It is quite common to ignore the efficiency costs imposed on foreign countries through US protection. This approach does not reflect the reality that US protection, like that of other industrial countries, occurs at quite restrictive levels in a small number of industries, and also discriminates against particular supplying countries. The US is not a "small" country in the large world market, and its highly selective pattern of protection generates substantial deadweight losses both at home and abroad.

This paper begins from a US perspective, examining the costs to both the US and other countries from US protectionism. It then moves to a more global policy perspective. The emerging free trade areas in Europe, North America and Asia raise the prospect of gains from trade within each region, but also the possibility of global costs from protectionist actions across the regions. To quantify this, Krugman (1990) considers a world split onto

The Effect of an Import Quota on the U.S. Market
Figure 1

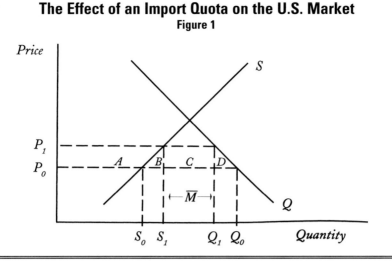

three trading regions, where under a hypothetical trade war each region restricts trade with the other regions by one-half. Using a simple triangle calculation, he suggests that the global efficiency losses from this dramatic reduction in trade may be only 2.5 percent of world GNP.

This calculation does not reflect the highly selective pattern of current protection, however, where trade barriers are maintained against specific goods rather than uniformly. Under this form of protection, reducing trade across regions can mean eliminating trade in the varieties of certain goods imported from outside the region, while other internal varieties are still available. This approach is particularly relevant to differentiated manufactured goods such as cars, consumer electronics, footwear, textiles and apparel, and so on. When the range of product varieties is reduced in this manner, the global losses can easily be several times larger than Krugman's estimate.

From a policy perspective, our discussion emphasizes the importance of limiting the use of selective and discriminatory trade protection whenever possible. Of course, the General Agreement on Tariffs and Trade aims at this goal, but GATT may be undercut by the movement towards regional free trade areas. The most important determinant of trade protection in the years ahead is likely to be a choice between the GATT approach of multilateral negotiations

to lower all trade barriers, and the more recent shift toward agreements which offer free trade within a region, but also risk discriminatory trade barriers against those outside the region.

Costs of U.S. Import Protection

Figure 1 illustrates the effect of an import quota on the US market. Let S be the US supply curve for a particular good, and let Q be the US demand curve. Suppose that imports are initially available at the free trade price of P_0, so that the quantity imported is $M_0 = Q_0 - S_0$. Then if the US limits the amount imported to M using a quota, the equilibrium price in the US would rise to P_1. Domestic producers would benefit, of course, and their rise in producer surplus is measured by the area A. In contrast, US consumers would suffer from the increase in the price, and their drop in consumer surplus is measured by the entire area A + B + C + D.

If the US were a "small" country, so that its purchases had no effect on the international price P_0, then the area C would be the "rents" associated with the quota M. In nearly all the cases of US import quotas we shall consider, the quotas are allocated to foreign exporters by their own governments. Under this system, it is the foreign firms that earn area C in Figure 1, so that the net US loss from the quota is areas B + C + D. In contrast, the

When U.S. Protectionism Affects World Prices
Figure 2

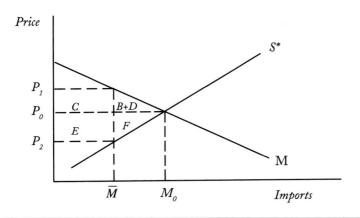

<hr>

global efficiency loss is only B + D, since the quota rents C are a redistribution from the United States to the foreign firms.

However, if protectionist actions by the US have some effect on the world prices, then the measurement of global losses is quite different. This is illustrated in Figure 2, where we incorporate the exporting countries. Let M be the US excess demand curve for imports of the good in question (which is the horizontal difference between domestic demand Q and supply S), and let S* be the excess supply curve from all foreign countries. Under free trade the equilibrium price and quantity of imports are again at P_0 and M_0. With the quota limit of M, the US price rises to P_1, as before. Foreign firms would have been willing to supply this amount at the reduced price P_2, so that $(P_1 - P_2)$ is the "quota premium" they earn on each unit sold. Then the quota rents they earn are measured by $(P_1 - P_2)M$ = area C + E in Figure 2.

However, not all of the quota rent is a welfare improvement abroad. The drop in foreign producer surplus due to the reduced US sales would be calculated as the area E + F, which represents the losses of those pushed out of the US market as a result of the quota.[1] These losses must be counted against the rents that the foreign firms earn. The net change in the welfare of the supplying countries is therefore $(C + E) - (E + F) = C - F$.

The area F represents the deadweight loss to the foreign countries. These countries are worse off due to the import restriction if this deadweight loss exceeds C, which will certainly occur if the quota M is set at a very restrictive level. The efficiency losses to the world as a whole are measured by the areas B + D + F.

In summary, the costs of US import protection in the United States can be measured as the sum of deadweight losses (B + D) and that part of the quota rents which represent the increase in US prices (area C). The measurement of the global losses due to US protectionism would need to subtract the quota rents from US losses, and add the efficiency losses created in the countries supplying to the US (area F). Table 1 offers estimates of these three categories: US deadweight loss (B + D), quota rents (C or C + E), and foreign deadweight losses (F).

U.S. Deadweight Loss

The first column of Table 1 displays estimates of the deadweight loss to the US economy from the major instances of import protection. Other cases of import protection include machine tools and meat, though the losses involved are much less than those in Table 1, and would not substantially affect the totals. The estimates shown are annual costs

Annual Cost of U.S. Import Protection (billion dollars, years around 1985)
Table 1

	U.S. Deadweight Loss (B+D)	Quota Rents (C or C+E)	Foreign Deadweight Loss (F)
Automobiles	0.2 - 1.2 [a,b]	2.2 - 7.9 [a,c]	0 - 3 [d]
Dairy*	1.4 [b]	0.25 [c]	0.02 [e]
Steel	0.1 - 0.3 [a,b]	0.7 - 2.0 [a,c]	0.1 [f]
Sugar	0.1 [b]	0.4 - 1.3 [c,g]	0.2 [g]
Textiles & Apparel	4.9 - 5.9 [a,b]	4.0 - 6.1 [a,c]	4 - 15.5 [h]
Average Tariffs	1.2- 3.4 [i]	0	n.a.
Total	7.9 - 12.3	7.3 - 17.3	4.3 - 18.8

*In dairy the quota rents are earned by U.S. importers, and so are not included in the total.

n.a.— not available

Source:

a. de Melo and Tarr (1990)

b. Hufbauer, Berliner and Elliot (1986)

c. Bergsten et al (1987,. Table 3.3)

d. Feenstra (1988)

e. Anderson (1985)

f. Boorstein (1987)

g. Leu, Schmitz and Knutson (1987)

h. Trela and Whalley (1988, 1990, 1991)

i. Rousslang and Tokarick (1991)

for years ranging between 1983 and 1987, and are centered around 1985. For each industry, imports are primarily restricted by quotas, though small tariff rates also apply.

The estimates in column one are obtained from two sources: partial equilibrium models estimating the deadweight loss triangles for US consumers and producers (Hufbauer, Berliner and Elliott, 1986); and computable general equilibrium models (de Melo and Tarr, 1990). Both of these methods rely on a wide range of literature for estimates of the demand elasticities, supply elasticities, and the value of the import quota. In some cases the value of the import quotas, or quota premium, is directly observed, while in other cases it is inferred from the reduction in trade and the supply and demand elasticities; some examples will be provided below. The range of estimates in Table 1 is intended to emphasize that the losses are subject to error from both the parameters used and the assumptions imposed.

A few details on each industry should be mentioned. The "voluntary" export restraint on Japanese auto imports was negotiated in 1981, and limited the US sales of each Japanese company. These quotas were increased in 1987, and are still in place today. However, they are not currently binding for most companies, partly because many Japanese firms have established plants in the United States, and sales from these plants are not limited by the agreement. The estimate of the deadweight loss in column one does not reflect this foreign investment, though we shall discuss later the effect of including it.

Dairy products subject to import restrictions include cheese, butter and powdered milk. These restrictions are used in conjunction with domestic support prices, and are intended to preserve income for US farmers, as is the case with sugar. The deadweight loss of $1.4 billion in dairy is primarily due to the restrictive quotas on cheese imports.

The US steel industry has lobbied for various forms of protection during the past two decades, and since 1985 a "voluntary" export restraint has been in place with nearly every trading partner. The complexity of this arrangement is surpassed only by the Multi-Fiber Arrangement, governing world trade in textiles and apparel. Initiated in 1974, this arrangement imposes extremely detailed quotas on every country and product imported to the United States. The distortionary cost of these restrictions to the US is estimated at $4-6 billion, the largest of the industry deadweight losses shown in Table 1.

While tariffs are low in many industries, there are important exceptions. For example, since 1980 there has been a tariff of 25 percent on compact trucks imported from Japan.[2] Estimates of the cost of the tariffs are not available for most industries, so the last row of column one includes a range of estimates for the deadweight loss due to the average tariff rate (3.7 percent) in the US economy.

Summing the estimates in column one, we obtain $8-12 billion. This estimate should be treated as a lower bound to the actual loss, however, since we have ignored many factors that could lead to additional costs for the US For example, the increase in producer surplus as a result of US protection (area A in Figure 1) is many times greater than the deadweight losses, and we might expect some waste of resources as firms attempt to secure this increase in surplus. This waste could occur through lobbying and other "rent-seeking" activities, or more subtly, as firms neglect to modernize their capital equipment to demonstrate the need for continued protection (Matsuyama, 1990).

In addition, it is quite likely that the quotas applied in industries such as autos and steel have allowed US firms to exercise greater market power in setting prices, with associated deadweight losses for US consumers.[3] A simulation model incorporating this idea has been applied to the European car market by Smith and Venables (1991), who find significant costs due to the change in market conduct. Dinopoulos and Kreinin (1988) found that European firms selling cars in the United States increased their prices simultaneously with the US quota on Japanese car imports. This effect is quite plausibly the result of a change in market conduct.

Other areas of US trade legislation can also create deadweight losses. For example, a number of US dumping investigations are settled out of court, thereby allowing the US and foreign firms to raise their prices jointly (Prusa, 1991; Staiger and Wolak, 1991). This outcome should have some added cost to the United States though its magnitude is not known. Finally, the recent literature on trade and growth suggests that protection can have adverse affects on a country's growth rate, leading to welfare losses. While these effects are no doubt important, reliable estimates for the US are not yet available.

Quota Rents

The second column of Table 1 shows estimates of the quota rents. For all the industries shown except dairy products, these rents are earned by foreign firms who are allocated the quotas by an agency of their government. For example, in autos the total number of cars intended for export from Japan to the US is determined by the Japanese government, and then the Ministry of International Trade and Industry allocates the quotas to Japanese firms. For textiles, the quotas for each country are determined under the Multi-Fiber Arrangement (MFA), which are then allocated to firms by their governments. In Hong Kong, the firms are permitted to trade these quotas on a secondary market (Hamilton, 1986). In contrast, for dairy products the quotas are allocated by the Department of Agriculture to US importers, who then earn the rents.

In some cases, the studies we draw on measure only the quota rents leading to US losses (that is, only area C in Figures 1 and 2). For example, Hufbauer, Berliner and Elliott (1986) assume that the US is a "small" country facing a horizontal foreign supply curve at the price P_0, though they recognize that this assumption may not be realistic.[4] For a number of industries, the quota premiums they use are inferred from the reduction in trade and domestic supply and demand elasticities under this "small" country assumption, so that only area C is measured. In contrast, de Melo and Tarr (1990) allow for upward sloping foreign supply curves in some industries, and appear to measure the area C + E by using quota premiums that reflect the full difference between the US price and foreign marginal cost. This is certainly the case for textiles, where their estimate of the quota premium is taken from the observed market price for the quotas (in Hong Kong), and arguably also the case for autos.[5] These authors obtain higher estimates of the quota rents in column two, which is explained partly by the quota premium that they use.[6]

Summing the quota rents in column two, we obtain a range of $7-17 billion. Adding the deadweight losses from the column of Table 1, we obtain an estimate of $15-30 billion as the cost to the US of its own protection, which can be compared to 1985 US GNP of $4 trillion. Thus, the costs we have identified do not exceed three-quarters of one percent of GNP. Despite the fact that the quota rents we have used may overstate the US costs in some cases, we would still treat three-quarters of one percent as a lower bound to the actual losses from protection in the US, for the reasons discussed above: rent-seeking, market power, effects on growth, and so on. To this list, we can add one other factor often resulting from the application of quotas, with potential costs to the US: the upgrading of imports.

Since US import quotas apply to the quantity sold by foreign firms, a common reaction of the firms is to increase the value of the goods which they send. There are two different arguments for why this phenomena might occur. Under the first (Falvey, 1979), a foreign firm selling multiple types of a product – say, steel – will face a limit on the total tonnage sold in the United States. To maximize profits, the firm will ensure that it earns the same quota premium on the marginal ton of each product sold, regardless of whether that ton is steel bars or specialty steel. This means that each ton will have the same dollar premium due to the quota, which corresponds to a lower percentage price increase on the highly-processed units. Under reasonable assumptions about the elasticity of demand for various products, relative sales will shift towards the more highly-processed units after the quota.

In principle, the US welfare costs of the quota could be measured by applying Figure 1 to each type of steel imported, and no special adjustment for the upgrading would be needed. In practice, however, the US costs are always measured at a more aggregate level (that is, for total steel imported from each country), and this approach misses entirely the shift in the composition of demand across imports types. Boorstein and Feenstra (1991) have argued that an additional welfare cost can be attributed to this upgrading, and that for US import restrictions on steel from 1969-74, the losses due to upgrading are comparable in magnitude to the conventional deadweight loss. Since changes in the composition of imports due to US quotas have been observed in a number of other industries, including footwear and textiles and apparel, we would expect losses in these cases as well.

A second argument for why upgrading might occur focuses on the quality choice for each particular product, rather than the composition across products. For example, US imports of autos from Japan experienced very dramatic increases in their size, horsepower, and luxury equipment as a result of the "voluntary" export restraint. Feenstra (1988) finds that these additional features added about $1,500 to the average value of Japanese cars over the period 1981-1985. Note that this quality upgrading has been omitted from the quota premium used in column two of Table 2, and also from the losses in column one. Winston and Associates (1987) find that the deadweight loss to the United States due to the import restriction was abpout $2 billion, where this amount includes the loss caused by both the price and quality changes. Unfortunately, an estimate of the loss due to quality upgrading alone is not reported.

When imports are upgraded through the addition of quality characteristics, it is difficult to make a sharp distinction between the efficiency costs to US consumers and to foreign firms: the upgrading can also be viewed as a form of rent-seeking activity by foreign firms. We shall return to a discussion of the auto case below, after considering the foreign deadweight losses in other industries.

Foreign Deadweight Losses

While foreigners earn the rents from nearly all US quotas, it does not necessarily follow that these firms prefer to have the restrictions in place. When the quota limits are very tight, the premium that foreign firms earn on sales to the US may not compensate for the sales they have lost, as was explained earlier in Figure 2.

The textile and apparel industry is one case where countries supplying to the United States do suffer from US import restrictions, despite collecting the quota rents. Trela and Whalley (1990) calculate that all developing countries lose $8 billion from the quotas and tariffs applied to textiles by the industrial countries. The reason for this very large loss is the restrictiveness of the MFA quota and tariffs. In earlier work, Trela and Whalley (1988) report that the losses to developing countries from just the US import restrictions are about one-half as large, or $4 billion.[7] This amount represents the area F - C in Figure 2, and therefore underestimates the deadweight loss F.

Moreover, the loss to the developing countries grows if the calculation includes the internal costs of allocating the quotas among suppliers. Trela and Whalley (1991) describe how the allocation schemes within the developing countries create losses by not granting export licenses to the most efficient producers, and by requiring that exporters with licenses send some of their product to non-quota countries.[8] Including these efficiency costs, the total losses to the developing countries of the Multi-Fiber Arrangement are estimated as $31 billion. The costs from US restrictions alone might be half this amount (as in Trela and Whalley, 1988), which is the basis for the estimate in the third column of Table 1.

The US quotas on sugar may also be so restrictive that foreign countries do not gain, despite receiving the quota rents. Leu, Schmitz, and Knutson (1987) calculate that the foreign deadweight loss is about $200 million. Again, the drop in foreign producer surplus roughly equals the quota rents, so that supplying countries are not gaining from existing quotas. As the authors note (p. 597): "Interestingly, while countries holding sugar quotas once favored a restrictive US sugar policy which generated high quota rents, in lobbying activities related to the 1985 farm bill, they joined with sugar users and consumers groups in support of lower sugar prices as a means of maintaining a market for sugar in the United States."

For both sugar and textiles and apparel, foreign countries do not benefit from US import quotas; in fact, the losses from greater inefficiency may even exceed the quota rents they receive. For other industries listed in Table 1, there is evidence of costs to foreigners through the upgrading of imports, or through the allocation of quotas which attempts to control this upgrading. Rodriguez (1979) argues that the upgrading of imports has an efficiency cost on foreign firms, for the following reasons.

Consider a firm that is choosing the level of some quality characteristic (such as horsepower) to include in its product. In a competitive market with free trade, it can be argued that the firm will choose the level of quality that can be produced with minimum average cost.[9] If the sales of the firm are restricted by an import quota, however, it will have an incentive to raise the quality level, since this will allow it to increase the sales value and quota rents earned on each unit. This means that the quality level is no longer chosen to minimize average costs, and so the firm has some technological inefficiency. This inefficiency is caused by the attempt to increase rents, and in this sense, is analogous to other forms of rent-seeking activity.

To quantify this efficiency cost for Japanese auto imports, we would need to have evidence on the cost function of Japanese producers, and the extent to which the quality upgrading raised the average costs of producing each characteristic. In the absence of this information, we simply use the total amount of upgrading–$1,500 per car (Feenstra, 1988) times 2 million imports–as an upper bound on the waste of resources associated with adding the extra equipment. Thus, the range $0-3 billion is included as a foreign efficiency cost in the third column. As discussed above, it is difficult to separate the foreign and US losses due to upgrading in this case. The important point is that some additional cost from column three should be added to the US deadweight loss in column one to obtain the global efficiency cost.

Costs of upgrading have also been estimated for the quotas on US cheese imports by Anderson (1985). He finds that the US deadweight loss due to the quota-induced shift in the composition of demand across products (the first reason for upgrading discussed above) is very small at $0.4 million. However, he also finds that the allocation of the quotas across countries promotes supplies from less efficient producers, which results in an excess cost of $22 million, as reported in Table 1. This amount should be treated as a foreign efficiency cost, and would need to be added to the US deadweight loss to obtain the global cost.

In the steel industry, Boorstein (1987) finds that the very detailed, country-by-country allocation of these quotas by the US has led to an increase in the share of supplies from less efficient producers. She argues that this allocation can be seen as an attempt to prevent the upgrading of steel imports which had occurred earlier, particularly in product lines competing closely with US production. Over the 1983-85 period an index of supplier prices rose by 2.3 percent due to this (mis)allocation of quotas. These price increases correspond to a foreign efficiency cost of $110 million, as shown in Table 1, which is also a global loss.[10]

Summing the foreign losses in column three we obtain $4-19 billion, which is comparable to the range of the total quota rents. The implication is that total global losses (columns 1 + 3) are no smaller than the total US losses (columns 1 + 2). Of course, the foreign losses are dominated by the estimates in textiles and apparel, and need to be treated as more tentative than other losses in Table 1. Nevertheless, from the evidence we have presented it is apparent that foreign losses due to US protection are pervasive, and cannot be ignored in any estimate of the global losses.

Foreign Investment

No discussion of the costs of protection would be complete without mentioning the increasing levels of investment by foreign firms within the US economy. The annual value of US businesses acquired or established by foreign investors reached $72.7 billion in 1988, while declining slightly to $64.4 billion in 1990. Japan has now replaced the United Kingdom as the largest source country of new direct investment, with 1990 outlays of $20.5 billion (Fahim-Nader, 1991). A rise in foreign investment is intertwined with the costs of protectionism for several reasons.

Most obviously, foreign investment can be motivated by anticipated or actual trade restrictions, as a means of "defusing" the protectionist sentiment. From a global point of view, of course, this sort of "quid pro quo" foreign investment (Bhagwati, 1986, 1988) would not reflect the most efficient choice of location, and so would have some deadweight loss for this reason. The evidence that investment with this motive has occurred in a number of US industries during the 1980s is anecdotal at present, but plausible.[11]

On the positive side, however, investment attracted into industries protected by quotas will increase supplies within the United States, reduce import demand, and thus lower the quota premium earned by firms exporting to the United States.[12] In the auto industry, for example, de Melo and Tarr (1991) reduce their estimated cost of protection by $0.5 billion due to Japanese investment up to 1984. In addition, foreign investment would have additional benefits if it raises local wages or employment, regardless of protection in the domestic industry.

Increasing foreign investment in the US also raises the issue of special regulations applying to these firms. Beyond rules for the reporting of acquisitions, it may seem obvious that foreign-owned firms would be subject to essentially the same regulations as their US counterparts. However, in one surprising and little known case, an import tariff was applied to a foreign-owned firm producing within the United States. This case illustrates the potential for manipulation of US trade laws to suit the goals of domestic firms and regulators.

The case involves the temporary tariff on heavyweight motorcycle imports to the United States that was in effect from 1983-87. This tariff was put in place to protect the only US producer—Harley Davidson—on the grounds that several Japanese producers had large US inventories, and this was judged to be a "threat of serious injury" to the domestic industry (US International Trade Commission, 1983). Since several countries other than Japan supplied heavyweight motorcycles to the United States, the tariff was applied to all of them, but only for imports in excess of a quota limit specified for each country. However, only for Japan was the quota set low enough to result in any tariff duties being collected.

Moreover, even production by Japanese firms within the United States came under the tariff. During this time, Honda and Kawasaki operated plants in the Midwest to produce motorcycles, both for the United States and abroad. Like much other foreign investment in the United States, these plants were in Foreign Trade Zones, which is a tax status allowing producers to import parts duty-free when the final goods are intended for export. If instead the final goods are sold in the United States, the firms are normally allowed to pay either the tariff on the imported parts, or the tariff on the final good, whichever is less. However, for the US sales of heavyweight motorcycles from the Honda and Kawasaki plants, the US Trade Representative directed that these firms pay the full tariff on the sales of every motorcycle (US International Trade Commission, 1987, Appendix E).

While this is only one case, it does illustrate the potential for discriminatory policy against foreign producers in the United States. Other examples of how US regulations can be manipulated around the issue of foreign investment include: the differential treatment of cars as either domestic or imported, to satisfy US fuel-economy standards and the import quota with Japan; and the recent squabble over whether cars imported from Canada

have 50 percent "North American content," and are therefore entitled to duty-free access.[13] The usual view of protection as applying to imports needs to be broadened to incorporate foreign investment. The magnitude and growth of foreign investment has led some to suggest that it will be a more important focus of trade policy than import competition in the years ahead.

Trading Regions

A founding principle of the General Agreement on Tariffs and Trade (GATT) was that all signatories should have "most-favored-nation" status, which means that they should be treated equally when a member country applies any trade restriction. However, exceptions to this principle are becoming more frequent. GATT includes exceptions for agriculture and textiles and apparel, and the quotas in these areas discriminate across supplying countries. The use of "voluntary" export restraints in autos and steel by the US and European countries also discriminates against particular suppliers, with Japan and other Asian exporters frequently being singled out. These export restraints are outside of the GATT framework, but even for actions which follow the GATT guidelines discrimination against particular importers is sometimes achieved, as illustrated by the discussion of US motorcycle imports.

Against the backdrop of these protectionist actions in specific industries, certain groups of countries have been moving toward freer trade within regional areas: Canada and the United States agreed to a free trade area in 1988 and negotiations are now underway to extend this agreement to Mexico, creating a North America Free Trade Area; barriers to trade within Europe are being dismantled by 1992; and Japan may be creating an economic sphere of influence among its Asian neighbors. While reduced trade barriers in each of the regional areas hold the prospect of gain for the member countries, significant costs may also result if the regional trading areas take steps to reduce or eliminate trade with outside countries.

Trade Shares and Costs of Trade War
(percent of income in each region)
Table 2

	Trade with Other Regions	Elasticity of Substitution		
		1.5	2	3
North and South America	7.2	7.2	3.6	1.8
Europe & Asia	6.4	6.4	3.2	1.8
Asia & Oceania	11.7	11.7	5.8	2.9
World Average	8.0	8.0	4.0	2.0

Source: Trade shares calculated from Summers and Hesto (1991), and General Agreement on Tariffs and Trade (1990).

There are two reasons why the formation of trade regions may lead to efficiency losses. First, as described some years ago by Viner (1950), if two countries form a free trade area but maintain tariffs against the rest of the world, their combined income can fall rather than rise. This is because the additional trade from a partner country can occur at higher costs than the goods were formerly produced at abroad: Viner called this "trade diversion," and it would also imply a loss for the outside country that has reduced demand. In contrast, if the free trade area leads to increased trade from a partner country when the goods were formerly produced at higher costs domestically, then "trade creation" has occurred, and it is likely that both countries gain.

A second reason that the formation of trading regions can be harmful is that each region will have greater influence over world prices than did the individual countries, and may be tempted to apply an external tariff to exploit this monopoly power in trade. Krugman (1991a, b) finds that the potential for protectionist action is greatest when the number of trading regions falls in an intermediate range, and for the simulations he presents, the number that minimizes world welfare is three regions! Despite this negative result, he argues that the costs from protectionist actions across the regions may not be that large.

As an example, Krugman (1990) considers a hypothetical trade war between three trading regions, one centered on the United States, one on Europe, and one on Japan. If each region applied a 100 percent tariff on imports from the other, and this restricted trade by one-half, he then suggests the following calculation of global deadweight losses (p. 105):

"With a 100% tariff, some goods would be produced domestically even though they could have been imported at half the price. For these goods, there is thus a waste of resources equal to the value of the original imports…Our three hypothetical trading blocs would, however, import only about 10 percent of the goods and services they use from abroad even under free trade. A trade war that cut international trade in half, and which caused an average cost of wasted resources for the displaced production of, say, 50 percent, would therefore cost the world economy only 2.5 percent of its income (50 percent x 5 percent = 2.5 percent)."[14]

However, this calculation contains an implicit assumption: that the tariff applies to all goods imported from the other trading regions. In view of the selective pattern of current protection against particular industries and supplying countries, it is more relevant to consider a case where trade in one-half of the products from other trading regions is eliminated, while the other half of trade is unaffected. Under this scenario, what would the costs of the trade war be?

To tackle this question, we can use a model of trade with monopolistic competition, as in Krugman (1980). We suppose that each good is produced in many different varieties, which can be either imported or purchased from domestic firms. Consumers do not treat these product varieties as identical, but the expenditure on each variety does fall as its price increases. A decrease in the number of varieties imported from outside the region, as could occur through a trade war, lowers the welfare of each consumer. Our approach is to compare the initial equilibrium with a situation where the import varieties for one-half of the traded goods are not available, but the prices and availability of all other goods are unchanged. [15]

In this framework, the size of the welfare loss will depend on what proportion of income is spent on the varieties that are eliminated, and on the degree of substitution between the imported and domestic varieties. One can derive a simple expression in which the change in the cost of living due to the elimination of import varieties is proportional to the share of income originally spent on those varieties, and inversely proportional to the elasticity of substitution minus one. [16] The elasticity of substitution measures the degree to which consumers are willing to substitute between varieties of traded goods as their prices change, and various estimates are available. For US and imported varieties of autos, Levinsohn (1988) finds elasticities from 1.3 to 2.3. Using data for disaggregated steel and textiles products, elasticities from 1.2 to 4.5 are obtained (Grossman, 1982; Feenstra, 1991), where each country importing to the US is treated as a distinct variety. [17]

Measuring the elasticity of substitution for every variety of every good and calculating the amount of variety eliminated by various trade barriers is obviously an enormous task. The simple calculations presented in this section use two shortcuts. First, I use a single elasticity of substitution for the product varieties of every import, although presenting a range of estimates. Second, I suppose that imports from various countries represent different product varieties, which ignores the possibility that some countries produce more similar product varieties than others.

Using only the member countries of GATT, the world was divided into three trading regions: North and South America; Europe and Africa; Asia and Oceania. [18] The share of regional income spent on trade with the other regions for 1988 was calculated using the system of Real National Accounts from Summers and Heston (1991) and the "direction of trade" statistics in GATT (1990). With the world divided in this way, more than half of international trade is internal to the three regions: total trade is 20 percent of world income, while trade with other regions comprises 8 percent of world income. The extent of trade between regions, as a share of each region's income, is shown in column one of Table 2.

The rest of Table 2 presents estimates based on eliminating one-half of the trade between regions, and considering values of 1.5, 2 and 3 for the elasticity of substitution. These calculations give a range 2 to 8 percent for the decline in world welfare caused by the reduction in product varieties available. [19] Thus, estimates at the lower end of this range are close to Krugman's (1990) 2.5 percent loss, but at the upper end of the range the costs are several times larger. Of course, the exact magnitude is quite sensitive to the elasticity of substitution that is used, with lower costs corresponding to the case where consumers gain little from additional product variety.

The estimates presented in Table 2 probably understate the costs of a trade war, however, since they include only the impact on consumers of reduced product variety. There would also be efficiency losses on the production side, and these losses could be substantial if there were economies of scale in production. Computable models incorporating economies of scale were developed to assess the gains from the Canada-US Free Trade Agreement, and the results from these can give us some idea of the order of magnitude of the production efficiency effects.

The initial work of Harris (1984) gave dramatic estimates of the effect on Canadian welfare; national income rose by 6.2 to 8.6 percent due to the expansion of outputs and resulting fall in average costs due to economies of scale: the so-called rationalization of production. These gains were obtained by avoiding the duplication of fixed costs across firms, as would occur in a protected market, but did not rely on the presence of product differentiation. Instead, the model used a "focal point" pricing rule, under which Canadian firms set their prices equal to the US price plus any tariff.

Later work has relied on the more familiar monopolistically competitive pricing behavior (or segmented markets across the countries), which lowers the estimates of the Canadian efficiency gains. The Canadian Department of Finance (1988) obtained 2.5 percent of Canadian real income as the calculated gains, while subsequent researchers have obtained estimates of 0.6 percent or less (Brown and Stern, 1989). The message from these studies is that the potential gains due to the expansion of firm outputs in larger markets are substantial, though the exact magnitude of this effect is quite sensitive to the assumptions of the model.

Bilateralism or Multilateralism?

This paper has emphasized the substantial costs imposed on foreign countries by US protectionism. These costs result from the highly selective nature of protection in particular industries and against particular exporting countries. Despite rules to the contrary in the General Agreement on Tariffs and Trade, the use of these discriminatory trade restrictions has been increasing in recent years. Perhaps as a result of the perceived failure of GATT to regulate these actions, the US and other countries have been moving towards the establishment of regional free trade areas, negotiated bilaterally with chosen countries. While holding the promise of significant gains to the countries included in each agreement, this path holds the risk of greater discrimination and losses for the countries excluded.

Economists differ strongly as to whether bilateral negotiations should, or will, be followed. For example, Krugman (1990, p. 131) foresees "the prospect of a fragmentation of the world into mutually protectionist trading blocs – a costly outcome though not a tragic one. Is there a middle way? Perhaps not. It seems likely that the bashers will more or less have their way, and that this decade will be one of growing economic nationalism." In contrast, Bhagwati (1991) argues for incorporating regional agreements more fully into GATT, which would provide some check on the adverse impact on other countries. On the prospects for the current round of multilateral negotiations, he concludes optimistically (p. 96): "The promise of the Uruguay Round is so considerable, and the downside from its failure would be so unfortunate, that it is hard to see an agreement not finally emerging."

A pragmatic path is one that continues to pursue multilateral agreements as a primary strategy, while adding bilateral agreements whenever needed. Richardson (1991) calls this approach "minilateralism," and describes how it has influenced US trade policy in the 1980s. The bilateral agreements should not be seen as an end in themselves, however, since they are not necessarily better from a global point of view than the current system. Indeed, Bergsten (1991) argues that "trade diversion" is actually a goal of recent proposals for trading areas rather than an unintended consequence, and that the costs from reduced world efficiency are substantial. The incentives for regional trading areas to restrict trade from outside countries would very likely lead other nations to pursue free trade areas themselves (as the Asian nations are now being led to consider). The challenge for economists is to ensure that the movement towards regional trading areas also creates the dynamics for a multilateral agreement

Robert C. Feenstra is Professor of Economics, University of California, Davis, California. The author thanks Jagdish Bhagwati, Severin Borenstein, Jim Levinsohn, Peter Lindert, Andy Rose, Robert Staiger, and the editors for very helpful comments, and Wen Hai for research assistance.

Notes

[1] Note that the foreign excess supply curve S^* is the difference between the supply curve of foreign firms and the demand curve of foreing consumers. Strictly speaking, then the area E + F represents the difference between the gain to foreign consumers as their prices are reduced from P_0 to P_2 and the loss to foreign producers.

[2] This unusually high tariff originally applied to truck imports from West Germany, and was a form of US retaliation against the tariff on poulty sales there, in what became known as the "Chicken War" of 1962-63.

[3] The impact of quotas on market conduct is examined in a monopoly model by Bhagwati (1965), and in oligopoly models by Harris (1985) and Krishna (1989). It is noteworthy that these models of imperfect competition lead to additional costs of protectionist actions, in contrast to the idea of "strategic trade policy" that tariffs or export subsidies might be in the national interest. At least for the industries listed in Table1, there is no evidence that US trade policies have provided them with any strategic advantage.

[4] As they state (p.33): "In real life, foreign supply curves may not be perfectly elastic... Since the measurement of gains or losses to foreign supplies is not our main focus, we will adhere to assumption of perfectly elastic foreign supply curves."

[5] Feenstra (1988) estimates the quota premium in autos by pooling data on car and truck from Japan, where the latter were subject to a 25 percent tariff. He finds that annual changes in the truck prices, net of the tariff, provide an acceptable estimate of the quota-free changes in car prices. In addition, the evidence from Feenstra (1989) is that Japanese firms absorbed about one-third of the tariff in trucks, meaning that the net of tariff price (P_2 in Figure 2) was lower than that of the free trade price (P_0).

[6] In addition, de Melo and Tarr (1990) include "rents" earned by foreign suppliers of autos who were not covered by the quota agreements, but who nevertheless increased their prices to the United States. Such price increases by "uncovered" suppliers can be explained by a rise in their costs as they expand production for sale to the US or as an exercise of their market power in the quota-restricted market. In either case, the price increase should be counted as a cost to the US economy.

[7] The figure reported in Trela and Whalley (1988) for the losses to developing countries from the US MFA restrictions is actually $6.9 billion, while the losses due to the MFA restrictions in all developed countries was $11.3 billion. The latter estimate was revised downward to $8 billion in subsequent work, but the effect of the US restrictions alone was not calculated again.

[8] This scheme creates an efficiency cost through encouraging firms to sell to a non-quota countires at less than marginal cost. See Bark and de Melo (1988), who also cite evidence that this type of scheme applies to Korean exports of footwear and steel to the United States.

[9] Of course, the competitive case may not be the most appropriate for autos, and the monopoly has been analyzed by Krishna (1987).

[10] The foreign supplier prices used by Boorstein (1987) actually include the quota rents, so for steel there is some double-counting between the losses in column three and the quota rents in column two.

[11] The following sort of press report is common and suggestive: "Fearful of trade friction, the Communications Industry Associations of Japan, a trade group, has cautioned its members to avoid explosive increases in exports and to build factories in the United States, according to Ozawa, its president. 'We have learned lessons in the experience with automobie exports to United States and semiconductor exports to the United States,' he said in an interview" (*The New York Times*, June 2, 1984).

[12] Note that this reasoning would not apply if the domestic industry was protected with a tariff, since foreign investment may then lower welfare of the host country; see Brecher and Diaz-Alejandro (1977).

[13] *The Wall Street Journal*, November 11, 1991, p.A1; and February 19,1992, p A18.

[14] In terms of Figure 2, suppose that the foreign supply curve S^* is horizontal. Then if the value of imports $P_0 M_0$ under free trade is 10 percent of world GNP, and the price P_1 is twice P_0 while M_1 is one-half of M_0, it follows that the global deadweight loss B+D equals 2.5 percent of world GDP.

[15] This second situation may not be an equilibrium, but can still be used to isolate the drop in welfare due to the elimination of the import varieties. In this second situation, there would be an incentive for domestic firms to expand the range of product varieties to sell in the protected regional market, but an offsetting incentive to contract the range of varieties due to lost export sales. We are ignoring both of these influences.

[16] At a more formal level, the calculation proceeds like this. A reduction in the number of varieties would raise the cost of living—or true price index—for consumers. Let P denote the

price index conrresponding to the preferences with a constant elasticity of substitution between varieties, denoted by ∂. Assume that $\partial > 1$. Suppose that the share of total expenditure going to the varieties which will no longer be available is S_m. Then the increase in the cost of living due to the reduction in product varieties is given by $P = (1 - S_m)^{-1/(\partial-1)}$ (Feenstra, 1991). Thus, the increase in the price index facing consumers is higher if the share of imports that are eliminated (S_m) is larger, or if the elasticity of substitution ∂ is smaller. Conversely, as the varieties become perfect substitues so that s is very large, then the price index P approaches one: the consumer is not affected by the elimination of imports when they are perfect substitutes with domestic varieties. A slightly simpler form of the equation is obtained by taking logarithms of both sides, and using an approximation which holds when s_m is small: ln $P=S_m/(S-1)$. This approximation is the one referred to in the text.

[17] Note that these estimates are higher than those compiled by Shiells, Stern and Deardorff (1986), which include many elasticities which are less than unity, and are therefore inconsistent with pricing under monopolistic competition. These low estimates may arise because many studies first aggregate import countries into groups, and then estimate the elasticity of substitution between the groups of countries. This procedure will lead to a downward bias if, in the language of Chamberlin, the elasticity of the DD curve rather than the dd curve is being estimated. I thank Avinash Dixit for this suggestion.

[18] Oceania includes Australia, New Zealand, and the Pacific Islands. Contrary to the way we divided up the regions, in preliminary proposals for an Asian free trade area, Australia and New Zealand have been excluded (Kreinin and Plummer, 1992).

[19] This calculation uses the formula in note 16, where the share of trade eliminated (s_m) equals one-half of the amounts in column one of Table 2.

References

Anderson, James E., "The Relative Inefficiency of Quotas," *American Economic Review*, March 1985, 75: 1, 178-90.

Bark, Taeho, and Jaime de Melo, "Export Quota Allocations, Export Earnings, and Market Diversification," *The World Bank Economic Review*, September 1988, 2:3, 341-48.

Bergsten, C. Fred, "Commentary: The Move Towards Free Trade Zones." In *Policy Implications of Trade and Currency Zones*, Federal Reserve Bank of Kansas City, 1991,43-57.

Bergsten, C. Fred, et al., eds., *Auction Quotas and United States Trade Policy*. Washington D.C.: Institute for International Economics, Policy Analyses in International Economics 19, September 1987.

Bhagwati, Jagdish, "On the Equivalence of Tariffs and Quotas." In Baldwin, R.E., et al., eds., *Trade, Growth and the Balance of Payments–Essays in Honor of Gottfried Haberler*. Chicago: Rand McNally, 1965, 52-67.

Bhagwati, Jagdish, "Investing Abroad." Esmee Fairbairn Lecture, University of Lancaster, 1986.

Bhagwati, Jagdish, *Protectionism*. Cambridge: MIT Press, 1988.

Bhagwati, Jagdish, *The World Trading at Risk*. Princeton: Princeton University Press, 1991.

Boorstein, Randi, "The Effect of Trade Restrictions on the Quality and Composition of Imported Products: An Empirical Analysis of the Steel Industry." Ph.D. dissertation. Columbia University, 1987.

Boorstein, Randi, and Robert C. Feenstra, "Quality Upgrading and Its Welfare Cost in US Steel Imports, 1969-74." In Helpman, Elhanan, and Assaf Razin, eds., *International Trade and Trade Policy*. Cambridge: The MIT Press, 1991, 167-86.

Brecher, Richard A., and Carlos F. Diaz-Alejandro, "Tariffs, Foreign Capital, and Immiserizing Growth," *Journal of International*, November 1977, 7:4, 317-22.

Brown, Drusilla K., and Robert M. Stern, "Computable General Equilibrium Estimates of the Gains from U.S.-Canadian Trade Liberalisation." In Greenaway, David, Thomas Hyclak, and Robert J. Thorton, eds., *Economic Aspects of Regional Trading Arrangements*. London: Harvester Wheatsheaf, 1989, 69-108.

de Melo, Jaime, and David Tarr, "Welfare Costs of U.S. Quotas in Textiles, Steel and Autos," *The Review of Economics and Statistics,* August 1990, 72:3, 489-97.

de Melo, Jaime, and David Tarr, "VERs under Imperfect Competition and Foreign Direct Investment: A Case Study of the U.S.-Japan Auto VER." Washington, D.C.: The World Bank, January 1991, mimeo.

Dinopoulos, Elias, and Mordechai E. Kreinin, "Effects of the U.S.-Japan Auto VER on European Prices and on U.S. Welfare," *The Review of Economics and Statistics,* August 1988, 70:3, 484-91.

Fahim-Nader, Mahnaz, "U.S. Business Enterprises Acquired or Established by Foreign Direct Investors in 1990," *Survey of Current Survey of Current Business,* U.S. Department of Commerce, May 1991, 30-39.

Falvey, Rodney E., "The Comparison of Trade within Import-Restricted Product Categories," *Journal of Political Economy,* Part I, October 1979, 87:5, 1105-14.

Feenstra, Robert C., "Quality Change Under Trade Restraints in Japanese Autos," *Quarterly Journal of Economics,* February 1988, 103:1, 131-46.

Feenstra, Robert C., "Symmetric Pass-through of Tariffs and Exchange Rates Under Imperfect Competition: An Empirical Test," *Journal of International Economics,* August 1989, 27: 25-46.

Feenstra, Robert C., "New Goods and Index Numbers: U.S. Import Prices," National Bureau of Economic Research Working Paper No. 3610, February 1991.

General Agreement on Tariffs and Trade, *International Trade International Trade 1989/90.* Geneva, 1990.

Government of Canada, Department of Finance, *The Canada-U.S. Free Trade Agreement: An Economic Assessment.* Ottawa, 1988.

Grossman, Gene M., "Import Competition from Developed and Developing Countries," *Review of Economics and Statistics,* May 1982, 64:2, 271-81.

Hamilton, Carl, "An Assessment of Voluntary Restraints on Hong Kong Exports to Europe and the U.S.," *Economica,* August 1986, 53:2 11, 339-50.

Harris, Richard G., "Why Voluntary Export Restrains are 'Voluntary'," *Canadian Journal of Economics,* November 1985, 18:4, 799-809.

Harris, Richard G., "Applied General Equilibrium Analysis of Small Open Economies with Scale Economies and Imperfect Competition," *American Economic Review,* December 1984, 74:5, 1016-32.

Hufbauer, Gary Clyde, Diane T. Berliner, and Kimberly Ann Elliott, *Trade Protection in the United States: 31 Case Studies.* Washington, D.C.: Institute for International Economics, 1986.

Kreinen, Mordechai E. and Michael G. Plummer, "Economic Effects of the North American Free-Trade Area on Australia and New Zealand," East-West Center, Institute for Economic Development and Policy, Honolulu, 1992.

Krishna, Kala, "Tariffs vs. Quotas with Endogenous Quality," *Journal of International Economics,* August 1987, 23:1/2, 97-112.

Krishna, Kala, "Trade Restrictions as Facilitating Practices," *Journal of International Economics,* May 1989, 26:3/4, 251-70.

Krugman, Paul, "Scale Economies, Product Differentiation, and the Pattern of Trade," *American Economic Review,* December 1980, 70:5, 950-59.

Krugman, Paul, *The Age of Diminished Expectations—U .S . Economic Policy in the 1990s.* Cambridge: The MIT Press, 1990.

Krugman, Paul, "Is Bilateralism Bad?" In Helpman, Elhanan and Assaf Razin, eds., *International Trade and Trade Policy.* Cambridge: MIT Press, 1991a, 9-23.

Krugman, Paul, "The Move Toward Free Trade Zones." *In Policy Implications of Trade and Currency Zones*, Federal Reserve Bank of Kansas City, 1991b, 43-57.

Leu, Gwo-Jiun M., Andrew Schmitz and Ronald D. Knutson, "Gains and Losses of Sugar Program Policy Options," *American Journal of Agricultural Economics*, August 1987, 69:3, 591-602.

Levinsohn, James A., "Empirics of Taxes on Differentiated Products: The Case of Tariffs in the U.S. Automobile Industry." In Baldwin, Robert E., ed., *Trade Policy Issues and Empirical Analysis*. Chicago: The University of Chicago Press, 1988, 11-40.

Matsuyama, Kiminori, " Perfect Equilibria in a Trade Liberalization Game," *American Economic Review*, June 1990, 80:3, 480-92.

Prussa, Thomas, "Why Are So Many Anti-dumping Petitions Withdrawn," State University of New York at Stony Brook, working paper, 1991, *Journal of International Economics*, forthcoming 1992.

Richardson, J. David, "U.S. Trade Policy in the 1980s: Turns and Roads not Taken," National Bureau of Economic Research Working Paper No. 3725, June 1991.

Rodriguez, Carlos A., "The Quality of Imports and the Differential Welfare Effects of Tariffs, Quotas, and Quality Controls as Protective Devices," *Canadian Journal of Economics*, August 1979, 12:3, 439-49.

Rousslang, Donald J., and Stephen P. Tokarick, "Estimating the Welfare Cost of U.S. Tariffs: The Role of the Work-Leisure Choice," Working Paper 91-O 1-G, Office of Economics, U.S. International Trade Commission, January 1991.

Shiells, Clinton R., Robert M. Stern, and Alan V. V. Deardorff, "Estimates of the Elasticies of Substitution between Imports and Home Goods for the United States," *Weltwirtschafliches* Archiv, 1986, 122:3, 497-519.

Smith, Alasdair, and Anthony J. Venables, "Counting the Cost of Voluntary Restrains in the European Car Market." In Helpman, Elhanan and Assaf Razin, eds., *International Trade and Trade Policy*. Cambridge: The MIT Press, 1991, 187-220.

Staiger, Robert W., and Frank A. Wolak, "The Determinants and Impacts of Antidumping Suit Petitions in the United States: An Industry Level Analysis," working paper, Stanford University, 1991.

Summers, Robert, and Alan Heston, "The Penn World Trade (Mark 5): An Expanded Set of International Comparisons, 1950-1988," *Quarterly Journal of Economics*, May 1991, 106:2, 327-68.

Trela, Irene, and John Whalley, "Do Developing Countries Lose from the MFA?" National Bureau of Economic Research Working Paper No. 2618, June 1988.

Trela, Irene, and John Whalley, "Global Effects of Developed Country Restrictions on Textiles and Apparel," *The Economic Journal*, December 1990, 100, 1190-1205.

Trela, Irene, and John Whalley, "Internal Quota Allocation Schemes and the Costs of the MFA," National Bureau of Economic Research Working Paper No. 3627, February 1991.

United States International Trade Commission, *Heavyweight Motorcycles, and Engines and Power Train Subassemblies Therefor*, USITC Publication 1342, Washington D.C., February 1983.

United States International Trade Commission, *Heavyweight Motorcycles*, USITC Publication 1988, Washington D.C., June 1987.

Viner, Jacob, *The Customs Union Issue*. New York: Carnegie Endowment for International Peace, 1950.

Winston, Clifford, and Associates, *Blind Intersection? Policy and the Automobile Industry*. Washington DC.: The Brookings Institution, 1987.

2

Toughest on the Poor
America's Flawed Tariff System

E D W A R D   **G R E S S E R**

The Bush administrations decision last March to impose tariffs of 8-30 percent on steel has been called everything from hypocrisy and stupidity to Machiavellian political brilliance. The reaction has been a remarkable demonstration of the strength of free-trade opinion in the United States -- but it has also been a bit puzzling.

The steel tariffs, even if one believes they are bad policy, are just temporary aberrations from the norm; they will be lifted in a couple of years. But for dozens of other products -- sneakers, spoons, bicycles, underwear, suitcases, drinking glasses, T-shirts, plates, and more -- tariffs of 8-30 percent are neither aberrant nor temporary. In fact, they are normal and permanent parts of US trade policy. Barring a deliberate change in policy, they will never be lifted -- and no one seems to care.

The reason is not simply that people care more about steel than about underwear. Rather, it is that the tariff system has become an obscure, little-studied topic. Those who debate trade and globalization view tariff policy as boring and out of date. Career trade negotiators who set tariff rates have little contact with the customs officers who collect the money. Journalists cover political debate and international disputes rather than the functioning of permanent policy. And government officials, aware that tariffs are generally low and raise little money compared to domestic taxes, rarely think about the system as a whole.

But if these groups were to look more closely, they would find a remarkable situation. Tariff policy, without any deliberate intent, has evolved into something astonishingly tough on the poor. Young single mothers buying cheap clothes and shoes now pay tariff rates five to ten times higher than middle-class or rich families pay in elite stores. Very poor countries such as Cambodia or Bangladesh face tariffs 15 times those applied to wealthy nations and oil exporters. Despite this dismal situation, however, fixing the system would be easier than many imagine.

Malign Neglect

The problem arises more from neglect than from malice. No US administration since the 1970s, or perhaps even since John Kennedy's, has had a specific vision for tariff policy. Regardless of party, administrations have instead seen tariffs as a series of discrete issues that are useful in building domestic support for, and co-opting potential opposition to, larger trade agreements.

In past trade negotiations, some domestic interests -- manufacturers of semiconductors, chemicals, capital goods, and so on -- sought export opportunities by advocating the elimination of overseas trade barriers and were willing to give up tariffs at home in exchange. Other industries -- shoes, textiles, cutlery, glassware -- feared foreign competition and fought to keep tariffs high. In the three big multilateral trade agreements since

Most Tariff Revenue Comes From Consumer Goods
Table 1

Product	Value of 2001 Imports[1]	Tariff Revenue[2]	Average Tariff
All goods	$1,132.6 100%	$18.6 100%	1.6%
Shoes & clothes	$76.3 6.7%	$8.7 46.7%	11.4%
Other high-tariff consumer goods	$21.6 1.9%	$1.6 8.4%	8.4%
Everything else	$1,038.7 91.4%	$8.4 44.9%	0.8%

Source: US International Trade Commission "dataweb," at dataweb.usitc.gov.
[1] In billions of dollars and as a percentage of the value of all imports.
[2] In billions of dollars and as a percentage of all tariff revenue.

1970 that have focused on manufactured goods -- the Tokyo and Uruguay Rounds of the General Agreement on Tariffs and Trade, and the Information Technology Agreement of the World Trade Organization (WTO) -- US administrations tried to satisfy both groups, and largely succeeded.

These accords, combined with free trade agreements with Canada, Mexico, Israel, and Jordan, and four duty-free programs for developing countries, have brought overall US tariffs to a historic low. In July, Robert Zoellick, the US trade representative, told the Bundestag Forum that the average trade-weighted tariff for the United States is now under 2 percent.

In making this point, Zoellick was not just accurate but modest. Last year, the US Customs Service collected $18.6 billion in tariff revenue on $1.1 trillion in goods imports—meaning the effective US tariff rate is 1.6 percent. But the low overall average masks something more troubling.

Tariffs on industrial imports are not just low but extremely low. For expensive consumer goods such as cars, appliances, and televisions, rates are also generally low and are further reduced in practice by trade agree-

ments with Mexico and Canada. But for light consumer goods, the story is different. Tariffs on these products (with a few exceptions, such as toys and furniture) remain at levels other industries last saw in the 1960s and 1970s: for instance, 8.7 percent for cutlery and tableware, 13.8 percent for suitcases and handbags, 10 percent for bicycles, and 11.4 percent for shoes and clothes, the largest category of consumer imports for the United States.

In effect, the United States now has two tariff systems. One, for low-tech consumer goods, has an average rate of 10.5 percent. The other, for everything else, has an average rate of 0.8 percent. As a result, most tariff revenue now comes from a very small number of goods. Shoes and clothes in particular, as Table 1 shows, make up less than 7 percent of imports but bring in nearly half of all tariff revenues.

Finally, tariffs also vary from one consumer good to the next. Most notably, they are much higher on cheap goods than on luxuries. This disparity occurs because elite firms, selling image and brand name, find small price advantages relatively unimportant. They have not pressed the government to keep tariffs high, and tariffs on luxury goods such as silk

Tariffs Are High on Cheap Goods, Low on Luxuries
Table 2

Product	2002 Rate
Women 's underwear	
Man-made fiber	16.2%
Cotton	11.3%
Silk	2.4%
Men 's knitted shirts	
Synthetic fiber	32.5%
Cotton	20.0%
Silk	1.9%
Drinking glasses	
30¢ or less	30.4%
$5 or more	5.0%
Leaded glass	3.0%
Forks	
Stainless steel, under 25¢	10.5 –18.5%
Gold or silver plated	0%
Handbags	
Plastic-sided	16.8%
Leather, under $20	10.0%
Reptile leather	5.3%

Source: ITC dataweb, harmonized tax schedule,at dataweb.usitc.gov/scripts/tariff/toc.html.
Note: For a few types of clothes, the United States has not yet completed Uruguay Round tariff cuts. In most cases this will widen the disparities; women's silk underwear, for example, will have a final tariff rate of 1.1%, but for man-made fiber the final rate will be 16%.

lingerie, silver-handled cutlery, leaded-glass beer mugs, and snakeskin handbags are now very low. But makers of nylon lingerie, stainless steel cutlery, cheap water glasses, and plastic purses benefit by adding a few percentage points to their competitors prices. So on the cheapest goods, as Table 2 shows, tariffs are even higher than overall averages for consumer goods suggest.

If The Shoe Fits

So the structure of the tariff system is simple: tariffs are low overall, high on consumer goods, and especially high on cheap goods. How does it work in real life? A convenient place to begin is with the justification for the tariff system: preservation of jobs in light manufacturing.

Here, the system seems ineffective. Employment in high-tariff industries now accounts for only about three percent of US manufacturing jobs. It has fallen by half since 1990, and the plunge is fastest in some of the most protected industries. In 1992, for example, 20,000 Americans worked making womens shoes. No shoe tariffs have been cut since the 1970s, but since 1992 employment in womens shoes has fallen by 90 percent, to only 2,000 workers. Likewise, the number of workers making childrens clothes is down from 44,000 to fewer than 7,000. For the manufacture of goods such as watches, bicycles, and drinking glasses, job totals are even lower.

In such fields, tariffs are evidently not preserving jobs. Instead they are operating more like large wholesale taxes. And although their effects are minor for domestic producers, they are considerable for people who buy and make such goods: poor families in the United States, and workers and businesses in poor countries.

One type of shoe provides an instructive example. Cheap sneakers valued at $3 or less per pair carry tariffs of 48 percent (a rate, incidentally, far above that of any product on the administrations steel list). Virtually none of these shoes is made in the United States. Last year, the United States imported 16 million pairs of these sneakers, at a total cost of $35 million. Thus the average price at the border was $2.20 per pair. The Treasury Department then collected $17 million in tariffs, adding another $1.06 per pair to the buyer's cost. The extra dollar and change is then magnified by retail markups of around 40 percent and state sales taxes of about 5 percent to raise the final consumer price of the sneakers from about $3.25 (without tariffs) to $4.80 per pair (with tariffs).

Such tariff-based overpricing exists, though at less dramatic levels, in store aisles stocking baby clothes, T-shirts, silverware, and other typical family products. Because it is most pronounced on the cheapest shoes and clothes, its effect falls most heavily on single-parent families.

Incomes for these families are very low: at an average of about $25,100 per year, they are about 40 percent of a typical two-parent family's income. But single-parent families face shoe and clothing bills nearly as high as those of wealthier families. In total, the average single-parent family spends nearly $2,000 a year on clothes and shoes. Depending on the mix of purchases, as much as $400 of this total may simply be price inflation due to tariffs. Budgets for other tariffed goods, though smaller, are still a larger expense relative to income for poor families than for rich families. And so single-parent families lose much more of their income to tariffs than do other families.

Punishing the Poor

Beyond US shores, the tariff system operates in a similar fashion. It hits countries that specialize in the cheapest goods, in particular very poor countries in Asia, much harder than others.

Average tariffs on European exports to the United States -- primarily cars, power equipment, computers, and chemicals -- now barely exceed one percent. Developing countries such as Malaysia, which specialize in information-technology products, get rates just as low. So do natural-resource exporters such as Saudi Arabia and Nigeria. Middle-income exporters that ship a broader variety of goods, such as China, Thailand, and Brazil, face rates typically between two percent and four percent -- above average but still not exorbitant. The least-developed Asian countries, however, take it on the chin.

For Bangladesh, Cambodia, Nepal, Mongolia, and a few others, clothes make up 90 percent of all exports to the United States. So they face average tariff rates of 14.6 percent -- nearly 10 times the world average, and 15 times the rate for wealthy Western countries. Translated into real dollars, the disparities can be remarkable.

As Table 3 notes, the US now collects more tariff revenue from Bangladeshi goods than from French goods, even though Bangladesh exports $2 billion in goods a year to the United States and France $30 billion.

Cambodia's exports to the United States total $900 million and Singapore's usually reach $15-$20 billion -- but the US government collects nearly twice as much revenue from Cambodian goods as from Singaporean goods. And struggling Nepal faces tariff rates on its skirts, scarves, and suits fully 60 times higher than those applied to Ireland's chemicals, pacemakers, and silicon chips.

In fairness, such disparities are not universal, and some attempts to ease tariff burdens have been successful. The African Growth and Opportunity Act, set up under the Clinton administration, is the best example. Since it was enacted two years ago, African clothing exports to the United States have nearly doubled, but tariff collection on African goods has dropped by more than half. The results of the Caribbean Basin Initiative are less dramatic, but Haiti, Honduras, and several other beneficiaries also face fairly low rates.

The US system is not uniquely bad. Europes tariffs on clothes and shoes -- not to mention food -- are also high, and European Union tariff collection is far less transparent and accessible than Americas. Some developing countries would also do well to look in the mirror.

Recent World Bank studies, in fact, indicate that the poorest countries would gain most from tariff reform in large developing economies. India is a case in point: as dispiriting as US treatment of Nepali goods may be, Nepal still exports more each year to the United States than to its giant southern neighbor, where clothing imports are often simply banned and tariffs on other goods regularly reach 40 percent.

Do the Right Thing

The fact that others have bad policies is no excuse for Americans to adopt them too. US trade policies should be defended on their own merits. And a system that hits the poor harder than anyone else is quite hard to defend.

Tariffs, especially on clothes, have tenacious advocates. But in fact, this system that protects so few and hurts so many can be fixed without much dislocation. The International

The Poor Pay More
Table 3

Country	Per Capita GDP	2001 Exports to US in billions	Tariffs Paid in millions	Rate
Nepal	$240	$0.20	$25	12.3%
Ireland	$22,660	$18.60	$29	0.2%
Bangladesh	$370	$2.35	$331	14.1%
France	$24,170	$30.02	$330	1.1%
Cambodia	$260	$0.96	$152	15.8%
Singapore	$30,170	$14.90	$96	0.6%

Sources: World Bank, World Development Indicators 2002; ITC dataweb.

Trade Commissions July 2002 study finds that employment in high-tariff industries is already so low that eliminating all US trade barriers would mean a net gain of about 35,000 jobs rather than a loss. And so, if the problems with the system were better understood, the solutions might be fairly simple.

One option, of course, would be simply to scrap tariffs on consumer goods for domestic policy reasons. Considered as a form of taxation, they are offensive to the principles of both parties -- Republicans always being enthusiastic for tax cuts, and Democrats being opposed to regressive taxation. A $10 billion annual tax cut would be substantial, but it seems moderate when compared to recent tax legislation.

Alternatively, with US trade credibility needing a boost after the steel and farm bill decisions (and since the tariff policies of US trading partners also need change), the administration could suggest a worldwide goal of zero tariffs on clothes, shoes, and other consumer goods. This would recapture whatever moral high ground on trade was lost in the past year and also create a powerful incentive for developing nations to seek a successful conclusion to the WTO negotiations begun at Doha last year.

But one point seems quite clear. A system that makes maids pay higher rates than corporate vice presidents, and hits Cambodians 15 times harder than Germans, is an ethical scandal and a problem far bigger than any temporary steel policy. The facts are plain, and reform is only a question of political will.

Edward Gresser is Director of the Project on Trade and Global Markets at the Progressive Policy Institute.

Steel Policy:
The Good, the Bad, and the Ugly

3

G ARY C LYDE **H UFBAUER**
AND B EN **G OODRICH**

Background

While the US steel industry has been in distress for decades, the "steel crisis" of 1999-2001 was particularly acute. More than 30 steel producing and steel processing firms fell into bankruptcy between 1997 and 2001, and most of the failures occurred after President Bush took office.[1] During his presidential campaign, Bush promised steelworkers that he would not neglect them. As the crisis worsened, the steel industry and the United Steel Workers of America (USWA) pressed the Bush administration to make good on its campaign promise.

In response, President Bush launched a three-pronged steel strategy in June 2001. The first prong sought to address global excess steel capacity. The second prong sought an end to subsidies and other market-distorting practices. These two prongs have been pursued under the auspices of the Organization for Economic Cooperation and Development (OECD).

The third prong was a Section 201 investigation to determine whether "safeguards" should be imposed against 33 types of steel imports. In October 2001, the US International Trade Commission (ITC) made affirmative or evenly divided determinations that 16 of the 33 types of steel "are being imported into the United States in such increased quantities that they were a substantial cause of serious injury or threat of serious injury" to US steel producers.[2] In contrast to the requirements for an antidumping or a

countervailing duty case, a safeguard investigation requires no demonstration that steel imports are sold unfairly. In December 2001, the commissioners gave their remedy recommendations to President Bush—remedies that took the form of tariffs, quotas, or tariff-rate quotas (TRQS) against the injurious imports.

In March 2002, President Bush chose to impose tariffs against 14 of the 16 products found by the ITC to be injuring the domestic steel industry.[3] President Bush imposed 30 percent tariffs on flat steel products, hot-rolled bars, and cold-finished bars, and tariffs up to 15 percent on other steel products. On steel slabs (unfinished steel that is processed in US integrated mills to make flat steel products), President Bush adopted a TRQ: all imports in excess of 6 million short tons are subject to a tariff of 30 percent, but all slab imports up to 6 million short tons face no additional duty.[4] The safeguard remedies are scheduled to be phased down each year and abolished completely after March 2005.

Canada, Mexico, and other countries that have preferential trade agreements with the United States are excluded from the Section 201 remedies, as are developing countries whose steel imports fall below a de minimis threshold.[5] In 2000, the United States imported 32.1 million short tons of steel, of which only 29 percent (9.3 million short tons) were subject to the safeguard tariffs levied by President Bush in March 2002. The remaining 71 percent were covered by ITC findings of no injury or by initial country exclusions.[6] This policy brief reviews the good, the bad, and the ugly dimensions of US steel policy in 2001 and 2002. On balance, the policy has not been nearly as helpful to the US steel industry as partisans hoped. At the same time, it is not nearly as bad as some steel consumers and foreign exporters may have feared. Nevertheless, the policy should be dramatically changed in the coming months to avoid potentially ugly consequences. In this policy brief, we offer recommendations geared both toward averting the ugly consequences and toward achieving a lasting solution to the problems that beset the steel industry. On balance, US steel policy in 2001 and 2002 has not been nearly as helpful to the US steel industry as partisans hoped.

The Good—Global Trade Liberalization Is Progressing

President Bush's decision to protect the US steel industry with Section 201 tariffs had no economic justification. Before relief was granted, we calculated that safeguard tariffs would cost over $400,000 annually per job saved in the steel industry.[7] Moreover, they would result in net job losses in the economy due to downstream layoffs, which is why most of President Bush's economic advisers expressed their opposition.

Few could argue that the US steel industry was not distressed, but objective observers certainly questioned whether trade was the problem and whether trade protection was the right solution. The administration's steel tariffs were driven not by an economic match between problems and solutions but by two political motivations. The first was the noble goal of passing Trade Promotion Authority (TPA) in Congress; the second was the less noble goal of buying the steel industry's support in congressional and presidential elections.

President Bush's steel decision had international ramifications. Foreign steel exporters and their governments threatened retaliation, which could have soured the atmosphere for global and regional trade negotiations (the Doha Round and the Free Trade Area of the Americas). The good news is that the steel tariffs have furthered the cause of global trade

liberalization by helping Bush obtain TPA. So far, the negative international consequences of the steel decision have led neither to trade retaliation nor to a breakdown of trade negotiations.

Trade Promotion Authority

For several years, trade negotiating authority was stalled in the House of Representatives. In November 1997, President Clinton and his congressional allies, fearing a loss, pulled their trade bill from the House floor. In September 1998, the House voted against "fast-track" by a margin of 243 to 180. In December 2001, the House passed its version of TPA (the new name for "fast track") by a single vote; in July 2002, the House approved the TPA conference report by just three votes.

Several factors contributed to the successful passage of TPA in 2002, and President Bush's steel policy was arguably among them. Of the 31 members of the House who voted against TPA in 1998 and for TPA in 2001 and 2002, 10 were members of the House Steel Caucus. No one has acknowledged an explicit deal between the Bush administration and Caucus members, but at a minimum the Section 201 steel investigation gave these 10 representatives "political cover" to vote for TPA. All 10 won their November 2002 elections with at least 60 percent of the vote, so with the benefit of hindsight, they probably could have afforded to vote for TPA regardless of the administration's steel decisions.[8] But the administration's actions certainly afforded these 10 Representatives comfort in the November elections.

The United States has historically resorted to protectionist measures in order to launch or implement major trade negotiations.[9] The "one step back, two steps forward" strategy is tolerable if the protectionist step backward is the minimum necessary to obtain the larger prize. In this case the larger prize is TPA and the resulting opportunity to complete regional and global trade deals (the FTAA and the Doha Round), which promise to improve US and global welfare by hundreds of billions of dollars annually. For example, one study estimates that a 33 per-cent reduction in world trade barriers could increase US welfare by $177 billion annually and world welfare by $613 billion annually.[10]

The TPA package included renewal and expansion of Trade Adjustment Assistance (TAA). The new TAA provides a 65 percent tax credit for health insurance as well as income maintenance and job training for displaced workers. The new TAA package also includes a wage insurance program for older workers, a concept advocated in previous Institute policy briefs.[11] The 65 percent tax credit for health insurance is extended to non-Medicare eligible retired workers over the age of 55 whose pensions are administered by the Pension Benefit Guarantee Corporation owing to the bankruptcy of their former employers. This provision to help retirees was motivated by the plight of retired steel workers, and it certainly counts among the "good" outcomes of US steel policy. Expanded TAA benefits partly assuage public fears about growing imports and may increase congressional sympathy for future trade liberalization. President Bush's decision to protect the US steel industry with Section 201 tariffs had no economic justification.

Product Exclusions

As soon as President Bush announced the steel tariffs, domestic steel consumers and foreign steel exporters complained that they were being forced to pay for Bush's gift to the steel industry. Leading the charge, the European Union and Japan publicly threatened to retaliate against hallmark US exports from politically sensitive congressional districts—such as textiles from Southeast states and citrus products from Florida—in advance of the November 2002 mid-term elections.

To deflect the foreign backlash, the administration immediately announced that it would exempt certain items from the steel tariffs if domestic firms were not able to produce adequate quantities of highly similar steel goods. In practice, the product exclusion process devolved into a balancing act: the Bush administration tried to grant just enough product exclusions to prevent foreign retalia-

tion, but not so many as to exhaust the goodwill previously garnered with the steel industry, the USWA, and congressional members of the Steel Caucus.

Some product exclusions were granted immediately, and others came in batches throughout the summer of 2002. Altogether, the 3.5 million short tons of exclusions granted to date cover 727 steel products and constitute 25 percent of the tonnage covered by Bush's Section 201 remedy. However, it should be noted that half the product exclusions (measured by volume) cover unfinished steel that is imported by integrated steel firms for further processing.[12] While product exclusions for unfinished steel clearly are not detrimental to integrated firms, the USWA resents the fact that its employers are essentially outsourcing the initial stages of production.[13]

We calculate that, of the steel imports that would ordinarily be subject to a 30 percent tariff increase in the second and third quarters of 2002, 46 percent (by value) entered with a product exclusion and faced a negligible tariff.[14] Furthermore, by our calculations only 31 percent of such imports can afford to "eat" a 30 percent tariff increase. Hence if not for the product exclusions on steel imports subject to a 30 percent tariff increase, an additional $233 million worth of steel imports (between 600,000 and 700,000 short tons) would have been displaced by the Section 201 remedies.

Foreign steel exporters gain much more from product exclusions than do domestic steel consumers. Some foreign steel exporters with product exclusions actually benefit from the overall system of Section 201 protection because the rest of their foreign competitors still face safeguard tariffs of up to 30 percent. Unlucky foreign competitors without exclusions operate at a distinct disadvantage in the US market. Meanwhile, US steel consumers have to pay the going price to all steel suppliers. Lucky foreign steel exporters with product exclusions can therefore raise the prices they charge US steel consumers by a substantial fraction of the 30 percent tariff and pocket the additional profits, technically known as "quota rents."[15]

US government-fostered largesse in the form of quota rents served to appease Japanese and European steel producers and their governments, which agreed to put off retaliation until after the World Trade Organization (WTO) hears the case against the US steel safeguards. We believe that the safeguard tariffs will be found inconsistent with WTO standards and thus liable to WTO-sanctioned retaliation. The legal case, including appeals, will likely be concluded in late 2003.

If Japan and the European Union had instead gone ahead with immediate retaliation—citing an ambiguous but untested provision of the WTO Agreement on Safeguards—the atmosphere for further global trade liberalization would have worsened.[16] The Bush administration deserves credit for avoiding this outcome.

Hence if not for the product exclusions on steel imports subject to a 30 percent tariff increase, an additional $233 million worth of steel imports (between 600,000 and 700,000 short tons) would have been displaced by the Section 201 remedies. US tonnage consumption of steel (inclusive of imports) was less in 2001 than in 1964, despite the fact that the real value of US durable goods consumption increased over 150 percent during this period.

Mixed Blessings—Steel Prices and Productivity Both Up

In this section, we examine two phenomena to illustrate that there is no such thing as a free lunch. First, productivity in the US steel industry has continued its upward trend in 2002, which is good for steel consumers and bad for the USWA, since the ranks of dues-paying members get downsized. Second, thanks in part to the Section 201 tariffs, steel prices are up, which is good for steel producers but bad for steel consumers.

Productivity in the US Steel Industry

Table 1 presents a snapshot of the US steel industry in 1964, 2001, and 2002. The most striking figure is that US tonnage consumption of steel (inclusive of imports) was less in 2001 than in 1964, despite the fact that

the real value of US durable goods consumption increased over 150 percent during this period.[17] The US economy is much less steel intensive today than in previous years, and US demand for steel has been essentially stagnant for four decades. Moreover, consumption of steel is projected to decline further in 2002, despite the moderate up-turn in the economy relative to 2001.

At the same time, competition on the supply side of the market has intensified dramatically, both from foreign and domestic sources. Although integrated steel producers and the USWA concentrate their blame on imports, over half the decline in traditional integrated steel production is attributable to the rise of domestic minimills, such as Nucor and Steel Dynamics. Traditional integrated steel production decreased by 62 million short tons between 1964 and 2001, while minimill production increased by 35 million short tons.

Moreover, US integrated steel mills are the sole importers of unfinished steel, which they further process and sell with markups; thus, unfinished steel imports help rather than harm integrated steel producers. When seen in these terms, the increase in finished steel imports (17 million short tons between 1964 and 2001)—the kind of steel imports that compete with the final output of domestic mills—was less than half the corresponding increase in minimill production. Minimills, not imports, are the main force crowding integrated steel firms.

The rise of minimills allows finished steel to be made more efficiently. To cite just one statistic, each employee in Nucor's minimills makes three times as many tons of steel as each employee at US Steel (the largest integrated steel producer in the United States and second to Nucor in absolute production).[18] To be sure, both input and output mixes differ between the two firms, but the differences do not cancel out the crude comparison of annual tons per worker. Over the past four decades, Nucor has been profitable every year, while US Steel has often incurred losses.

Improvements in labor productivity are good for steel consumers, because productive firms take market share from less productive

Snapshot of the US steel industry in 1964, 2001, and 2002 - Table 1
Millions of short tons Units   *Units*

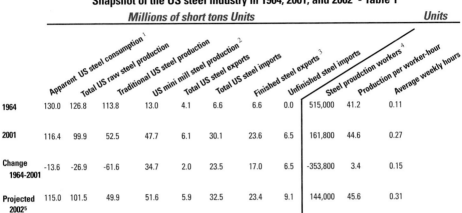

	Apparent US steel consumption[1]	Total US raw steel production	Traditional US steel production[2]	US mini mill steel production	Total US steel exports	Total US steel imports	Finished steel exports[3]	Unfinished steel imports	Steel production workers[4]	Production per worker-hour	Average weekly hours
1964	130.0	126.8	113.8	13.0	4.1	6.6	6.6	0.0	515,000	41.2	0.11
2001	116.4	99.9	52.5	47.7	6.1	30.1	23.6	6.5	161,800	44.6	0.27
Change 1964-2001	-13.6	-26.9	-61.6	34.7	2.0	23.5	17.0	6.5	-353,800	3.4	0.15
Projected 2002[5]	115.0	101.5	49.9	51.6	5.9	32.5	23.4	9.1	144,000	45.6	0.31

1. Apparent consumption is roughly equal to [production - exports + imports], but it is technically defined as [shipments - exports + finished imports + stock changes]. Data for shipments and stock changes are not reported here.
2. In 1964, traditional production included two types of integrated production: open hearth production and blast oxygen furnace production. Today, all integrated mill production uses blast oxygen furnaces.
3. All steel imports in 1964 are assumed to be finished.
4. Figures are for SIC 331 and are averaged based on monthly data.
5. 2002 figures are generally projected by utilizing the appropriate year-to-date through October 2002 data from the AISI. The three exceptions are the growth rate for apparent steel consumption, which is taken from the IISI, the growth rate for raw steel production, which was taken from the AISI's December 2002 data and the data on production workers and weekly hours, which was taken from the BLS's December 2002 data.

Notes: USGS figures are originally reported in metric tons. Components may not add to totals due to rounding.

Sources: USGS (2002a, 2002b) for most 1964 tonnage data; Barringer and Pierce (2000, p.260) for minimill production in 1964; AIIS (2002) for apparent steel consumption in 2001 and 2002; BLS (2002b) for labor data; and AISI (2002a, 2002b) for other data.

firms by offering better quality and reduced prices. As a result, however, less productive firms and their workers suffer and are eventually driven out of the steel industry. The combination of stagnant demand and rising productivity (especially in nonunionized minimills) is the greatest threat to the USWA—not imports.[19] At current levels of productivity and annual worker hours, the United States could make all the steel it made in 1964 with less than 175,000 production workers, which would increase the current production workforce by only 30,000. If all finished steel imports in 2002 were replaced with domestic production, about 32,000 additional steel production workers would be needed to fill this demand. An additional 30,000 to 32,000 production workers would bring the total industry production workforce to the actual number of steel production workers just two short years ago and the increase would still be

less than one-tenth of the steel production jobs lost since 1964 (some 343,000 jobs) solely due to increases in productivity and weekly hours.

In our previous policy brief, we predicted that a moderate Section 201 remedy would increase the gross number of jobs in the steel industry by a mere 3,500. The number of steel production workers in November 2002 was the same as in February 2002 and is almost the same as the monthly average for 2002. Although it is possible that the Section 201 remedy saved some jobs by preventing further lay-offs, we continue to be baffled by the willingness of unionized workers to believe that protection is a great benefit to them. When will they realize that their union leaders wrongly vilify imports and make false promises about the payoff from protection?...

The Bad—Many US Integrated Steel Firms Are Still in Trouble

Despite the recent increase in steel prices, many integrated mills are still incapable of making healthy profits. The reason why many integrated mills lose money even with higher steel prices is simple: their average costs are even higher. In this section, we examine the reasons why the performance of the US steel industry as a whole is consistently poor.

Sales, Profits, and Stock Prices

Figure 2 shows the revenue and after-tax profits for the US iron and steel industry along with the price of the Dow Jones Steel Index on a quarterly basis from 1993 to the third quarter of 2002. [29] Stock prices are largely a function of expected profits, and steel stocks had a bad year in 2002.

During the first three quarters of 2002, the Dow Jones Steel Index lost more value in percentage terms (27.7 percent) than the Dow Jones Industrial Average (24.2 percent), despite the absence of accounting scandals in the steel industry. [30] Stock markets are not always right, but figure 2 illustrates that change in the Dow Jones Steel Index has been a good leading indicator of steel revenue in subsequent quarters.

During the period from 1993Q1 to 2002Q3, the iron and steel industry as a whole has never made an after-tax quarterly profit of more than $1 billion. The steel industry lost $800 million after taxes through the first three quarters of 2002. Despite the Section 201 tariffs, all the antidumping orders, and increased capacity utilization, the steel industry as a whole will still take an after-tax loss for the year 2002.

Based on the sales figures for the second and third quarters of 2002 and assuming a 3.3 percent price increase, the Section 201 tariffs are responsible for only $1 billion in additional revenue for the steel industry. Although this figure may be conservative, it should be kept in mind that additional profits are considerably less because downstream steel producers must pay higher prices for raw steel.

In the "pre-crisis" period of 1996 to 1998, the industry earned $19.22 per short ton produced, a profit margin of less than 3 percent. In the "crisis" period of 1999 to 2001, the industry lost $16.30 per short ton produced, a loss of less than 3 percent. [31] Although average steel prices declined about 10 percent in the "crisis period" relative to the "pre-crisis" period, profit margins deteriorated only 5.5 percent, due to the shift in steel production away from high-cost integrated mills to minimills.

Figure 3 shows the annual operating margins for a sample of US integrated mills and a sample of US minimills between 1995 and 2002. [32] While the minimills remained profitable (even during 2001), integrated mills are still losing money in 2002. Although the competitive advantages of minimills have been in place for a long time, figure 3 illustrates an important point emphasized in our previous policy briefs: steel protection helps strong firms more than weak ones.

Capacity in the US Steel Industry

Figure 4 shows steel capacity and capacity utilization between 1980 and 2002 and the producer price index for steel since 1986. US steel capacity was rationalized substantially between 1983 and 1987 (dropping 25 percent) and remained essentially flat until 1994. Between 1994 and 2000, minimills increased capacity much faster than integrated mills shed capacity, so US steel capacity as a whole expanded by 20 percent. Since 2001, steel capacity has declined sharply, which has helped push capacity utilization up to 86 percent in August 2002. [33]

However, the US steel industry faces an important Catch-22: In order for the steel industry as a whole to turn a profit, prices need to be extremely high, but high prices encourage steel firms to increase capacity and output, which drives down steel prices. The capacity increases that started in 1988 and in 1995 both followed a period of rising steel prices. The same thing will probably happen in 2003. In 2001, eight flat-rolled mills that accounted for 16 million short tons of annual capacity were idled, but now four of them have restarted, adding 10 million short tons back to US steel-making capacity. LTV

Sales, profits, and stock price in the US iron and steel industry, 1993-2002
Figure 2

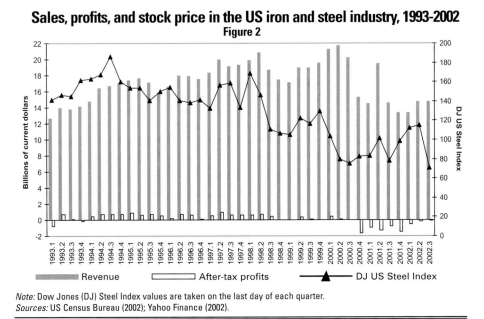

Note: Dow Jones (DJ) Steel Index values are taken on the last day of each quarter.
Sources: US Census Bureau (2002); Yahoo Finance (2002).

Corporation, whose idled assets were sold to new owners (the International Steel Group, ISG) in 2002, is the biggest component of the fluctuation in flat-rolled capacity (6 to 7 million short tons).[34] The stock market is astutely betting that this increase in steel supply will drive down steel prices and profits, which helps explain the poor performance of the Dow Jones Steel Index.

Pathetic efforts by the administration to induce US steel firms to restructure can also be considered among the "bad" aspects of US steel policy. To appear even-handed, the Bush administration required US steel producers to submit reports to the USTR by September 5, 2002, documenting how they planned to restructure. The steel firms were also asked to submit public versions of the report (i.e., deleting confidential business information) by the same deadline. Four months later there have been zero public reports. But the September press releases issued by the steel firms describing the confidential versions suggest that the reports are probably not worth reading.

The press releases have three common elements, which can be paraphrased as:

• We have been restructuring for many years resulting in many lost jobs.

• We plan to reduce costs and improve quality in the future.

• Safeguard tariffs need to remain in place for two more years in order to implement our plan.[35]

In a capitalist economy, nearly every firm—no matter the industry, country, or time period—has plans to reduce costs and improve quality. Nor do we believe the industry should be given "credit" for past restructuring that was forced upon it by market forces. The real question should be: What actions are US steel producers taking that would not be possible without tariffs? The press releases do not answer this question.

In our view, the steel industry should emphasize measures that reduce capacity permanently. Sadly, although Section 201 requires recipient industries to restructure in exchange for protection, the Bush administration lacks the gumption to ask hard questions about capacity reduction—much less to subject steel industry replies to public scrutiny. We do not believe tariffs are essential to keep the capitalist engine working; in fact, safeguards—in the absence of industry restructuring—only hurt the engine's performance.

Figure 3 Profit margins of minimills and integrated mills, 1995-2002

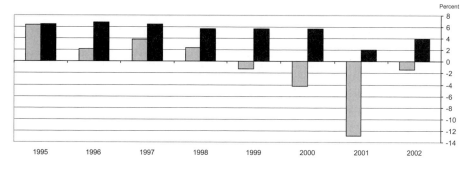

Note: Profit margin is calculated as net income (excluding unusual items) as a percent of revenue. See footnote 32 for the companies that constitute each sample.
Source: SEC (2002).

Figure 4 Performance of the US steel industry

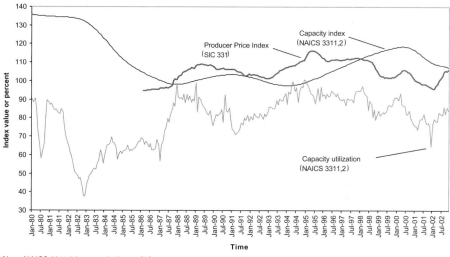

Note: NAICS 3311,2 is very similar to SIC 331.
Sources: BLS (2002 c) for Producer Price Index; FRB (2002) for capacity index and capacity utilization.

Legacy Costs

Legacy costs are health care and pension obligations that integrated steel firms owe to their retirees. These costs were estimated to run some $13 billion in net present value as of 1999.[36] In 1999, health expenditures for retirees at seven integrated steel firms amounted to $15 per ton of steel, and pension benefits added another $50 per ton. These seven integrated firms lost about $7 per ton in 1999 (and much more in 2000 and 2001), so legacy costs are a substantial obstacle to profitability.[37]

Bethlehem Steel, with its $9 billion in legacy costs, illustrates this dilemma.[38] Bethlehem filed for Chapter 11 bankruptcy in October 2001. Under Chapter 11, the firm continues to operate but can forestall debt payments (including legacy costs). Bethlehem wants to merge with another domestic steel producer to avoid liquidation under Chapter 7.

On January 6, 2003, it was announced that ISG (the company formed from the assets of LTV and Acme Metals) had offered to purchase substantially all of Bethlehem's assets and to assume a small fraction of Bethlehem's liabilities for a total cost of $1.5 billion. This offer will likely be approved soon by Bethlehem's management, the USWA, and the bankruptcy judge even though Bethlehem listed $2.7 billion worth of property, plant, and equipment as of November 30, 2002.[39]

What will happen to Bethlehem's workforce remains to be seen. ISG has a general agreement with the USWA that apparently will apply when ISG assumes control of Bethlehem's assets. The USWA generally supports ISG's efforts because ISG's cost-cutting strategy has focused on eliminating salaried employees and trimming benefits more so than cutting wages and eliminating job opportunities for hourly workers. But much of Bethlehem's total workforce (perhaps 40 percent) will likely be laid off. Late in 2002, Bethlehem planned on giving its older workers an early retirement proposal, but the Pension Benefit Guarantee Corporation (PBGC) foreclosed that option by assuming control of Bethlehem's pension plan in December 2002. Once the PBGC assumes control of a pension plan, the company cannot increase the PBGC's liability by offering more generous pension benefits as part of an early retirement package. ISG may be contemplating offering early retirement proposals to older workers that would expand upon the terms of its existing agreement with the USWA. However, any of Bethlehem's workers who are laid off would likely qualify for health benefits and wage insurance under the TAA program enacted by Congress in 2002 as part of the TPA package.

Since the US government is now picking up part of the legacy costs of liquidated firms via the enhanced TAA program, some say that Chapter 7 liquidation or Bethlehem-style asset sales are not such bad outcomes. Assets are sold in a competitive fashion and the new

owners escape the burden of legacy costs and restrictive union contracts. Under these circumstances, the new owners should be able to operate profitably. In individual cases, the capitalist system—underpinned by bankruptcy liquidation—is working just as Joseph Schumpeter prescribed!

The benchmark, however, should be whether the liquidation system as a whole—taking public and private actors together—performs efficiently, not whether it works for an individual steel firm. In a Chapter 7 liquidation, the firm's assets are sold to pay secured creditors to the extent possible and the remaining unsecured obligations (such as legacy costs) are simply not fulfilled. As a result, a substantial part of legacy costs, together with loan guarantees and adjustment costs, become a public obligation. Hard-nosed advocates of market capitalism might say that the right answer is to get the government out of the business of paying legacy and adjustment costs and making loan guarantees. We disagree with their prescription; more importantly, we do not think hard-nosed capitalism is about to become public policy—for steel or any other major sector. We think the sensible approach is to accept the government safety net, and then ask how to improve its efficiency over the medium term.

Seen as a system, private liquidation fosters public subsidization. A new private firm gets the benefit (steel assets at a cheap price) while the public budget is saddled with various costs (legacy obligations, loan guarantees, employment insurance, etc.). If public costs were a one-time event, that might be acceptable. However, the public burden is not just a one-time event. Instead ex post public assistance in all its guises feeds the cycle of overcapacity that leads to future firm failures.[40]

Two other factors compound this problem. First, the USWA contributes to the cycle of failure by insisting that all union contracts be roughly comparable. The buyer of liquidated assets is thus pressured to meet the unionized standard for salary, benefits, and work rules. This is a high standard in the face of nonunion competition and can lay the ground-work for future bankruptcies. Second, public support for the US steel industry provides a handy excuse for other countries to subsidize their steel industries, which they are inclined to do anyway. This in turn provokes trade remedies both in the United States and elsewhere. The pathological combination of private markets and public subsidies is not, of course, confined to the United States. It is an endemic feature of the steel industry in Europe and other parts of the world.[41]

The Bethlehem saga illustrates another aggravating circumstance to this cycle. In order to complete its deal with ISG, Bethlehem wanted to cut its workforce by offering early retirement to older workers. It is generally good to reduce the number of steel workers, but there is a moral hazard problem: Bethlehem and other failing steel firms have every incentive to offer overly generous terms to induce early retirement because they have no intention of fulfilling them and have every intention of passing the costs on to the government. The Pension Benefit Guarantee Corporation—whose financial resources are already stretched too thin—intervened to prevent additional early retirements, which in this case put capacity reduction and the renegotiation of restrictive union contracts in jeopardy, although in the end, it appears that ISG managed to overcome these hurdles.

We think the medium-term solution lies in reducing high-cost capacity rather than artificially limiting competition through trade protection. Minimills, which have low fixed costs, have been doing well for years. But reducing high-cost capacity will require a very difficult political decision: Congress will have to appropriate additional money without giving in to the temptation to use public money as a life-support system for failing steel firms. In our previous policy brief, we proposed a "Grand Bargain" where the government would assume a portion of the legacy costs of some integrated firms, if those firms were willing to reduce total capacity in a merger. The Bush administration shows no willingness to pursue this or any other legacy cost initiative (aside from its grudging acceptance of the enhanced TAA provisions). Thus, the various bills in Congress that address legacy costs

stand little chance of becoming law. Given the tenor of the bills as written, this may be a good outcome, because congressional sponsors generally attempt to preserve capacity rather than eliminate it.[42] However, as laid out in our recommendations, we think it is possible to condition legacy cost relief on capacity reduction and buy out rather than bail out high-cost steel producers. The legacy cost dilemma arises from the fact that legacy costs weaken the financial position of a firm but simultaneously act as a "poison pill" that prevents a merger with another firm that has a stronger balance sheet.

The Ugly—US Steel Policy Provokes International Trade Conflicts

The international dimensions of US steel policy are primarily debated in the OECD and the WTO. The first two prongs of President Bush's steel plan—to reduce excess capacity and market-distorting practices—are being pursued in leisurely fashion in quarterly OECD meetings. The third prong—Section 201 relief—has been challenged by seven countries and the European Union under WTO rules. US trading partners have also challenged the WTO legality of other US steel-related policies, notably the Byrd Amendment and the methodologies used to determine antidumping (AD) and countervailing duties (CVD).

Both the United States and the international community link these various issues, but do so in different ways. The United States argues that trade remedies are triggered by excess capacity resulting from public and private distortions and that AD, CVD, and safeguard measures are needed to force the international community to curtail the distortions, thereby reducing high-cost, excess capacity. The international community sees US penalty duties, especially AD tariffs, as thinly disguised protection, which should be put on the negotiating table as part of a comprehensive effort to eliminate market distortions. Both sides are correct in identifying each other's market-distorting practices, but the central failure of US steel policy has been to insist that foreign countries reform their practices without offering concessions of its own.

OECD Steel Meetings

The first few meetings of steel-producing countries at the OECD have focused on the elimination of excess capacity. There is no internationally accepted definition of what constitutes "excess" capacity. Among the worst definitions is one frequently used in US steel industry and USWA publications: Excess capacity equals domestic capacity minus domestic consumption. This flawed definition serves only to paint the United States as a victim and would be appropriate only in a fantasy world of 100 percent capacity utilization and balanced trade in the steel industry.

A better definition of excess capacity would be capacity that is habitually unprofitable (after deducting public subsidies from private revenues). Some form of this definition appears to be gaining ground in OECD talks. However, all habitually unprofitable steel firms assert that they would be profitable if only their habitually unprofitable competitors would shut down. As a result, the OECD capacity reduction talks have made little progress. The OECD participants did set a goal of eliminating 130 million short tons of gross steel-making capacity by 2005, and they established a peer-review mechanism to monitor each country's progress. Given this "soft" framework, the 130-million-ton goal will only be met to the extent that market forces dictate. Even if market forces take out 130 million short tons of old, high-cost capacity, nothing precludes the installation of 130 million (or more) tons of new low-cost capacity. Indeed, the recent worldwide steel price increase makes it less likely that old, high-cost capacity will be retired and more likely that new, low-cost capacity will be installed.

President Bush's safeguard tariffs—the third prong of his "comprehensive" steel plan—have served to undermine the first two prongs of his plan by inducing other countries to enact their own safeguards against steel imports. In our previous policy brief, we predicted a "domino effect"—other countries would enact protectionist barriers on both steel and other products if the United States went ahead with its steel safeguards. Our prediction has been more than vindicated. In the first nine months of 2002, there have been 116 non-US safeguard investigations (94 in the "steel and metals" industry including those by the European Union and Canada) as compared to 20 non-US safeguard investigations during the 12 months of 2001.[43] For the first time, the worldwide number of new safeguard investigations for all products is on track to exceed the number of new AD investigations (109 through the first nine months of 2002), and the number of exporters included in a safeguard investigation is always much larger than in an AD investigation.[44]

At the September 2002 OECD meeting, the United States proposed a four-part plan to eliminate the market distortions that give rise to excess steel capacity:

• Prohibit all subsides to the steel industry—except for subsidies intended to facilitate the closing of steel capacity (i.e., health and pension legacy costs, plus environmental legacy costs).

• Abolish all market access barriers—except safe-guards and AD/CVD duties.

• Enforce domestic laws that combat anticompetitive practices.

• Strictly limit new preferential financing to the steel sector, such as multilateral loans and export credits.

The European Union and other steel producers initially objected to the US proposal because it did not reform US trade remedy laws, which the international community believes are abused to the point of market distortion. In the OECD meetings in December 2002, the steel producing nations agreed to a compromise. They will first discuss the elimination of most subsidies and then discuss the reform of trade remedy laws—but in order to succeed the two sets of discussions would ultimately have to be tied together into a single agreement. In other words, other countries will insist that the United States reform its trade remedy laws (perhaps in the Doha negotiations) before they agree to limit their steel subsidies. Until the December OECD meeting,

Table 2   Overlap between Section 201 and AD/CVD tariffs

Section 201 Tariff Increase	Subject to AD/CVD No	Yes	Total	Percent share of "yes"
Slab TRQ	1	4	5	80
8%	6	1	7	14
13%	12	2	14	14
15%	21	37	58	64
30%	49	128	177	72
	89	172	261	66
	212	213	425	50
	301	385	686	56

Notes: Numbers represent the number of 10-digit classifications within chapters 72 and 73 of the Harmonized Tariff Schedule. We can reject the null hypothesis that Section 201 tariff increases and AD/CVD orders are independent under both a chi-squared test and a Fisher exact test.
Sources: US Customs Department (2002a, 2002b).

the United States adamantly refused to take the one step necessary to jumpstart international negotiations—putting its own protection on the negotiating table.[45] Now that the US stance has softened, we urge the Bush administration not to scuttle whatever progress is made on the subsidies front by taking a hard line on trade remedies. To this end, in the final section, we offer a proposal to reform the way the United States applies trade remedies.

US government and steel officials often dismiss the need for US concessions by asserting that the United States is the "world's steel dumping ground." This claim is specious. The United States does import a larger quantity and value of steel than any other country, but this is true of hundreds of products simply because the US economy is much larger than that of any other country. For the year 2001, if the value of iron and steel imports is taken as a share of GDP, Japan (0.07 percent) ranks as the most closed followed by the United States (0.15 percent), and the European Union (0.16 percent for extra-EU imports). Twelve other countries imported more steel as a share of GDP in 2001, and the average for these 15 importing nations was 0.41 percent.[46] Thus, the average importer in this sample had almost triple the US openness to iron and steel imports in 2001.

The primary reason why steel imports made up such a small share of US GDP in 2001 was the prevalence of AD and CVD orders and investigations. Of the 336 US AD

and CVD orders in place as of November 2002, 57 percent (191) were related to iron and steel.[47] Between 1980 and 2000, $18 billion of steel imports have been subject to an AD or a CVD investigation, and $10 billion of imports were penalized with an AD or CVD tariff.[48]

Moreover, there is a substantial overlap between US AD/CVD orders and US Section 201 tariffs, as is shown in table 2. There are 686 types of iron and steel products at the 10-digit level of the US Harmonized Tariff Schedule. Of these 686, 172 are affected by Section 201 remedies and 385 are affected by AD or CVD orders. Of the 425 iron and steel products not affected by Section 201 remedies, half are subject to an AD/CVD order and half are not. But, of the 261 iron and steel products affected by Section 201 remedies, two-thirds are also affected by an AD or CVD order. In other words, for the most part Section 201 remedies and AD/CVD orders are in practice, complementary measures, not alternative measures.[49]

This correlation between Section 201 remedies and AD/CVD orders suggests a legal dilemma for US steel import policy. One possibility is that petitioners in AD/CVD cases have been injured by steel imports not subject to the AD/CVD investigation, which raises the question of whether the ITC improperly blames steel imports subject to the AD/CVD investigation for materially injuring the domestic industry. Alternatively, the US safeguard decision may have been a primary function of steel import prices rather than a

Figure 5   Comparison of import surges preceding US steel and Argentine footwear safeguards

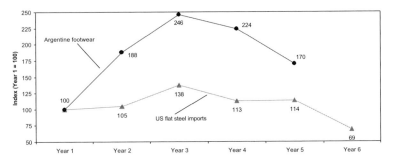

Note: Year 1 in the Argentine footwear case is 1991, while year 1 is 1996 in the US steel case. See footnote 53 for an explanation of how we treated data in year 6.
Sources: Ministry of Economy, Trade, and Industry of Japan (1992) and USITC (2002c).

primary function of steel import volume. Volume increases are an essential element of a safeguard case, both under the WTO Agreement on Safeguards and US law. Under either explanation of the observed correlation, US steel producers are "double-dipping" on protectionism and steel producers in other countries are not happy about it.

WTO Dispute Settlement

The WTO Agreement on Safeguards permits temporary protective tariffs for distressed industries, but the associated obligations are relatively strict. The United States simply ignored many of the obligations. Moreover, the coverage of US safeguard tariffs was substantial. President Bush applied tariffs to about $10 billion worth of steel imports—the equivalent of two decades worth of AD and CVD orders. With this background, it comes as no surprise that the international community is asking the WTO to condemn the safeguard tariffs.

The first problem with the US safeguard action is that the ITC included imports from Canada and Mexico (which constitute almost a fifth of total US steel imports) in its injury investigation, but President Bush did not subject NAFTA partners to his tariff remedies. In a previous case, the WTO Appellate Body rebuked the United States for this practice and required "parallelism"—that NAFTA partners be included in both the injury investigation and the remedy, or not be included at all.[50]

After the ITC made its remedy recommendations, USTR Robert Zoellick sent a letter to the ITC Commissioners asking (among other things) if their injury determinations would have been different had imports from Canada and Mexico been excluded from the injury investigation. The Commissioners said "no," but did not give extensive analysis nor did they hold further hearings. The WTO will probably find fault with the missing parallelism.

The second problem with the US Section 201 action is that increased imports of like or directly competitive steel products are not the principal cause of the domestic industry's distress. Article 2.1 of the WTO Agreement on Safeguards permits safeguards:

> ...*only if that Member has determined ... that such product is being imported into its territory **in such increased quantities,** absolute or relative to domestic production, and under such conditions as to cause or threaten to cause serious injury to the domestic industry that produces **like or directly competitive products** (emphasis added)* ...

The United States has been accused of violating each of the bold phrases. There is no dispute that US imports of most steel products increased between 1996 and 1998 and then declined between 1998 and 2001—in some cases to sub-1996 levels.[51] The WTO Appellate Body in a previous safeguard case involving footwear imports by Argentina deemed that "the increase in imports must have been recent enough, sudden enough, sharp enough, and significant enough, both quantitatively and qualitatively, to cause or threaten to cause 'serious injury'."[52]

The United States is making the heroic attempt to meet this burden by contending that low steel prices in 2000 and 2001 were largely caused by the increase in imports up through 1998. This argument will likely fall on deaf ears because steel import prices continued to fall between 1998 and 2001, even as the quantity of imports declined substantially. Thus, while the United States may be able to prove that, in 2001, steel was being imported "under such conditions" (low prices) as to cause serious injury, it will not be able to meet the two-pronged test that steel was being imported "in such increased quantities" and "under such conditions" as to cause serious injury to the domestic industry.

Figure 5 compares the percentage increases in imports in the safeguard cases involving both Argentine footwear imports and US imports of flat steel products.[53] The five years shown in the figure are 1991 to 1995 for Argentine footwear imports and 1996 to 2000 for US flat steel imports, with a projection for 2001 in order to simulate the evidence facing the ITC during the injury investigation.[54] Considering that the WTO Appellate Body found that the increase in footwear imports was insufficient to justify Argentina's safeguard, the United States has little hope of winning its case. The growth peak in the quantity of US flat steel imports was barely half that of Argentine footwear imports. Although the decline from the peak in the fourth and fifth years under safeguard investigation was steeper for Argentine footwear, US flat steel imports were projected to fall precipitously in 2001 to half their 1998 levels. Moreover, Argentine footwear imports were 70 percent above the original level in the fifth year as compared to a mere 14 percent increase in the US steel case by the fifth year (and an absolute decline when annualized data from the sixth year is taken into account).

Other WTO members also make persuasive arguments that the ITC failed to adequately separate the harm caused by increased imports from the harm caused by other factors, such as minimills, legacy costs, and changes in demand. Furthermore, other members contend that the ITC should not have considered four or five disparate flat steel products to be a single "like or directly competitive" product for the purpose of assessing injury. Indeed, considering unfinished steel slabs to be like or directly competitive with tin and other flat finished steel products, seems about as logical as filling a car with imported crude oil rather than gasoline.

Finally, even if the United States prevails on all these contested issues, it will have a difficult time meeting an additional WTO requirement—that the remedy be proportional to the harm caused by imports. In fact, there is a negative correlation between the products with the strongest Section 201 remedies and the products that experienced the largest percentage increases in import volume between 1996 and 2001. Put another way, the products with smaller percentage increases in import volume received stronger trade remedies.[55]

The Section 201 case is not the only instance where US steel policy has been challenged in the WTO. Recently the Commerce Department changed its methodology in response to adverse WTO rulings regarding the calculation of AD and CVD steel duties. Meanwhile, a WTO panel found that the Continued Dumping and Subsidy Offset Act (the Byrd Amendment) is inconsistent with WTO obligations. The United States is appealing the decision on the Byrd Amendment (the appeal will allow at least one more disbursement to petitioners while hearings take place).

Unlike the Section 201 tariffs, which can be rescinded unilaterally by the President, Congress would have to repeal the Byrd Amendment in order to best comply with the WTO Appellate Body ruling. Greg Mastel, Chief Trade Counsel in 2002 for the Senate Finance Committee, confidently predicted that the Senate would choose not to comply with the WTO rulings on the Byrd

Amendment.[56] If so, the precedent set in the recent WTO arbitration ruling in the Foreign Sales Corporation (FSC) case does not bode well for US exporters.[57] The Byrd Amendment shells out over $200 million annually to petitioning firms (inclusive of steel firms). Under the FSC precedent, each of the 11 trade partners that challenged the Byrd Amendment could impose prohibitive tariffs on $200 million of US exports each year.

If the United States chooses not to comply with adverse WTO rulings on the Section 201 tariffs, as well as the Byrd Amendment, other countries may feel forced to retaliate. A "steel war" will not advance the prospects for substantial trade liberalization in the FTAA or the WTO. On the other hand, if the United States does comply with WTO dispute settlement decisions, then Congress may be especially skeptical of any trade package coming out of the FTAA or WTO that reforms safeguard, AD, or CVD remedies. Putting all this together, despite the passage of TPA, difficult trade negotiations are made all that much harder—both at home and abroad—by conflicts over US steel policy. In the spirit of our earlier Grand Bargain, we propose that the US government offer to assume a percentage of a steel firm's total long-term legacy obligation (inclusive of environmental legacy costs) equal to the percentage of its capacity that the firm is willing to permanently shutter.

Recommendations

The administration needs to pursue a new steel strategy that can gain support from both Congress and the international community. Pressure is building on the domestic front from steel users who resent paying extra for steel in a weak economy. On the international front, pressure has waned slightly due to product exclusions and high world steel prices. However, declining steel prices in 2003 and WTO disapproval of US safeguard tariffs seem almost inevitable. When those two events occur, trade partners will again turn up the heat on the United States. Many steps need to be taken but most of them require at least tacit approval from the US Congress.

Here we offer recommendations that we think will be beneficial to the steel industry and possibly palatable to Congress.

International Dimension

The first step the United States should take is to offer to suspend the steel safeguards against any country that commits to the US plan to end market distortions in the steel industry. The Bush administration can take this step unilaterally. Since US safeguard tariffs will probably be disapproved by the WTO Appellate Body in late 2003, this bargaining chip should be used quickly before the panel and Appellate Body make their decisions.

In addition, the United States could propose to clarify the language in the WTO Agreement on Safeguards regarding the time frame for safeguard investigations. As written, nothing in the WTO Agreement explicitly prevents a country from imposing safeguards on the grounds that imports of a product have increased substantially since the Marrakesh Declaration was signed in 1994. The time frame could be tightened—for example, to the most recent 36-month period for which data is available at the time of the investigation.

Foreign steel producers fear AD investigations launched by the US steel industry as much if not more than safeguard measures. In the first stage of an AD case, the plaintiffs need only to prove that imports are being sold at less-than-fair-value (LTFV); the domestic industry does not need to show that low prices are the result of a less-than-fair-practice, such as a cartel, a subsidy, or predatory pricing.[58] This is akin to accusing students who earn high test scores of cheating without alleging (much less proving) that they improperly collaborated or had advance knowledge of the questions. Thus, unfair trade remedies purportedly combat a process (unfair competition) solely on the basis of an outcome (export prices that are either below average cost—the great majority of cases—or that are below prices charged in the home market or third country markets). In the second stage of an AD case, the petitioners must prove that imports sold at LTFV cause material injury or threat of material injury to a domestic industry. "Material injury" has come to be interpreted as slight injury.[59]

We propose a new system to replace the material injury test with a test that is directly aimed at the market-distortion issue. The administration should propose legislation that has the effect of applying a "smoking gun" test to cases involving industries (such as steel) that suffer from systemic market distortions. Once the Commerce Department finds LTFV sales, the ITC should determine, based on the preponderance of the evidence, whether the subject imports are sold at LTFV because of market-distorting practices. If so, then the existence of a less-than-fair-practice (LTFP) would suffice to prove that the domestic industry is threatened by material injury.[60] Under our proposal, in the absence of an LTFP, the United States would not impose AD tariffs. Of course, even if unfair practices are not distorting steel trade, the industry could seek safeguard tariffs, provided that imports are causing serious injury.[61]

We think that a proposal along these lines would be attractive to the international community. It offers a new approach to the market-distortion problem not by gutting the AD statute, but by focusing the statute on the unfair practices rather than the unfavorable outcomes.

Domestic Dimension

Pressure on the Bush administration to "do something" for the steel industry will intensify before the 2004 presidential election, especially once the WTO has disapproved the Section 201 tariffs. In the spirit of our earlier Grand Bargain, we propose that the US government offer to assume a percentage of a steel firm's total long-term legacy obligation (inclusive of environmental legacy costs) equal to the percentage of its capacity that the firm is willing to permanently shutter.[62] A firm could also reduce its legacy liability if it were willing to buy out and permanently shutter a portion of another firm's capacity. The capacity bought out would be added to the purchaser's total capacity for the purpose of determining the equivalent amount of legacy liability transferred to the government. This offer should stand regardless of any merger activity but would encourage mergers rather than Chapter 7 liquidation. After a predetermined date, say the end of 2004, the offer would be pulled from the table. This deadline would provide an incentive to high-cost steel producers to reduce their capacity quickly and would encourage stronger firms to merge with bankrupt firms before Chapter 7 liquidation. By offering not a bailout but a buyout, we think the pathological cycle fostered by the current public subsidy/private market system would be brought to an end.

Gary Clyde Hufbauer is Reginald Jones Senior Fellow at the Institute for International Economics. He is coeditor of The Ex-Im Bank in the 21st Century: A New Approach? (2000) and coauthor of World Capital Markets: Challenge to the G-10 (2001), Steel: Big Problems, Better Solutions, International Economics Policy Brief 01-9 (2001), and Time for a Grand Bargain in Steel? International Economics Policy Brief 02-1 (2002).

Ben Goodrich is a research assistant at the Institute. He is coauthor of Steel: Big Problems, Better Solutions, International Economics Policy Brief 01-9 (2001), and Time for a Grand Bargain in Steel? International Economics Policy Brief 02-1 (2002).

Endnotes

[1] For a list of bankruptcies, see USWA (2002).

[2] Under US law, evenly divided determinations (covering 4 types of steel) are tantamount to affirmative injury findings. See USITC (2002a) for the official ITC determinations.

[3] During the course of its investigation the majority of the ITC found that plate, hot-rolled sheet and strip, cold-rolled sheet and strip, and coated steel were a "like" product and could be treated as a single product for the purpose of determining injury and recommending relief. Two minority ITC commissioners considered tin to be included in the flat product group. Thus, some prefer to classify President Bush's remedy as covering 11 out of 13 types of steel imports. However, we think the decision to group the flat products is misleading and will likely be faulted by the WTO.

[4] The 6 million short-ton quota applies to non-NAFTA slab imports only. Mexico and Canada are permitted to export an unlimited amount of slab to the United States without triggering tariffs. Slab imports from non-NAFTA countries were on track as of August 2002 to approach 7.5 million short-tons in 2002, so the 30 percent tariffs may have been triggered sometime in the fourth quarter of 2002.

[5] The steel industry is pressing the Bush administration to revoke the exclusions of countries such as India and Turkey for some steel products on the grounds that their exports to the US market now exceed the de minimis thresholds.

[6] These figures come from Hillman (2002).

[7] See Hufbauer and Goodrich (2002).

[8] Unofficial campaign results from CNN (2002).

[9] See Bergsten (2002).

[10] See Brown, Deardorff, and Stern (2001).

[11] See Hufbauer and Goodrich (2001, 2002). The wage insurance proposal in those policy briefs was based on the policy brief of Kletzer and Litan (2001).

[12] Figures come from USTR (2002a).

[13] Unfinished imports are detrimental to minimills, and Nucor led the charge to impose 40 percent tariffs against unfinished imports for the sole purpose of driving up the operating costs of roller mills (a type of integrated mill that produces finished goods by rolling imported slab), which represent an emerging threat to minimill dominance in the steel industry.

[14] The products that would ordinarily face a tariff increase of 30 percent are plated steel, hot-rolled flat steel, cold-rolled steel, coated steel, tin, hot-rolled bars and light shapes, and cold-finished steel from countries that are subject to the remedies for these products. Other types of steel, as well as steel imports from Canada, Mexico, and developing countries are not considered in this calculation.

[15] The CEO of POSCO, Korea's quasi-public steel producer, which received an 826,720 short ton exception to supply U.S. Steel, recently said in the *Chicago Tribune* (2002), "I would like to extend personal gratitude to Mr. Bush for putting in place the steel safeguards and other initiatives," adding that "I am extremely skeptical that this kind of protectionist measures for U.S. steelmakers will contribute to the industry restructuring and reviving itself." The tendency of protection to create quota rents is further analyzed in Hufbauer and Wada (1999).

[16] Article 8.3 of the WTO Agreement on Safeguards states: "The right of suspension referred to in paragraph 2 shall not be exercised for the first three years that a safeguard measure is in effect, provided that the safeguard measure has been taken as a result of an absolute increase in imports ..." The legal controversy is whether affected parties are permitted to unilaterally judge that US steel imports are not increasing in absolute terms. The United States said "no." The European Union and Japan said "yes," but agreed to refrain from retaliation due to the product exclusions and the quota rents they enjoyed.

[17] Data for the consumption of durable goods comes from the BEA (2002) and is deflated using the Consumer Price Index published by the BLS (2002a).

[18] Based on 2001 annual reports, see US Steel (2002) and Nucor (2002). US Steel Corporation operates a foreign mill in Slovakia, but the Slovakian output and employees are not included in this calculation.

[19] There has been considerable discussion recently about the value of the dollar, the effect of the exchange rate on imports, and the health of the US manufacturing sector, particularly industries like steel. For contrasting views on the issue, see Baily (2002) and Blecker (2002).

[29] The Dow Jones Steel Index consists of seven US firms: AK Steel, Allegheny Technologies, Carpenter Technology, Nucor, Ryerson Tull, US Steel, and Worthington Industries.

[30] Data comes from Yahoo (2002).

[31] Production data (not shown) is from USGS (2002a).

[32] 2002 data includes the first three quarters if available and is taken from SEC (2002). The samples closely correspond to the sample used by the International Trade Commission in its Industry, Trade, and Technology Review, which regularly includes a similar chart. In this

paper, the integrated mill sample includes ACME Metals, AK Steel, Bethlehem Steel, LTV, Ispat Inland, US Steel, Weirton, and National Steel. The minimill sample includes AmeriSteel, Nucor, Oregon Steel, and Steel Dynamics. Some firms are not included in some years due to closings and mergers.

[33] Utilization of raw steel capacity, as reported by the AISI (2002b), has been 90 percent for the period January-October 2002. The data in figure 4 pertain to the steel industry as a whole. In contrast, capacity utilization for durable goods manufacturing as a whole has hovered around 70 percent in 2002 and has not reached the 90 percent range since 1967, according to data from the FRB (2002).

[34] Figures come from Steel Business Briefing (2002), quoting Mark Parr of McDonald Investments.

[35] The press releases also usually endorse the continued use of antidumping tariffs and countervailing duties.

[36] Figure comes from Klinefelter (2002). Another potential "legacy cost" is the cost of future environmental cleanup; however, we set this issue aside (as many others do) mainly for lack of even ballpark estimates.

[37] Data on pension and health care costs is from USWA (2001). Net loss per ton is derived from this data as well as annual reports maintained by the SEC (2002). The seven major integrated steel firms are U.S. Steel, Bethlehem, LTV, AK Steel, National Steel, Ispat-Inland, and Wheeling-Pittsburgh. LTV has since been liquidated.

[38] See Crenshaw (2002).

[39] SEC (2002)

[40] The Emergency Steel Loan Guarantee Act of 1999 offers loan guarantees to the steel industry, but has only been utilized once. Since the Act did not induce creditors to loan money to LTV and Geneva Steel despite the 85 percent (or more) guarantee, several House bills contain language to make the program even more generous. We think this is a very bad idea. See Cooney (2002) for additional details on the House bills.

[41] Nor is the cycle confined to the steel industry. Shipbuilding is another pathological case.

[42] See Cooney (2002) for a summary and status report for these various bills.

[43] The United States initiated 33 steel safeguard investigations bringing the total number of safeguard investigations worldwide to 53 in 2001. The United States has not initiated any safeguard investigations in 2002, except for one against China under a special safeguard provision.

[44] Data from Stevenson (2002).

[45] The same attitude— "It's your fault, not mine. You reform first."—cramped the US negotiating stance in the run-up to the failed Seattle Summit in October 1999.

[46] The data comes from the WTO (2002b) and IMF (2002). These 15 importing nations were the only ones that imported more than $1 billion worth of iron and steel imports in 2001.

[47] USITC (2002b).

[48] Figures come from Hillman (2002).

[49] The null hypothesis between Section 201 and AD/CVD orders has a less than one in ten thousand chance of being true under both a chi-squared test and a Fisher exact test.

[50] The text of NAFTA requires that the United States exclude Canada and Mexico from safeguard remedies or provide them with immediate compensation. This provision of NAFTA is probably inconsistent with WTO obligations, although no country has directly challenged the NAFTA provision.

[51] Technically, the ITC only considered the first half of 2001 in its injury investigation but imports on a year-to-date basis were still declining relative to the same period in 2000.

[52] WTO (1999, paragraph 131).

[53] For this calculation, flat steel imports are defined as slabs, plate, hot-rolled steel, cold-rolled steel, and coated steel according to the definition used by the majority of the ITC. Tin and grain-oriented electrical steel are not included in this definition.

[54] We annualized data for 2001 by multiplying the growth rate of imports for flat steel products in the first six months of 2001 compared to the same period in 2000 by the annual data for 2000 to produce a seasonally adjusted projection for 2001 flat steel imports. Simply doubling imports for the first six months of 2001 would result in an upwardly biased projection because steel imports generally peak in the second quarter.

[55] The data comes from the USITC (2002c). We annualized data for 2001 by multiplying the growth rate of imports for each steel product in the first six months of 2001 compared to the same period in 2000 by the annual data for 2000 to produce a seasonally adjusted projection for 2001 imports, in order to replicate the evidence facing the ITC at the time of the investigation. Simply doubling imports for the first six months of 2001 would result in an upwardly biased projection because steel imports generally peak in the second quarter. The 33 products were ranked by the percentage increase in import quantity from 1996 to 2001 (annual projection) and by the magnitude of the tariff

remedy. The Spearman rank correlation is statistically significant at the 98 percent confidence level and has a value of –0.43.

[56] Quoted in Inside US Trade (2002).

[57] See Hufbauer (2002).

[58] Under current law, the Commerce Department can find that imports are sold at LTFV on the basis of predation (exporting to the United States at prices below the marginal cost of production) but in practice this clause is rarely invoked. Predation would obviously be deemed an LTFP under our proposal.

[59] Congress has statutorily defined "material injury" as "harm that is not inconsequential, immaterial, or unimportant," language that gives the ITC maximum latitude to find injury.

[60] Article 3.7 of the WTO Anti-Dumping Agreement requires that "A determination of a threat of material injury shall be based on facts and not merely on allegation, conjecture or remote possibility. The change in circumstances which would create a situation in which the dumping would cause injury must be clearly foreseen and imminent ... [t]he totality of the factors considered must lead to the conclusion that further dumped exports are imminent and that, unless protective action is taken, material injury would occur." We believe our proposal is WTO-consistent because if a LTFP is identified, then the threat is "clearly foreseen and imminent".

[61] In the Doha Round, the United States should work to generalize this proposal to other industries and negotiate language in the WTO Anti-Dumping Agreement that requires this alternative methodology.

[62] For example, if a steel firm is willing to permanently close half its capacity (and not sell it to another firm), the government would take half the firm's legacy costs.

References

American Institute for International Steel (AIIS). 2002. US Steel Market Analysis. http://www.aiis.org/chairmans_us/?file=statement.htm (accessed December 11). American Iron and Steel Institute (AISI). 2002a. Selected Steel Industry Data. http://www.steel.org/stats (accessed January 6).

American Iron and Steel Institute (AISI). 2002b. *Raw Steel Production through Week Ended 12/14/02* http://www.steel.org/stats/weekly/2002/021214.htm (accessed December 17).

American Metal Market. 2002. "NAM committee to rethink policy on '201' tariffs." October 17. http://www.amm.com/index2.htm (accessed November 4).

Baily, Martin Neil. 2002. Persistent Dollar Swings and the US Economy in *The Overvalued Dollar in the World Economy*, ed. C. Fred Bergsten and John Williamson. International Economics Special Report 15. Washington: Institute for International Economics. December.

Barringer, William H. and Kenneth J. Pierce. 2000. *Paying the Price for Big Steel*. Washington: American Institute for International Steel. http://www.aiis.org/pdfs/book.pdf (accessed November 6).

Bergsten, C. Fred. 2002. "A Renaissance for United States Trade Policy?" Foreign Affairs November/December. http://www.iie.com/papers/bergsten1002.htm.

Blecker, Robert A. 2002. *Let It Fall: The Effects of the Over-valued Dollar on U.S. Manufacturing and the Steel Industry*. http://www.steel.org/images/pdfs/blecker.pdf (accessed November 5).

Broderick, Thomas J. 2002. *Testimony Before the House Subcommittee on Commerce, Trade, and Consumer Protection*. Washington: House Subcommittee on Commerce, Trade, and Consumer Protection.

Brown, Drusilla K., Alan V. Deardorff, and Robert M. Stern. 2001. *Impacts on NAFTA Members of Multilateral and Regional Trading Arrangements and Initiatives and Harmonization of NAFTA's External Tariffs*. Ford School Discussion Paper 471. November 4, 2002.

Bureau of Economic Analysis. 2002. Gross Domestic Product. Washington: BEA.

Bureau of Labor Statistics (BLS). 2002a. *Consumer Price Index*. Washington: BLS.

Bureau of Labor Statistics (BLS). 2002b. *Current Employment Statistics*. Washington: BLS.

Bureau of Labor Statistics (BLS). 2002c. *Producer Price Indexes*. Washington: BLS.

Cable News Network (CNN) 2002. *Election Results: House of Representatives.* http://www.cnn.com/ELECTION/2002/ pages/house/index.html (accessed November 6).

Chicago Tribune. 2002. "South Korea steelmaker could export lessons." October 30.

Cooney, Stephen. 2002. *Steel Industry and Trade Issues*. Congressional Research Service Report for Congress RL31107. October 10. Washington: CRS.

Crandall, Robert W. 2002. *The Futility of Steel Trade Protection*. http://www.criterioneconomics.com/documents/crandall_report.pdf (accessed November 6).

Crenshaw, Albert B. 2002. "U.S. Targets Steel Firm's Pension Plan." *The Washington Post*, December 17, p.E01.

Federal Reserve Board (FRB). 2002. *Capacity Utilization and Industrial Capacity*. Washington: FRB. http:// www.federalreserve.gov/releases/g17/caputl.htm (accessed December 17).

Francois, Joseph F. and Laura M. Baughman. 2002. *Estimated Economic Effects of Proposed Import Relief Remedies for Steel*. http://www.citac.info/remedy/index.htm (accessed November 6).

Hillman, Jennifer. 2002. *Perspectives on the Global Metals Trade*. Presentation to the Metal Service Center Institute (MSCI), May 2002. Chicago, IL: MSCI.

Hufbauer, Gary Clyde. 2002. *The Foreign Sales Corporation: Reaching the Last Act?* International Economics Policy Brief 02-10. Washington: Institute for International Economics. November.

Hufbauer, Gary Clyde and Ben Goodrich. 2001. *Steel: Big Problems, Better Solutions*. International Economics Policy Brief 01-09. Washington: Institute for International Economics. July.

Hufbauer, Gary Clyde and Ben Goodrich. 2002. *Time for a Grand Bargain in Steel?* International Economics Policy Brief 02-01. Washington: Institute for International Economics. January.

Hufbauer, Gary Clyde and Erika Wada. 1999. *Steel Quotas: A Rigged Lottery*. International Economics Policy Brief 99-05. Washington: Institute for International Economics.

Inside US Trade. 2002. "Senate Aide Sees Congress Refusing to Address Adverse WTO Rulings." September 30.

International Iron and Steel Institute. 2002. *Report of the Secretary General.* http://www.worldsteel.org/media/ iisi36/shortrangeoutlook.pdf (accessed November 6).

International Monetary Fund (IMF). 2002. *World Economic Outlook Database*. September. http://www.imf.org/external/ pubs/ft/weo/2002/02/data/index.htm (accessed November 4).

Ministry of Economy, Trade and Industry of Japan (METI). 2002. First Written Submission of the Government of Japan. WTO Case WT/DS249. Tokyo: METI.

Kletzer, Lori G. and Robert E. Litan. 2001. *A Prescription to Relieve Worker Anxiety*. International Economics Policy Brief 01-02. Washington: Institute for International Economics and The Brookings Institution. February.

Klinefelter, Bill. 2002. Testimony Before the House Sub-committee on Commerce, Trade, and Consumer Protection. September 10. Washington: House Subcommittee on Commerce, Trade, and Consumer Protection.

Morici, Peter. 2002. The Impact of Steel Import Relief on US and World Steel Prices: A Survey of Some Counterintuitive Results. http://www.steel.org/images/Morici_Paper. pdf (accessed November 4).

Mueller, Hans. 2002. The Impact of 201 Tariffs on US Steel Users and Foreign Steelmakers: A Critique of Peter Morici's Survey of Some Counterintuitive Results. http://www.aiis.org /speeches/muellerstudy_0702.pdf (accessed November 4).

Nucor. 2002. 2001 Annual Report. November 4.

Purchasing Magazine. 2002. *Steel Flash Report.* October 31. http:// www.manufacturing.net /PUR/index.asp?layout=articleWebzine&articleid=CA256185 (accessed November 6).

Steel Business Briefing. 2002. *Daily Email Newsletter.* September 24.

Steel Manufacturers Association. 2002. *Statement on Recent Press Comments on Steel Prices.* http://www.steelnet.org/new /20020606_statement_prices.htm (accessed November 6).

Stevenson, Cliff. 2002. *Global Trade Protection Report 2002* Update. Received by email on October 25, 2002.

Tomz, Michael, Jason Wittenberg and Gary King. 2000. "Making the Most of Statistical Analyses: Improving Interpretation and Presentation." *American Journal of Political Science* 44, no. 2, April.

Tomz, Michael, Jason Wittenberg, and Gary King. 2001. CLARIFY: Software for Interpreting and Presenting Statistical Results. Version 2.0. Cambridge, MA: Harvard University.

United States Census Bureau. 2002. *Quarterly Financial Report Past Press Releases.* Washington: United States Census Bureau.

United States Customs Service. 2002a. Steel 201 Remedy Coverage Guide. Washington: United States Customs Service. September. http://www.customs.gov/impoexpo/ steel_docs/remedy_pub.xls   (accessed December 11).

United States Customs Service. 2002b. *Steel 201 Remedy Coverage* Guide. Washington: United States Customs Service. October. http://www.customs.gov/impoexpo/steel_do cs/steel_remedy_guide-updated_public_ version.xls (accessed December 11).

United States Geological Survey (USGS). 2002a. *Iron and Steel Statistics.* Reston, VA: USGS.

United States Geological Survey (USGS). 2002b. *Mineral Commodity Summaries: Iron and Steel.* Reston, VA: USGS.

United States Geological Survey (USGS). 2002c. *Historical Data for Metal Industry Indicators.* Reston, VA: USGS.

United States International Trade Commission (USITC). 2001. *Staff Report: Volume III.* Publication 3479. Washington: USITC.

United States International Trade Commission (USITC). 2002a. ITC Details Its Determinations Concerning Impact of Imports of Steel on US Industry. http: //www.usitc.gov/er/nl2001/ER1023Y1.PDF (November 4).

United States International Trade Commission (USITC). 2002b. *Antidumping and Countervailing Duties in Place.* Washington: USITC.

United States International Trade Commission (USITC). 2002c. US *Imports of Steel Products.* Washington: USITC.

United States International Trade Commission (USITC). 2002d. USITC Interactive Tariff and Trade DataWeb. Washington: USITC.

United States Securities and Exchange Commission (SEC). 2002. *EDGAR Company Search.* http://www.sec.gov/ edgar/searchedgar/companysearch.html (accessed November 4).

United States Trade Representative (USTR). 2002a. *Follow-Up To Request for Information on Steel Exclusion Process.* Content received by e-mail (accessed November 4).

United States Trade Representative (USTR). 2002b. *Developing Countries with Products Not Excluded From the Remedies.* http://www.ustr.gov/sectors/industry/ steel201/2002-03-05-exclusions.PDF (accessed November 5).

United Steelworkers of America (USWA). 2001. *The Crisis in American Steel.* http://www.uswa.org/sra/pdf/Steel Update Presentation8-14-01.pdf (accessed November 4).

United Steelworkers of America (USWA). 2002. *Steel Companies Filing for Bankruptcy.* http://www.uswa.org/sra/pdf/SteelBankruptc ies 8-16-02.pdf (accessed November 4).

U.S. Steel. 2002. 2001 Annual Report. November 4, 2002.

World Trade Organization (WTO). 1999. *Argentina– Safeguard Measures on Imports of Footwear Report of the Appellate Body.* WT/DS121/AB/R. http://docsonline.wto.org/ DDFDocuments/t/WT/DS/121ABR.DOC (accessed November 4).

World Trade Organization (WTO). 2002a. *Agreement on Safeguards.* http:// www.wto.org/ english/docs_e/legal_e/25safeg.pdf (accessed November 4).

World Trade Organization (WTO). 2002b. *Leading exporters and importers of iron and steel, 2001.* http:/www.wto.orgenglish/res_estatis_e/its2002_e/ section4_e/iv34.xls (November 4).

World Trade Organization (WTO). 2002c. *Agreement on Implementation of Article VI of the General Agreement on Tariffs and Trade 1994.* http://www.wto.org/english/docs_e/legal_e/19-adp.pdf (accessed November 4).

Yahoo. 2002. *Yahoo! Finance.* http://finance.yahoo.com (accessed in December 11).

America's Bittersweet Sugar Policy

4

MARK A. GROOMBRIDGE

Nowhere is there a larger gap between the U.S. government's free-trade rhetoric and its protectionist practices than in the sugar program. Through preferential loan agreements and tariff-rate quotas, the U.S. government thwarts price competition to maintain an artificially high domestic price for sugar—a price that can be twice the world market price or higher.

The program benefits a small number of sugar producers, but virtually every governmental and nongovernmental survey concludes that the program results in a net loss of welfare for the U.S. economy, with U.S. consumers suffering the most. Direct costs to consumers due to higher prices could be as much as $1.9 billion a year and the net welfare loss to the U.S. economy nearly $1 billion. Moreover, the U.S. government spends close to $1.68 billion a year buying and storing excess sugar to maintain those artificially high domestic prices.

U.S. sugar consumers would not be the only winners if U.S. price supports and quotas were removed. Poor nations would benefit as well. Freeing just the U.S. market would boost global demand and raise world prices by 17 percent, increasing the annual export earnings of developing nations by $1.5 billion.

America's sugar quotas pose a threat to multilateral and regional trade negotiations. U.S. trading partners routinely and rightly point to quotas as being inconsistent with U.S. demands for more open markets abroad. The sugar program has become an obstacle to lowering foreign trade barriers to U.S. exports.

The U.S. sugar program is a classic case of concentrated benefits and dispersed costs: a very small number of sugar growers receive enormous benefits, while the costs of providing those benefits are spread across the U.S. economy, specifically to consumers and confectioners. Repealing the sugar quota program will require more vigorous leadership from the president and the many members of Congress who represent far more people who suffer from the U.S. sugar program than who benefit.

Introduction

The United States has long championed itself as the world leader of the free-trade movement. Recognizing that protectionist trade barriers hurt consumers as well as exporters and import-consuming industries, the United States has been at the forefront of trade liberalization since World War II. But that leadership has been missing in several politically sensitive sectors of the U.S. economy. Despite the economic arguments in favor of free trade, some industries remain highly protected because of the strength of powerful interest groups and the absence of counter-vailing consumer pressure to reform. Those barriers hurt the domestic economy and undermine U.S. efforts to launch successful multilateral and regional trade negotiations to promote more open markets around the world.

Perhaps there is no more egregious example of the U.S. government's hypocrisy in this regard than its sugar policy. Through policies such as preferential loan agreements and tariff-rate quotas, the U.S. sugar industry is highly effective at keeping foreign sugar out. By guaranteeing a minimum price for sugar, the U.S. government forces the price of sugar in our market to go up substantially.

Who pays the price for our sugar programs? The answer is U.S. industries that rely on sugar as an input and, ultimately, of course, U.S. consumers. Sugar programs raise prices for consumers through restricted competition and impose costs on taxpayers because the U.S. government must buy and store excess sugar to maintain those artificially high domestic prices.

It is not just U.S. consumers that suffer from trade protections in the sugar industry— the foundations of the multilateral trading system suffer as well. A number of countries point to the U.S. policy on sugar as a justification for not lowering their own trade barriers. Given the number of Latin American nations involved in the production of sugar, U.S. sugar policy will likely make it difficult to successfully conclude a free-trade agreement of the Americas (FTAA), which would establish the entire western hemisphere as a free-trade zone. U.S. sugar policy will also complicate efforts to launch a new round of global trade talks through the World Trade Organization.

Advocates of trade barriers in the U.S. sugar industry argue that other countries protect their own sugar industries far more than does the United States. In some cases that is true, but it is a very weak excuse for keeping foreign sugar out of the U.S. market. Lowering trade barriers in the U.S. sugar industry, even unilaterally, is a favor that we can bestow upon ourselves.

Yet the sugar program endures. The U.S. House of Representatives, in February 1996, came within five votes of abolishing the U.S. sugar program; five years later, on October 4, 2001, the House could only muster 177 votes for a modest amendment to cut the sugar loan rate by 1 cent per pound. The U.S. sugar program is a failure by every measure except its political support in Congress.

Sugar Policy in the United States

The United States is the world's fourth largest producer of sugar (behind Brazil, India, and China) and the fourth largest importer.[1] Since 1981 the U.S. government has operated a price support program for sugar beet and sugar cane producers and processors. The ostensible goal is to maintain high prices by limiting imports. Unlike other agricultural sectors in the United States, there are no restrictions on domestic sugar production. There were cosmetic changes to sugar policy in the Federal Agriculture Improvement and Reform (FAIR) Act of 1996, but no substantive reforms were made.[2]

Historically, the United States produced about 55 percent of the sugar it consumed and imported 45 percent. Largely as a result of current U.S. sugar protections, today the United States produces 88 percent of domestic consumption and imports only 12 percent.[3]

The U.S. sugar program has two primary facets. The first is price support loans. Unlike other farm loan programs, the U.S. sugar program makes loans available to millers and processors, which are generally corporations or cooperatives, rather than directly to individual farmers. Under a system of "non-recourse" loans, processors agree to pay growers the government established minimum price based on loan rates for cane and beet sugar, pledging the sugar as collateral. When the loan matures, processors must decide whether to pay off the loan, plus interest, and sell the pledged sugar on the domestic market, or forfeit the sugar and keep the money paid to them by the U.S. government. If domestic sugar prices fall below the loan rate, sugar processors may forfeit up to 10 percent of their sugar to the U.S. government, with a 1-cent per pound penalty, rather than repay the loans.

Of course, if the U.S. sugar market were open to unrestricted imports, the artificially high domestic price would attract lower-priced imported sugar, driving down the domestic price and forcing the government to acquire huge amounts of sugar as processors decided to forfeit their sugar to the U.S. Department of Agriculture. To avoid that scenario, the U.S. government intervenes in the market a second time: through a system of tariff-rate quotas (TRQ).

Tariff-rate quotas for raw cane sugar are allocated on a country-by-country basis among 41 countries in total, while those for refined sugar are allocated on a global first-come, first-served basis. If demand for sugar outstrips supply in the United States, the USDA can alter the quota as needed. Although sugar can enter our market in excess of the TRQ, a prohibitive duty of close to 16 cents per pound is imposed.[4]

Government intervention is somewhat limited by international agreement. In accordance with the 1994 Uruguay Round Agreements (which established the WTO), the United States is committed to importing roughly 1.25 million tons of sugar annually. Similarly, under the North American Free Trade Agreement, the United States must accept an increasing amount of sugar imports from Mexico and grant Mexican producers full access to the U.S. sugar market by 2008.[5] Despite those mild constraints, the U.S. sugar program remains highly interventionist.

Who Pays the Price for Protectionism?

Documenting the exact cost of trade protectionism in any industry is no easy task, and the sugar industry is no exception. Virtually every governmental and nongovernmental survey, however, concludes that the U.S. sugar program results in a net loss of welfare for the U.S. economy, with U.S. consumers suffering the most.

A Huge Consumer Tax

Although there is some fluctuation in price, U.S. consumers over the past 20 or so years have typically paid roughly twice the world market price (Table 1). Currently, the number is higher, with U.S. consumers paying 22 cents a pound for sugar, while the world price (as of October 15, 2001) is just under 7 cents a pound.[6] World market prices will likely remain low as well in light of expanding production. Global sugar production has increased 22 percent in the last six years, with Brazil accounting for the largest gain.[7]

The U.S. General Accounting Office, which does not take a policy position in the debate, estimated in its latest analysis that the sugar program cost domestic sweetener users $1.9 billion in 1998. By "users" the GAO means sugar cane refiners, food manufacturers, and consumers.[8] Complementing the GAO report, the U.S. International Trade Commission concluded that abolishing the U.S. program would result in a net annual welfare gain to the U.S. economy of $986 million.[9]

Other studies have also found that significant economic costs are imposed by U.S. sugar protectionism. One study by the Australian Bureau of Agriculture and Resource Economics concluded that U.S. government support accounts for around 40 percent of American sugar producers' revenue. According to the ABARE study, if the United States unilaterally removed its trade barriers on sugar, U.S. consumers would save an estimated $1.6 billion a year, and the U.S. economy as a whole would gain an additional net $456 million per year.[10]

Regardless of the exact cost to U.S. sugar refiners, food manufacturers, and, most important, U.S. consumers, it is naive to think that there is not at least some cost imposed. The entire rationale underpinning trade protectionism is to raise domestic prices by limiting supply—in this case from overseas markets. Obviously, that cost is passed on to consumers and sugar-using producers. And although dismantling the U.S. sugar program may or may not lead directly to lower prices for consumers (evidence on this is mixed), the bulk of the data shows that it will slow price increases.[11] At a minimum, the U.S. sugar program results in a

U.S. and World Prices for Raw and Refined Sugar, 1985–98
(cents per pound)
Table 1

Year	U.S. Raw Cane Sugar[a]	U.S. Wholesale Refined Beet Sugar	U.S. Retail Refined Sugar	World Raw Sugar[b]	World Refined Sugar[c]
1985	20.34	23.18	35.34	4.04	6.79
1986	20.95	23.38	35.08	6.05	8.47
1987	21.83	23.60	35.28	6.71	8.75
1988	22.12	25.44	36.60	10.17	12.01
1989	22.81	29.06	40.03	12.79	17.16
1990	23.26	29.97	42.78	12.55	17.32
1991	21.57	25.65	42.80	9.04	13.41
1992	21.31	25.44	41.53	9.09	12.39
1993	21.62	25.15	40.54	10.03	12.79
1994	22.04	25.15	39.99	12.13	15.66
1995	22.96	25.83	39.83	13.44	17.99
1996	22.40	29.20	41.79	12.24	16.64
1997	21.96	27.09	43.26	12.06	14.33
1998	22.06	26.12	42.98	9.68	11.59

Source: Economic Research Service, USDA, Sugar and Sweetener Situation and Outlook (Washington: USDA September 1999); and the New York Coffee, Sugar, and Cocoa Exchange, as displayed in U.S. General Accounting Office, "Sugar Programs: Supporting Sugar Prices Has Increased Users' Costs While Benefiting Producers," June 2000, p. 14.

Note: U.S. and world prices are in nominal dollars.

[a] U.S. prices are based on futures contract prices for number 14 raw cane sugar on the New York Coffee, Sugar, and Cocoa Exchange.

[b] World prices are based on bulk spot contracts for number 11 raw cane sugar on the New York Coffee, Sugar, and Cocoa Exchange (free on board stowed Caribbean port, including Brazil). To compare the world and U.S. prices, 1.5 cents per pound needs to be added to the world price to account for the cost of transporting raw sugar from the Caribbean to New York.

[c] World prices are based on spot contracts for number 5 refined sugar, London daily price (free on board Europe).

---

misallocation of investment in the confection industry. It creates artificial distortions by forcing confectioners to allocate more money for one of their most important inputs. That makes the industry less profitable, hurting its shareholders and workers alike.

U.S. sugar consumers and sugar-consuming industries are not the only losers. Sugar producers in poor nations also pay a price for U.S. policy. Freeing just the U.S. sugar market would result in an increase in world prices of 17 percent, increasing the annual export earnings of developing nations by $1.5 billion.[12]

The "It Could Be Worse" Argument

Proponents of the status quo argue that U.S. sugar protections are justified in light of protectionism in other countries. It is true that sugar is one of the most highly protected commodities in the world. Nearly 40 percent of world production is highly subsidized, and over 90 percent of world sugar supplies are sold at prices above world spot market prices.[13] It is also true that U.S. retail sugar prices are lower by 20 and 50 percent than prices in Western Europe and Japan, respectively.[14]

It is disingenuous, though, to argue as some people do that this "saves" Americans $2 billion per year.[15] Proponents of sugar protectionism use sugar prices in Western Europe and Japan as benchmarks and argue that, since our sugar prices are lower, this constitutes a savings. That is ridiculous on its face. The benchmark should be the world market price. That Western Europe and Japan have even worse sugar programs in place than does the United States is a poor excuse for continuing to protect the U.S. market.

What the U.S. sugar industry does not want people to know is that a number of countries are expanding their sugar production capabilities at a relatively low cost with little to no subsidies. Countries such as Australia and Thailand have doubled their production and exports at the world market price.[16] The reason for their expanded production is relatively straightforward—comparative advantage stemming from favorable climatic conditions and lower labor costs.

Jobs Lost and Jobs Gained

Proponents of the U.S. sugar program advance the specious argument that reform of the program would jeopardize 420,000 American jobs, but that number is wildly exaggerated.[17] According to the USITC, only about 16,400 American workers were employed in raw cane sugar, beet sugar, and cane sugar refining in 1996.[18] Of those workers, fewer than 3,000 would lose their jobs if quotas were repealed—a miniscule number in an economy of 140 million workers. The USITC model also predicts that an equal number of jobs would be created in other sectors of the economy that would benefit from lower sugar prices.[19]

Most of the jobs supposedly jeopardized by opening the sugar market are not involved in producing sugar at all, but in producing other sweeteners. Of the 420,000 figure cited by defenders of the sugar program, 250,000 are employed in corn sweetener production in the Midwestern farm belt.[20] Corn growers benefit from the U.S. sugar program because inflated sugar prices create an artificial incentive for confectioners, soft drink

makers, and the like to switch to corn syrup, which serves as a substitute for sugar.[21] But the 250,000 figure contrasts with some 520,000 workers in the food processing industry who would benefit from repeal of sugar protectionism. Cities such as Chicago, which have a large number of confection industries, are feeling the pinch, prompting Chicago's mayor, Richard M. Daley, to release a statement condemning U.S. sugar policy.[22] Daley noted that the confection industry had lost 11 percent of its Chicago-based jobs since 1991 and that, "the continuation of domestic sugar price supports . . . is a key reason these companies [confectioners] are considering leaving Chicago and relocating their facilities outside of U.S. borders."[23] The U.S. sugar program is protecting jobs in the sugar and related industries only by destroying jobs in sugar-using industries.

The Cost to Taxpayers and the Environment

The cost of the sugar program is more than higher prices at the grocery store. An artificially induced oversupply of domestic sugar has forced the U.S. government to store sugar or in some cases to have sugar fields plowed under. Because of new technologies, preferential government policies, and favorable weather conditions for much of the 1990s through the present, production of U.S. sugar has surged ahead of demand. In the late 1990s production increased, on average, 6 percent per year, while demand grew at less than 2 percent per year.[24] In 1999 a record 8.5 million tons of sugar were produced, pushing domestic prices to their lowest levels in 20 years (although they remain far above the world price). Oversupply problems have continued into 2001 (Figure 1).

In response to this oversupply averaging 1 million tons per year, USDA took two further steps in 2000 to boost U.S. prices. First, it bought a record amount of sugar in May 2000 and stuck it in a warehouse at the cost of $1.4 million a month.[25] Originally, USDA planned to allow the stockpiled sugar to be sold for processing into ethanol, but the agency was forced to retreat on that policy

U.S. Sugar Production (in millions of short tons), Fiscal Years 1990–2000
Figure 1

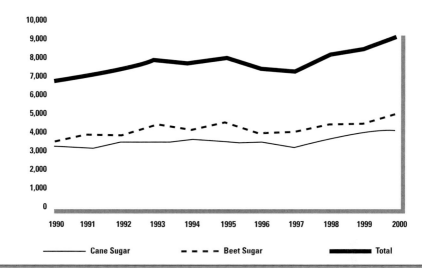

when ethanol producers argued that they would be adversely affected.

Second, in August 2000, USDA actually paid sugar growers to plow under some of their sugar beet crop in order to reduce output. Neither action succeeded in raising prices sufficiently high to allow producers to pay back all of their loans. Consequently, USDA had to pay out significant sums for the sugar program for the first time since 1986.[26] These payouts are likely to continue given estimates of future production trends. USDA estimates the program will cost the government an additional $2 billion over the next 10 years.[27] Currently, roughly 9 percent of the 1999-2000 domestic crop (some 793,000 tons) is sitting in warehouses, paid for by the U.S. government, or more to the point, U.S. taxpayers.[28]

The U.S. sugar program also affects the environment by encouraging sugar production in such ecologically sensitive places as the Florida Everglades. In 2000 Congress passed a $7.8 billion Everglades restoration package in an attempt to reverse the damage caused in large part by sugar farming. Sugar production in southern Florida has disturbed the fragile Everglades ecosystem by disrupting water flow and dumping pol-

lutants such as phosphorus into the waterways.[29] Attempts to shift from sugar to other crops have failed because of the guaranteed high price for sugar. It is contradictory, to say the least, for the U.S. government to establish a fund to protect the Everglades and at the same time encourage the region's destruction through the U.S. sugar program.

Undermining Free Trade Worldwide

In a host of sectors, the United States has lowered trade barriers unilaterally, regardless of the actions of other countries. In terms of multilateral liberalization, the United States has been the principal architect of the global trading system in the post-World War II era, first with the General Agreement on Tariffs and Trade and then with the WTO since 1995. That system, based on the principles of free trade, has strengthened the world economy by encouraging nations to realize the productivity gains to be had from international trade.

Most countries protect at least some sectors of their economy from foreign competition, and the United States is no exception.

Traditionally, agriculture has been one of the most highly subsidized and regulated sectors in the U.S. economy. The 1996 farm bill mentioned earlier was an important step forward in reducing government interference in the farm sector. While there was some backsliding, the United States has done a better job in opening its farm sector to global competition than have Europe and Japan.[30]

Despite agricultural subsidies and barriers overseas, the U.S. agricultural sector remains competitive in global export markets. According to USDA, during the first half of fiscal year 2001 agricultural exports increased almost $2 billion more than in the same period the previous year.[31] Forecasts for the next 10 years support continued growth as well.[32] That other agricultural sectors have competed effectively both domestically and on global markets, even with barriers overseas, undermines the argument of the U.S. sugar industry that U.S. government protections are necessary to create a "level playing field."

A more disturbing consequence of the U.S. sugar program is its impact on advancing the broader U.S. free trade agenda. Other countries routinely point out the hypocrisy of the U.S. sugar policy. The United States is engaged in a series of negotiations aimed at lowering trade barriers in sectors in which the United States is highly competitive, notably services and knowledge-based industries. Countries that are less competitive in such sectors (and maintain monopolies in many cases) argue that the United States protects its own "sensitive" industries as well. It is not uncommon to hear criticisms, such as those leveled by Australian ambassador Michael Thawley, that the United States "talks out of both sides of its mouth" with regard to agriculture policy.[33]

U.S. policymakers agree, commenting that the sugar program is "the Achilles heel of U.S. trade policy" and that it "stands as one of the principal impediments to our hopes for continuing agricultural trade liberalization."[34] Even U.S. trade representative Charlene Barshefsky remarked that the United States will have to tackle some of its own "Achilles' heels, such as textiles and sugar,"[35] if it is serious about new trade talks.

For decades now the United States has been the leader in building a multilateral trading system based on the principles of free trade. The U.S. sugar program is a mockery of those principles. By undermining America's broader agenda of trade expansion, sugar quotas have reduced the chance of successfully negotiating bilateral agreements with such trading partners as Australia, or an FTAA, or a new agreement with other members of the WTO. Unilaterally dismantling our sugar program and protections would put the United States in a much more powerful position to advance the free-trade agenda that has served our economic interests so well.

Resistance to Change

In light of the overwhelming evidence that the U.S. sugar program creates serious economic distortions and hurts U.S. consumers, it seems reasonable to ask: Why does the U.S. government continue to support such a bad policy? Despite the obvious flaws of the U.S. sugar program, substantial obstacles stand in the way of its removal—notably, the powerful and well-funded sugar lobby.

The U.S. sugar program is a classic case of concentrated benefits and diffused costs. Put differently, a very small number of sugar growers receive enormous benefits, while the costs of providing those benefits are spread across the U.S. economy, specifically, to consumers and confectioners. Consequently, U.S. sugar producers have a very strong incentive to lobby and fund campaigns of U.S. policymakers. And they have done so.

Dominated largely by two companies in Florida (Flo-Sun and U.S. Sugar), the sugar lobby has been a major financial contributor to incumbent politicians. In the 2000 election cycle, for example, Flo-Sun contributed $690,750 in "soft money" contributions to both the Democrats and the Republicans and $78,200 in direct funds to candidates and the parties.[36] By the time the committees began to consider the 1996 farm bill, the campaigns of 49 members of the House Agriculture Committee had received an average of $16,000 apiece in sugar campaign money in the preceding five years. Much of that money came from Florida's two big growers.[37] Overall, the U.S. sugar industry contributed $7.2 million to political action committees and $5.7 million in soft money donations, for a total of $13.0 million.[38]

That is not an argument to further control lobbying or political speech through restrictions on campaign finance. Sugar producers have a right to lobby the government to protect what they perceive to be their interests. But elected officials have an offsetting duty to protect the public interest and the principles of limited, constitutional government against those who would disregard them in pursuit of their own private gain. Standing up to the sugar lobby will require more vigorous leadership from the president and many members of Congress who represent far more people who suffer from the U.S. sugar program than who benefit. It will also require journalists to shine a light on this program because "sunshine is the best disinfectant." It is simply bad policy to force the mass of U.S. consumers to pay higher prices at the grocery store to make a small number of sugar farmers richer.

Conclusion

In many sectors the United States has championed free trade by unilaterally dismantling its own barriers and standing as a strong advocate for change at the multilateral level. In the sugar sector, however, it has not, and the payoff for sugar companies has been huge. As one consumer group representative noted, "Sugar is the only major agriculture program that hasn't taken a hit."[39]

It is true that the U.S. sugar program is not the world's most egregious, but it ranks within the top three (behind those of the European Union and Japan).[40] That other countries' policies are worse, however, is a poor excuse for saddling our consumers with higher food costs. And, given the upward trend in global sugar production, those costs are only going to rise.

On its face, the U.S. sugar program is an easy target for ridicule. The U.S. government protects the domestic sugar market from foreign competition, and it is now paying farmers to not grow sugar and is buying sugar only to store it indefinitely in a warehouse. Of course, it is not the U.S. government that is ultimately picking up the tab but U.S. consumers and taxpayers. These expenditures will only rise given future production trends—and it is American families that will pay. And by compromising America's free-trade leadership, the sugar program stands as a barrier to market access abroad for U.S. exports.

U.S. sugar policy does not serve the national interest. It benefits a small group of sugar producers at the expense of American families, sugar-using industries and their workers, and a broad swath of U.S. exporters. It is time for our rhetoric on free trade to be reflected in all of our policies, even those dominated by powerful lobbies.

Notes

1 American Sugar Alliance, "Sugar Policy," 2001, www.sugaralliance.org/sugarpolicy/index.htm.

2 Specifically, the authority of the secretary of agriculture to impose domestic marketing allotments, which would allow more domestic production if imports fell below 1.5 million tons, was repealed. The agreement terminates marketing allotments and implements a 1-cent penalty on forfeited sugar. In the past, the secretary could assign allotments whereby U.S. farmers would make up the shortfall. See Mel Skold, Agriculture and Business Notes, *The Federal Agriculture Improvement and Reform Act of 1996: Title by Title—Summary of Major Provisions of the Conference Agreement*, September 21, 2001, www.colostate.edu/Depts/CoopExt/NWR/ABM/abm.htm.

3 Remy Jurenas, "IB95117: Sugar Policy Issues," Congressional Research Service Issue Brief for Congress, April 13, 2001, www.cnie.org/nle/ag-27.html.

4 Coalition for Sugar Reform, "How the Government's Sugar Program Works," July 2001, www.sugar-reform.org/myths.htm.

5 Andrea Mandel-Campbell, "Debt Mountain Threatens Mexican Sugar," *Financial Times*, June 28, 2001, www.ft.com.

6 The world market price for raw cane sugar is published daily in the *Wall Street Journal*. See, for example, "Cash Prices: Food," *Wall Street Journal*, October 15, 2001, p. C11.

[7] International Trade Data System, *Sugar Industry,* July 3, 2001, www.itds.treas.gov/Sugar_Industry.html.

[8] U.S. General Accounting Office, "Sugar Program: Supporting Sugar Prices Has Increased Users' Costs While Benefiting Producers," GAO/RCED-00-126, June 2000, p. 5. Despite the fact that the study was peer reviewed by leading academics and submitted for prior review to USDA, the GAO study was criticized sharply by both USDA and the American Sugar Alliance, which represents sugar cane and sugar beet growers. Those criticisms and responses are reprinted in the final report.

[9] U.S. International Trade Commission, "The Economic Effects of Significant U.S. Import Restraints: Second Update," Investigation no. 332–325, publication 3201, May 1999, p. 65.

[10] Terry Sheales et al., "Sugar: International Policies Affecting Market Expansion," Australian Bureau of Resource and Agricultural Economics Research Report 99.14, 1999, p. 3.

[11] In 1990 and 1994, for example, when raw sugar prices declined 6 percent, retail sugar prices also declined 6 percent. Other years do not show decreases, but increases have not taken place either. (See Coalition for Sugar Reform.) That a decrease in raw sugar prices does not directly translate into a decline in retail prices for such items as candies or sodas is not surprising. Consumers are unlikely to switch brands of sugar over relatively small price differences, but the data suggest lower input prices do give an incentive to processors and refiners of sugar not to raise prices.

[12] Sheales et al., p. 2.

[13] Brent Borell and David Pearce, "Sugar: The Taste Test of Liberalisation," Center for International Economics Report, 1999, p. 3.

[14] Ibid., p. 4.

[15] See Rep. Patsy T. Mink (D-Hawaii), Testimony before the Senate Agriculture Committee, 106th Cong., 2d sess., July 31, 2000, www.house.gove/apps/list/press/hi02_ming/sugar73100.html.

[16] Borrell and Pearce, p. 6.

[17] Coalition for Sugar Reform, "Myths vs. Reality," July 2001, www.sugar reform.org/myths.htm.

[18] USITC, p. 60.

[19] Ibid., pp. 66–67.

[20] Larry Lipman, "New Battle Is Brewing over U.S. Sugar Program," Cox Washington Bureau, June 17, 2001, www.coxnews.com/washingtonbureau/staff/lipman/061701SUGAR17.html.

[21] Kelly Whitman, "Who's Your Sugar Daddy?" *Dismal Scientist,* June 2, 2000.

[22] Dave Carpenter, "Sweet-Talking Mayor Bitter over Sugar," *Oregonian,* June 6, 2001, p. C3.

[23] Quoted in Lipman.

[24] Ira S. Shapiro, Coalition for Sugar Reform, Testimony before the Senate Committee on Agriculture, 106th Cong., 2d sess., July 26, 2000.

[25] David Barboza, "Free Trade Frontier: U.S. Sugar Policy," *International Herald Tribune,* May 7, 2001, p. 11.

[26] Jurenas.

[27] Lipman.

[28] Jurenas.

[29] Green Scissors, *A Sweet Deal: Sugar Program,* 2000, www.greenscissors.org/agriculture/sugar.htm.

[30] Brink Lindsey et al., "Seattle and Beyond: A WTO Agenda for the New Millennium," Cato Institute Trade Policy Analysis no. 8, November 4, 1999, p. 11.

[31] USDA, "U.S. Ag Trade Surplus up Significantly During First Half of FY 2001," News Release No. 0119.01, www.usda.gov/news/releases/2001/07/0119.htm.

[32] Economic Research Service, USDA, Baseline Projections, February 2001, www.ers.usda.gov/briefing/baseline/.

[33] Quoted in Evelyn Iritani, "Payback Time As Countries Protest U.S. Trade Policies," *Los Angeles Times,* January 25, 2001, www.wtowatch.org.

[34] Shapiro. See also, David Barboza, "Sugar Rules Defy Free-Trade Logic," *New York Times,* May 7, 2001, p. 28A.

[35] Quoted in Iritani.

[36] Lipman.

[37] PBS Online Newshour, "Sugar Daddy," *Money Trail,* March 25, 1997, www.pbs.org/newshour/bb/congress/march97/sugar_3-25.html.

[38] Common Cause, "The $1 Billion PB&J Sandwich," *Pocketbook Politics: How Special-Interest Money Hurts the American Consumer,* 1998, www.commoncause.org/publications/pocketbook5.htm.

[39] Center for Responsive Politics, "White Gold: The Politics of Sugar," 1998, www.opensecrets.org/pubs/cashingin_sugar/sugar01.html.

[40] Borell and Pearce, p. 3.

Using Sanctions to Fight Terrorism

5

G ARY C LYDE **H UFBAUER**
J EFFERY J. **S CHOTT**
B ARBARA **O EGG**

Introduction

Following the September 11 attacks on the World Trade Center and Pentagon, President Bush prepared the country for a "war on terrorism." As outlined in his speech before the joint session of Congress on September 20, the war on terrorism will be fought on many fronts: diplomatic, intelligence, covert action, economic sanctions, law enforcement as well as military. Diplomacy, intelligence, covert action, and economic sanctions have historically served as auxiliary measures in wartime. Economic sanctions, in particular, have routinely foreshadowed or accompanied broader war efforts.

What sets the campaign against international terrorism apart from other wars is the emphasis on economic tools. Several senior US officials, including Secretary of Defense Donald Rumsfeld, have suggested that economic and financial efforts will be as important in winning the war on terrorism as the military campaign. Determined to bring US economic as well as military power to bear in the fight against terrorism, the Bush administration has deployed a variety of economic tools such as preferential trade measures, the removal of existing sanctions coupled with loans to reward allies, and new sanctions to intimidate adversaries. In this war, sanctions policy is being used both as a stick and a carrot, which is a new and welcome twist.

That said, the history of economic sanctions in the past century reveals very few instances where economic weapons achieved major foreign policy goals.[1] Striking terror is the raison d'être of terrorist groups. To eliminate these groups, or persuade them to abandon their objective, would rank as a major policy triumph. The history of economic sanctions amply demonstrates that only military force and covert action can play a decisive role in a battle of this magnitude. At best, economic sanctions can play only a supporting role with respect to terrorist groups.

While economic sanctions alone may not dissuade terrorist groups, they may cause states that harbor and support terrorist groups to reconsider the extent of their support. The Libyan extradition of the two Pan Am suspects illustrates an important shift in state policy induced in part by economic sanctions.

One of the first measures implemented by President Bush in the war on terrorism was aimed at disrupting terrorist finances. On September 23, he issued an executive order freezing the assets of named terrorists, terrorist groups, and terrorist fundraising organizations in an effort to weaken the financial lifeline of the al Qaeda network.[2] To coordinate the activities of the various US agencies on the financial front, the administration created the Foreign Terrorist Asset Tracking Center in the Treasury Department.

These measures carry on the tradition of past US counterterrorism efforts. Indeed, US counterterrorism policy, dating back to the early 1970s, has been heavily sanctions oriented. US counterterrorism sanctions policy rests on two primary legislative tools— the designation of state sponsors of terrorism and Foreign Terrorist Organizations (FTOs), and the presidential determination of Specially Designated Terrorists (SDTs).

State Sponsors

In the 1970s and 1980s, US counterterrorism policy primarily focused on state sponsorship of international terrorism. State sponsors of terrorism are countries designated by the Secretary of State under Section 6 (j) of the Export Administration Act of 1979 as countries that have "repeatedly provided state support for acts of international terrorism." Currently the list of state sponsors includes seven countries: Cuba, Iran, Iraq, Libya, North Korea, Sudan, and Syria.

Naming a country on the terrorism list triggers a series of economic sanctions under different US laws. These sanctions include:

- restrictions on export licenses (or a general ban) for dual-use items or critical technology (under the Export Administration Act of 1979)
- ban on sales or licenses for items on the US Munitions Control List (under the Arms Export Control Act)
- ban on US foreign assistance including Export-Import Bank credits and guarantees (under the Foreign Assistance Act of 1961)
- authorization for the president to restrict or ban imports of goods and services from designated terrorist countries (under the International Security and Development Cooperation Act of 1985)
- prohibition of financial transactions by US persons with the governments of designated terrorist countries (under the Antiterrorism and Effective Death Penalty Act of 1996)

- requirement that US representatives at international financial institutions vote against loans or other financial assistance to that country (under the International Financial Institutions Act of 1977)
- ineligibility for the Generalized System of Preferences (GSP, under the Trade Act of 1974)

Although naming a country as a state sponsor does not automatically trigger a total economic embargo, with the exception of Syria, all countries currently designated as state sponsors—Cuba, Iran, Iraq, Libya, Sudan, and North Korea—are also subject to comprehensive trade and financial sanctions imposed by the executive branch under the International Emergency Economic Powers Act (IEEPA). In some of these cases—particularly Cuba and North Korea—US sanctions policy is less determined by concerns over terrorism than broad foreign policy conflicts.

Case Studies

Iran. Iran was added to the list of state sponsors of terrorism in 1984 in response to the alleged Iranian involvement in the bombing of the US Marine base in Lebanon. Export controls imposed following Iran's initial designation as state sponsor were tightened twice. In 1987, under pressure from Congress, President Reagan invoked Section 505 of the International Security and Development Act and banned all imports from Iran and prohibited exports of several potentially militarily useful goods. In 1992, Congress passed the Iran-Iraq Arms Non-Proliferation Act prohibiting the export of defense items, nuclear material, and certain dual-use goods under the Export Administration Act.

Concerned about nuclear proliferation and Iran's continued support for terrorist groups, President Clinton issued a series of executive orders beginning in 1995. These eventually banned all US trade, investment, and financial dealings with Iran. In addition,

US residents and companies are barred from financing, supervising, and managing oil development projects in Iran under the Iran-Libya Sanctions Act of 1996 (which was extended for 5 years in August 2001).

In 1999 and 2000, the Clinton administration lifted selected sanctions on Iran to signal support for reforms by moderate President Mohammad Khatami. In April 1999, the administration modified the trade ban to allow for the sale of food and medicine on a case-by-case basis, and a year later the administration lifted the ban on certain nonoil imports such as carpets, caviar, pistachios, and dried fruit.

However, according to the State Department's annual report on "Patterns of Global Terrorism 2000" (hereafter cited as Patterns 2000), Iran remained the "most active" state sponsor of international terrorism in 2000. In other words, two decades of US economic sanctions failed to reduce Iran's willingness to sponsor terrorism.

Iraq. Iraq was first placed on the terrorism list in December 1979 and removed in 1982. After Iraq's invasion of Kuwait in 1990, the State Department again placed Iraq on the terrorism list. Meanwhile, Iraq has been subject to the most comprehensive US and UN trade and financial sanctions regime mounted since the Second World War. US and UN sanctions probably curbed Iraq's ability to instigate very high-tech terror, such as suitcase nuclear weapons and sophisticated biological weapons, by reducing resources available to Saddam Hussein. But Patterns 2000 reports that Iraq continues to plan and sponsor international terrorism focused on Iraqi dissident groups abroad and continues to offer safe haven to various expatriate terrorist groups such as the Palestine Liberation Front and the Abu Nidal organization. Furthermore, post-September 11 investigations revealed Iraqi contacts with one of the lead hijackers (Mohammed Atta) and possible links between Iraq and anthrax. These offenses, together with US-Iraq differences over Iraq's regional ambitions and its record of non-compliance with UN weapons inspectors,

will probably keep Iraq on the terrorism list for the foreseeable future.

Libya. Libya has a long history of sponsoring international terrorism and was placed on the first terrorism list in December 1979. Export controls were followed by a ban on crude oil imports from Libya, restrictions on exports of sophisticated oil and gas equipment and technology, and later a ban on imports of refined oil products. In response to Libyan involvement in the terrorist attacks on airports in Rome and Vienna, President Reagan invoked IEEPA to implement comprehensive trade and financial controls in 1986. The Reagan administration barred most exports and imports of goods, services, and technology, prohibited all loans or credits to the Libyan government, and froze Libyan government assets in US banks.

Following the bombings of Pan Am flight 103 in December 1988 and France UTA flight 772 in September 1989, US policy toward Libya was dominated by efforts to extradite two Libyan intelligence agents accused of the Pan Am bombing. Libyan intransigence in the face of extradition demands led to greater multilateral cooperation. In 1992, the UN Security Council imposed an arms embargo on Libya and prohibited all travel to and from Libya. A year later, the United Nations banned the sale of petroleum equipment to Libya and froze all nonpetroleum-related Libyan government assets abroad.

According to Patterns 2000, Libyan terrorism was sharply reduced after the imposition of UN sanctions. Pressure from the international community was credited as a deterrent to Libyan sponsorship. Mandatory UN sanctions, the first to be imposed in response to government involvement in an act of terrorism, ultimately secured the extradition of the two Libyan Pan Am suspects in April 1999. This led to the suspension of UN sanctions. The suspects were subsequently tried and one was convicted and imprisoned for life, but conviction and punishment were not conditions for lifting UN sanctions.

In continued efforts to improve its international standing, Libya not only expelled the radical Palestinian terrorist group Abu Nidal but also compensated the victims of the France UTA flight. Libya also accepted "general responsibility" for the 1984 shooting of a policewoman outside the Libyan embassy in London and agreed to compensate her family. While Libya has made progress toward meeting US demands, the Bush administration insists that US unilateral sanctions will remain in place until Libya accepts responsibility for the Pan Am bombing, compensates the victims, and renounces all support for terrorism.

The success of UN sanctions in the case of Libya suggests that economic sanctions, if imposed multilaterally, can achieve clearly defined and relatively modest policy goals, illustrated by the extradition of the two mid-level Pan Am suspects.

Syria. Like Libya, Syria has been on the terrorism list since its inception in December 1979. Although subject to strict export controls and other economic restrictions due to its position on the terrorism list, most US trade and investment with Syria is allowed. Despite its designation as a state sponsor, Syria enjoys comparatively normal relations with the United States. According to State Department sources, there is no evidence of direct Syrian involvement in or support for terrorist actions since 1986. However, Syria continues to support and provide safe haven to Hezbollah and Hamas, among other Palestinian terrorist groups.

Sudan. According to Patterns 2000, Sudan signaled its willingness to cooperate with international counterterrorism efforts shortly after the State Department added Sudan to the list of state sponsors in August 1993. In 1994, Sudan extradited "Carlos the Jackal" to France. Under US pressure, Sudan also expelled Osama bin Laden in 1996. Nevertheless, the United States imposed comprehensive sanctions on Sudan because of the persecution of Christians in southern Sudan. Preempting congressional action, President Clinton issued Executive Order 13067 in November 1997, blocking all property of the Sudanese government in the United States, imposing a trade embargo, and prohibiting any transactions with Sudan.[3]

By the end of 2000, Sudan had signed all 12 international conventions for combating terrorism and taken several other positive steps. However, Sudan has yet to comply with three UN Security Council Resolutions passed in 1996. These resolutions demand the extradition of three suspects in the assassination attempt on Egyptian President Hosni Mubarak in 1995 and ask that Sudan end all support to terrorists. The resolutions impose limited travel and diplomatic sanctions, and (in theory only) restrict international flights in and out of Sudan.

Cuba. Cuba, which has been under comprehensive US sanctions since 1960, was added to the list of state sponsors in 1982, primarily because of its support for the M-19 guerrilla organization in Colombia. Although the Castro regime was very active in providing arms and training to leftist terrorist organizations during the Cold War, Cuba is no longer active in supporting armed struggles around the world. Cuba, however, remains on the terrorist list because it continues to provide safe haven to individual terrorists and maintains ties to Latin American insurgents.

North Korea Similar to Cuba, North Korea has been subject to comprehensive US sanctions for several decades (indeed since the Korean War). North Korea was added to the list of countries sponsoring terrorism because of its implication in the bombing of a South Korean airline in November 1987. Although North Korea has on several occasions publicly condemned all forms of terrorism, it remains on the state sponsor list because it continues to provide refuge to international terrorists.

Afghanistan. The State Department characterized Afghanistan in 1999 as "the primary safe haven for terrorists." But the country was never designated as a state sponsor of terrorism because of the State

Department's concern that this determination would constitute a de facto recognition of the Taliban as the legitimate government of Afghanistan. However, the Antiterrorism and Effective Death Penalty Act of 1996 created a new designation category—noncooperation. Section 330 prohibits sale of arms to any country the president determines and certifies is not cooperating fully with US antiterrorism efforts. In May 1997, the Clinton administration certified Afghanistan for the first time as not cooperating with US antiterrorism efforts. Apart from the seven state sponsors, Afghanistan is the only country currently certified as not fully cooperating with US antiterrorism efforts.[4]

Because Islamic fundamentalist terrorists continued to train and operate out of Afghanistan, and more specifically because the Taliban continued to harbor Osama bin Laden and his terrorist networks that were believed to be responsible for bombing two US embassies in Africa, the Clinton administration imposed comprehensive sanctions on the Taliban in 1999. The executive order banned all trade with the areas in Afghanistan under Taliban control, froze Taliban assets in the United States, and prohibited financial contributions to the Taliban by US persons.

The United Nations supported US efforts, imposed a flight ban, and froze overseas Taliban assets. A year later, the United Nations also imposed an arms embargo and ordered the freeze of the assets of bin Laden and his associates.

Somalia. Although Somalia is not listed as a state sponsor of terrorism, the Bush administration is concerned about terrorist centers in Somalia and regards the country as a likely alternative safe haven for Osama bin Laden and his associates—if they leave Afghanistan. Somalia has been without a central government since its last president Mohamed Siad Barre fled the country in 1991 and interfactional fighting then led to national disintegration. The United Nations intervened in 1992 and imposed a weakly enforced arms embargo. The United States

closed its embassy and ended its participation in the UN mission in Somalia in 1994. According to US intelligence reports Somalia has served as a regional base for operations of al Qaeda since 1993, when Osama bin Laden first provided assistance to warlord Mohamed Aideed. (Aideed's forces killed 18 US soldiers serving in a UN peacekeeping mission.) Al Qaeda also maintains close ties with the radical Somali Islamic group al-Itahaad.

Summary of State Sponsors

This brief review of US policy toward state sponsors of terrorism suggests that unilateral US sanctions, by themselves, have not deterred countries from engaging in terrorist activities. Despite several decades of economic sanctions, the majority of designated state sponsors have continued to shelter and harbor international terrorists and terrorist groups in their territories. According to the annual reports, sanctions contributed to the negotiated compromise that led to the extradition and subsequent trial of the suspects in the bombing of the Pan Am flight. Multilateral economic sanctions also succeeded in convincing Sudan to cooperate with US terrorism efforts. These are the only two terrorism-related cases where the United States succeeded in garnering multilateral support for economic sanctions.

Modest success in these two cases corresponds with general trends we have observed. In a survey of about 180 cases of economic sanctions imposed after the Second World War, we found that the success rate of US unilateral sanctions has sharply declined over the last several decades. Between 1960 and 1970 the success rate of unilateral US sanctions dropped from 62 percent to a mere 17 percent. Low success rates for unilateral sanctions continued in the 1980s and 1990s. Meanwhile, the success rate of all US sanctions cases where the United States was part of a sanctions coalition remained in the 25 percent range over the period from the 1970s to 1990s.

The US approach in dealing with state sponsors has differed from the approach favored by its allies. While the European Union believes in "constructive engagement" with countries such as Iran, the United States is inclined to isolate and punish these countries. Frustrated by the lack of international cooperation, the US Congress sought to extend the reach of unilateral US measures by imposing secondary sanctions on firms located in third countries. In 1996, Congress passed the Helms-Burton Act targeting foreign companies that invest in Cuba, and a few months later, Congress passed the Iran-Libya Sanctions Act (ILSA) seeking to prevent European companies from investing in the oil sector in Iran and Libya. The extraterritorial scope of these measures irritated key US allies, but Presidents Clinton and Bush have waived key provisions of each bill to avoid imposing sanctions against allied industrial nations. As a result, these US laws only block activities by US firms.

Other secondary measures imposed in the 1990s include an amendment to the Foreign Assistance Act of 1961 that prohibits selected US government foreign assistance to any country that provides economic assistance or lethal military assistance to the designated terrorist countries, and the Iran Non-Proliferation Act of 2000, which allows for the imposition of economic sanctions to entities in third countries that contribute to Iranian weapons proliferation. The threat of secondary sanctions in these instances did not lead to greater international cooperation with US counterterrorism policies.

Historically, most major acts of terrorism against American citizens and other targets abroad were supported and, in some cases, instigated by state sponsors. Accordingly, US policy in the 1970s and 1980s focused on state sponsors and the groups they support. However, in the last decade, as the State Department has indicated in its annual reports, signs point to declining state sponsorship of terrorist activities and a rising threat posed by independent terrorist networks such as Osama bin Laden's al Qaeda network. In response to these new threats, US counterterrorism initiatives were expanded to incorporate restrictions on foreign terrorist groups and individuals.

Foreign Terrorist Organizations and Specially Designated Terrorists

In 1995, President Clinton issued an executive order that prohibits transfers of funds, goods, and services to any individual or organization that threatens to disrupt the Middle East peace process.[5] The order also blocked all property and interests in property of persons designated by the Secretary of Treasury, in coordination with the Secretary of State and the Attorney General, as opposing the Middle East peace process ("Specially Designated Terrorist"). The "Specially Designated Terrorist" (SDT) label, and the associated freeze of US-held assets, also included persons and entities designated to "be owned or controlled by, or to act for or on behalf of" any Specially Designated Terrorist.

The central legislative initiative with respect to US counterterrorism policy in the 1990s is the Antiterrorism and Effective Death Penalty Act of 1996. This Act provides for the designation of "Foreign Terrorist Organizations" (FTOs) by the Secretary of State, a designation equivalent to the state sponsor designation. The Act also included provisions aimed at disrupting financial flows to FTOs: Section 303 makes it a crime for US residents to knowingly provide material support or resources to a designated FTO. In addition, financial institutions are required to block funds in "which a foreign terrorist organization, or its agent, has an interest"[6] and report the existence of these funds to the Treasury. The Treasury may require US financial institutions to freeze assets of a designated FTO.

The provision of the Act that received great publicity was the so-called "Farrakhan Amendment." In its broadest interpretation, the Amendment prohibits financial transactions by US persons with the governments of designated terrorist countries. The administration, in issuing the regulations, chose to interpret the provision more narrowly—restricting donations or transactions when a US person has reason to believe it will be used to support terrorist acts in the United States. The 1990s saw the emergence of Osama bin Laden and the al Qaeda network on the international scene. After the United States successfully pressured Sudan into expelling Osama bin Laden in 1996, bin Laden found refuge in Afghanistan. From there, he is believed to have masterminded the bombing of US embassies in Nairobi and Dar es Salaam in 1998, and the suicide attack on the USS Cole in October 2000. In response to the embassy attacks, President Clinton issued Executive Order 13099 on 21 August 1998 determining that Osama bin Laden and his al Qaeda network constitute a threat to the Middle East peace process, thereby adding them to the list of SDTs and FTOs. The order banned US financial transactions with bin Laden's organization and allowed US law enforcement to freeze any bin Laden assets in the United States that can be identified. However, prior to September 11, the US Treasury was unable to link any assets in the United States firmly to bin Laden or his terrorist network.

Despite the substantial experience of the US Treasury Department Office of Foreign Assets Control (OFAC) in administering financial sanctions, its pre-September 11 efforts to stop the money flow to terrorist organizations were not particularly successful. The 2000 Treasury Department annual report on terrorist assets reveals that only $301,146 in assets of designated Foreign Terrorist Organizations or Specially Designated Terrorists in the United States were frozen. A major challenge for an asset freeze program is to identify funds belonging to the individuals, governments, and organizations targeted. Although the means of tracking financial assets have greatly improved, so have the means of deception. Even when individual funds can be identified, secrecy and speed are critical in preventing targets from moving assets to numbered accounts in offshore banking centers. Unfortunately, secrecy and speed are not easily reconciled with the need to coordinate efforts with allies or within the UN Security Council.[7] The importance of improved cooperation is illustrated by recent press reports that UN, US, and EU lists of targeted individuals and organizations associated with the Taliban and Osama bin Laden do not match up.

Post-September 11 Initiatives

Following the attack on September 11, law enforcement focused sharply on the financial trails of terrorist networks. Declaring a national emergency with respect to acts of terrorism, President Bush used his power under the IEEPA on 23 September 2001 to broaden existing authorities in several ways. First, the new executive order expanded the coverage of past executive orders from terrorism in the Middle East to global terrorism. Second, it expanded the class of targeted groups to include all those who are "associated with" designated terrorist groups. Third, it established the ability to block US assets, and deny access to US markets, of foreign banks that refuse to freeze terrorist assets.

Broadening the scope of current laws and regulations with respect to terrorist assets is crucial. Prior laws and regulations gave the government less authority to seize assets of terrorists than the assets of drug lords. The "Specially Designated Narcotics Traffickers" (SDNT) program administered by OFAC has been modestly successful precisely because its targets included those that provide material, technological, or financial assistance to designated narcotics traffickers. The White House reported on October 11 that about $40 million of assets linked to Taliban and al Qaeda have been frozen worldwide since September 11. Some press reports suggested that frozen terrorist assets are closer to $100 million. However, it is not clear if these estimates include assets belonging only to the al Qaeda network or to other terrorist groups as well. By 1999, the United

States had already frozen a reported $254 million of Taliban assets. These numbers suggest that inclusion of entities "associated with" terrorist groups may prove to be important for disrupting access to funding.

While no data is available on the amount of money frozen under OFAC's "Specially Designated Narcotics Traffickers" program, OFAC reports emphasize that since the inception of the program in 1995 more than 10 drug kingpins and about 568 other SDNTs have been identified. OFAC also reports that about 60 companies linked to drug traffickers have been liquidated or are in the process of liquidation. These companies had a combined net worth of about $45 million and combined annual income of about $230 million[8]—tiny amounts considering that estimates place the retail value of illicit drug trade between $300 billion and $500 billion annually.[9] Interpreting the seizure figures very generously, in the case of narcotics, asset freezes have disrupted less than 1 percent of the annual money flow. If the antiterrorist program is 10 times as successful, and disrupts 10 percent of terrorist funding, that unfortunately would leave 90 percent of terrorist money free to spread destruction and disease.

Another difficulty in freezing terrorist assets is that these groups may transfer money outside the banking system either in cash or through street-corner money exchange systems. Further, unlike drug traffickers who control legitimate businesses to launder illegal profits, in the case of terrorism money, legitimate businesses and charities may divert a part of their funds to support terrorist groups. Solid evidence that money is being diverted for terrorist activities is hard to come by. Also, the amounts involved in terrorist activities are much smaller than in drug trafficking and are therefore less likely to attract attention.

Following September 11, the administration worked closely with Congress on broad new antiterrorism legislation. The "USA Patriot Act" passed by Congress at the end of October 2001 strengthens the criminal laws against terrorism and expands the ability of US law enforcement and intelligence agencies to track and detain suspected terrorists. The act also includes several measures to disrupt money laundering and other methods of terrorist financing. The bill requires that foreign banks with corresponding accounts in US banks designate a point person to receive subpoenas related to these accounts. Furthermore, US banks are barred from doing business with banks that have no physical facility or operate outside the regulated banking system. The Treasury also has the authority to require banks to scrutinize deposits from residents of nations that do not cooperate with US officials. The bill also includes a provision that allows the Treasury to impose sanctions on banks that refuse to provide information to law enforcement agencies.

The threat of US sanctions sends an important message about the level of US commitment to foreign banks. Nevertheless, previous efforts to extend the force of US sanctions to third countries have always been contentious. Coordination of efforts within the G-7 and the United Nations Security Council may ultimately prove to be more successful in securing international cooperation than the threat of secondary economic sanctions.

Indeed, dramatically improved international cooperation with US efforts in the wake of September 11 may have made the biggest difference in terms of tracking down terrorist assets so far. According to an October 11 press release by the Treasury Department, 102 countries have committed themselves to joining the effort to disrupt terrorist assets, and 62 countries have already put blocking orders into effect. Terrorist assets frozen abroad include:[10]

• Germany: $3.7 million
• Bahamas: $20 million
• The Netherlands: $550,000
• United Kingdom: $88 million (including Taliban assets frozen prior to September 11)

Despite these early successes, formidable challenges remain. For one, terrorist activities are in most cases low-budget operations. Identifying and tracking accounts (especially small amounts) require a tremendous amount of intelligence and coordination. The new Foreign Terrorist Asset Tracking Center, which for the first time coordinates all intelligence sources and efforts with cooperating governments, together with the provisions of the US Patriot Act and increased international cooperation, may greatly improve the US ability to track terrorist finances and locate targeted accounts. To further increase the effectiveness of financial sanctions, other measures that might be considered include: (1) placing covert agents in banks in countries that do not cooperate with US law enforcement and reporting requirements; (2) more aggressive tracking of even modest money transfers ($20,000 or less) to immigrants living in the United States; and (3) the provision of large bounties to reward disclosure of terrorist funds.

In a Heritage Foundation Backgrounder, Brett Schaefer has argued that America's allies, as well as the International Monetary Fund and the World Bank, should stop providing grants and loans to all seven countries identified by the US State Department as sponsors of terror (Cuba, Iran, Iraq, Libya, North Korea, Sudan, and Syria). If the US government could accomplish this objective in a cooperative rather than confrontational manner with its allies, and in a way that allowed some of the state sponsors to "switch sides" in the war against terror, that would be a notable achievement. However, it would set the coalition back if the US government attempted to browbeat its allies and the international financial institutions into cutting off all their grants and loans in short order.

Appraisal

In the aftermath of September 11, the Bush administration took all the right initiatives in deploying economic sanctions. It used existing statutory powers to the fullest extent. It enlisted multilateral cooperation in freezing the assets of terrorist groups and their supporters. Notably, on November 18, all G-20 finance ministers (including Saudi Arabian and Indonesian) at US urging agreed to forceful financial measures against terrorist groups. Imaginatively, the Bush administration used the large reservoir of existing US sanctions to supply carrots for newly discovered allies-of-convenience. It worked diligently to speed other financial assistance for these same allies through the halls of the IMF, the World Bank, and similar institutions.

Even though the administration did everything right and with considerable flair, it would be illusory to expect that the arsenal of economic sanctions can play more than a modest role in the war against terrorism. There are several reasons to suggest that even the best-conceived measures will have limited effect.

• First, the history of sanctions against state sponsors shows a very modest record in achieving limited goals (Libya and Sudan are the only success cases and the achievements with those countries are modest).

• Second, the history of sanctions in the past decade records no instance of success against terrorist groups, such as Hezbollah, Hamas, Abu Nidal, or for that matter, al Qaeda. Since terrorism is their raison d'être, using sanctions to stop these groups amounts to seeking a major policy objective with economic tools. Economic sanctions have almost never succeeded in such cases.

• Third, in the financial war against drug lords, probably less than 1 percent of a vast ocean of cash has been captured by various asset freezes. Terrorist groups command a far smaller stream of resources than drug lords, and thus present a more elusive target. Even if the economic success rate against terrorists is 10 times as large, that would leave a substantial fraction of resources at their disposal.

To say that economic sanctions will play an auxiliary role to intelligence, covert action, and military strikes is not to denigrate their importance. In all of America's wars during the past century—the First and

Second World Wars, the Korean War, the Vietnam War, and the Gulf War—sanctions made worthy, if auxiliary, contributions. In the war against terrorism, asset freezes, and other sanctions will pinch. But we cannot count on economic sanctions to bring bin Laden and al Qaeda to heel. Nevertheless, the judicious combinations of sanctions and positive measures (including the selective waiver of existing sanctions) can help build support among the frontline states in the global war against terrorism.

Notes

[1] See Gary Clyde Hufbauer, Jeffrey J. Schott, Kimberly Ann Elliott, assisted by Barbara Oegg. Forthcoming. *Economic Sanctions Reconsidered*. 3rd edition. Washington: Institute for International Economics.

[2] For a detailed list of targeted entities, see New York Times, 25 September 2001, B4; *Washington Post*, 25 September 2001, A9.

[3] Although Congress passed the International Religious Persecution Act in 1998, no additional sanctions were imposed on Sudan. The State Department argued that existing measures meet the requirements of the Act.

[4] Afghanistan was certified for the first time under Section 40A of the Arms Export Control Act on 22 May 1997. In 1996, the State Department's Office of Defense Trade Controls amended the International Traffic in Arms Regulations to indicate that the United States will not issue licenses authorizing transactions involving Afghanistan.

[5] Executive Order 12947, 23 January 1995.

[6] Antiterrorism and Effective Death Penalty Act of 1996, Title III, Section 303, PL 104-132.

[7] See "First Interlaken Expert Seminar on Targeting UN Financial Sanctions" (March 17-19, 1998), at http://www.smartsanctions.ch/interlaken1.htm; and "Second Interlaken Seminar on Targeting UN Financial Sanctions" (March 29-31, 1999), at http://www.smart-sanctions.ch/interlaken2.htm

[8] R. Richard Newcomb, Testimony before the Senate Appropriations Committee, Subcommittee on Treasury and General Government, 10 May 2001.

[9] United Nations International Drug Control Program, Fact Sheet: Economic and Social Consequences of Drug Abuse and Illicit Trafficking, http://www. undcp.un.or.th/econ_soc. Note that the retail value of drugs intercepted at the US border ranged between $1 billion and $2 billion annually in the 1990s. See Statistical Abstract of the United States 2000, table 349. This figure is probably less than 1 percent of the retail value of annual flows across the US border.

[10] USIS, 11 October 2001; Financial Times, 3 October 2001, 4; *Financial Times*, 16 October 2001, 5; *Washington Post*, 2 October 2001, A12.

References

Hufbauer, Gary Clyde, Jeffrey J. Schott, Kimberly Ann Elliott, assisted by Barbara Oegg. Forthcoming. *Economic Sanctions Reconsidered*, 3rd edition. Washington: Institute for International Economics.

Katzman, Kenneth. 2001. *Terrorism: Near Eastern Groups and State Sponsors*, 2001. Congressional Research Service. Washington: Congressional Research Service, Library of Congress, September 10.

Perl, Raphael F. 2001. *Terrorism, the Future, and U.S. Foreign Policy.* Congressional Research Service. Washington: Congressional Research Service, Library of Congress, March 23.

Schaefer, Brett D. 2001. *Stop Subsidizing Terrorism*. Heritage Foundation Backgrounder No. 1485. Washington: Heritage Foundation, October 4.

US Department of State, Office of the Coordinator for Counterterrorism. 2000. Patterns of Global Terrorism 2000. Washington: Department of State.

US Department of State, Office of the Coordinator for Counterterrorism. 1999. Patterns of Global Terrorism 1999. Washington: Department of State.

Discussion Questions

I

1. In the estimates of the total welfare losses due to protectionism, why are the losses estimated for the US different from the estimates for global welfare loss?

2. Do you think that the losses Feenstra presents are significant?
   What other types of losses are left out of the analysis?

3. Why are US trade policies toughest on the poor?
   Who is Gresser talking about when he refers to the poor?

4. Can you make an argument that US trade policies also hurt the poor in the US?

5. What mistakes do Huffbauer and Goodrich think the Bush administration made in proposing to protect the steel industry?

6. One traditional argument for protecting an industry like steel is that steel is critical for national defense. Using what you have learned from Huffbauer and Goodrich, do you think failing to protect the US steel industry would harm the US defense? Why or why not?

7. What are legacy costs? Why are they important in dealing with the steel industry? Devise a non-protectionist national policy to deal with these costs.

8. If the US abandoned its sugar subsidies, what do you think would be the effect on the US sugar industry? Who would benefit and who would lose? Overall, what do you think would be the economic impact? What policy would you favor?

9. Have sanctions been an effective policy against terrorism?
   Can you think of other economic policies that might work?

WTO, Trade Labor, and the Environment

II

When the first edition of this reader came out in 1990 the World Trade Organization (WTO) had not yet been created and many of the issues of debate today were barely perceptible. With the (somewhat) successful completion of the Uruguay round in the 1990s, the focus of the WTO has shifted towards a number of new topics. In some cases, these issues are those, like agriculture, that festered in the Uruguay round for a lack of consensus. However, some issues that were less important in earlier rounds are now gaining increasing importance. This section attempts to identify each of the most important issues and delineate what the key issues and areas of contention are.

The first article, "The Doha Development Agenda," gives an overview of the main issues of concern in the upcoming round of WTO negotiations in Doha. As the article points out, agriculture, services, intellectual property rights and the environment are all key issues.

In "Bridging the Trade-Environment Divide," Daniel Esty presents a thorough overview of the issues involved in the debate between environmentalists and free-traders. One key issue is the environmental "Kuznets curve," an empirical generalization that poor countries pollute more when they first start to grow, and only reduce their pollution when they become high-income countries. To the extent that trade encourages economic growth, pollution rates could increase in the

short run. Another issue is "transboundary externalities" which encompass concerns such as fishing rights, global warming, and CFC pollution which affect more than one country. Finally, the author addresses the "race to the bottom issue"—a major concern of environmentalists—that poor countries will compete to host polluting industries by lowering their standards. While Esty rejects this hypothesis, he does believe that countries may act in a strategic fashion and create environmental policies which are not in the best interests of the planet.

A key issue in the upcoming Doha round and in the future of trade negotiations is labor standards. Proponents of stricter labor standards argue that it is unfair for companies like Nike to produce in low wage countries with sweat shop conditions and then sell these products in wealthy countries. These practices, they argue, promote unemployment in the US and other industrialized countries and do little to promote economic growth in developing countries. In "Labor Standards: Where Do They Belong on the International Trade Agenda?" Drusilla Brown examines the debate from both sides. She points out, as most economists do, that a one-size-fits-all labor standards policy will not work since wages and working hours are much longer in poor countries than in rich countries. However, she argues that some labor standards may benefit all, particularly child labor standards, since children who work many hours will have reduced educational opportunities. She also notes that since poor countries are labor abundant, policies that restrict labor supply may, in fact, benefit poor countries.

In "Borders Beyond Control," Jagdish Bhagwati examines another key issue that has mostly been ignored by the WTO—immigration. He argues that there is little that developed countries can do to stop the flow of immigrants and that countries should adopt policies to adjust to this reality.

"Willing Workers: Fixing the Problem of Illegal Immigration" examines one specific aspect of immigration—illegal migration into the US from Mexico and other Latin American countries. The article argues that legalizing immigration, in particular creating a guest-worker system to allow temporary migration, would not exacerbate the problem, but would instead make it easier for migrants to return and be with their families and would rationalize a system out of control.

"Intellectual Property Rights and the WTO," written by one of the editors of this reader, examines the issues in Doha concerning intellectual property rights (IPRs). The article points out that the interests of developed and developing countries are often at odds in these negotiations. While industrialized countries argue that IPRs benefit everyone, there is much evidence that developing countries benefit far more from free-riding off of patents and trademarks, and that allowing poor countries easy access to drugs and other patented products may be beneficial in the long run. The article also examines new areas of IPRs, such as the protection of traditional cultures and practices.

Finally, in "Reducing America's Dependence on Foreign Oil," noted economist Martin Feldstein examines a key trade issue for the US—its increasing dependence upon imported oil. Feldstein points out that the US imports 60% of its total oil consumption and that the reason for this high level is clear—gas is cheap and Americans have little incentive to conserve. Feldstein examines a number of fuel-saving technologies such as hybrid vehicles, that could be adopted, but points out that there is currently little incentive to adopt these policies since gas is cheap. He proposes a tradable voucher permit scheme that he believes would be acceptable and would encourage energy conservation.

6

The Doha Development Agenda

ANNE MCGUIRK

The launch of a new trade round in Doha last November was a major breakthrough following the debacle in Seattle in 1999. The new round places the needs and interests of developing countries at the heart of its work, but a successful outcome for rich and poor nations alike is by no means a foregone conclusion.

Trade has been an engine of growth for the past 50 years, owing in part to eight successive rounds of multilateral trade liberalization. Over the past 20 years, world trade has grown twice as fast as world real GDP (6 percent versus 3 percent), deepening economic integration and raising living standards. Many developing countries have shared in this process, narrowing the gap with rich countries and becoming—as a group—key players in world trade. Their trade has grown the fastest and their trade relations have changed markedly from the traditional north-south pattern. They now account for nearly a third of world trade; many have substantially increased their exports of manufactures and services; and 40 percent of their exports now go to other developing countries. But even after successive trade rounds, many lower-income countries have failed to integrate into the global economy—reflecting both external and internal constraints—and the poorest countries have seen their share of world trade decline (see chart).

The last trade round, the Uruguay Round launched over 15 years ago, was the most ambitious thus far, and some of its agreements are still being implemented (see table).

Tariff cuts covered a greater percentage of world trade than under previous rounds, and quantitative restrictions will be virtually eliminated by 2005. The round also established the World Trade Organization (WTO)—the successor to the General Agreement on Tariffs and Trade (GATT); brought international trade rules to areas previously excluded or subject to weak rules (agriculture, textiles and clothing, services, trade-related investment measures, and trade-related intellectual property rights (TRIPS); and strengthened the dispute settlement mechanism. Developing countries played a more active role than in previous rounds and adopted the same WTO agreements as other members as part of the round's "single undertaking"—nothing is agreed until everything is agreed.

Yet despite these achievements, the global trading system faces major challenges. First, even after Uruguay Round commitments are fully implemented, protection will remain high and concentrated in areas of particular interest to developing countries. In agriculture, only limited progress has been made in reducing high tariffs and trade-distorting subsidies. In manufacturing, the rules for phasing out quotas under the Agreement on Textiles and Clothing allow most liberalization to be postponed until 2005. And in both agriculture and manufacturing, tariff peaks (tariffs at or over 15 percent) and escalation (tariffs rising with the degree of processing of imports) persist, impeding the diversification of developing country exports.

Moreover, developing countries themselves maintain high protection in these same areas; their tariffs on industrial products are three to four times as high as those of industrial countries. And use of contingent protection such as antidumping measures is now widespread among both developed and developing countries.

Second, with the deepening of economic integration and the decline in tariffs and quantitative import restrictions, attention has shifted to other obstacles to trade that touch on domestic policies, such as industrial subsidies and intellectual property rights (incorporated in past negotiations) and, more recently, investment and competition policies. While some find this shift necessary for the trading system to remain relevant, others believe that pressures to bring domestic regulatory policies into the WTO could hurt the interests of developing countries, in part by diverting attention from more pressing needs.

Third, many poorer developing countries feel that they are bearing the costs of implementing difficult and complex Uruguay Round agreements (for example, customs valuation, intellectual property rights) without seeing the benefits of improved market access or obtaining adequate technical and financial assistance to ease their integration into the global economy. Given the constraints on their capacity to negotiate and undertake needed supply-side investments, they are reluctant to engage in further multilateral negotiations.

Outcome of Doha

Against this backdrop, the Ministerial Conference in Doha in November 2001 adopted the Development Agenda, which calls for a more coherent approach to trade and development and puts the needs and interests of the developing countries at the heart of the WTO's work program. The agenda includes new trade talks; an action program to resolve developing countries' complaints about the implementation of Uruguay Round agreements; and, in a major breakthrough, an accord on TRIPS ensuring that

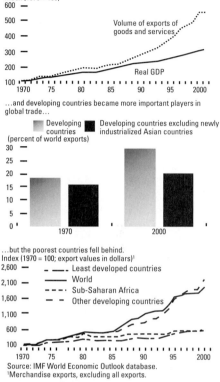

Going global

During the past 30 years, exports grew much faster than output...

Index (1970 = 100)

Volume of exports of goods and services.

Real GDP

...and developing countries became more important players in global trade...

Developing countries
Developing countries excluding newly industrialized Asian countries
(percent of world exports)

...but the poorest countries fell behind.
Index (1970 = 100; export values in dollars)[1]

— — — Least developed countries
———— World
— — — Sub-Saharan Africa
— — Other developing countries

Source: IMF World Economic Outlook database.
[1]Merchandise exports, excluding all exports.

patent protection does not block developing countries' access to affordable medicines. The conference also paved the way for China and Taiwan Province of China to get full membership in the WTO.

What do the new trade talks cover? They are actually quite broad, giving negotiators a chance to tackle both old and new areas. The timetable is ambitious—negotiations are scheduled to conclude no later than January 1, 2005, as part of a single undertaking (see box next page). The trade negotiations that began in 2000 on agriculture and services will be expanded to cover industrial goods (including textiles and clothing). Negotiators will also review and update trade rules—a major part of the work program—and delve into new areas, including the environment and the so-called Singapore issues (investment, competition policy, transparency in government procurement, and trade facilitation).

The GATT/WTO Trade Rounds

1947	Geneva	Tariffs	12
1949	Annecy	Tariffs	13
1951	Torquay	Tariffs	38
1956	Geneva	Tariffs	26
1960-61	Geneva (Dillon Round)	Tariffs	26
1964-67	Geneva (Kennedy Round)	Tariffs & antidumping measures	62
1973-79	Geneva (Tokyo Round)	Tariffs, nontariff measures, rules, services, intellectual property, dispute settlement, textiles, agriculture, creation of WTO.	123
2002-2004	Doha	All goods and services, tariffs, non-tariff measures, antidumping and subsidies, regional trade agreements. Intellectual property, environment, dispute settlement, Singapore issues	144

Scope of Doha trade negotiations

Hard bargaining was required for participants to reach a consensus on the scope of negotiations. Objectives in key areas are highlighted below, but they do not prejudge the outcome.

Agriculture: substantially improve market access; reduce all forms of export subsidies, with a view to phasing them out; and substantially reduce trade-distorting domestic support.

Services: further liberalize all categories of services and modes of supply.

Industrial goods: further reduce tariffs, including tariff peaks, high tariffs, and tariff escalation, as well as nontariff barriers, particularly on products of export interest to developing countries.

Antidumping measures and subsidies: clarify and improve disciplines, while preserving the basic concepts, principles, and effectiveness of these agreements and their instruments and objectives.

Regional trade agreements: clarify and improve disciplines and procedures under existing WTO rules applying to regional trading agreements.

TRIPS: establish a multilateral system of notification and registration of geographical indications for wines and spirits. Protection of geographical indications of other products addressed under review of implementation of TRIPS agreement.

Dispute settlement mechanism: improve the implementation of rulings and participation of the developing countries.

The environment: negotiations limited to the relationship between existing WTO rules and specific trade obligations set out in multilateral environmental agreements and to the reduction or elimination of tariff and nontariff barriers to environmental goods and services.

Possible negotiations on Singapore issues: (investment, competition policy, transparency in government procurement, and trade facilitation) subject to a decision on the negotiating modalities at the Fifth Ministerial Conference, in 2003.

While the broad scope of the negotiations will facilitate trade-offs, it could overwhelm even the more advanced developing countries. Thus, as part of the bargain, trade ministers made extensive commitments to provide technical assistance and capacity-building programs to help ensure that developing countries can defend their interests and respond to trade opportunities. However, because much of the capacity-building agenda lies outside the competence of the WTO, its credibility will depend critically on the response of the international community and whether developing countries move aggressively to help themselves.

What's at Stake

Is the successful outcome of this new trade round really that critical? The answer is an unqualified yes, for three main reasons. First, the remaining trade barriers impose costs on all countries and provide an opportunity for substantial gains from reciprocal trade liberalization. Estimates by the World Bank and others suggest that the static welfare gains from removing barriers to merchandise trade would amount to between $250 billion and $620 billion a year—with developing countries capturing one-third to one-half of these gains, largely by opening their own markets. This is far more than the annual flow of aid to these countries. Removing barriers to trade in services would increase global welfare by even more, given the dominant role of the service sectors in most economies and the still large trade barriers typical of these sectors.

Second, removing the barriers to poor countries' exports is key to the success of the international community's strategy for achieving the Millennium Development Goals—including halving poverty by 2015. Opening markets would not only boost trade and global growth over time, it would also bring greater stability and predictability to the global economy and thereby help ensure a healthier international financial system.

Third, further strengthening and developing trade rules is vital to improve the security of market access and establish favorable conditions for trade and long-term capital flows. In particular, trade rules need to be clarified and strengthened in areas susceptible to capture by protectionist interests (for example, antidumping and other safeguard measures, and health and safety standards). A more effective dispute settlement mechanism is essential to maintain confidence in the rules-based system, which ultimately protects the weak against the powerful. Constructive ways must also be found to deal with new issues such as investment and competition policy, where developing countries are reluctant to make new commitments. Cooperative (rather than legalistic) approaches, such as those developed to strengthen the international financial system (for example, the IMF-World Bank Financial Sector Assessment Program) could be explored to promote good practices in these areas.

But overcoming the strength of protectionist forces will not be easy. This was evident from the Doha Conference, where some of the most contentious issues were the phasing out of agricultural export subsidies and quotas on textiles and clothing, and the tightening of disciplines on antidumping actions. To build support for liberalization, countries need to do much more to facilitate structural change and to help their citizens adapt to it—for example, by providing more effective adjustment assistance for those hurt in the short run. This is particularly true of industrial countries, where vested interests have long resisted the changes required when certain sectors lose their comparative advantage. Developing countries also need to convince their citizens that the benefits of multilateral liberalization outweigh transient trade preferences and special treatment that shield their economies from competition.

However, for the developing countries to become full partners in the global trading system, trade measures alone will not suffice. That is why the Doha Declaration invited the Bretton Woods institutions and the broader international community to join forces with the WTO as part of a coherent approach to global policymaking. Efforts by the WTO to open markets and strengthen trade rules must be reinforced at the global level by sound macroeconomic and financial policies and financial market stability. And to benefit from open markets, developing countries will need to strengthen their own policies. They will also need much greater aid for trade from their development partners to build the capacity to engage in trade and participate effectively in the WTO.

One promising approach to the challenge of coordinating such assistance is the Integrated Framework for Trade-Related Technical Assistance for Least-Developed Countries. The IMF is working with the World Bank and others within this framework to help poor countries strengthen their own policies and institutions and make trade a strategic component of their poverty reduction strategies. By prioritizing and coordinating the delivery of trade-related technical assistance within these strategies, the aim is to improve the relevance and effectiveness of such assistance. Areas where the IMF is providing trade-related technical assistance include revenue systems, customs administration, trade facilitation, social safety nets, and financial sector soundness—which is particularly relevant to the liberalization of financial services.

Realizing the Promise

As the global community searches for ways to ensure brighter prospects for all people, the new trade round, which embraces industrial and developing countries, holds the greatest promise of making inroads where protection remains concentrated and of developing a trade architecture that both meets the needs of global commerce and supports economic development. The advantage of multilateral negotiations is the leverage they provide over domestic protectionist interests; by opening other markets on a nondiscriminatory basis, they magnify the gains. Moreover, ownership and effectiveness require that the shortcomings of the trading system be tackled at the multilateral level with the full participation of developing and developed countries

alike. The WTO, as it approaches universal membership, provides the appropriate forum for governments representing their citizens' interests to grapple with these issues.

Whether the promise of Doha can be realized, however, will depend on the extent to which trade barriers and trade-distorting subsidies are substantially reduced; both developed and developing countries cooperate in further reforming the trading system in ways that foster development; the international community supports the round through complementary efforts to provide resources for technical assistance and capacity building; and developing countries strengthen their own policies and institutions, so their citizens can respond to the opportunities for trade and investment.

Anne McGuirk is Assistant Director in the IMF's Policy Development and Review Department.

References:

Bernard Hoekman, 2002, "*Strengthening the Global Trade Architecture for Development,*" World Trade Review, Vol. 1 (March), pp. 23-46.

International Monetary Fund, 2001, World Economic Outlook, October 2001 (Washington).

——— and World Bank, 2001, "*Market Access for Developing Countries' Exports,*" joint IMF-World Bank staff study; http://www.imf.org/external/np/madc/eng/0 42701.htm.

Jeffrey Schott, 2002, "*Reflections on the Doha Ministerial,*" Economic Perspectives, Vol. 7, No. 1 (January).

Alan L. Winters, 2002, "*Doha and the World Poverty Targets,*" paper presented at the World Bank's Annual Conference on Development Economics, Washington, D.C., April 29-30.

Bridging the Trade-Environment Divide

DANIEL C. ESTY

Protection. For free traders, this word represents the consummate evil. For environmentalists, it is the ultimate good. Of course, for the trade community, "protection" conjures up dark images of Smoot and Hawley, while the environmental camp sees clear mountain streams, lush green forests, and piercing blue skies. One cannot blame all of the tensions at the trade environment interface on linguistic differences, but these competing perspectives are emblematic of a deep clash of cultures, theories, and assumptions.

Trade officials often seek to limit efforts to link trade and environmental policymaking, and sometimes to prohibit such efforts altogether. In this regard, the narrow focus and modest efforts of the World Trade Organization's Committee on Trade and Environment are illustrative.[1] The launch of negotiations for a Free Trade Area of the Americas with an express decision to exclude environmental issues from the agenda provides an even starker example of the trade community's hostility toward serious environmental engagement. Economists have been prominent among those arguing that pollution control and natural resource management issues are best kept out of the trade policymaking process (Cooper, 1994; Bhagwati, 1999). Other economists, however, have tried to set trade policymaking in a broader context and to build environmental sensitivity into the international trading system (Runge, 1994; Rodrik, 1997; Summers, 2000).

In fact, there is no real choice about whether to address the trade and environment linkage; this linkage is a matter of fact. The only choice is whether the policies put in place to respond will be designed openly, explicitly, and thoughtfully, with an eye to economic and political logic—or implicitly and without systematic attention to the demands of good policymaking. This article seeks to explain why trade liberalization and environmental protection appear to be in such tension and to push economists to explore more aggressively what economic theory and practice might do to address the concerns being raised.

Trade and Environmental Linkages

Potential Conflicts Between Domestic Regulations and Trade

In recent years, the focus of trade liberalization has shifted from lowering tariffs, which have come down considerably around the world, to the elimination of non-tariff barriers to trade (Jackson, 1992). Since many kinds of domestic regulations can potentially be construed as non-tariff barriers, the extent and impact of the market access commitment and other regulatory disciplines negotiated in the trade domain have expanded.

A number of the most prominent international trade disputes in the last decade have concerned the clash between domestic regulations and trade rules. In the well-known tuna-dolphin case, the United States banned Mexican tuna imports because the fishing methods resulted in incidental dolphin deaths. In 1991, Mexico obtained a GATT panel decision declaring the United States to be in violation of its GATT obligations for imposing such a ban. In the ongoing beef hormone dispute, the European Union has refused to adjust its "no added hormones in beef" food safety standards despite a series of WTO rulings that its regulations had no scientific foundation and were in contravention of the rules of international trade. The U.S. sanctions against Thai shrimp caught using methods that killed endangered sea turtles were recently deemed to be GATT-illegal. Trade and environment friction can be found outside the WTO, as well. Witness the enormous effort that the European Union has put into harmonizing environmental standards over the past several decades (Vogel, 1994).

There is no end in sight to "trade and environment" cases. If anything, the number of disputes seems to be rising (Sampson, 2000). As global economic integration intensifies, so does the potential for conflict (Lawrence et al., 1996; Dua and Esty, 1997). Public health standards, food safety requirements, emissions limits, waste management and disposal rules, packaging and recycling regulations, and labeling policies all may shape trade flows. Trade disciplines may also affect national-scale environmental efforts, especially to the extent that WTO dispute settlement procedures are used to challenge pollution control or natural resource management programs.

Thus, while fearmongering about lost "sovereignty" (Perot, 1993; Wallach and Sforza, 1999) can be dismissed, the suggestion that trade liberalization constrains regulatory flexibility rings true. With new issues like biotechnology and climate change emerging, the potential for significant and divisive battles between trade policy and regulatory choices—including environmental rules—looms large.

Increasing Trade, Economic Growth, and Environmental Risks

The literature on the interaction between economic growth and pollution points to what has been called an environmental "Kuznets curve." The Kuznets curve is a inverted-U relationship which shows that environmental conditions tend to deteriorate in the early stages of industrialization and then improve as nations hit middle-income levels, at a per capita GDP of about $5000 to $8000 (Grossman and Krueger, 1993, 1995; Shafik and Bandyopadhyay, 1992; Seldon and Song, 1994). Since the primary purpose of liberalizing trade is to increase economic growth, trade unavoidably affects the level of environmental protection through its impact on the Kuznets curve.

A first concern stemming from the Kuznets curve is that air and water pollution problems tend to worsen in the early stages of development. Many developing countries are living through the part of the Kuznets curve in which environmental conditions deteriorate. In addition, some problems, especially those that are spread spatially or temporally (such as greenhouse gas emissions), do not yet appear to have reached the downward-sloping part of the Kuznets curve in any country. This empirically derived pattern of ongoing deterioration perhaps reflects the fact that, absent reciprocity, the benefit-cost ratio for policy interventions in response to diffuse problems is always negative from a national perspective.

A second concern is that even if expanded trade and economic growth need not hurt the environment, there is no guarantee that it will not (Harbaugh, Levinson and Wilson, 2000; Hauer and Runge, 2000). The effects of economic growth on trade can be broken down into three effects. "Technique" effects arise from the tendency toward cleaner production processes as wealth increases and trade expands access to better technologies and environmental "best practices." "Composition" effects involve a shift in preferences toward cleaner goods. "Scale" effects refer to increased pollution due to expanded economic activity and greater consumption made possible by more wealth (Grossman and Krueger 1993; Lopez, 1994). Thus, the claim that growth improves the quality of environment can be rephrased as a claim that, above a certain level of per capita income, technique and composition effects will outweigh scale effects. Empirical evidence on the relative sizes of these effects is limited. But at least some of the time, it appears that expanded trade may worsen environmental conditions (Antweiler, Copeland and Taylor, 1998).

Finally, the odds that increased trade will have net negative environmental impacts rise if resources are mispriced (Anderson, 1998; Panayotou, 1993). Around the world, many critical resources like water, timber, oil, coal, fish, and open space are underpriced (or overpriced) (World Bank, 1997; Earth Council, 1997). Even the WTO acknowledges in its most recent "Trade and Environment Special Report" that expanded trade can exacerbate pollution harms and natural resource management mistakes in the absence of appropriate environmental policies (Nordstrom and Vaughan, 1999).

Transboundary Externalities

Transboundary pollution spillovers make attention to trade-environment linkages a matter of normative necessity as well as descriptive reality. Perhaps the most discussed issues involve emissions of ozone-layer-depleting chlorofluorocarbons and greenhouse gases, which threaten global climate change. But recent advances in tracing the movement of pollutants have also demonstrated long-distance impacts from particulates (Grad, 1997), sulfur dioxide and other precursors of acid rain (Howells, 1995), DDT and other pesticides (Lawler, 1995; Rappaport et al., 1985), mercury and other heavy metals (Fitzgerald, 1993), and bioaccumulative toxics (Francis, 1994). Other transboundary issues involve rules governing shared resources such as fisheries in the open ocean and biodiversity.

The need to control transboundary externalities makes trade-environment linkages essential from the point of view of good economic policy-making. After all, uninternalized externalities not only lead to environmental degradation, but also threaten market failures that will diminish the efficiency of international economic exchanges, reduce gains from trade, and lower social welfare. National governments, no matter how well intended, cannot address inherently international problems such as climate change or fisheries depletion unilaterally. A functioning Global Environmental Organization, operating in parallel with the trading system, might be a "first-best" policy option in response to these challenges (Esty, 2000a). But no such regime exists. Thus, the World Trade Organization along with regional trade agreements cannot avoid some shared responsibility for managing ecological interdependence.

The Political Economy of Trade Liberalization

Taking environmental issues seriously must also be understood as a political necessity for free traders. Forward momentum in the trade realm is difficult to sustain (Bergsten, 1992). In this regard, the trade community cannot risk diminishing further the already narrow coalition in favor of freer trade, especially in the United States. Dismissing environmental concerns, which results in broad environmental community opposition to trade agreements, generates unnecessary and avoidable political resistance to liberalized trade (Esty, 1998a).

Certain environmentalists will always be opposed to trade liberalization because they adhere to a "limits to growth" philosophy. But the environmental community is neither monolithic nor uniformly protectionist. Many mainstream environmentalists believe in "sustainable development" and will support freer trade if they feel that pollution and natural resource management concerns are being taken seriously. For example, the congressional vote in favor of the NAFTA depended critically on the fact that a number of environmental groups came out in favor of the agreement, which translated into support from politicians who define themselves as both pro–free trade and environmentally oriented (Audley, 1997). Concomitantly, the several recent failures to obtain a majority for new fast track negotiating authority can be attributed to this swing group voting against the legislation because the proposals lacked environmental credibility (Destler and Balint, 1999).

In practice, moreover, there is no empirical support for the suggestion that environmental linkages detract from trade agreements or trade liberalization. The North American Free Trade Agreement, often considered the "greenest" trade pact ever, contains a number of environmental elements and was adopted with an Environmental Side Agreement. There is no evidence that these provisions have in any way diminished the post-NAFTA U.S.-Canada-Mexico trade flows (Araya, 2002; Hufbauer et al., 2000).

One might argue that this political analysis has little to do with economists' role in the trade and environment debate. To the contrary, if the arguments of economists become disconnected from the reality of political pressures and policy imperfections, then economic logic is unlikely to prevail in trade policy-making.

The Arguments for Separating Trade and Environmental Policy

While many "no linkage" economists and trade officials understand the arguments for taking up environmental issues in the trade context, they fear a scenario in which protectionist wolves find their way into the trading system in environmental sheep's clothing (Bhagwati, 1988; Subramanian, 1992).[2] The sight at the 1999 WTO Ministerial Meeting in Seattle of green activists marching arm-in-arm with avowed protectionists confirmed for many, especially in the developing world, the suspect motives of those advancing the environmental agenda. A related argument for keeping the environment out of the WTO turns on the fear that trade liberalization will grind to a halt under the weight of environmental burdens. Why, ask trade economists, must trade measures be used to enforce international environmental agreements? Shouldn't environmental policy problems be solved with environmental policy tools? Those who wish to separate trade and environmental policy-making also fear that high-income countries will impose lofty environmental standards on low-income countries, depriving them of one aspect of their natural comparative advantage and subjecting them to trade barriers if they fail to perform up to developed country standards (Bhagwati, 1999; 2000).

But while these worries have some basis in reality, they do not provide a justification for complete separation of trade and environmental policies. Certainly, environmentalism should not be used as a cover to disguise trade barriers. Certainly, the tactical partnerships of some environmental groups have been misguided. Certainly, better environmental regulation at both the national and global levels could markedly reduce trade environment tensions.[3] Certainly, global scale environmental efforts should not mean a reduction in the standard of living for people in low-income countries.

But these are not arguments for ignoring the inescapable linkages between trade and the environment. They are arguments for trying to integrate trade and environmental policies in sensible ways. The following sections discuss key areas for research and policy analysis that could help to narrow the divide between trade and environmental policy goals and practices. The next section focuses on strengthening the foundations of environmental policy, while the next two sections focus on issues of economic theory and trade policy.

Strengthening Environmental Policy Foundations

A battle rages among environmentalists over how best to address (and even understand) environmental challenges. Many environmentalists support the concept of "sustainable development" (World Commission on Environment and Development, 1987) and believe that economic growth can, if managed properly, support environmental improvements. A significant number of environmental advocates remain committed, however, to a "limits to growth" paradigm in which trade liberalization contributes to more economic activity and therefore more pollution and unsustainable consumption of natural resources (Meadows et al., 1972; Daly, 1993). But even those who find the promise of sustainable development attractive worry that, in practice, environmental policy tools are not up to the pressures of globalization.

Economists are likely to have little in common with the advocates of lower consumption levels, especially when the burdens of such a policy choice would fall most heavily on those in the poorest countries of the world. But economists can play a role in answering certain persistent environmental research and policy questions which could, in turn, help to expand the common ground between free traders and environmentalists.

Clarifying Concerns about Sustainable Development

Sustainable development has proven hard to define and even harder to put into practice. It is clear that poverty can force people to make short-term choices that degrade the environment, like cutting down nearby trees for firewood despite the likelihood of future soil erosion. But the hope that trade liberalization will lead to economic growth that will alleviate poverty and generate resources for environmental investments sometimes seems to rely on a tenuous chain of events which may well unravel under real-world conditions.

It is useful to examine these issues in terms of the inverted-U environmental Kuznets curve discussed earlier, which shows a general pattern of increasing environmental degradation up to a certain level of per capita GDP and environmental improvements beyond that point.

Environmentalists will always be worried about societies which are living through the portion of the Kuznets curve where growth is accompanied by environmental degradation, even if it can be shown that people are receiving other welfare gains. Economists could, however, significantly bridge the gap with green groups if they were to find ways to reduce the duration and intensity of environmental deterioration as low-income countries grow to middle income. Economists might also confirm that ignoring pollution altogether until middle-income levels are reached is a serious policy mistake. Some environmental investments, like protecting drinking water or siting polluting factories downwind of urban areas, have such high benefit-cost ratios that even the poorest countries should undertake them.

As regards the portion of the environmental Kuznets curve in which growth and environmental quality are both improving, many mainstream environmentalists express concerns that either rising wealth or increased population will drive up consumption in ways that undermine prospects for sustainable development. Both economic theory and recent empirical evidence could help to assuage these apprehensions. Development economists have demonstrated that population growth diminishes with wealth. Economists might do more to demonstrate that poverty alleviation is critical for population control, which in turn offers significant potential environmental benefits. More generally, the economics field has had little to say about how to minimize scale effects and maximize the chances that growth will improve environmental quality.

Finally, as noted earlier, certain environmental harms do not appear to diminish with increases in income. Carbon dioxide emissions, for instance, continue to rise, albeit at a decreasing rate, as GDP per capita goes up. It may be that, even for carbon dioxide emissions, the downward portion of the environmental Kuznets curve would be reached at some income level, but no society has achieved the exalted wealth required. If or until that occurs, economists could gain credibility by agreeing that wealth is not an environmental cure all.

The common theme in this discussion is that the environmental Kuznets curve need not be destiny. The present shape of the curve, as estimated from historical experience, reflects a political economy interaction among trade, growth, and the environment. Trade has a positive effect on the environment (and perhaps a net welfare benefit more broadly) only if environmental policy advances alongside trade liberalization (Anderson, 1992, 1998; Esty, 1994). However, institutional failures in the environmental realm often mean that the requisite strengthening of environmental performance in parallel with trade liberalization may not occur (Chichilnisky, 1994; Zhao, 2000). In this regard, economists should take more seriously the need to find policy strategies that lead to a shorter and flatter Kuznets curve.

Disciplining Free Riders

Economists and environmental policy-makers generally agree on the wisdom of enforcing the "polluter pays" principle, which holds that those who cause environmental degradation should bear the costs. But as a matter of policy, this goal remains elusive. While economists have demonstrated the value of market-based environmental strategies, they have by and large not managed to convince the environmental and political worlds that pollution fees, emissions allowances, or other economic incentives will work in practice. Environmental policy remains underdeveloped in terms of economic sophistication and largely mired in "command and control" approaches. The collapse of the international negotiations over climate change, in part because of disputes over how far to go in using market mechanisms, demonstrates the persistence within the environmental policy community of anti-economics sentiment.

Figuring out how to enact policies that embody the polluter pays principle becomes even more difficult when the scope of the environmental harm is broader than the vista of the regulators. Dua and Esty (1997) argue that "super-externalities," which spill beyond the defined jurisdiction of regulatory authorities in either space or time, aggravate the collective action problem.[4] A small number of scholars have looked at the spatial distribution of issues in the trade domain (Krugman, 1991; Bloom and Sachs, 1998) and at the geographic dimensions of the trade and environment problem (Hauer and Runge, 2000; Esty, 1994), but more work needs to be done in the realm of economic geography.

Transboundary environmental spillovers create a risk of allocative inefficiency and market failure in the international economy. Some mechanism for promoting collective action and for disciplining free riders is therefore required (Baumol and Oates, 1988). Whether free traders like it or not, trade measures are one potential candidate for this function. Admittedly, trade sanctions are imperfect, costly to those who impose them, and may backfire. But at least in some cases, trade penalties have worked (Brack, 1996; Barrett, 1997). Moreover, better tools to discipline free riders in the international environmental domain do not seem readily available. As environmentalists point out, the weakness of the extant global environmental regime cannot be wished away nor dismissed as irrelevant to the question of how environmental goals get squared with the trade liberalization agenda.

There are a number of issues to be investigated which could shed light on the use of trade policy as a tool for enforcement of environmental standards. First, refined theory on the use of trade measures to support environmental cost internalization in the international realm is needed, advancing the preliminary analyses of Charnovitz (1993), Chang (1995), and Barrett (1997). Second, more work to find ways to strengthen the international environmental regime, which could relieve the pressure on the World Trade Organization to play a major environmental role, would be useful (Esty, 1994, 2000a). Such work might build on efforts to investigate the political economy of environmental protection (for example,

Keohane, Revesz and Stavins, 1998). Third, the advantages and disadvantages of policy linkages need to be more fully explored. Concerns are sometimes expressed that if trade policy becomes entangled with environmental policy, either or both sets of policies may be unable to advance. Yet the potential benefits of cross-issue policies and trade-offs have been repeatedly demonstrated (Haas, 1958; Carrero and Siniscalco, 1994). Finally, those who wish to limit the trade system's role in enforcing international environmental agreements would find their case greatly strengthened if they could point to workable alternative enforcement mechanisms.[5]

Refining Trade Theory

Environmental perspectives on trade often clash with the settled views of economists. Frequently, the problem reflects a degree of economic misunderstanding by those in the environmental community. But often, there is a kernel (or more) of truth in the environmental position with which the economic community has failed to grapple. In these areas, there are intriguing research opportunities for economists.

Level Playing Fields

Environmentalists often worry that expanded trade will lead to competitive pressures which will push down environmental standards. They fear a regulatory "race toward the bottom" as jurisdictions with high environmental standards relax their rules so as to avoid burdening their industries with pollution control costs higher than competitors operating in low-standard jurisdictions. Thus, they call for harmonization of pollution control regulations at stringent levels, the imposition of "eco-duties" on those with subpar rules, or other policy interventions to "level the playing field."

Economists point out that the existence of divergent circumstances, including variations in societal preferences about the optimal level of environmental protection, is what makes gains from trade possible. If environmental rules vary because of differences in climate, weather, geography, existing pollution levels, population density, risk preferences, level of development, or other "natural" factors, the variation in standards should be considered welfare enhancing and appropriate. Clearly, a sweeping presumption in favor of uniform standards fails to grasp the insight of comparative advantage and makes no sense (Burtless et al., 1998). More generally, economists tend to find arguments in favor of regulatory harmonization in a context of economic integration unpersuasive (Bhagwati, 1996, 2000).

Diversity in circumstances generally makes uniformity less attractive than standards tailored to the heterogenous conditions that exist (Mendelsohn, 1986; Anderson, 1998). But not always. Divergent standards across jurisdictions may impose transaction costs on traded goods that exceed any benefits obtained by allowing each jurisdiction to maintain its own requirements. Sykes (1995, 1999) has demonstrated that market forces will tend, over time, to eliminate such problems. Vogel (1994) argues, in fact, that upward harmonization (a "race to the top") often occurs. But this logic only applies to product standards, and standards that relate to production processes or methods are not subject to the same market pressures.

Some theoretical work has been done to try to understand the different harmonization dynamics (Bhagwati and Hudec, 1996; Esty and Geradin, 1998, 2001), but more would be useful, as would empirical evidence on what happens to environmental standards in the process of trade liberalization. For example, how often do free trade agreements include commitments to lower environmental standards and how often to higher standards?

Environmentalists also fear that the rules of international trade are biased against their interests. They believe that within the trading system—both WTO and regional trade agreements—free trade principles always trump other policy goals such as environmental protection. Some recent analyses suggest that such a tilt in GATT jurisprudence might once have existed, but is now less pronounced (Char-novitz, 2000; Wofford, 2000). Efforts to illuminate the facts might diminish fears that trade liberalization runs roughshod over environmental issues. Some efforts have been made in this regard (Trachtman, 2000; Burtless et al., 1998), but more would be welcome.

Psychological Spillovers and Ethical Preferences

Most economists acknowledge, at least in theory, that transboundary pollution externalities need to be addressed, but economists tend to be skeptical about claims of psychological spillovers (Blackhurst and Subramanian, 1992; Cooper, 1994). What are we to make of complaints about environmental degradation in China or campaigns to save the rain forest? As long as the harms are localized, shouldn't environmental policy choices (even "mistakes") in other jurisdictions be accepted? Maybe so from a perspective of economic theory, but most people do not see the world this way. The fact that Chinese workers produce goods under adverse environmental conditions is not celebrated, even if the low standards in China translate into cheaper products in export markets. Why not?

Perhaps economists assume a utilitarianism that is oversimplified. Sen (1977) and others have noted the narrow behavioral assumptions on which most of economics builds, ignoring human realities such as the existence of interdependent welfare functions. In fact, many people consider themselves, at least to some extent, to be part of a global community. In addition, economists may too readily accept as a given that the policy choices in places like China are locally optimal and do not stop to ask whether Chinese environmental standards truly reflect the will of the people.[6] By gliding past "choice of public" questions (Esty, 1996), economists simplify their models but diminish the policy traction of their arguments.

Environmentalist concerns about extraterritorial policy choices frequently seem to be paternalistic or even imperialistic. Green groups often think that they know better than the people or governments of other countries, especially developing nations, what constitutes the "right" environmental standard or policy program. Economists have been quick to condemn those who "are keen to impose their own ethical preferences on others, using trade sanctions to induce or coerce acceptance of such preferences" (Bhagwati, 1993).

But trade, like any realm of human endeavor, cannot exist without baseline rules, defined by community standards and values. One such set of rules concerns what constitutes a fair and legitimate basis for comparative advantage. From nineteenth century British hesitation about trading with the slave holding American south to Article XX(e) of the GATT, which permits trade restrictions on products made by prison labor, the international trading system has always circumscribed the bounds of acceptable commercial behavior.

The issue becomes one of line drawing. When is a divergent policy in another jurisdiction just a "choice," worthy of respect and acceptance in a world of diversity? When does it become a violation of moral minimum standards that should not be abided?

A conservative answer here would be that when environmental harms are purely local in scope, then preservationist demands from abroad are overreaching. In such a case, trade policy should not be the primary tool for international environmental policy, and instead environmental advocates should find a way to pay for their preferences in other countries. But if localized environmental harms are vast and there is reason to doubt whether the will of the people is being fairly represented, it makes sense to leave open the possibility that international pressure for a cleaner environment may be justified.

Is There a Race Toward the Bottom?

Economists have strongly rejected suggestions that country-versus-country competitiveness pressures degrade environmental standards.[7] They argue that the idea that jurisdictions with low environmental standards will become pollution havens, luring industries from high-standard jurisdictions and triggering a back-and-forth downward spiral in environmental standards finds little basis in theory (Revesz, 1992; Drezner, 2000) and lacks empirical support (Kalt, 1988; Low and Yeats, 1992; Repetto, 1995). For example, it does not appear that U.S. pollution control standards have dropped in the aftermath of NAFTA nor following the various rounds of GATT and WTO negotiations over time.

But the real concern is not about a race literally to the bottom. Rather, the concern arises from the possibility that economic integration will create a regulatory dynamic in which standards are set strategically with an eye on the pollution control burdens in competing jurisdictions. The result may be a "political drag" that translates into suboptimal environmental standards in some places.[8] These effects might involve not only weakened environmental laws, but perhaps more importantly, environmental standards not strengthened as much as they would otherwise have been or environmental enforcement cases not brought.

The evidence here is by no means as one-sided as many economists have come to believe. Some recent empirical studies find races to the bottom (Mani and Wheeler, 1999; van Beers and van den Bergh, 1997). Moreover, a growing theoretical literature, largely published in law journals, suggests that if the market in "locational rights" is flawed, regulatory races toward the bottom may occur (Klevorick, 1996; Engel and Rose-Ackerman, 2001; Esty and Geradin, 2001). A mismatch between the scope of pollution harms and the jurisdiction of regulators, as well as information gaps or technical deficiencies in the regulatory process, or public choice distortions (such as the fact that politicians may be more influenced by highly visible job effects and may overlook more subtle environmental impacts) may lead jurisdictions to set their environmental standards too low (or too high) (Esty, 1996). Moreover, once a trade competitor has deviated from optimal regulatory levels, a welfare maximizing government may benefit by strategically adjusting its own environmental standards.

Within economics, the welfare effects of inter-jurisdictional regulatory competition have been carefully analyzed (Fischel, 1975; Oates and Schwab, 1988). However, the application of the theory to the race-toward-the-bottom question in the international trade and environment context has only recently begun to get attention (Levinson, 1997; Fredriksson and Millimet, 2000). New work is beginning to specify those settings in which regulatory competition will improve outcomes and when some degree of harmonization (not necessarily uniform standards) will improve results.[9]

The Development and Evolution of Trade Policy-Making

Advances in both the procedures and substantive rules of the international trading system could help to alleviate some trade environment tensions. A good bit of the environmentalist animosity toward freer trade arises from the closed process by which trade liberalization has historically proceeded and the sense that any expression of environmental concerns, no matter how valid, would not be taken seriously. The World Trade Organization, like GATT before it, has usually done its business through negotiations between governments. Mechanisms for participation by nongovernmental organizations including environmental groups and other elements of civil society have been limited. But the obscure nature of the process and the attempt to channel all political debate to the national level has created an image of the WTO as a star chamber or "black box" where insiders take advantage of their access to the levers of power.

The closed nature of the system had a logic; it shielded the trade regime from special interest manipulation and "capture" (Bhagwati, 1988; Subramanian, 1992). But the organization's future now depends on it becoming more transparent. Beyond building public understanding and acceptance, a more open WTO policy-making process has other virtues. Notably, nongovernmental organizations provide critical "intellectual competition" for both national and intergovernmental decision makers (Esty, 1998b). In presenting alternative perspectives, data, policy analyses, and options, these non-government organizations force officials to explain and justify their policy choices. There remains, however, work to be done to find ways to maximize the benefits of the interchange while limiting the risk that access will give special interests undue power to manipulate or block outcomes. In this quest, the learning from public choice theory may be helpful.

Economists could also help the trade community to modernize the WTO's substantive rules on a basis of greater analytic rigor. In this regard, several issues stand out at the trade-environment interface.

First, the reliance on a distinction between product standards imposed on imports (generally acceptable) and production process or methods restrictions (generally unacceptable) makes little sense in a world of ecological interdependence.[10] How things are produced matters. Production related externalities cannot be overlooked. For example, semiconductors manufactured using chlorofluorocarbons destroy everyone's ozone layer. Where international environmental agreements are in place, such as the 1987 Montreal Protocol phasing out chlorofluorocarbons, trade rules should be interpreted to reinforce the agreed upon standards. Indeed, such a principle can be found in Article 104 of the North American Free Trade Agreement.

A recrafted trade principle that accepts the legitimacy of environmental rules aimed at transboundary externalities would eliminate the risk of the trade regime providing cover for those shirking their share of global responsibilities. A number of economists, including some who have been skeptical about trade-environment linkages, have now come around to view that trade rules must not permit free riding on global environmental commitments (Cooper, 2000; Bhagwati, 2000). But how this agreement in principle should be translated into actual trade policies has not been clarified. Economists are in a good position to think through the efficiency and equity implications of the issues and options.

Another opportunity for updating of the trade system centers on the traditional rule that, when trade and environment principles clash, only the "least GATT inconsistent" environmental policies are acceptable. Such an approach lacks balance, because clever policymakers can always come up with a possible policy alternative that is less restrictive to trade. A more neutral decision rule would focus on whether the environmental standards are arbitrary, unjustifiable, or a disguised restriction on trade. Such a principle seems to be emerging in recent WTO dispute settlement cases, notably the 1998 shrimp turtle Appellate Body decision (Wofford, 2000).

Final Thoughts

A traditional piece of received wisdom about trade policy-making is that more can be accomplished by operating in a closed "club system" beneath the radar of public scrutiny rather than through open debate (Keohane and Nye, 2001). Whether this hypothesis was ever correct is now moot. The World Trade Organization has gained a very high profile, and it will never again be able to operate in the policy shadows (Esty, 2000b). When the trade agenda was perceived to be narrow and technical, the trade regime's performance was of interest only to the trade cognoscenti. But today the WTO's work has much broader impacts, and the trade agenda encompasses nontariff barriers and other issues which impinge on commercial and governmental activities beyond the trade domain. Where once the WTO's legitimacy turned on its capacity to produce good results from a trade perspective, the organization is now subject to much wider scrutiny. If the WTO is to play its designated role as one of the key international organizations managing economic interdependence, it must find a new center of gravity (Schott, 2000).

Going forward, the WTO's authority and public acceptance will have to be founded on a more democratic basis and on a refined ability to reflect the political will of the global community. Such a transformation entails a commitment to transparency and an open trade policy-making process that provides access to non-government organizations across the spectrum of civil society. The WTO's future legitimacy requires a more robust trade and environment dialogue, not artificial separation of these policy-making realms. Special interest lobbies will have to be disciplined by exposure and argument, not exclusion (Esty, 1998b).

Environmental rules cannot be seen as simple pollution control or natural resource management standards; they also provide the ground rules for international commerce and serve as an essential bulwark against market failure in the international economic system. Building environmental sensitivity into the trade regime in a thoughtful and systematic fashion should therefore be of interest to the trade community as well as environmental advocates. In working toward a world of effective environmental protection that is simultaneously free of trade protectionism, economists could play a substantial role.

Thanks to Monica Araya and Brian Fletcher for research assistance and to the Global Environment and Trade Study (GETS) and its funders, especially the Ford Foundation. Thanks also to INSEAD, Stephan Schmidheiny, and Alqueria for support.

Daniel C. Esty is Associate Dean and Professor of Environmental Law and Policy, Yale School of Forestry and Environmental Studies, New Haven, Connecticut. He has a joint appointment at the Yale Law School and serves as Director of the Yale Center for Environmental Law and Policy. His e-mail address is (daniel.esty@yale.edu)

Endnotes

[1] For a full review of the work of the WTO Committee on Trade and Environment, see (http://www.wto.org/WT/CTE).

[2] Some trade officials, however, seem not to have learned their economics very well. Many of the comments of the trade leaders who spoke at the WTO's 1999 "Trade and Environment Symposium" reflected serious deficiencies in the understanding of core principles, such as the implications of externalities or the Olsonian logic of collective action. See, for example, the speech of de la Calle (WTO, 1999).

[3] Momentum for a revitalized international environmental regime, perhaps including a new Global Environmental Organization to serve as a counterpart and counterbalance to the WTO, seems to be building (Esty, 1994; Ruggiero, 1999; Barrett, 2000; Jospin, 2000).

[4] Issues that cross jurisdictional boundaries create a risk of "structural" failure in the regulatory cost-benefit calculus (Esty, 1996). Related problems arise with long-term environmental issues in which there is a risk of market failure because future citizens are not present to cast their "market votes." Some thinking has gone into how to manage problems with long time horizons (Cline, 1993; Revesz, 1999). But if economic theories are to be persuasive to environmentalists, they will have to deal explicitly with the broader set of issues such as threshold effects, nonlinear cost curves, and irreversibility (for example, species destruction).

[5] The suggestion that there be more use of carrots (financial rewards for compliance) and less of sticks (trade measures) may be useful in some circumstances. But in other cases, transboundary pollution spillovers represent a serious infringement on property rights, making a "victim pays" strategy inappropriate (Esty, 1996).

[6] A number of economists (Sachs, 1998; Sen, 1999) and others (Esty and Porter, 2000) have begun to argue that a society's underlying legal, political, and economic structure critically affects economic growth trajectories, environmental performance, and other variables. The extent to which economic and trade theory even applies in a nation may therefore depend on these structural conditions.

7 Economists see any such pressures that emerge as mere market clearing or "pecuniary" effects, not real externalities that distort allocative efficiency (Baumol and Oates, 1988). Interestingly, the legal literature leans in a different direction on this point. Elliott, Ackerman and Millian (1985), for example, explain that real economic externalities will arise if the scope of the cost-bearers and beneficiaries of regulation are not coterminous.

8 In many instances, the result will be lower standards (Esty, 1994, 1996). But note that, where NIMBYism (that is, not in my back-yard–ism) is pervasive, strategic behavior may create pressures for suboptimally high standards as a way of discouraging local development (Levinson, 1999).

9 For a recent study, drawing on the work of economists, lawyers, political scientists, and business professors, and looking at this issue across regulatory domains (environment, labor, tax, banking) and economic integration experiences (United States versus European Union versus WTO), see Esty and Geradin (2001).

10 A potentially groundbreaking WTO decision in the asbestos case has shown more sensitivity regarding restrictions based on process and production methods (World Trade Organization, 2001).

References

Anderson, Kym. 1992. "The Standard Welfare Economics of Policies Affecting Trade and the Environment," in *The Greening of World Trade Issues*. Kym Anderson and Richard Blackhurst, eds. Ann Arbor: University of Michigan Press, pp. 25–48.

Anderson, Kym. 1998. "Environmental and Labor Standards: What Role for the WTO?" in *The WTO as an International Organization*. Anne O. Krueger, ed. Chicago: University of Chicago Press, pp. 231–55.

Anderson, Kym and Richard Blackhurst. 1992. "Trade, the Environment and Public Policy," in *The Greening of World Trade Issues*. Kym Anderson and Richard Blackhurst, eds. Ann Arbor: University of Michigan Press, pp. 3–18.

Antweiler, Werner, Brian R. Copeland and M. Scott Taylor. 1998. "Is Free Trade Good for the Environment?" National Bureau of Economic Research Working Paper No. W6707. August.

Araya, Monica. 2002. "Trade and Environment Lessons from NAFTA for the FTAA," in *Trade and Sustainability in the Americas: Lessons from NAFTA*. Carolyn Deere and Daniel C. Esty, eds. Cambridge: MIT Press, forthcoming.

Audley, John. 1997. *Green Politics and Global Trade: NAFTA and the Future of Environmental Politics*. Washington: Georgetown University Press.

Barrett, Scott. 1997. "The Strategy of Trade Sanctions in International Environmental Agreements." *Resource and Energy Economics*. 19:4, pp. 345–61.

Barrett, Scott. 2000. "Trade and Environment: Local Versus Multilateral Reforms." *Environment and Development Economics*. 5, pp. 349–59.

Baumol, William J. and Wallace E. Oates. 1988. *The Theory of Environmental Policy*. Cambridge: Cambridge University Press.

Beckerman, Wilfred. 1992. "Economic Growth and the Environment: Whose Growth? Whose Environment?" *World Development*. 20, pp. 481–96.

Bergsten, C. Fred. 1992. "The Primacy of Economics." *Foreign Policy*. Summer, 87, 3–24.

Bhagwati, Jagdish. 1988. *Protectionism*. Cambridge: MIT Press.

Bhagwati, Jagdish. 1993. "The Case for Free Trade." *Scientific American*. November, pp. 42–49.

Bhagwati, Jagdish. 1996. "Trade and the Environment: Does Environmental Diversity Detract from the Case for Free Trade?" in *Fair Trade and Harmonization: Prerequisites for Free Trade?* Jagdish Bhagwati and Robert Hudec, eds. Cambridge: MIT Press, pp. 159–223.

Bhagwati, Jagdish. 1999. "Third World Intellectuals and NGOs Statement Against Linkage." Letter drafted by Bhagwati and signed by several dozen academics, circulated on the Internet; copy on file with author.

Bhagwati, Jagdish. 2000. "On Thinking Clearly About the Linkage Between Trade and the Environment." *Environment and Development Economics*. 5:4, pp. 485–96.

Bhagwati, Jagdish and Robert E. Hudec. 1996. *Fair Trade and Harmonization: Prerequisites for Free Trade?* Cambridge: MIT Press.

Blackhurst, Richard L. and Arvind Subramanian. 1992. "Promoting Multilateral Cooperation on the Environment," in T*he Greening of World Trade Issues.* Kym Anderson and Richard L. Blackhurst, eds. Ann Arbor: University of Mich-igan Press, pp. 247–68.

Bloom, Dave E. and Jeffrey Sachs. 1998. "Geography, Demography, and Economic Growth in Africa." (Revised) CID/HIID Working Paper. October. Available online at <http//www2.cid.harvard.edu/cidpapers/brookafr.pdf>

Brack, Duncan. 1996. *International Trade and the Montreal Protocol.* London: Chatham House.

Burtless, Gary et al. 1998. *Globaphobia: Confronting Fears About Open Trade.* Washington: Brookings Institution.

Carrero, C. and D. Siniscalco. 1994. "Policy Coordination for Sustainability," in *The Economics of Sustainable Development.* Goldin and Winters, eds. Cambridge: Cambridge University Press, pp. 264–82.

Chang, Howard F. 1995. "An Economic Analysis of Trade Measures to Protect the Global Environment." *Georgetown Law Journal.* 83, pp. 2131–213.

Charnovitz, Steve. 1993. "Environmentalism Confronts GATT Rules." Journal of World Trade. April, 27:2, pp. 37–52.

Charnovitz, Steve. 2000. "World Trade and the Environment: A Review of the New WTO Report." *Georgetown International Environmental Law Review.* 12:1, pp. 523–41.

Chichilnisky, Graciela. 1994. "North-South Trade and the Global Environment." *American Economic Review.* September, 84:5, pp. 851–75.

Cline, William R. 1993. *The Economics of Global Warming.* Washington: Institute for International Economics.

Cooper, Richard N. 1994. *Environment and Resource Policies for the World Economy.* Washington: Brookings Institution.

Cooper, Richard N. 2000. "Trade and the Environment." *Environment and Development Economics.* 5:4, pp. 501–4.

Daly, Herman E. 1993. "The Perils of Free Trade." *Scientific American.* November, pp. 51–55.

Destler, I.M. and Peter J. Balint. 1999. *The New Politics of American Trade: Trade, Labor and the Environment.* Washington: Institute for International Economics.

Drezner, Daniel W. 2000. "Bottom Feeders." *Foreign Policy.* November/December, 29:6, pp. 64–70.

Dua, Andre´ and Daniel C. Esty. 1997. *Sustaining the Asia Pacific Miracle: Environmental Protection and Economic Integration.* Washington: Institute for International Economics.

Earth Council. 1997. *Subsidizing Unsustainable Development.* Vancouver: Earth Council.

Elliott, E. Donald, Bruce A. Ackerman and John C. Millian. 1985. "Toward a Theory of Statutory Evolution: The Federalization of Environmental Law." *Journal of Law Economics and Organization.* Fall, 1:2, pp. 313–40.

Engel, Kirsten and Susan Rose-Ackerman. 2001. "Environmental Federalism in the United States: The Risks of Devolution," in *Regulatory Competition and Economic Integration: Comparative Perspectives.* Daniel C. Esty and Damien Geradin, eds. Oxford: Oxford University Press.

Esty, Daniel C. 1994. *Greening the GATT: Trade, Environment and the Future.* Washington: Institute for International Economics.

Esty, Daniel C. 1996. "Revitalizing Environmental Federalism." *Michigan Law Review.* 95:3, pp. 570–653.

Esty, Daniel C. 1998a. "Environmentalists and Trade Policy-making," in *Constituent Interests and U.S. Trade Policies.* Alan W. Deardorff and Robert M. Stern, eds. Ann Arbor: University of Michigan Press.

Esty, Daniel C. 1998b. "NGOs at the World Trade Organization: Cooperation, Competition or Exclusion." *Journal of International Economic Law.* 1:1, pp. 123–48.

Esty, Daniel C. 2000a. "Global Environment Agency Will Take Pressure off WTO." *Financial Times*. July 13, p. 12.

Esty, Daniel C. 2000b. "Environment and the Trading System: Picking up the Post-Seattle Pieces," in *The WTO After Seattle*. Jeffrey J. Schott, ed. Washington: Institute for International Economics.

Esty, Daniel C. and Damien Geradin. 1998. "Environmental Protection and International Competitiveness: A Conceptual Framework." *Journal of World Trade*. 32:3, p. 5.

Esty, Daniel C. and Damien Geradin. 2001. "Regulatory Co-opetition," in *Regulatory Competition and Economic Integration: Comparative Perspectives*. Daniel C. Esty and Damien Geradin, eds. Oxford: Oxford University Press.

Esty, Daniel C. and Michael E. Porter. 2000. "Measuring National Economic Performance and its Determinants," in *The Global Competitiveness* Report 2000. Michael E. Porter, Jeffrey D. Sachs, et al., eds. New York: Oxford University Press.

Fischel, William A. 1975. "Fiscal and Environmental Considerations in the Location of Firms in Suburban Communities," in *Fiscal Zoning and Land Use Controls*. Edwin S. Mills and Wallace E. Oates, eds. Lexington, Mass.: Lexington Books, pp. 119–74.

Fitzgerald, William F. 1993. "Mercury as a Global Pollutant." *The World and I*. October, 8, pp. 192–223.

Francis, B. Magnus. 1994. *Toxic Substances in the Environment*. New York: John Wiley.

Fredriksson, Per, ed. 2000. *Trade, Global Policy, and the Environment*. World Bank Discussion Paper no. 402. Washington: World Bank.

Fredriksson, Per G. and Daniel L. Millimet. 2000. "Strategic Interaction and the Determination of Environmental Policy and Quality Across the US States: Is There a Race to the Bottom?" Unpublished working paper.

Grad, Franklin P. 1997. *Treatise on Environmental Law*. New York: M. Bender.

Grossman, Gene M. and Alan B. Krueger. 1993. "Environmental Impacts of a North American Free Trade Agreement," in *The Mexico-US Free Trade Agreement*. Peter M. Garber, ed. Cam-bridge: MIT Press, pp. 13–56.

Grossman, Gene M. and Alan B. Krueger. 1995. "Economic Growth and the Environment." *Quarterly Journal of Economics*. CX:2, pp. 353–77.

Haas, Ernst B. 1958 *The Uniting of Europe: Political, Social and Economic Forces*. Stanford: Stanford University Press.

Harbaugh, William, Arik Levinson and David Wilson. 2000. "Re-examining the Empirical Evidence for an Environmental Kuznets Curve." NBER Working Paper No. 7711, May.

Hauer, Grant and C. Ford Runge. 2000. "Transboundary Pollution and the Kuznet's Curve in the Global Commons." Unpublished manuscript.

Howells, Gwyneth P. 1995. *Acid Rain and Acid Waters*. New York: E. Horwood.

Hufbauer, Gary C. et al. 2000. *NAFTA and the Environment: Seven Years Later*. Washington: Institute for International Economics.

Jackson, John. 1992. *The World Trading System: Law and Policy of International Economic Relations*. Cambridge: MIT Press.

Jospin, Lionel. 2000. "Development Thinking at the Millennium." Speech to the Annual Bank Conference on Development Economics (World Bank), Paris. June 26.

Kalt, Joseph. 1988. "The Impacts of Domestic Environmental Regulatory Policies on US International Competitiveness," in *International Competitiveness*. A. Michael Spence and Heather A. Hazard, eds. Cambridge: Ballinger, pp. 221–62.

Keohane, Robert O. and Joseph S. Nye. 2001. "The Club Model of Multilateral Cooperation and the World Trade Organization: Problems of Democratic Legitimacy," in *Efficiency, Equity and Legitimacy: The Multilateral Trading System at the Millennium*. Robert O. Keohane and Joseph S. Nye, eds. Cambridge: Harvard University Press, pp. 313–67.

Keohane, Nathaniel, Richard L. Revesz, and Robert N. Stavins. 1998. "The Choice of Regulatory Instruments in Environmental Policy." *Harvard Environmental Law Review.* 22, pp. 313–67.

Klevorick, Alvin K. 1996. "The Race to the Bottom in a Federal System: Lessons from the World of Trade Policy." *Yale Law and Policy Review* and *Yale Journal on Regulation.* Symposium Issue, 14, pp. 177–86.

Krugman, Paul R. 1991. *Geography and Trade.* Cambridge: MIT Press.

Lawler, Andrew. 1995. NASA Mission Gets Down to Earth. *Science.* September, 1, pp. 1208–10.

Lawrence, Robert et al. 1996. *A Vision for the World Economy.* Washington: Brookings Institution.

Levinson, Arik. 1997. "A Note on Environmental Federalism: Interpreting some Contradictory Results." *Journal of Environmental Economics and Management.* 33, pp. 359–66.

Levinson, Arik. 1999. "NIMBY Taxes Matter: The Case of State Hazardous Waste Disposal Taxes." *Journal of Public Economics.* 74, pp. 31–51.

Lopez, Ramon. 1994. "The Environment as a Factor of Production: The Effects of Economic Growth and Trade Liberalization." *Journal of Environmental Economics and Management.* 27, pp. 163–84.

Low, Patrick and Alexander Yeats. 1992. "Do 'Dirty' Industries Migrate?" in *International Trade and the Environment.* Patrick Low, ed. World Bank Discussion Paper 159. Washington: World Bank, pp. 89–103.

Mani, Muthukumara and David Wheeler. 1999. "In Search of Pollution Havens? Dirty Industry in the World Economy 1960–1995," in *Trade, Global Policy and the Environment.* Per G. Fredriksson, ed. Washington: World Bank, pp. 115–27.

Meadows, Donella H. et al. 1972. *The Limits to Growth.* New York: Universe Books.

Mendelsohn, Robert. 1986. "Regulating Heterogeneous Emissions." *Journal of Environmental Economics and Management.* December, 13:4, pp. 301–13.

Nordstrom, Hakan and Scott Vaughan. 1999. *Special Studies: Trade and Environment.* Geneva: World Trade Organization.

Oates, Wallace E. and Robert M. Schwab. 1988. "Economic Competition Among Jurisdictions: Efficiency Enhancing or Distortion Inducing?" *Journal of Public Economics.* 35:1, pp 333–62.

Panayotou, Theodore. 1993. *Green Markets: The Economics of Sustainable Development.* San Francisco: ICS Press.

Perot, Ross. 1993. *Save Your Job, Save Our Country: Why NAFTA Must Be Stopped Now!* New York: Hyperion.

Rappaport, R.A. et al. 1985. "'New' DDT Inputs to North America Atmospheric Deposition." *Chemosphere.* 14, pp. 1167–73.

Repetto, Robert. 1995. *Jobs, Competitiveness and Environmental Regulation: What Are the Real Issues?* Washington: World Resources Institute.

Revesz, Richard L. 1992. "Rehabilitating Interstate Competition: Rethinking the 'Race-to-the-Bottom' Rationale for Federal Environmen-tal Regulation." *New York University Law Review.* December, 67, pp. 1210–54.

Revesz, Richard L. 1999. "Environmental Regulation, Cost-Benefit Analysis and the Discounting of Human Lives." *Columbia Law Review.* May, 99, pp. 941–1017.

Rodrik, Dani. 1997. *Has Globalization Gone Too Far?* Washington: Institute for International Economics.

Ruggiero, Renato. 1999. "Opening Remarks to the High Level Symposium on Trade and the Environment." Speech at the WTO High Level Symposium on Trade and the Environment. Geneva Switzerland. March 15.

Runge, C. Ford. 1994. *Freer Trade, ProtectedEnvironment: Balancing Trade Liberalization and Environmental Interests.* New York: Council on Foreign Relations.

Sachs, Jeffrey. 1998. "Globalization and the Rule of Law." Yale Law School Occasional Papers, 2d ser., no. 4.

Sampson, Gary P. 2000. *Trade, Environment and the WTO: The Post-Seattle Agenda.* Washington: Johns Hopkins University Press.

Schott, Jeffrey. 2000. "The WTO After Seattle, in *The WTO After Seattle.* Jeffrey Schott, ed. Washington: Institute for International Economics, pp. 3–40.

Seldon, Thomas M. and Daqing Song. 1994. "Environmental Quality and Development: Is There a Kuznets Curve for Air Pollution Emissions." *Journal of Environmental Economics and Management.* September, 27:2, pp. 147–52.

Sen, Amartya K. 1977. "Rational Fools." *Philosophy and Public Affairs.* 6:4, pp. 317–44.

Sen, Amartya K. 1999. *Development as Freedom* New York: Knopf.

Shafik, Nemat and Sushenjit Bandyopadhyay. 1992. "Economic Growth and Environmental Quality: Time Series and Cross-Country Evidence." Background Paper prepared for WorldBank, *World Development Report 1992: Development and the Environment.* New York: Oxford University Press.

Subramanian, Arvind. 1992. "Trade Measures for Environment: A Nearly Empty Box?" *World Economy.* 15:1, pp.135–52.

Summers, Lawrence. 2000. Speech to the Confederation of Indian Industry, Bombay. January 18.

Sykes, Alan O. 1995. *Product Standards for Internationally Integrated Goods Markets.* Washington: Brookings Institution.

Sykes, Alan O. 1999. "Regulatory Protectionism and the Law of International Trade." *University of Chicago Law Review.* 66, pp. 1.

Trachtman, Joel. 2000. "Assessing the Effects of Trade Liberalization on Domestic Environmental Regulation: Towards Trade-Environment Policy Integration," in *Assessing the Environmental Effects of Trade Liberalization Agreements: Methodologies.* Paris: OECD.

van Beers, Cees and Jeroen C.J.M. van den Bergh. 1997. "An Empirical Multi-Country Analysis of the Impact of Environmental Regulations on Foreign Trade Flows." *Kyklos.* 50:1, pp. 29–46.

Vogel, David. 1994. *Trading Up: Consumer and Environmental Regulation in a Global Economy.* Cambridge: Harvard University Press.

Wallach, Lori and Michelle Sforza. 1999. *Whose Trade Organization: Corporate Globalization and the Erosion of Democracy.* Washington: Public Citizen.

Wofford, Carrie. 2000. "A Greener Future at the WTO: The Refinement of WTO Jurisprudence on Environmental Exceptions to the GATT." *Harvard Environmental Law Review.* 24:2, pp. 563–92.

World Bank. 1997. *Expanding the Measure of Wealth: Indicators of Environmentally Sustainable Development.* Washington: World Bank.

World Commission on Environment and Development (WCED). 1987. *Our Common Future.* Oxford: Oxford University Press. Commonly known as the "Brundtland Report."

World Trade Organization (WTO). 1999. High Level Symposium on Trade and Environment. Proceedings available online (visited 12/10/00) at www.wto.org/english/tratop_e/envir_e/hlspeech.htm.

World Trade Organization (WTO). 2001. Report of the Appellate Body on Measures affecting asbestos and asbestos-containing products. AB-2000-11. WTO/DS/135/AB/R/. March 12, 2001.

Zhao, Jinhua. 2000. "Trade and Environmental Distortions: Coordinated Intervention." *Environmental and Development Economics.* October, 5:4, pp. 361–76.

Labor Standards: Where Do They Belong on the International Trade Agenda?

DRUSILLA K. BROWN

During the past decade, universal labor standards have become the focus of intense debate among policymakers, international agencies, nongovernmental organizations, college campus activists and the general public. Tension over labor standards has sometimes erupted into violent conflict between police and demonstrators, as it recently did during the spring 2001 Conference of the Americas in Quebec.

Labor rights activists argue that the nations of the world ought to be able to agree on some set of universally accepted human rights regarding working conditions that would apply in all nations. In addition, trade with countries in which labor is protected poorly may create an incentive to lower wages in industrialized countries and weaken existing labor law in order to maintain competitiveness in international trade. As a remedy, some proponents seek to protect the interests of labor by incorporating labor rights into international trade law.

Opponents of internationally established labor standards respond that the regulation of labor markets, as a matter of national sovereignty, should remain primarily in the domain of domestic policy and should not be a topic in international trade negotiations. The promulgation of standards internationally ought to be delegated to the International Labour Organization (ILO) and advanced exclusively through dialogue, monitoring and technical advice.

Our purpose here is to analyze the arguments concerning the value of coordinating labor standards internationally, the arena in which international labor standards ought to be established, and the instruments that can be used constructively to bring about compliance. We will examine the analytical underpinnings of universal rules for labor rights; the evidence on whether labor practices in developing countries have adverse consequences for workers in industrialized countries; and the question of whether labor standards should be introduced formally into the negotiations of the World Trade Organization (WTO) or remain primarily in the purview of the ILO.

Labor Standards Defined: Rights, Outcomes, Efficiency

The regulation of labor markets originally emerged before the fourteenth century in Europe with laws generally written to serve the interests of the elite rather than to protect labor.[1] However, with the onset of the industrial revolution, social activists began advocating labor protections that might mitigate the more brutal aspects of industrialization. Engerman (2001) marks the beginning of the modern labor rights movement with the English Factory Act of 1802. This act regulated the working conditions of pauper apprentices by establishing a twelve-hour day, prohibiting night work and providing for basic academic and religious training.

From its inception, the debate over labor rights addressed the legitimate right of the government to intrude upon market outcomes and the free choices of workers. Thus, most of the labor legislation in Europe and North America throughout the nineteenth century focused only on regulating the working conditions of women and children, with the intention of offsetting their weak bargaining power with employers. Legislation typically controlled the length of the workday and night work, and prohibited the employment of women in hazardous conditions such as underground mines.

There is also a long tradition of concern over the international coordination of labor law to mitigate the effects of labor protections on trade competitiveness.[2] The drive to coordinate labor practices internationally began during the second half of the nineteenth century. However, success was limited largely to the prohibition of production and importation of white phosphorous matches and night work by women.

The international labor rights agenda broadened dramatically at the end of World War I with the creation of the International Labour Organization. The ILO was established in 1919 as an offshoot of the League of Nations and originally had 44 member countries from Europe, Asia, Africa and Latin America.[3] Initially, discussions in the ILO focused on the eradication of slavery and all forms of forced labor. However, a broader labor rights agenda also included the rights to freedom of association and collective bargaining, nondiscrimination in employment, and the elimination of child labor (ILO, 1999).

As part of building an international consensus on labor standards, the ILO promulgates certain "Conventions" and "Recommendations" that member nations may choose to ratify. The early Conventions adopted between 1919 and 1939 included a long list of labor market practices targeted for international standards. For example, Convention 1 establishes the 8-hour day/48-hour workweek, and Convention 5 establishes a minimum work age of 14 years (although children working with family members are excluded). Additional Conventions and Recommendations pertained to wages, occupational health and safety, retirement compensation, severance pay, survivor's benefits and other topics.

The Critique of International Labor Standards

In the face of the lengthy list of labor standards contemplated by the ILO, critics of international labor standards point out the unfairness of attempting to establish standards in all of these areas without regard for the level of economic development and cultural norms. While most countries may be willing to embrace the broad caveat-filled language typical of ILO Conventions, that does not imply that the same countries will be able to agree on specific language pertaining to labor standards that would then be subject to trade disciplines in the World Trade Organization.

For example, there is strong empirical evidence that the optimal length of the workweek is negatively correlated with a nation's level of income; that is, high-income countries have a shorter workweek than many low-income countries. For example, Table 1 reports on typical workweeks, wages and labor costs for a select group of countries for manufacturing, agriculture and wearing apparel. In Costa Rica, a typical worker in manufacturing earned $1.54/hour and worked 49.1 hours a week in 1999. Some textile and wearing apparel workers earning less than $1/hour worked 50 or more hours per week. By contrast, a typical manufacturing worker in the United States earned $13.91/hour and worked 41.7 hours a week in 1999. Similarly, a suitable minimum wage cannot be set uniformly since its effects will depend critically on how high it is relative to the productivity of less-skilled labor.

Child labor practices, which receive the most intensive scrutiny in the public discussions, clearly depend on the level of economic development, and for many families the income earned by their children is a matter of the family's survival. Krueger (1997) finds a very strong negative correlation between child

Labor Market Characteristics for Select Countries: Hours Worked, Wages and Labor Costs, 1999
Table 1

Country	Manufacturing			Agriculture[a]			Wearing Apparel[a]		
	Hrs. Worked (week)	Wages (US$/hr)	Labor Cost (US$/hr)	Hours/Week Worked	Hours/Week Normal	Wages (US$/hr)	Hours/Week Worked	Hours/Week Normal	Wages (US$/hr)
Africa									
Mauritius				41.0		1.57	43.0		0.70
Latin America									
Costa Rica	49.1	1.54							
El Salvador							44.0		0.81
Mexico	45.4	1.27	3.94						
Peru				49.0	48.0	0.96	50.0	48.0	0.94
Europe									
Cyprus	41.0	6.23							
Estonia	33.8	1.92							
Hungary	34.5	2.02	3.27						
Slovenia	40.5	4.17							
Spain	36.3		18.45						
Middle East									
Israel	41.7	10.11							
Asia									
Hong Kong							45.0		4.69
New Zealand	41.0	8.80							
United States	41.7	13.91	19.20						

Sources: ILO (2000a, b), IMF (2000).
[a]Data for typical production workers in each sector

labor force participation and per capita GDP. Children 14 years and younger are not completely withdrawn from the labor force until GDP approaches $5000 per capita.

Virtually every country in the world attempts to regulate child labor by setting minimum educational requirements and minimum age of employment, though with limited success. National regulations on minimum ages for work and compulsory education, along with child labor force participation rates for a select group of countries, are reported in Table 2. For countries in the poorest parts of the world, more than 40 percent of children aged 5–14 work. This is the case even though the legal minimum age of work is typically 14 years old or higher, and in no case is the minimum work age less than 12 years.

Core Labor Standards as Basic Human Rights

Several responses have been offered to the concerns raised by the critics of labor standards. First, even if a global minimum wage applying across all countries seems nonsensical, there are still certain "core standards" that should be imposed universally because they are arguably independent of national income and reflect natural rights or broadly held values. A second line of argument holds that certain basic labor standards will have positive economic effects and can be justified on these grounds.

Cast in these terms, the discussion of core labor standards is closely related to the ongoing debate in political science and philosophy over the notion of natural rights. Some prefer to avoid the language of "rights," but

Child Labor and Education Labor Force Participation Rates, Minimum Age of Work and Compulsory Education

Table 2

Region	Child Labor Force Participation		Minimum Age for Work		Compulsory Education Ages
	Age Range	Rate	Basic	Hazardous	
Africa	5–14	41.0			
Egypt	6–14	12.0	14	15–17	6–13
Kenya	10–14	41.3	16	16–18	
South Africa	10–14	4.3	15	18	7–13
Tanzania	10–14	39.5	12–18	18	7–13
Asia	5–14	21.0			
Bangladesh	5–14	19.1	12–15	18	6–10
India	5–14	5.4	14	14–18	
Nepal	5–14	41.7	14	16	
Pakistan	5–14	8.0	14	14–21	
Philippines	5–14	10.6	15	18	6–11
Thailand	10–14	16.2	15	18	6–11
Latin America	5–14	17.0			
Brazil	5–14	12.8	14	18–21	7–14
Guatemala	7–14	4.1	14	16	6–15
Mexico	12–14	17.3	14	16–18	6–15
Nicaragua	10–14	9.9	14	18	7–12
Peru	6–14	4.1	12–16	18	6–16
Europe	5–14				
Turkey	6–14	12.6	15	18	6–13

Source: Adapted from U.S. Department of Labor (1998).

instead argue that something of a consensus has emerged on a broader set of values that are derived from the notion of individual freedom (Maskus, 1997).

Such rights-based or value-based language appears in the charters and declarations of several international organizations that include nearly all countries in the world in their membership. For example, the ILO Conventions pertaining to core labor standards, listed in Table 3, have been ratified by well over 100 countries. Furthermore, the 1998 ILO Declaration on Fundamental Principles at Work binds all 175 ILO members and states that

"...all Members, even if they have not ratified the Conventions in question, have an obligation arising from the very fact of membership in the Organization, to respect, to promote and to realize, in good faith and in accordance with the Constitution, the Principles concerning the fundamental rights which are the subject of those Conventions, namely:

1. freedom of association and the effective recognition of the right to collective bargaining,
2. the elimination of all forms of forced or compulsory labor,
3. the effective abolition of child labor, and
4. the elimination of discrimination in respect of employment and occupation."

Thus, proponents argue that the ILO and UN language can be viewed as a near universally accepted set of humanitarian principles concerning the treatment of labor (Eddy, 1997).

ILO Core Conventions
Table 3

Convention	Number	Year	Ratification Status	
			Total Members Ratifying Convention[a]	**United States**
Suppression of Forced Labor	29	1930	153	no
The Abolition of Forced Labor	105	1957	145	yes
Freedom of Association and Protection of the Right to Organize	87	1948	130	no
The Application of the Principles of the Right to Organize	98	1949	146	no
Equal Remuneration for Men and Women Workers for Work of Equal Value	100	1951	147	no
Discrimination in Respect of Employment and Occupation	111	1958	143	no
Minimum Age for Admission to Employment	138	1973	93	no
The Prohibition and Immediate Action for the Elimination of the Worst Forms of Child Labor	182	1999	72	yes

Source: (http://www.ilo.org/public/english/standards/norm/whatare/fundam/index.htm).
[a]As of 2001.

Of course, the fact that an ILO document refers to "fundamental rights" does not end the discussion. Bhagwati (1995) has been a prominent voice among those arguing that in the area of labor standards, there is little universal agreement. We have a near-universal consensus only in favor of prohibiting forced labor.[4] On other issues, like the appropriate rules to regulate collective bargaining or child labor or discrimination, we have a mixture of good intentions, some blood-curdling stories about undoubted abuses in extreme cases, and great uncertainty over what the appropriate labor standard should be.

Some statements about labor standards may be attractive general goals, but they vary too much across countries to be defined as rights. Even the United States, which has been a driving force behind the recent international labor standards initiative, has not ratified any of the ILO Conventions pertaining to nondiscrimination, forced labor, or the right to free association and collective bargaining, as can be seen from Table 3. Similarly, the debate over what constitutes "the elimination of discrimination" has proceeded for decades inconclusively. At this point there appears little closure on the issue.

Labor Process Standards

To avoid the intellectual quagmire of natural rights, other organizing principles have been proposed. For example, Aggarwal (1995) distinguishes labor market standards that are focused on outcomes from those that are focused on processes. Outcome-related standards, like a minimum wage, will always depend on levels of productivity and economic development and, thus, are poor candidates for international standards. By contrast, the core labor standards listed in the 1998 ILO Declaration are largely process-related; that is, they concern the organization of the labor market without specifying any particular market outcome. If we adopt the "process" approach, the question becomes what labor standards should be regulated and how?

An OECD (1996) report isolates labor standards that either reflect (near) universally held values and/or play a role in supporting the efficient function of labor markets. According to this view, standards such as freedom of association, the right to collective bargaining, prohibition of forced labor, the principle of nondiscrimination and prohibition of "exploitative" child labor can be imposed without regard to the degree of development and can actually promote economic growth.

While it would be convenient if efficiency-enhancing labor standards could be linked to humanitarian values, these connections are often ambiguous and controversial. Consider first the prohibition against forced labor. The consensus against slavery or labor contracts that lead to slave-like conditions is one point on which there is virtually no debate. Although it is possible to make an efficiency argument supporting the prohibition of forced labor—for an example, see Swinnerton (1997)—humanitarian concerns typically dwarf any discussion of efficiency.

The grey area concerns bonded labor contracts prohibited under ILO Convention 105. The act of choosing to be bonded may be voluntary, but once bonded, the worker is no longer free (Singh, 2001). Genicot (2000) emphasizes the role of capital market failure in bonded labor contracts. Extremely poor workers frequently have no access to formal capital markets and so are forced to offer their own labor as collateral to obtain a loan. Such arrangements may be mutually agreed upon by the worker and the employer, at least before the bonding contract is signed. Nevertheless, banning such contracts may be justified if they result from limited information or rationality on the part of the worker.

Genicot (2000) further argues that the legality of bonded labor contracts may actually inhibit the development of formal capital markets. He points out that a bank may be unwilling to extend a loan if the worker has the option of obtaining a second loan by bonding his labor. Presumably, the bondholder has greater power to enforce the loan agreement than the bank, thereby raising the default risk for the bank. In such cases, outlawing bonded labor contracts can actually improve the options for the worker by lowering the default risk for formal credit institutions.

Standard efficiency arguments are also weakened when we are constrained by political feasibility. Take, for example, discrimination in employment. Discrimination discourages workers from entering the job to which they are best-suited, thereby lowering the value of output. However, Rodrik (1999) offers a striking example in which discrimination was Pareto-improving for political economy reasons.

Mauritius set out on a development strategy that depended on operating an export-processing zone. To generate a consensus in support of the export-oriented development strategy, the interests of those benefiting from long-standing protection had to be preserved. This was accomplished by following a two-part development strategy: protection for existing industries that hired males was continued, while the export-processing zones employed females. Rodrik (1999) argues that the segmentation of the labor force along gender lines was critical to the policy's success. Male workers and import-competing producers continued to produce under the same conditions as before the introduction of the export-promotion plan, while women and capital owners in the export-processing zones had new opportunities opened to them. In Rodrik's words (p. 21): "New profit opportunities were created at the margin, while leaving old opportunities undisturbed." Thus, the Pareto-improving step was rendered politically feasible by segmenting the labor market along gender lines. Dealing with entrenched cultural patterns that have favored one group over another may sometimes lead to advocacy of policies— either preserving some of the benefits to the favored group or assuring benefits to the disfavored group—that would not pass a strict nondiscrimination test.

The expected outcome of collective bargaining is similarly uncertain. As argued by Freeman (1994), unionism has two faces. In many cases, a union can improve dispute resolution, provide a channel of information from worker to employer, and coordinate the differing views among workers concerning the trade-off between working conditions and wages (for views of unions along these lines, see Stiglitz, 2000; Piore, 1994; and Marshall, 1994). However, if a union behaves like a monopoly in an otherwise competitive market, favoring the interests of a small elite at the expense of a large group of excluded workers, then the efficiency effects are negative (Bhagwati, 1995; Srinivasan, 1997).

Finally, the OECD (1996) report seeks to include the prohibition of "exploitative" child labor as a core standard. Indeed, the specter of small children working long hours in appalling conditions motivates most analysts to find some analytical basis on which to circumscribe, at the very least, labor practices concerning children.

Bonded child labor is frequently put forward as the most egregious and offensive form of exploitative child labor. Not only do families depend on the income earned by their children for survival, but in some traditional households, children are bonded to finance a dowry or funeral ceremony. Children delivered into bonded servitude are sometimes clothed, housed and fed by their employer, and they may receive only a very small wage. The excess product generated by the child's work that is not devoted to the child's support is paid to the parent, who receives a lump sum at the time the child is delivered into servitude. That is, the child must be subsidizing the standard of living of the rest of the family and thus is exploited in this sense (Brown, Deardorff and Stern, 2001).

Although the OECD (1996) report focuses on "exploitative" child labor, it is possible to make an argument for banning child labor more broadly defined on both equity

and efficiency grounds.[5] Basu and Van (1998) analyze the case of families who put their children to work only when the adult wage is below some critical level at which the family's survival is threatened. When child labor decisions depend on the adult wage in this manner, two labor market equilibria may emerge.

In the low-wage child-labor equilibrium, both children and their parents work because the adult wage is below the critical level at which children are withdrawn from the labor market. A ban on child labor that requires parents to withdraw their children from the labor force contracts the supply of labor and may give rise to a second equilibrium with an adult wage above the critical level at which children no longer work. The ban on child labor is effective when it redistributes income from capital to labor in such a way as to alter the family's child-labor decisions.

Although much attention is focused on poverty as the root cause of child labor, Baland and Robinson (2000) refocus on the role of capital market failure. Presumably, poor families analyze the trade-off between work and schooling in part by comparing the present discounted value of an education relative to the income from current work. It is arguably the case that the relative return to education is as high or higher for a poor child than for children generally. However, poor parents may still choose to put their child to work if they cannot borrow against their educated child's future income.[6] In this situation, a ban on child labor may be part of a strategy for improving the efficiency of the labor market when combined with a program that provides poor families access to capital markets or otherwise repairs the capital market failure. Brown (2001) offers a review of policies that combine education and capital market reform.

Taking steps to reduce forced labor, child labor, and discriminatory behavior, or to support free association and collective bargaining will often have a mixture of effects. Realizing the potential efficiency, equity and humanitarian benefits of core standards may depend on first correcting ancillary market or political failures. Further, we cannot make a general statement that universal labor standards derived from commonly held moral values will always produce positive economic outcomes. The effect on economic performance and the lives of workers and their families of legally imposed labor market constraints of the sort contemplated by labor rights activists cannot be presumed to be positive, but instead must be empirically investigated on a country-by-country basis.

Divergent Labor Standards, Trade and Wages of Unskilled Workers in High-Income Countries

While humanitarian concerns have played a prominent role in the debate over international labor standards, a complementary motivation rests on the view that trade with low-wage countries has increased unemployment and slowed the growth in wages of unskilled workers in high-income countries over the past three decades. To the extent that low labor cost in developing countries is the result of poorly protected core labor rights, trade based on low wages is sometimes seen as unfair or illegitimate.

As a matter of theory, poorly protected worker rights in one country can assuredly lower the wages in its trade partner. According to the Stolper-Samuelson (1941) theorem, international trade between a high-wage and a low-wage country will lower the return to unskilled labor in the high-wage country. But to what extent is the decline in the return to unskilled labor in the United States in the last few decades the result of international trade with low-wage countries? Further, to what extent is such trade the consequence of low labor standards?

Has Trade Lowered the Return to Unskilled Labor in the United States over the Past Two Decades?

There appear to be two primary candidates driving the rise in inequality between skilled and unskilled labor in the United States in recent decades. Skill-biased technical change, presumably associated with the new information and communications technologies, would shift up the demand for skilled workers. However, labor rights activists focus on the expansion of international trade with low-wage economies, which they argue has tended to reduce the demand for low-skilled labor in the United States.

A number of pieces of evidence suggest that an important shift toward skill-biased technological change has indeed occurred. For example, the relative supply of skilled labor did expand throughout the 1980s even as the relative wage of skilled labor increased, which suggests that firms were moving up along the skilled-labor supply curve, paying higher wages and adopting a more skill-intensive technique of production (Bound and Johnson, 1992). Similarly, throughout the 1980s, U.S. manufacturing consistently substituted toward skilled labor in spite of its rising costs (Lawrence and Slaughter, 1993). Such a pattern of behavior is cost-minimizing only if there has been a technological change rendering skilled labor relatively more productive. The greater demand for skilled labor seems to have occurred more as a broad-based shift within many sectors of the economy rather than arising only in certain labor-intensive sectors. Such evidence is consistent with skill-biased technological change that drives up the demand for skill in all sectors (Berman, Bound and Griliches, 1994). Finally, there is little evidence that the relative price of labor-intensive goods fell during the 1980s, as one would expect if imports from low-income countries were undercutting less-skilled U.S. labor (Leamer, 1996).

Nevertheless, a number of economists continue to believe that international trade is responsible, at least in part, for the recent decline in the relative wages of unskilled workers in the United States. As one example, Borjas, Freeman and Katz (1992) calculate the factor supplies embodied in U.S. international trade and immigration. They find that for 1985–1986, trade and immigration implicitly increased the supply of workers with a skill level equivalent to a high school dropout in the United States by 27 percent, whereas the comparable number for college graduates was 9 percent. They use a wage equation to relate the implicit change in relative factor supplies to a change in relative wages and conclude that trade and immigration gave rise to a 2 percent increase in the college graduate wage premium, which was 20 percent of the total change in the college premium during the period.[7]

Choosing between skill-biased technology and trade as explanations for the rise in income inequality is further complicated by the reality that these factors may be intertwined; that is, technological improvements may both increase the demand for skilled labor and also increase imports from low-wage countries by making it easier to manage far-flung supply chains.

The controversy over trade and the distribution of income continues.[8] However, at this point, the bulk of the evidence supports the argument that skill-biased technological change is more important than trade as an explanation of wage inequality in the United States, although rising levels of trade with low-income countries may have played a secondary role.

Do National Labor Standards Alter Exports, Competitiveness or Comparative Advantage?

With regard to the issue of international labor standards, the question is whether poorly protected labor rights have played a role in determining comparative advantage and increasing exports from developing countries.

Several studies have examined a simple correlation between the existence and/or observance of core labor standards and various measures of trade performance. For example, Mah (1997) analyzes the trade performance of 45 developing countries and finds that each country's export share of GDP is strongly negatively correlated with rights to nondiscrimination, negatively correlated with freedom-of-association rights, and weakly negatively correlated with the right to organize and collective bargaining.

However, to gauge the marginal contribution of core labor standards, one must compare each country's trade performance against a baseline expectation as to what such a country should be trading given its factor endow-

ments and other determinants of trade. Rodrik (1996) provides an excellent example of how such analysis can be undertaken. He first considers the impact of core labor standards on labor costs per worker in manufacturing. He does this by calculating a regression using labor cost as the dependent variable and per capita income and various measures of labor standards as the independent variables. In this framework, per capita income is being used as a proxy for productivity in the economy. Labor standards are measured in a variety of ways: total number of ILO Conventions ratified; number of ILO Conventions ratified pertaining to labor standards; Freedom House indicators of civil liberties and political rights; statutory hours worked; days of paid annual leave; the unionization rate; and an indicator of child labor.

Rodrik (1996) finds that for the period 1985-88, labor costs are overwhelmingly determined by labor productivity. However, the number of ILO Conventions ratified, Freedom House indicators of democracy, and the index of child labor are large and statistically significant, with laws regulating child labor playing a particularly important role in determining labor costs.

Rodrik (1996) then turns to the determinants of comparative advantage in labor-intensive goods. He uses the fraction of textiles and clothing exports in total exports as a proxy for measuring comparative advantage in labor-intensive goods. As a theoretical matter, comparative advantage is primarily determined by factor endowments. Therefore, the comparative advantage variable is regressed on the independent variables of population-to-land ratio (a measure of the labor endowment), average years of schooling in the population over 25 (a measure of the stock of human capital) and the labor standards variables. The population and human capital variables have the expected signs and are statistically significant. However, generally the labor standards variables, while having the expected sign, are not statistically significant. The lone exception is statutory hours worked. The longer the workweek, the stronger is the comparative advantage in textiles and clothing.

Overall, the link from low labor standards in low-income countries to the wage of unskilled workers in industrialized countries is not especially strong. Increased global trade is at most a secondary cause of income inequality in high-income countries, and labor standards are at most a secondary determinant of wages in low-income countries. Moreover, this evidence begs the question as to whether externally imposed labor standards will actually affect labor market practices in developing countries (Brown, 2000). Some evidence on this question is discussed below.

Competition between Labor Standards and the Risk of a Race to the Bottom

Proponents of international coordination of core labor standards argue that, in the absence of coordination, each country might lower its own standards in an attempt to be more attractive to foreign investment or to gain a competitive advantage over foreign exporters. The possibility of a prisoner's dilemma outcome arises, in which each country has an individual incentive to adopt low labor standards, but all nations could benefit from a coordinated choice of higher labor standards.

This scenario raises several questions. How powerful is this incentive to diminish labor standards? Must core labor standards be harmonized according to a universal guideline or will some more limited coordination be more effective? Should the responsibility of promulgating standards and monitoring labor practices remain with the ILO or should the trade disciplines of the WTO be brought to bear on countries with low labor standards?

The Race to the Bottom

Those most concerned with a prisoner's dilemma in labor protections couch their arguments in terms of a "race to the bottom" in which governments may be pressured to loosen labor protections so as not to hamper domestic firms that are competing in the international arena. This line of argument implies that international trade and labor standards are inextricably linked

and, therefore, should be negotiated simultaneously within the WTO.

To understand the political economy of this race to the bottom, consider in the spirit of Brown, Deardorff and Stern (1996) the situation of a country that wishes to impose new labor standards on an import-competing sector of the economy. For a small country, the price of the good is fixed on world markets. Consequently, the cost of the labor standard must be borne solely by domestic producers, who have no power to pass the cost of the regulation on to consumers. However, if all countries impose the new labor standard, global supply for the product declines, allowing firms in this sector worldwide to raise their price. In this case, consumers end up bearing some of the cost. Thus, with coordination, the political objection to the labor standards legislation by domestic producers will be less intense, enhancing the chances of passage.

It is important to note for the purposes of the following discussion that this country pays a price for relying on international coordination to discipline the domestic political process. Harmonization is effective in transferring some of the cost of the labor standard from the producer to the consumer precisely because it raises the international price of the imported good. In other words, this country suffers a deterioration in its terms of trade with harmonization—specifically, higher prices for its imports and lower prices for its exports.

International Trade and Some Surprising Incentives for Higher Labor Standards

At first blush, the forces driving a race to the bottom in international standards may seem obvious. However, all countries have an incentive at least to consider the efficiency properties of their labor market policies. We need to consider, then, how international trade alters the political and economic incentives to pursue efficiency-enhancing domestic policies, such as labor standards (Srinivasan, 1998). As it turns out, trade provides at least some incentives for both high- and low-income countries to choose higher labor standards.

Consider first standards-setting in a high-income country. Bagwell and Staiger (2000) analyze a situation in which a government's rationale for establishing labor standards is, at least in part, driven by the true social benefits and costs of such standards. For example, the decision to raise the minimum age of employment by one year reflects an attempt to balance the social benefits of greater educational attainment and the social cost of the forgone production of young workers.

In this situation, when a high-income economy opens to trade, goods formerly produced by inexperienced and low-skilled young workers can now be replaced with low-priced imports. Thus, opening to trade creates an incentive, because of the reduced opportunity cost, to tighten rather than relax labor standards in the high-income country.

Next, consider the effect that international trade has on the incentives to set labor standards in developing countries. Brown, Deardorff and Stern (1996) point out that low-income countries are, typically, labor abundant. They make the plausible assumption that higher labor standards are "labor using," which means that a tightening of world labor standards will contract the world supply of labor. Wages worldwide rise, pushing up the price of labor-intensive goods exported by developing countries. The change in the terms of trade serves the interests of the labor-abundant developing countries at the expense of industrialized countries that are physical and human capital abundant. Therefore, developing countries, as a group, have an incentive to overprotect labor.

This analysis does not suggest that labor standards in developing countries will be higher than in industrialized countries, but only that developing countries with market power in international trade might have higher-than-expected labor standards given their level of economic development. More importantly, when labor standards are used in this way to gain a strategic advantage over the terms of trade, the policy is welfare reducing from a world point of view. A low-income country that uses labor standards for strategic purposes is surrendering efficiency to bring about higher export prices. However, from a world point of view, the terms-of-trade effects are zero-sum. The terms-of-trade gain for the labor-abundant country comes at the expense of their labor-scarce trade partners. Thus, on balance, the efficiency effect is negative.

The Race to the Bottom Revisited

Given the conflicting incentives, where can we find a race to the bottom that is broadly consistent with optimizing behavior on the part of governments? Bagwell and Staiger (1999) point out that lower labor standards may be used to gain a strategic advantage in international trade or to accomplish domestic political objectives when tariffs are also being used to restrict trade. Labor standards, like tariffs, have implications for the international terms of trade and for the well-being of import-competing firms and, thus, are policy substitutes.

For example, an import tariff provides relief to import-competing producers from the pressure of foreign imports by raising the price of imports. A reduction in labor standards similarly provides relief by lowering labor cost for import-competing producers. Both policies expand production by import-competing firms, which has the additional effect of lowering the demand for imports. If the country has international market power, the contraction in the demand for imports will also reduce the world price of imports, giving rise to a terms-of-trade improvement.

When countries remove tariffs and other barriers to trade in the context of international trade negotiations, they give up the policy tools normally used to turn the terms of trade to their advantage and to protect their import-competing producers. These protectionist urges are thus deflected onto domestic policies such as labor standards. Consequently, some mechanism for controlling subsequent competition in domestic policies is necessary if WTO members are to realize the full benefits of trade liberalization.

Labor Standards in International Negotiations

The strategic interaction between tariffs and labor standards raises the question of whether or how labor standards might be included in the negotiations of the WTO. A recent review of trade law by the OECD (1996) considered various ways of trying to link labor standards to existing WTO rules.[9] However, the OECD report found that in each case, either low labor standards do not meet the technical requirements of the article and/or the WTO does not provide for an enforcement mechanism. As a consequence, some revision to the WTO charter will be required if low labor standards are to be addressed directly.

Opponents of a "social clause" in the WTO warn of a morass that will emerge if governments attempt to negotiate trade and domestic policy simultaneously. Concerns for domestic autonomy, to say nothing of complexity, could bring the WTO process to its knees. However, because of the strategic interaction between tariffs and labor standards discussed in the previous section, the "benign neglect" of labor standards in the WTO is also a potential source of inefficient bargaining over trade policy (Bagwell and Staiger, 2000).

Remarkably, Bagwell and Staiger (2000) find a clever device for implicitly drawing domestic policies into the WTO framework without having to negotiate over domestic policies directly. As they argue in this symposium, when governments negotiate over tariffs in the WTO, they are implicitly making a commitment to a particular level of market access. This is the case because, under GATT Article XXIII, any country in the WTO is entitled to "right of redress" for changes in domestic policy that systematically erode market access commitments even if no explicit GATT rule has been violated. Such a "nonviolation" complaint entitles the aggrieved party either to compensation in the form of other tariff concessions to "rebalance" market access commitments or the complaining partner may withdraw equivalent concessions of its own.

In the context of labor standards, any country that attempts to undo its market access commitments made in a round of WTO negotiations may be required to provide additional trade concessions to restore the originally agreed-upon market access commitments. As a consequence, no government has the ability to pass the cost or benefit of their labor standards onto the rest of the world or to achieve a strategic advantage by altering its labor standards.

Of course, a change in labor standards policy may expand, as well as contract, market access. Thus, to achieve symmetry, GATT Article XXIII would have to be amended to allow countries that expand market access as a consequence of changes in domestic policy to retract subsequently some tariff concessions that restore the original market access commitments.

We can gain an intuitive feel for the Bagwell-Staiger mechanism by returning to the race to the bottom presented above. Recall that some governments have a political economy incentive to seek stricter labor standards internationally to offset the cost of domestic labor standards for their import-competing producers. An internationally coordinated labor standard could provide relief to domestic producers, since it reduces worldwide production of the labor-intensive good, thereby raising its price on the world market. However, under the tariff negotiating scenario envisioned by Bagwell and Staiger, a country that raises its labor standards, thereby increasing import demand, would be entitled to a tariff increase that returns market access to the originally agreed-upon level.

Note that a high-income country will prefer the Bagwell-Staiger mechanism to the strategy of harmonizing labor standards internationally. Both provide relief to domestic producers by raising the landed price of imports. However, harmonization entails a deterioration in the terms of trade and requires all countries to agree upon a single standard. By contrast, the Bagwell-Staiger mechanism does not alter the terms of trade and leaves all countries with the option of setting their labor standards in the manner that serves their own economic and domestic political interests.

The essential feature of the Bagwell-Staiger mechanism is that it requires each country to neutralize the international economic repercussions of its domestic policy decisions. As a consequence, countries are not tempted to sacrifice socially desirable labor market policies in order to achieve zero-sum terms-of-trade gains. Perhaps more importantly, each government is also given the ability to offset some of the distributional effects of efficiency-enhancing domestic policies. By internalizing to each country all of the external effects of domestic policy, legislators are free to choose optimizing domestic policies without regard for their strategic consequences for international trade.

Labor Protections and Humanitarian Concerns

The analysis to this point has probably not been particularly satisfying for those motivated by humanitarian concerns. It is morally meaningless to prohibit the domestic production of goods by our own children if the end result is simply to import goods produced by illiterate children in a neighboring country. A similar argument can also be made, albeit in a lower tone, about goods produced by workers who receive low wages or work long hours.

While it is undoubtedly the case that consumers in high-income countries are genuinely concerned with the welfare of foreign workers, it is not at all clear that these concerns can be constructively addressed in the WTO by applying trade disciplines. To understand the role that the WTO might play in mediating humanitarian concerns with the process of production, it is important to distinguish between two different forms in which these moral concerns might manifest themselves.

First, moral distaste may be a private good. For example, a consumer might prefer not to consume goods produced by children or under poor working conditions. In this case, consumers ought to have an opportunity to avoid goods produced in this manner,

provided that they are willing to pay the additional cost of production. In some cases, this might be accomplished by attaching a product label detailing the conditions under which the good was produced (Freeman, 1994). But one can also make a case that countries that wish to do so should be allowed to include a broad definition of immoral working conditions and, acting as a country, refuse to import such goods.

However, this particular moral stance focuses only on alleviating the bad feeling consumers have in knowing they have consumed a good produced under unpleasant circumstances. The welfare of the foreign workers themselves is not necessarily at issue. But if consumers in high-income countries can exhaust their moral commitments simply by avoiding consumption of goods produced in ways that they dislike contemplating, without regard for the welfare of the workers involved, then the humanitarian argument begins to lose some of its moral gravity. If, by contrast, humanitarian and moral concerns focus on the welfare of the workers themselves, rather than on the discomfort of the consumer, then the ability of trade sanctions imposed through the WTO to address these concerns is highly limited.

In fact, trade sanctions in the face of low labor standards are as likely or even more likely to harm workers as they are to improve working conditions. Maskus (1997) provides a detailed discussion of this point, which I draw upon throughout this section.

Consider the problem of child labor in the case of a small open economy in which the export sector is adult labor-intensive, the import sector is capital-intensive, and a non-traded intermediate input to the export sector is produced using child labor. The child's labor supply is increasing in the child's wage and decreasing in the adult wage. The marginal child worker is the youngest, since the opportunity cost in terms of forgone education falls as the child ages.

In this setting, a foreign tax imposed on goods produced by children can lead to the social optimum in the sense of internalizing the external effect of child work on the well-being of western consumers. Those children no longer working who receive an education are also better off. However, if, as a consequence of the tax, the newly unemployed children live in a household with lower income, less nutrition, and otherwise diminished life alternatives, the trade sanction has probably been counterproductive. Children who continue to work after the imposition of the tax are definitely worse off, since the firms who employ children have to pay a tax. In a small open economy, a tax must lower the after-tax wage of the working child.

A similar type of analysis can be applied to discrimination in employment. Suppose, for example, that the supply of female workers is upward-sloping but there is a legally mandated ceiling on the wages paid to female workers in the export sector. A foreign tariff imposed as a sanction against the offending practice will lower the demand for the offending country's exports. By implication, the demand for female labor in the export sector also declines. Since the equilibrium wage for female workers is now lower than before the sanctions were imposed, firms will find it less costly than before to engage in discrimination, thus making discrimination more likely. Women, of course, are made worse off in the process relative to male workers since both their employment and wages have declined.

The foreign tariff will only be successful if the government responds to the threat of sanctions by eliminating the discriminatory practice. However, the threat itself lacks credibility in view of the fact that the tariff harms precisely the group of workers who are already victimized.

A threat with such adverse consequences could hardly be credible. The threat of sanctions will be particularly ineffective if the targeted country simply lacks the resources to respond to the threat. For example, Rogers and Swinnerton (1999) estimate that if GDP per worker falls below $5020, families are so poor that they cannot survive without contributions to family income from children. Thus, no matter how intense the demand for a reduction in child labor, child labor practices will continue.

Furthermore, trade sanctions do little to address the underlying market failure that gives rise to offending labor practices. For example, capital market failure arguably lies at the heart of the most egregious forms of child labor exploitation. If parents had access to capital markets, they would school their children while transferring wealth from the future to the present by borrowing against their own future income or the future income of their children (Baland and Robinson, 2000). However, lacking collateral and facing other capital market pathologies, the only device parents have available to them is to put their children to work. The end result, of course, is inadequate human capital formation.

Nor does it appear that legislating labor practices is likely to be particularly effective when standards are not sensitive to local community conditions. For example, Krueger (1996) examines the relationship between mandatory education and the actual age at which children leave school. In 1947, the United Kingdom raised the age at which children could leave school from 14 to 15 years. In 1973 the age was raised again from 15 to 16 years. In both cases, the modal age at which students left school adjusted with the law. By contrast, in Brazil, 80 percent of students leave school before the age of 13, even though school attendance is mandatory through age 14. In Mexico and Portugal, 25 percent of students leave school before the legal age. More generally, none of the developing countries studied showed a spike in leaving school at the compulsory age for doing so.

The decline in child labor in the United States between 1880 and 1910 suggests a similar pattern (Moehling, 1999). In 1900, twelve states had a minimum age law prohibiting work by children under the age of 14 years. By 1910, 32 states had enacted similar legislation. However, a review of the censuses taken in 1880, 1900 and 1910 suggests that the legislation had little effect on the incidence of child labor.

More broadly, the difficulty in enforcing agreed-upon labor standards has plagued the ILO since its inception. Many countries have ratified ILO Conventions pertaining to both core and other labor practices, but have ultimately lacked the intention or the resources to change their labor market conditions.

For example, many countries that have ratified ILO Conventions pertaining to the right to organize and collective bargaining maintain tight political control over union activity (OECD, 1996). The main union federations in Jordan, Kenya, Singapore and Taiwan are closely linked with the ruling parties. More extremely, China, Egypt, Iran, Kuwait, Syria and Tanzania effectively permit only a single union structure, and the right to strike is severely circumscribed in many countries.

Thus, while international pressure can lead to the passage of stricter labor law, it is unclear to what extent the newly enacted legislation will change the realities of the labor market in low-income countries. If trade sanctions are actually employed in pursuit of higher labor standards, the effect will often be to hurt precisely those who are the focus of humanitarian concerns. Of course there are some cases in which sanctions by the international community can be brought to bear against some more egregious violations of broadly held humanitarian values. However, the routine use of trade sanctions or the threat of sanctions imposed through the WTO does not seem an especially promising mechanism for helping workers in low-income countries.

International Enforcement of Labor Standards

The weight of the argumentation above militates against direct negotiation over labor standards in the WTO, leaving the ILO as the main forum for discussion. Labor rights activists nevertheless argue in favor of some link between the ILO and the WTO on labor issues in order to provide the ILO with enforcement power beyond its current practice of monitoring and providing members with advice and technical support.

Countries who have ratified ILO Conventions are obligated to report regularly on their compliance activities. In addition, ILO Article 24 allows employers' and workers' organizations to report to the ILO on a state's compliance, and under ILO Article 26, another member of the ILO can bring evidence of a state's failure to comply with ratified Conventions. Moreover, freedom-of-association complaints can be brought even against countries that have not ratified the specific Conventions 87 and 98. In cases where problems exist with compliance, the ILO begins a consultative process with the member government, providing technical support and drawing press attention to the matter.

While the ILO may be effective in promoting discussion between workers and member governments, it has none of the remedies available to members of the WTO. For this reason, linkage between the ILO and the WTO has been suggested as a way of transferring some enforcement power on trade policy to labor standards.

It is possible to link two separate issues in a single agreement and, through that linkage, improve enforcement of both issues. Spagnolo (1999) considers the case in which two governments are attempting to cooperate over two separate policy issues. For our purposes, these two policy issues can be viewed as tariffs and labor standards. Both policy issues are characterized by a prisoner's dilemma; that is, both countries would gain if they could find a sustainable mechanism to cooperate on lower tariffs and higher labor standards, but an inferior outcome emerges in the absence of cooperation.

In a repeated prisoner's dilemma game, cooperation can be self-enforcing if the benefit of defecting in any round of the game is smaller than the cost of the punishment in all succeeding rounds. Thus, one strategy for sustaining cooperation in a repeated prisoner's dilemma game is a "trigger" strategy: cooperate as long as the other party cooperates, but make clear that if the other party ever defects, then there will be no future cooperative behavior. When policy issues become linked in an international agreement, defection on either tariff or labor standards commitments will cause the entire agreement to collapse. Employing linkage to raise the cost of defecting from either tariff or labor standards commitments should help to sustain compliance on both dimensions.

However, it is important to realize that linking trade and labor standards could slow the process of trade liberalization. Limao (2000) considers a case in which the international community has found it relatively easy to achieve a nearly optimal agreement on tariffs but has had greater difficulty finding a self-enforcing agreement on labor standards. If tariffs and labor standards are linked together, the likely agreement would consist of less trade liberalization but tighter labor standards than would have occurred in a partitioned agreement. Nevertheless, in this example world welfare is higher than in the absence of linkage because the gains from improving the relatively inadequate labor standards are larger than the losses from raising the already close-to-optimal tariff levels.

As with most conclusions in economics, the outcome depends on the underlying assumptions. Limao (2000) points out that linkage can become counterproductive in the face of a powerful lobby, which advocates in favor of producers in the import-competing sector. In this scenario, defection on the tariff agreement by raising tariffs makes the import-competing sector larger. The larger is the import-competing sector, the greater the gain in producer surplus from subsequently relaxing labor standards. That is, when it comes to cheating, cheating in labor standards and cheating in tariffs are complements when producer surplus in the import-competing sector plays an important role in the political process. The consequent increase in the returns to cheating makes defection on a linked agreement more attractive when compared to two separate agreements. In this case, the enforcement power of two separate agreements can be destroyed by linkage.

Conclusion

There is clearly a trend in global trade talks to extend coverage beyond traditional tariffs, quotas and subsidies. During the Uruguay round of multilateral trade negotiations, the purview of the GATT process extended well past debate over tariffs to include issues previously relegated to the domestic agenda, such as intellectual property rights, competition policy, and investment regulations. In each case, the argument is that trade policies and domestic policies need to be negotiated simultaneously if all policy tools are to be set optimally.

Labor standards have proved to be one of the most contentious of the domestic policies considered for introduction into the WTO. In spite of the "trade-relatedness" of labor market practices, the case for international labor standards mediated by the WTO is ultimately problematic.

For those whose goal is to protect the wages of low-skilled workers in high-income countries from import competition, it seems unlikely that trade is the primary factor that has caused the stagnant wages of low-skilled workers in recent decades. Nor does it appear that harmonizing labor standards is a powerful tool for improving the distribution of income in industrialized countries.

For those concerned with a race to the bottom in labor standards, there is a strong case that efficiency can be achieved without negotiating over labor standards directly. As long as countries are required to adhere to market access commitments made in a round of tariff negotiations, any subsequent change in domestic policy that erodes that commitment must be offset with additional tariff concessions. If GATT Article XXIII is interpreted and enforced in this way, it can be used to short-circuit any motivation for setting labor standards strategically.

For those motivated by humanitarian concern over the plight of workers in low-income countries, it is an uncomfortable reality that trade sanctions leveled against countries with poor labor practices may well hurt the very workers who are the intended beneficiaries. Moreover, it is by no means clear that attempts to use trade sanctions to enforce labor standards will strengthen either trade or labor standards, at least not in a world of strong political lobbies.

Heterogeneous labor standards across the world are a legitimate source of policy concern. But it seems unlikely that the appropriate policy response is to seek a single set of universal labor rules.

Drusilla K. Brown is Associate Professor of Economics, Tufts University, Medford, Massachusetts. Her e-mail address is <Drusilla.Brown@tufts.edu>.

Endnotes

[1] See Engerman (2001) for a discussion of the history of international labor standards

[2] See in particular the 1818 writings of Robert Owen (Engerman, 2001).

[3] Specifics concerning the ILO and ILO Conventions can be found at http://www.ILO.org.

[4] Portes (1994) offers a four-part taxonomy of labor standards: basic rights, which include the rights against the use of child labor, involuntary servitude, physical coercion and discrimination; civic rights, including free association, collective representation and expression of grievances; survival rights, including a living wage, accident compensation and a limited workweek; and security rights, which protect against arbitrary dismissal and provide for retirement compensation and survivors' compensation.

[5] See Basu (1999) for a review of the literature concerning child labor.

[6] In fact, there is considerable evidence that the presence of household assets lowers the probability of child labor above and beyond their impact on family income. See Psacharopoulos (1994) for a discussion.

[7] The factor content approach relies on certain underlying assumptions that are controversial. For critiques, see Panagariya (2000), Bhagwati and Dehejia (1994) and Leamer (2000). For a defense of the approach, see Krugman (2000).

[8] For discussions of the state of the literature on trade and wages, readers are referred to the "Symposium on Income Inequality and Trade" in the Summer 1995 issue of this journal, with articles by Richard B. Freeman, J. David Richardson, and Adrian Wood. More recently, see Cline (1997), Slaughter and Swagel (1997), and Panagariya (2000).

[9] Specifically, some possible sources of linkage from labor standards to trade in the WTO, based on the articles of the original GATT, include: the prohibition on dumping products at less than normal value (GATT Article VI); the prohibition on export subsidies (GATT Article XVI); the prohibition on goods produced by prison labor (GATT Article XX(e)); the Nullification and Impairment Provision (GATT Article XXIII); the Opt-Out Provision (GATT Article XXXV); and the Trade Policy Review Mechanism. See OECD (1996) for a detailed discussion.

References

Aggarwal, Mita. 1995. "International Trade, Labor Standards, and Labor Market Conditions: An Evaluation of Linkages." USITC, Office of Economics Working Paper No. 95-06-C (June).

Bagwell, Kyle and Robert W. Staiger. 1999. "Domestic Policies, National Sovereignty and International Economic Institutions." NBER Working Paper 7293.

Bagwell, Kyle and Robert W. Staiger. 2000. "The Simple Economics of Labor Standards and the GATT," in *Social Dimensions of U.S. Trade Policy*. A. V. Deardorff and R.M. Stern, eds. Ann Arbor, MI: University Press, pp. 195–231.

Baland, Jean-Marie and James Robinson. 2000. "A Model of Child Labor." *Journal of Political Economy*. 108:4, pp. 663–79.

Basu, Kaushik. 1999. "Child Labor: Cause, Consequence, and Cure, with Remarks on International on Labor Standards." *Journal of Economic Literature*. September, 37, pp. 1083–1119.

Basu, Kaushik and Pham Hoang Van. 1998. "The Economics of Child Labor." *American Economic Review*. 88:3, pp. 412–27.

Berman, Eli, John Bound and Eli Griliches. 1994. "Changes in the Demand for Skilled Labor within U.S. Manufacturing: Evidence from Annual Survey of Manufacturers." *Quarterly Journal of Economics.* 109:2, pp. 367–97.

Bhagwati, Jagdish. 1995. "Trade Liberalisation and 'Fair Trade' Demands: Addressing the Environmental and Labour Standards Issues." *World Economy.* 18:6, pp. 745–59.

Bhagwati, Jagdish and V. Dehejia. 1994. "Freer Trade and Wages of the Unskilled? Is Marx Striking Again?" in *Trade and Wages: Leveling Wages Down?* J. Bhagwati and M. Kosters, eds. Washington, D.C.: AEI, pp. 36–75.

Borjas, George J., Richard B. Freeman and Lawrence F. Katz. 1992. *Immigration and the Work Force: Economic Consequences for the United States and Source Areas.* Chicago: University of Chicago Press.

Bound, John and George Johnson. 1992. "Changes in the Structure of Wages in the 1980s: An Evaluation of Alternative Explanations." *American Economic Review.* 82:3, pp. 371–92.

Brown, Drusilla K. 2000. "International Trade and Core Labour Standards: A Survey of the Recent Literature." Labour Market and Social Policy Occasional Papers No. 43, Organization for Cooperation and Development, Paris.

Brown, Drusilla K. 2001. "Child Labor in Latin America: Policy and Evidence." *World Economy,* forthcoming.

Brown, Drusilla K., Alan V. Deardorff and Robert M. Stern. 1996. "International Labor Standards and Trade: A Theoretical Analysis," in *Fair Trade and Harmonization: Prerequisites for Free Trade? Economic Analysis, Vol. 1.* Jagdish Bhagwati and Robert Hudec, eds. Cambridge and London: MIT Press, pp. 227–80.

Brown, Drusilla K., Alan V. Deardorff and Robert M. Stern. 2001. "U.S. Trade and Other Policy Options and Programs to Deter Foreign Exploitation of Child Labor," in *Topics in Empirical International Economics.* Bagnus Blomstrom and Linda S. Goldberg, eds. Chicago and London: The University of Chicago Press.

Cline, William R. 1997. *Trade and Income Distribution.* Washington, D.C.: Institute for International Economics.

Eddy, Lee. 1997. "Globalization and Labour Standards: A Review of Issues." *International Labour Review.* 136:2, pp. 173–89.

Engerman, Stanley L. 2001. "The History and Political Economy of International Labor Standards," mimeo.

Freeman, Richard. 1994. "A Hard-Headed Look at Labour Standards," in *International Labour Standards and Economic Interdependence.* Werner Sengenberger and Duncan Campbell, eds. Geneva: International Institute for Labour Studies, pp. 79–92.

Genicot, Garance. 2000. "Bonded Labor and Serfdom: A Paradox of Choice." Working Paper, University of California, Irvine.

International Labour Organization. 1999. *Promoting Social Justice.* Geneva: International Labour Office.

International Labour Organization. 2000a. *Statistics on Occupational Wages and Hours of Work and on Food Prices.* Geneva: International Labour Office.

International Labour Organization. 2000b. *LABOURST.* Geneva: Bureau of Labour Statistics.

International Monetary Fund. 2000. *International Financial Statistics Yearbook.* Washington, D.C.: International Monetary Fund.

Katz, Lawrence F. and Kevin M. Murphy. 1992. "Changes in Relative Wages, 1963–1987: Supply and Demand Factors." *Quarterly Journal of Economics.* 107:428, pp. 35–78.

Krueger, Alan. 1997. "International Labor Standards and Trade," in *Annual World Bank Conference on Development Economics.* Michael Bruno and Boris Pleskovic, eds. Washington, D.C.: The World Bank, pp. 281–302.

Krugman, Paul R. 2000. "Technology, Trade and Factor Prices." *Journal of International Economics.* 50, pp. 51–71.

Lawrence, Robert Z. and Matthew Slaughter. 1993. "Trade and U.S. Wages in the 1980s: Giant Sucking Sound or Small Hiccup?" *Brookings Papers on Economic Activity: Microeconomics,* pp. 161–210.

Leamer, Edward E. 1996. "A Trial Economist's View of U.S. Wages and Globalization," in *Imports, Exports, and the American Worker.* Susan Collins, ed. Washington, D.C.: Brookings Institution.

Leamer, Edward E. 2000. "What's the Use of Factor Contents?" *Journal of International Economics.* 50, pp. 17–49.

Limao, Nuno. 2000. "Trade Policy, Cross-Border Externalities and Lobbies: Do Linked Agreements Enforce More Cooperative Outcomes?" Mimeo.

Mah, J.S. 1997. "Core Labor Standards and Export Performance in Developing Countries." *World Economy.* September, 20:6, pp. 773–85.

Marshall, Ray. 1994. "The Importance of International Labour Standards in a More Competitive Global Economy," in *International Labour Standards and Economic Interdependence.* Werner Sengenberger and Duncan Campbell, eds. Geneva: International Institute for Labour Studies, pp. 65–78.

Maskus, Keith. 1997. "Should Core Labor Standards Be Imposed through International Trade Policy?" World Bank Policy Research Working Paper No. 1817, August.

Moehling, Carolyn M. 1999. "State Child Labor Laws and the Decline of Child Labor." *Explorations in Economic History.* January, 36, pp. 72–106.

Organization for Economic Cooperation and Development. 1996. *Trade, Employment and Labour Standards: A Study of Core Workers' Rights and International Trade.* Paris: OECD.

Panagariya, Arvind. 2000. "Evaluating the Factor-Content Approach to Measuring the Effect of Trade on Wage Inequality." *Journal of International Economics.* 50, pp. 91–116.

Piore, Michael. 1994. "International Labor Standards and Business Strategies," in *International Labor Standards and Global Economic Integration: Proceedings of a Symposium.* Washington, D.C.: U.S. Department of Labor, Bureau of International Labor Affairs.

Portes, Alejandro. 1994. "By-Passing the Rules: The Dialectics of Labour Standards and Informalization in Less-Developed Countries," in *International Labour Standards and Economic Interdependence.* Werner Sengenberger and Duncan Campbell, eds. Geneva: International Institute for Labour Studies, pp. 159–76.

Psacharopoulos, George. 1994. "Returns to Investment in Education: A Global Update." *World Development.* 22:9, pp. 1325–43.

Rodrik, Dani. 1996. "Labor Standards in International Trade: Do They Matter and What Do We Do About Them," in *Emerging Agenda For Global Trade: High States for Developing Countries.* Robert Z. Lawrence, Dani Rodrik and John Walley, eds. Overseas Development Council Essay No. 20, Washington, D.C.: Johns Hopkins University Press.

Rodrik, Dani. 1999. "Institutions for High-Quality Growth: What They Are and How to Acquire Them," manuscript.

Rogers, Carol Ann and Kenneth A. Swinnerton. 1999. "Inequality, Productivity, and Child Labor: Theory and Evidence," mimeo, Georgetown University.

Singh, Nirvikar. 2001. "The Impact of International Labor Standards: A Survey of Economic Theory," mimeo, University of California, Santa Cruz.

Slaughter, Matthew J. and Philip Swagel. 1997. "The Effect of Globalization on Wages in the Advanced Economies." IMF Working Paper WP/97/43.

Spagnolo, Giancarlo. 1999. "Issue Linkage, Delegation, and International Policy Cooperation." Cambridge, DEA Working Paper no. 9913.

Srinivasan, T.N. 1997. "Trade and Human Rights," in *Representation of Constituent Interests in Design and Implementation of U.S. Trade Policies.* Alan V. Deardorff and Robert M. Stern, eds. Ann Arbor: University of Michigan Press.

Srinivasan, T.N. 1998. *Developing Countries and the Multilateral Trading System: From the GATT to the Uruguay Round and the Future.* Boulder and Oxford: Harper Collins, Westview Press.

Stiglitz, Joseph. 2000. "Democratic Development as the Fruits of Labor." Keynote Address of the Annual Meetings of the Industrial Relations Research Association, Boston, MA, January.

Stolper, Wolfgang F. and Paul A. Samuelson. 1941. "Protection and Real Wages." *Review of Economic Studies.* 9, pp. 58–73.

Swinnerton, Kenneth A. 1997. "An Essay on Economic Efficiency and Core Labour Standards." *World Economy.* 20:1, pp. 73–86.

U.S. Department of Labor. 1998. *By the Sweat and Toil of Children, Efforts to Eliminate Child Labor, Vol. V.* Washington, D.C.: Bureau of International Labor Affairs.

Borders beyond Control

J AGDISH **B HAGWATI**

A Door That Will Not Close

International migration lies close to the center of global problems that now seize the attention of politicians and intellectuals across the world. Take just a few recent examples: Prime Ministers Tony Blair of the United Kingdom and Jose Mar'a Aznar of Spain proposed at last year's European Council meeting in Seville that the European Union withdraw aid from countries that did not take effective steps to stem the flow of illegal emigrants to the EU. Blair's outspoken minister for development, Clare Short, described the proposal as "morally repugnant" and it died amid a storm of other protests; Australia received severe condemnation worldwide last summer when a special envoy of the UN high commissioner for human rights exposed the deplorable conditions in detention camps that held Afghan, Iranian, Iraqi, and Palestinian asylum seekers who had landed in Australia.

Following the September 11 attacks in New York City and Washington, D.C., US Attorney General John Ashcroft announced several new policies that rolled back protections enjoyed by immigrants. The American Civil Liberties Union (ACLU) and Human Rights Watch fought back. So did Islamic and Arab ethnic organizations. These groups employed lawsuits, public dissent, and congressional lobbying to secure a reversal of the worst excesses.

The *Economist* ran in just six weeks two major stories describing the growing outflow of skilled citizens from less developed countries to developed countries seeking to attract such immigrants. The "brain drain" of the 1960s is striking again with enhanced vigor.

These examples and numerous others do not just underline the importance of migration issues today. More important, they show governments attempting to stem migration only to be forced into retreat and accommodation by factors such as civil-society activism and the politics of ethnicity. Paradoxically, the ability to control migration has shrunk as the desire to do so has increased. The reality is that borders are beyond control and little can be done to really cut down on immigration. The societies of developed countries will simply not allow it. The less developed countries also seem overwhelmed by forces propelling emigration. Thus, there must be a seismic shift in the way migration is addressed: governments must reorient their policies from attempting to curtail migration to coping and working with it to seek benefits for all.

To demonstrate effectively why and how this must be done, however, requires isolating key migration questions from the many other issues that attend the flows of humanity across national borders. Although some migrants move strictly between rich countries or between poor ones, the most compelling problems result from emigration from less developed to more developed countries. They arise in three areas. First, skilled workers are legally emigrating, temporarily or permanently, to rich countries. This phenomenon predominantly concerns the less developed countries that are losing skilled labor. Second, largely unskilled migrants are entering developed countries illegally and looking for work. Finally, there is the "involuntary" movement of people, whether skilled or unskilled, across borders to seek asylum. These latter two trends mostly concern the developed countries that want to bar illegal entry by the unskilled. All three problems raise issues that derive from the fact that the flows cannot be effectively constrained and must instead be creatively accommodated. In designing such accommodation, it must be kept in mind that the illegal entry of asylum seekers and economic migrants often cannot be entirely separated. Frustrated economic migrants are known to turn occasionally to asylum as a way of getting in. The effective tightening of one form of immigrant entry will put pressure on another.

Software Engineers, Not Huddled Masses

Looking at the first problem, it appears that developed countries' appetite for skilled migrants has grown – just look at Silicon Valley's large supply of successful Indian and Taiwanese computer scientists and venture capitalists. The enhanced appetite for such professionals reflects the shift to a globalized economy in which countries compete for markets by creating and attracting technically skilled talent. Governments also perceive these workers to be more likely to assimilate quickly into their new societies. This heightened demand is matched by a supply that is augmented for old reasons that have intensified over time. Less developed countries cannot offer modern professionals the economic rewards or the social conditions that they seek. Europe and the United States also offer opportunities for immigrant children's education and career prospects that are nonexistent at home. These asymmetries of opportunity reveal themselves not just through cinema and television, but through the immediacy of experience. Increasingly, emigration occurs after study abroad. The number of foreign students at US universities, for example, has grown dramatically; so has the number who stay on. In 1990, 62 percent of engineering doctorates in the United States were given to foreign-born students, mainly Asians. The figures are almost as high in mathematics, computer science, and the physical sciences. In economics, which at the graduate level is a fairly math-intensive subject, 54 percent of the Ph.D.'s awarded went to foreign students, according to a 1990 report of the American Economic Association.

Many of these students come from India, China, and South Korea. For example, India produces about 25,000 engineers annually. Of these, about 2,000 come from the Indian Institutes of Technology (IITS), which are modeled on MIT and the California Institute of Technology. Graduates of IITS accounted for 78 percent of US engineering Ph.D.'s granted to Indians in 1990. And almost half of all Taiwanese awarded similar Ph.D.'s had previously attended two prestigious institutions: the National Taiwan University and the National Cheng Kung University. Even more telling, 65 percent of the Korean students who received science and engineering Ph.D.'s in the United States were graduates of Seoul National University. The numbers were almost as high for Beijing University and Tsinghua University, elite schools of the People's Republic of China.

These students, once graduated from American universities, often stay on in the United States. Not only is US graduate education ranked highest in the world, but it also offers an easy way of immigrating. In fact, it has been estimated that more than 70 percent of newly minted, foreign-born Ph.D.'s remain in the United States, many becoming citizens eventually. Less developed countries can do little to restrict the numbers of those who stay on as immigrants. They will, particularly in a situation of high demand for their skills, find ways to escape any dragnet that their home country may devise. And the same difficulty applies, only a little less starkly, to countries trying to hold on to those citizens who have only domestic training but are offered better jobs abroad.

A realistic response requires abandoning the "brain drain" approach of trying to keep the highly skilled at home. More likely to succeed is a "diaspora" model, which integrates present and past citizens into a web of rights and obligations in the extended community defined with the home country as the center. The diaspora approach is superior from a human rights viewpoint because it builds on the right to emigrate, rather than trying to restrict it. And dual loyalty is increasingly judged to be acceptable rather than reprehensible. This option is also increasingly feasible. Nearly 30 countries now offer dual citizenship. Others are inching their way to similar options. Many less developed countries, such as Mexico and India, are in the process of granting citizens living abroad hitherto denied benefits such as the right to hold property and to vote via absentee ballot.

However, the diaspora approach is incomplete unless the benefits are balanced by some obligations, such as the taxation of citizens living abroad. The United States already employs this practice. This author first recommended this approach for developing countries during the 1960s, and the proposal has been revived today. Estimates made by the scholars Mihir Desai, Devesh Kapur, and John McHale demonstrate that even a slight tax on Indian nationals abroad would substantially raise Indian government revenues. The revenue potential is vast because the aggregate income of Indian-born residents in the United States is 10 percent of India's national income, even though such residents account for just 0.1 percent of the American population.

Unstoppable

The more developed countries need to go through a similar dramatic shift in the way they respond to the influx of illegal economic immigrants and asylum seekers. Inducements or punishments for immigrants' countries of origin are not working to stem the flows, nor are stiffer border-control measures, sanctions on employers, or harsher penalties for the illegals themselves.

Three sets of factors are behind this. First, civil-society organizations, such as Human Rights Watch, the ACLU, and the International Rescue Committee, have proliferated and gained in prominence and influence. They provide a serious constraint on all forms of restrictive action. For example, it is impossible to incarcerate migrants caught crossing borders illegally without raising an outcry over humane treatment. So authorities generally send these people back across the border, with the result that they cross again and again until they finally get in. More than 50 percent of illegals, however, now enter not by crossing the Rio Grande but by legal means, such as tourist visas, and then stay on illegally. Thus, enforcement has become more difficult without invading privacy through such measures as identity cards, which continue to draw strong protests from civil liberties groups. A notable example of both ineffectual policy and successful civil resistance is the 1986 Sanctuary movement that surfaced in response to evidence that US authorities were returning desperate refugees from war-torn El Salvador and Guatemala to virtually certain death in their home countries. (They were turned back because they did not meet the internationally agreed upon definition for a refugee.) Sanctuary members, with the aid of hundreds of church groups, took the law into their own hands and organized an underground railroad to spirit endangered refugees to safe havens. Federal indictments and convictions followed, with five Sanctuary members given three- to five-year sentences. Yet, in response to a public outcry and an appeal from Senator Dennis DeConcini (D-Ariz.), the trial judge merely placed the defendants on probation.

Sanctions on employers, such as fines, do not fully work either. The General Accounting Office, during the debate over the 1986 immigration legislation that introduced employer sanctions, studied how they had worked in Switzerland and Germany. The measures there failed. Judges could not bring themselves to punish severely those employers whose violation consisted solely of giving jobs to illegal workers. The US experience with employer sanctions has not been much different.

Finally, the sociology and politics of ethnicity also undercut enforcement efforts. Ethnic groups can provide protective cover to their members and allow illegals to disappear into their midst. The ultimate constraint, however, is political and results from expanding numbers. Fellow ethnics who are US citizens, legal immigrants, or amnesty beneficiaries bring to bear growing political clout that precludes tough action against illegal immigrants. Nothing matters more than the vote in democratic societies. Thus the Bush administration, anxious to gain Hispanic votes, has embraced an amnesty confined solely to Mexican illegal immigrants, thereby discarding the principle of nondiscrimination enshrined in the 1965 Immigration and Nationality Act.

Minding the Open Door

If it is not possible to effectively restrict illegal immigration, then governments in the developed countries must turn to policies that will integrate migrants into their new homes in ways that will minimize the social costs and maximize the economic benefits. These policies should include children's education and grants of limited civic rights such as participation in school-board elections and parent-teacher associations. Governments should also assist immigrants in settling throughout a country, to avoid depressing wages in any one region. Greater development support should be extended to the illegal migrants' countries of origin to alleviate the poor economic conditions that propel emigration. And for the less developed countries, there is really no option but to shift toward a diaspora model.

Some nations will grasp this reality and creatively work with migrants and migration. Others will lag behind, still seeking restrictive measures to control and cut the level of migration. The future certainly belongs to the former. But to accelerate the progress of the laggards, new institutional architecture is needed at the international level. Because immigration restrictions are the flip side of sovereignty, there is no international organization today to oversee and monitor each nation's policies toward migrants, whether inward or outward bound.

The world badly needs enlightened immigration policies and best practices to be spread and codified. A World Migration Organization would begin to do that by juxtaposing each nation's entry, exit, and residence policies toward migrants, whether legal or illegal, economic or political, skilled or unskilled. Such a project is well worth putting at the center of policymakers' concerns.

Jagdish Bhagwati is University Professor at Columbia University and Andre Meyer Senior Fellow at the Council on Foreign Relations.

Intellectual Property Rights and the WTO

PHILIP G. **KING**

As the scope of the World Trade Organization (WTO has increased, one key issue in each successive round of negotiations is intellectual property rights (IPRs). IPRs came to the fore in the Uruguay round and lead to an agreement on Trade Related Aspects of Intellectual Property Rights (TRIPs). IPRs remain a contentious issue in the Doha round, often pitting the interests of developed countries against those of developing countries. There is also disagreement on the extent and scope of the WTO's involvement in IPRs, as well as the extent to which the WTO should enforce these rights. This article will define IPRs more precisely and discuss key issues in the Doha Round.

What are IPRs?

Traditionally, Intellectual Property Rights are designed to encourage individuals or companies to engage in innovative activities like research and development, artistic creation, or other activities that generate value in society. Like property rights for other assets, intellectual property rights allow owners to restrict use of the property and earn a return on ownership. Typically IPRs can be bought, sold, licensed or used in production. However, IPRs differ from other types of property in that they are intangible and, typically, they are non-rival in consumption—that is, one's use of an IPR does not interfere with someone else's use. This last characteristic of IPRs generates some of the tension between developing and developed countries, since developing countries argue that they can use IPRs without hurting the developed world.

IPRs are often divided into two types, industrial IPRs, such as patents and trademarks, and artistic and literary property, most frequently protected by copyrights. In the past decade, however, many of these lines have been blurred as computer software has earned copyrights. Another traditional characteristic of IPRs is that they represent a specific discovery, invention, or other (human) creative activity, but this criteria has also been adapted as traditional cultures and folklore and genes from specific species of plants and animals have also come under scrutiny for IPRs.

Traditional IPRs

Patents are perhaps the best known IPR. A patent allows the inventor to prevent others from using the process or product without specific permission of the patent holder. Patents have a limited duration, which varies by country, but the minimum period of protection in the TRIPs agreement is 20 years. Patents are protected by national law, not international law, and thus they must be enforced within the country where the violation occurs. US patent law allows owners of the patent to sue in civil court for violation and collect damages. In recent years, plant varieties have also been subject to patents, though the rules here may differ.

Rights to Industrial Design protect the design and other aesthetic aspects of a commercial property such as an Apple McIntosh computer. Under the TRIPs agreement, industrial designs must be protected for at least 10 years.

Trademarks or Service Marks confer a specific name or mark on a product, designed to distinguish it from other similar products. Coca-Cola and Coke are two specific trademarks known throughout the world. Most economists agree that trademarks encourage companies to maintain product quality since they confer a specific reputation. Unlike patents, trademarks have no specific expiration date and, theoretically, can last forever. The rationale here is that other companies or individuals can create their own trademarks and compete in the marketplace in this manner.

Geographical Indications are similar in some ways to trademarks in that they confer specific information to consumers. For example, a wine labeled Bordeaux should only come from the Bordeaux region in France. Unlike trademarks and patents, however, geographical indications are not owned by one individual or company and cannot be transferred or licensed. Instead they are conferred on a region and may be used by approved producers in the region. Some countries, like France, restrict the use of these geographical indications to specific users, or distinguish further the type or grade of the product, for example a Bordeaux Superior, or Premier Cru (first growth) confers a higher valued product within the region. Other common geographical indications are: "Scotch," "Tequila," "Champagne," and "Roquefort" (cheese). Note that some titles which originated as geographical indications can be conferred on products from other areas, for example, "Cheddar" or "Chablis."

Copyrights are conferred to individuals or companies for creative work such as a book, movie or a song. They are typically conferred for 50-70 years after the death of the author. While Copyrights traditionally protect artistic endeavors of individuals, computer software can also be copyrighted.

Trade Secrets involve specific processes that are used to produce a (usually trademarked) product such as the formula for Coke. Whereas patents must be made public and have limited duration trade secrets are not protected as an IPR.

The TRIPS agreement

The TRIPs agreement began on January 1, 1995, after almost ten years of negotiation (1986-1994) of the Uruguay round, which established the WTO. TRIPs was created to coordinate policies on IPRs between WTO member countries and to allow for the settlement of disputes over IPRs between countries. According to the WTO, TRIPs cover five main issues:

- "how basic principles of the trading system and other international intellectual property agreements should be applied.
- how to give adequate protection to intellectual property rights.
- how countries should enforce those rights adequately in their own territories
- how to settle disputes on intellectual property between members of the WTO special transitional arrangements during the period when the new system is being introduced.
- special transitional arrangements during the period when the new system is being introduced."

The TRIPs agreement covers all traditional IPRs, but recent discussions have allowed the incorporation of newer types of IPRs (to be discussed below) to be covered as well. In essence, the purpose of TRIPs is to promote a common set of standards that all members should follow including agreement on what constitute IPRs and reciprocity between countries over specific IPRs. For IPRs to be effective, they also must be enforced. Enforcement generally occurs at the national level and currently (especially in developing countries) enforcement is quite uneven. TRIPs allow for disputes between countries to be settled under the WTO's dispute settlement mechanism. One area of particular concern in the current (Doha) round of negotiations is the transition period that should be allowed before developing countries must harmonize their policies with those of richer countries.

Issues of Concern in the Doha Round

Many of the current concerns in the Doha round of negotiations stem from the inherent conflict between developing and developed countries. As one would expect, most IPRs are held by individuals and businesses in the developing world, and thus further extension of IPRs could result in a transfer of resources from poor to rich countries. Developing countries counter that IPRs allow for the transfer of technology which may not occur otherwise, though evidence of this effect is meager or non-existent. The other contentious issue involves the extension of IPRs to traditional cultures and to traditional and newly created plant species.

While copyright laws allow artists to earn royalties on specific creative works, no such royalty can be earned on traditional industries, such as traditional music, crafts, rug designs, etc. Representatives of developing countries argue that such a system is inherently unfair to them and essentially allows their own culture to be exploited with no compensation. Further, a failure to define specific rights here diminishes the incentive to preserve and codify these traditions as many of them face marginalization in the face of an increasingly global modern culture. In some cases, popular (and lucrative) songs have been derived from traditional music. For example, the song "The Lion Sleeps Tonight" has been recorded by a number of commercial artists in the west and was recently used in the Walt Disney movie, *The Lion King*. The song was originally composed and recorded in 1939 by Solomon Linda, a Zulu singer, in Africa. It is estimated that the song has earned $10 to $20 million in royalties, yet its creator, Mr. Linda, earned just one pound in cash and died in poverty.[1]

Incorporating folklore into a system of IPRs is, however, fraught with a number of problems. First, unlike typical copyrights, no one individual can be credited with the creation. Thus the property rights must be conferred on a community. Many traditional cultures have evolved over time, though, and it may be extremely difficult to codify what are the key characteristics of the tradition, what group is responsible for the creation, and who should benefit from its use (and how will these benefits be distributed). Some artists have even argued that such a codification is ultimately unproductive, since it may inhibit further development of the medium or only allow the "correct" people to make these changes. In general, courts in developing countries have not recognized a traditional community's right to own specific designs even where these designs are widely recognized to have originated within that community. Despite these obstacles, some traditions are already protected by individual countries. Australia allows for certification of crafts and other artifacts created by aboriginal artists in order to protect and promote indigenous crafts and other countries are following suit. The US International Trade Commission estimates that these industries are estimated to be worth over $30 billion a year worldwide.

Genetic Resources

One of the most controversial issues in the field of IPRs is the issue of genetic resources. The pharmaceutical and biotechnology industry has lobbied hard to allow specific plant varieties to be patented. They argue that the creation of a specific organism, such as a crop which is resistant to the herbicide Roundup or a variety of rice that produces its own vitamin A, confers benefits to users and does not infringe upon the use of more traditional types of organisms. Developing these new genetic varieties is similar to creating new inventions or new pharmaceuticals in that the research and development costs, as well as the costs of testing and winning approval for these new varieties approved by government agencies, is extremely costly and would not occur without an incentive such as a patent.

Critics argue that the development of genetic resources represents a completely different type of activity because the genes being manipulated were developed by nature, not by humans. Many critics of Genetically Modified Organisms (GMOs) also believe that the environmental consequences of these new organisms have not been properly defined and could potentially be devastating.

Traditional varieties and uses of foods and spices have also come under scrutiny. In one controversial case, an American firm applied for a patent on the spice turmeric, specifically for healing wounds. The government of India protested, arguing that turmeric was a traditional herb and that its healing properties have been known for centuries. The applicant argued that India had failed to document these advantages and to apply for patent protection, while Indian government argued that the use was traditional and should not be inhibited by this type of "biopiracy." The government of India won the case.

In a somewhat similar case, an American firm, RiceTec, developed a new strain of basmati rice, a traditional, and widely sought after, strain of rice grown in a specific region of India. RiceTec argued that it had improved on the traditional grain and developed a superior product. The government of India again filed suit claiming that basmati rice was not just a specific strain of rice, but had to be grown in a specific region to have the full taste and texture associated with basmati rice. Thus, the name basmati was a geographical indication like Champagne and should not be used by producers outside of India. They argued that allowing an American firm to use the term basmati would confuse consumers and presented evidence that basmati rice produced in India was indeed different from the American version. In this case, the courts allowed the American firm to use the appellation "Texmati" to distinguish their version from the traditional one. The case in interesting in a number of ways but also indicates that developing countries must use their scarce resources to defend traditional crops and practices in a national court or in the WTO through the TRIPs agreement. Developing countries have proposed a digital library cod-

ifying traditional practices and plant varieties to help address some of the issues created by these and other cases.

Pharmaceuticals

While drugs have been protected by patents for decades, the current practice of licensing and distributing drugs worldwide has come under great scrutiny, particularly as the epidemic of HIV/AIDS has spread throughout Africa. Critics have pointed out that the costs of drugs to treat HIV are prohibitively expensive for African countries. For low income countries, the average spent per capita on health care is $23, whereas therapies to treat HIV cost $200. Even though this amount is far lower than it costs in the US to treat HIV, it is still beyond the resources of most African countries and thus the disease generally goes untreated. In the case of HIV, US drug companies have responded to public pressure to sell the drugs at cost, but they are still beyond the means of most developing countries.

Another important issue with respect to pharmaceuticals is that virtually all the new development of drugs is oriented to dealing with diseases that affect citizens of rich countries, who can afford to pay the high cost of patented pharmaceuticals. According to the World Bank, "It has been estimated that less than 5% of the money spent worldwide on pharmaceutical R&D is for diseases that predominately affect developing countries."[2] Diseases such as malaria and tuberculosis, which are endemic in many developing countries have received little attention since the potential profit from the development of new drugs for these diseases is small, while a great deal of research in developing countries is devoted to new drugs only marginally better for chronic conditions such as high blood pressure and allergies.

In the case of pharmaceuticals, however, it is difficult to see how changes to the way IPRs are enforced would encourage the development of new drugs for disease like malaria. Instead, countries must somehow devote the resources to develop these new drugs. In many ways this type of research falls under the rubric of what economists call "public goods" since treating these diseases benefits everyone, yet, since those most affected are generally poor, the incentives provided by the marketplace fail to bring about an efficient allocation of resources.

In the case of pharmaceuticals widely used in the third world, such as antibiotics, however, a case can be made for relaxing the restrictions on their use since IPRs effectively raise the price of these drugs and thus make it difficult for the poor to use the best medicine. It should be pointed out that pharmaceutical companies widely practice differential pricing, and thus sell drugs at much lower prices in poor countries than in rich countries. Even so, many of these drugs remain beyond the grasp of the poorest. It is hard to make a cogent argument that this practice benefits developing countries or that the WTO should become a mechanism for restricted the use of life-saving drugs to developing countries.

Do Developing Countries Benefit from IPRs?

As was stated at the beginning of this article, the key issue regarding IPRs ahead involved the conflict between developing and developed countries. While no definitive work has been completed in this area, the World Bank estimates that enforcement of the current TRIPS agreement will increase revenues to the US by about $19 billion and cost developing countries about $7.5 billion.[3] Clearly the two sides have very different views on how the next round of negotiations should proceed. While the US can point to piracy of software and entertainment in China and Southeast Asia through bootlegged CDs and DVDs, one can also point to the increased cost of pharmaceuticals and other benefits of technology that will become more expensive, and thus less frequently used, in the third world if TRIPS is fully enforced. A British panel, the *Commission on Intellectual Property Rights*, published a report[4] which concluded that developed countries should relax the enforcement of IPRs and delay the enforcement of the TRIPS agreement in the developing

world. They cite evidence that the benefits of letting developing countries benefit from these IPRs far exceed the costs and that the transfer of income from the rich countries to the poorest countries was desirable. The Commission further noted that currently developed countries, such as the US, obtained technology from other countries without an elaborate system of enforcement and that the lack of IPR enforcement allowed these countries to acquire and develop new technology more easily and at less expense.

Endnotes

[1] See http://www.wto.org/english/thewto_e /whatis_ e/tif_e/agrm6_e.htm#special.

[2] Intellectual Property Rights and Economic Development, The World Bank, 2002, p.38.

[3] Intellectual Property Rights and Economic Development, The World Bank, 2001, p.21.

[4] See The British Commission on Intellectual Property Rights Report, 2003, http://www.iprcommission.org

References

Commission on Intellectual Property Rights, Final Report," 2002, available at http://www.iprcommission.org.

World Bank, Intellectual Property Rights and Economic Development, by Carlos A. Primo Braga, Carsten Fink, Claudia Paz Sepulveda, 2002.

World Trade Organization, "Intellectual Property, Protection and Enforcment," 2003, available at http://www.wto.org /english/thewto_e/whatis_e/tif_e/special.

Reducing America's Dependence on Foreign Oil Supplies

MARTIN FELDSTEIN

The United States now imports nearly 60 percent of the oil that we consume. This dependence on foreign supplies makes us vulnerable to disruptions in world oil markets and to fluctuations in world oil prices. It is significant that a rise in the price of oil preceded each of the economic downturns of the past four decades.

Our dependence on imported oil has profound effects on U.S. foreign relations and on our defense policy. In the September 2002 National Security statement[1] the White House asserted the importance of increasing U.S. energy security and described a policy of doing so by expanding the geographic sources of energy supply.

Other policies being pursued by the U.S. government, like building up the size of the strategic petroleum reserve, focus on dampening the short-run price fluctuations that could result from temporary damage to foreign production. Yet others, like increasing automobile fuel efficiency and opening new domestic sources of oil production, deal with the long-term dependence of the U.S. on foreign oil.

My aim in these remarks is to consider how the extent to which the United States could in principle be able to reduce our economic vulnerability to changes in foreign oil supplies and how such a reduction in dependence might be brought about.

Reducing our vulnerability to changes in foreign oil supplies is not the same as reducing our imports of foreign oil. Nor is it the same as diversifying the geographic sources of that oil.[2] Even completely eliminating oil imports would not insulate American consumers and businesses from fluctuations in the global oil price as long as U.S. domestic producers of crude oil are free to export. A rise in the world oil price would induce an increase in U.S. oil exports until domestic and global prices were equal. Although the government could in principle prevent this by limiting oil exports as a matter of national security, we are unlikely to achieve the condition of oil self-sufficiency that would ever make such a policy relevant. As a practical matter, we are likely to require oil imports for the indefinite future.

But even if we cannot completely eliminate the need for oil imports, it is possible to reduce substantially the role of oil in the economy with the technology that now exists and even more so with the technology that will be operational during the next two or three decades.

Reducing our consumption of oil would make the U.S. economy less sensitive to global oil prices and therefore to shocks in foreign global supplies. If oil plays a smaller role in the economy, changes in world oil prices would have less of an impact on the domestic price level and on domestic economic output. Reducing the sensitivity of the U.S. economy to foreign oil markets by decreasing oil consumption relative to GDP would also reduce the pressure to bend our foreign policy and our military actions to the geopolitics of oil supply. Reducing the consumption of oil can also have favorable effects on the emission of carbon dioxide and other specific forms of air pollution. The extent to which it does so would depend on the nature of the alternative energy sources that replace gasoline and other petroleum products.

Some Basic Facts

A few basic facts will indicate both the potential and the limits for reducing oil imports. The United States consumed 20 million barrels of oil per day in the year 2000 of which nearly 60 percent was imported. The U.S. Department of Energy estimates that by 2020 oil consumption will rise by 30 percent while domestic oil production will decline by 15 percent, raising the share of imports to nearly 75 percent of consumption.

Although the technology exists for sharply reducing and eventually eliminating the use of oil to fuel cars, a subject to which I will return in a few moments, that would not be enough to eliminate the need for oil imports. Oil consumption in automobiles and light trucks amounts to only 40 percent of the total consumption of petroleum products. Residential and commercial use of oil for heating is now down to only 6 percent of oil consumption and oil for electricity production is only 1.5 percent. Thus, converting these three uses of oil to some other source of energy would not be sufficient to eliminate oil imports.

Half of the remaining 50 percent of oil consumption is used by industry, primarily as an input into petrochemical products like plastics rather than as a source of energy. This use of oil would be very difficult to reduce. Moreover, existing technologies for reducing gasoline use by automobiles cannot be applied to airplanes, railroads and commercial trucks.

Nevertheless, cutting our oil imports in half would have a major favorable affect on the sensitivity of the U.S. economy to global oil conditions. To do that would require cutting gasoline consumption substantially, with the possibility of additional help from a further reduction in the use of oil for residential and commercial heating. I will comment first on some of the new technologies that are or will be available to reduce gasoline consumption and will then discuss the incentives that could be used to bring changes about with or without new technology.

New Technologies

Three classes of technology that are now operational (even if not fully commercial) would permit dramatic reductions in gasoline consumption per passenger mile: non-petroleum carbon fuels (i.e., using natural gas or a mixture of ethanol and gasoline), hybrid electric vehicles that combine small gasoline engines with electricity from batteries, and cars powered by hydrogen fuel cells.[3] I do not include pure electric cars on this list because the batteries must be charged from ordinary electric sources and their mileage range is very limited, something that could of course change if battery technology is substantially improved.

Non-petroleum Carbon Fuels

Shifting the stock of US cars from gasoline to a compressed natural gas (CNG) technology would eliminate all of the petroleum used by automobiles. This is a feasible technology. There are more than 100,000 vehicles on U.S. roads powered by CNG. All three of the major U.S. auto firms sell cars that use CNG in full sized cars and vans. These include the Chevy Silverado, the Ford Crown Victoria, and the Daimler-Chrysler Ram Wagon.

Natural gas is not the only non-petroleum carbon fuel. All three major US car manufacturers also make full size cars and/or SUVs powered by engines that use a combination of 85 percent ethanol and 15 percent gasoline.[4] Shifting the stock of US cars to such an ethanol-gasoline mixed fuel would eliminate about 60 percent of the current use of oil for motor vehicle fuel. The overall net reduction in oil use would, however, depend on the extent to which oil was used as fuel for the fermentation and distillation of alcohol from corn or agricultural waste. The net reduction in oil use would be much greater if the ethanol is produced from agricultural waste, a feasible process but one that is not yet fully developed as a commercial technology.[5]

The Hybrid Car

The hybrid car uses a wholly different approach to reducing gasoline consumption. These cars, such as the Toyota Prius, are powered by a combination of electric batteries and a small internal combustion engine powered by gasoline. The batteries are charged in the operation of the car, particularly during braking. The Prius, which feels to the driver like any ordinary car, is rated as achieving 52 miles per gallon in cities and 45 MPG on the highway, nearly twice the average for all new cars that are now being sold. With a 12 gallon fuel capacity, it can go more than 500 miles on a tank of gas. It is a five passenger vehicle and weighs about 2800 pounds, similar to other popular Toyota models. The list price is $20,480, about 20 percent more than the list price of a comparable Toyota with a traditional gasoline engine. With normal driving, however, the lower fuel cost can offset the extra purchase price over the life of the car. Although the Prius is now the largest selling hybrid car, the other major auto makers in the U. S. will be bringing such cars to the market within one or two years.

Hydrogen Fuel

The auto technology of the future, according to many experts, is the fuel cell car that uses hydrogen to generate electricity to power the car. Unlike the hybrid car, no petroleum at all is used to power such a car. Electric energy is created when the hydrogen that is carried by the car is combined with oxygen from the air.[6] Ford, General Motors, Daimler-Chrysler and BMW are all developing such cars. Prototype models have been demonstrated to the public based on large SUV vehicles.

Hydrogen can now be extracted from natural gas, leaving carbon dioxide as a residual. In the longer run, the technology that is now being developed should be able to extract hydrogen from water by an electrolysis process. The electricity needed for this process could come from nuclear power or renewable sources like wind and hydro. Using the hydrogen for automobile fuel cells would then require establishing a network of hydrogen stations to supply hydrogen to cars on the road just as gasoline stations now supply gasoline. Unlike current electric cars, the range of hydrogen powered cars would be as great as that of current gasoline cars.

The U.S. government is supporting research on fuel cell technology and the European Union has recently committed more than $2 billion for research on this technology over the next few years. Even so, widespread use of fuel cells is likely to be at least twenty years away and could be much further into the future. How quickly policies are adopted to move toward this oil-free technology will depend on how concerned governments are about the risks associated with oil dependence.

Creating the Incentives to Reduce Gasoline Consumption

Even without the adoption of any of the new fuel technologies it is possible to reduce oil consumption. Individuals can drive fewer miles by using public transportation more or by increased car pooling. Moderate speeds and better tires can also increase the miles per gallon of existing cars. New smaller or lighter or more energy efficient cars will also consume less fuel per mile.

Changing behavior requires changing incentives. One of the reasons for the high level of gasoline consumption per capita and per mile in the United States is that gasoline prices are relatively low by international standards and have declined substantially in real terms since the early 1980s. The real price of a gallon of gasoline is the same as it was in 1950 (when incomes and car fuel efficiency were both much lower than they are today) and less than half of the typical price in most European countries.

In order to reduce gasoline consumption, the U.S. government in 1978 imposed gas mileage standards for new cars and now levies fines on those auto manufacturers who do not meet the standard. In practice these Corporate Average Fuel Economy rules (known as CAFÉ standards) succeeded in raising gasoline mileage on the fleet of cars but also induced individuals who prefer larger and heavier vehicles to shift their purchases to sports utility vehicles and light trucks that are permitted to have lower gasoline efficiency. The net effect has been essentially no overall increase in the total miles per gallon of all vehicles.

Tightening CAFÉ standards would do nothing to encourage less driving or more fuel efficient driving habits. Doing so would also discourage scrapping existing cars and shifting to new and more fuel efficient vehicles.

The same objections apply to the proposal for so-called cap-and-trade rules that would impose average fuel standards on car manufacturers but would allow individual manufacturers to "sell" extra fuel savings to other companies that choose not to produce enough fuel efficient vehicles.[7]

Raising the price of gasoline to European levels by increasing the gasoline tax by about $2 a gallon could achieve substantial reductions in gasoline demand through changes in driving styles and by encouraging the demand for new and more fuel efficient vehicles. But such an increase in the existing gasoline tax has been shown to be politically unacceptable to the American public and our representatives in Congress. Although economists may reason that the resulting extra tax revenue of more than $200 billion a year (about one-fifth of the total personal income tax revenue) could in principle be returned to the tax payers in the form of lower income taxes, voters rightly fear that much of the extra revenue would remain in Washington where, as in Europe, it would finance increased government spending on a wide range of activities.[8]

The same objection applies to the proposal for an oil company cap-and-trade policy that would limit the amount of gasoline that the petroleum companies as a whole could sell.[9] Each company would require a permit per gallon of gasoline that it sells.

Regardless of whether they are given these permits by the government or required to buy them from the government, the permits would have a market value that would have to be reflected in the price that consumers pay for gasoline. Reducing overall gasoline demand by the same amount as a $2 a gallon tax would make the permits worth $2 each and would therefore raise the price of gasoline by two dollars a gallon. Since selling the permits to the oil companies would also generate as much revenue as a $2 retail gasoline tax, this form of oil company cap-and-trade policy should be seen as nothing more than a way of thinly disguising an increase in the gasoline tax.

The alternative of giving the permits to the oil companies instead of selling them is also politically impossible; it would still raise the price to consumers by $2 a gallon and would generate a $200 billion a year windfall to the oil companies.

It is possible however to achieve all of the favorable incentive effects of an increased gasoline tax without any actual tax increase by using a system of tradeable personal "voucher points."[10] In such a system, the government would give each adult a number of voucher points, with the number of voucher points varying to reflect urban-rural geographic differences that are likely to affect driving miles. Individuals would be required to use one voucher point for each gallon of gasoline that he or she purchases. The total number of voucher points given to all individuals would be set equal to the maximum amount of gasoline that the government wants to have purchased in the year. Individuals who do not need their full quota of voucher points could sell them to individuals who need more than their quota of points. Thus individuals who economize on their use of gasoline would be directly rewarded.

The mechanics of this tradeable voucher system could be simplified by giving each individual a gasoline voucher debit card. When the individual purchases gasoline, he would pay the money price and would also debit his gasoline voucher card by one point per gallon. Gasoline pumps could be modified to read these cards just as they now read credit and debit cards for regular money payment. The pumps could also allow the individual to sell or buy voucher points for cash if he has excess points or inadequate points. A separate allocation of voucher points could be given to truck owners who would also be required to "pay" voucher points as well as money to purchase gasoline.

The key feature of this system of tradeable personal voucher points is that each invidual would face a "combined price" for each gallon of gasoline (i.e., the sum of the cash price and the value of the voucher point that he must buy or can sell) that would be determined in the market in a way that limits total national gasoline consumption to the annual level determined by the government. No taxes would be collected and no money would go to Washington as part of this plan. Announcing a series of annual targets for decreasing future gasoline consumption would provide experts with a basis for predicting future costs of gasoline to consumers and would therefore provide a guide for planning future oil consumption strategies.

Strong incentives to reduce oil consumption now and to shift over time to a different technology that does not rely on oil would reduce U.S. economic vulnerability to changes in world oil conditions and in the world price of oil. Although we can never expect to achieve full independence from the conditions in global oil markets, any reductions in our use of oil will increase our national security and enhance our freedom of action in military planning and foreign policy.

Martin Feldstein is Professor of Economics, Harvard University, and President of the National Bureau of Economic Research. These remarks were prepared for presentation at the annual meeting of the American Economic Association on December 3, 2003.

Endnotes

1 The White House, *The National Security Strategy of the United States,* September 2002

2 Encouraging the existence of several oil producers with excess capacity would however contribute to price stability by providing alternative sources of "swing capacity" that could respond to shortages elsewhere. Now Saudi Arabia is the primary swing producer. Russia might become another.

3 Ford and Nissan also make pure electric vehicles. These have relatively limited ranges and have not been popular with customers, with fewer than 5000 private owners even after being on the market for at least five years.

4 There are also more than 250,000 vehicles powered by propane. Since propane is derived as a by-product in refining oil and natural gas, it cannot be scaled up to a much larger share of the market.

5 Compressed natural gas could also be used as a fuel in the production of ethanol, but this may be a less efficient use of CNG than its direct use as a fuel in cars.

6 There are several variations on the basic theme of the hydrogen-powered car. Instead of fuel cells, the internal combustion engines in cars could be designed or converted to run on hydrogen instead of gasoline.

7 The net effect of such a cap-and-trade approach to CAFÉ rules would be to achieve the desired overall fuel efficiency in new cars without forcing each company to alter its product mix in inefficient ways. See Congressional Budget Office, *Reducing Gasoline Consumption: Three Policy Options* (2002).

8 The existing 18-cent federal gasoline tax was originally earmarked for a trust fund to be used only for federal highways. That restriction has since been changed to allow spending on mass transit.

9 The proposal is described in Congressional Budget Office, *Reducing Gasoline Consumption: Three Policy Options* (2002).

10 The current discussion is a modified version of the idea presented in my "Oil Dependence and National Security: A Market-based System for Reducing U.S. Vulnerability," *The National Interest,* November 2001 (http://www.nber.org/feldstein/oil.html) and discussed also in my Vouchers Can Free U.S. From Foreign Oil," *The Wall Street Journal,* December 27th 2001 (http://www.nber.org /feldstein/wj122701.pdf).

Discussion Questions

II

1. Esty argues that "transboundary externalities" are a key issue in upcoming trade talks. What are "transboundary externalities"? Give three examples not mentioned in the article. Why do they matter? What institutions do you believe are necessary to deal with "transboundary externalities"?

2. Most environmentalists argue that, absent restrictions, free trade will lead to a "race to the bottom." What do they mean by that? Give an example. Does Esty agree with this assessment? Does he see other issues in coordinating policies?

3. What is the Environmental Kuznet's curve? What are its implications in terms of trade and development?

4. What are the key labor issues that need to be addressed in trade talks? Of these which does Brown think are the most important?

5. Why does Brown argue that child labor laws might encourage economic growth?

6. Devise a set of labor standards for the upcoming Doha round—what issue do you think is key?

7. Do sweatshops exploit the poor?

8. Why does Bhagwati believe that immigration cannot be stopped? If the US tried to stem the flow what do you think would happen?

9. What is Bhagwati's solution?

10. One problem Bhagwati mentions only briefly is the "brain drain"—the flow of highly educated people to the US and other developed countries. Why is this a concern? Given Bhagwati's belief that restricting immigration won't work, propose another solution. Could changes made to tax laws help deal with this problem?

11. What are the key issues facing the upcoming Doha round with regard to Intellectual Property Rights?

12.   Why are the interests of developed countries different than those of developing countries when it comes to Intellectual Property Rights?

13.   Would you agree with a rule that abolished patent protection for drugs in developing countries? What problems would this type of law create? What benefits would it have?

14.   Explain how Feldstein's voucher system works. Do you agree with it?
      Do you think it is feasible politically?

15.   Why are we dependent on foreign oil?

16.   After reading all the articles above, what do you believe are the most pressing and least pressing issues in the Doha round ahead?

Trade and Development: NAFTA

III

The final trade section in this reader examines trade and development. While a number of articles in previous sections examine some of the issue involving developing countries, this section focuses specifically on these issues.

In "The Global Governance of Trade as if Development Really Mattered," Dani Rodrik argues that most of the multilateral institutions set up to protect the international order, in particular the WTO, have fostered policies that benefit the industrialized world over the developing world. He believes that each country needs to develop separate institutions to encourage capital formation and efficient allocation of resources—there is no one-size-fits-all policy such as US style capitalism. Rodrik presents a detailed overview of trade and development policies over the last 30 years and argues that the development of stable institutions to reduce conflict within a country was of paramount importance, and that the relatively small gains from completely free trade were secondary effects, not worthy of the attention that has been devoted to these effects from economists. He argues that a careful examination of the evidence does not reveal a strong correlation between free trade policies and growth; in short a reevaluation of the policies that has governed the last 50 years of trade negotiations is in order.

"Farm Fallacies That Hurt the Poor" argues that trade subsidies in the industrialized world do a great deal to hurt the poor and that if developed countries really cared, they would reduce these subsidies. The article examines one such policy that has been intensely scrutinized lately, cotton subsidies. American cotton producers receive a $3.6 billion subsidy to grow cotton, three times US aid to Africa, which hurts Africa.

Finally, "Economic Developments during NAFTA's First Decade" presents an overview of NAFTA and its impact on the US, Canadian, and Mexican economies.

12

The Global Governance of Trade as if Development Really Mattered

D A N I **R O D R I K**

Introduction

What objectives does (or should) the World Trade Organization (WTO) serve? The first substantive paragraph of the Agreement establishing the WTO lists the following aspirations:

> raising standards of living, ensuring full employment and a large and steadily growing volume of real income and effective demand, and expanding the production of and trade in goods and services, while allowing for the optimal use of the world's resources in accordance with the objective of sustainable development, seeking both to protect and preserve the environment and to enhance the means for doing so in a manner consistent with their respective needs and concerns at different levels of economic development. (WTO 1995:9)

A subsequent paragraph cites 'mutually advantageous arrangements directed to the substantial reduction of tariffs and other barriers to trade and to the elimination of discriminatory treatment in international trade relations' as a means of 'contributing to these objectives' (ibid.). It is clear from this preamble that the WTO's framers placed priority on raising standards of living and on sustainable development. Expanding trade was viewed as a means towards that end, rather than an end in itself. Recently, promoting economic development has acquired an even higher standing in the official rhetoric of the WTO, partly in response to its critics.[1]

That the purpose of the world trade regime is to raise living standards all around the world—rather than to maximize trade per se—has never been controversial. In practice, however, these two goals—promoting development and maximizing trade— have increasingly come to be viewed as synonymous by the WTO and multilateral lending agencies, to the point where the latter easily substitutes for the former. As the WTO's Mike Moore (2000) puts it, 'the surest way to do more to help the poor is to continue to open markets.' This view has the apparent merit that it is backed by a voluminous empirical literature that identifies trade as a key determinant of economic growth. It also fits nicely with traditional modus operandi of the WTO, which is to focus predominantly on reciprocal market access (instead of development-friendly trade rules). However, the net result is a confounding of ends and means. Trade becomes the lens through which development is perceived, rather than the other way around.

Imagine a trading regime that is true to the WTO preamble, one in which trade rules are determined so as to maximize development potential, particularly of the world's poorest nations. Instead of asking, 'How do we maximize trade and market access?' negotiators would ask, 'How do we enable countries to grow out of poverty?' Would such a regime look different from the one that exists currently?

The answer depends on how one interprets recent economic history and the role that trade openness plays in the course of economic development. The prevailing view in G7 capitals and multilateral lending agencies is that integration into the global economy is an essential determinant of economic growth. Successful integration in turn requires both enhanced market access in the advanced industrial countries and a range of institutional reforms at home (ranging from legal and administrative reform to safety nets) to render economic openness viable and growth promoting. This can be regarded as the 'enlightened standard view'—enlightened because of its recognition that there is more to integration than simply lowering tariff and non-tariff barriers to trade, and standard because it represents the prevailing conventional wisdom (see World Bank/IMF 2000). In this conception, today's WTO represents what the doctor ordered: the focus on expanding market access and deepening integration through the harmonization of a wide range of 'trade related' practices is precisely what development requires.

This paper presents an alternative account of economic development, one that questions the centrality of trade and trade policy and emphasizes instead the critical role of domestic institutional innovations that often depart from prevailing orthodoxy. In this view, transitions to high economic growth are rarely sparked by blueprints imported from abroad. Opening up the economy is hardly ever a key factor at the outset. The initiating reforms instead tend to be a combination of unconventional institutional innovations with some of the elements drawn from the orthodox recipe. These combinations tend to be country-specific, requiring local knowledge and experimentation for successful implementation. They are targeted on domestic investors and tailored to domestic institutional realities.

In this alternative view, a development-friendly international trading regime is one that does much more than enhance poor countries' access to markets in the advanced industrial countries. It is one that enables poor countries to experiment with institutional arrangements and leaves room for them to devise their own, possibly divergent solutions to the developmental bottlenecks that they face. It is one that evaluates the demands of institutional reform not from the perspective of integration ('What do countries need to do to integrate?') but from the perspective of development ('What do countries need to do achieve broad-based, equitable economic growth?'). In this vision, the WTO would no longer serve as an instrument for the harmonization of economic policies and practices across countries, but become an organization that manages the interface between different national practices and institutions.

This paper argues that a renewed focus on development and poverty reduction, along with an empirically-based understanding of the development process, would have far-reaching implications for the way in which the international trading regime and the WTO function. It focuses on broad principles, rather than specific recommendations, because it is only through a change in the overall perspective of trade negotiations that significant change can be accomplished.

One of the key propositions is that developing countries are shortchanging themselves when they focus their complaints on specific asymmetries in market access (tariff peaks against developing country exports, industrial country protection in agriculture and textiles, etc.). This approach reflects acceptance of a market–access perspective that does developing countries limited good. They would be far better served by pressing for changes that enshrine development at the top of the WTO agenda, and correspondingly provide them with a better mix of enhanced market access and manoeuvring room to pursue appropriate development strategies.

Since this paper is as much about the approach to development that should inform views about the international trade regime as it is about the WTO itself, much of the discussion is devoted to the empirical content of these ideas. The paper begins with an assertion that the distinction between development strategies that focus on growth versus those that focus on poverty reduction is a false one, since in practice, the two ends are inseparable. The main strike against existing trade rules is not that they over-emphasize trade and growth at the expense of poverty reduction, but that they over-emphasize the expense of poverty reduction and growth. It then argues that the enlightened standard development model encompasses an impossibly broad and unfocused development agenda, and one that is biased towards a particular set of institutional arrangements. It emphasizes instead the centrality of domestic institutional innovations (comprising a mix of orthodoxy with 'local heresies') and of investment strategies that are tailored to the circumstances of each country.

Much of the paper focuses on the link between trade policy and economic performance. The voluminous literature in this area, which forms the basis for the oft-heard claims to the benefits of trade openness, is, upon examination, less unequivocal. A close look reveals that there is no convincing evidence that trade liberalization is predictably associated with subsequent economic growth. This raises serious questions about the priority that the integrationist policy agenda typically receives in orthodox reform programmes. The problem is not trade liberalization per se, but the diversion of financial resources and political capital from more urgent and deserving developmental priorities.

Finally, the paper offers some general principles for a world trade regime that puts development first. First, the trade regime must accept, rather than seek to eliminate, institutional diversity along with the right of countries to 'protect' their institutional arrangements. However, the right to protect one's own social arrangements is distinct from, and does not extend to, the right to impose it on others. Once these simple principles are accepted and internalized in trade rules, developmental priorities of poor nations and the needs of the industrial countries can be rendered compatible and mutually supportive.

Growth versus Poverty Reduction: A Meaningless Debate

Should governments pursue economic growth first and foremost, or should they focus on poverty reduction? Recent debate on this question has become embroiled in broader political controversies on globalization and its impact on developing economies. Critics of the WTO often take it to task for being overly concerned about the level of economic activity (and its growth) at the expense of poverty reduction. Supporters argue that expanded trade and higher economic growth are the best ways to reduce poverty. This largely sterile debate merely diverts attention from the real issues. In practice, economic growth and poverty reduction do tend to correlate very closely. However, the real question is (or ought to be) whether open trade policies are a reliable mechanism for generating self-sustaining growth and poverty reduction, the evidence for which is far less convincing.

Regarding the relationship between growth and poverty reduction, let's take some of the easier questions. Does growth benefit the poor? Yes, in general. The absolute number of people living in poverty has dropped in all of the developing countries that have sustained rapid growth over the past few decades. In theory, a country could enjoy a high average growth rate without any benefit to its poorest households if income disparities grew significantly—that is, if the rich got richer while the incomes of the poor stagnated or declined. This is unlikely, however; income distribution tends to be stable over time, and rarely changes so much that the poor would experience an absolute decline in incomes while average incomes grow in a sustained fashion.

Moreover, to the extent that income distribution changes, its relationship to economic growth varies from country to country. Growth has been accompanied by greater equality of income in the Taiwan Province of China, Bangladesh and Egypt, for example, but by greater inequality in Chile, China and Poland. This suggests that the magnitude of the poverty reduction payoff from growth depends, in part, on a country's specific circumstances and policies.

Is poverty reduction good for growth? Again, yes, in general. It is hard to think of countries where a large decrease in the absolute number of people living in poverty has not been accompanied by faster growth. Just as we can imagine growth occurring without any reduction of poverty, we can also imagine a strategy of poverty reduction that relies exclusively on redistributing wealth from the rich and the middle classes to the poor. In principle, a country pursuing redistributive policies could reduce poverty even if its total income did not grow. But we would be hard-pressed to find real-world examples. Policies that increase the incomes of the poor, such as investments in primary education, rural infrastructure, health and nutrition, tend to enhance the productive capacity of the whole economy, boosting the incomes of all groups.

What does a high correlation between growth and the incomes of the poor tell us? Practically nothing, for the reasons outlined above. All it shows is that income distribution tends to be stable and fairly unresponsive to policy changes. Moreover, a strong correlation between economic growth and poverty reduction is compatible with both of the following arguments: (1) only policies that target growth can reduce poverty; and (2) only policies that reduce poverty can boost overall economic growth. Therefore, the observed correlation between growth and poverty reduction is of little interest as far as policy choices and priorities are concerned.

A somewhat different question is whether the well-being of the poor should enter as an independent determinant of policy choices, in addition to the usual focus on macroeconomic stability, macroeconomic efficiency, and institutional quality. In other words, should economic reform strategies have a poverty focus? Yes, for at least three reasons. First, in considering social welfare, most people in general, and most democratically elected governments in particular, would give more weight to the well-being of the poor than to that of the rich. An economy's growth

rate is not a sufficient statistic for evaluating welfare because it ignores the distribution of the rewards of growth. A policy that increases the income of the poor by one rupee can be worthwhile at the margin even if it costs the rest of society more than a rupee. From this perspective, it may be entirely rational and proper for a government considering two competing growth strategies to choose the one that has greater potential payoff for the poor even if its impact on overall growth is less assured.

Second, even if the welfare of the poor does not receive extra weight, interventions aimed at helping the poor may still be the most effective way to raise average incomes. Poverty is naturally associated with market imperfections and incompleteness. The poor remain poor because they cannot borrow against future earnings to invest in education, skills, new crops and entrepreneurial activities. They are cut off from economic activity because they are deprived of many collective goods (e.g., property rights, public safety, infrastructure) and lack information about market opportunities. It is a standard tenet of economic theory that raising real average incomes requires interventions targeted at closing gaps between private and social costs. There will be a preponderance of such opportunities where there is a preponderance of poverty.

Third, focusing on poverty is also warranted from the perspective of an approach to development that goes beyond an exclusive focus on consumption or income to embrace human capabilities. As Amartya Sen (1999) has emphasized, the overarching goal of development is to maximize people's capabilities—that is, their ability to lead the kind of life they value. The poor face the greatest hurdles in this area and are therefore the most deserving of urgent policy attention.

Policy-makers make choices and determine priorities all the time. The lens through which they perceive development profoundly affects their choices. Keeping poverty in sight ensures that their priorities are not distorted. Consider some illustrative tradeoffs.

• *Fiscal policy.* How should a government resolve the trade-off between higher spending on poverty-related projects (rural infrastructure, say) and the need for tight fiscal policies? Should it risk incurring the disapproval of financial markets as the price of better irrigation? How should it allocate its educational budget? Should more be spent on building primary schools in rural areas or on training bank auditors and accountants?

- *Market liberalization.* Should the government maintain price controls on food crops, even if such controls distort resource allocation in the economy? Should it remove capital controls on the balance of payments, even if that means fiscal resources will be tied up in holding additional foreign reserves—resources that could otherwise have been used to finance a social fund?

- *Institutional reform.* How should the government design its anti-corruption strategy? Should it target the large-scale corruption that foreign investors complain about or the petty corruption in the police and judicial systems that affect ordinary citizens? Should legal reform focus on trade and foreign investment or domestic problems? Whose property rights should receive priority, peasants or foreign patent holders? Should the government pursue land reform, even if it threatens politically powerful groups?

As these examples illustrate, in practice, even the standard, growth-oriented desiderata of macroeconomic stability, microeconomic efficiency and institutional reform leave considerable room for manoeuvre. Governments can use this room to better or worse effect. A poverty focus helps ensure that the relevant trade-offs are considered explicitly.

Since growth and poverty reduction go largely hand in hand, the real questions are: What are the policies that yield these rewards? How much do we know about policy impacts? The honest answer is that we do not know nearly enough. We have evidence that land reforms, appropriately targeted price reforms and certain types of health and education expenditures benefit the poor, but we are uncertain about many things. It is one thing to say that development strategies should have a poverty focus, another to identify the relevant policies.

But this is not a strike against poverty-oriented programmes, since we are equally uncertain about growth-oriented programmes. The uncomfortable reality is that our knowledge about the kinds of policies that stimulate growth remains limited. We know that large fiscal and macroeconomic imbalances are bad for growth. We know that 'good' institutions are important, even though we have very little idea about how countries can acquire them. And, despite a voluminous literature on the subject, we know next to nothing about the kinds of trade policies that are most conducive to growth (see below).

For all of these reasons, it is not productive to make a sharp distinction between policies that promote growth and those that target the poor directly. These policies are likely to vary considerably depending on institutional context, making it difficult to generalize with any degree of precision. Our real focus should be on what works, how, and under what circumstances.

Achieving Economic Growth: What Really Matters?

The enlightened standard view of development policy grew out of dissatisfaction with the limited results yielded by the Washington Consensus policies of the 1980s and 1990s. The disappointing growth performance and increasing economic insecurity in Latin America—the region that went furthest with policies of privatization, liberalization and openness—the failures in the former Soviet Union, and the Asian financial crisis of 1997-98 all contributed to a refashioning, resulting in the 'augmented Washington Consensus' (shown in Table 1). This goes beyond liberalization and privatization to emphasize the need to create the institutional underpinnings of market economies. Reforms now include financial regulation and prudential supervision governance and anti-corruption, legal and administrative reform, labour-market 'flexibility' and social safety nets.

Operationally, these institutional reforms are heavily influenced by an Anglo-American conception of what constitutes

Table 1

The Original Washington Consensus	The Augmented Washington Consensus
Fiscal discipline	*The original list plus:*
Reorientation of public expenditures	Legal/political reform
Tax reform	Regulatory institutions
Financial liberalization	Anti-corruption
Unified and competitive exchange rates	Labour market flexibility
Unified and competitive exchange rates	WTO agreements
Trade liberalization	Financial codes and standards
Openness to DFI	'Prudent' capital-account opening
Privatization	Non-intermediate exchange rate regimes
Deregulations	Social safety nets
Secure property rights	Poverty reduction

desirable institutions (as in the preference for arms-length finance over 'development banking' and flexible labour markets over institutionalized labour markets). In addition, they are driven largely by the requirements of integration into the world economy: hence the emphasis on the international harmonization of regulatory practices, as in the case of financial codes and standards and of the WTO agreements.

Market economies rely on a wide array of non-market institutions that perform regulatory stabilization and legitimizing functions (see Rodrik 2001a). Cross-national econometric work shows that the quality of a country's public institutions is a critical and perhaps the most important, determinant of a country's long-term development (Acemoglu et al. 2000). While the recent emphasis on institutions is thus highly welcome, it needs to be borne in mind that the institutional basis for a market economy is not uniquely determined. There is no single mapping between a well-functioning market and the form of non-market institutions required to sustain it, as is clear from the wide variety of regulatory, stabilizing and legitimizing institutions in today's advanced industrial societies. The American style of capitalism is very different from the Japanese style of capitalism. Both differ from the European style. And even within Europe, there are large differences between the institutional arrangements in, say, Sweden and

Germany. Over the long term, each of these have performed equally well.[2]

The point about institutional diversity has in fact a more fundamental implication. As Roberto Unger (1998) argues, the institutional arrangements in operation today, varied as they are, themselves constitute a subset of the full range of potential institutional possibilities. There is no reason to suppose that modern societies have exhausted all useful institutional variations that could underpin healthy and vibrant economies. We must avoid thinking that a specific type of institution—mode of corporate governance, social security system or labour market legislation, for example—is the only one compatible with a well-functioning market economy.

Leaving aside the question of long-term choice over institutional forms, the enlightened standard view, insofar as it is presented as a recipe for stimulating economic growth, also suffers from a fatal flaw: it provides no sense of priorities among a long and highly demanding list of institutional prerequisites. This kitchen-sink approach to development strategy flies in the face of practical reality and is at odds with the historical experience of today's advanced industrial economies. What are today regarded as key institutional reforms in areas such as corporate governance, financial supervision, trade law and social safety nets did not take place in Europe or Northern America until quite late in the economic development process (Chang 2000). Indeed, many of the items on the augmented Washington Consensus agenda (Table 1) should be properly viewed as outcomes of successful economic development rather than its prerequisites.

The reality of growth transformations is that they are instigated by an initially narrow set of policy and institutional initiatives, which might be called 'investment strategies' (Rodrik 1999). Adequate human resources, public infrastructure, social peace and stability are all key enabling elements of an investment strategy. But often the critical factor is a set of targeted policy interventions that kindle the animal spirits of domestic investors. These investment strategies set off a period of economic growth, which in turn facilitates a cycle of institutional development and further growth. The initiating reforms are rarely replicas of each other, and they bear only partial resemblance to the requirements highlighted by the enlightened standard view. Typically, they entail a mix of orthodoxy with unconventional domestic innovations. An analysis of three sets of investment strategies will elucidate this central point and highlight the different paths taken to greater prosperity: import-substitution, East Asian-style outward orientation and two-track reform strategies. The list is not meant to be exhaustive, and in the future successful strategies are likely to differ from all three.

Import-Substituting Industrialization (ISI)

Import-substituting industrialization is based on the idea that domestic investment and technological capabilities can be spurred by providing home producers with (temporary) protection against imports. Although this approach has fallen into disgrace since the 1980s, it actually did quite well for a substantial period of time in scores of developing nations. Until the first oil shock hit in 1973, no fewer than 42 developing countries grew at rates exceeding 2.5 per cent per capita per annum (see Rodrik 1999: ch. 4). At this rate, incomes would double every 28 years or less.

The list of countries which followed ISI policies include 12 countries in South America, six in the Middle East and North Africa, and 15 in Sub-Saharan Africa. In fact, there were no less than six Sub-Saharan African countries among the 20 fastest-growing developing countries in the world prior to 1973: Swaziland, Botswana, Côte d' Ivoire, Lesotho, Gabon and Togo, with Kenya ranking 21st. There can be little doubt that economic growth led to substantial improvements in the living conditions of the vast majority of the house-holds in these countries. Between 1967 and 1977, life expectancy at birth increased by four years in Brazil (from 58 to 62), by five years in Cote d' Ivoire (from 43 to 48), by five years in Mexico (from 60 to 65), and by five years in Pakistan (from 48 to 53). In Kenya, infant mortality fell from 112 (per 1,000 live births) in 1965 to 72 in 1980.

ISI policies spurred growth by creating protected and therefore profitable home markets for domestic entrepreneurs to invest in. Contrary to received wisdom, ISI-driven growth did not produce technological lags and inefficiency on an economy-wide scale. In fact, the productivity performance of many Latin American and Middle Eastern countries was, in comparative perspective, exemplary. According to estimates produced by Collins and Bosworth (1996), not only was average total factor productivity (TFP) growth during the period preceding the first oil shock quite high in the Middle East and Latin America (at 2.3 and 1.8%, respectively), it was actually significantly higher than in East Asia (1.3%)! Countries such as Brazil, the Dominican Republic and Ecuador in Latin America; Iran, Morocco and Tunisia in the Middle East; and Côte d' Ivoire and Kenya in Africa all experienced more rapid TFP growth than any of the East Asian countries in this early period (with the possible exception of Hong Kong, for which comparable data are not available). Mexico, Bolivia, Panama, Egypt, Algeria, Tanzania and Zaire experienced higher TFP growth than all but Taiwan. Of course, not all countries following ISI policies did well: Argentina is a striking counterexample, with an average TFP growth of only 0.2% from 1960 to 1973.

The dismal reputation of ISI is due partly to the subsequent economic collapse experienced by many of the countries pursuing it in the 1980s, and partly to the extremely influential studies of Little, Scott and Scitovsky (1970) and Bela Balassa (1971). What these two studies did was to document in detail some of the static economic inefficiencies generated by high and extremely dispersed effective rates of protection (ERP) in the manufacturing sectors of the countries under study. The discovery of cases of negative value-added at world prices—that is, cases where countries would have been better off by throwing away the inputs than by processing them as they did in highly protected plants—was particularly shocking. However, neither study claimed to show that countries which had followed 'outward oriented' strategies had been systematically immune from the same kind of inefficiencies. In fact, their evidence can be read as suggesting that there was no such clear dividing line.[3] In addition, the evidence on TFP growth reviewed above shows that the idea that ISI produced more dynamic inefficiency than did 'outward orientation' is simply incorrect.

Hence, as an industrialization strategy intended to raise domestic investment and enhance productivity, import substitution apparently worked pretty well in a very broad range of countries until at least the mid-1970s. However, starting in the second half of the 1970s, a disaster befell the vast majority of the economies that had been doing well. Of the 42 countries with growth rates above 2.5% prior to 1973, less than a third (12) managed the same record over the next decade. The Middle East and Latin America, which had led the developing world in TFP growth prior to 1973, not only fell behind, but actually began to experience negative TFP growth on average. Only East Asia held its own, while South Asia actually improved its performance (see Collins and Bosworth 1996).

Was this a result of the 'exhaustion' of import-substitution policies? As I have argued elsewhere (Rodrik 1999), the common timing implicates the turbulence experienced in the world economy following 1973—the abandonment of the Bretton Woods system of fixed exchange rates, two major oil shocks, various other commodity boom-and-bust cycles, plus the U.S. Federal Reserve interest-rate shock of the early 1980s. The fact that some of the most ardent followers of ISI policies in South Asia—especially India and Pakistan—managed to either hold on to their growth rates after 1973 (Pakistan) or increase them (India) also suggests that more than just ISI was involved.[4]

The actual story implicates macroeconomic policies rather than the trade regime. The proximate reason for the economic collapse was the inability to adjust macroeconomic policies appropriately in the wake of these external shocks. Macroeconomic maladjustment gave rise to a range of syndromes associated with macroeconomic instability—high or repressed inflation, scarcity of foreign exchange and large black-market premiums, external payments imbalances and debt crises—which greatly magnified the real costs of the shocks. Countries that suffered the most were those with the largest increases in inflation and black-market premiums for foreign currency. The culprits were poor monetary and fiscal policies and inadequate adjustments in exchange-rate policy, sometimes aggravated by shortsighted policies of creditors and the Bretton Woods institutions. The bottom line is that in those countries that experienced a debt crisis, the crisis was the product of monetary and fiscal policies that were incompatible with sustainable external balances: there was too little expenditure reducing and expenditure switching. Trade and industrial policies had very little to do with bringing on the crisis.

Why were some countries quicker to adjust their macroeconomic policies than others? The real determinants of growth performance after the 1970s are rooted in the ability of domestic institutions to manage the distributional conflicts triggered by the external shocks of the period. Social conflicts and their management—whether successful or not—played a key role in transmitting the effects of external shocks on to economic performance. Societies with deep social cleavages and poor institutions of conflict management proved worse at handling shocks (see Rodrik 1999).

'Outward-Oriented' Industrialization

The experience of the East Asian tigers is often presented as one of export-led growth, in which opening up to the world economy unleashed powerful forces of industrial diversification and technological catch-up. However, the conventional account overlooks the active role taken by the governments of Taiwan Province of China and the Republic of Korea (and Japan before them) in shaping the allocation resources. In neither of these countries was there significant import liberalization early in the process of growth. Most of their trade liberalization took place in the 1980s, when high growth was already firmly established.

The key to these and other East Asian countries' success was a coherent strategy of raising the return to private investment, through a range of policies that included credit subsidies and tax incentives, educational policies, establishment of public enterprises, export inducements, duty-free access to inputs and capital goods and actual government coordination of investment plans. In the Republic of Korea, the chief form of investment subsidy was the extension of credit to large business groups at negative real interest rates. Korean banks were nationalized after the military coup of 1961, and consequently the government obtained exclusive control over the allocation of investible funds in the economy. Another important manner in which investment was subsidized in Korea was through the socialization of investment risk in selected sectors. This emerged because the government—most notably President Park—provided an implicit guarantee that the state would bail out entrepreneurs investing in 'desirable' activities if circumstances later threatened the profitability of those investments. In Taiwan, investment subsidies took the form of tax incentives. In both the Republic of Korea and Taiwan, public enterprises played a very important role in enhancing the profitability of private investment by ensuring that key inputs were available locally for private producers downstream. Not only did public enterprises account for a large share of manufacturing output and invest-

ment in each country, their importance actually increased during the critical take-off years of the 1960s. Singapore also heavily subsidized investment, but this country differs from the Republic of Korea and Taiwan in that its investment incentives centred heavily on foreign investors.

While trade policies that spurred exports were part of this complex arsenal of incentives, investment and its promotion was the key goal in all countries. To that end, governments in the Republic of Korea and Taiwan freely resorted to unorthodox strategies: they protected the home markets to raise profits, implemented generous export subsidies, encouraged their firms to reverse-engineer foreign patented products, and imposed performance requirements such as export-import balance requirements and domestic content requirements on foreign investors (when foreign companies were allowed in). All of these strategies are now severely restricted under the WTO agreements.

The Two-Track Strategy

A relatively minimal set of reforms in China in the late 1970s set the stage for the phenomenal economic performance that has been the envy of any poor country since. Initial reforms were relatively simple: they loosened the communal farming system and allowed farmers to sell their crops in free markets once they had fulfilled their quota obligations to the state. Subsequent reforms allowed the creation of township and village enterprises and the extension of the 'market track' into the urban and industrial sectors. Special economic zones were created to attract foreign investments. What stands out about these reforms is that they are based on dual tracks (state and market), on gradualism and on experimentation.

One can interpret Chinese-style gradualism in two ways. One perspective, represented forcefully in work by Sachs and Woo (2000) underplays the relevance of Chinese particularism by arguing that the successes of the economy are not due to any special aspects of the Chinese transition to a market economy, but instead are largely due to a convergence of Chinese institutions with those in non-socialist economies. In this view, the faster the convergence, the better the outcomes: 'favorable outcomes have emerged not because of gradualism, but despite gradualism' (ibid: 3). The policy message that follows is that countries that look to China for lessons should focus not on institutional experimentation but on harmonizing their institutions with those abroad.

The alternative perspective, perhaps best developed in work by Qian and Roland, is that the peculiarities of the Chinese model represent solutions to particular political or informational problems for which no blueprint-style solution exists. Hence Lau, Qian and Roland (1997) interpret the dual-track approach to liberalization as a way of implementing Pareto-efficient reforms: an alteration in the planned economy that improves incentives at the margin, enhances efficiency in resource allocation, and yet leaves none of the plan beneficiaries worse off. Qian, Roland and Xu (1999) interpret Chinese-style decentralization as all owing to the development of superior institutions of coordination: when economic activity requires products with matched attributes, local experimentation is a more effective way of processing and using local knowledge. These analysts find much to praise in the Chinese model because they think the system generates the right incentives for developing the tacit knowledge required to build and sustain a market economy, and therefore, they are not overly bothered by some of the economic inefficiencies that may be generated along the way.

A less well-known instance of a successful two-track strategy is that of Mauritius, where superior economic performance has been built on a peculiar combination of orthodox and heterodox strategies. An export processing zone (EPZ), operating under free-trade principles, enabled an export boom in garments to European markets and an accompanying investment boom at home. Yet the island's economy has combined the EPZ with a domestic sector that was highly protected until the mid-1980s: the IMF gave the Mauritian economy the highest (i.e., worst)

score on its 'policy restrictiveness' index for the early 1990s, reckoning it was one of the world most protected economies even by the late 1990s (see Subramanian 2001). Mauritius is essentially an example of an economy that has followed a two-track strategy not too dissimilar to that followed by China, but which was underpinned by social and political arrangements that encouraged participation, representation and coalition building.

The circumstances under which the Mauritian EPZ was set up in 1970 are instructive, and highlight the manner in which participatory political systems help design creative strategies for building locally adapted institutions. Given the small size of the home market, it was evident that Mauritius would benefit from an outward-oriented strategy. But as in other developing countries, policy-makers had to contend with the import substituting industrialists who had been propped up by the restrictive commercial policies of the early 1960s prior to independence, and who were naturally opposed to relaxing the trade regime.

A Washington economist would have advocated across-the-board liberalization without regard to what that might do the precarious ethnic and political balance of the island. The EPZ scheme provided a neat way around the political difficulties. The creation of the EPZ generated new opportunities of trade and of employment, without taking protection away from the import-substituting groups and from the male workers who dominated the established industries. The segmentation of labour markets early on between male and female workers—with the latter predominantly employed in the EPZ—was particularly crucial as it prevented the expansion of the EPZ from driving wages up in the rest of the economy, thereby disadvantaging import-substituting industries. New employment and profit opportunities were created at the margin, while leaving old opportunities undisturbed. This in turn paved the way for the more substantial liberalizations that took place in the mid-1980s and in the 1990s. By the 1990s, the female-male earning ratio was higher in the EPZ than in the rest of the economy (ILO 2001, table 28). Mauritius found its own way to economic development because it was able to devise a strategy that was unorthodox, yet effective.

The Bottom Line

These examples suggest that while market incentives, macroeconomic stability and sound institutions are critical to economic development, they can be generated in a number of different ways—by making the best use of existing capabilities in light of resource and other constraints. There is no single model of a successful transition to a high-growth path. Each country has to figure out its own investment strategy. Once the appropriate strategy is identified (or stumbled upon), the institutional reforms needed may not be extensive. Most of the institutional development occurs alongside economic development, not as a prerequisite to it.

Trade Liberalization, Growth and Poverty Reduction: What Do the Facts Really Show?

Consider two countries, A and B. Country A engages in state trading, maintains import monopolies, retains quantitative restrictions and high tariffs (in the range of 30-50 per-cent) on imports of agricultural and industrial products and is not a member of the WTO. Country B, a WTO member, has slashed import tariffs to a maximum of 15 percent and removed all quantitative restrictions, earning a rare recommendation from the U. S. State Department that 'there are few significant barriers to US exports' (US State Department 1999). One of the two economies has experienced GDP growth rates in excess of 8 percent per annum, has sharply reduced poverty, has expanded trade at double-digit rates, and has attracted large amounts of foreign investment. The other economy has stagnated and suffered deteriorating social indicators, and has made little progress in integrating with the world economy as judged by trade and foreign investment flows.

Country A is Viet Nam, which since the mid-1980s has followed Chinese-style gradu-

alism and a two-track reform programme. Country B is Haiti. Viet Nam has been phenomenally successful, achieving not only high growth and poverty reduction but also a rapid pace of integration into the world economy despite high barriers to trade. Haiti's economy has gone nowhere, even though the country undertook a comprehensive trade liberalization in 1994-95.

The contrasting experiences of these two countries highlight two important points. First, a leadership committed to development and standing behind a coherent growth strategy counts for a lot more than trade liberalization, even when the strategy departs sharply from the enlightened standard view on reform. Second, integration with the world economy is an outcome, not a prerequisite of a successful growth strategy. Protected Viet Nam is integrating with the world economy significantly more rapidly than is open Haiti, because Viet Nam is growing and Haiti is not.

This comparison illustrates a common misdiagnosis. A typical World Bank exercise consists of classifying developing countries into 'globalizers' and 'non-globalizers' based on their rates of growth of trade volumes. The analyst asks whether globalizers (i.e., those with the highest rates of trade growth) have experienced faster income growth, greater poverty reduction and worsened income distribution (see Dollar and Kraay 2000). The answers tends to be yes, yes, and no. As the Viet Nam and Haiti cases show, however, this is a highly misleading exercise. Trade volumes are the outcome of many different things, including most importantly an economy's overall performance. They are not something that governments control directly. What governments control are trade policies: the level of tariff and no-tariff barriers, membership in the WTO, compliance with its agreements and so on. The relevant question is: Do open trade policies reliably produce higher economic growth and greater poverty reduction?

Cross-national comparison of the literature reveals no systematic relationship between a country's average level of tariff and non-tariff restrictions and its subsequent economic growth rate. If anything, the evidence for the 1990s indicates a positive (but statistically insignificant) relationship between tariffs and economic growth (see Figure 1). The only systematic relationship is that countries dismantle trade restrictions as they get richer. That accounts for the fact that today's rich countries, with few exceptions, embarked on modern economic growth behind protective barriers, but now have low trade barriers.

The absence of a robust positive hip between open trade policies and economic growth may come as a surprise in view of the ubiquitous claim that trade liberalization promotes higher growth. Indeed, the literature is replete with cross-national studies concluding that growth and economic dynamism are strongly linked to more liberal trade policies. For example, an influential study by Sachs and Warner (1995) found that economies that are open, by their definition, grew 2.4 percentage points faster annually than did those that are not—an enormous difference. Without such studies, organizations such as the World Bank, IMF and the WTO could not have been so vociferous in their promotion of trade concentric development strategies.

Upon closer look, however, these studies turn out to be flawed. The classification of countries as 'open' or 'closed' in the Sachs-Warner study, for example, is not based on actual trade policies but largely on indicators related to exchange rate policy and location in Sub-Saharan Africa. Their classification of countries in effect conflates macroeconomics, geography and institutions with trade policy. It is so correlated with plausible groupings of alternative explanatory variables—macroeconomic instability, poor institutions, location in Africa—that one cannot draw from the subsequent empirical analysis any strong inferences about the effects of openness on growth (see Rodriguez and Rodrik 2001).

The problem is a general one. In a review of the best-known literature (Dollar 1992; Ben-David 1993; Edwards 1998; Frankel and Romer 1999; Sachs and Warner 1995), Francisco Rodriguez and I found a major gap between the policy clusions that are typically drawn and what the research has actually shown. A common

problem has been the misattribution of macroeconomic phenomena (e.g., overvalued currencies or macroeconomic instability) or geographic location (e.g., in the tropical zone) to trade policies. Once these problems are corrected, any meaningful relationship across countries between the level of trade barriers and economic growth evaporates (see also Helleiner 1994).

In practice, the relationship between trade openness and growth is likely to be a contingent one, dependent on a host of internal and external characteristics. The fact that practically all of today's advanced countries embarked on their growth behind tariff barriers, and reduced protection only subsequently, surely offers a clue of sorts. Moreover, the modern theory of endogenous growth yields an ambiguous answer to the question of whether trade liberalization promotes growth, one that depends on whether the forces of comparative advantage push the economy's resources towards activities that generate long-run growth (research and development, expanding product variety, upgrading product quality, etc.) or divert them from such activities.

No country has developed successfully by turning its back on international trade and long-term capital flows. Very few countries have grown over long periods of time without experiencing an increase in the share of foreign trade in their national product. In practice, the most compelling mechanism that links trade with growth in developing countries is that imported capital goods are likely to be significantly cheaper than those manufactured at home. Policies that restrict imports of capital equipment, raise the price of capital goods at home and thereby reduce real investment levels have to be viewed as undesirable on the face of it—although this does not rule out the possibility of selective infant industry policies in certain segments of capital-goods industries. Exports, in turn, are important since they permit the purchase of imported capital equipment.

But it is equally true that no country has developed simply by opening itself up to foreign trade and investment. The trick has been to combine the opportunities offered by world

Low Import Tariffs Are Good For Growth? Think Again.
Figure 1

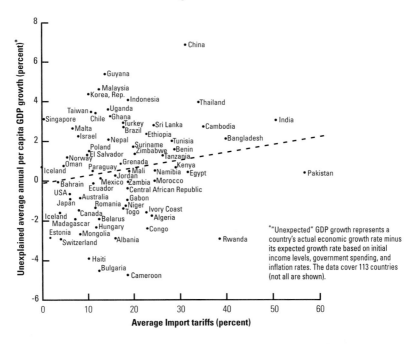

Sources: All data are averages for the 1990s, and come from the Dollar and Kraay (2000) data set. Specifications are based on Dollar and Kraay (2000), replacing trade/GDP with tariff levels and controlling separately for initial income, government consumption/GDP and inflation rate.

markets with a domestic investment and institution-building strategy to stimulate the animal spirits of domestic entrepreneurs. Almost all of the outstanding cases—East Asia, China, India since the early 1980s—involve partial and gradual opening up to imports and foreign investment.

The experiences of China and India are particularly noteworthy, as they are two huge countries that have done extremely well recently, and are often cited as examples of what openness can achieve (see Stern 2000: 3). The reality, once again, is more complicated. In both India and China, the main trade reform took place about a decade after the onset of higher growth. Moreover, these countries' trade restrictions remain among the highest in the world. As noted briefly above, the increase in China's growth started in the late 1970s with the introduction of the household responsibility system in agriculture and of two-tier pricing. Trade liberalization did

not start in earnest until much later, during the second half of the 1980s and especially during the 1990s, once the trend growth rate had already increased substantially.

The case of India is shown in Figure 2. As the figure makes clear, India's trend growth rate increased substantially in the early 1980s (a fact that stands out particularly clearly when it is compared against other developing countries), while serious trade reform did not start until 1991-93. The tariff averages displayed in the chart show that tariffs were actually higher in the rising growth period of the 1980s than in the low-growth 1970s. To be sure, tariffs hardly constitute the most serious trade restrictions in India, but they nonetheless display the trends in Indian trade policy fairly accurately.

Of course, both India and China did 'participate in international trade,' and by that measure they are both globalizers. But the relevant question for policy-makers is not

Tariffs and Growth in India
Figure 2

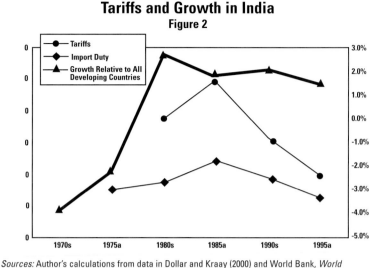

Sources: Author's calculations from data in Dollar and Kraay (2000) and World Bank, *World Development Indicators 2000*, CD-Rom.

whether trade per se is good or bad—countries that do well also increase their trade/GDP ratios as a by-product—but what the correct sequence of policies is and how much priority deep trade liberalization should receive early in the reform process. With regard to the latter questions, the experiences of India and China are suggestive of the benefits of a gradual, sequenced approach.

To repeat, the appropriate conclusion is not that trade protection is inherently preferable to trade liberalization; certainly, there is scant evidence from the last 50 years that inward looking economies experience systematically faster economic growth than open ones. But the benefits of trade openness are now greatly oversold. Deep trade liberalization cannot be relied on to deliver high rates of economic growth and therefore does not deserve the high priority it typically receives in the development strategies pushed by leading multilateral organizations.[5]

As Helleiner (2000: 3) puts it, there are 'few reputable developing country analysts or governments who question the positive potential roles of international trade or capital inflow in economic growth and overall development. How could they question the inevitable need for participation in, indeed a considerable degree of integration with, the global economy?' The real debate is not over whether integration is good or bad, but over matters of policy and priorities: 'It isn't at all obvious either (1) that further external liberalization ("openness") is now in every country's interest and in all dimensions or (2) that in the overarching sweep of global economic history what the world now most requires is a set of global rules that promote or ease the path to greater freedom for global market actors, and are universal in application' (ibid: 4).

The Integrationist Agenda and the Crowding Out of Development Priorities

Priorities are important because in the enlightened standard view, insertion into the world economy is no longer a matter of simply removing trade and investment barriers. Countries have to satisfy a long list of institutional requirements in order to maximize the gains and minimize the risks of participation in the world economy. Global integration remains the key prerequisite for economic development, but there is now a lot more to it than just throwing the borders open. Reaping the gains from openness requires a full complement of institutional reforms.

So trade liberalization entails not only the lowering of tariff and non-tariff barriers, but also compliance with WTO requirements on subsidies, intellectual property, customs procedures, sanitary standards and policies vis-à-vis foreign investors. Moreover, these legal requirements have to be complemented with additional reforms to ensure favourable economic outcomes: tax reform to make up for lost tariff revenues; social safety nets to compensate displaced workers; credibility enhancing institutional innovations to quell doubts about the permanence of the reforms; labour-market reform to enhance labour mobility across industries; technological assistance to upgrade firms adversely affected by import competition; training programmes to ensure that export-oriented firms and investors have access to skilled workers; and so on. Reading World Bank reports on trade policy, one can be excused for thinking that the list of complementary reforms is virtually endless.

Not withstanding the overly Anglo-American conception of institutional possibilities reflected in the Washington agenda for integrationist reform, many of the proposed institutional reforms are perfectly sensible ones, and in a world without financial, administrative or political constraints, there would be little argument about the need to adopt them. But in the real world, fiscal resources, administrative capabilities and political capital are all scarce, and choices need to be made about how to deploy them. In such a world, viewing institutional priorities from the vantage point of insertion in the global economy has real opportunity costs.

Some trade-offs are illustrative. It has been estimated that it costs a typical developing country $150 million to implement requirements under just three of the WTO agreements: customs valuation, sanitary and phytosanitary measures (SPS) and intellectual property rights (TRIPs). As the World Bank's Michael Finger points out, this is a sum equal to a year's development budget for many of the least-developed countries (Finger and Schuler 1999).

In the area of legal reform, should the government focus its energies on 'importing' legal codes and standards, or on improving existing domestic legal institutions? In Turkey, a weak coalition government spent several months gathering political support for a bill that would provide foreign investors the protection of international arbitration. Wouldn't it have been a better strategy, for the long run, to reform the existing legal regime for the benefit of foreign and domestic investors alike?

In public health, should the government pursue tough policies on compulsory licensing and/or parallel importation of basic medicines, even if that means running afoul of existing WTO rules? The United States has charged that Brazil's highly successful treatment programme for HIV/AIDS violates WTO rules because it allows the government to seek compulsory licensing when a foreign patent holder does not 'work' the patent locally.

In industrial strategy, should the government simply open up and let the chips drop wherever they might, or should it emulate East Asian experience of industrial policies through export subsidies, directed credit and selective protection?

How should the government focus its anti-corruption strategy? Should it target the 'grand' corruption that foreign investors complain about, or the petty corruption that affects the poor the most? Perhaps, as proponents of permanent normal trade relations with China argued in the recent US Congressional debate, a government that is forced to protect the rights of foreign investors becomes more inclined to protect the human rights of its own citizens too. But isn't this at best a trickle-down strategy of institutional reform? Shouldn't institutional reform be targeted on the desired ends directly—whether those ends are the rule of law, improved observance of human rights or reduced corruption?

The rules for admission into the world economy not only reflect little awareness of development priorities, they are often completely unrelated to sensible economic principles. WTO rules on anti-dumping, subsidies and countervailing measures, agriculture, textiles, trade related investment measures (TRIMs) and trade related intellectual property rights (TRIPs) are utterly devoid of any economic rationale beyond the mercantilist interests of a narrow set of powerful groups in the advanced industrial countries. The developmental pay-off of most of these requirements is hard to see.

Bilateral and regional trade agreements are often far worse, as they impose even tighter prerequisites on developing countries in return for crumbs of enhanced 'market access' in the larger partners. The Africa Growth and Opportunity Act passed by the U. S. Congress in 2000, for example, contains a long list of eligibility criteria, including the requirement that African governments minimize interference in the economy. It provides free access to U.S. markets only under strict rules of origin, thereby ensuring that few economic linkages are generated in the African countries themselves. The U.S.-Jordan Free Trade Agreement imposes more restrictive intellectual property rules on Jordan than exist under the WTO.

In each of these areas, a strategy focused on integration crowds out more development-friendly alternatives. Many of the institutional reforms needed for insertion in the world economy can be independently desirable, or produce broader spillovers. But these priorities do not necessarily coincide with the priorities of a broader development agenda. A strategy that focuses on getting the state out of the way of the market overlooks the important functions that the state must play during the process of economic transformation. What belongs on the agenda of institutional reform is building up state capacity—not diminishing it (Evans 2000).

World markets are a source of technology and capital; it would be silly for the developing world not to exploit these opportunities. But, as I have argued above, successful development strategies have always required a judicious blend of imported practices with domestic institutional innovations. Policy-makers need to forge a domestic growth strategy, relying on domestic investors and domestic institutions. The most costly downside of the integrationist agenda is that it is crowding out serious thinking and efforts along such lines.

An International Trade Regime That Puts Development First: General Principles

Access to the markets of the industrial countries matters for development. But so does the autonomy to experiment with institutional innovations that diverge from orthodoxy. The exchange of reduced policy autonomy in the South for improved market access in the North is a bad bargain where development is concerned.

Consider the old GATT system, under which the international trade regime did not reach much beyond tariff and non-tariff barriers to trade. The developing countries were effectively exempt from prevailing disciplines. The 'most favoured nation' principle ensured that they benefited from the tariff cuts negotiated among the industrial countries, while they themselves 'gave up' little in return. The resulting pattern of liberalization may have been asymmetric (with many products of interest to developing countries either excluded or receiving less beneficial treatment, but the net effect for the developing world was still highly salutary.

It is in such an environment that the most successful 'globalizers' of an earlier era—the East Asian tigers—managed to prosper. These countries were free to do their own thing, and did so, combining trade reliance with unorthodox policies—export subsidies, domestic-content requirements, import-export linkages, patent and copyright infringement restrictions on capital flows (including direct foreign investment), directed credit and so on—that are largely precluded by today's rules.[6] In fact, such policies were part of the arsenal of today's advanced industrial countries until quite recently (see Scherer and Watal 2001). The environment for today's globalizers is significantly more restrictive (see Amsden 2000).

For the word's poorest economies, the so-called least developed countries (LLSDCs), something along the old GATT lines is still achievable, and would constitute a more development-friendly regime than the one that exists currently. LLSDCs are economies that are individually and collectively small enough that 'adjustment' issues in the advanced countries are not a serious obstacle to the provision of one-sided free-market access in the North to the vast majority of products of interest to them. Instead of encumbering these countries with all kinds of institutional requirements that come attached to a 'single undertaking,' it would be far better to leave them the room to follow their own institutional priorities, while providing them with access into northern markets that is both duty free and free of quantitative restrictions. In practice, this can be done either by extending existing 'phase-in' periods until certain income thresholds are reached, or incorporating a general LLSDC exception.

In the case of middle-income and other developing nations, it is unrealistic to expect that advanced industrial countries would be willing to accept a similar arrangement. The amount of political opposition that imports from developing countries generate in the advanced industrial countries is already disproportionate to the volume of trade in question. Some of these objectives have a legitimate core, and it is important that developing nations understand and accept this (see Mayda and Rodrik 2001). Under a sensible set of global trade rules, industrialized countries would have as much right to protect their own social arrangements—in areas such as labour and environmental standards, welfare-state arrangements, rural communities, or industrial organization—as developing nations have to adopt divergent institutional practices. Countries such as India, Brazil, or China, whose exports can have a sizable impact on, say, labour-market institutions and employment relations within the advanced countries, cannot ask importing countries to overlook these effects while demanding at the same time that the constraints on their own developmental agenda be lifted. Middle-income developing countries have to accept a more balanced set of rights and obligations.

Is it possible to preserve developing countries' autonomy while also respecting the legitimate objectives of advanced industrial countries to maintain high labour, social and environmental standards at home? Would such a regime of world trade avoid collapsing into protectionism, bilateralism or regional trade blocs? Would it in fact be development-friendly? The answer to all these questions is yes, provided we accept five simple principles.

Trade is a means to an end, not an end in itself. Step number one is to move away from attaching normative significance to trade itself. The scope of market access generated by the international trade regime and the volume of trade thereby stimulated are poor measures of how well the system functions. As the WTO's preamble emphasizes, trade is useful only insofar as it serves broader developmental and social goals. Developing countries should not be obsessed with market access abroad, at the cost of overlooking more fundamental developmental challenges at home. Industrial countries should balance the interests of their exporters and multinational companies with those of their workers and consumers.

Advocates of globalization lecture the rest of the world incessantly about the adjustments countries have to undertake in their policies and institutions in order to expand their international trade and become more attractive to foreign investors. This is another instance of confusing means for ends. Trade serves at best as an instrument for achieving the goals that societies seek: propriety, stability, freedom and quality of life. Nothing enrages WTO bashers more than the suspicion that, when push comes to shove, the WTO allows trade to trump the environment or human rights. And developing countries are right to resist a system that evaluates their needs from the perspective of expanding world trade instead of poverty reduction.

Reversing our priorities would have a simple but powerful implication. Instead of asking what kind of multilateral trading system maximizes foreign trade and investment opportunities, we would ask what kind of multilateral system best enables nations around the world to pursue their own values and developmental objectives.

Trade rules have to allow for diversity in national institutions and standards. As I have emphasized above, there is no single recipe for economic advancement. This does not mean that anything and everything works: market-based incentives, clear property-control rights, competition and macroeconomic stability are essential everywhere. But even these universal requirements can be and have been embodied in diverse institutional forms. Investment strategies, needed to jump-start economies, can also take different forms.

Moreover, citizens of different countries have varying preferences over the role of government regulations or provision of social welfare, however imperfectly these preferences are articulated or determined. They differ over the nature and extent of regulations to govern new technologies (such things as genetically modified organisms) or protect the environment, of policies to extend social safety nets and, more broadly, about the entire relationship between efficiency and equity. Rich and poor nations have very different needs in the areas of labour standards or patent protection. Poor countries need the space to follow developmental policies that richer countries no longer require. When countries use the trade system to impose their institutional preferences on others, the result is erosion of the system's legitimacy and efficacy. Trade rules should seek peaceful co-existence among national practices, not harmonization.

Non-democratic countries cannot count on the same trade privileges as democratic ones. National standards that deviate from those in trade partners and thereby provide 'trade advantages' are legitimate only to the extent that they are grounded in free choices made by citizens. Think of labour and environmental standards, for example. Poor countries argue that they cannot afford to have the same stringent standards in these areas as the advanced countries. Indeed, tough emission standards or regulations against the use of child labour can easily backfire if they lead to fewer jobs and greater poverty. Democratic countries such as India and Brazil can legitimately argue that their practices are consistent with the wishes of their own citizens, and that therefore it is inappropriate for labour groups or NGOs in advanced countries to tell them what standard they should

have. Of course, democracy never works perfectly (in either developing countries or in advanced countries), and one would not want to argue that there are no human rights abuses in the countries just mentioned. The point is simply that the presence of civil liberties and political freedoms provides a presumptive cover against the charge that labour, environmental and other standards in the developing nations are inappropriately low.

But in non-democratic countries, such as China, the assertion that labour rights and the environment are trampled for the benefit of commercial advantage cannot be as easily dismissed. Consequently, exports of non-democratic countries deserve greater scrutiny when they entail costly dislocations or adverse distributional consequences in importing countries. In the absence of the presumptive cover provided by democratic rights such countries need to make a 'devlopmental' case for policies that generate adjustment difficulties in the importing countries. For example, minimum wages that are significantly lower than in rich countries or health and other benefits that are less generous can be justified by pointing to lower labour productivity and living standards in poor nations. Lax child labour regulations can sometimes be justified by the argument that under conditions of widespread poverty it is not feasible or desirable to withdraw young workers from the labour force. In other cases, the 'affordability' argument carries less weight: non-discrimination, freedom of association, collective bargaining, prohibition of forced labour do not 'cost' anything; compliance with these 'core labour rights' does not harm, and indeed possibly benefits, economic development. The latter are examples that do not pass the 'development test.'

Countries have the right to protect their own institutions and development priorities. Opponents of today's trade regime argue that trade sets off a 'race to the bottom,' with nations converging towards the lowest levels of environmental, labour and consumer protections. Advocates counter that there is little evidence that trade leads to the erosion of national standards. Developing nations complain that current trade laws are too intrusive, and leave little room for development-friendly policies. Advocates of the WTO reply that these rules provide useful discipline to rein in harmful policies that would otherwise end up wasting resources and hampering development.

One way to cut through this impasse is to accept that countries can uphold national standards and policies, by withholding market access or suspending WTO obligations if necessary, when trade demonstrably undermines domestic practices that enjoy broad popular support. For example, poor nations might be allowed to subsidize industrial activities (and indirectly, their exports) when this is part of a broadly supported development strategy aimed at stimulating technological capabilities. Advanced countries might seek temporary protection against imports originating from countries with weak enforcement of labour rights when such imports serve to worsen working conditions at home. The WTO already has a 'safeguards' system in place to protect firms from import surges. An extension of this principle to protect developmental priorities or environmental, labour and consumer-safety standards at home—with appropriate procedural restraints against abuse—might make the world trading system more development-friendly, more resilient and less resistant to ad-hoc protectionism.

Currently, the Agreement on Safeguards allows (temporary) increases in trade restrictions under a very narrow set of conditions (see Rodrik 1997). It requires a determination that increased imports 'cause or threaten to cause serious injury to the domestic industry,' that causality be firmly established and that if there are multiple causes, injury not be attributed to imports. Safeguards cannot be applied to developing country exporters unless their share of imports of the product concerned is above a threshold. A country applying safeguard measures has to compensate the affected exporters by providing 'equivalent concessions,' lacking which the exporter is free to retaliate.

A broader interpretation of safeguards would acknowledge that countries may legiti-mately seek to restrict trade or suspend existing WTO obligations—to exercise what I call 'opt-outs'—for reasons going beyond competitive threats to their industries. Among such reasons are, as I have discussed, developmental priorities as well as distributional concerns or conflicts with domestic norms or social arrangements in the industrial countries. We could imagine recasting the current agreement into an Agreement on Developmental and Social Safeguards, which would permit the application of opt-outs under a broader range of circumstances. This would require re-casting the 'serious injury' test and replacing it with the need to demonstrate broad domestic support, among all concerned parties, for the proposed measure.

To see how that might work in practice, consider what the current agreement says:

> A Member may apply a safeguard measure only following an investigation by the competent authorities of that Member pursuant to procedures previously established and made public in consonance with Article X of the GATT 1994. This investigation shall include reasonable public notice to all interested parties and public hearings or other appropriate means in which *importers, exporters and other interested parties could present evidence and their views,* including the opportunity to respond to the presentations of other parties and to submit their views, inter alia, as to *whether or not the application of a safeguard measure would be in the public interest.* The competent authorities shall publish a report setting forth their findings and reasoned conclusions reached on all pertinent issues of fact and law. (WTO 1995: 9; emphasis added)

The main shortcoming of this clause is that while it allows all relevant groups, and exporters and importers in particular, to make their views known, it does not actually compel them to do so. Consequently, it results in a strong bias in the domestic investigative process towards the interests of import-competing groups, who are the petitioners for import relief and its obvious beneficiaries. Indeed, this is a key problem with hearings in anti-dumping proceedings, where testimony from other groups besides the import-competing industry is typically not allowed.

The most significant and reliable guarantee against the abuse of opt-outs is informed deliberation, at the national level. A critical reform, then, would be to require the investigative process in each country to: (1) gather testimony and views from all relevant parties, including consumer and public-interest groups, importers and exporters, civil society organizations, and (2) determine whether there exists sufficiently broad support among these groups for the exercise of the opt-out or safeguard in question. The requirements that groups whose incomes might be adversely affected by the opt-out—importers and exporters—be compelled to testify, and that the investigative body trade off the competing interests in a transparent manner would help ensure that protectionist measures that benefit a small segment of industry at a large cost to society would not have much chance of success. When the opt-out in question is part of a broader development strategy that has already been adopted after broad debate and participation, an additional investigative process need not be launched. This last point deserves to be highlighted in view of the emphasis placed on 'local ownership' and 'participatory mechanisms' in strategies of poverty reduction and growth promoted by the international financial institutions.

The main advantage of this procedure is that it would force a public debate on the legitimacy of trade rules and when to suspend them, ensuring that all sides would be heard. This is something that rarely happens even in the industrial countries, let alone in developing nations. This procedure could be complemented with a strengthened monitoring and surveillance role for the WTO, to ensure that domestic opt-out procedures are in compliance with the expanded safeguard clause. An automatic sunset clause could ensure that trade restrictions and opt-outs do not become entrenched long after their perceived need has disappeared.

Allowing opt-outs in this manner would not be without its risks. The possibility that the new procedures would be abused for protectionist ends and open the door to unilateral action on a broad front, despite the high threshold envisaged here, has to be taken into account. But as I have already argued, the current arrangements also have risks. The 'more of the same' approach embodied in the industrialized countries' efforts to launch a comprehensive new round of trade negotiations is unlikely to produce benefits for developing nations. Absent creative thinking and novel institutional designs, the narrowing of the room for institutional divergence harms development prospects. It may also lead to the emergence of a new set of 'grey area' measures entirely outside multilateral discipline. These are consequences that are far worse than the expanded safeguard regime I have just described.

But countries do not have the right to impose their institutional preferences on others. The exercise of opt-outs to uphold a country's own priorities has to be sharply distinguished from using them to impose these priorities on other countries. Trade rules should not force Americans to consume shrimp that are caught in ways that most Americans find unacceptable; but neither should they allow the United States to use trade sanctions to alter the way that foreign nations go about their fishing business. Citizens of rich countries who are genuinely concerned about the state of the environment or of workers in the developing world can be more effective through channels other than trade—via diplomacy or foreign aid, for example. Trade sanctions to promote a country's own preferences are rarely effective, and have no moral legitimacy (except for when they are used against repressive political regimes).

This and the previous principle help us draw a useful distinction between two styles of 'unilateralism'—one that is aimed at protecting differences, and the other aimed at reducing them. When the European Union drags its feet on agricultural trade liberalization, it is out of a desire to 'protect' a set of domestic social arrangements that Europeans, through their democratic procedures, have decided are worth maintaining. When, on the other hand, the United States threatens trade sanctions against Japan because its retailing practices are perceived to harm American exporters or against South Africa because its patent laws are perceived as too lax, it does so out of a desire to bring these countries' practices into line with its own. A well-designed world trade regime would leave room for the former, but prohibit the latter.

Other development-friendly measures. In addition to providing unrestricted access to least developed countries' exports and enabling developing countries to exercise greater autonomy in the use of subsidies, 'trade-related' investment, patent regulations and other measures, a development-friendly trade regime would do the following (see UNCTAD 2000; Raghavan 1996):

- Greatly restrict the use of anti-dumping (AD) measures in advanced industrial countries when exports originate from developing countries. A small, but important step would be to require that the relevant investigating bodies take fully into account the consumer costs of anti-dumping action.
- Allow greater mobility of workers across international boundaries, by liberalizing for example the movement of natural persons connected to trade in labour-intensive services (such as construction).
- Require that all existing and future WTO agreements be fully costed out (in terms of implementation and other costs). It would condition the phasing in of these agreements in the developing countries on the provision of commensurate financial assistance.
- Require additional compensation when a dispute settlement panel rules in favour of a developing country complainant, or (when compensation is not forthcoming) require that other countries join in the retaliation.

- Provide expanded legal and fact-finding assistance to developing country members of the WTO in prospective dispute settlement cases.

Conclusions: From a Market-Exchange Perspective to a Development Perspective

Economists think of the WTO as an institution designed to expand free trade and thereby enhance consumer welfare, in the South no less than in the North. In reality, it is an institution that enables countries to bargain about market access. 'Free trade' is not the typical outcome of this process; nor is consumer welfare (much less development) what the negotiators have chiefly in mind. Traditionally, the agenda of multilateral trade negotiations has been shaped in response to a tug-of-war between exporters and multinational corporations in the advanced industrial countries (which have had the upper hand), on the one hand, and import-competing interests (typically, but not solely, labour) on the other. The chief textbook beneficiaries of free trade—consumers—do not sit at the table. The WTO can best be understood, in this context, as the product of intense lobbying by specific exporter groups in the United States or Europe or of specific compromises between such groups and other domestic groups. The differential treatment of manufactures and agriculture, or of clothing and other goods within manufacturing, the anti-dumping regime, and the intellectual property rights (IPR) regime, to pick some of the major anomalies, are all results of this political process. Understanding this is essential, as it underscores the fact that there is very little in the structure of multilateral trade negotiations to ensure that their outcomes are consistent with development goals, let alone that they be designed to further development.

Hence there are at least three sources of slippage between what development requires and what the WTO does. First, even if free trade were optimal for development in its broad sense, the WTO does not fundamentally pursue free trade. Second, even if it did, there is no guarantee that free trade is the best trade policy for countries at low levels of development. Third, compliance with WTO rules, even when these rules are not harmful in themselves, crowds out a more fully developmental agenda—at both the international and national level.

My main argument has been that the world trading regime has to shift from a 'market access' perspective to a 'development' perspective (see Helleiner 2000:19). Essentially, the shift means that we should stop evaluating the trade regime from the perspective of whether it maximizes the flow of trade in goods and services, and ask instead, 'Do the trading arrangements—current and proposed—maximize the possibilities of development at the national level?' I have discussed why these two perspectives are not the same, even though they sometimes overlap, and have outlined some of the operational implications of such a shift. One is that developing nations have to articulate their needs not in terms of market access, but in terms of the policy autonomy that will allow them to exercise institutional innovations that depart from prevailing orthodoxies. A second is that the WTO should be conceived of not as an institution devoted to harmonization and the reduction of national institutional differences, but as one that manages the interface between different national systems.

This shift to a development perspective would have several important advantages. The first and more obvious is that it would provide for a more development friendly international economic environment. Countries would be able to use trade as a means for development, rather than being forced to view trade as an end in itself (and being forced to sacrifice development goals in the bargain). It would save developing countries precious political capital by obviating the need to bargain for 'special and differential treatment'—a principle that in any case is more form than substance at this point.

Second, viewing the WTO as an institution that manages institutional diversity (rather than imposing uniformity) provides developing countries a way out of a conun-

drum inherent in their current negotiating stance. The problem arises from the inconsistency between their demands for space to implement their development policies on the one hand, and their complaints about northern protectionism in agriculture, textiles and labour and environmental standards, on the other. As long as the issues are viewed in market-access terms, developing countries will be unable to make a sound and principled defense of their legitimate need for space. And the only way they can gain enhanced market access is by restricting their own policy autonomy in exchange. Once the objective of the trading regime is seen as letting different national economic systems prosper side by side, the debate can become one about each nation's institutional priorities and how they may be rendered compatible in a development friendly way.

The third advantage of this shift in perspective is that it provides a way out of the impasse that the trading system finds itself in post-Seattle. At present, two groups feel particularly excluded from the decision-making machinery of the global trade regime: developing country governments and northern NGOs. The former complain about the asymmetry in trade rules, while the latter charge that the system pays inadequate attention to values such as transparency, accountability human rights and environmental sustainability. The demands of these two disenfranchised groups are often perceived to be conflicting — over questions such as labour and environmental standards or the transparency of the dispute settlement procedures—allowing the advanced industrial countries and the WTO leadership to seize the 'middle' ground. It is the demands of these two groups, and the apparent tension between them, that has paralyzed the process of multilateral trade negotiations in recent years.

But once the trade regime—and the governance challenges it poses—is seen from a development perspective, it becomes clear that developing country governments and many of the northern NGOs share the same goals: policy autonomy to pursue independent values and priorities, poverty reduction, and human development in an environmentally sustainable manner. The tensions over issues such as labour standards become manageable if the debate is couched in terms of development processes—broadly defined—instead of the requirements of market access. On all counts, then, the shift in perspective provides a better foundation for the multilateral trading regime.

Dani Rodrik is the Rafiq Hariri Professor of International Political Economy at the John F. Kennedy School of Government, Harvard University. He has published widely in the areas of international economics, economic development, and political economy. Rodrik is the research coordinator of the Group of 24 (G-24), and is also affiliated with the National Bureau of Economic Research and the Centre for Economic Policy Research (London). He is the recipient of a Carnegie Scholar award for 2001, and his work has been supported also by the Ford and Rockefeller Foundations. He is the faculty chair of the new MPA in International Development (MPAID) degree programme at Harvard. He holds a Ph.D. in economics and an MPA from Princeton University, and an A.B. from Harvard College.

Endnotes

[1] See, for example, Mike Moore (2000) or his speech at the London Ministerial roundtable 19 March 2001 (www.wto.org/english/news).

[2] The supposition that one set of institutional arrangements must dominate in terms of overall performance has produced the fads of the decade: Europe, with its low unemployment, high growth and thriving culture, was the continent to emulate throughout much of the 1970s; during the trade-conscious 1980s, Japan became the exemplar of choice; and the 1990s have been the decade of US-style free-wheeling capitalism.

[3] For example, although Taiwan and Mexico are commonly regarded as following diametrically opposed development paths, figures provided by Little et al. (1970:174-90) show that long after introducing trade reforms, Taiwan had a higher average ERP in manufacturing and greater variation in ERPs than did Mexico.

[4] Although India did gradually liberalize its trade regime after 1991, its relative performance began to improve a full decade before these reforms went into effect (in the early 1980s).

[5] The same is true of the promotion and subsidization of inward flows of direct foreign investment (see Hanson 2001).

[6] A recent illustration is the dispute between Brazil and Canada over Brazil's subsidization of its aircraft manufacturer, Embraer. Brazil lost this case in the WTO, and will either remove the subsidies or have to put up with retaliation from Canada. The Republic of Korea, the Taiwan province of China and Mauritius subsidized their export industries for years without incurring similar sanctions.

References

Acemoglu, Daron, Simon Johnson and James A. Robinson. 2000 'The Colonial Origins of Comparative Development: An Empirical Investigation,' unpublished paper, Massachusetts Institute of Technology, Cambridge, MA.

Amsden, Alice. 2000. 'Industrialization Under New WTO Law,' paper prepared for the High-Level Round Table on Trade and Develoment, UNCTAD X, Bankok, February 12.

Balassa, Bela. 1971. *The Structure of Protection in Developing Countries*. Baltimore: Johns Hopkins University Press.

Ben-David, Dan. 1993. 'Equalizing Exchange: Trade Liberalization and Income Convergence,' *Quarterly Journal of Economics*, 108, no. 3.

Chang, Ha-Joon. 2000. 'Institutional Development in Developing Countries in a Historical Perspective,' unpublished paper, Faculty of Economics and Politics, Cambridge University.

Collins, Susan and Barry Bosworth. 1996. 'Economic Growth in East Asia: Accumulation versus Assimilation.' Brookings Papers on Economic Activity 2: 135-191.

Dollar, David. 1992. 'Outward-Oriented Developing Economies Really Do Grow More Rapidly: Evidence from 95 LDCs, 1976-85.' *Economic Development and Cultural Change*, pp. 523-44.

Dollar, David and Aart Kraay. 2000. 'Trade, Growth, and Poverty,' World Bank, Washington, DC, October.

Edwards, Sebastian. 1998. 'Openness, Productivity and Growth: What Do We Really Know?' *Economic Journal* 108 (March): 383-98.

Evans, Peter. 2000. 'Economic Governance Institutions in a Global Political Economy: Implications for Developing Countries.' Paper prepared for the High-Level Round Table on Trade and Development, 'UNCTAD X, Bankok, February 12.

inger, Michael J. and Philip Schuler. 1999. 'Implementation of Uruguay Round Commitments: the Development Challenge,' World Bank policy research working paper no. 2215, September.

Frankel, Jeffrey and David Romer. 1999. 'Does Trade Cause Growth?' *American Economic Review* 89, no.3 (June): 379-99

Hanson, Gordon. 2001. 'Should Countries Promote Foreign Direct Investment,' Group of 24 Discussion Paper no. 9, February.

Helleiner, Gerald K. 2000. 'Markets, Politics, and the Global Economy: Can the Global Economy Be Civilized?' Prebisch Lecture, UNCTAD, Geneva.

——————. 1994. *Trade Policy and Industrialization in Turbulent Times*. New York: Routledge.

International Labour Office. 2001. Mauritius. Studies on the Social Dimensions of Globalization. Geneva: ILO.

Lau, Lawrence J., Yingyi Quian and Gerard Roland. 1997. 'Reform Without Losers: An Interpretation of China's Dual-Track Approach to Transition,' unpublished paper, November.

Little, Ian, Tibor Scitovsky and Maurice Scott. 1970. *Industry and Trade in Some Developing Countries*. London and New York: Oxford University Press for OECD.

Mayda, Anna Maria and Dani Rodrik. 2001 'Why Are Some People (or Countries) More Protectionist than Others? Harvard University, Cambridge, MA. http://www.harvard.edu/rodrik.

Moore, Mike. 2000. 'The WTO Is a Friend of the Poor,' *Financial Times*, June 19, 2000.

Qian, Yingi, Gerare Roland and Chenggang Xu.

1999. 'Coordingating Changes in M-Form and U-Form Organizations,' paper prepared for the Nobel Symposium, August.

Raghavan, Chakravarthi. 1996. "The New Issues and Developing Countries,' TWN Trade & Development Series, no. 4, Third World Network, Penang, Malaysia

Rodriguez, Francisco and Dani Rodrik. 2001. "Trade Policy an Economic Growth: A Skeptic's Guide to the Cross-National Literature.' Forthcoming in Ben Bernanke and Kenneth S. Rogoff, eds., NBER Macro Annual 2000. Cambridge, MA:NBER. (http://www1.ksg.harvard.edu/rodrik/skepti1299.pdf)

Rodrik, Dani. 2001a. 'Institutions for High-Quality Growth: What They Are and How to Acquire Them,' *Studies in Comparative International Development,* forthcoming.

——————. 2001b. "Trading in Illusions,' *Foreign Policy.* March-April.

——————. 2000a. 'Five Simple Principles for World Trade," *The American Prospect,* January 17.

——————. 2001b 'Trading in Illusions' *Foreign Policy,* March – April..

——————. 2000b. "Growth versus Poverty Reduction: A Hollow Debate,' *Finance & Develoment* 37, no. 4 (December)

——————. 1999. 'The New Global Economy and the Developing Countries: Making Openness Work,' Overseas Development Council, Washington, DC, 1999.

——————. 1997. 'Has Globalization Gone Too Far?' Institute for International Economics, Washington, DC 1997.

Sachs, Jeffrey D., and Wing Thye Woo. 2000. 'Understanding China's Economic Performance,' *Journal of Policy Reform* 4, no. 1.

Sachs, Jeffrey, and Andrew Warner, 1995. 'Economic Reform and the Process of Global Integration,' Brookings Papers on Economic Activity. No. 1:1-118.

Scherer, F.M. and Jayashree Watal. 2001. 'Post-TRIPS Options for Access to Patented Medicines in Developing Countries,' John F. Kennedy School of Government, Harvard University.

Sen, Amartya. 1999. *Development As Freedom.* New York: Alfred Knopf.

————. 1993. "Capability and Well-being.' In Martha Nussbaum and Amartya Sen, eds., *The Quality of Life.* Oxford: Clarendon Press.

Stern, Nicholas. 2000. "Globalization and Poverty.' Presented at the Institute of Economic and Social Research, Faculty of Economics, University of Indonesia, December 15.

Subramanian, Arvind. 2001. 'Mauritius' Trade and Development Strategy: What Lessons Does It Offer?' paper presented at the IMF High-Level Seminar on Globalization and Africa, March.

UNCTAD. 2000. Positive Agenda and Future Trade Negotiations. Geneva: UNCTAD.

Unger, Roberto Mangabeira. 1998. *Democracy Realized: The Progressive Alternative.* London and New York: Verso Books.

United States, Department of State. 1999. '1999 Country Report on Economic Policy and Trade Practices: Haiti,' http://www.state.gov /www/issues/economic/trade_reports/1999/ haiti.pdf.

World Bank. 2000. World Development Indicators 2000. Washington, DC: World Bank.

World Bank and IMF. 2000. "Trade, Development and Poverty Reduction,' joint paper prepared for the consideration of the Development Committee, March 31.

World Trade Organization (WTO). 1995. 'Agreement Establishing the World Trad Organization.' WTO Information and Media Relations Divisions, Geneva. http://wto.org/english/docs_e/legal_e/ 04-wto.pdf.

Farm Fallacies That Hurt the Poor

13

KEVIN **WATKINS**

Apart from wringing their hands, endorsing human development goals, and promising more aid, what can governments in rich countries do about poverty in poor ones? Answer: get serious about reforming their farm policies. Industrial country agricultural support is destroying the livelihoods of poor farmers across the developing world, reinforcing an unequal pattern of globalization in the process.

Two years ago developing countries joined the Doha round of World Trade Organization (WTO) negotiations on the clear understanding that it would create the conditions for agricultural trade reform. Northern governments solemnly promised to improve access to their own markets, cut support to agriculture, and stop the subsidized dumping of agricultural surpluses. Keeping that promise is vital if the WTO talks are to live up to their billing as a 'development round'. Unfortunately, one of two less benign outcomes now looks likely: no deal at all, or a deal that perpetuates the present distortions and inequalities.

Why does this matter to the world's poor? Partly because three-quarters of them—about 900 million people—live and work in rural areas, most of them as small farmers. And partly because northern agricultural policies are destroying the markets on which they depend.

Devastating subsidies

The underlying problem is this. Each year, industrialized countries provide over $300 billion in support to agricultural producers—roughly six times the amount they spend on aid. To put this figure in context, it is more than the total income of the 1.2 billion people in the world living on less than $1 a day.

High levels of agricultural support translate into increased output, fewer imports, and more exports than would otherwise be the case. Small farmers in developing countries suffer damage through various channels. Subsidized exports undercut them in global, and even local, markets, driving down household incomes. Meanwhile, those seeking access to northern markets have to negotiate some of the world's highest trade barriers.

The US and the EU are the 'subsidy superpowers', accounting for over 60 percent of rich country agricultural support spending. Europe spends more in absolute terms—and its subsidies represent a larger share of the value of farm output. However, the US spends more per farmer. It also concentrates subsidies on a narrower range of commodities. EU and US subsidies matter to the rest of the world because of their dominant position in global markets.

Whatever their wider differences, the US and the EU have one thing in common: political leaders that like to justify agricultural support by reference to worthy social objectives. President Bush signed the controversial

GINI Coefficients for Agricultural Support and National Income
(Selected countries)
Figure 1

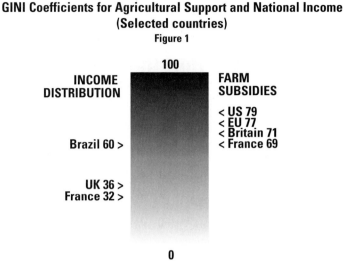

100

INCOME DISTRIBUTION	FARM SUBSIDIES
	< US 79
	< EU 77
	< Britain 71
Brazil 60 >	< France 69
UK 36 >	
France 32 >	

0

Source: World Bank, World Development Indicators (2002); Oxfam calculations

---

2002 Farm Act claiming that it would protect small family farmers. The French minister for agriculture, Henri Gaymard, has made even more grandiose claims on behalf of the Common Agricultural Policy (CAP). He recently declared it an integral part of the 'European model' for a social market.

All of which is abject nonsense. In the real world, farm subsidies are tightly linked to output and the size of landholdings, not to social need. That is why the biggest 7 per cent of farms receive over 50 per cent of farm subsidies, both in the US and the EU. Subsidy distribution to agricultural producers in Europe and America is more unequal than income distribution in Brazil, one of the world's most unequal countries. To make matters worse, many of the benefits end up with corporate exporters or get capitalized into rising land values and input prices.

If industrial country farm subsidies were purely of domestic concern they could be written off as an act of reckless extravagance guided by perverse economics. Sadly, the subsidy fest for the world's richest agricultural producers hurts some of its poorest.

Take the case of cotton. When it comes to harvesting subsidies, America's 25,000 cotton barons are first among equals. In 2001

they received $3.6 billion in government support—three times US aid to Africa. Because the US is the world's largest cotton exporter, accounting for 40 percent of the world market, these subsidies lowered world prices: by around one quarter according to the International Cotton Advisory Committee. Farmers in Africa have suffered the consequences.

In West Africa alone 10-11 million people depend on cotton cultivation as a source of income. The crop is also a major source of foreign exchange and government revenue. Lower world prices caused by American subsidies mean that desperately poor households have seen their incomes fall, with attendant consequences for poverty. In Benin, the price decline associated with American subsidies translates into a 4 percent increase in the incidence of poverty, or 250,000 people falling below the poverty line. Meanwhile, foreign exchange losses have eroded the benefits of development assistance: Burkina Faso loses more because of US subsidies than it gets in debt relief.

What makes the cotton case so egregious is that West Africa is a far more efficient producer than the US. Fewer than 10 per cent of America's producers would be competitive on world markets without support. But in 2001/2002 the subsidy provided to American cotton farmers exceeded the total national income of countries like Burkina Faso and Mali. In a bizarre throwback to the principles of Bolshevik state planning, it also exceeded the value of cotton output. In cotton, as in other areas of agricultural trade, market outcomes owe less to comparative advantage than to comparative access to subsidies.

To be fair, even the US is hard-pressed to match the EU's capacity for double standards in agriculture. Consider the CAP sugar regime. Europe is among the world's highest cost producers of sugar. It is also the world's biggest exporter of white sugar. The reason: subsidies and tariffs. EU farmers are paid three times the world price for sugar, and EU taxpayers and consumers then foot the bill for dumping the resulting surplus—7 million tons of it—on world markets. Non-subsidizing exporters such as Malawi and Thailand suffer the twin consequences of lower prices and lost market shares. Meanwhile, high tariffs keep the EU's own market firmly out of bounds.

Unfair tariffs and export dumping

Import restrictions in agriculture deny developing countries an opportunity to exploit an obvious area of comparative advantage. Average agricultural tariffs in the EU and the US are some five times higher for agricultural goods than for manufactured goods. And tariff peaks in excess of 100 per cent are common, notably in tariff lines such as sugar, beef, dairy produce and processed fruit.

Escalating tariffs—duties that rise with each stage of processing—are another standard feature of the agricultural policy landscape. If Latin American tomato exporters make the mistake of processing the vegetable into sauce, the tariff they face rises by a factor of six percent. Average EU tariffs on fully processed foods are twice as high as on products in the first stage of processing. Tariff escalation serves the deeply pernicious purpose of keeping poor countries trapped in low value-added segments of the agricultural trading system.

Excluded from rich country markets, small farmers also suffer in domestic markets. In their development rhetoric, most northern governments recognize that smallholder agriculture is vital to poverty reduction. Yet the same governments systematically undermine the local markets of food producers through subsidized export dumping.

In Africa, farmers are being pushed out of urban markets by heavily subsidized EU wheat and dairy exports, undermining incentives for production and creating a dangerous dependence on imports. But the problems are not confined to the world's poorest countries. Mexico has some 2 million maize farmers working on land in rain-fed areas, many on ecologically fragile hillsides. Regional integration is exposing these farmers to competition for US maize imports. Many are losing their livelihoods. This outcome owes less to market realities than to market subsidies. Last year, US maize farmers received $3.2 billion in government support—more than double the total agricultural budget for Mexico.

The Doha round opportunity

The Doha round provides a real opportunity to establish new rules of the game in agricultural trade. There are four basic requirements: a prohibition on export dumping, deep cuts in production subsidies, improved market access, and a provision allowing developing countries to protect their agricultural systems for food security reasons.

Prohibiting export dumping ought to be the most straightforward objective. Unfortunately, the EU's lamentable proposals for a 45 percent export subsidy cut would leave it with some $4 billion in the dumping arsenal. For its part, the US has refused to bring either its $7 billion-plus subsidized export credit program, or the commercial dumping components of its food aid program, under WTO export disciplines.

The EU has single-handedly dashed hopes for early progress towards improved market access. It has proposed that tariff cuts be based on the failed formula adopted in the Uruguay Round, with average tariffs cut by 36 per cent. Applied to a sector with many tariff peaks exceeding 100 percent, it is hard to see how this will facilitate the "substantial improvement in market access" promised at Doha.

On the question of subsidy cuts there is every prospect of a EU-US deal—but not one that will benefit developing countries. Efforts to reform the CAP have been stymied by political differences between member states. Meanwhile, the 2002 US Farm Act not only increases budget support for agriculture, but also strengthens the links between farm support and production.

Instead of cutting support, both the EU and the US are repackaging subsidies into payments permitted under WTO rules (which they wrote). Nominally, these payments have to be 'non-trade distorting', or decoupled from production decisions. But these multi-billion programs will generate production by providing farmers with three key benefits: liquidity, capital, and guarantees against risk.

Another source of Trans-Atlantic consensus is the view that developing countries should have only limited rights to protect their farmers through import controls. Both sides want to see any special WTO provisions in this area restricted to the poorest countries, and to a narrow range of specified 'food security' crops. The problem here is that the EU and the US continue to see the WTO as a useful vehicle for prizing open developing country markets, providing outlets for export dumping.

So where does this all leave us? One possible outcome is that the latest bout of EU-US brinkmanship in agriculture will block any deal, jeopardizing the entire Doha round. This would have devastating consequences for poverty reduction efforts—not to mention the future of the rules-based multilateral system. The other, more likely, scenario is a deal that fails to address the real problems facing poor farmers in developing countries. It all calls to mind the old Swahili proverb: 'When the elephants fight, the grass gets crushed; when the elephants make love, the grass gets crushed'.

Kevin Watkins is Head of Research at Oxfam.

Economic Developments during NAFTA's First Decade

14

J O A N N A **M O S S**

When the NAFTA agreement was debated in the fall of 1993, both proponents and opponents took their cause to the public and to Congress with intense passion. Those in favor projected significant U.S. job expansion and golden business opportunities south of the border. NAFTA was going to cement the market liberalization that Mexico had previously begun. NAFTA's opponents unleashed a torrent of economic doomsday projections. The NAFTA agreement was going to take away U.S. jobs, decrease investment and cause environmental degradation. Ross Perot popularized the "sucking sound" of two million jobs going south of the border. The debate reached a furor reminiscent of the free silver debate of the late 19th century, as anti-NAFTA commentators fulminated that American jobs and livelihood should not be sacrificed on the altar of regional free trade.

Nearly ten years have passed since the agreement went into force. NAFTA has been neither as bad nor as good as was projected, however, the NAFTA debate still rages on in the economic literature and popular media. While there is no denying the more than 2 million jobs created per year form 1994 through 2000 in the US economy, critiques of NAFTA point to job loss among the unskilled. The NAFTA debate has become intertwined with the controversy on the effects of increased globalization.

This article has three goals. First, to acquaint the reader with NAFTA as an exten-sion of pre-NAFTA economic and institutional exchanges between the U.S. and Mexico.[1] Second, to take a look at the major economic developments during NAFTA's first decade, and third, to review the recent literature on the "NAFTA effect."

Chronology of Events Leading to NAFTA

In the early 60's the U.S. canceled the bracero program, which had permitted Mexican workers to cross the border to do seasonal work in the U.S. Thus cut off from an important source of foreign exchange, the Mexican government initiated the *maquiladora* program in 1965. Roughly translated, *maquiladora* means an industrial park comprised of foreign-owned plants. This program was consistent with Mexico's then current model of import substitution. Under the maquiladora program foreign-owned firms could set up operations in Mexico and import inputs duty-free as long as the final products were exported out of Mexico. Foreign firms (mostly U.S.) operating in Mexico were allowed to utilize duty-free imports as long as at least 80% of the plant's output was exported.[2]

Concurrent with the maquiladora program, changes took place in the U.S. Tariff code in the mid-sixties. The 1966 Offshore Assembly Provisions[3] (OAP) allowed U.S. manufacturers to ship American-made components overseas for assembly. On their return to the U.S., the import duties imposed on them applied only to the value added in the foreign assembly plant. Together, these two programs spurred Mexican manufactured exports to the U.S. and employed Mexican labor.

As an oil exporter during the 1970's, Mexico benefited from higher oil prices and from the consequent increase in its ability to borrow in international capital markets. However by 1982 Mexico was unable to service its foreign debt and the ensuing peso crisis of 1982-83 forced a huge devaluation of the peso. An international financial rescue mission by the U.S. and the IMF was necessary to help Mexico meet its obligations.

Under President Miguel de la Madrid (1982-1988) Mexico began an extraordinary, decade-long process of economic reform. Previously, inward-oriented development policies had emphasized import substitution and close regulation of commercial ties with other countries. The de la Madrid administration initiated a dramatic shift toward "outward-looking" economic policies which included privatizing some industries, promoting exports, and trimming deficits. Since the mid-1980's Mexico has promoted a policy of economic liberalization, sharply reducing restrictions on external trade and expanding the role of private markets. It began to embrace what has come to be called the "neo-liberal model."

Mexico joined the General Agreement on Trade and Tariffs (GATT) in 1986. Consistent with GATT rules that require curtailment of tariff and non-tariff barriers, and well before NAFTA, Mexico acted unilaterally to cut tariffs in half, to an average of about 12%. Similarly, the proportion of domestic output protected by import licenses was reduced from 75% to 20%. In addition, controls on cross-border financial transactions were almost completely eliminated. Mexico brought its inflation rate down, reduced its budget deficit and embarked on an extensive program of privatization and deregulation of domestic economic institutions.

In 1989 the Canadian-U.S. Free Trade Agreement entered in force. Under the agreement, a free trade area was formed over a 10 year period, with the purpose that by 1998 all items should be traded duty-free between the two countries.

Mexican President Carlos Salinas proposed a "North American Free Trade Area," In 1990 to be negotiated between Mexico, Canada and the U.S., modeled after the Canada-U.S. Free Trade Agreement. For Mexico, NAFTA was the culmination of its decade-long shift away from its earlier import substitution model. The Agreement was the logical endgame of a process of economic reform that had started ten years earlier. Many of its advocates perceived NAFTA as a means of solidifying and protecting these reforms from any tampering by future generations.[4]

The NAFTA Agreement went into effect January 1, 1994. It provides for the elimination of tariffs in stages over periods of between 10 and 15 years, including a phase-out of tariffs on textiles and apparel. Side agreements were later negotiated on labor and environmental issues.

Main Provisions of NAFTA

- NAFTA creates a Free Trade Area between the three North American countries: Goods and services will eventually be exchanged without tariffs or non-tariff barriers in the entire North American area. This eventual tariff elimination extends to traditionally protected sectors such as agriculture, textiles and autos.

- Agriculture: NAFTA phases in free trade in agricultural products between Mexico and the U.S over a 15-year period.

- Textiles: The agreement establishes freer trade in textiles.

- Autos: The treaty eliminates Mexican tariffs on autos and auto parts and establishes a 62.5% North American content requirement in order to qualify for duty-free status.

- Investment: NAFTA liberalizes cross-border investment. Gone are the export performance requirements that compelled foreign companies to export a certain percentage of their output. Also gone are domestic or local content rules that forced companies to purchase inputs from local or domestic sources. U.S., Mexican and Canadian investors are free to invest in most sectors of all three countries.

• Rules of Origin: Products manufactured with materials or labor from outside North America qualify for NAFTA treatment only if they undergo substantial transformation within Canada, U.S., or Mexico. For example in autos 62.5% of the car's value must be added in the NAFTA region for the car to be exempt from duties. NAFTA's strict rules of origin requirements are designed to assure favorable export platforms within the region.

NAFTA Side Agreements

Three side agreements were added before the U.S. Congress passed the treaty. An Environmental Protocol was added, the North American Development Bank was set up and funded to help with border area environmental problems, and a Labor Protocol was created as an agency to investigate and fine labor abuses. Finally the Snap-Back Provision serves as a safety net against import surges.

• *Environmental Protocol* - Under this side agreement an agency was created in Canada to investigate environmental abuses. If two of the three countries agree, fines and sanctions can be imposed if a country fails to enforce its own environmental laws. Separate funds were set aside for cleanup along the U.S.-Mexican border.

• *Labor Protocol* - The second side agreement created an agency to investigate and levy fines for labor abuses in any of the three countries. Fines or trade sanctions can be imposed if countries fail to enforce minimum-wage standards, child-labor laws or worker-safety rules. The same two-country majority rule prevails.

• *Snap-back Provision* - The third side agreement provides a safety net for industries

imperiled by a surge of imports. Under the snap-back provision, tariffs equal to pre-NAFTA levels can be reimposed for three to four years to offset import surges.

Discussion

NAFTA is, strictly speaking, a free trade area with additional provisions for dealing with other issues such as cross-border investment, environmental issues, and labor protocols. It is not a European-style customs union. From an economic theory perspective, one expects the integration process to be furthered and trade to increase between the partners, as tariffs are lowered. Trade creation will hopefully replace higher cost producers with lower cost suppliers. However, some trade diversion can also be expected as the rules of origin favor member producers over non-members.[5]

One of the most important implications of NAFTA is that it has locked in market-oriented policies in Mexico. In addition, regional trade and investment rules are explicit in a single document, signed and ratified by all three participants. These are two fundamental contributions of NAFTA to the long-term improvement of the bilateral trading relationship between the partners.[6]

In practice, while the long process of opening markets has proceeded fairly smoothly since its inception before NAFTA, adjustment difficulties and trade disputes have persisted. One contentious area has been agriculture. In the beginning of 2003, Mexican tariffs were eliminated on agricultural products. Mexican farmers have been struggling and finding it nearly impossible to compete with the cheaper, heavily subsidized U.S. foodstuffs flowing into Mexico. Agricultural groups in Mexico have staged protests and there have been calls for a renegotiation of the NAFTA agreement. Although all three governments have resisted any formal renegotiation of NAFTA, the Fox administration has temporarily suspended some of the tariff reductions in agriculture to assist the beleaguered agricultural industry.[7]

In the area of poultry trade Mexico and the U.S. agreed to modify the NAFTA tariff

Comparative Statistics of the Three NAFTA Countries
Table 1

	Canada	Mexico	U.S.	Total
Population (2001, millions)	31.1	101.8	284.8	417.6
GDP (2002, billions of U.S. dollars)	727.8	641.5	10,445.6	11,814.9
Per Capita GDP (2002, U.S. dollars)	23,204.5	6,199.9	36,209.6	--
Exports (2002, billions of U.S. dollars)	632.8	173.4	974.1	1,780.3
As a percent of NAFTA Total:	35.5%	9.7%	54.7%	100.0%
Imports (2002, billions of U.S. dollars)	269.2	186.3	1392.1	1,847.6
As a percent of NAFTA Total:	14.6%	10.1%	75.3%	100.0%
Share of Employment in Agriculture, Forestry & Fishing (2000)	1.9%[a]	18.1%	1.7%	--
Secondary School Enrollment (1999)	97.87%	57.37%	87.44%	--
Income/Highest 20 Percent of Population[b] (ca. 2000)	39.3	58.2	46.4%	--

[a] Agricultural employment only.
[b] Proportion of wealth held by the wealthiest 20% of the population.
Sources:
• International Financial Statistics, International Monetary Fund, June 2003 issue (data for population, Canadian and Mexican exports and imports).
• "U.S. International Transactions: First Quarter 2003," U.S. Department of Commerce, Bureau of Economic Analysis (U.S. exports and imports).
• World Economic Outlook: Growth and Institutions, April 2003, International Monetary Fund (data for GDP and Per Capita GDP).
• The World Bank Group Data and Statistics, http://www.worldbank.org/data/dataquery.html (data for secondary school enrollment).
• Statistics Canada, U.S. Department of Labor, Bureau of Labor Statistics
• Mexican Survey of Employment, Secretaria del Trabajo y Prevision Social (for share of employment in agriculture data).
• OECD in Figures 2000 (data for income/highest 20 percent of population).

elimination schedule. The agreement reached in January of 2002 postpones a NAFTA provision that would have fully opened up Mexico's poultry market to U.S. imports. Instead Mexico can continue to impose tariffs, though they will be gradually reduced, reaching zero by 2008.

On the other hand, Auto sector liberalization is expected to proceed on schedule. In January of 2004, Mexico will be obliged to eliminate all or most tariffs on imports of new motor vehicles from the U.S. and Canada. The major motor-vehicle assembly plants in Mexico are subsidiaries of either the three giant US automobile manufacturers Ford, DaimlerChrysler, and General Motors or Japanese or European competitors like Nissan and Volkswagen.[9]

Comparative Economic Conditions of U.S., Canada and Mexico

The North American economy in 2002 included over 417 million people, over 300 million workers, and $11.8 trillion of annual GDP. This continental economy is staggeringly unequal. Less than 4% of Canadian workers and less than 3% of U.S. workers are involved in primary sectors such as agriculture, fisheries, mineral extraction and forestry. But nearly 20% of the Mexico's workers are in primary sectors. Table 1 presents comparative statistics on the three NAFTA countries while Figure 1 shows some of the same numbers in graphic form. Not surprisingly, the U.S. is the dominant player. Within the grouping, it accounts for two thirds of the population, 75% of the exports & imports and 88% of the GDP. The U.S.'s per capita

Comparative Statistics of the Three NAFTA Countries
Figure 1

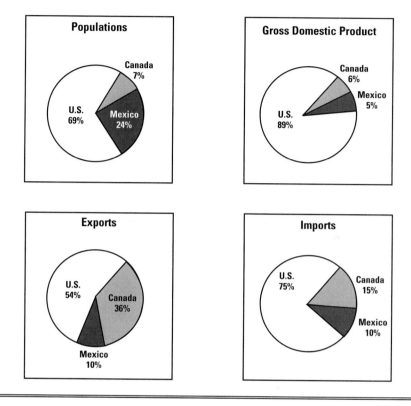

GNP is almost 50% higher than Canada's and almost eight times that of Mexico.

Table 2 and Table 3 illustrate the relative importance of the three countries' trade with each other. In Table 2 we see that the U.S. is the primary trading partner for both Mexico and Canada. Both countries send more than 80% of their exports to the U.S. and acquire over two thirds of their imported items from the U.S. Table 3 shows that from the U.S. economic perspective, Mexico and Canada are less important. Canada, while our largest single trading partner, accounts for about a fifth of U.S. two-way trade. Mexican-US trade has grown dramatically since before NAFTA went into effect. Mexico importance as a U.S. import source almost doubled from the early 1990's to 2002, increasing from 6.3% to 11.6% and moving Mexico into place as the second most important U.S. trading partner.

The Evolution of the Maquiladora Program

As mentioned earlier, the maquiladora program was originally designed to favor exports. Initially, only 20% of an industrial plant's product could be sold in Mexico and, at first, production could occur only along a narrow strip near the U.S.-Mexican border. With advancing economic liberalization in Mexico during the 1980's the program was liberalized to allow more maquiladora production to be sold in Mexico and to allow maquiladora plants to be located further south.

Canadian and Mexican Exports to and Imports from the United States as a Percentage of Total Exports and Imports
Table 2

	Canada		Mexico	
Year	Exports	Imports	Exports	Imports
1992	77.8%	63.5%	81.1%	71.3%
1993	81.3%	65.0%	83.3%	71.2%
1994	82.5%	65.8%	85.3%	71.8%
1995	80.4%	66.7%	83.6%	74.5%
1996	82.3%	67.4%	84.0%	75.6%
1997	83.2%	67.5%	85.6%	74.8%
1998	86.5%	68.0%	87.9%	74.5%
1999	87.6%	67.0%	88.3%	74.1%
2000	87.4%	64.4%	88.7%	73.1%
2001	87.6%	63.7%	88.5%	67.6%
2002[a]	87.2%	70.5%	84.0%	70.5%

[a]Data are trade estimates based on data through the third quarter of 2002.
Source: Computed from data in Direction of Trade Statistics Yearbook, 2002, and Direction of Trade Statistics Quarterly, March 2003.

Table 4 presents employment and export trends at the maquiladora plants. Between 1980 and 1992 the number of plants increased more than threefold and spurred trade between the two countries. Employment rose to a half million workers and net exports approached $5 billion annually. Since the imported inputs enter Mexico duty-free, net exports are a measure of the value added by the plants.

During the NAFTA years, the maquiladoras have continued to expand. Maquiladora plants now account for half of all Mexican manufactured exports and for over 40% of all Mexican exports to the U.S., as well as for 26% of all Mexican labor employed in manufacturing.[10] As evidenced in Table 4 and Figure 4, from 1994 to 2000 the number of Maquiladora plants grew by about 60% while employment and exports more than doubled.

The Maquiladora Program has been changed under NAFTA. New rules for maquiladoras are taking effect in two phases. During the first phase from 1994 through 2000, the maquiladoras' access to the domestic market has been gradually liberalized culminating in 2001 with the Maquiladoras fully able to sell to the domestic market. During the second phase beginning in 2001 the duty-free status of imported inputs is being abandoned. As a free trade area, the advantage of paying duties only on value added is gone. Instead, North American rules of origin will determine duty-free status for a given import. Effectively, the Maquiladora Program is being merged into the NAFTA trade provisions.[11]

Did NAFTA assist in the rapid expansion of Maquiladora plants, employment and exports, since its inception in 1994? While there is no doubt that the NAFTA guarantees have provided a stable framework for commerce and that they have made Mexico more advantageous to invest in as compared to other low-wage areas like Asia, studies show that other important factors were influential. Gruben finds that during the 1990's the U.S. economic boom stimulated demand for Mexican export products and made investment necessary to continue to meet these higher demand levels. Supply factors also made Mexico a desirable location. With the peso devaluation in 1994, Mexican labor costs were low in comparison to U.S. wage rates or to wages in Hong Kong, Korea, Singapore and Taiwan. Gruben concludes that it is these factors, rather than NAFTA, that were responsible for the rapid maquiladora sector expansion.[12]

U.S. Exports and Imports, Balance of Payments Basis
(billions of $ and percent of total U.S. exports and imports)
Table 3

	1990	1992	1994	1995	1996	1997	1998	1999	2000	2001	2002
Canada:											
Exports	83.4	91.1	114.7	127.4	134.3	151.9	156.7	166.7	178.9	163.3	160.9
	21.5%	20.7%	22.8%	22.1%	21.9%	22.4%	23.4%	24.4%	23.2%	22.7%	23.6%
Imports	93.1	100.9	131.2	146.9	158.5	170.1	175.8	201.3	233.7	218.7	211.8
	18.7%	18.8%	19.6%	19.6%	19.7%	19.4%	19.2%	19.5%	19.1%	19.1%	18.2%
Mexico:											
Exports	28.1	40.4	50.6	46.2	56.7	71.2	78.6	86.8	111.2	101.2	97.3
	7.3%	9.2%	10.1%	8.0%	9.3%	10.5%	11.7%	12.7%	14.4%	14.1%	14.3%
Imports	30.5	35.6	50.1	62.8	75.1	86.7	95.4	110.6	136.8	132.2	135.5
	6.1%	6.6%	7.5%	8.4%	9.4%	9.9%	10.4%	10.7%	11.2%	11.5%	11.6%

Source: U.S. Department of Commerce, Bureau of Economic Analysis, U.S. International Transaction Accounts Data. http://www.bea.gov/bea/international/bp_web/list.cfm?anon=99

The NAFTA Debate Continues

NAFTA was heatedly debated in 1992 and 1993 prior to its ratification. The discussion centered on issues of job loss, investment loss, labor abuse and the environment. Optimists saw net job growth through increased trade in the region. They foresaw increased GDP and exports and, in general, improved business opportunities from the agreement. Pessimists focused on job loss, new investment going abroad, plant closures, increased environmental degradation and labor abuses. Each side produced economic studies and statistics to support their point of view.

Perhaps the most contentious issue in the NAFTA debate was the potential loss of U.S. jobs to workers south of the border. Estimates varied wildly. Optimists such as Hufbauer and Schott predicted net job gains upward of 170,000. Academic pessimists like Koechlin and Larudee foresaw possible job losses of up to 490,000. Politicians such as Ross Perot aided by Pat Choate warned of "job losses in the millions." They foresaw the sacrifice of the U.S. standard of living and at the same time, the exploitation of Mexican workers. Central to their fears was the assumption that U.S. business would leave, going south for cheap labor and lax environmental standards.[13]

In the years since its enactment, the debate over the NAFTA agreement has evolved and been melded into the broader debate over the effects of increasing globalization. NAFTA has become a metaphor for discontentment with the current economic situation or for satisfaction with it.[14]

Advocates talk about the tremendous success resulting from NAFTA in boosting Mexican exports and increasing foreign investment in Mexico. Griswold, writing for the Cato Institute's Free Trade Bulletin,[15] highlights the unmitigated successes that NAFTA has had on trade. He further argues that not only were the critics of NAFTA very incorrect in saying that the effects would be catastrophic for the US economy, but they were also wrong about Mexico's political economy in the aftermath of the NAFTA agreement. He concludes that, "By every reasonable measure, NAFTA has been a public policy success in the decade since it was signed. It has deepened and institutionalized Mexico's drive to modernize and liberalize its economy and political system."[16]

The El Paso Business Frontier, published by Federal Reserve Bank of Dallas, El Paso Branch, hails NAFTA as a successful agreement. NAFTA has increased trade

Maquiladoras: Employment and Net Exports
Table 4

Year	Number of Plants	Employment (thousands)	Net Exports (millions)
1980	578	119.5	$772
1982	585	127.0	851
1984	722	199.7	1,155
1986	844	249.8	1,295
1988	1,441	369.5	2,337
1990	1,938	460.3	3,611
1992	2,075	505.0	4,808
1994	2,085	579.4	5,944
1995	2,104	639.9	4,930
1996	2,553	754.8	6,429
1997	2,717	898.7	8,834
1998	2,983	1008.0	10,307
1999	3,297	1,143.2	13,444
2000	3,590	1,291.2	17,759
2001	3,684	1,201.6	19,282
2002	3,251	1,081.7	18,745

Sources:
• Gary C. Hufbauer and Jeffrey J. Schott, NAFTA: An Assessment, revised edition (Washington, DC: Institute for International Economics, 1993), Copyright ©1993 by the Institute for International Economics. All rights reserved. Table A3, p. 172. Data for 1994 - 1997 courtesy of the Research Department, El Paso Branch of Federal Reserve Bank of Dallas.
• 1998 data for number of plants and employment: El Paso Branch of the Federal Reserve Bank of Dallas.
• 1997 and 1998 data for Net Exports of Maquiladoras: Indicadores Economicos, Banco de Mexico, Febrero 1999.

markedly in the trilateral zone because the tariffs have fallen markedly. This does not mean that there have not been continuous trade disputes. However, trade disputes are now resolved in a more amicable fashion, through a dispute resolution mechanism. Finally, the advent of NAFTA has meant that a lot of trade that was not taking place between Canada and Mexico has now begun, flourishing where it languished before.[17]

Of course the U.S. Trade Representative considers NAFTA "an engine of trade."[18] NAFTA's record is clear: By lowering trade barriers, the agreement has expanded trade in all three countries. This has led to increased employment, more choices for consumers at competitive prices, and rising prosperity.[19]

Detractors employ hyperbole of their own, a sort of road rage against globalization vented against NAFTA. According to Scott[20] NAFTA has contributed to stagnant real wages, and eliminated 766,000 jobs in the United States between 1994 and 2000. It has contributed to the worsening distribution of income in all three countries, has increased the insecurity of 70% of the American labor force, and has diminished job prospects and wage rates for unemployed, unskilled, and less skilled workers. Furthermore, in boosting Mexican and Canadian exports, NAFTA has contributed to the U.S. balance of trade deficit. Scott contends with mercantilist logic that since NAFTA promised increased U.S. export to Mexico and a U.S. trade surplus with Mexico, this would have translated into increased employment. Instead, a U.S. trade deficit with Mexico means a loss of jobs.[21] In addition, still according to Scott, NAFTA has

Maquiladoras Trends before and during NAFTA
Figure 2

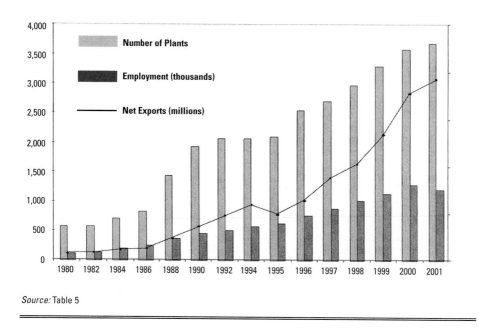

Source: Table 5

contributed to the reduction in manufacturing employment in the U.S. and has pushed manufacturing workers into lower paying service sector jobs. Finally, the increased import competition and capital mobility resulting from globalization has increased "threat effects" in bargaining between employers and workers, further contributing to stagnant wages and job insecurity.[22]

Anderson[23] is very critical of the effect of NAFTA on Mexico's macroeconomic outlook. She argues that although there are positive indicators, such as a large foreign investment boom, a large rise in employment in maquiladoras, and a huge increase in exports to the United States, these could not outweigh the numerous "negative indicators." Anderson cites among those negative indicators a fall in real wages in the manufacturing sector despite higher productivity. Mainstream economists argue that an increase in productivity should be accompanied by a requisite increase in the level of income. Yet, this is not happening. Moreover, the level of

poverty and the level of industry-related pollution has increased markedly, in concert with the destruction of Mexico's natural resources. Although investment has certainly increased, so has volatility. When coupled with a staggering debt burden and harm to Mexico's rural sector, things are not going well.

Rosenberg has written a number of articles critical of industrial countries' trade policies towards developing countries. In a recent article Rosenberg[24] argues that the massive subsidies that United States gives to farmers mean that Mexican farmers are unable to compete, meaning that they are forced to either sell off their land and move to the cities or live a starvation-threatened subsistence lifestyle. We can't fully blame the U.S. government's agriculture policies of course. Mexico has done virtually nothing to improve the situation for Mexico's huge rural population. This will have an impact on Mexico's cities, too, because they can't even cope with the current levels of migration to urban centers. NAFTA is implicitly a culprit since it has allowed lowering of tariffs on agricultural products and simultaneously reduced subsidies to Mexican farmers.

How do we explain these markedly different interpretations of the NAFTA agreement? Are there valid points on both sides or is one or the other group ideologically driven to construe the facts to fulfill their vision? The following sections of this paper attempt to present information through statistics and through review of NAFTA studies that will be helpful in analyzing the agreement's results, as well as responding to the differing points of view.

Developments during the Decade of NAFTA

Capturing the "NAFTA effect" is a complex undertaking. Many major economic and institutional forces affecting trade and investment in the region were well underway before the signing of the agreement. Mexico's trade liberalization policies and the country's dramatic steps towards a more open economy were started back in the 1980's. The maquiladora program's trade and employment effects began even further back in the 1960's. Finally the peso crisis of 1994-95 clouds the picture even more.

While many of the provisions such as those in agriculture have been, or will be, phased in over a number of years, a number of changes went into effect immediately upon NAFTA's effective date of January 1, 1994. For example NAFTA provided for immediate tariff reductions on 68% of U.S. exports to Mexico and 49% of U.S. imports from Mexico.

The Peso Crisis

The results of Mexican economic reforms begun before NAFTA were mixed. Lower inflation had obvious benefits. Mexico's foreign trade with other nations rose sharply with the removal of trade restrictions. Aided by an overvalued exchange rate, Mexicans went on a spending spree. By 1994, Mexico's current account deficit was 8% of GDP![25] The widening current account deficit was covered by increasingly larger infusion of foreign capital. These inflows were for a time supported by the optimism surrounding NAFTA and by a favorable interest rate differential. However, as these funds began to dry up, the Mexican government met the outflows by drawing down reserves and by issuing "Tesobonos," bonds denominated in pesos but indexed to the dollar. The outstanding stock of Tesobonos rose from $3 billion to $20 billion between March and December of 1994. During the same period, Mexico's international reserves fell from $26 billion to $6 billion.[26]

Meanwhile, weaknesses in Mexico's political and economic systems manifested themselves in 1994—e.g., the peasant uprising in Chiapas and the assassination of presidential candidate Luis Donaldo Colosio. The Mexico government, which had been luring foreign investors with Tesobonos in order to cover the current account deficit, had not adjusted the exchange rate. By mid to late 1994 investors got nervous and began pulling their money out of Mexico. The same financial market actors who had been excessively euphoric about Mexico in previous years overreacted in the opposite direction and Mexico's problems ballooned to dangerous proportions.

The crisis was in full swing by December of 1994. The loss of investor confidence and the exhaustion of reserves forced a devaluation of the peso. Mexico abandoned the fixed exchange rate and let the peso depreciate from 3.4 pesos to the dollar in November of 1994 to 5.7 pesos to the dollar in January of 1995.

In 1995 the U.S., Canada, and several international institutions put together a bailout package of loans and credits worth $50 billion. Successfully recovering from the crisis, Mexico was by mid-1996 in the process of repaying the loans. The outstanding balances with the U.S. and Canada were repaid by 1997 and the $8.2 billion of credits from the IMF is being repaid over a five-year period.

Despite the efforts to contain the crisis and its effects, Mexico suffered. GDP dropped by 7% during the year 1995. Real income fell. Wages declined to their 1980 level. In 1996 the economy leveled out and began to grow; by 1997 real GDP was growing about 5% and exports were booming. Nevertheless the economic hardships brought on by the crisis are still being felt to date.

NAFTA's Role in the Peso Crisis

What role did NAFTA play in this drama? Did NAFTA contribute to the 1994-95 crisis? The hype surrounding NAFTA may have contributed to reckless financial flows. Unrealistic expectations may have generated short-term speculative capital flows where long-term real private domestic investment was needed. On the whole, political shocks, a current account deficit and misalignment of macroeconomic policies, all unrelated to NAFTA, are among the more important causes of the 1994 peso crisis.

In the aftermath of the crisis, NAFTA may have been a positive force. As Williamson points out, Mexico has a history of financial catastrophes, including a default on international debt in 1932. After each crisis, it took years for foreign capital to flow back into Mexico. For example, after the 1982 debt episode it took seven years before lending revived. In contrast, creditworthiness was reestablished in a matter of little more than a year after the 1994-95 crisis. The fact that NAFTA was signed, sealed and operative, may well have assuaged investors' concerns about Mexico's future.[28]

Mexico's recovery from the peso crisis has been aided by a rapid expansion of exports to the United States. In fact, exports have been the engine of recovery, increasing over 15% a year since 1995. Mexico took full advantage of NAFTA's market opening effects. In addition, Lustig points out that the sectors showing the highest rates of growth were those where the regional integration was fairly advanced even before NAFTA: autos and auto parts, as well as textiles and apparels, food and beverages, agriculture and cattle products.[29] By Mexico's adhering to the NAFTA trade rules, even during financial crisis these areas continued to expand.

NAFTA may have also ameliorated the deleterious effects of the pesos crisis on U.S. goods destined for Mexico. During the crisis and its aftermath in 1995 and 1996 Mexico did not retrench from its NAFTA commitment. There were some tariff increases temporarily put in place for some countries, mainly the European Union. But because of NAFTA the U.S., Canada and other countries that had signed free-trade agreements with Mexico were spared these increases. Moreover, as we will see below, U.S. exports to Mexico, stumbled in 1995, dropping by 2% but quickly rebounded, whereas non-NAFTA countries (such as Japan and the European Union) experienced drop-offs of as much as 25% in their exports to Mexico. As Lustig comments, some of the U.S. success in retaining the Mexican market must be ascribed to the expanded market access for U.S. exporters and the growing importance of intra-industry bilateral trade, both strengthened by NAFTA.[30]

Trade Developments during the NAFTA Years

Most students of the subject would agree that the full effects derived from the formation of a free trade area take a long time to mature, since structural adjustment within the member countries takes time. Capacity and employment need to be reduced in some sectors, as additional investments and new jobs are added in others. Moreover, the effects of trade liberalization are often progressive by their very nature. Some gradualism is deliberately built into the agreement itself. Time is given for phase-out periods for the full elimination of tariffs and the dismantling of non-tariff barriers. All of these factors suggest that although NAFTA has been in operation for nearly a decade, it is still too early to make definitive conclusions about the effects of the agreement.

Furthermore, it is difficult to sort out empirically the impact of the formation of a regional trade agreement from other concurrent shocks and trends. As noted earlier, any studies on NAFTA trade effects must try to take into account the trade liberalization measures undertaken by Mexico and the relative importance of the U.S. in Mexican trade before the agreement went into effect. Also, the peso crisis and the ensuing peso devaluation changed the competitive position of Mexico vis-à-vis Asian and other competitors. Macroeconomic forces, as well, can have a significant effect on trade; witness the current (2001-2003) economic slowdown and the resulting moderation in U.S. demand for imports.

Trade creation and trade diversion are also potential outcomes of NAFTA; hence the agreement's trade effects need to be assessed in the context of trade with the rest of the world.[31] Did NAFTA create new trade opportunities within North America or did it simply divert trade from countries outside NAFTA? Are non-NAFTA countries' exports being replaced by NAFTA country goods because they are cheaper or because of tariffs which make third-party exports more expensive?

Overview of NAFTA Trade Studies

Not unexpectedly, Tables 2 and 3 display evidence of continuously strong trade performance between the three NAFTA countries. From the U.S. perspective, both countries increased in relative importance both as export markets and as import providers. Mexico's relative standing as a source of imports grew almost 50% from the early 1990's to 2002. Its relative importance as an export market doubled during the same time period. Canada also grew in relative importance as a trading partner, although the increases are not as dramatic.

These overall percentage increases are clearly positive, but how do we isolate the "NAFTA effect"? Since many of the trade liberalizations measures were already in place when NAFTA began, would this trade expansion have taken place anyway, even without NAFTA? Research is beginning to shed light on these questions.

Gould set out to measure how NAFTA has affected North American trade during the first three years of operation.[33] He finds that U.S. exports to Mexico grew faster than they would have in the absence of a trade agree-

ment. On average, U.S. export growth to Mexico is about 16.3% higher per year with the NAFTA agreement. Similarly, U.S. imports from Mexico on average grew about 16.2% higher per year with NAFTA. U.S.-Canadian trade did not appear to be significantly affected by the NAFTA agreement. This result was expected given the existing free trade agreement between the two countries, which was already in force at the time of NAFTA's inception.

In a confirmation of these studies, Sarkar looks at the five-year "pre-NAFTA" period and compares it to the first five years of NAFTA. He finds a statistically significant increase in U.S.-Mexican trade increases in export/import trade during NAFTA as compared to the period before NAFTA.[34]

There appears to be limited evidence of significant trade diversion. Gould finds that while trade grew within the NAFTA grouping, their trade with non-NAFTA countries also grew after the agreement's implementation. The share of total trade between North American countries increased because trade within North America grew faster than did trade with countries outside of North America. Consequently, he finds that although trade diversion is a possibility, it is unlikely to be a large problem.[35]

Krueger[36] also concludes that there is no evidence that for the first five years since inception NAFTA diverted trade from non-NAFTA countries. Krueger's[37] overall conclusion provides a good summary of the results from empirical work since NAFTA came into force in 1994 through 1999. She notes, "the evidence to date bears out most economists' initial predictions: that for the US, the impact of NAFTA has been relatively small, and that for Mexico, changes in trade flows to date do not give much support to the view that NAFTA might be seriously trade diverting."

A number of economists have noted NAFTA's role in insulating the U.S. from the Peso Crisis effects. Both Lustig and Gould comment on the importance of Mexico's commitment to NAFTA during the crisis.[38]

Figure 3 examines data on trade from 1990 to 1996 and captures developments dur-

Growth of Imports to Mexico from the U.S. and from Non-NAFTA Countries
Figure 3

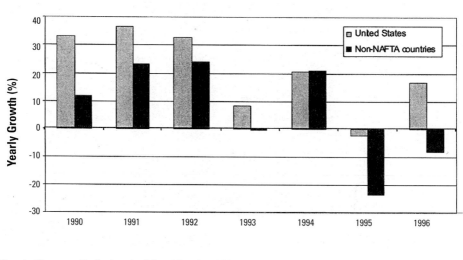

Growth of Imports to Mexico from the U.S. and from Non-NAFTA Countries
Source: SECOFL data as cited in Espinosa and Noyola (1997).

ing and after the peso crisis. While there was a brief fall-off in American goods destined for Mexico in 1995, it was more than offset by a subsequent rebound in 1996. The brunt of the crisis was borne by non-NAFTA countries, whose exports to Mexico fell more than 20% and did not recover. The expanded access acquired by U.S. exporters in Mexico as a result of NAFTA, and the growing importance of intra-industry trade that emerged before, and was enhanced by, NAFTA played a role in this trade shift.[39]

Burfisher, Robinson and Thierfelder[40] in their 2001 work, develop a thesis that despite the naysayers, the impact of liberalizing trade in the NAFTA zone has been overwhelmingly positive both for the United States and Mexico. The authors say that "NAFTA has had a relatively small positive effect on the U.S. economy and relatively large positive effects on Mexico." Notably, Ross Perot's predictions of a "giant sucking sound" did not come true, despite the huge disparities in

income between the U.S. and Canada on the one hand, and Mexico on the other, and despite the different structural attributes of the three economies. For example, both the United States and Canada have economies that are based around services and manufacturing, whereas Mexico is still largely agrarian, albeit with a growing manufacturing base. The authors reached several implications in their study. The first is that measurements of trade gains have appeared to be correct—that there was a "small positive effect" for the Americans and a "large positive" benefit to Mexico. Secondly, the authors believe that what is important in the measurements is how resources were reallocated and patterns of trade diversion and creation, rather than concentrating on such numbers as the trade balance. Emphasis on the trade balance number is nothing more than a short-hand number that can actually do more harm than good in the policy arena. Thirdly, even though the predictions of widespread displacement of workers in the United States were not entirely untrue, the number of people affected was nowhere near the predicted numbers and most of those individuals received adjustment training so that they could get other jobs. Finally, because of the increased competition amongst the three countries, artificial, rent-accruing distortions in the market have been eliminated because policymakers and industrial leaders must reform to compete. As a result, the authors contend that consumers benefit with lower prices and a wider range of products.

Hillberry and McDaniel studied NAFTA's trade effects through 2001.[41] Their work found that total trade with NAFTA partners increased 78% in real terms between 1993 and 2001, compared to 43% with the rest of the world. Their work compared the nature of U.S. trade growth with Canada and Mexico, to that with non-NAFTA partners. By analyzing the composition of this growth they provided insights into whether the United States has been trading more of the same goods with NAFTA partners, trading new products, or upgrading the quality and variety of products. They found that quality upgrading and variety upgrading explain part of U.S.-Mexican trade growth. Commodities that were not exported to NAFTA markets in 1993 are exported now, and industries that did not face competition from specific markets are facing it now. The largest changes are seen in U.S. imports from Mexico, suggesting that a new set of industries has had to face competition from an increased variety of Mexican imports. At the same time, consumers and manufacturers have been given a broader set of suppliers, which reduces prices and improves the selection of goods available.

Another study by Wall[42], analyzed NAFTA trade looking at specific geographic areas of North America. He found that NAFTA had a significant effect on expansion of Canadian-Mexican trade as well as on U.S.-Mexican trade. However the central and western provinces of Canada benefited the most from this trade expansion. He also found both a trade creation effect on a region-by-region and on a country-by-country basis,

as well as a trade diversion with respect to European and Asian exports to the North American continent.

After reviewing all of the traditional statistical techniques for studying the economic effects of NAFTA integration, Hinojosa-Ojeda and McCleery proposed looking at the problem as a process of positive and negative cumulative causation, an idea first developed a half century ago by Gunnar Myrdal.[43]

They find that the economic integration between Mexico and the U.S. is having both positive and negative effects on Mexican economic development; however the positive effects outweigh the negative.

Developments of U.S. Investment in Mexico during the NAFTA Years

The process of economic integration initiated through a free trade agreement might be expected to have positive effects on investment among its parties.[44] In the case of the NAFTA countries, given the asymmetry of development and industrial structure, there is some expectation that investment flows from the U.S. to Mexico would increase over time. As Krueger points out, increased trade through NAFTA is likely to lead to increased investment in Mexico.[45]

Table 5 looks at U.S. foreign direct investment in Mexico. The flow of U.S. investment to Mexico appears to have increased in 1994, but fallen off in 1995 and 1996. Investors may well have been scared off by the uncertainties created by the peso crisis. Other research suggests that this was a windfall from an anticipatory buildup of U.S. investment in Mexico immediately prior to NAFTA. U.S. investment in Mexico rebounded in 1997 and by 1998 U.S. investment in Mexico was back to the 3% range as a portion of U.S. overseas investment which characterized the past 10 years,[46] with the glaring exception being 2001, when U.S. foreign direct investment tripled.

However, this tremendous increase was due to liberalization of investment laws which went into effect in that year and to a very large acquisition wherein Citibank purchased Banamex for $12.9 billion.

U.S. Direct Investment in Mexico
Table 5

U.S. Capital Outflows to Mexico

	Flow of U.S. Foreign Direct Investment to Mexico	Mexican Share of U.S. Direct Foreign Investment
1993[a]	$2.5 Billion	3.3%
1994	$3.7 Billion	5.3%
1995	$3.0 Billion	3.2%
1996	$2.4 Billion	2.8%
1997	$5.6 Billion	5.8%
1998	$4.6 Billion	3.5%
1999	$6.0 Billion	3.4%
2000	$5.3 Billion	3.2%
2001	$15.1 Billion	13.2%
2002	$3.6 Billion	3.3%

Sources:

[a] 1993-94, The Impact of the North American Free Trade Agreement on the U.S. Economy and Industries: A Three Year Review, June 1997, International Trade Commission

- 1995-2000: http://www.bea.doc.gov/bea/di/di1usdbal.htm
- 2001-2002: http://www.bea.doc.gov/bea/di/usdiacap.prn
- U.S. Department of Commerce, Bureau of Economic Analysis

Like export expansion, foreign investment has increased during the NAFTA years, albeit only until the recent economic slowdown in the U.S. in 2002. Foreign investment is critical to Mexico's development. As Lustig[47] points out, Mexican firms with foreign direct investment employ around 20 percent of all workers in the formal sector, with wages 48% higher than the national average. The growth rate of employment in these firms was double that of the overall economy during the second half of the 1990s. Further Lustig indicates that the rate of employment in these firms is double that of the overall economy; in fact, between 1994 and 1998 firms with foreign direct investment generated one of every four jobs created in the country. The United States is the largest source of foreign investment in Mexico. Between 1994 and 2000, more than 11,000 US firms invested $35.1 billion in Mexico. European Union countries, Japan, and Canada are the other major foreign investors in Mexico.[48]

While there have been plant closures and movement to Mexican at the expense of American workers, it would be hard to argue that Mexico has siphoned off a significant portion of new investment in the United States. The staggering U.S. current account deficits of over $400 billion annually are offset by capital and financial inflows of similar amounts. The U.S. remains has the dubious honor of being the world's largest recipient of foreign direct investment, and it has been in first place since 1996.[50]

Nevertheless, U.S. investment in Mexico has grown significantly over the past ten years. From 1994 to 2002 roughly 1351 businesses have relocated to Mexico and 334 have relocated to Canada. This equates to about 200 per year, or about 1% of U.S. business relocations annually. Relocation of businesses between regions is a familiar characteristic of modern advanced economies. For example, in the United States between 1996 and 1999, about 16,000 firms moved between states.[51]

U.S. Labor Market Developments during the NAFTA Years

As with other areas of the agreement, studying the "NAFTA effect" on the U.S. labor market is difficult. Concerns about NAFTA's effects on the U.S. labor market need to be tempered by the recognition that the overwhelming relative size of the U.S. economy and other economic characteristics that set it off from Mexico are bound to limit any profound impact. That being said, NAFTA does have some economic consequence.

Job Losses

Unfortunately, "job counting" has become a popular way to evaluate NAFTA and bilateral trade agreements in general. Logic dictates that the net effect on employment would be very small relative to the size of the U.S. economy. Furthermore, the main determinants of employment and unemployment are macroeconomic phenomena, not trade agreements. Nevertheless, before the agreement was ratified, several studies attempted to predict the impact of the NAFTA on employment. Predictions ranged from a net gain of 170,000 U.S. jobs by 1995—calculated by multiplying projected U.S. net exports to Mexico by Department of Commerce estimates of jobs supported by exports—to as many as 490,000 U.S. jobs lost between 1992 and 2000, resulting from an expected $20 billion reduction in the U.S. capital stock provoked by a shift of investment from the United States to Mexico.[52]

A simplistic interpretation of these estimates would regard them as jobs gained or lost in the overall labor force. A more nuanced approach would regard them as

jobs directly impacted by additional imports or exports, even if the direct impact would be neutralized by offsetting forces in the U.S. economy such as job creation or job displacement in other sectors.

Nearly a decade into NAFTA, estimates of its impact on U.S. jobs continue to be far apart. On the negative side, one study recently claimed that "NAFTA eliminated 766,030 actual and potential jobs between 1994 and 2000," an assertion that amounts to around 110,000 U.S. jobs lost on account of NAFTA each year.[53]

On the positive side, another study found that new exports to Canada and Mexico during NAFTA's first five years created 709,988 jobs, or about 140,000 jobs annually. This number was calculated by multiplying increased merchandise exports to Mexico and Canada during NAFTA's first five years by the Department of Commerce average figure of jobs supported per billion dollars of exports.[54] Yet another group of researchers concluded that trade with Mexico has a net positive effect on U.S. employment.[55] There is clearly a wide variation in the job creation or destruction effects of NAFTA, due to the assumptions utilized and the statistical technique and data employed.[56]

Fortunately, the NAFTA-Transitional Adjustment Assistance (TAA) Program, created as a part of NAFTA implementing legislation, provides actual data about workers adversely affected by trade with and investment in Mexico and Canada. "Adversely affected" means workers "who lose their jobs or whose hours of work and wages are reduced as a result of trade with, or a shift in production to, Canada or Mexico.[57] So-called "secondary workers" (upstream and downstream workers who are indirectly affected by trade with or shifts in production to Canada and Mexico) are eligible as well. NAFTA does not have to be the cause of the job loss to qualify for NAFTA-TAA.[58] For example, as of December 2001, the U.S. Department of Labor had certified 370,137 workers, about 50,000 workers per year, as adversely affected and thus eligible for NAFTA-TAA. Of the total number of workers certified under

NAFTA-TAA, over 100,000 come from the apparel industries. Another 130,000 certifications stem mostly from the categories of fabricated metal products, machinery, and transport equipment. NAFTA-TAA certification may overestimate the pain of job losses because not all workers certified actually lose their jobs, and some who did lose their jobs were quickly reemployed. On the other hand, the NAFTA-TAA figures might well underestimate the number of job losses because the program was unknown to many workers, because workers indirectly displaced are likely to be unaware that NAFTA is at the origin of their woes, and because the application process is cumbersome. Despite these limitations, the NAFTA-TAA is probably the best record of the direct impact of additional NAFTA imports on U.S. labor. No comparable certification process exists for the direct impact of additional NAFTA exports on U.S. employees.[59]

Although the heated debate over the numbers continues, the reality is that the effect of NAFTA is small when compared to even the normal turnover of the U.S. labor market. In a boom year like 1999, with unemployment at a 30-year low, the US economy displaced 2.5 million workers.[60] This means that these workers were laid off due to closure or substantial restructuring of a plant. Suppose that the most pessimistic estimate is correct—an adverse NAFTA impact of 110,000 jobs lost annually, the figure comes to less than 5 percent of total annual displacement in the labor force and much less than annual gross job creation.

Stagnant Real Wages and Rising Inequality

Those who oppose NAFTA contend that competition from cheap unskilled Mexican labor will depress real wages of unskilled American workers, and widen the earnings gap between skilled and unskilled workers. NAFTA supporters discount this effect on the argument that the nominal cost advantage of low Mexican wages is largely or entirely offset by the higher productivity of U.S. workers, unskilled as well as skilled.

Numbers on U.S. real wages show that, compared with high-skilled workers, unskilled workers did poorly during most of the past 30 years. As a result, average real wage growth in the United States was sluggish between the 1970s and the mid-1990s. This trend changed in the mid-1990s, when economic expansion started effecting significant real wage growth for unskilled workers, and a sustained rise in the average real wage. Indeed, between 1993 and 1999, 81 percent of the newly created US jobs were in industry and occupation categories paying above-median wages.[61]

Technological change is the major force driving real wages in the United States, both relative and average levels. U.S. output per worker in the 1950s and 1960s grew at an average annual rate of 2.8 percent, but slowed to only 1.2 percent between the 1970s and the early 1990s. This sluggish performance came to an end in the mid-1990s, and U.S. labor productivity grew at around 2.4 percent a year from 1995 through 2000.[62] The spurt reflected information technology and other "new economy" forces.[63]

To the extent that real wage gains are determined by higher output per worker (a long-term explanation), weaker increases in productivity, not an expansion of trade, would explain the slower growth of real wages between 1970 and the mid-1990s.[64] Buttressing the productivity explanation, real wage stagnation was most pronounced in the service sectors, which are mostly non tradeables and have little Foreign Direct Investment (FDI) activity.

Another issue in the NAFTA debate is its effect on the distribution of income, i.e. notable changes in relative wages. Earnings inequality in the United States is strongly associated with skill differences and educational differences. The growth of the U.S. skill premium was a major feature of the wage story between 1970 and 2000. In the early 1980s non-production (more skilled) workers earned 50 percent more than production (less skilled) workers; by the mid-1990s the skill premium was over 70 percent.[65] Technological change explains about half of the rising U.S. skill premium while trade and immigration forces account for around 10 and 5 percent respectively.[66] Other influences on the growing wage disparity are a stagnant minimum wage in real terms and declining unionization. U.S. data on relative product prices also supports the hypothesis that trade was not a major factor driving relative wages. If trade were the explanation for changing relative wages,[67] either between industries or between skill categories, relative product prices in the United States should have fallen in import-competing sectors, especially those that employ large numbers of low-skilled workers. Recent research could uncover no such movement in U.S. relative product prices. Another point which confirms the small impact of NAFTA on U.S. wages and inequality is that greater wage inequality is not evident in states with more NAFTA-TAA certified workers.[69]

Although the overall effect of NAFTA on wages is small, the effect on those directly impacted by increased trade is not negligible. About a quarter of manufacturing workers displaced by trade suffer considerable wage losses--not unlike other manufacturing workers separated from their jobs for reasons having nothing to do with trade. However, not all trade-displaced workers end up in low-paying retail service jobs. According to a recent study of US manufacturing workers, only about 10 percent of reemployed displaced workers go into retail trade. While the average wage loss of reemployed displaced workers is sizable at about 13 percent, there are great disparities within the group. Roughly 36 percent of displaced workers find new jobs with equal or higher levels of earnings and at the other extreme, about 25 percent suffer wage losses of over 30 percent. Once again workers with lower skill levels suffer the largest percentage losses.[70]

The Maquiladora Industry and US Labor

The maquiladora system, as discussed above, has allowed American firms to perform all or part of a manufacturing process in Mexico and bring the item back to the United States, paying duty only on value added (typically the Mexican labor). Despite NAFTA's negation of the tariff advantage of maquiladoras, American manufacturers still seek the cheaper labor which the plants across the border offer. Has the maquiladora system been harmful to U.S. employment and earnings?

Hufbauer and Schott assess the effect of maquiladora growth on U.S. employment and earnings. They conclude that global imports reduce employment, but the magnitude of the effect is very small. However, employment in maquiladoras shows no statistically significant effect on U.S. employment or U.S. earnings levels.[71]

This finding should not come as a great surprise. Prior to NAFTA, U.S. firms used maquiladoras to take advantage of cheap labor without paying tariffs at the border. NAFTA actually makes maquiladoras less economically important because almost all manufactured goods can now be traded duty free. Furthermore, maquiladoras use inputs that are produced in the United States, and this reduces the overall effect of maquiladoras on U.S. employment. Critics of NAFTA seem to believe that if maquiladoras did not exist, the entire manufacturing process would take place in the United States and thus generate more U.S. jobs. The economic reality is that if maquiladoras did not exist, the entire manufacturing process, in many cases, would take place outside the United States and the finished product would be imported.

As we have seen NAFTA plays a very limited role in the overall determination of real and relative wages in the United States; however, some unskilled workers who are laid off as a consequence of trade with Mexico and Canada do suffer a significant loss of earnings. NAFTA-TAA is designed to help them but it has a limited effect and more is needed to help displaced workers.[72] The recently passed Trade Act of 2002 roughly tripled the level of adjustment assistance available to workers from ($400 million to $1.2 billion annually), extended coverage to some secondary workers (those indirectly impacted) and provided a health insurance subsidy for laid-off workers. As an alternative to trade adjustment assistance, older dislocated workers can claim wage insurance for up to 50 percent of the wage gap between old and new jobs (with a $5,000 cap per worker).

Labor and Environmental Accords

As mentioned earlier, the final NAFTA document passed by Congress included Labor and Environmental Protocols. On the labor side of the agreement, the North American Agreement on Labor Cooperation (NAALC) set out to ensure labor rights such as the right to organize and to strike, equal pay and safety standards, etc. in all three countries.[74] NAALC has no authority to enforce these rights as each country maintains its own labor codes and standards. It has a modest budget of about $2 million per year currently and it hears complaints and provides a framework for discussion of labor issues.

The Environmental Protocol, formally the North American Agreement for Environmental Cooperation (NAAEC), established several new institutions for dealing with environmental issues. The Commission for Environmental Cooperation, made up of all three countries serves to enhance cooperation and public participation in the preservation, protection and enrichment of North America's natural environment. The broad goals of the commission are implemented through specific projects attempting to address multilateral environmental issues, prevent potential trade and environmental conflicts, and ensure the effective monitoring of environmental laws.

The North American Development Bank (NADB) and the Border Environment Cooperation Commission (BECC) were created as independent institutions, but are now linked in a joint effort to preserve and promote the health and welfare of border residents and their environment in the United States and Mexico. The primary goals and functions of the two institutions are to respond to concerns of water supply, wastewater treatment and municipal solid waste management within a 62-mile (100 kilometer) region surrounding the border. Specifically, the BECC handles oversight of the initial project development, while the NADB is in charge of long-term project supervision.[75]

The NAAEC has a current modest budget of about $14,000 per year. Despite all of the problems associated with the resource constraints of both the CEC and the CLC, the side agreements do seem to work in a small way to help alleviate some of the problems associated with NAFTA's liberalization of trade. The CEC is especially beneficial to the border regions where the Tijuana River and Rio Grande watershed have been made less polluted than before thanks to the work of the Border Environment Cooperation Commission and other institutions that have been funded through the environmental side agreement (The North American Environment 1998). The CEC also has real teeth which can be used to ameliorate otherwise unhealthy situations stemming from free trade.[76]

Other Aspects of the "NAFTA Effect"

As a free trade agreement, NAFTA is nearly a decade old. Many of the trade-liberalizing measures are still being phased in. NAFTA has the potential to affect many aspects of the economic interchanges between the members. For example, in the trade area, researchers are continuously trying to establish connections between trade liberalization measures and trade expansion, as well as effects on compositional changes in trade. NAFTA also has the potential to influence other, more subtle changes. The very existence of a free trade agreement can bring about economic adjustments in the region. As Gould points out, changing expectations for the sustainability of free trade under NAFTA are potentially among the most important aspects of the agreement. With a credible commitment to free trade on the part of governments, new investment is likely to flow into export industries to take advantage of reduced trade barriers. Expectations for a more stable and open trading environment also affect trade by providing the incentive for firms to make long-term capital commitments, both at home and in the member countries.[77]

There are also benefits by omission, what did not happen because a free trade agreement was in force. During the peso crisis, Mexico did not erect trade barriers against its NAFTA partners, while it did increase tariff rates against other industrial countries temporarily. Trade with NAFTA countries was relatively unimpeded during the peso crisis. By enhancing the economic ties between the North American countries, NAFTA may have limited a protectionist response and helped to facilitate a return of foreign investment and economic growth to Mexico that occurred much quicker than after previous financial crises.

United States–Mexican Migration Issues and the NAFTA Agreement

Under NAFTA, the U.S., Mexico and Canada agreed to dismantle barriers to trade and investment across their border. This has resulted in increased economic integration between the NAFTA members. Mexico is now the second largest trading partner of the U.S., as well as a recipient of significant sums of U.S. and Canadian direct foreign investment. Improvements in communication and infrastructure are facilitating the flow of economic resources. The one glaring exception to this general economic liberalization trend is immigration policy. While the U.S. labor market beckons to Mexicans to take the chance and cross the border illegally, the U.S. government has been resistant to any official change in U.S. policy towards Mexican workers.

Before the terrorist attacks of September 11, 2001, discussions were underway between the U.S. and Mexico exploring changes in immigration policy that would include "matching willing workers with willing employers; serving the social and economic needs of both countries…." However, little progress has been made since that time.

There are currently an estimated 4.5 million Mexicans living in the United States illegally. Each year about 250,000 more immigrants enter illegally or overstay their visas.

More than half of those entering come from Mexico.[79] Since the mid-1980's, in its effort to stop illegal immigration, the U.S. government has imposed new and burdensome regulations on American employers and dramatically increased spending on border patrol. The various new programs to stop illegal border crossing—Operation Blockage, Operation Gatekeeper and Operation Hold the line—have all failed to stop illegal border crossing. Instead, getting from Mexico to the U.S. illegally has become more expensive and more dangerous, but it continues unabated.[80]

The presence of so many undocumented workers creates political and economic problems on both sides of the border. In the U.S. illegal workers contribute to a black market in labor, which in turn causes smuggling, fraudulent document creation, and wage distortions. It exposes illegal immigrant workers to unsafe (unregulated) working conditions and abuse. In Mexico the treatment of their countrymen in the U.S. is often presented as a human rights abuse.

Despite the risks, Mexicans continue to come to the U.S. for higher wages and because of a complex process driven by other factors such as risk diversification, social networks and the relative underdevelopment of capital markets and social insurance in their own country. To enhance the lives of their families back home, they send back "workers remittances," which are cash transfers sent across the border. The remittances allow their families to live better lives and often provide capital where bank loans and other forms of credit are not easily available. These worker's remittances have become an important source of foreign exchange for Mexico. In 2002 Mexicans sent $9.81 billion home, whereas foreign investment in that year was about $13.6 billion![81]

Ironically, most Mexicans who migrate illegally do not intend to settle permanently in the U.S. They come to solve a temporary problem of family finances. However since the border crossing is expensive and dangerous, they tend of stay longer than they would otherwise. Studies show that during periods of less border scrutiny before 1986, 80% of the

Mexicans entering illegally eventually returned to their homeland.[82]

Proponents of a more open immigration policy with Mexico stress the benefits which might result from legitimization of the now illegal human flows. According to the "segmented hypothesis" immigrants are generally in demand for the highest and lowest-skilled jobs, and the do not typically compete for the kinds of jobs held by the vast majority of Americans. Immigration can serve as a safety valve for the U.S. labor market, allowing in foreign workers when they are needed, while discouraging the same workers during periods of economic downturn because of fewer jobs being available. Immigration does lower the wages of the lowest skilled labor groups, but this translates into lower production costs and cheaper products for consumers. Finally, America's recent economic history confirms that our economy can prosper with immigration. Witness the 1990's when the unemployment rate fell to 4%, real wages grew, income distribution improved and immigration (legal and illegal) hit record levels. [83]

Opponents of freer immigration fear that legalizing Mexican migration will unleash a flood of new immigrants to the U.S., hurt native born low-skilled workers, burden taxpayers, create a permanent unassimilated underclass, reward law-breaking and compromise border security as we fight the war on terrorism.

Of course, it is hard to know exactly what would happen with a freer border. Many illegal migrants may choose to go home, while other more skilled Mexicans may take the opportunity to be rewarded with higher wages. Legalization of Mexican migrants would mean that they and their employers pay more taxes and might well reduce the welfare burden of taxpayers. As to the argument of a permanent unassimilated underclass, Mexicans are already branching out to points north and east to find jobs in the United States. As concerns border security and the war on terrorism, most of the hijackers came in legally or through Canada, not Mexico.[84]

One solution to the problems of creating a freer North American labor market might be a system of temporary work visas granted to Mexicans for limited periods of time. This would allow workers to move freely between the U.S. and Mexico and change jobs if employment conditions changed. The market for "coyotes," or human smugglers, would be seriously eroded and Mexican people could return to their families as economic conditions in Mexico improve, without confronting formidable barriers if they chose to work in the U.S. again.

Conclusions

1. NAFTA hasn't confirmed the dire predictions of its detractors, nor has it fulfilled the dreams of its supporters. The agreement seems to have had a stabilizing effect on economic relations in allowing them to grow in an otherwise tumultuous period.

2. There is evidence that following the peso crisis, Mexico's trade with the U.S. recovered faster than with non-NAFTA countries. This can be partially explained by a "NAFTA effect" of trade ties forging intra-industry links.

3. Aided by NAFTA-guaranteed market access, Mexican exports poured into the U.S. after the peso crisis, assisting Mexico in its speedy recovery, and in turn buoying renewed investor confidence. Investment funds flowed back into Mexico faster than after previous peso crises.

4. U.S. direct foreign investment in Mexico has grown throughout the NAFTA period. However, correcting for one unusually large financial acquisition in 2001, Mexico has received roughly the same percentage of all U.S. investment overseas throughout the last decade.

5. NAFTA does not appear to have had any significant effect on the U.S. labor market. The unskilled segment continues to suffer from competition with cheap labor abroad, part of which is in Mexico.

6. While cross-border labor movements are not part of the NAFTA agreement, the large number of Mexicans living in the United States, legally and illegally, contribute to the Mexican economy through workers' remittances.

The author wishes to acknowledge Govind Acharya and Anne R. Wenzel for their tireless and patient assistance in the research and preparation of this article.

Endnotes

[1] The main focus of this article is on U.S.-Mexican economic relations. Canada is mentioned only in passing.

[2] Walter (1997)

[3] Carbaugh (1998)

[4] Bosworth and Lustig (1997)

[5] Carbaugh (1998) and Klein and Salvatore (1995)

[6] Espinosa and Noyola (1997)

[7] Internet Securities (2003)

[8] SourceMex Economic News & Analysis on Mexico (2003)

[9] SourceMex Economic News & Analysis on Mexico (2003b); Walter (1997)

[10] Walter (1997)

[11] Vargas (1995)

[12] Gruben (2001)

[13] Espinosa and Noyola (1997) and Hufbauer and Schott (1993), Table 4A

[14] Hinojosa-Ojeda and McCleery (2002)

[15] Griswold (2002b)

[16] Griswold (2002b) p. 2

[17] Vargas (1999)

[18] United States Trade Representative (2003)

[19] United States Trade Representative (2003) p. 1

[20] Scott, (2001)

[21] Scott (2001), pp. 7-8

[22] Bronfenbrenner 1997 as cited in Scott, (2001) p. 8

[23] Anderson (2001)

[24] Rosenberg (2003)

[25] Williamson (1997)

[26] Bosworth and Lustig (1997)

[27] Bosworth and Lustig (1997)

[28] Williamson (1997)

[29] Lustig (1997)

[30] Lustig (1997)

[31] For a full discussion of trade creation and trade diversion see Chapter 9, Carbaugh (1998)

[32] For a detailed sectoral analysis see United States International Trade Commission (1997). NAFTA's reduction in tariff and non-tariff barriers contributed to increased U.S. exports of motor vehicles, electronic components, textiles and apparel, computers, chemicals and a range of agricultural products, and they were a factor in increased U.S. imports of Mexican textiles, apparel and light trucks.

[33] Gould (1998)

[34] Sarkar (1998)

[35] Gould (1998)

[36] Krueger (1999)

[37] Krueger (1999b), p. 3

[38] Gould (1998) and Lustig (1997)

[39] Espinosa and Noyola (1997)

[40] Burfisher, Robinson and Thierfelder (2001)

[41] Hillberry and McDaniel (2002)

[42] Wall (2003)

[43] Myrdal (1957)

[44] Carbaugh (1998), Chapter 9

[45] Krueger (1999b)

[46] Stevens (1998)

[47] Lustig (2001)

[48] Internet Securities (2003b)

[49] Meant that foreign direct investment inflows to the United States have exceeded outflows in recent years.

[50] Carbaugh (2004), Chapter 11

[51] Bandow (1999)

[52] Koechlin and Larudde (1992).

[53] Scott (2001). This study uses three-digit SIC trade data and the BLS 192-sector employment table to estimate the impact of changes in merchandise trade flows on labor requirements in these 192 industries. The figure of 766,030 jobs lost was calculated by allocating imports and exports to individual states on the basis of their share of industry-level employment in each three-digit industry.

[54] Bolle (2000). The number of jobs supported by new exports was calculated by multiplying the value of export growth each year expressed in billions of dollars times the corresponding estimate for the number of workers supported by each additional billion of exports correcting for productivity changes and inflation. In 1994 the number of workers supported by an addi-

tional billion dollars in exports was estimated at 14,361 jobs, in 1995 13,774 jobs, in 1996 13,258 jobs, and so on. The number declines each year because of productivity gains and inflation.

[55] Hinojosa-Ojeda et al. (2000).

[56] Hufbauer and Schott (2002) provide a full discussion of the different approaches, statistical techniques and results, pages 5-6.

[57] US Department of Labor (2002a).

[58] Public Citizen (2002).

[59] NAFTA-TAA discussion adapted from Hufbauer and Schott (2002)

[60] Kletzer (2001). Displacement is defined as a layoff resulting from the closure or substantial restructuring of a plant.

[61] Council of Economic Advisers (1999).

[62] Council of Economic Advisers (2001).

[63] Baily (2001).

[64] Scheve and Slaughter (2001).

[65] Scheve and Slaughter (2001, figure 4).

[66] Economic Report of the President 1997, as quoted in Scheve and Slaughter (2001). See also Cline (1992)who finds slightly different sensitivities of the skill premium to trade and immigration.

[67] The relationship between goods prices and factor prices was spelled out in 1941 by Stolper and Samuelson in their landmark article, "Protection and Real Wages." According to the Stolper-Samuelson theorem, trade liberalization should raise wages of workers employed relatively intensively in sectors where relative prices are rising (export sectors), and reduce wages for workers employed relatively intensively in sectors with declining prices (import-competing sectors).

[68] Lawrence and Slaughter (1993).

[69] Kletzer (2001)

[70] Kletzer (2001).

[71] Hufbauer and Schott (2002), pages 11-12

[72] Kletzer and Litman (2001)

[73] http://www.cbsnews.com/stories /2002/05/23/politics/main510041.shtml

[74] http://www.naalc.org/english/infocentre.htm

[75] http://www.ustr.gov/regions/whemisphere/organizations.shtml#environmental

[76] Kirton and Maclaren (2002)

[77] Carbaugh (2004) and Gould (1998)

[78] The White House, "Joint Statement between the United States and the United Mexican States," Washington, D. C, September 6, 2001, www.whitehouse.gov/news/releases /2001/09/20010906-8html.

[79] Griswold (2002), p. 1

[80] In recent years over 300 Mexicans per year have died crossing the border illegally in remote locations. Griswold (2002) p. 3

[81] Bank of Mexico release as cited in www.latamnews.com/mexicans_e051203.html

[82] Massey, Durand and Malone (2002), p. 45

[83] Griswold (2002), pp. 8-9

[84] Griswold (2002), p. 11

References

Anderson, Sarah. 2001. "Seven Years Under NAFTA," Institute for Policy Studies, Washington, D.C.

Baily, Martin Neil. 2001. "Macroeconomic Implications of the New Economy," Institute for International Economics Working Paper 01-9, as cited in Hufbauer & Schott, 2002.

Banco de Mexico, 1999. "The Mexican Economy 1998." http://www.banxico.org.mx/public_html/doyai/publica.html (April 28, 1999).

Bandow. 1999. "Bandow Company Releases US Business Migration Report." September 3. http://www.preweb.com/releases/1999/9/preweb9093.php (June 24, 2002)

Bosworth, B., S. Collins, and N. Lustig. 1997. Coming Together? Mexico-U.S. Relations. Washington: Brookings Institute.

Bronfenbrenner, Kate. 2000. "Uneasy Terrain: The Impact of Capital Mobility on Workers, Wages, and Union Organizing," commissioned research paper for the U.S. Trade Deficit Review Commission, http://www.ustdrc.gov/research/research.html.

Burfisher, Mary E., Sherman Robinson and Karen Thierfelder. 2001. "The Impact of NAFTA on the United States," *Journal of Economic Perspectives*, Volume 15, Number 1, Winter 2001, pp 125-144.

Cañas, Jesus and Roberto Coronado. 2002. "Maquiladora Industry: Past, Present and Future," El Paso Business Frontier 2, El Paso Branch, Federal Reserve Bank of Dallas.

Carbaugh, R. 2004. *International Economics.* Cincinnati, Ohio: South-Western College Publishing Co.

Casario, M. 1996. "North American Free Trade Agreement Bilateral Trade Effects." *Contemporary Economic Policy* 14 (January) 36-57.

Cavanagh, John, Sarah Anderson, Jaime Serra and J. Enrique Espinosa. 2002. "Happily Ever NAFTA?" *Foreign Policy,* Washington, Sep/Oct 2002.

CBS News. 2002. "Trade Bill Clears Senate," Washington: May 24, 2002, http://www.cbsnews.com/stories/2002/05/23/politics/main510041.shtml.

Chambers, Edward J. and Peter H. Smith. 2002. NAFTA in the New Millenium, The University of Alberta Press, October 2002.

Cline, William R. 1992. Trade and Income Distribution, Washington: Institute for International Economics, as cited in Hufbauer and Schott, 2002.

Commission for Environmental Cooperation. 2003. http://www.cec.org

Commission for Labor Cooperation. 2003. http://www.naalc.org.

Council of Economic Advisors. 1999. "20 Million Jobs: January 1993-November 1999," December 3, 1999.

Council of Economic Advisors. 2001. Economic Report of the President 2001, June 24, 2002.

De Long, J. Bradford. 2001. "A Symposium on the North American Economy," *Journal of Economic Perspectives,* Volume 15, number 1, Winter 2001, pp. 81, 83.

Dow Jones Newswires. 1999. "Mexico Foreign Sec: Relations With U.S. Strong, But Need Work." April 23, 1999. http://interactive.wsj.com/archive/retrieve.cgi?id=DI-CO-19990423-00098.djml.

Dow Jones Newswires. 1999. "US, Canada, Mexico Announce New NAFTA Initiatives." April 26, 1999. http://interactive.wsj.com/archive/retrieve.cgi?id=BT-CO-19990426-000907.djml.

Dow Jones Newswires. 1999. "USTR Fischer: Nafta Aids U.S. Econ Growth, Creates More Jobs." April 13, 1999. http://interactive.wsj.com/archive/retrieve.cgi?id=DI-CO-19990413-005877.djml.

The Economist. 1998. "Alphabet Spaghetti." October 3, 1998.

Espinosa, J., and P. Noyola. 1997. "Emerging Patterns in Mexico-U.S. Trade," in *Coming Together? Mexico-U.S. Relations.* Edited by B. Bosworth, S. Collins, and N. Lustig. Washington: Brookings Institute.

Federal News Service, Washington D.C. 1999. "Clinton's Trip to Mexico: A Brookings Press Briefing." Tuesday, February 9, 1999, 10:00 a.m. [EST]. http://www.brook.edu/cppe/hmpages/mexico/SPP0.HTM#AB11235.

Garber, P., ed. 1993. *The Mexico-U.S. Free Trade Agreement.* Cambridge, MA.: MIT Press.

Gereffi, Gary, David Spener and Jennifer Bair, editors. 2002. *Free Trade and Uneven Development: The North American Apparel Industry After NAFTA.* Temple University Press, September 2002.

Gould, D. 1998. "Has NAFTA Changed North American Trade," Federal Reserve Bank of Dallas. Economic Review. (October, 1998) 12-22.

Griswold, Daniel T. 2002. "Willing Workers: Fixing the Problem of Illegal Mexican Migration to the United States," Trade Policy Analysis, Washington: The Cato Institute, October 15, 2002.

Griswold, Daniel T. 2002b. "NAFTA at 10: An Economic and Foreign Policy Success," Free Trade Bulletin, December 2002, Center for Trade Policy Studies, Cato Institute.

Gruben, Vargas and Welsh. 1993. "The Benefits of NAFTA for Jobs, Wages, and the Future of America." Dallas. *The Southwest Economy.* (December 1993) 3-8.

Gruben, William C. 2001. "Was NAFTA Behind Mexico's High Maquiladora Growth?" *Economic and Financial Review,* Third Quarter 2001.

Hillberry, Russell and Christine McDaniel. 2002. "A Decomposition of North American Trade Growth Since NAFTA," *International Economic Review,* USITC Publication 3527, U.S. International Trade Commission, Office of Economics, May/June 2002.

Hinojosa-Ojeda, R. 1996. "North American Integration Three Years After NAFTA: A Framework for Tracking, Modeling and Internet Accessing the National and Regional Labor Market Impacts." Los Angeles: North American Integration and Development Center.

Hinojosa-Ojeda, Raul and Robert K. McCleery. 2002. "NAFTA as Metaphor: The Search for Regional and Global Lessons for the United States," *NAFTA in the New Millenium,* Edward J. Chambers and Peter H. Smith, editors, The University of Alberta Press.

Hufbauer, G. and J. Schott. 1991. "North American Free Trade: Issues & Recommendations." Washington: Institute for International Economics.

Hufbauer, G. and J. Schott. 1993. "NAFTA: An Assessment." Washington: Institute for International Economics.

Hufbauer, Gary Clyde and Gustavo Bega-Cánovas. 2003. "Whither NAFTA: A Common Frontier?" *The Rebordering of North America? Integration and Exclusion In a New Security Context,* edited by Peter Andreas and Thomas J. Biersteker, Routledge, 2003.

Hufbauer, Gary Clyde and Jeffrey J. Schott. 2002. "North American Labor Under NAFTA," Institue for International Economics, September 2002.

Internet Securities. 2003, "Fox and His Cabinet Evaluate Progress with Farmers," February 5, 2003.

Internet Securities. 2003b, "Mexico Attracts US$13.63bn in FDI in 2002," February 25, 2003.

Kamel, Rachael, and Anya Hoffman, editors. 1999. The Maquiladora Reader: Cross-Border Organizing Since NAFTA, American Friends Service Committee, 1999.

Kirton, John J. and Virginia W. Maclaren. 2002. "Forging the Trade-Environment-Social Cohesion Link: Glboal Challenges, North American Experiences," *Linking Trade, Environment, and Social Cohesion,* Ashgate Publishing Company, Hampshire, England, 2002.

Klein, L. and D. Salvatore. 1995. "Welfare Effects of the North American Free Trade Agreement." *Journal of Policy Modeling* (Volume 17, Number 2, April) 163-176.

Kletzer, Lori G. 2001. "Job Loss from Imports: Measuring the Costs," Washington: Institute for International Economics.

Kletzer, Lori G. and Robert E. Litan. 2001. "A Prescription to Relieve Worker Anxiety," Institute for International Economics Policy Brief 01-2, Washington: Institute for International Economics.

Koechlin, Timothy and Mehrene Larudde. 1992. "The High Cost of NAFTA," Challenge. September/October 2002, as cited in Hufbauer and Schott, "North American Labor Under NAFTA," Institue for International Economics, September 2002.

Kouparitsas, M. 1995. "Dynamic Trade Liberalization Analysis: Steady State, Transitional and Inter-Industry Effects," Federal Reserve Bank of Chicago. (December 1998).

Krueger, Anne O. 1999a. "Are Preferential Trading Arrangements Trade-Liberalizing or Protectionist?" *Journal of Economic Perspecives,* Volume 13, Number 4, Fall 1999, pp. 105-124.

Krueger, Anne O. 1999b. "Trade Creation and Trade Diversion Under NAFTA," NBER Working Paper Series, http://www.nber. org/papers/w7429 (December 1999).

Krugman, P. 1993. "The Uncomfortable Truth about NAFTA." *Foreign Affairs.* Council on Foreign Relations 75 (November/December) 13-19.

Krugman, P. 1996. "How Is NAFTA Doing?." *The New Democrat* (May/June) 18-21.

Lawrence, Robert Z. and Mathew J. Slaughter. 1993. "International Trade and American Wages in the 1980s: Giant Sucking Sound or Small Hiccup?" Brookings Papers on Economic Activity, Microeconomics 2: 161-211, as cited in Hufbauer & Schott, 2002.

Lustig, Nora 1997. "Brookings Institution." NAFTA: Setting the Record Straight. June 1997. http://www.brookings.org./comm /policybriefs/pb0200/pb20.htm (May 10, 1999).

Lustig, Nora. 2001. "Life Is Not Easy: Mexico's Quest for Stability and Growth," *Journal of Economic Perspeitives,* Volume 15, no. 1, Winter 2001.

Massey, Douglas S., Jorge Durand and Nolan J. Malone. 2002. *Beyond Smoke and Mirrors: Mexican Immigration in an Era of Economic Integration,* New York: Russell Sage Foundation, as cited in Griswold, 2002.

Myrdal, Gunner. 1957. *Economic Theory and Underdeveloped Regions* (London: Duckworth, 1957).

Nazmi, N. and M. Ramirez. 1998. "Public and Private Investment and Economic Growth in Mexico." *Contemporary Economic Policy* 15 (January) 65-75.

Orme, W. 1993. "Myth versus Facts, the Truth about the Half Truths." *Foreign Affairs.* Council on Foreign Relations 75 (November/December) 2-12.

Orenius, Pia M. 2001. "Illegal Immigration and Enforcement Along the U.S.-Mexico Border: An Overview," Economic and Financial Review, First Quarter 2001, Federal Reserve Bank of Dallas.

Pastor, R., 1993. "NAFTA as the Center of an Integration Process." Washington. *The Brookings Review.* (Winter 1993) 40-45.

Public Citizen. 2002. http://www.citizen.org/trade/forms/search_taa.cfm as cited in Hufbauer & Schott, 2002.

Reichard, Robert S. 1998 "Another Fair Year Ahead for U.S. Textiles." *Textile World.* January 1998.

Rosenberg, Tina. 2003. "Why Mexico's Small Corn Farmers Go Hungry," *The New York Times,* March 3, 2003.

Rothstein, J. and R. Scott. 1997. "NAFTA's Casualties." Washington, Issue Brief # 120. Economic Policy Institute.

Sanchez, Roberto A. 2002. "Governance, Trade, and the Environment in the Context of NAFTA," *The American Behavioral Scientist,* Thousand Oaks, Calif., May 2002.

Sarkar, Shyamalendu. 1998. "Impact of the North American Free Trade Agreement (NAFTA) on the U.S. Trade With Mexico." Presented at the 73rd Annual WEA International Conference, June-28-July 2, 1998, at Harveys Resort Hotel, Lake Tahoe, U.S.A.

Scheve, Kenneth F. and Matthew J. Slaughter. 2001. "Globalization and the Perceptions of American Workers," Washington: Institute for International Economics, as cited in Hufbauer and Schott, 2002.

Scott, Robert E. 2001. "NAFTA's Hidden Costs: Trade Agreement Results in Job Losses, Growing Inequality, and Wage Suppression for the United States," *NAFTA at Seven,* Economic Policy Institute, Washington, D.C. (2001).

SourceMex Economic News & Analysis on Mexico. 2003a. "Mexico, U.S. Agree to Modify NAFTA Tariff-Elimination Provision for Poultry," January, 29, 2003.

SourceMex Economic News & Analysis on Mexico. 2003b. "Auto Industry Prepares for Elimination of Import Tariffs Under NAFTA in 2004," February 5, 2003.

Stevens, G. 1998. "U.S. Direct Investment in Mexico: Politics, Economics and NAFTA." *Contemporary Economic Policy* 16 (April) 197-209.

Torres, C. 1997. "Foreigners Snap Up Mexican Companies; Impact is Enormous." *Wall Street Journal* (September 30, 1997).

Truett, L. and D. Truett. 1993. "Maquiladora Response to U.S. and Asian Relative Wage Rate Changes." *Contemporary Economic Policy* 11 (January) 18-27.

United States Department of Labor. 2002. Division of Trade Adjustment Assistance, http://www.dllr.state.md.us/employment/nafta.htm#whatis.

United States International Trade Commission. 1997. Study on the Operation and Effects of the North American Free Trade Agreement. Washington. (July, 1997).

United States Trade Representative. 2001. "Fact Sheet: Accomplishments of the Free Trade Area of the Americans (FTAA)," presented at the Trade Negotiations Committee (TNC) meeting, September 26-28, 2001, Managua, Nicaragua (http://www.ustr.gov/regions/whemisphere/2001-09-26_TNC.PDF).

United States Trade Representative. 2003. Free Trade Agreement Negotiations, http://www.ustr.gov/new/fta/.

United States Trade Representative. 2002. NAFTA at Eight, (8 Year Report – May 2002), http://ustr.gov/naftareport/nafta8_brochure-eng.pdf

Vargas, L. 1995. "Maquiladoras: Mexico's Bright Spot," Federal Reserve Bank of Dallas. The Southwest Economy 5. (1995) 9-19.

Vargas, L. 1996. "The Maquiladora Industry: Still Going Strong (Part 1)," El Paso Business Frontier 3, El Paso Branch, Federal Reserve Bank of Dallas, (1996).

Vargas, L. 1997. "NAFTA and Jobs," El Paso Business Frontier 1, El Paso Branch, Federal Reserve Bank of Dallas, (1997).

Vargas, L. 1999. "NAFTA's First Five Years (Part 1)," El Paso Business Frontier 2, El Paso Branch, Federal Reserve Bank of Dallas, (1999).

Wall, Howard, J. 2003, "NAFTA and the Geography of North American Trade," Review, Federal Reserve Bank of St. Louis, March/April 2003.

Walter, T. 1997. *The World Economy.* New York: John Wiley & Sons Inc.

Williamson, J. 1997. "Mexican Policy toward Foreign Borrowing," in *Coming Together? Mexico-U.S. Relations.* Edited by B. Bosworth, S. Collins, and N. Lustig. Washington: Brookings Institute.

Discussion Questions

III

1. Is Rodrik against free trade?

2. Why does Rodrik argue that institutions are so important? Why does he believe that the WTO and other institutions can inhibit development?

3. Does Rodrik point to a specific set of policies for trade and development? Explain.

4. Why do farm subsidies hurt the poor? Why do developed countries adopt these policies if they are harmful to the poor?

5. Has NAFTA been a success for the US? For Canada? For Mexico? What country do you believe has benefited the most?

6. Where will NAFTA go from here?

Globalization

The debate over globalization has become increasingly important to the public, to protestors, and to policy makers, and in this edition we have decided it warrants an entire section. Each of these articles examines a different aspect of the phenomenon and each offers a specific viewpoint on globalization.

The first article, "Trading in Illusions," by Dani Rodrik is critical not so much of globalization as of the policies that are foisted upon poor countries by multilateral institutions in the name of free trade and globalization. He points out that China, often used as a poster child for globalization, has violated almost all of the scriptures for free trade and globalization and Rodrik believes China has prospered precisely because it has created a system of gradual reform. Rodrik argues that countries that open up their economies completely to free trade have often not fared as well. He concludes that, "while global markets are good for poor countries, the rules according to which they are being asked to play the game are often not. Caught between WTO agreements, World Bank strictures, IMF conditions, and the need to maintain the confidence of financial markets, developing countries are increasingly deprived of the room they need to devise their own paths out of poverty."

The article "Five Wars of Globalization" examines other issues often not discussed in academic debates on the issue. The article examines what one might call the side-effects of globalization that global society must tackle. These are drugs, arms trafficking, intellectual property, alien smuggling, and money laundering. Naim believes that these issues cannot be dealt with until new institutions are developed to tackle these issues and cooperation between countries increases.

In "Spreading the Wealth," Dollar and Kraay defend globalization against the claims of its critics. They point out that as globalization increases apace global inequality has fallen. Countries that have embraced trade, such as China and (recently) India, have seen their growth rates increase (though see the Rodrik article for a different perspective) and the foreign investment accompanying globalization has reduced poverty.

The final article in this section, and the longest, entitled "The New Wave of Globalization and its Economic Effects," looks at globalization in historic perspective. A number of scholars have pointed out that globalization is not a new phenomenon at all and that, in fact, it can be argued that the wave of globalization in the late 19th century was more significant than the one today. This article examines three waves of globalization and the impact of each wave.

Trading in Illusions

D ANI **R ODRIK**

Advocates of global economic integration hold out utopian visions of the prosperity that developing countries will reap if they open their borders to commerce and capital. This hollow promise diverts poor nations' attention and resources from the key domestic innovations needed to spur economic growth

senior U.S. Treasury official recently urged Mexico's government to work harder to reduce violent crime because "such high levels of crime and violence may drive away foreign investors." This admonition nicely illustrates how foreign trade and investment have become the ultimate yardstick for evaluating the social and economic policies of governments in developing countries. Forget the slum dwellers or campesinos who live amidst crime and poverty throughout the developing world. Just mention "investor sentiment" or "competitiveness in world markets" and policymakers will come to attention in a hurry.

Underlying this perversion of priorities is a remarkable consensus on the imperative of global economic integration. Openness to trade and investment flows is no longer viewed simply as a component of a country's development strategy; it has mutated into the most potent catalyst for economic growth known to humanity. Predictably, senior officials of the World Trade Organization (WTO), International Monetary Fund (IMF),

and other international financial agencies incessantly repeat the openness mantra. In recent years, however, faith in integration has spread quickly to political leaders and policymakers around the world.

Joining the world economy is no longer a matter simply of dismantling barriers to trade and investment. Countries now must also comply with a long list of admission requirements, from new patent rules to more rigorous banking standards. The apostles of economic integration prescribe comprehensive institutional reforms that took today's advanced countries generations to accomplish, so that developing countries can, as the cliché goes, maximize the gains and minimize the risks of participation in the world economy. Global integration has become, for all practical purposes, a substitute for a development strategy.

This trend is bad news for the world's poor. The new agenda of global integration rests on shaky empirical ground and seriously distorts policymakers' priorities. By focusing on international integration, governments in poor nations divert human resources, administrative capabilities, and political capital away from more urgent development priorities such as education, public health, industrial capacity, and social cohesion. This emphasis also undermines nascent democratic institutions by removing the choice of development strategy from public debate.

World markets are a source of technology and capital; it would be silly for the developing world not to exploit these opportunities. But globalization is not a shortcut to development. Successful economic growth strategies have always required a judicious blend of imported practices with domestic institutional innovations. Policymakers need to forge a domestic growth strategy by relying on domestic investors and domestic institutions. The costliest downside of the integrationist faith is that it crowds out serious thinking and efforts along such lines.

Excuses, Excuses

Countries that have bought wholeheartedly into the integration orthodoxy are discovering that openness does not deliver on its promise. Despite sharply lowering their barriers to trade and investment since the 1980s, scores of countries in Latin America and Africa are stagnating or growing less rapidly than in the heyday of import substitution during the 1960s and 1970s. By contrast, the fastest growing countries are China, India, and others in East and Southeast Asia. Policymakers in these countries have also espoused trade and investment liberalization, but they have done so in an unorthodox manner—gradually, sequentially, and only after an initial period of high growth—and as part of a broader policy package with many unconventional features.

The disappointing outcomes with deep liberalization have been absorbed into the faith with remarkable aplomb. Those who view global integration as the prerequisite for economic development now simply add the caveat that opening borders is insufficient. Reaping the gains from openness, they argue, also requires a full complement of institutional reforms.

Consider trade liberalization. Asking any World Bank economist what a successful trade-liberalization program requires will likely elicit a laundry list of measures beyond the simple reduction of tariff and nontariff barriers: tax reform to make up for lost tariff revenues; social safety nets to compensate displaced workers; administrative reform to bring trade practices into compliance with WTO rules; labor market reform to enhance worker mobility across industries; technological assistance to upgrade firms hurt by import competition; and training programs to ensure that export-oriented firms and investors have access to skilled workers. As the promise of trade liberalization fails to materialize, the prerequisites keep expanding. For example, Clare Short, Great Britain's secretary of state for international development, recently added universal provision of health and education to the list.

In the financial arena, integrationists have pushed complementary reforms with even greater fanfare and urgency. The prevailing view in Washington and other Group of Seven (G-7) capitals is that weaknesses in banking systems, prudential regulation, and corporate governance were at the heart of the Asian financial crisis of the late 1990s. Hence the ambitious efforts by the G-7 to establish international codes and standards covering fiscal transparency, monetary and financial policy, banking supervision, data dissemination, corporate governance, and accounting standards. The Financial Stability Forum (FSF)—a G-7 organization with minimal representation from developing nations—has designated 12 of these standards as essential for creating sound financial systems in developing countries. The full FSF compendium includes an additional 59 standards the agency considers "relevant for sound financial systems," bringing the total number of codes to 71. To fend off speculative capital movements, the IMF and the G-7 also typically urge developing countries to accumulate foreign reserves and avoid exchange-rate regimes that differ from a "hard peg" (tying the value of one's currency to that of a more stable currency, such as the U.S. dollar) or a "pure float" (letting the market determine the appropriate exchange rate).

A cynic might wonder whether the point of all these prerequisites is merely to provide easy cover for eventual failure. Integrationists can conveniently blame disappointing growth performance or a financial crisis on "slippage" in the implementation of complementary reforms rather than on a poorly designed liberalization. So if Bangladesh's freer trade policy does not produce a large enough spurt in growth, the World Bank concludes that the problem must involve lagging reforms in public administration or continued "political uncertainty" (always a favorite). And if Argentina gets caught up in a confidence crisis despite significant trade and financial liberalization, the IMF reasons that structural reforms have been inadequate and must be deepened.

Free Trade-offs

Most (but certainly not all) of the institutional reforms on the integrationist agenda are perfectly sensible, and in a world without financial, administrative, or political constraints, there would be little argument about the need to adopt them. But in the real world, governments face difficult choices over how to deploy their fiscal resources, administrative capabilities, and political capital. Setting institutional priorities to maximize integration into the global economy has real opportunity costs.

Consider some illustrative trade-offs. World Bank trade economist Michael Finger has estimated that a typical developing country must spend $150 million to implement requirements under just three WTO agreements (those on customs valuation, sanitary and phytosanitary measures, and trade-related intellectual property rights). As Finger notes, this sum equals a year's development budget for many least-developed countries. And while the budgetary burden of implementing financial codes and standards has never been fully estimated, it undoubtedly entails a substantial diversion of fiscal and human resources as well. Should governments in developing countries train more bank auditors and accountants, even if those investments mean fewer secondary-school teachers or reduced spending on primary education for girls?

In the area of legal reform, should governments focus their energies on "importing" legal codes and standards or on improving existing domestic legal institutions? In Turkey, a weak coalition government spent several months during 1999 gathering political support for a bill providing foreign investors the protection of international arbitration. But wouldn't a better long-run strategy have involved reforming the existing legal regime for the benefit of foreign and domestic investors alike?

In public health, should governments promote the reverse engineering of patented basic medicines and the importation of low-cost generic drugs from "unauthorized" suppliers, even if doing so means violating WTO rules against such practices? When South Africa passed legislation in 1997 allowing imports of patented AIDS drugs from cheaper sources, the country came under severe pressure from Western governments, which argued that the South African policy conflicted with WTO rules on intellectual property.

How much should politicians spend on social protection policies in view of the fiscal constraints imposed by market "discipline"? Peru's central bank holds foreign reserves equal to 15 months of imports as an insurance policy against the sudden capital outflows that financially open economies often experience. The opportunity cost of this policy amounts to almost 1 percent of gross domestic product annually—more than enough to fund a generous antipoverty program.

How should governments choose their exchange-rate regimes? During the last four decades, virtually every growth boom in the developing world has been accompanied by a controlled depreciation of the domestic currency. Yet financial openness makes it all but impossible to manage the exchange rate.

How should policymakers focus their anticorruption strategies? Should they target the high-level corruption that foreign investors often decry or the petty corruption that affects the poor most? Perhaps, as the proponents of permanent normal trade relations with China argued in the recent U.S. debate, a government that is forced to protect the rights of foreign investors will become more inclined to protect the rights of its own citizens as well. But this is, at best, a trickledown strategy of institu-

High Tariffs Don't Mean Low Growth
Gross Domestic Product (GDP) Growth & Tariff Rates, 1990s

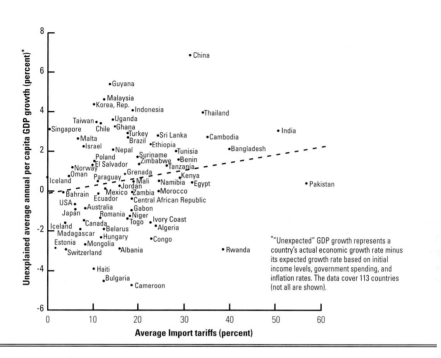

*"Unexpected" GDP growth represents a country's actual economic growth rate minus its expected growth rate based on initial income levels, government spending, and inflation rates. The data cover 113 countries (not all are shown).

tional reform. Shouldn't reforms target the desired ends directly—whether those ends are the rule of law, improved observance of human rights, or reduced corruption?

The rules for admission into the world economy not only reflect little awareness of development priorities, they are often completely unrelated to sensible economic principles. For instance, WTO agreements on antidumping, subsidies and countervailing measures, agriculture, textiles, and trade-related intellectual property rights lack any economic rationale beyond the mercantilist interests of a narrow set of powerful groups in advanced industrial countries. Bilateral and regional trade agreements are typically far worse, as they impose even tighter prerequisites on developing countries in return for crumbs of enhanced "market access." For example, the African Growth and Opportunity Act signed by U.S. President Clinton in May 2000 provides increased access to the U.S. market only

if African apparel manufacturers use U.S.-produced fabric and yarns. This restriction severely limits the potential economic spillovers in African countries.

There are similar questions about the appropriateness of financial codes and standards. These codes rely heavily on an Anglo-American style of corporate governance and an arm's-length model of financial development. They close off alternative paths to financial development of the sort that have been followed by many of today's rich countries (for example, Germany, Japan, or South Korea).

In each of these areas, a strategy of "globalization above all" crowds out alternatives that are potentially more development-friendly. Many of the institutional reforms needed for insertion into the world economy can be independently desirable or produce broader economic benefits. But these priorities do not necessarily coincide with the priorities of a comprehensive development agenda.

Asian Myths

Even if the institutional reforms needed to join the international economic community are expensive and preclude investments in other crucial areas, pro-globalization advocates argue that the vast increases in economic growth that invariably result from insertion into the global marketplace will more than compensate for those costs. Take the East Asian tigers or China, the advocates say. Where would they be without international trade and foreign capital flows?

That these countries reaped enormous benefits from their progressive integration into the world economy is undeniable. But look closely at what policies produced those results, and you will find little that resembles today's rule book.

Countries like South Korea and Taiwan had to abide by few international constraints and pay few of the modern costs of integration during their formative growth experience in the 1960s and 1970s. At that time, global trade rules were sparse and economies faced almost none of today's common pressures to open their borders to capital flows. So these countries combined their outward orientation with unorthodox policies: high levels of tariff and nontariff barriers, public ownership of large segments of banking and industry, export subsidies, domestic-content requirements, patent and copyright infringements, and restrictions on capital flows (including on foreign direct investment). Such policies are either precluded by today's trade rules or are highly frowned upon by organizations like the IMF and the World Bank.

China also followed a highly unorthodox two-track strategy, violating practically every rule in the guidebook (including, most notably, the requirement of private property rights). India, which significantly raised its economic growth rate in the early 1980s, remains one of the world's most highly protected economies.

All of these countries liberalized trade gradually, over a period of decades, not years. Significant import liberalization did not occur until after a transition to high economic growth had taken place. And far from wiping the institutional slate clean, all of these nations managed to eke growth out of their existing institutions, imperfect as they may have been. Indeed, when some of the more successful Asian economies gave in to Western pressure to liberalize capital flows rapidly, they were rewarded with the Asian financial crisis.

That is why these countries can hardly be considered poster children for today's global rules. South Korea, China, India, and the other Asian success cases had the freedom to do their own thing, and they used that freedom abundantly. Today's globalizers would be unable to replicate these experiences without running afoul of the IMF or the WTO. The Asian experience highlights a deeper point: A sound overall development strategy that produces high economic growth is far more effective in achieving integration with the world economy than a purely integrationist strategy that relies on openness to work its magic. In other words, the globalizers have it exactly backwards. Integration is the result, not the cause, of economic and social development. A relatively protected economy like Vietnam is integrating with the world economy much more rapidly than an open economy like Haiti because Vietnam, unlike Haiti, has a reasonably functional economy and polity.

Integration into the global economy, unlike tariff rates or capital-account regulations, is not something that policymakers control directly. Telling finance ministers in developing nations that they should increase their "participation in world trade" is as meaningful as telling them that they need to improve technological capabilities—and just as helpful. Policymakers need to know which strategies will produce these results, and whether the specific prescriptions that the current orthodoxy offers are up to the task.

Too Good to Be True

Do lower trade barriers spur greater economic progress? The available studies reveal no systematic relationship between a country's average level of tariff and nontariff barriers and its subsequent economic growth rate. If anything, the evidence for the 1990s indicates a positive relationship between import tariffs and economic growth [see chart]. The only clear pattern is that countries dismantle their trade restrictions as they grow richer. This finding explains why today's rich countries, with few exceptions, embarked on modern economic growth behind protective barriers but now display low trade barriers.

The absence of a strong negative relationship between trade restrictions and economic growth may seem surprising in view of the ubiquitous claim that trade liberalization promotes higher growth. Indeed, the economics literature is replete with cross-national studies concluding that growth and economic dynamism are strongly linked to more open trade policies. A particularly influential study finds that economies that are "open," by the study's own definition, grew 2.45 percentage points faster annually than closed ones—an enormous difference.

Upon closer look, however, such studies turn out to be unreliable. In a detailed review of the empirical literature, University of Maryland economist Francisco Rodríguez and I have found a major gap between the results that economists have actually obtained and the policy conclusions they have typically drawn. For example, in many cases economists blame poor growth on the government's failure to liberalize trade policies, when the true culprits are ineffective institutions, geographic determinants (such as location in a tropical region), or inappropriate macroeconomic policies (such as an overvalued exchange rate). Once these misdiagnoses are corrected, any meaningful relationship across countries between the level of trade barriers and economic growth evaporates.

The evidence on the benefits of liberalizing capital flows is even weaker. In theory, the appeal of capital mobility seems obvious: If capital is free to enter (and leave) markets based on the potential return on investment, the result will be an efficient allocation of global resources. But in reality, financial markets are inherently unstable, subject to bubbles (rational or otherwise), panics, shortsightedness, and self-fulfilling prophecies. There is plenty of evidence that financial liberalization is often followed by financial crash—just ask Mexico, Thailand, or Turkey—while there is little convincing evidence to suggest that higher rates of economic growth follow capital-account liberalization.

Perhaps the most disingenuous argument in favor of liberalizing international financial flows is that the threat of massive and sudden capital movements serves to discipline policymakers in developing nations who might otherwise manage their economies irresponsibly. In other words, governments might be less inclined to squander their societies' resources if such actions would spook foreign lenders. In practice, however, the discipline argument falls apart. Behavior in international capital markets is dominated by mood swings unrelated to fundamentals. In good times, a government with a chronic fiscal deficit has an easier time financing its spending when it can borrow funds from investors abroad; witness Russia prior to 1998 or Argentina in the 1990s. And in bad times, governments may be forced to adopt inappropriate policies in order to conform to the biases of foreign investors; witness the excessively restrictive monetary and fiscal policies in much of East Asia in the immediate aftermath of the Asian financial crisis. A key reason why Malaysia was able to recover so quickly after the imposition of capital controls in September 1998 was that Prime Minister Mahathir Mohamad resisted the high interest rates and tight fiscal policies that South Korea, Thailand, and Indonesia adopted at the behest of the International Monetary Fund.

Growth Begins at Home

Well-trained economists are justifiably proud of the textbook case in favor of free trade. For all the theory's simplicity, it is one of our profession's most significant achievements. However, in their zeal to promote the virtues of trade, the most ardent proponents are peddling a cartoon version of the argument, vastly overstating the effectiveness of economic openness as a tool for fostering development. Such claims only endanger broad public acceptance of the real article because they unleash unrealistic expectations about the benefits of free trade. Neither economic theory nor empirical evidence guarantees that deep trade liberalization will deliver higher economic growth. Economic openness and all its accouterments do not deserve the priority they typically receive in the development strategies pushed by leading multilateral organizations.

Countries that have achieved long-term economic growth have usually combined the opportunities offered by world markets with a growth strategy that mobilizes the capabilities of domestic institutions and investors. Designing such a growth strategy is both harder and easier than implementing typical integration policies. It is harder because the binding constraints on growth are usually country specific and do not respond well to standardized recipes. But it is easier because once those constraints are targeted, relatively simple policy changes can yield enormous economic payoffs and start a virtuous cycle of growth and additional reform.

Unorthodox innovations that depart from the integration rule book are typically part and parcel of such strategies. Public enterprises during the Meiji restoration in Japan; township and village enterprises in China; an export processing zone in Mauritius; generous tax incentives for priority investments in Taiwan; extensive credit subsidies in South Korea; infant-industry protection in Brazil during the 1960s and 1970s—these are some of the innovations that have been instrumental in kick-starting investment and growth in the past. None came out of a Washington economist's tool kit.

Few of these experiments have worked as well when transplanted to other settings, only underscoring the decisive importance of local conditions. To be effective, development strategies need to be tailored to prevailing domestic institutional strengths. There is simply no alternative to a homegrown business plan. Policymakers who look to Washington and financial markets for the answers are condemning themselves to mimicking the conventional wisdom du jour, and to eventual disillusionment.

Dani Rodrik is professor of international political economy at the John F. Kennedy School of Government at Harvard University.

Want to Know More?
This article appeared in the March/April 2001 Issue of *Foreign Policy Magazine*

16

The Five Wars of Globalization

MOISÉS NAÍM

The illegal trade in drugs, arms, intellectual property, people, and money is booming. Like the war on terrorism, the fight to control these illicit markets pits governments against agile, stateless, and resourceful networks empowered by globalization. Governments will continue to lose these wars until they adopt new strategies to deal with a larger, unprecedented struggle that now shapes the world as much as confrontations between nation-states once did.

The persistence of al Qaeda underscores how hard it is for governments to stamp out stateless, decentralized networks that move freely, quickly, and stealthily across national borders to engage in terror. The intense media coverage devoted to the war on terrorism, however, obscures five other similar global wars that pit governments against agile, well-financed networks of highly dedicated individuals. These are the fights against the illegal international trade in drugs, arms, intellectual property, people, and money. Religious zeal or political goals drive terrorists, but the promise of enormous financial gain motivates those who battle governments in these five wars. Tragically, profit is no less a motivator for murder, mayhem, and global insecurity than religious fanaticism.

In one form or another, governments have been fighting these five wars for centuries. And losing them. Indeed, thanks to the changes spurred by globalization over the last decade, their losing streak has become even more pronounced. To be sure, nation-states have benefited from the information revolution, stronger political and economic linkages, and the shrinking importance of geographic distance. Unfortunately, criminal networks have benefited even more. Never fettered by the niceties of sovereignty, they are now increasingly free of geographic constraints. Moreover, globalization has not only expanded illegal markets and boosted the size and the resources of criminal networks, it has also imposed more burdens on governments: Tighter public budgets, decentralization, privatization, deregulation, and a more open environment for international trade and investment all make the task of fighting global criminals more difficult. Governments are made up of cumbersome bureaucracies that generally cooperate with difficulty, but drug traffickers, arms dealers, alien smugglers, counterfeiters, and money launderers have refined networking to a high science, entering into complex and improbable strategic alliances that span cultures and continents.

Defeating these foes may prove impossible. But the first steps to reversing their recent dramatic gains must be to recognize the fundamental similarities among the five wars and to treat these conflicts not as law enforcement problems but as a new global trend that shapes the world as much as confrontations between nation-states did in the past. Customs officials, police officers, lawyers, and judges alone will never win these wars. Governments must recruit and deploy more spies, soldiers, diplomats, and economists who understand how to use incentives and regulations to steer markets away from bad social outcomes. But changing the skill set of government combatants alone will not end these wars. Their doctrines and institutions also need a major overhaul.

The Five Wars

Pick up any newspaper anywhere in the world, any day, and you will find news about illegal migrants, drug busts, smuggled weapons, laundered money, or counterfeit goods. The global nature of these five wars was unimaginable just a decade ago. The resources—financial, human, institutional, technological—deployed by the combatants have reached unfathomable orders of magnitude. So have the numbers of victims. The tactics and tricks of both sides boggle the mind. Yet if you cut through the fog of daily headlines and orchestrated photo ops, one inescapable truth emerges: The world's governments are fighting a qualitatively new phenomenon with obsolete tools, inadequate laws, inefficient bureaucratic arrangements, and ineffective strategies. Not surprisingly, the evidence shows that governments are losing.

Drugs

The best known of the five wars is, of course, the war on drugs. In 1999, the United Nations' "Human Development Report" calculated the annual trade in illicit drugs at $400 billion, roughly the size of the Spanish economy and about 8 percent of world trade. Many countries are reporting an increase in drug use. Feeding this habit is a global supply chain that uses everything from passenger jets that can carry shipments of cocaine worth $500 million in a single trip to custom-built submarines that ply the waters between Colombia and Puerto Rico. To foil eavesdroppers, drug smugglers use "cloned" cell phones and broadband radio receivers while also relying on complex financial structures that blend legitimate and illegitimate enterprises with elaborate fronts and structures of cross-ownership.

The United States spends between $35 billion and $40 billion each year on the war on drugs; most of this money is spent on interdiction and intelligence. But the creativity and boldness of drug cartels has routinely outstripped steady increases in government resources. Responding to tighter security at the U.S.-Mexican border, drug smugglers built a tunnel to move tons of drugs and billions of dollars in cash until authorities discovered it in March 2002. Over the last decade, the success of the Bolivian and Peruvian governments in eradicating coca plantations has shifted production to Colombia. Now, the U.S.-supported Plan Colombia is displacing coca production and processing labs back to other Andean countries. Despite the heroic efforts of these Andean countries and the massive financial and technical support of the United States, the total acreage of coca plantations in Peru, Colombia, and Bolivia has increased in the last decade from 206,200 hectares in 1991 to 210,939 in 2001. Between 1990 and 2000, according to economist Jeff DeSimone, the median price of a gram of cocaine in the United States fell from $152 to $112.

Even when top leaders of drug cartels are captured or killed, former rivals take their place. Authorities have acknowledged, for example, that the recent arrest of Benjamin Arellano Felix, accused of running Mexico's most ruthless drug cartel, has done little to stop the flow of drugs to the United States. As Arellano said in a recent interview from jail, "They talk about a war against the Arellano brothers. They haven't won. I'm here, and nothing has changed."

Arms Trafficking

Drugs and arms often go together. In 1999, the Peruvian military parachuted 10,000 AK-47s to the Revolutionary Armed Forces of Colombia, a guerrilla group closely allied to drug growers and traffickers. The group purchased the weapons in Jordan. Most of the roughly 80 million AK-47s in circulation today are in the wrong hands. According to the United Nations, only 18 million (or about 3 percent) of the 550 million small arms and light weapons in circulation today are used by government, military, or police forces. Illict trade accounts for almost 20 percent of the total small arms trade and generates more than $1 billion a year. Small arms helped fuel 46 of the 49 largest conflicts of the last decade and in 2001 were estimated to be responsible for 1,000 deaths a day; more than 80 percent of those victims were women and children.

Small arms are just a small part of the problem. The illegal market for munitions encompasses top-of-the-line tanks, radar systems that detect Stealth aircraft, and the makings of the deadliest weapons of mass destruction. The International Atomic Energy Agency has confirmed more than a dozen cases of smuggled nuclear-weapons-usable material, and hundreds more cases have been reported and investigated over the last decade. The actual supply of stolen nuclear-, biological-, or chemical-weapons materials and technology may still be small. But the potential demand is strong and growing from both would-be nuclear powers and terrorists. Constrained supply and increasing demand cause prices to rise and create enormous incentives for illegal activities. More than one fifth of the 120,000 workers in Russia's former "nuclear cities"—where more than half of all employees earn less than $50 a month—say they would be willing to work in the military complex of another country.

Governments have been largely ineffective in curbing either supply or demand. In recent years, two countries, Pakistan and India, joined the declared nuclear power club. A U.N. arms embargo failed to prevent the reported sale to Iraq of jet fighter engine parts from Yugoslavia and the Kolchuga anti-Stealth radar system from Ukraine. Multilateral efforts to curb the manufacture and distribution of weapons are faltering, not least because some powers are unwilling to accept curbs on their own activities. In 2001, for example, the United States blocked a legally binding global treaty to control small arms in part because it worried about restrictions on its own citizens' rights to own guns. In the absence of effective international legislation and enforcement, the laws of economics dictate the sale of more weapons at cheaper prices: In 1986, an AK-47 in Kolowa, Kenya, cost 15 cows. Today, it costs just four.

Intellectual Property

In 2001, two days after recording the voice track of a movie in Hollywood, actor Dennis Hopper was in Shanghai where a street vendor sold him an excellent pirated copy of the movie with his voice already on it. "I don't know how they got my voice into the country before I got here," he wondered. Hopper's experience is one tiny slice of an illicit trade that cost the United States an estimated $9.4 billion in 2001. The piracy rate of business software in Japan and France is 40 percent, in Greece and South Korea it is about 60 percent, and in Germany and Britain it hovers around 30 percent. Forty percent of Procter & Gamble shampoos and 60 percent of Honda motorbikes sold in China in 2001 were pirated. Up to 50 percent of medical drugs in Nigeria and Thailand are bootleg copies. This problem is not limited to consumer products: Italian makers of industrial valves worry that their $2 billion a year export market is eroded by counterfeit Chinese valves sold in world markets at prices that are 40 percent cheaper.

The drivers of this bootlegging boom are complex. Technology is obviously boosting both the demand and the supply of illegally copied products. Users of Napster, the now defunct Internet company that allowed anyone, anywhere to download and reproduce copyrighted music for free, grew from zero to 20 million in just one year. Some 500,000 film files are traded daily through file-sharing services such as Kazaa and Morpheus; and in late 2002, some 900 million music files could be downloaded for free on the Internet—that is, almost two and a half times more files than those available when Napster reached its peak in February 2001.

Global marketing and branding are also playing a part, as more people are attracted to products bearing a well-known brand like Prada or Cartier. And thanks to the rapid growth and integration into the global economy of countries, such as China, with weak central governments and ineffective laws, producing and exporting near perfect knockoffs are both less expensive and less risky. In the words of the CEO of one of the best known Swiss watchmakers: "We now compete with a product manufactured by Chinese prisoners. The business is run by the Chinese military, their families and friends, using roughly the same machines we have, which they purchased at the same industrial fairs we go to. The way we have rationalized this problem is by assuming that their customers and ours are different. The person that buys a pirated copy of one of our $5,000 watches for less than $100 is not a client we are losing. Perhaps it is a future client that some day will want to own the real thing instead of a fake. We may be wrong and we do spend money to fight the piracy of our products. But given that our efforts do not seem to protect us much, we close our eyes and hope for the better." This posture stands in contrast to that of companies that sell cheaper products such as garments, music, or videos, whose revenues are directly affected by piracy.

Governments have attempted to protect intellectual property rights through various means, most notably the World Trade Organization's Agreement on Trade-Related Aspects of Intellectual Property Rights (TRIPS). Several other organizations such as the World Intellectual Property Organization, the World Customs Union, and Interpol are also involved. Yet the large and growing volume of this trade, or a simple stroll in the streets of Manhattan or Madrid, show that governments are far from winning this fight.

Alien Smuggling

The man or woman who sells a bogus Hermes scarf or a Rolex watch in the streets of Milan is likely to be an illegal alien. Just as likely, he or she was transported across several continents by a trafficking network allied with another network that specializes in the illegal copying, manufacturing, and distributing of high-end, brand-name products.

Alien smuggling is a $7 billion a year enterprise and according to the United Nations is the fastest growing business of organized crime. Roughly 500,000 people enter the United States illegally each year—about the same number as illegally enter the European Union, and part of the approximately 150 million who live outside their countries of origin. Many of these backdoor travelers are voluntary migrants who pay smugglers up to $35,000, the top-dollar fee for passage from China to New York. Others, instead, are trafficked—that is, bought and sold internationally—as commodities. The U.S. Congressional Research Service reckons that each year between 1 million and 2 million people are trafficked across borders, the majority of whom are women and children. A woman can be "bought" in Timisoara, Romania, for between $50 and $200 and "resold" in Western Europe for 10 times that price. The United Nations Children's Fund estimates that cross-border smugglers in Central and Western Africa enslave 200,000 children a year. Traffickers initially tempt victims with job offers or, in the case of children, with offers of adoption in wealthier countries, and then keep the victims in subservience through physical violence, debt bondage, passport confiscation, and threats of arrest, deportation, or violence against their families back home.

Governments everywhere are enacting tougher immigration laws and devoting more time, money, and technology to fight the flow of illegal aliens. But the plight of the United Kingdom's government illustrates how tough that fight is. The British government throws money at the problem, plans to use the Royal Navy and Royal Air Force to intercept illegal immigrants, and imposes large fines on truck drivers who (generally unwittingly) transport stowaways. Still, 42,000 of the 50,000 refugees who have passed through the Sangatte camp (a main entry point for illegal immigration to the United Kingdom) over the last three years have made it to Britain. At current rates, it will take 43 years for Britain to clear its asylum backlog. And that country is an island. Continental nations such as Spain, Italy, or the United States face an even greater challenge as immigration pressures overwhelm their ability to control the inflow of illegal aliens.

Money Laundering

The Cayman Islands has a population of 36,000. It also has more than 2,200 mutual funds, 500 insurance companies, 60,000 businesses, and 600 banks and trust companies with almost $800 billion in assets. Not surprisingly, it figures prominently in any discussion of money laundering. So does the United States, several of whose major banks have been caught up in investigations of money laundering, tax evasion, and fraud. Few, if any, countries can claim to be free of the practice of helping individuals and companies hide funds from governments, creditors, business partners, or even family members, including the proceeds of tax evasion, gambling, and other crimes. Estimates of the volume of global money laundering range between 2 and 5 percent of the world's annual gross national product, or between $800 billion and $2 trillion.

Smuggling money, gold coins, and other valuables is an ancient trade. Yet in the last two decades, new political and economic trends coincided with technological changes to make this ancient trade easier, cheaper, and less risky. Political changes led to the deregulation of financial markets that now facilitate cross-border money transfers, and technological changes made distance less of a factor and money less "physical." Suitcases full of banknotes are still a key tool for money launderers, but computers, the Internet, and complex financial schemes that combine legal and illegal practices and institutions are more common. The sophistication of technology, the complex web of financial institutions that crisscross the globe, and the ease with which "dirty" funds can be electronically morphed into legitimate assets make the regulation of international flows of money a daunting task. In Russia, for example, it is estimated that by the mid-1990s organized crime groups had set up 700 legal and financial institutions to launder their money.

Faced with this growing tide, governments have stepped up their efforts to clamp down on rogue international banking, tax havens, and money laundering. The imminent, large-scale introduction of e-money—cards with microchips that can store large amounts of money and thus can be easily transported outside regular channels or simply exchanged among individuals—will only magnify this challenge.

Why Goverments Can't Win

The fundamental changes that have given the five wars new intensity over the last decade are likely to persist. Technology will continue to spread widely; criminal networks will be able to exploit these technologies more quickly than governments that must cope with tight budgets, bureaucracies, media scrutiny, and electorates. International trade will continue to grow, providing more cover for the expansion of illicit trade. International migration will likewise grow, with much the same effect, offering ethnically based gangs an ever growing supply of recruits and victims. The spread of democracy may also help criminal cartels, which can manipulate weak public institutions by corrupting police officers or tempting politicians with offers of cash for their increasingly expensive election campaigns. And ironically, even the spread of international law—with its growing web of embargoes, sanctions, and conventions—will offer criminals new opportunities for providing forbidden goods to those on the wrong side of the international community.

These changes may affect each of the five wars in different ways, but these conflicts will continue to share four common characteristics:

They are not bound by geography.

Some forms of crime have always had an international component: The Mafia was born in Sicily and exported to the United States, and smuggling has always been by definition international. But the five wars are truly global. Where is the theater or front line of the war on drugs? Is it Colombia or Miami? Myanmar (Burma) or Milan? Where are the battles against money launderers being fought? In Nauru or in London? Is China the main theater in the war against the infringement of intellectual property, or are the trenches of that war on the Internet?

They defy traditional notions of sovereignty.

Al Qaeda's members have passports and nationalities—and often more than one—but they are truly stateless. Their allegiance is to their cause, not to any nation. The same is also true of the criminal networks engaged in the five wars. The same, however, is patently not true of government employees—police officers, customs agents, and judges—who fight them. This asymmetry is a crippling disadvantage for governments waging these wars. Highly paid, hypermotivated, and resource-rich combatants on one side of the wars (the criminal gangs) can seek refuge in and take advantage of national borders, but combatants of the other side (the governments) have fewer resources and are hampered by traditional notions of sovereignty. A former senior CIA official reported that international criminal gangs are able to move people, money, and weapons globally faster than he can move resources inside his own agency, let alone worldwide. Coordination and information sharing among government agencies in different countries has certainly improved, especially after September 11. Yet these tactics fall short of what is needed to combat agile organizations that can exploit every nook and cranny of an evolving but imperfect body of international law and multilateral treaties.

They pit governments against market forces.

In each of the five wars, one or more government bureaucracies fight to contain the disparate, uncoordinated actions of thousands of independent, stateless organizations. These groups are motivated by large profits obtained by exploiting international price differentials, an unsatisfied demand, or the cost advantages produced by theft. Hourly wages for a Chinese cook are far higher in Manhattan than in Fujian. A gram of cocaine in Kansas City is 17,000 percent more expensive than in Bogotá. Fake Italian valves are 40 percent cheaper because counterfeiters don't have to cover the costs of developing the product. A well-funded guerrilla group will pay anything to get the weapons it needs. In each of these five wars, the incentives to successfully overcome government-imposed limits to trade are simply enormous.

They pit bureaucracies against networks.

The same network that smuggles East European women to Berlin may be involved in distributing opium there. The proceeds of the latter fund the purchase of counterfeit Bulgari watches made in China and often sold on the streets of Manhattan by illegal African immigrants. Colombian drug cartels make deals with Ukrainian arms traffickers, while Wall Street brokers controlled by the U.S.-based Mafia have been known to front for Russian money launderers. These highly decentralized groups and individuals are bound by strong ties of loyalty and common purpose and organized around semiautonomous clusters or "nodes" capable of operating swiftly and flexibly. John Arquilla and David Ronfeldt, two of the best known experts on these types of organizations, observe that networks often lack central leadership, command, or headquarters, thus "no precise heart or head that can be targeted. The network as a whole (but not necessarily each node) has little to no hierarchy; there may be multiple leaders . . . . Thus the [organization's] design may sometimes appear acephalous (headless), and at other times polycephalous (Hydra-headed)." Typically, governments respond to these challenges by forming interagency task forces or creating new bureaucracies. Consider the creation of the new Department of Homeland Security in the United States, which encompasses 22 former federal agencies and their 170,000 employees and is responsible for, among other things, fighting the war on drugs.

Rethinking the Problem

Governments may never be able to completely eradicate the kind of international trade involved in the five wars. But they can and should do better. There are at least four areas where efforts can yield better ideas on how to tackle the problems posed by these wars:

Develop more flexible notions of sovereignty.

Governments need to recognize that restricting the scope of multilateral action for the sake of protecting their sovereignty is often a moot point. Their sovereignty is compromised daily, not by nation-states but by stateless networks that break laws and cross borders in pursuit of trade. In May 1999, for example, the Venezuelan government denied U.S. planes authorization to fly over Venezuelan territory to monitor air routes commonly used by narcotraffickers. Venezuelan authorities placed more importance on the symbolic value of asserting sovereignty over air space than on the fact that drug traffickers' planes regularly violate Venezuelan territory. Without new forms of codifying and "managing" sovereignty, governments will continue to face a large disadvantage while fighting the five wars.

Strengthen existing multilateral institutions.

The global nature of these wars means no government, regardless of its economic, political, or military power, will make much progress acting alone. If this seems obvious, then why does Interpol, the multilateral agency in charge of fighting international crime, have a staff of 384, only 112 of whom are police officers, and an annual budget of $28 million, less than the price of some boats or planes used by drug traffickers? Similarly, Europol, Europe's Interpol equivalent, has a staff of 240 and a budget of $51 million.

One reason Interpol is poorly funded and staffed is because its 181 member governments don't trust each other. Many assume, and perhaps rightly so, that the criminal networks they are fighting have penetrated the police departments of other countries and that sharing information with such compromised officials would not be prudent. Others fear today's allies will become tomorrow's enemies. Still others face legal impediments to sharing intelligence with fellow nation-states or have intelligence services and law enforcement agencies with organizational cultures that make effective collaboration almost

impossible. Progress will only be made if the world's governments unite behind stronger, more effective multilateral organizations.

Devise new mechanisms and institutions.

These five wars stretch and even render obsolete many of the existing institutions, legal frameworks, military doctrines, weapons systems, and law enforcement techniques on which governments have relied for years. Analysts need to rethink the concept of war "fronts" defined by geography and the definition of "combatants" according to the Geneva Convention. The functions of intelligence agents, soldiers, police officers, customs agents, or immigration officers need rethinking and adaptation to the new realities. Policymakers also need to reconsider the notion that ownership is essentially a physical reality and not a "virtual" one or that only sovereign nations can issue money when thinking about ways to fight the five wars.

Move from repression to regulation.

Beating market forces is next to impossible. In some cases, this reality may force governments to move from repressing the market to regulating it. In others, creating market incentives may be better than using bureaucracies to curb the excesses of these markets. Technology can often accomplish more than government policies can. For example, powerful encryption techniques can better protect software or CDs from being copied in Ukraine than would making the country enforce patents and copyrights and trademarks.

In all of the five wars, government agencies fight against networks motivated by the enormous profit opportunities created by other government agencies. In all cases, these profits can be traced to some form of government intervention that creates a major imbalance between demand and supply and makes prices and profit margins skyrocket. In some cases, these government interventions are often justified and it would be imprudent to eliminate them—governments can't simply walk away from the fight against trafficking in heroin, human beings, or weapons of mass destruction. But society can better deal with other segments of these kinds of illegal trade through regulation, not prohibition. Policymakers must focus on opportunities where market regulation can ameliorate problems that have defied approaches based on prohibition and armed interdiction of international trade.

Ultimately, governments, politicians, and voters need to realize that the way in which the world is conducting these five wars is doomed to fail—not for lack of effort, resources, or political will but because the collective thinking that guides government strategies in the five wars is rooted in wrong ideas, false assumptions, and obsolete institutions. Recognizing that governments have no chance of winning unless they change the ways they wage these wars is an indispensable first step in the search for solutions.

Moisés Naím is editor of FOREIGN POLICY magazine.

Spreading the Wealth

17

DAVID D. DOLLAR
AND AART KRAAY

A Rising Tide

One of the main claims of the antiglobalization movement is that globalization is widening the gap between the haves and the have-nots. It benefits the rich and does little for the poor, perhaps even making their lot harder. As union leader Jay Mazur put it in these pages, "globalization has dramatically increased inequality between and within nations" ("Labor's New Internationalism," January/February 2000). The problem with this new conventional wisdom is that the best evidence available shows the exact opposite to be true. So far, the current wave of globalization, which started around 1980, has actually promoted economic equality and reduced poverty.

Global economic integration has complex effects on income, culture, society, and the environment. But in the debate over globalization's merits, its impact on poverty is particularly important. If international trade and investment primarily benefit the rich, many people will feel that restricting trade to protect jobs, culture, or the environment is worth the costs. But if restricting trade imposes further hardship on poor people in the developing world, many of the same people will think otherwise.

Three facts bear on this question. First, a long-term global trend toward greater inequality prevailed for at least 200 years; it peaked around 1975. But since then, it has stabilized and possibly even reversed. The chief reason for the change has been the accelerated growth of two large and initially poor countries: China and India.

Second, a strong correlation links increased participation in international trade and investment on the one hand and faster growth on the other. The developing world can be divided into a "globalizing" group of countries that have seen rapid increases in trade and foreign investment over the last two decades -- well above the rates for rich countries -- and a "nonglobalizing" group that trades even less of its income today than it did 20 years ago. The aggregate annual per capita growth rate of the globalizing group accelerated steadily from one percent in the 1960s to five percent in the 1990s. During that latter decade, in contrast, rich countries grew at two percent and nonglobalizers at only one percent. Economists are cautious about drawing conclusions concerning causality, but they largely agree that openness to foreign trade and investment (along with complementary reforms) explains the faster growth of the globalizers.

Third, and contrary to popular perception, globalization has not resulted in higher inequality within economies. Inequality has indeed gone up in some countries (such as China) and down in others (such as the Philippines). But those changes are not systematically linked to globalization measures such as trade and investment flows, tariff rates, and the presence of capital controls. Instead, shifts in inequality stem more from domestic education, taxes, and social policies.

World Income Inequality, 1820–1995
(in percent)

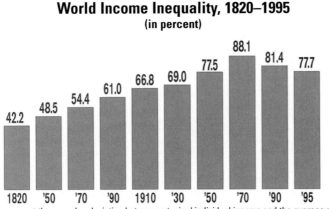

Note: Figures represent the mean log deviation between a typical individual income and the average per capita income.
Sources: F.Bourguignon and C.Morrisson,"Inequality Among World Citizens,1820 –1992," working paper 2001-25 (Paris: Department of Applied and Theoretical Economics, 2001); and David Dollar,"Globalization, Inequality, and Poverty Since 1980," World Bank background paper,available at http://www.worldbank.org/research/global.

In general, higher growth rates in globalizing developing countries have translated into higher incomes for the poor. Even with its increased inequality, for example, China has seen the most spectacular reduction of poverty in world history -- which was supported by opening its economy to foreign trade and investment.

Although globalization can be a powerful force for poverty reduction, its beneficial results are not inevitable. If policymakers hope to tap the full potential of economic integration and sustain its benefits, they must address three critical challenges. A growing protectionist movement in rich countries that aims to limit integration with poor ones must be stopped in its tracks. Developing countries need to acquire the kinds of institutions and policies that will allow them to prosper under globalization, both of which may be different from place to place. And more migration, both domestic and international, must be permitted when geography limits the potential for development.

The Great Divide

Over the past 200 years, different local economies around the world have become more integrated while the growth rate of the global economy has accelerated dramatically. Although it is impossible to prove causal link-age between the two developments -- since there are no other world economies to be tested against -- evidence suggests the arrows run in both directions. As Adam Smith argued, a larger market permits a finer division of labor, which in turn facilitates innovation and learning by doing. Some of that innovation involves transportation and communications technologies that lower costs and increase integration. So it is easy to see how integration and innovation can be mutually supportive.

Different locations have become more integrated because of increased flows of goods, capital, and knowledge. From 1820 to 1914, international trade increased faster than the global economy. Trade rose from about 2 percent of world income in 1820 to 18 percent in 1914. The globalization of trade took a step backward during the protectionist period of the Great Depression and World War II, and by 1950 trade (in relation to income) was lower than it had been in 1914. But thanks to a series of multilateral trade liberalizations under the General Agreement on Tariffs and Trade (GATT), trade dramatically expanded among industrialized countries between 1960 and 1980. Most developing countries remained largely isolated from this trade because of their own inward-focused policies, but the success of such notable exceptions as Taiwan and South Korea eventually helped encourage other developing economies to open themselves up to foreign trade and investment.

International capital flows, measured as foreign ownership of assets relative to world income, also grew during the first wave of globalization and declined during the Great Depression and World War II; they did not return to 1914 levels until 1980. But since then, such flows have increased markedly and changed their nature as well. One hundred years ago, foreign capital typically financed public infrastructure projects (such as canals and railroads) or direct investment related to natural resources. Today, in contrast, the bulk of capital flows to developing countries is direct investments tied to manufacturing and services.

The change in the nature of capital flows is clearly related to concurrent advances in economic integration, such as cheaper and faster transportation and revolutionary changes in telecommunications. Since 1920, seagoing freight charges have declined by about two-thirds and air travel costs by 84 percent; the cost of a three-minute call from New York City to London has dropped by 99 percent. Today, production in widely differing locations can be integrated in ways that simply were not possible before.

Another aspect of integration has been the movement of people. Yet here the trend is reversed: there is much more international travel than in the past but much less permanent migration. Between 1870 and 1910, about ten percent of the world's population relocated permanently from one country to another; over the past 25 years, only one to two percent have done so.

As economic integration has progressed, the annual growth rate of the world economy has accelerated, from 1 percent in the mid-nineteenth century to 3.5 percent in 1960-2000. Sustained over many years, such a jump in growth makes a huge difference in real living standards. It now takes only two to three years, for example, for the world economy to produce the same amount of goods and services that it did during the entire nineteenth century. Such a comparison is arguably a serious understatement of the true difference, since most of what is consumed today -- airline travel, cars, televisions, synthetic fibers, life-extending drugs -- did not exist 200 years ago. For any of these goods or services, therefore, the growth rate of output since 1820 is infinite. Human productivity has increased almost unimaginably.

All this tremendous growth in wealth was distributed very unequally up to about 1975, but since then growing equality has taken hold. One good measure of inequality among individuals worldwide is the mean log deviation -- a measure of the gap between the income of any randomly selected person and a general average. It takes into account the fact that income distributions everywhere are skewed in favor of the rich, so that the typical person is poorer than the group average; the more skewed the distribution, the larger the gap. Per capita income in the world today, for example, is around $5,000, whereas a randomly selected person would most likely be living on close to $1,000 -- 80 percent less. That gap translates into a mean log deviation of 0.8.

Taking this approach, an estimate of the world distribution of income among individuals shows rising inequality between 1820 and 1975. In that period, the gap between the typical person and world per capita income increased from about 40 percent to about 80 percent. Since changes in income inequality within countries were small, the increase in inequality was driven mostly by differences in growth rates across countries. Areas that were already relatively rich in 1820 (notably, Europe and the United States) grew faster than poor areas (notably, China and India). Global inequality peaked sometime in the 1970s, but it then stabilized and even began to decline, largely because growth in China and India began to accelerate.

Another way of looking at global inequality is to examine what is happening to the extreme poor -- those people living on less than $1 per day. Although the percentage of the world's population living in poverty has declined over time, the absolute number rose fairly steadily until 1980. During the Great Depression and World War II, the number of poor increased particularly sharply, and it declined somewhat immediately thereafter. The world economy grew strongly between 1960 and 1980, but the number of poor rose because growth did not occur in the places where the worst-off live. But since then, the most rapid growth has occurred in poor locations. Consequently the number of poor has declined by 200 million since 1980. Again, this trend is explained primarily by the rapid income growth in China and India, which together in 1980 accounted for about one-third of the world's population and more than 60 percent of the world's extreme poor.

Upward Bound

The shift in the trend in global inequality coincides with the shift in the economic strategies of several large developing countries. Following World War II, most developing regions chose strategies that focused inward and discouraged integration with the global economy. But these approaches were not particularly successful, and throughout the 1960s and 1970s developing countries on the whole grew less rapidly than industrialized ones. The oil shocks and U.S. inflation of the 1970s created severe problems for them, contributing to negative growth, high inflation, and debt crises over the next several years. Faced with these disappointing results, several developing countries began to alter their strategies starting in the 1980s.

For example, China had an extremely closed economy until the mid-1970s. Although Beijing's initial economic reform focused on agriculture, a key part of its approach since the 1980s has involved opening up foreign trade and investment, including a drop in its tariff rates by two-thirds and its nontariff barriers by even more. These reforms have led to unprecedented economic growth in the country's coastal provinces and more moderate growth in the interior. From 1978 to 1994 the Chinese economy grew annually by 9 percent, while exports grew by 14 percent and imports by 13 percent. Of course, China and other globalizing developing countries have pursued a wide range of

reforms, not just economic openness. Beijing has strengthened property rights through land reform and moved from a planned economy toward a market-oriented one, and these measures have contributed to its integration as well as to its growth.

Other developing countries have also opened up as a part of broader reform programs. During the 1990s, India liberalized foreign trade and investment with good results; its annual per capita income growth now tops four percent. It too has pursued a broad agenda of reform and has moved away from a highly regulated, planned system. Meanwhile, Uganda and Vietnam are the best examples of very low-income countries that have increased their participation in trade and investment and prospered as a result. And in the western hemisphere, Mexico is noteworthy both for signing its free-trade agreement with the United States and Canada in 1993 and for its rapid growth since then, especially in the northern regions near the U.S. border.

These cases illustrate how openness to foreign trade and investment, coupled with complementary reforms, typically leads to faster growth. India, China, Vietnam, Uganda, and Mexico are not isolated examples; in general, countries that have become more open have grown faster. The best way to illustrate this trend is to rank developing countries in order of their increases in trade relative to national income over the past 20 years. The top third of this list can be thought of as the "globalizing" camp, and the bottom two-thirds as the "nonglobalizing" camp. The globalizers have increased their trade relative to income by 104 percent over the past two decades, compared to 71 percent for rich countries. The nonglobalizers, meanwhile, actually trade less today than they did 20 years ago. The globalizers have also cut their import tariffs by 22 percentage points on average, compared to only 11 percentage points for the nonglobalizers.

How have the globalizers fared in terms of growth? Their average annual growth rates accelerated from 1 percent in the 1960s to 3 percent in the 1970s, 4 percent in the 1980s, and 5 percent in the 1990s. Rich countries' annual

GDP Growth and Poverty Reduction in Uganda, India, Vietnam, and China, 1992–98 in percent per year

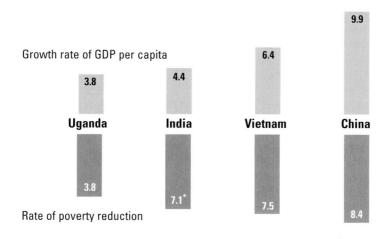

*India poverty reduction figure is for 1993–99.
Source:* David Dollar, "Globalization, Inequality, and Poverty Since 1980," World Bank background paper, available at http://www.worldbank.org/research/global.

growth rates, by comparison, slowed to about 2 percent in the 1990s, and the nonglobalizers saw their growth rates decline from 3 percent in the 1970s to 1 percent in the 1980s and 1990s.

The same pattern can be observed on a local level. Within both China and India, the locations that are integrating with the global economy are growing much more rapidly than the disconnected regions. Indian states, for example, vary significantly in the quality of their investment climates as measured by government efficiency, corruption, and infrastructure. Those states with better investment climates have integrated themselves more closely with outside markets and have experienced more investment (domestic and foreign) than their less-integrated counterparts. Moreover, states that were initially poor and then created good investment climates had stronger poverty reduction in the 1990s than those not integrating with the global economy. Such internal comparisons are important because, by holding national trade and macroeconomic policies constant, they reveal how important it is to complement trade liberalization with institutional reform so that integration can actually occur.

The accelerated growth rates of globalizing countries such as China, India, and Vietnam are consistent with cross-country comparisons that find openness going hand in hand with faster growth. The most that these studies can establish is that more trade and investment is highly correlated with higher growth, so one needs to be careful about drawing conclusions about causality. Still, the overall evidence from individual cases and cross-country correlation is persuasive. As economists Peter Lindert and Jeffrey Williamson have written, "even though no one study can establish that openness to trade has unambiguously helped the representative Third World economy, the preponderance of evidence supports this conclusion." They go on to note that "there are no anti-global victories to report for the postwar Third World."

Contrary to the claims of the antiglobalization movement, therefore, greater openness to international trade and investment has in fact helped narrow the gap between rich and poor countries rather than widen it. During the 1990s, the economies of the globalizers, with a combined population of about 3 billion, grew more than twice as fast as the

Net Investment Rates in India, 1999
(in percent)

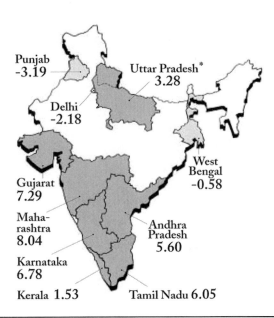

*In September 2000,a new state, Uttaranchal,was created out of the northwestern section of Uttar Pradesh. *Note*: Net investment rates represent the annual rate of growth of the capital stock of domestic and international firms. A negative rate implies that firms are pulling out.

Source: O.Goswami et al., "Competitiveness of Indian Manufacturing: Results of a Firm-Level Survey " (New Delhi: Confederation of Indian Industry, 2001).

Punjab -3.19
Uttar Pradesh* 3.28
Delhi -2.18
West Bengal -0.58
Gujarat 7.29
Maharashtra 8.04
Andhra Pradesh 5.60
Karnataka 6.78
Kerala 1.53
Tamil Nadu 6.05

---

rich countries. The nonglobalizers, in contrast, grew only half as fast and nowadays lag further and further behind. Much of the discussion of global inequality assumes that there is growing divergence between the developing world and the rich world, but this is simply not true. The most important development in global inequality in recent decades is the growing divergence within the developing world, and it is directly related to whether countries take advantage of the economic benefits that globalization can offer.

The Path of Poverty

The antiglobalization movement also claims that economic integration is worsening inequality within countries as well as between them. Until the mid-1980s, there was insufficient evidence to support strong conclusions on this important topic. But now more and more developing countries have begun to conduct household income and consumption surveys of reasonable quality. (In low-income countries, these surveys typically track what households actually consume because so much of their real income is self-produced and not part of the money economy.) Good surveys now exist for 137 countries, and many

go back far enough to measure changes in inequality over time.

One way of looking at inequality within countries is to focus on what happens to the bottom 20 percent of households as globalization and growth proceed apace. Across all countries, incomes of the poor grow at around the same rate as GDP. Of course, there is a great deal of variation around that average relationship. In some countries, income distribution has shifted in favor of the poor; in others, against them. But these shifts cannot be explained by any globalization-related variable. So it simply cannot be said that inequality necessarily rises with more trade, more foreign investment, and lower tariffs. For many globalizers, the overall change in distribution was small, and in some cases (such as the Philippines and Malaysia) it was even in favor of the poor. What changes in inequality do reflect are country-specific policies on education, taxes, and social protection.

It is important not to misunderstand this finding. China is an important example of a country that has had a large increase in inequality in the past decade, when the income of the bottom 20 percent has risen much less rapidly than per capita income. This trend may be related to greater openness, although domestic liberalization is a more likely cause. China started out in the 1970s with a highly equal distribution of income, and part of its reform has deliberately aimed at increasing the returns on education, which financially reward the better schooled. But the Chinese case is not typical; inequality has not increased in most of the developing countries that have opened up to foreign trade and investment. Furthermore, income distribution in China may have become more unequal, but the income of the poor in China has still risen rapidly. In fact, the country's progress in reducing poverty has been one of the most dramatic successes in history.

Because increased trade usually accompanies more rapid growth and does not systematically change household-income distribution, it generally is associated with improved well-being of the poor. Vietnam nicely illustrates this finding. As the nation has opened up, it has experienced a large increase in per capita income and no significant change in inequality. Thus the income of the poor has risen dramatically, and the number of Vietnamese living in absolute poverty dropped sharply from 75 percent of the population in 1988 to 37 percent in 1998. Of the poorest 5 percent of households in 1992, 98 percent were better off six years later. And the improved well-being is not just a matter of income. Child labor has declined, and school enrollment has increased. It should be no surprise that the vast majority of poor households in Vietnam benefited immediately from a more liberalized trading system, since the country's opening has resulted in exports of rice (produced by most of the poor farmers) and labor-intensive products such as footwear. But the experience of China and Vietnam is not unique. India and Uganda also enjoyed rapid poverty reduction as they grew along with their integration into the global economy.

The Open Societies

These findings have important implications for developing countries, for rich countries such as the United States, and for those who care about global poverty. All parties should recognize that the most recent wave of globalization has been a powerful force for equality and poverty reduction, and they should commit themselves to seeing that it continues despite the obstacles lying ahead.

It is not inevitable that globalization will proceed. In 1910, many believed globalization was unstoppable; they soon received a rude shock. History is not likely to repeat itself in the same way, but it is worth noting that antiglobalization sentiments are on the rise. A growing number of political leaders in the developing world realize that an open trading system is very much in their countries' interest. They would do well to heed Mexican President Vicente Fox, who said recently,

> "We are convinced that globalization is good and it's good when you do your homework, ... keep your fundamentals in line on the economy, build up high levels of education, respect the rule of law... When you do your part, we are convinced that you get the benefit."

But today the narrow interests opposed to further integration -- especially those in the rich countries -- appear to be much more energetic than their opponents. In Quebec City last spring and in Genoa last summer, a group of democratically elected leaders gathered to discuss how to pursue economic integration and improve the lives of their peoples. Antiglobalization demonstrators were quite effective in disrupting the meetings and drawing media attention to themselves. Leaders in developed and developing countries alike must make the proglobalization case more directly and effectively or risk having their opponents dominate the discussion and stall the process.

In addition, industrialized countries still raise protectionist measures against agricultural and labor-intensive products. Reducing those barriers would help developing countries significantly. The poorer areas of the world would benefit from further openings of their own markets as well, since 70 percent of the tariff barriers that developing countries face are from other developing countries.

If globalization proceeds, its potential to be an equalizing force will depend on whether poor countries manage to integrate themselves into the global economic system. True integration requires not just trade liberalization but wide-ranging institutional reform. Many of the nonglobalizing developing countries, such as Myanmar, Nigeria, Ukraine, and Pakistan, offer an unattractive investment climate. Even if they decide to open themselves up to trade, not much is likely to happen unless other reforms are also pursued. It is not easy to predict the reform paths of these countries; some of the relative successes in recent years, such as China, India, Uganda, and Vietnam, have come as quite a surprise. But as long as a location has weak institutions and policies, people living there are going to fall further behind the rest of the world.

Through their trade policies, rich countries can make it easier for those developing countries that do choose to open up and join the global trading club. But in recent years, the rich countries have been doing just the opposite. GATT was originally built around agreements concerning trade practices. Now, institutional harmonization, such as agreement on policies toward intellectual property rights, is a requirement for joining the WTO. Any sort of regulation of labor and environmental standards made under the threat of WTO sanctions would take this requirement for harmonization much further. Such measures would be neoprotectionist in effect, because they would thwart the integration of developing countries into the world economy and discourage trade between poor countries and rich ones.

The WTO meeting in Doha was an important step forward on trade integration. More forcefully than in Seattle, leaders of industrial countries were willing to make the case for further integration and put on the table issues of central concern to developing nations: access to pharmaceutical patents, use of antidumping measures against developing countries, and agricultural subsidies. The new round of trade negotiations launched at Doha has the potential to reverse the current trend, which makes it more difficult for poor countries to integrate with the world economy.

A final potential obstacle to successful and equitable globalization relates to geography. There is no inherent reason why coastal China should be poor; the same goes for southern India, northern Mexico, and Vietnam. All of these locations are near important markets or trade routes but were long held back by misguided policies. Now, with appropriate reforms, they are starting to grow rapidly and take their natural place in the world. But the same cannot be said for Mali, Chad, or other countries or regions cursed with "poor geography" -- i.e., distance from markets, inherently high transport costs, and challenging health and agricultural problems. It would be naive to think that trade and investment alone can alleviate poverty in all locations. In fact, for those locations with poor geography, trade liberalization is less important than developing proper health care systems or providing basic infrastructure -- or letting people move elsewhere.

Migration from poor locations is the missing factor in the current wave of globalization that could make a large contribution to reducing poverty. Each year, 83 million people are added to the world's population, 82 million of them in the developing world. In Europe and Japan, moreover, the population is aging and the labor force is set to shrink. Migration of relatively unskilled workers from South to North would thus offer clear economic benefits to both. Most migration from South to North is economically motivated, and it raises the living standard of the migrant while benefiting the sending country in three ways. First, it reduces the South's labor force and thus raises wages for those who remain behind. Second, migrants send remittances of hard currency back home. Finally, migration bolsters transnational trade and investment networks. In the case of Mexico, for example, ten percent of its citizens live and work in the United States, taking pressure off its own labor market and raising wages there. India gets six times as much in remittances from its workers overseas as it gets in foreign aid.

Unlike trade, however, migration remains highly restricted and controversial. Some critics perceive a disruptive impact on society and culture and fear downward pressure on wages and rising unemployment in the richer countries. Yet anti-immigration lobbies ignore the fact that geographical economic disparities are so strong that illegal immigration is growing rapidly anyway, despite restrictive policies. In a perverse irony, some of the worst abuses of globalization occur because there is not enough of it in key economic areas such as labor flows. Human traffic, for example, has become a highly lucrative, unregulated business in which illegal migrants are easy prey for exploitation.

Realistically, none of the industrialized countries is going to adopt open migration. But they should reconsider their migration policies. Some, for example, have a strong bias in their immigration rules toward highly skilled workers, which in fact spurs a "brain drain" from the developing world. Such policies do little to stop the flow of unskilled workers and instead push many of these people into the illegal category. If rich countries would legally accept more unskilled workers, they could address their own looming labor shortages, improve living standards in developing countries, and reduce illegal human traffic and its abuses.

In sum, the integration of poor economies with richer ones over the past two decades has provided many opportunities for poor people to improve their lives. Examples of the beneficiaries of globalization can be found among Mexican migrants, Chinese factory workers, Vietnamese peasants, and Ugandan farmers. Many of the better-off in developing and rich countries alike also benefit. After all the rhetoric about globalization is stripped away, many of the policy questions come down to whether the rich world will make integrating with the world economy easy for those poor communities that want to do so. The world's poor have a large stake in how the rich countries answer.

David Dollar and Aart Kraay are economists at the World Bank's Development Research Group. The views expressed here are their own.

18

The New Wave of Globalization and Its Economic Effects

THE WORLD BANK

Since about 1980 there has been unprecedented global economic integration. Globalization has happened before, but not like this. Economic integration occurs through trade, migration, and capital flows. Figure 1.1 tracks these flows. World trade is measured relative to world income. Capital flows are proxied by the stock of foreign capital in developing countries relative to their GDP. Migration is proxied by the number of immigrants to the United States. Historically, before about 1870 none of these flows was sufficiently large to warrant the term globalization.

For about 45 years, starting around 1870, all these flows rapidly became substantial, driven by falling transport costs. What had been many separate national economies started to integrate: the world's economies globalized. However, globalization is not an inevitable process; this first wave was reversed by a retreat into nationalism. Between 1914 and 1945 transport costs continued to fall, but trade barriers rose as countries followed beggar-thy-neighbor policies. By the end of that period trade had collapsed back to around its 1870 level. After 1945 governments cooperated to rein in protectionism. As trade barriers came down, and transport costs continued to fall, trade revived. This second wave of globalization, which lasted until around 1980, was approximately a return to the patterns of the first wave.

Since 1980 many developing countries—the "new globalizers"—have broken into world markets for manufactured goods and services. There has been a dramatic rise in the share of manufactures in the exports of developing countries: from about 25 percent in 1980 to more than 80 percent today. There has also been a substantial increase in FDI. This marks an important change: low-income countries are now competing head-on with high-income countries while previously they specialized in primary commodities. During this new wave of global market integration, world trade has grown massively. Markets for merchandise are now much more integrated than ever before.

In this chapter we contrast this new third wave of globalization with the two previous waves. We analyze its main processes and show how it is affecting poverty and inequality.

Previous Waves of Globalization and Reversals

Most developing countries have two potential sources of comparative advantage in international markets: abundant labor and abundant land. Before about 1870 neither of these potentials was realized and international trade was negligible.

The first wave of globalization: 1870 – 1914

The first wave of global integration, from 1870 to 1914, was triggered by a combination of falling transport costs, such as the

Three waves of globalization
Figure 1.1

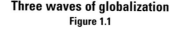

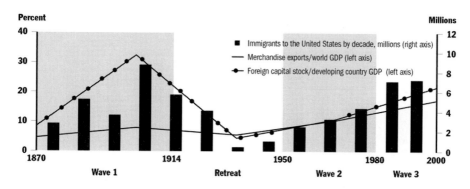

Source: Foreign capital stock/developing country GDP: Maddison (2001), table 3.3; Merchandise exports/world GDP: Maddison (2001), table F-5; Migration: Immigration and Naturalization Service (1998).

switch from sail to steamships, and reductions in tariff barriers, pioneered by an Anglo-French agreement. Cheaper transport and the lifting of man-made barriers opened up the possibility of using abundant land. New technologies such as railways created huge opportunities for land-intensive commodity exports. The resulting pattern of trade was that land-intensive primary commodities were exchanged for manufactures. Exports as a share of world income nearly doubled to about 8 percent (Maddison 2001).

The production of primary commodities required people. Sixty million migrated from Europe to North America and Australia to work on newly available land. Because land was abundant in the newly settled areas, incomes were high and fairly equal, while the labor exodus from Europe tightened labor markets and raised wages both absolutely and relative to the returns on land. South-South labor flows were also extensive (though less well documented). Lindert and Williamson (2001b) speculate that the flows from densely populated China and India to less densely populated Sri Lanka, Burma, Thailand, the Philippines, and Vietnam were of the same order of magnitude as the movements from Europe to the Americas.[1] That would make the total labor flows during the first wave of globalization nearly 10 percent of the world's population.

The production of primary commodities for export required not just labor but large amounts of capital. As of 1870 the foreign capital stock in developing countries was only about 9 percent of their income (figure 1.1). However, institutions needed for financial markets were copied. These institutions, combined with the improvements in information permitted by the telegraph, enabled governments in developing countries to tap into the major capital markets. Indeed, during this period around half of all British savings were channeled abroad. By 1914 the foreign capital stock of developing countries had risen to 32 percent of their income.

Globally, growth accelerated sharply. Per capita incomes, which had risen by 0.5 percent per year in the previous 50 years, rose by an annual average of 1.3 percent. Did this lead to more or less equality? The countries that participated in it often took off economically, both the exporters of manufactures, people and capital, and the importers. Argentina, Australia, New Zealand, and the United States became among the richest countries in the world by exporting primary commodities while importing people, institutions, and capital. All these countries left the rest of the world behind.

Between the globalizing countries them-

Worldwide household inequality, 1820–1910

Figure 1.2

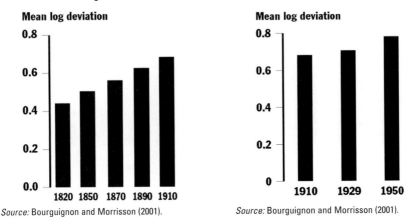

Mean log deviation

1820 1850 1870 1890 1910

Source: Bourguignon and Morrisson (2001).

Worldwide household inequality, 1910–50

Figure 1.3

Mean log deviation

1910   1929   1950

Source: Bourguignon and Morrisson (2001).

selves there was convergence. Mass migration was a major force equalizing incomes between them. "Emigration is estimated to have raised Irish wages by 32 percent, Italian by 28 percent and Norwegian by 10 percent. Immigration is estimated to have lowered Argentine wages by 22 percent, Australian by 15 percent, Canadian by 16 percent and American by 8 percent." Indeed, migration was probably more important than either trade or capital movements (Lindert and Williamson 2001b).

The impact of globalization on inequality within countries depended in part on the ownership of land. Exports from developing countries were land-intensive primary commodities. Within developing countries this benefited predominantly the people who owned the land. Since most were colonies, land ownership itself was subject to the power imbalance inherent in the colonial relationship. Where land ownership was concentrated, as in Latin America, increased trade could be associated with increased inequality. Where land was more equally owned, as in West Africa, the benefits of trade were spread more widely. Conversely, in Europe, the region importing land-intensive goods, globalization ruined landowners. For example, Cannadine (1990) describes the spectacular economic

collapse of the English aristocracy between 1880 and 1914. In Europe the first wave of globalization also coincided with the establishment for the first time in history of the great legislative pillars of social protection— free mass education, worker insurance, and pensions (Gray 1998).

Ever since 1820—50 years before globalization—world income inequality as measured by the mean log deviation had started to increase drastically (figure 1.2).[2] This continued during the first wave of globalization. Despite widening world inequality, the unprecedented increase in growth reduced poverty as never before. In the 50 years before 1870, the incidence of poverty had been virtually constant, falling at the rate of just 0.3 percent per year. During the first globalization wave, the rate of decline more than doubled to 0.8 percent. Even this was insufficient to offset the increase in population growth, so that the absolute number of poor people increased.

The retreat into nationalism: 1914–45

Technology continued to reduce transport costs: during the inter-war years sea freight costs fell by a third. However, trade policy went into reverse. As Mundell (2000) puts it: "The twentieth century began with a highly efficient international monetary system that was destroyed in World War I, and its bungled recreation in the inter-war period brought on the great depression." In turn, governments responded to depression by protectionism: a vain attempt to divert demand into their domestic markets. The United States led the way into the abyss: the Smoot-Hawley tariff, which led to retaliation abroad, was the first: between 1929 and 1933 U.S. imports fell by 30 percent and, significantly, exports fell even more, by almost 40 percent.

Globally, rising protectionism drove international trade back down. By 1950 exports as a share of world income were down to around 5 percent—roughly back to where it had been in 1870. Protectionism had undone 80 years of technical progress in transport.

During the retreat into nationalism capital markets fared even worse than merchandise markets. Most high-income countries imposed controls preventing the export of capital, and many developing countries defaulted on their liabilities. By 1950 the foreign capital stock of developing countries was reduced to just 4 percent of income—far below even the modest level of 1870.

Unsurprisingly, the retreat into nationalism produced anti-immigrant sentiment and governments imposed drastic restrictions on newcomers. For example, immigration to the United States declined from 15 million during 1870–1914 to 6 million between 1914 and 1950.

The massive retreat from globalization did not reverse the trend to greater world inequality. By 1950 the world was far less equal than it had been in 1914 (figure 1.3). Average incomes were, however, substantially lower than had the previous trend been maintained: the world rate of growth fell by about a third. The world's experiment with reversing globalization showed that it was entirely possible but not attractive. The economic historian Angus Maddison summarizes it thus: "Between 1913 and 1950 the world economy grew much more slowly than in 1870–1913, world trade grew much less than world income, and the degree of inequality between regions increased substantially" (Maddison

2001, p. 22).

The combination of a slowdown in growth and a continued increase in inequality sharply reduced the decline in the incidence of poverty— approximately back to what it had been in the period from 1820 to 1870. The decline in the incidence was now well below the rate of population growth, so that the absolute number of poor people increased by about 25 percent. Despite the rise in poverty viewed in terms of income, this was the great period of advances in life expectancy, due to the global spread of improvements in public health. Poverty is multi-dimensional, and not all its aspects are determined by economic performance.

The second wave of globalization: 1945–80

The horrors of the retreat into nationalism gave an impetus to internationalism. The same sentiments that led to the founding of the United Nations persuaded governments to cooperate to reduce the trade barriers they had previously erected. However, trade liberalization was selective both in terms of which countries participated and which products were included. Broadly, by 1980 trade between developed countries in manufactured goods had been substantially freed of barriers, but barriers facing developing countries had been substantially removed only for those primary commodities that did not compete with agriculture in the developed countries. For agriculture and manufactures, developing countries faced severe barriers. Further, most developing countries erected barriers against each other and against developed countries.

The partial reduction in trade barriers was reinforced by continued reductions in transport costs: between 1950 and the late 1970s sea freight charges again fell by a third. Overall, trade doubled relative to world income, approximately recovering the level it had reached during the first wave of globalization. However, the resulting liberalization was very lopsided. For developing countries it restored the North-South pattern of trade— the exchange of manufactures for land-intensive primary commodities—but did not

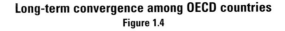

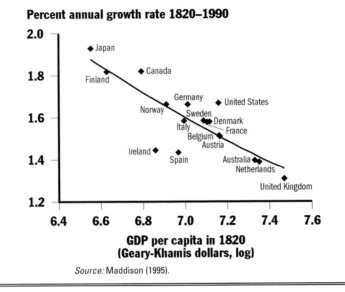

Long-term convergence among OECD countries
Figure 1.4

Percent annual growth rate 1820–1990

GDP per capita in 1820
(Geary-Khamis dollars, log)

Source: Maddison (1995).

restore the international movements of capital and labor.

By contrast, for rich countries the second wave of globalization was spectacular. The lifting of barriers between them greatly expanded the exchange of manufactures. For the first time international specialization within manufacturing became important, allowing agglomeration and scale economies to be realized. This helped to drive up the incomes of the rich countries relative to the rest.

Economies of agglomeration. The second wave introduced a new type of trade: rich country specialization in manufacturing niches that gained productivity from agglomerated clusters. Most trade between developed countries became determined not by comparative advantage based on differences in factor endowments but by cost savings from agglomeration and scale. Because such cost savings are quite specific to each activity, although each individual industry became more and more concentrated geographically, industry as a whole remained very widely dispersed to avoid costs of congestion.

Firms cluster together, some producing the same thing and others connected by verti-

cal linkages (Fujita, Krugman, and Venables 1999). Japanese auto companies, for example, are well known for wanting certain of their parts suppliers to locate within a short distance of the main assembly plant. As Sutton (2000) describes it: "Two-thirds of manufacturing output consists of intermediate goods, sold by one firm to another. The presence of a rich network of manufacturing firms provides a positive externality to each firm in the system, allowing it to acquire inputs locally, thus reducing the costs of transport, of coordination, of monitoring and of contracting."

Clustering enables greater specialization and thus raises productivity. In turn, it depends upon the ability to trade internationally at low cost. The classic statement of this was indeed Adam Smith's: "The division of labor is limited only by the extent of the market" (*The Wealth of Nations*). Smith argued that a larger market permits a finer division of labor, which in turn facilitates innovation. For example, Sokoloff (1988) shows that as the Erie Canal progressed westward in the first half of the 19th century, patent registrations rose county by county as the canal reached them. This pattern suggests that ideas that

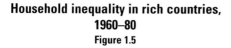

Household inequality in rich countries, 1960–80
Figure 1.5

Household inequality in the developing world, 1960–80
Figure 1.6

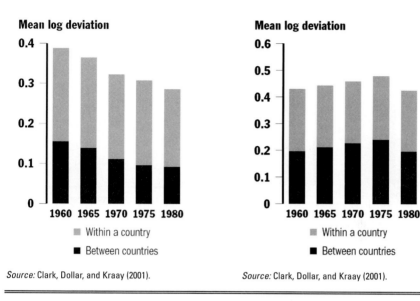

Source: Clark, Dollar, and Kraay (2001).

Source: Clark, Dollar, and Kraay (2001).

were already in people's heads became economically viable through access to a larger market.

However, while agglomeration economies are good news for those in the clusters, they are bad news for those left out. A region may be uncompetitive simply because not enough firms have chosen to locate there. As a result "a 'divided world' may emerge, in which a network of manufacturing firms is clustered in some 'high wage' region, while wages in the remaining regions stay low" (Sutton 2000).

Firms will not shift to a new location until the gap in production costs becomes wide enough to compensate for the loss of agglomeration economies. Yet once firms start to relocate, the movement becomes a cascade: as firms re-base to the new location, it starts to benefit from agglomeration economies.

During the second globalization wave most developing countries did not participate in the growth of global manufacturing and services trade. The combination of persistent trade barriers in developed countries, and poor investment climates and anti-trade policies in developing countries, confined them to

dependence on primary commodities. Even by 1980 only 25 percent of the merchandise exports of developing countries were manufactured goods.

Cascades of relocation did occur during the second wave, but they were to low-wage areas within developed countries. For example, until 1950 the U.S. textile industry was clustered in the high-wage Northeast. The cost pressure for it to relocate built up gradually as northern wages rose and as institutions and infrastructure improved in southern states. Within a short period in the 1950s the whole industry relocated to the Carolinas.

The effect on inequality and poverty. During globalization's second wave there were effectively two trading systems: the old North-South system, and the new intra-North system.

The intra-North system was quite powerfully equalizing: lower-income industrial countries caught up with higher-income ones. Figure 1.4 shows this pattern of long-term convergence among OECD economies.

Second wave globalization coincided with the growth of policies for redistribution

Worldwide household inequality, 1960 – 79

Figure 1.7

Mean log deviation

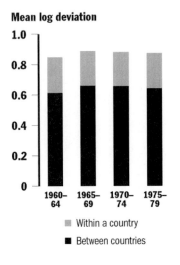

- ▨ Within a country
- ■ Between countries

Source: Clark, Dollar, and Kraay (2001).

Shares in merchandise exports in developing country exports

Figure 1.8

Source: Martin (2001).

and social protection within developed societies. Not only did inequalities reduce between countries—probably an effect of globalization—but inequality was reduced within countries, probably as a result of these social programs. Figure 1.5 shows the dramatic reduction both in between-country and within-country inequality that occurred in developed countries during the period. The second wave of globalization was thus spectacularly successful in reducing poverty within the OECD countries. Rapid growth coincided with greater equity, both to an extent without precedent. For the industrial world it is often referred to as the "golden age."

Second wave globalization was not golden for developing countries. Although per capita income growth recovered from the inter-war slowdown, it was substantially slower than in the rich economies. The number of poor people continued to rise. Non-income dimensions of poverty improved—notably rising life expectancy and rising school enrollments. In terms of equity, within developing countries in aggregate there was

little change either between countries or within them (figure 1.6). As a group, developing countries were being left behind by developed countries.

World inequality was thus the sum of three components: greater equity within developed countries, greater inequality between developed and developing countries, and little net change in developing countries. The net effect of these three very different components was broadly no change. World inequality was about the same in the late 1970s as it had been a quarter of a century earlier (figure 1.7).

The New Wave of Globalization

The new wave of globalization, which began about 1980, is distinctive. First, and most spectacularly, a large group of developing countries broke into global markets. Second, other developing countries became increasingly marginalized in the world economy and suffered declining incomes and rising poverty. Third, international migration and capital movements, which were negligible

GNP density
Map 1.1

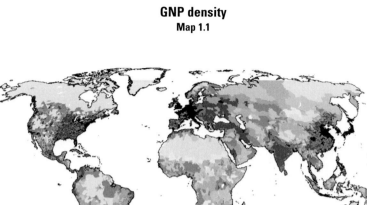

GNP per square kilometer
- $0–499
- $500–1,099
- $1,100–2,999
- $3,000–8,099
- $8,100–21,199
- $22,000–59,999
- $60,000–162,999
- $163,000–441,999
- $442,000–546,000,000

Source: Sachs, Mellinger, and Gallup (2001)

during second wave globalization, have again become substantial. We take these features of the new global economy in turn.

The changing structure of trade: The rise of the new globalizers

The most encouraging development in third wave globalization is that some developing countries, accounting for about 3 billion people, have succeeded for the first time in harnessing their labor abundance to give them a competitive advantage in labor-intensive manufactures and services. In 1980 only 25 percent of the exports of developing countries were manufactures; by 1998 this had risen to 80 percent (figure 1.8). Davis and Weinstein (forthcoming) show that developing country exports are indeed now labor-intensive.

This is an astonishing transformation over a very short period. The developing countries that have shifted into manufactures trade are quite diverse. Relatively low-income countries such as China, Bangladesh, and Sri Lanka have manufactures shares in their exports that are above the world average of 81 percent. Others, such as India, Turkey, Morocco, and Indonesia, have shares that are nearly as high as the world average. Another important

change in the pattern of developing country exports has been their substantial increase in exports of services. In the early 1980s, commercial services made up 17 percent of the exports of rich countries but only 9 percent of the exports of developing countries. During the third wave of globalization the share of services in rich country exports increased slightly—to 20 percent—but for developing countries the share almost doubled to 17 percent.

What accounted for this shift? Partly it was changing economic policy. Tariffs on manufactured goods in developed countries continued to decline, and many developing countries undertook major trade liberalizations. At the same time many countries liberalized barriers to foreign investment and improved other aspects of their investment climate. Partly it was due to continuing technical progress in transport and communications (Venables 2001). Containerization and airfreight brought a considerable speeding up of shipping, allowing countries to participate in international production networks. New information and communications technologies mean it is easier to manage and control geographically dispersed supply chains. And information-based activities are "weightless"

Characteristics of more globalized and less globalized developing economies (population-weighted averages)
Table 1.1

Socioeconomic characteristics	More globalized (24)	Less globalized (49)
Population, 1997 (billions)	2.9	1.1
Per capita GDP, 1980	$1,488	$1,947
Per capita GDP, 1997	$2,485	$2,133
Inflation, 1980 (percent)	16	17
Inflation, 1997 (percent)	6	9
Rule of law index, 1997 (world average = 0)	−0.04	−0.48
Average years primary schooling, 1980	2.4	2.5
Average years primary schooling, 1997	3.8	3.1
Average years secondary schooling, 1980	0.8	0.7
Average years secondary schooling, 1997	1.3	1.3
Average years tertiary schooling, 1980	0.08	0.09
Average years tertiary schooling, 1997	0.18	0.22

Source: Dollar (2001)

Change in trade/GDP for selected countries, 1977–97
Figure 1.9

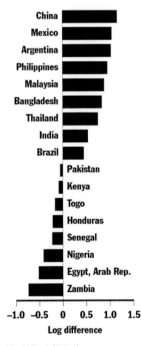

Source: World Bank (2001d).

so their inputs and outputs (digitized information) can be shipped at virtually no cost.

Some analysts have suggested that new technologies lead to the "death of distance" (Cairncross 1997) undermining the advantage of agglomeration. This is likely true in a few activities, while for other activities distance seems to be becoming even more important—for example, the proximity requirements of "just-in-time" technologies. The OECD agglomerations continue to have massive cost advantages and technological change may even be increasing these advantages. Even within well-located countries there will be clustering as long as agglomeration economies are important, and hence wage pressure to migrate to towns and cities. For example, within the United States, which has similar institutions across the country, there has been a clear trend for economic activity and labor to migrate away from the center of the country. One hundred years ago the Mississippi River and the Great Lakes provided reasonably good transport links. But recent increases in the scale of ocean-going ships and related declines in ocean shipping rates have increased the competitiveness of U.S. coastal locations compared to the center.

**Decline in average import tariffs,
mid-1980s to late-1990s**
Figure 1.10

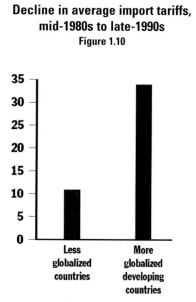

Source: Dollar and Kraay (2001b).

Results from a better rule of law
Figure 1.11

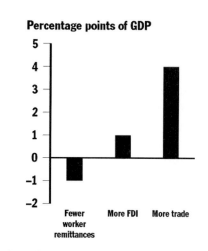

Source: Dollar and Zoido-Lobatón (2001).

It is cheaper to ship iron ore from Australia to Japan than the much shorter distance across the Great Lakes from Minnesota to the steel mills of Illinois and Indiana. For large countries such as China and India we can expect to see more migration toward coastal areas as development proceeds.

By the end of the millennium economic activity was highly concentrated geographically (map 1.1). This reflects differences in policies across countries, natural geographic advantages and disadvantages, and agglomeration and scale economy effects. As the map shows, Africa has a very low output density and this is unlikely to change through a uniform expansion of production in every location. Africa has the potential to develop a number of successful manufacturing/service agglomerations, but if its development is like that of any other large region, there will be several such locations around the continent and a need for labor to migrate to those places. Africa is much less densely populated than Europe, and the importance of migration to create agglomerations is therefore greater.

However, most countries are not just victims of their location. The newly globalizing developing countries helped their firms to

break into industrial markets by improving the complementary infrastructure, skills and institutions that modern production needs. So, to some extent those developing countries that broke into world markets just happened to be well located, and to some extent they shaped events by their own actions. To get some understanding of this distinction it is useful to look at the characteristics of the post-1980 developing globalizers. We rank developing countries by the extent to which they increased trade relative to income over the period, and compare the top third with the remaining two-thirds. The one-third/two-thirds distinction is of course arbitrary. We label the top third "more globalized" without in any sense implying that they adopted pro-trade policies.[3] The rise in trade may have been due to other policies or even to pure chance. By construction, the "more globalized" had a large increase in trade relative to income: 104 percent, compared to 71 percent for the rich countries. The remaining two-thirds of developing countries have actually had a decline in trade compared to GDP over this period. The variation in export performance is illustrated in figure 1.9.

Openness and growth: Regression evidence
Box 1.1

IT IS DIFFICULT TO ESTABLISH A LINK BETWEEN openness and growth in a rigorous manner. The specific trade liberalization actions that are important often include non-tariff measures such as eliminating licensing schemes or allowing access to foreign exchange for current account transactions, and it is difficult to quantify these policies. Further, countries tend to pursue a broad package of reforms at the same time so that identifying the separate effect of one reform may not be possible. Recognizing these limitations, what does the cross-country literature find? Sachs and Warner (1995) claim that liberal trade policies cause growth. They develop a measure of openness based on tariff rates for capital equipment, the extent of non-tariff barriers, and the degree of distortion in the foreign exchange market (proxied by the parallel market premium). Dollar (1992) creates an index of the price level adjusted for factor endowments, arguing that high prices for tradable goods reflect high levels of import protection, and finds a significant effect on growth. Both measures have been criticized (by Rodriguez and Rodrik 1999, among others) on the grounds that they are more a measure of good institutions and policies in general than of trade policy narrowly defined. This points up an important identification problem: the countries with more open trade and investment policies tend to be ones with more reliable property rights and better economic institutions more generally. Frankel

and Romer (1999) find that openness as measured by the share of trade in income is robustly related to long-term growth. They are able to rule out the possibility of reverse causation from growth to trade by "instrumenting" for trade with geography variables. While this is supportive of models in which access to markets accelerates growth, there is no easy way to rule out the possibility that geography matters for growth through other channels. A different approach to measuring openness is taken by Ades and Glaeser (1999) in their study of 19th century America. They focus on openness in the sense of access to seaports and rail services, and find that backward, open regions tend to grow fast and converge on more advanced regions. Specifically, they interact their openness measure with the initial level of development and find that the combination of openness and backwardness is associated with especially rapid development. Finally, there are some recent studies that focus on changes in growth rates and changes in trade and FDI. This approach has the advantage that all of the variables that do not change over time drop out of the analysis (geography, ethnolinguistic fractionalization, institutional measures that show no time variation), reducing the multicollinearity problems. Dollar and Kraay (2001b) show that both increased trade and increased FDI are related to accelerated growth. They control for changes in other policies and address reverse causation with internal instruments.

The more globalized were not drawn from the higher-income developing countries. Indeed, in 1980 they were poorer as a group.[4] The two groups had very similar educational attainment in 1980 (table 1.1). Since 1980, the more globalized have made very significant gains in basic education: the average years of primary schooling for adults increased from 2.4 years to 3.8 years. The less globalized made less progress and now lag behind in primary attainment. The spread of basic education tends to reduce inequality and raise health standards, as well as being complementary to the process of raising productivity. It can also be seen in table 1.1 that both groups reduced inflation to single digits over

Per capita GDP growth rates: More globalized developing countries
Figure 1.12

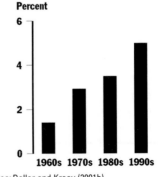

Source: Dollar and Kraay (2001b).

the past two decades. Finally, as of 1997 the more globalized fared moderately better on an index of property rights and the rule of law.[5] The same measure is not available for 1980, but clearly countries such as China and Hungary have strengthened property rights as they have reformed.

During third wave globalization, the new globalizers also cut import tariffs significantly, 34 points on average, compared to 11 points for the countries that are less globalized (figure 1.10). However, policy change was not exclusively or even primarily focused on trade. The list of post-1980 globalizers includes such well-known reformers as Argentina, China, Hungary, India, Malaysia, Mexico, the Philippines, and Thailand, which undertook reforms involving investment liberalization, stabilization, and property rights. The outcome of increased integration into the world economy need not be due to changes in trade policy. Dollar and Zoido-Lobatón (2001) find that reliable property rights, strong rule of law, and macroeconomic stability are all associated with more trade and FDI. A one standard deviation increase on an index of the rule of law (roughly the difference between Kenya and Uganda) is associated with 4 percentage points of GDP more in trade and 1 percentage point more FDI (figure 1.11). They also find that it is associated with lower emigration.

As they reformed and integrated with the world market, the "more globalized" developing countries started to grow rapidly, accelerating steadily from 2.9 percent in the 1970s to 5 percent through the 1990s (figure 1.12). They found themselves in a virtuous circle of rising growth and rising penetration of world markets. It seems likely that growth and trade reinforced each other, and that the policies of educational expansion, reduced trade barriers, and strategic sectoral reforms reinforced both growth and trade.

Whether there is a causal connection from opening up trade to faster growth is not the issue. In those low-income countries that have broken into global markets, more restricted access to those markets would be damaging to growth, regardless of whether industrialization was triggered by opening up.

However, opening up integrates an economy into a larger market, and from Adam Smith on economists have suggested that the size of the market matters for growth. A larger market gives access to more ideas, allows for investment in large fixed-cost investments and enables a finer division of labor. A larger market also widens choice. Wider choice for high-income consumers is irrelevant for poverty reduction, but wider choice may have mattered more for firms than for consumers. For example, as India liberalized trade, companies were able to purchase better-quality machine tools. Similar effects have been found for the Chinese import liberalization. Finally, a larger market intensifies competition and this can spur innovation. There is some evidence that integration with the world economy is more important for small and poor economies than it is for large economies like India and China (Sachs and Warner 1995; Collier and Gunning 1999).

There is also a large amount of cross-country regression evidence on openness and growth (see box 1.1). This should be treated with caution but not dismissed altogether. Lindert and Williamson (2001a, pp. 29–30) summarize it:

The doubts that one can retain about each individual study threaten to block our view of the overall forest of evidence. Even though no one study can establish that openness to trade has unambiguously helped the representative Third World economy, the preponderance of evidence supports this conclusion. One way to see the whole forest more clearly is to consider two sets, one almost empty and one completely empty. The almost empty set consists of all statistical studies showing that protection has helped Third World economic growth, and liberalization has harmed it. The second, and this time empty, set contains those countries that chose to be less open to trade and factor flows in the 1990s than in the 1960s and rose in the global living-standard ranks at the same time. As far as we can tell, there are no anti-global victories to report for the postwar Third World. We infer that this is because freer trade stimulates growth in Third World economies today, regardless of its effects before 1940. (pp. 29–30)

To conclude, since 1980 the global integration of markets in merchandise has enabled those developing countries with reasonable locations, policies, institutions, and infrastructure to harness their abundant labor to give themselves a competitive advantage in some manufactures and services. The initial advantage provided by cheap labor has sometimes triggered a virtuous circle of other benefits from trade. For example, when Bangalore initially broke into the world software market, it did so by harnessing its comparative advantage in cheap, educated labor. As more firms gravitated to the city it began to reap economies of agglomeration. The increased export earnings financed more imports, thereby both intensifying competition and widening choice. There is some evidence that between them these four effects of trade raise not only the level of real income, but also its rate of growth. However, the growth process is complex. Trade is certainly not sufficient for growth.

Marginalization:
Why has the experience of many poor countries been the opposite of the globalizers?

Countries with total populations of around 2 billion people have not integrated strongly into the global industrial economy. They include most of Africa and many of the economies of the FSU. These countries often suffered deteriorating and volatile terms of trade in the markets for their primary commodity exports. In aggregate their per capita income actually declined during the third wave. Why did these countries diverge so drastically from the globalizers? Can they belatedly emulate the globalizers in harnessing their comparative advantage in abundant labor, thereby diversifying their exports toward services and manufactures? There are three views:

The "Join the Club" view. This view argues that weak globalizers have failed to harness their comparative advantage in abundant labor because of poor economic policies.

If, for example, infrastructure is poor, education is inadequate, corruption is rampant, and trade barriers are high, then the cost advantage from abundant labor might be more than offset by these disadvantages. According to this view, as and when policies, institutions, and infrastructure are improved, then countries will integrate into world markets for manufactures and services.

The "Geographic Disadvantage" view. This view argues that many of the countries that have failed to enter global manufacturing markets suffer from fundamental disadvantages of location. Even with good policies, institutions, and infrastructure, a landlocked, malaria-infested country simply will not be competitive in manufacturing or in services such as tourism. It is sometimes argued that it is precisely because the benefits of good policies, institutions, and infrastructure in such environments are so modest that they are not reformed. For many developing countries, transport costs to OECD markets are higher than the tariffs on their goods, so that transport costs are even more of a barrier to integration than the trade policies of rich countries. Sometimes the explanation for high transport costs is indeed adverse geography. But transport costs are also heavily influenced by the quality of infrastructure as implied by the "Join the Club" view. Limão and Venables (2000) find that "African economies tend to trade less with the rest of the world and with themselves than would be predicted by a simple gravity model, and the reason for that is their poor infrastructure" (p. 25). That includes inefficient seaports, but even more importantly the internal infrastructure of roads, rail, and telecommunications. Collier and Gunning (1999, pp. 71–72) document these infrastructure deficiencies in Africa:

where, for example, the density of the rural road network is only 55 kilometers per thousand square kilometers, compared to over 800 in India, and there are only one-tenth the telephones per capita of Asia. The quality of infrastructure is also lower. The telephone system has triple the level of faults to Asia's and the proportion of diesel trains in use is 40 percent lower. Prices of infrastructure use are much higher. Freight rates by rail are on average around double those in Asia. Port charges are higher (for example, a container costs $200 in Abidjan as opposed to $120 in Antwerp). Air transportation is four times more costly than in East Asia. Much of international transport is cartelized, reflecting the regulations of African governments intended to promote national shipping companies and airlines. As a result of these high costs, by 1991 freight and insurance payments on trade amounted to 15 percent of export earnings, whereas the average for developing countries is only 6 percent. Further, the trend has been rising for Africa whereas it has been falling elsewhere: the comparable figures for 1970 were 11 percent and 8 percent.

Thus, many of the weak globalizers have high transport costs to world markets partly due to intrinsically poor location and partly due to bad infrastructure. As a result they will have low wages, and even when trade is free of barriers it will not bring those wages into line with wages in more favored locations.

The "Missed the Boat" view. This view accepts the argument of the "Join the Club" view that, if any of these countries had had good policies it would have broken into world manufacturing and services, but it further argues that most of them have now missed the boat. World demand for manufactures is limited by world income, and because of agglomeration economies firms will locate in clusters. Although there is room for many clusters, firms already have satisfactory locations in labor-abundant countries and so the latecomers have nothing to offer.

Who's right?

Most plausibly, each view is right to some extent. It seems highly likely that there will be room for some new entrants to the market for global manufactures and services, and some well-located cities in countries that reform their policies, institutions, and infrastructure will surely develop successful clusters. Equally, it seems plausible that if all countries reformed, there would be more well located

sites than new clusters, so some would indeed have missed the boat. Finally, some countries are indeed badly located and will simply not industrialize. Such countries might become competitive in international services, but at present markets in services are far less integrated than markets in merchandise. This is partly because until very recently trade negotiations have focused on reducing barriers to merchandise trade.

Regardless of whether the disadvantages faced by the weak globalizers were intrinsic or could have been altered by better policy, their growth rates were even lower during third wave globalization than during second wave. One reason is that many countries dependent on primary commodities suffered declining prices for their exports. This was probably related to the slowdown in growth in developed countries. Could globalization itself have contributed to the economic marginalization of some countries? One way it might have adversely affected the weak globalizers is through the growth of international capital markets. Most marginalized countries integrated into world capital markets not through attracting capital inflows but through capital flight. By 1990 Africa, the region where capital is most scarce, had about 40 percent of its private wealth held outside the continent, a higher proportion than any other region. This integration was not a policy choice: most African governments erected capital controls, but they were ineffective. The main drivers of capital flight have been exchange rate misalignment, poor risk-ratings, and high indebtedness (Collier, Hoeffler, and Patillo 2001). However, capital flight was probably eased by the growth of international banking, some of it offshore, with poor practices of disclosure. A second way that globalization may have affected the weak globalizers adversely is through a rising risk of civil war. The incidence of civil war has declined sharply in the globalizing developing regions, but has risen sharply in Africa. Dependence on primary commodity exports is a powerful risk factor in civil conflict, probably because it provides easy sources of finance for rebel groups. Whereas most regions have diversified their exports, Africa

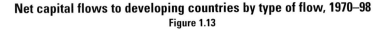

Net capital flows to developing countries by type of flow, 1970–98
Figure 1.13

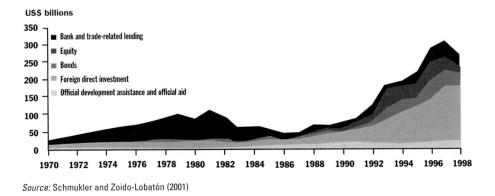

US$ billions

Legend:
- Bank and trade-related lending
- Equity
- Bonds
- Foreign direct investment
- Official development assistance and official aid

Source: Schmukler and Zoido-Lobatón (2001)

has remained heavily dependent on primary commodities. Furthermore, conflicts tend to last longer: the chances of reaching peace are much lower during third wave globalization than during the second wave.

The re-emergence of international capital flows

Controls on capital outflows from high-income countries were gradually lifted: for example, the United Kingdom removed capital controls in 1979. Governments in developing countries have also gradually adopted less hostile policies toward investors. Partly as a result of these policy changes and partly due to the oil shock of the 1970s, significant amounts of private capital again began to flow to developing countries.

Total capital flows to developing countries went from less than $28 billion in the 1970s to about $306 billion in 1997, in real terms (figure 1.13), when they peaked. In the process, their composition changed significantly. The importance of official flows of aid more than halved, while private capital flows became the major source of capital for a number of emerging economies. The composition of private capital flows also changed markedly. FDI grew continuously throughout the 1990s. Mergers and acquisitions were the most important source of this increase, especially those resulting from the privatization of

public companies. Net portfolio flows grew from $0.01 billion in 1970 to $103 billion in 1996, in real terms. New international mutual funds and pension funds helped to channel the equity flows to developing countries. The importance of syndicated bank loans and other private flows decreased steadily in relative terms throughout this period, especially after the debt crises of the 1980s.

Even though net private capital flows to developing countries increased during the third wave of globalization, by one measure they remained more modest than during the first wave. By 1998 the foreign capital stock was 22 percent of developing country GDP, roughly double what it had been in the mid-1970s but still well below the 32 percent reached in 1914 (Maddison 2001). Some countries receive large inflows, while other countries receive little. The top 12 emerging markets are receiving the overwhelming majority of the net inflows—countries such as Argentina, Brazil, China, India, Malaysia, Mexico, and Thailand. Much the most successful developing countries in attracting FDI were Malaysia and Chile, both with stocks of FDI of about $2,000 per capita.

FDI brings not just capital, but also advanced technology and access to international markets. It is critical for participating in international production networks. Dollar and Kraay (2001b) find that FDI has a powerful growth effect, whereas the overall level of investment by itself does not have a significant effect on growth—other factors are more important.

Capital flows to developing countries are just a tiny proportion of the global capital market. Because capital owners are concerned about risk, most global capital flows are between developed countries rather than from developed to developing countries. Even Malaysia and Chile have less FDI per capita than any of the major developed economies. FDI per capita in the United States is more than $3,200 per capita, while in Africa it is only $124 (Maddison 2001). This is despite the fact that differences in capital per member of the labor force between developed and developing countries are now far larger than they were during the first wave of globalization. World capital markets could clearly do more to raise growth in low-income countries.

Migration pressures are building

The massive gaps in income that had built up by the end of globalization's second wave created intense economic pressures for people to migrate out of poor areas—both rural-urban migration within countries and international migration. These pressures were largely frustrated by immigration controls, but in some rich countries controls were somewhat relaxed during the third wave, with powerful effects on wages in poor countries.

Recall that in the first great wave of modern globalization, from 1870 to 1910, about 10 percent of the world's population relocated permanently. Much of this flow was driven by economic considerations, the desire to find a better life in a more favorable location. The same forces operate today, though policies toward international migration are much more restrictive than in the past. About 120 million people (2 percent of the world's population) live in foreign countries (that is, not in the country of their citizenship). Roughly half of this stock of migrants is in the industrial countries and half in the developing world. However, because the population of developing countries is about five times greater than the population of the developed countries, migrants comprise a larger share of the population in rich countries (about 6 percent) than in poor countries (about 1 percent).

The main economic rationale for migration is that wages for the same skills differ vastly in different locations, especially between developing countries and rich ones. The average hourly labor compensation in manufacturing is about $30 per hour in Germany, and one one-hundredth of that level (30 cents) in China and India (figure 1.14). That gap is particularly extreme, but even between the United States and newly industrialized countries such as Thailand or Malaysia the compensation gap is ten-fold. Now, some of that difference results from the fact that the typical German worker has quite a bit more education and training than the typical Chinese or Indian. However, skill differences can only explain a small amount of the wage differential. A study following individual, legal immigrants found that on average they left jobs in Mexico paying $31 per week and on arrival in the United States could immediately earn $278 per week (a nine-fold increase). Similarly, Indonesian workers in Indonesia earn 28 cents per day, compared to $2 per day or more in next-door Malaysia. Clearly there are huge real gains to individual workers who migrate to more developed economies.

These large wage differentials across countries lead to mounting migration pressures, although the actual scale of migration depends upon the entry restrictions that migrants face. Hatton and Williamson (2001) study emigration from Africa. They find that both widening wage differentials and a demographic bulge of 15–29-year-olds are producing large and growing economic pressure for migration, although so far much of this has been bottled up by entry restrictions. Emigration from Mexico has been less restricted. There are about 7 million legal Mexican migrants living in the United States, and an additional estimated 3 million undocumented workers. This means that about 10 percent of Mexico's population is living and working in the United States. Emigration on this scale has a significant effect on developing country labor markets. Hatton and

Hourly labor costs in manufacturing
Figure 1.14

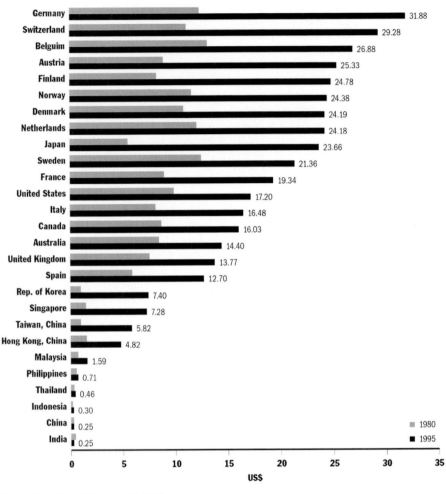

Germany — 31.88
Switzerland — 29.28
Belguim — 26.88
Austria — 25.33
Finland — 24.78
Norway — 24.38
Denmark — 24.19
Netherlands — 24.18
Japan — 23.66
Sweden — 21.36
France — 19.34
United States — 17.20
Italy — 16.48
Canada — 16.03
Australia — 14.40
United Kingdom — 13.77
Spain — 12.70
Rep. of Korea — 7.40
Singapore — 7.28
Taiwan, China — 5.82
Hong Kong, China — 4.82
Malaysia — 1.59
Philippines — 0.71
Thailand — 0.46
Indonesia — 0.30
China — 0.25
India — 0.25

■ 1980
■ 1995

US$

Source: Schmukler and Zoido-Lobatón (2001)

Williamson estimate the effect of out-migration from Africa on the wages of those who remain behind. They find that emigration powerfully raises the wages of remaining unskilled workers. It is likely that emigration from Mexico has substantially raised Mexican wages.

The benefits of migration to the sending region go beyond the higher wages for those who remain behind. Migrants send a large volume of remittances back to relatives and this is an important source of capital inflows (figure 1.15). India receives six times as much in remittances from its workers overseas every year as it gets in foreign aid.

Further, much trade and investment depends on personal and family networks. To take a significant historical example, a large number of Chinese have emigrated from China to other Asian countries (especially Thailand,

Workers' remittances, 1999
Figure 1.15

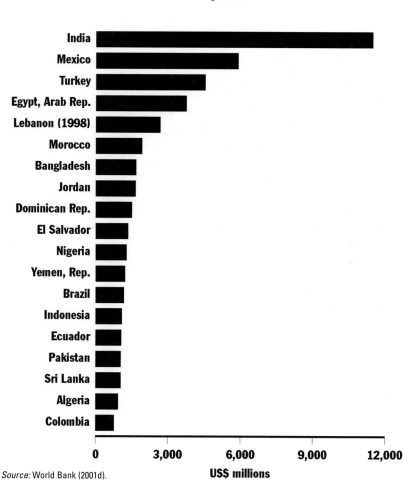

Source: World Bank (2001d).   **US$ millions**

Malaysia, Indonesia, and Singapore). The Chinese family networks play a significant role in trade and investment between these countries and China. It is inherently difficult to study and quantify this phenomenon, but there is more general evidence that language plays a large role in explaining trade and investment flows, and it makes sense that the stronger tie of family and kinship would have an even greater effect. The point here is that migration can facilitate the other flows of globalization—trade, capital, and ideas. Take, for example, the recent surge in Indian immigration to the United States. It happens that this immigration is particularly related to the high-tech sectors. It will support greater flows of technology and information between the United States and India, and also encourage more U.S. investment in India. Some successful Indian entrepreneurs in the United States may themselves open plants back in their home country, or U.S. companies may hire Indian engineers to work in India. And because much of manufacturing and services trade is associated with these kinds of networks, trade between the two countries is likely to increase.

Household inequality in rich countries, 1980–95
Figure 1.16

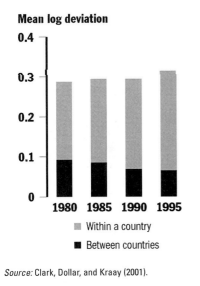

Mean log deviation

Within a country
Between countries

Source: Clark, Dollar, and Kraay (2001).

Household inequality in the globalizing world, 1975–95
Figure 1.17

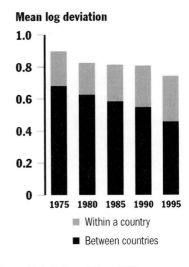

Mean log deviation

Within a country
Between countries

Source: Clark, Dollar, and Kraay (2001).

What have been the effects of third wave globalization on income distribution and poverty?

The breakthrough of developing countries into global markets for manufactures and services, and the reemergence of migration and capital flows, have affected poverty and the distribution of income between and within countries. Domestic policy choices unrelated to globalization also affect income distribution.

Among developed countries globalization has continued to generate the convergence of the first and second waves. By 1995 inequality between countries was less than half what it had been in 1960 and substantially less than it had been in 1980. However, as figure 1.16 shows, there was a serious offsetting increase in inequality within individual countries, reversing the trend seen during the second wave. A part of this may have been due to immigration. However, it may also have been due to policy changes on taxation and social spending unconnected to globalization. Global economic integration is consistent with wide differences in domestic distributional policies: inequality differs massively

between equally globalized economies. For the OECD economies taken as a whole, globalization has probably been equalizing as inequality between countries has radically decreased.

Among the new globalizers the same pattern of convergence has been evident as has occurred among the OECD economies over a longer period. Sachs and Warner (1995) find that this is indeed a general phenomenon among open economies. Treating the OECD and the new globalizers as a common group of integrated economies, overall inequality has declined (figure 1.17).

As in the OECD countries, within-country inequality has increased in the new globalizers. However, this is entirely due to the rise in inequality in China, which alone accounts for one-third of the population of the new globalizers. China started its modernization with an extremely equal distribution of income and extremely high poverty. Intra-rural inequality in China has actually decreased. The big growth in inequality has been between the rural areas and the rising urban agglomerations (figure 1.18), and

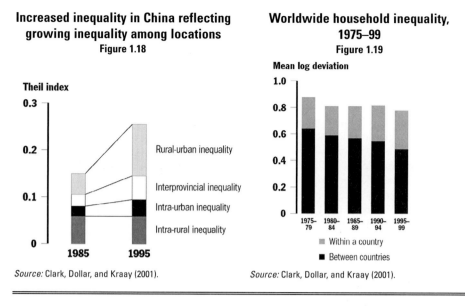

Increased inequality in China reflecting growing inequality among locations
Figure 1.18

Theil index

Rural-urban inequality

Interprovincial inequality

Intra-urban inequality

Intra-rural inequality

1985   1995

Source: Clark, Dollar, and Kraay (2001).

Worldwide household inequality, 1975–99
Figure 1.19

Mean log deviation

1975–79   1980–84   1985–89   1990–94   1995–99

■ Within a country
■ Between countries

Source: Clark, Dollar, and Kraay (2001).

between those provinces with agglomerations and those without them.

A closer investigation of the changes in inequality within countries is provided in Dollar and Kraay (2001a) and Ravallion (forthcoming). There are substantial difficulties in comparing income distribution data across countries. Countries differ in the concept measured (income versus consumption), the measure of income (gross versus net), the unit of observation (individuals versus households), and the coverage of the survey (national versus subnational). Dollar and Kraay restrict attention to distribution data based on nationally representative sources identified as high-quality by Deininger and Squire (1996), and perform some simple adjustments to control for differences in the types of surveys. These data cover a total of 137 countries. They focus on what has happened to the income of the poorest 20 percent of the population. They find that on average there is a one-to-one relationship between the growth rate of income of the poor and the growth rate of average income in society. However, there is much variation around that average relationship. They then investigate whether changes in trade account for any of this variation. They find no relationship between changes in openness and changes in inequality, whether openness is

measured by the share of trade in income, the Sachs-Warner measure of openness, average tariff rates, or capital controls. Ravallion qualifies this result. He finds that although on average openness does not affect inequality, in low-income countries it is associated with greater inequality. Regardless of its net effect, there are winners and losers from trade policies.

The combination of rapid growth with no systematic change in inequality has dramatically reduced absolute poverty in the new globalizing countries. Between 1993 and 1998 (the most recent period for which we have data) the number of people in absolute poverty declined by 14 percent to 762 million. For them, the third wave of globalization is indeed the golden age. Poverty is predominantly rural. As the new globalizers have broken into world markets their pace of industrialization and urbanization has increased. People have taken the opportunity to migrate from risky and impoverished rural livelihoods to less vulnerable and better paid jobs in towns and cities. Not only has poverty declined viewed in terms of income, but other dimensions of poverty have rapidly improved. Both average years of schooling and life expectancy have improved to levels close or equal to levels reached by the rich countries in 1960. Vietnam illustrates this experience. As it has integrated into the world economy, it has had a large increase in per capita income and no significant change in inequality. The income of the poor has risen dramatically, and the level of absolute poverty has dropped sharply, from 75 percent of the population in 1988 to 37 percent in 1998. Poverty was cut in half in only 10 years. We can be unusually confident of this information because a representative household survey was conducted early in the reform process (1992–93), and the same 5,000 households were visited again six years later. Of the poorest 5 percent of households in 1992, 98 percent had higher incomes six years later. Vietnam was unusually successful in entering global markets for labor-intensive products such as footwear, and the increased employment might be expected to benefit poor households. Uganda had a similar experience: dramatic poverty reduction and no increase in inequality.

While the more globalized economies grew and converged, the less globalized developing economies declined and diverged. Their growth experience was worse than during the second wave, but their divergence has been longstanding. Ades and Glaeser (1999) find that at least since 1960, less globalized developing countries, defined by the share of trade in income, have tended to diverge. Decline and divergence had severe consequences for poverty in its various dimensions. Between 1993 and 1998 the number of people in absolute poverty in the less globalized developing countries rose by 4 percent to 437 million. Not only were per capita incomes falling, but in many countries life expectancy and school enrollments declined.

During the second wave of globalization the rich countries diverged from the poor countries, a trend that had persisted for a century. During the third wave the new globalizers have started to catch up with the rich countries, while the weak globalizers are falling further behind.

The change in the overall distribution of world income and the number of poor people are thus the net outcomes of offsetting effects. Among rich countries there has been convergence: the less rich countries have caught up with the richest, while within some rich countries there has been rising inequality. Among the new globalizers there has also been convergence and falling poverty. Within China there has also been rising inequality, but not on average elsewhere. Between the rich countries and the new globalizers there has been convergence. Between all these groups and the weak globalizers there has been divergence. The net effect is that the long trend of rising global inequality and rising numbers of people in absolute poverty has been halted and even reversed (figure 1.19). Bourguignon and Morrisson (2001) estimate that the number of people in absolute poverty fell by about 100 million between 1980 and 1992 (the endpoint of their analysis). Chen and Ravallion (2001) estimate that there was a further fall of about 100 million between 1993 (the closest date for comparison) and 1998. Thus, globalization clearly can be a force for poverty reduction.

Endnotes

[1] Much of the emigration from India was forced, rather than voluntary.

[2] The mean log deviation has the advantage that it can be decomposed into inequality between locations and inequality within locations. It also has an intuitive interpretation. Income distributions everywhere are skewed in favor of the rich, so that the "typical" person (one chosen randomly from the population) has less income than the average for the whole group. Roughly speaking, the mean log deviation (times 100) is the percent gap between the typical person and the average income. The more skewed the distribution in favor of the rich, the larger is this gap. So, for example, if per capita income in the world is around $5,000 and the median person is living on $1,000 (80 percent less), the mean log deviation will be around 0.8.

[3] For this calculation we separated out rich economies (the original members of the OECD plus Chile; Korea; Singapore; Taiwan, China; and Hong Kong, China). The "more globalized"—the top third of developing countries in terms of increased trade to GDP between the 1970s and the 1990s—are Argentina, Bangladesh, Brazil, China, Colombia, Costa Rica, Côte d'Ivoire, the Dominican Republic, Haiti, Hungary, India, Jamaica, Jordan, Malaysia, Mali, Mexico, Nepal, Nicaragua, Paraguay, the Philippines, Rwanda, Thailand, Uruguay, and Zimbabwe. The "less global-

ized" are all other developing countries for which we have data. The less globalized group is a very diverse set of countries. It includes failed states whose economic performance has been extremely poor. It also includes some countries of the former Soviet Union that went through a difficult transition in the 1990s. Some of the less globalized countries have had stable but not increasing trade, and positive but slow growth.

4 The more globalized had per capita GDP, at purchasing power parity, of $1,488 in 1980, compared to $1,947 for other developing countries (table 1.1). These are population-weighted averages so that relatively poor China and India have a large weight. However, even a simple average of GDP per capita was significantly lower for the globalizers in 1980.

5 The rule of law index has a standard deviation of 1.0. The 0.44 advantage of the globalizers is roughly the same as Uganda's advantage over Zambia on this measure.

Discussion Questions

IV

1. Why is Rodrik critical of globalization? Are his arguments in this section's article consistent with his arguments in the article in section 3 of this text?

2. What are the five wars of globalization? Do we currently have the mechanisms available to deal with these problems? What does the author propose to deal with these issues?

3. Why do Dollar and Kraay argue that critics of globalization have gotten it wrong? Do you agree?

4. Do you believe Dollar and Kraay and Rodrik are on opposite sides of the globalization debate? Where do they agree and disagree?

5. What are the three main waves of globalization? Which one do you believe is most important? What characterizes each wave?

6. Do we need a new institutional framework to deal with globalization in the 21st century? If so, what would these new institutions look like?

7. What are the main strengths and weaknesses of globalization, in your opinion? On balance, has globalization been good for the poor?

8. Are developing countries well represented in international institutions such as the WTO, the IMF or the World Bank? Why or why not?

9. Do you think globalization will continue into the first two decades of the 21st century? What new trends do you perceive?

Balance of Payments

This section examines two related issues: what causes large current account deficits, and is the US current account deficit unsustainable. The current account is a financial statement summarizing all transactions involving the flow of goods, services, income, and net unilateral current transfers between the US and the rest of the world. The US government's Bureau of Economic Analysis reports that the estimated US current account deficit for the first quarter of 2003 was $136.1bn. The current account balance is the difference between domestic saving and domestic investment. If domestic saving falls, the US must borrow from abroad to finance domestic investment. Some economists have been uncomfortable with rising US foreign indebtedness. However, US foreign indebtedness is not necessarily bad if foreign funds are used towards investment. The following articles in this section address these concerns.

"What Drives Large Current Account Deficits?" by Cletus Coughlin and Patricia Pollard investigates whether government budget deficits and changes in domestic saving behavior can explain the US current account deficit. During the 1970's and 1980's, the US experienced twin deficits; both a government budget deficit and current account deficit. The authors find that rising current account deficits are associated with rising investment, and that simply focusing on saving behavior is insufficient in explaining the large US current account deficit. They conclude that invest-ment spending plays a key role in determining the current account balance.

In "Does the US Have a Current Account Deficit Disorder?" William Poole argues that the issue of US indebtedness to foreigners matters, not because the US will be plunged into financial crisis if foreigners liquidate their US assets, but rather because the debt has to be repaid in the future. Poole points out that if the US borrows to finance capital goods, which increase future production, repayment of the debt is not a problem. Repayment of the debt is potentially a problem if foreign funds are used to purchase consumption goods since future generations will bear the burden of debt. Poole presents evidence to suggest that the rising current account deficit is associated with rising domestic investment, and a significant share of foreign investment in the US is equity investment, which does not have to be repaid. He concludes that the US does not have a current account disorder.

What Drives Large Current Account Deficits?

C L E T U S   C .   **C O U G H L I N**   &
P A T R I C I A   S .   **P O L L A R D**

In recent years, the U.S. current account balance has declined sharply, falling from –1.7 percent of gross domestic product (GDP) in 1997 to –4.4 percent in 2000. Similarly, the current account balance declined from a surplus of 0.2 percent of GDP in 1981 to –3.3 percent in 1986. These two episodes, as well as episodes involving other developed countries, suggest that investment spending plays a key role in determining the path of a country's current account balance.

During the 1980s, the United States experienced rising deficits in both its current account and government budget balances. This "twin deficit" relationship led many analysts to conclude that government budget deficits were driving current account deficits. As shown in the table, many developed countries experiencing current account deficits of 3 percent of GDP or higher in the 1970s and early 1980s fit the twin deficit pattern, as indicated by a positive correlation between these balances (both as percentages of GDP). Since the mid-1980s, however, the two balances generally have been negatively correlated.

How can government deficits be linked with current account deficits? The current account balance equals the difference between domestic saving and investment. A country's total investment spending must be financed by a combination of domestic and foreign saving. Domestic saving consists of saving by households, businesses and the government. If government deficits reduce domestic saving, then the only way for a country to maintain investment spending is by borrowing from abroad (foreign saving). This is what occurred in the U.S. in the 1980s.

The last column in the table illustrates the incompleteness of the twin deficit explanation. In nearly every episode, the current account balance as a percent of GDP was negatively correlated with investment spending as a percent of GDP. Rising current account deficits were associated with rising domestic investment.

The most recent U.S. example of a falling current account balance shows the importance of investment. Between 1993 and 1997, the current account balance generally stayed in the range of –1.0 to –1.5 percent of gross domestic product, as a rising saving rate, caused primarily by declining federal budget deficits, kept pace with rising domestic investment. In 1998, this pattern changed: investment continued to rise, but a drop in the household saving rate resulted in a slight fall in domestic saving, producing a rise in the current account deficit.

Changes in domestic saving behavior provide, at most, a partial explanation of changes in current account balances. More importantly, large current account deficits in the developed economies are associated with increases in investment, not merely a shift in the funding of the investment from domestic to foreign savers.

Correlation with the Current Account

Country	Period	Government Budget	Investment
Austria	1975-82	-0.54	-0.87
Belgium	1976-85	0.37	-0.05
Canada	1973-80	0.49	-0.20
	1984-95	0.19	0.15
Finland	1972-77	-0.07	-0.83
	1984-94	-0.28	-0.37
Ireland	1967-90	0.79	-0.81
Italy	1972-77	-0.34	-0.94
Norway	1972-80	0.62	-0.88
	1985-90	0.27	-0.87
Portugal	1972-85	0.44	-0.35
Spain	1972-78	0.36	-0.62
	1986-95	-0.51	-0.77
Sweden	1978-84	0.40	-0.54
	1987-94	-0.32	-0.49
United Kingdom	1971-77	0.55	-0.69
	1985-94	-0.55	-0.68
United States	1980-89	0.31	-0.12
	1993-00	-0.91	-0.91

Note: The periods chosen begin prior to the start of the rising current account deficit and end (except the recent U.S. case) following the shrinkage of this deficit.
Sources: OECD, IMF and U.S. Bureau of Economic Analysis

Does the United States Have a Current Account Deficit Disorder?

20

W I L L I A M   **P O O L E**
PRESIDENT
FEDERAL RESERVE BANK OF ST. LOUIS

Since the beginning of 1998, the U.S. current account balance has declined sharply. In 2000, the current account deficit reached 4.4 percent of U.S. gross domestic product, which has caused much concern about the sustainability of this large deficit. Clearly, if this deficit is not sustainable, questions arise as to how the United States' current account balance would return to levels that could be maintained. One specific question concerns the implications of a sudden reversal of investor sentiment about the desirability of holding U.S. assets. Some commentators have raised the specter of a financial crisis with predictions of capital flight, sharp declines in the foreign exchange value of the dollar, higher interest rates and numerous bankruptcies and defaults. Such a scenario could produce consequences for the U.S. economy similar to those experienced by a number of countries in East Asia during the late 1990s.

My remarks focus on how to interpret recent developments in the U.S. current account. I plan to examine four related topics. First, I think some of the analysis and commentary discussing the U.S. current account is misinformed. Using some terminology from balance of payments accounting, which I will discuss later, many commentators have expressed the mistaken view that the capital and financial account "finances" the current account. In fact, for the United States, changes in the capital and financial account have been driving changes in the current account for many years. That is, the current account "finances" the capital and financial account. Second, and consequently, an understanding of changes in the capital and financial account requires an understanding of the reasons for the large financial flows to the United States in recent years. Third, I will explore what might cause a reversal of financial inflows into the United States. Fourth, I will examine evidence from other countries that have run large current account deficits to see how such evidence might add to our understanding of the U.S. situation today.

Before proceeding, I want to emphasize that the views I express here are mine and do not necessarily reflect official positions of the Federal Reserve System. This speech is a joint product with Cletus C. Coughlin, Vice President in the Research Division of the Federal Reserve Bank of St. Louis; I greatly appreciate his assistance. However, I retain full responsibility for errors.

Some Balance of Payments Accounting

Prior to developing my key points, I'll discuss a few concepts from balance of payments accounting to be sure we are all on the same wavelength. A country's balance of payments is a systematic account of all the exchanges of value between residents of that country and the rest of the world during a given period of time. For my discussion I will focus on two particular accounts within the balance of payments – the current account and the capital and financial account.

The U.S. current account summarizes all transactions involving flows of goods, services, income and unilateral transfers that take place between U.S. and foreign entities, which include private individuals, businesses and governments. The current account balance is simply the difference between U.S. receipts from the rest of the world and U.S. payments to the rest of the world as a result of these transactions. If U.S. payments exceed receipts, then the U.S. is said to be running a current account deficit. During 2000, U.S. payments exceeded receipts by $435 billion.

U.S. receipts arise from exports of goods and services, interest and dividends received by U.S. owners of foreign stocks and bonds, the reinvested earnings of the foreign affiliates of U.S. corporations and gifts to the United States from foreign residents and governments. Conversely, U.S. payments result from imports of goods and services, interest and dividends received by foreign owners of U.S. stocks and bonds, the reinvested earnings of U.S. affiliates of foreign corporations and gifts from the United States to foreign residents and governments.

This definition highlights a number of important facts. First, the receipts and payments encompass much more than the movement of merchandise across national borders. Second, the current account reflects the interaction of numerous decisions by individuals, firms, and governments both in the United States and abroad. Third, when receipts exceed payments, the United States, on net, is acquiring assets abroad. When U.S. payments exceed receipts, foreigners, on net, are acquiring assets in the United States.

When either U.S. residents acquire assets abroad or foreign residents acquire assets in the United States, the transactions are recorded in the capital and financial account of the balance of payments. A key accounting identity is that the capital and financial account balance must be exactly the opposite of the current account balance for any given period of time. In other words, a current account deficit must be matched by a capital and financial account surplus and vice versa. The balance of payments must balance!

There is, however, a more subtle point that is crucial to my analysis. The accounting balance measures, or accounts for, an economic equilibrium. The sum total of all purchases of U.S. dollars equals the sum total of all sales of U.S. dollars. Purchases and sales are simply the opposite sides of the transactions in which dollars are traded for goods, services, and assets. Markets reach equilibrium through changes in prices of goods, exchange rates, interest rates and other variables that determine the supplies and demands for goods, services and assets. The issue of the sustainability of the U.S. current account deficit -- or its counterpart, the capital and financial account surplus -- is, then, the issue of the sustainability of the combination of prices, interest rates, exchange rates, and so forth that give rise to the current account deficit.

Interpreting the Current Account

A common interpretation of the current account is that an increasing current account deficit is bad. One reason for such an interpretation is psychological -- we tend to view deficits as bad and surpluses as good. Thus, it is understandable that our initial instinct is to view an increasing deficit as bad. The possible error of this view is obvious: If the current account deficit is bad, so also is the capital and financial account surplus.

Concerns about current account deficits, however, are not strictly psychological. Several economic arguments suggest that an increasing current account deficit can be bad. A common argument begins by noting that to finance a current account deficit, the United States must borrow from abroad. Many perceive the accumulation of indebtedness to foreigners as a problem. In fact, the cumulative effect of U.S. current account deficits has made the net international asset position of the United States the largest such negative position in the world.

Some worry that if foreign nations suddenly attempted to liquidate their assets in the

United States, they might precipitate a financial crisis here. Such actions, however, are unlikely because foreign investors would be driving down their own wealth. Others are concerned about the sustainability of substantial levels of borrowing from abroad. Markets, however, will provide clear signals about sustainability by means of higher interest rates, lower exchange rates and reduced credit availability. At this point, there are no signals indicating such a problem.

Related to the issue of sustainability is the fact that the debt must be repaid. If most of the foreign financing is for capital goods, such as factories and equipment, that will allow for increased U.S. production in the future, then foreign debt is not necessarily a problem. If the foreign financing is for consumption goods, however, it may be undesirable because future generations will bear the burden of the debt. Accordingly, there are some reasonable arguments to support the view that an increasing current account deficit can be bad.

An Alternative View

There is another view, based on analyzing current account changes from a different perspective, that suggests in the present circumstances that the U.S. current account deficit is far from bad. This view starts from the position that capital and financial account transactions induce changes in the current account. To emphasize this alternative perspective, I'll now focus on the capital and financial account surplus. However, keep in mind that whenever I refer to the "capital and financial account surplus" you can substitute "current account deficit" because their dollar values are identical by the rules of accounting.

To illustrate: Assume that a foreign firm decides to build or expand a production facility in the United States. Two recent examples related to Dyersburg are Quebecor World's purchase and installation of a specialized printing press for high-quality magazines and catalogs and Northdown Industries' purchase of a building that will be converted to manufacture cat litter. In each of these cases, foreign residents are increasing their claims on assets in the United States. In terms of balance of payments accounting, these transactions would tend to increase the U.S. capital and financial account surplus, which, in turn, means that the U.S. current account deficit would increase.

An important question is what would induce foreign residents to increase their ownership of assets in the United States. It is reasonable to think that these investors would be looking at a rate of return, adjusted for risk, that is high enough relative to investing in other locations that makes the United States attractive. It is clear that in recent years the United States has been an attractive investment location. Low and stable inflation rates, rapid productivity growth and flexible labor markets are a few of the characteristics that have made the United States a rapidly growing economy and, therefore, an appealing investment location.

The preceding discussion suggests that we can gain a deeper insight into changes in the U.S. current account by examining saving and investment behavior both here and abroad. Our total investment spending as a country must be financed by a combination of domestic and foreign saving. Domestic saving consists of private saving and government saving. Until recently, government "saving" was actually dissaving because government spending exceeded tax revenue. Meanwhile, foreign saving directed to the United States is reflected in the magnitude of our current account deficit.

During the 1980s, the United States experienced rising deficits in both its current account and government budget balances. Chart 1 shows both of these balances relative to gross domestic product. It shows that these twin deficits moved in tandem in some years. Some economic analysts argued that the federal budget deficit was driving the current account. But that argument clearly breaks down during the 1990s. Chart 2 shows that these balances have tended to move in opposite directions since 1993. Moreover, based on research by Patricia Pollard, an economist at the Federal Reserve Bank of St. Louis, it is

US Current Account of Govt. Budget Balances: 1980s (% of GDP)
Chart 1

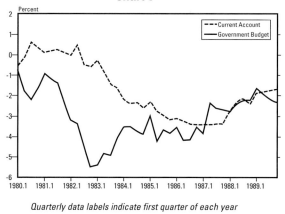

Quarterly data labels indicate first quarter of each year

Recent US Current Account of Govt. Budget Balances (% of GDP)
Chart 2

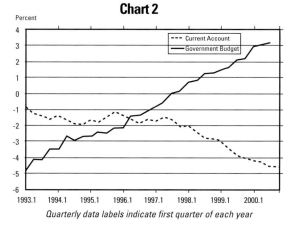

Quarterly data labels indicate first quarter of each year

clear that the twin deficit phenomenon is not a historical regularity in many advanced countries. She found that the changes in these two accounts are as likely to be moving in opposite directions as the same direction.

Now let's turn our attention to saving, both private and government, and investment. The current account deficit increases if either saving increases less than investment increases or if saving decreases more than investment decreases. Generally speaking, saving and investment are both desirable. Saving frees up resources that can be used for investment either

here or abroad. Gross private domestic investment, which includes the purchases of durable goods, such as business equipment, is essential for expanding both productive capacity and productivity. Such expansion permits more output to be produced in the future.

Chart 3 shows that the rising current account deficit in recent years has been accompanied by a rising rate of U.S. domestic investment. Between 1993 and 1997, the current account generally stayed in the range of 1.0 to 1.5 percent of gross domestic product, as a rising national saving rate, caused primarily by

Recent US Account Balance, Savings & Investment (% of GDP)
Chart 3

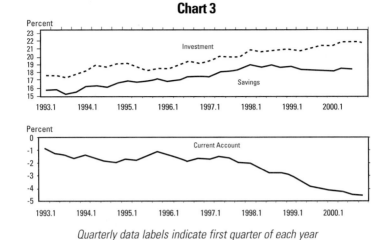

Quarterly data labels indicate first quarter of each year

US Current Account Balance & Real Trade Weighted Exchange Rate
(% of GDP)   Chart 4

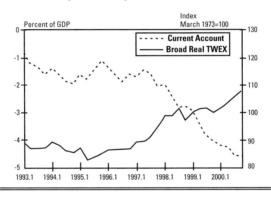

declining federal budget deficits, kept pace with rising domestic investment. In 1998, this pattern changed: Investment continued to rise, but saving stagnated and then fell slightly.

Chart 4 illustrates another fact that bolsters the contention that an increasing current account deficit is evidence of a strong and healthy economy. Since 1995, the foreign exchange value of the dollar has trended upward as shown by the solid line in the chart. If the current account were driving the capital account, then a weakening dollar would likely result. This reasoning is straightforward. A current account deficit means that the quantity of dollars demanded by foreign citizens to buy

U.S. goods is less than the quantity of dollars supplied by U.S. citizens to buy foreign goods. We might expect that this excess supply of dollars would put downward pressure on the foreign exchange value of the dollar. Alternatively, if the capital and financial account is driving the current account, then a strengthening dollar is possible. The reason is that the quantity of dollars demanded to make investments in the United States relative to the quantity of dollars supplied to make investments abroad can more than offset the excess supply of dollars for current account transactions. Given the attractiveness of U.S. assets, the dollar strengthens as international investors buy U.S. assets.

In fact, the relationship between investment and the current account for the United States appears to be a broad empirical regularity. Across developed countries that have experienced large current deficits, Pollard finds that the current account deficit systematically tends to increase as investment rises and tends to shrink as investment declines.

A return to smaller current account deficits requires a rise in saving and/or a fall in investment as a share of gross domestic product. Both of these changes took place during the late 1980s in the United States. Exactly when and how, or even whether, the present U.S. current account will shrink remains to be seen.

My investment discussion makes clear another critically important point. It is misleading to refer to the United States as a "debtor" nation. A significant share of international investment in the United States is equity investment. International investors who purchased shares of "dot-com" companies do not have to be repaid. Obviously, both domestic and international investors buy assets with the expectation of adequate returns, but may be disappointed after the fact. The important question is not whether investments made in 1999 will have to be repaid, but whether the U.S. investment climate this year and in the future will remain attractive to all investors, both domestic and international.

To date, my conclusion continues to be that the U.S. investment climate remains robust, perhaps surprisingly so given the extent of the stock market decline. Weaker near-term prospects seem not to have dimmed the long-run outlook of robust growth. Moreover, the dollar remains strong on the foreign exchange markets. It does not appear to me that the U.S. capital and financial account surplus is about to decline sharply. And that is good news rather than bad news.

Concluding Comments

What is clear from my discussion is that the capital and financial account drives the current account. The large U.S. current account deficit in recent years is the result of a large capital and financial account surplus. These annual surpluses reflect a healthy and growing U.S.

economy that has provided an excellent environment for investment. A similar comment applies more generally to developed economies that have experienced large current account deficits. An examination of the evidence shows that increased gross private domestic investment is systematically associated with increasing current account deficits. If longer-run U.S. economic growth declines, then it is reasonable to expect the U.S. current account deficit to shrink. However, as long as the fundamentals of the U.S. economy do not deteriorate rapidly, the prospects of a financial crisis are very slim. Thus, my answer to the question posed in the title of this presentation is that the United States certainly does not have a current account deficit disorder.

With respect to my own responsibilities, one fundamental that I see as crucial for a healthy U.S. economy is the control of inflation. An increasing inflation rate complicates the decisions of all economic actors and raises doubts about the real returns on U.S. assets -- one of the consequences being that the attractiveness of acquiring and holding U.S. assets relative to foreign assets is reduced. Such a development would cause the capital and financial account surplus to decrease and, thus, the current account deficit would also decrease. Even though some might view such a change in the current account as desirable, the key to assessing the desirability of such a change hinges on the reason for the change. Rising inflation is not a desirable event condition for the U. S. economy.

I hope the perspective I've offered on the U.S. current account deficit is useful to you. If nothing else, remember that it makes no sense to be concerned about that deficit unless you are also concerned about the capital account surplus, because one is a necessary implication of the other. A little accounting can take us far in the direction of focusing on the real issues and not just on that scary word "deficit"!

Remarks before the Business and Community Leaders Luncheon, The Lannom Center, Dyersburg, Tennessee. April 10, 2001

Discussion Questions

V

1. Explain how a government budget deficit can cause a current account deficit.

2. What reasons do Cletus Coughlin and Patricia Pollard cite for concluding that savings behavior is insufficient in explaining the US current account deficit?

3. Do you think the large US current account deficit is a serious problem?
    Why or why not?

4. According to William Poole is the US current account deficit bad?
    Explain why or why not.

Exchange Rates

This section examines a selection of topics involving the foreign exchange market. "The Structure of the Foreign Exchange Market" by Sam Cross presents an overview of the foreign exchange market. As the article indicates, the foreign exchange market is the largest and most liquid market in the world. In this market, transactions take place 24 hours a day. The market comprises an international network of dealer institutions that are geographically dispersed. Access to the foreign exchange market is open to participants from all countries and information is transmitted simultaneously. Hence at any one moment, the exchange rates of major countries are identical in all the financial centers. Further, the market's most widely traded currency is the US dollar because it is a "vehicle" currency.

The second article, "What Determines the Exchange Rate: Market Factors or Market Sentiment," by Gregory Hopper, presents the leading theories of exchange rate determination. Most economists believe that economic forces such as the money supply, the trade balance, or output influence the exchange rate. Hopper argues that the three major models of exchange rate determination (monetary model, overshooting model, and portfolio balance approach) are unsatisfactory in explaining movements in the exchange rate. He proposes an alternate view; that "market sentiment" could cause short-run exchange rate movements. Under this view

the exchange rate is influenced by a self-fulfilling prophecy.

Richard Cooper in "Exchange Rate Choices" presents the history of thought about exchange rates choices and explains the movement from flexible rates to fixed rates during the first half of the 20th century, and the movement from fixed to flexible rates from 1970. Cooper finishes the article by examining which exchange rate regimes are best for developing and developed countries. He argues that flexible exchange rates are not necessarily compatible for countries with small or poorly developed domestic capital markets.

Peter Kenen from Princeton University provides the case in favor and against fixed exchange rates in "Fixed versus Floating Exchange Rates." Kenen concludes that all countries, except the smallest, should adopt flexible exchange rates because the reasons for a fixed exchange rate have limited validity. He further argues that pegged but adjustable exchange rates are not viable. "Does the Exchange Rate Regime Matter for Inflation and Growth?" by Ghosh, Osry, Gulde, and Wolf discusses how various exchange rate regimes affect inflation and growth. They find there is a strong link between fixed exchange rates and low inflation because of monetary discipline. However, they also find evidence that productivity growth rates are higher for countries with flexible exchange rates. This correlation is valid despite higher net investment under fixed exchange rates.

The sixth article in this section, on "Currency Boards" by Sharmila King, presents arguments for and against a currency board. Countries that adopt a currency board arrangement are required to back local currency with foreign reserves denominated in "hard" currency. The article concludes with a discussion on Hong Kong's currency board arrangement, which is in its 20th year.

Following the collapse of Argentina's currency board, many economists debated dollarization as an alternate arrangement. Dollarization occurs when a country replaces its national currency with another currency (as the name implies, this is typically the US dollar) as legal tender. The final article, "Dollarization as a Monetary Arrangement for Emerging Market Economies" by Gaetano Antinolfi and Todd Keister, focuses on the reasons why countries consider dollarization and the costs and benefits associated with dollarization.

21

The Structure of the Foreign Exchange Market

SAM Y. CROSS

It Is the World's Largest Market

The foreign exchange market is by far the largest and most liquid market in the world. The estimated worldwide turnover of reporting dealers, at around $1.5 trillion a day, is several times the level of turnover in the U.S. Government securities market, the world's second largest market. Turnover is equivalent to more than $200 in foreign exchange market transactions, every business day of the year, for every man, woman, and child on earth!

The breadth, depth, and liquidity of the market are truly impressive. Individual trades of $200 million to $500 million are not uncommon. Quoted prices change as often as 20 times a minute. It has been estimated that the world's most active exchange rates can change up to 18,000 times during a single day. Large trades can be made, yet econometric studies indicate that prices tend to move in relatively small increments, a sign of a smoothly functioning and liquid market.

While turnover of around $1.5 trillion per day is a good indication of the level of activity and liquidity in the global foreign exchange market, it is not necessarily a useful measure of other forces in the world economy. Almost two-thirds of the total represents transactions among the reporting dealers themselves—with only one-third accounted for by their transactions with financial and non-financial customers. It is important to realize that an initial dealer transaction with a customer in the foreign exchange market often leads to multiple further transactions, sometimes over an extended period, as the dealer institutions readjust their own positions to hedge, manage, or offset the risks involved. The result is that the amount of trading with customers of a large dealer institution active in the interbank market often accounts for a very small share of that institution's total foreign exchange activity.

Among the various financial centers around the world, the largest amount of foreign exchange trading takes place in the United Kingdom, even though that nation's currency – the pound sterling – is less widely traded in the market than several others. As shown in Figure 1, the United Kingdom accounts for about 32 percent of the global total; the United States ranks a distant second with about 18 percent, and Japan is third with 8 percent. Thus, together, the three largest markets—one each in the European, Western Hemisphere, and Asian time zones—account for about 58 percent of global trading. After these three leaders comes Singapore with 7 percent.

The large volume of trading activity in the United Kingdom reflects London's strong position as an international financial center where a large number of financial institutions are located. In the 1998 foreign exchange market turnover survey, 213 foreign exchange dealer institutions in the United Kingdom reported trading activity to the Bank of England, compared with 93 in the United States reporting to the Federal Reserve Bank of New York.

Shares of Reported Global Foreign Exchange Turnover 1998
Figure 1

Source: Bank of International Settlements.
Note: Percent of total reporting foreign exchange turnover, adjusted for intra-country double-counting.

In foreign exchange trading, London benefits not only from its proximity to major Eurocurrency credit markets and other financial markets, but also from its geographical location and time zone. In addition to being open when the numerous other financial centers in Europe are open, London's morning hours overlap with the late hours in a number of Asian and Middle East markets; London's afternoon sessions correspond to the morning periods in the large North American market. Thus, surveys have indicated that there is more foreign exchange trading in dollars in London than in the United States, and more foreign exchange trading in marks than in Germany. However, the bulk of trading in London, about 85 percent, is accounted for by foreign-owned (non-U.K. owned) institutions, with U.K.-based dealers of North American institutions reporting 49 percent, or three times the share of U.K.-owned institutions there.

It Is a Twenty-Four Hour Market

During the past quarter century, the concept of a twenty-four hour market has become a reality. Somewhere on the planet, financial centers are open for business, and banks and other institutions are trading the dollar and other currencies, every hour of the day and night, aside from possible minor gaps on weekends. In financial centers around the world, business hours overlap; as some centers close, others open and begin to trade. The foreign exchange market follows the sun around the earth.

The international date line is located in the western Pacific, and each business day arrives first in the Asia-Pacific financial centers – first Wellington, New Zealand, then Sydney, Australia, followed by Tokyo, Hong Kong, and Singapore. A few hours later, while markets remain active in those Asian centers, trading begins in Bahrain and elsewhere in the Middle East. Later still, when it is late in the business day in Tokyo, markets in Europe open for business. Subsequently, when it is early afternoon in Europe, trading in New York and other U.S. centers starts. Finally, completing the circle, when it is mid- or late-afternoon in the United States, the next day has arrived in the Asia-Pacific area, the first markets there have opened, and the process begins again.

The twenty-four hour market means that exchange rates and market conditions can change at any time in response to developments that can take place at any time. It also means that traders and other market participants must be alert to the possibility that a sharp move in an exchange rate can occur during an off hour, elsewhere in the world. The large dealing institutions have adapted to these conditions, and have introduced various arrangements for monitoring markets and trading on a twenty-four hour basis. Some keep their New York or other trading desks open twenty-four hours a day, others pass the torch from one office to the next, and still others follow different approaches.

However, foreign exchange activity does not flow evenly. Over the course of a day, there is a cycle characterized by periods of very heavy activity and other periods of relatively light activity. Most of the trading takes place when the largest number of potential counterparties is available or accessible on a global basis. (Figure 2 gives a general sense of participation levels in the global foreign exchange market by tracking electronic conversations per hour.) Market liquidity is of great importance to participants. Sellers want to sell when they have access to the maximum number of potential buyers, and buyers want to buy when they have access to the maximum number of potential sellers.

Business is heavy when both the U.S. markets and the major European markets are open – that is, when it is morning in New York and afternoon in London. In the New York market, nearly two-thirds of the day's activity typically takes place in the morning hours. Activity normally becomes very slow in New York in the mid- to late afternoon, after European markets have closed and before the Tokyo, Hong Kong, and Singapore markets have opened.

Given this uneven flow of business around the clock, market participants often will respond less aggressively to an exchange rate development that occurs at a relatively inactive time of day, and will wait to see whether the development is confirmed when the major markets open. Some institutions pay little attention to developments in less active markets. Nonetheless, the twenty-four hour market does provide a continuous "real-time" market assessment of the ebb and flow of influences and attitudes with respect to the traded currencies, and an opportunity for a quick judgment of unexpected events. With many traders carrying pocket monitors, it has become relatively easy to stay in touch with market developments at all times – indeed, too easy, some harassed traders might say. The foreign exchange market provides a kind of never-ending beauty contest or horse race, where market participants can continuously adjust their bets to reflect their changing views.

The Market Is Made Up of an International Network of Dealers

The market consists of a limited number of major dealer institutions that are particularly active in foreign exchange, trading with customers and (more often) with each other. Most, but not all, are commercial banks and investment banks. These dealer institutions are geographically dispersed, located in numerous financial centers around the world. Wherever located, these institutions are linked to, and in close communication with, each other through telephones, computers, and other electronic means.

There are around 2,000 dealer institutions whose foreign exchange activities are covered by the Bank for International Settlements' central bank survey, and who, essentially, make up the global foreign exchange market. A much smaller subset of those institutions accounts for the bulk of trading and market-making activity. It is estimated that there are 100-200 market-making banks worldwide; major players are fewer than that.

At a time when there is much talk about an integrated world economy and "the global village," the foreign exchange market comes closest to functioning in a truly global fashion, linking the various foreign exchange trading centers from around the world into a single, unified, cohesive, worldwide market. Foreign

The Cicadian Rhythms of the FX Market
Electronic conversations per hour (Monday - Friday, 1992-93)
Figure 2

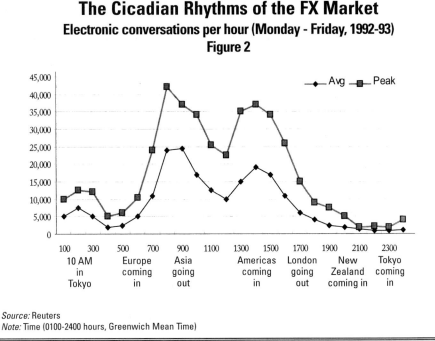

Source: Reuters
Note: Time (0100-2400 hours, Greenwich Mean Time)

exchange trading takes place among dealers and other market professionals in a large number of individual financial centers – New York, Chicago, Los Angeles, London, Tokyo, Singapore, Frankfurt, Paris, Zurich, Milan, and many, many others. But no matter in which financial center a trade occurs, the same currencies, or rather, bank deposits denominated in the same currencies, are being bought and sold.

A foreign exchange dealer buying dollars in one of those markets actually is buying a dollar-denominated deposit in a bank located in the United States, or a claim of a bank abroad on a dollar deposit in a bank located in the United States. This holds true regardless of the location of the financial center at which the dollar deposit is purchased. Similarly, a dealer buying Deutsche marks, no matter where the purchase is made, actually is buying a mark deposit in a bank in Germany or a claim on a mark deposit in a bank in Germany. And so on for other currencies.

Each nation's market has its own infrastructure. For foreign exchange market operations as well as for other matters, each country enforces its own laws, banking regulations, accounting rules, and tax code, and, as noted above, it operates its own payment and settlement systems. Thus, even in a global foreign exchange market with currencies traded on essentially the same terms simultaneously in many financial centers, there are different national financial systems and infrastructures through which transactions are executed, and within which currencies are held.

With access to all of the foreign exchange markets generally open to participants from all countries, and with vast amounts of market information transmitted simultaneously and almost instantly to dealers throughout the world, there is an enormous amount of cross-border foreign exchange trading among dealers as well as between dealers and their customers. At any moment, the exchange rates of major currencies tend to be virtually identical in all of the financial centers where there is active trading. Rarely are there such substantial price differences among major centers as to provide major opportunities for arbitrage. In pricing, the various financial centers that are open for business and active at any one time are effectively integrated into a single market.

Accordingly, a bank in the United States is likely to trade foreign exchange at least as frequently with banks in London, Frankfurt, and other open foreign centers as with other banks in the United States. Surveys indicate that when major dealing institutions in the United States trade with other dealers, 58 percent of the transactions are with dealers located outside the United States. The United States is not unique in that respect. Dealer institutions in other major countries also report that more than half of their trades are with dealers that are across borders; dealers also use brokers located both domestically and abroad.

The Market's Most Widely Traded Currency Is the Dollar

The dollar is by far the most widely traded currency. According to the 1998 survey, the dollar was one of the two currencies involved in an estimated 87 percent of global foreign exchange transactions, equal to about $1.3 trillion a day. In part, the widespread use of the dollar reflects its substantial international role as: "investment" currency in many capital markets, "reserve" currency held by many central banks, "transaction" currency in many international commodity markets, "invoice" currency in many contracts, and "intervention" currency employed by monetary authorities in market operations to influence their own exchange rates.

In addition, the widespread trading of the dollar reflects its use as a "vehicle" currency in foreign exchange transactions, a use that reinforces, and is reinforced by, its international role in trade and finance. For most pairs of currencies, the market practice is to trade each of the two currencies against a common third currency as a vehicle, rather than to trade the two currencies directly against each other. The vehicle currency used most often is the dollar, although by the mid-1990s the Deutsche mark also had become an important vehicle, with its use, especially in Europe, having increased sharply during the 1980s and 1990s.

Thus, a trader wanting to shift funds from one currency to another, say, from Swedish krona to Philippine pesos, will probably sell krona for U.S. dollars and then sell the U.S. dollars for pesos. Although this approach results in two transactions rather than one, it may be the preferred way, since the dollar/Swedish krona market, and the dollar/Philippine peso market are much more active and liquid and have much better information than a bilateral market for the two currencies directly against each other. By using the dollar or some other currency as a vehicle, banks and other foreign exchange market participants can limit more of their working balances to the vehicle currency, rather than holding and managing many currencies, and can concentrate their research and information sources on the vehicle.

Use of a vehicle currency greatly reduces the number of exchange rates that must be dealt with in a multilateral system. In a system of 10 currencies, if one currency is selected as vehicle currency and used for all transactions, there would be a total of nine currency pairs or exchange rates to be dealt with (i.e., one exchange rate for the vehicle currency against each of the others), whereas if no vehicle currency were used, there would be 45 exchange rates to be dealt with. In a system of 100 currencies with no vehicle currencies, potentially there would be 4,950 currency pairs or exchange rates [the formula is: $n(n-1)/2$]. Thus, using a vehicle currency can yield the advantages of fewer, larger, and more liquid markets with fewer currency balances, reduced informational needs, and simpler operations.

The US dollar took on a major vehicle currency role with the introduction of the Bretton Woods par value system, in which most nations met their IMF exchange rate obligations by buying and selling U.S. dollars to maintain a par value relationship for their own currency against the U.S. dollar. The dollar was a convenient vehicle, not only because of its central role in the exchange rate system and its widespread use as a reserve currency, but also because of the presence of large and liquid dollar money and other financial markets, and, in time, the Euro-dollar markets where dollars needed for (or resulting from) foreign exchange transactions could conveniently be borrowed (or placed).

Changing conditions in the 1980s and 1990s altered this situation. In particular, the Deutsche mark (dem) began to play a much more significant role as a vehicle currency and, more importantly, in direct "cross trading."

As the European Community moved toward economic integration and monetary unification, the relationship of the European Monetary System (EMS) currencies to each other became of greater concern than the relationship of their currencies to the dollar. An intra-European currency market developed, centering on the mark and on Germany as the strongest currency and largest economy. Direct intervention in members' currencies, rather than through the dollar, became widely practiced. Events such as the EMS currency crisis of September 1992, when a number of European currencies came under severe market pressure against the mark, confirmed the extent to which direct use of the dem for intervening in the exchange market could be more effective than going through the dollar.

Against this background, there was very rapid growth in direct cross rate trading involving the Deutsche mark, much of it against European currencies, during the 1980s and 1990s. (A "cross rate" is an exchange rate between two non-dollar currencies—e.g., dem/Swiss franc, dem/pound, and dem/yen.) There are derived cross rates calculated from the dollar rates of each of the two currencies, and there are direct cross rates that come from direct trading between the two currencies—which can result in narrower spreads where there is a viable market. In a number of European countries, the volume of trading of the local currency against the Deutsche mark grew to exceed local currency trading against the dollar, and the practice developed of using cross rates between the dem and other European currencies to determine the dollar rates for those currencies.

With its increased use as a vehicle currency and its role in cross trading, the Deutsche mark was involved in 30 percent of global currency turnover in the 1998 survey. That was still far below the dollar (which was involved in 87 percent of global turnover), but well above the Japanese yen (ranked third, at 21 percent), and the pound sterling (ranked fourth, at 11 percent).

It Is an "Over-The-Counter" Market with an "Exchange-Traded" Segment

Until the 1970s, all foreign exchange trading in the United States (and elsewhere) was handled "over-the-counter," (OTC) by banks in different locations making deals via telephone and telex. In the United States, the OTC market was then, and is now, largely unregulated as a market. Buying and selling foreign currencies is considered the exercise of an express banking power. Thus, a commercial bank in the United States does not need any special authorization to trade or deal in foreign exchange. Similarly, securities firms and brokerage firms do not need permission from the Securities and Exchange Commission (SEC) or any other body to engage in foreign exchange activity. Transactions can be carried out on whatever terms and with whatever provisions are permitted by law and acceptable to the two counterparties, subject to the standard commercial law governing business transactions in the United States.

There are no official rules or restrictions in the United States governing the hours or conditions of trading. The trading conventions have been developed mostly by market participants. There is no official code prescribing what constitutes good market practice. However, the Foreign Exchange Committee, an independent body sponsored by the Federal Reserve Bank of New York and composed of representatives from institutions participating in the market, produces and regularly updates its report on Guidelines for Foreign Exchange Trading. These Guidelines seek to clarify common market practices and offer "best practice recommendations" with respect to trading activities, relationships, and other matters. The report is a purely advisory document designed to foster the healthy functioning and development of the foreign exchange market in the United States.

Although the OTC market is not regulated as a market in the way that the organized exchanges are regulated, regulatory authorities examine the foreign exchange market activities of banks and certain other institutions participating in the OTC market. As with other business activities in which these institutions are engaged, examiners look at trading systems, activities, and exposure, focusing on the safety and soundness of the institution and its activities. Examinations deal with such matters as capital adequacy, control systems, disclosure, sound banking practice, legal compliance, and other factors relating to the safety and soundness of the institution.

The OTC market accounts for well over 90 percent of total U.S. foreign exchange market activity, covering both the traditional (pre-1970) products (spot, outright forwards, and FX swaps) as well as the more recently introduced (post-1970) OTC products (currency options and currency swaps). On the "organized exchanges," foreign exchange products traded are currency futures and certain currency options.

Trading practices on the organized exchanges, and the regulatory arrangements covering the exchanges, are markedly different from those in the OTC market. In the exchanges, trading takes place publicly in a centralized location. Hours, trading practices, and other matters are regulated by the particular exchange; products are standardized. There are margin payments, daily marking to market, and cash settlements through a central clearinghouse. With respect to regulation, exchanges at which currency futures are traded are under the jurisdiction of the Commodity Futures Trading Corporation (CFTC); in the case of currency options, either the CFTC or the Securities and Exchange Commission serves as regulator, depending on whether securities are traded on the exchange.

Steps are being taken internationally to help improve the risk management practices of dealers in the foreign exchange market, and to encourage greater transparency and disclosure. With respect to the internationally active banks, there has been a move under the auspices of the Basle Committee on Banking Supervision of the BIS to introduce greater consistency internationally to risk-based capital adequacy requirements. Over the past decade, the regulators of a number of nations have accepted common rules proposed by the Basle Committee with respect to capital adequacy requirements for credit risk, covering exposures of internationally active banks in all activities, including foreign exchange. Further proposals of the Basle Committee for risk-based capital requirements for market risk have been adopted more recently. With respect to investment firms and other financial institutions, international discussions have not yet produced agreements on common capital adequacy standards.

22

What Determines the Exchange Rate: Market Factors or Market Sentiment?

GREGORY P. **HOPPER**

Readers of the financial press are familiar with the gyrations of the currency market. No matter which way currencies zig or zag, it seems there is always an analyst with a quotable, ready explanation. Either interest rates are rising faster than expected in some country, or the trade balance is up or down, or central banks are tightening or loosening their monetary policies. Whatever the explanations, the underlying belief is that exchange rates are affected by fundamental economic forces, such as money supplies, interest rates, real output levels, or the trade balance, which, if well forecasted, give the forecaster an advantage in predicting the exchange rate.

What is not so well known outside academia is that exchange rates don't seem to be affected by economic fundamentals in the short run. Being able to predict money supplies, central bank policies, or other supposed influences doesn't help forecast the exchange rate. Economists have found instead that the best forecast of the exchange rate, at least in the short run, is whatever it happens to be today.

In this article, we'll review exchange-rate economics, focusing on what is predictable and what isn't. We'll see that exchange rates seem to be influenced by market sentiment rather than by economic fundamentals, and we'll examine the practical implications of this fact. Sometimes, there are situations in which market participants may be able to forecast the direction but not the timing of the movement. We'll also see that volatility of exchange rates and correlations between exchange rates are predictable, and we'll examine the implications for currency option pricing, risk management, and portfolio selection.

The Exchange Rate and Economic Fundamentals

The earliest model of the exchange rate, the monetary model, assumes that the current exchange rate is determined by current fundamental economic variables: money supplies and output levels of the countries. When the fundamentals are combined with market expectations of future exchange rates, the model yields the value of the current exchange rate. The monetary model might also be dubbed the "newspaper model." When analyzing movements in the exchange rate, journalists often use the results of the monetary model. Similarly, when Wall Street analysts are asked to justify their exchange-rate predictions, they will typically resort to some variant of the monetary model. This model is popular because it provides intuitive relationships between the economic fundamentals and it's based on standard macroeconomic reasoning.

The reasoning behind the monetary model is simple: the exchange rate is determined by the relative price levels of the two countries. If goods and services cost twice as much, on average, in U.S. dollars as they do in a foreign currency, $2 will fetch one unit of the foreign currency. That way, the same goods and services will cost the same whether they are bought in the U.S. or in the foreign country.[1]

But what determines the relative price levels of the two countries? The monetary model focuses on the demand and supply of money. If the money supply in the United States rises, but nothing else changes, the average level of prices in the United States will tend to rise. Since the price level in the foreign country remains fixed, more dollars will be needed to get one unit of foreign currency. Hence, the dollar price of the foreign currency will rise: the dollar will depreciate—it's worth less in terms of the foreign currency.

Money supplies are not the only economic fundamentals in the monetary model. The level of real output in each country matters as well because it affects the price level. For example, if the level of output in the United States rises, but other fundamental factors, such as the U.S. money supply, remain constant, the average level of prices in the United States will tend to fall, producing an appreciation in the dollar.[2] Future economic fundamentals also matter because they determine the market's expectations about the future exchange rate. Not surprisingly, market expectations of the future exchange rate matter for the current exchange rate. If the market expects the dollar price of the yen to become higher in the future than it is today, the dollar price of the yen will tend to be high today. But if the market expects the dollar price of the yen to be lower in the future than it is today, the dollar price of the yen will tend to be low today.

Here's an example of how to use the monetary model: suppose we wanted to predict the dollar-yen exchange rate. The first thing we need to do is think about the relationships between the fundamentals and the exchange rate. The monetary model implies that if the U.S. money supply is growing faster than the Japanese money supply, the dollar price of the yen will rise: the dollar will depreciate and the yen will appreciate. So, the analyst needs to assess monetary policy in the two countries. The monetary model also implies that if output is growing faster in the United States than it is in Japan, the dollar price of the yen will tend to fall: the dollar will appreciate and the yen will depreciate. Finally, the analyst must assess expectations about the future exchange rate. If the market's expectation of the future exchange rate were to change, the current exchange rate would move in the same direction. When making an exchange-rate forecast based on the monetary model, the analyst must consider the effect of all the fundamentals simultaneously. He can do this by using a statistical model or by combining judgment with the use of a statistical model.

In practice, using the monetary model to make exchange-rate forecasts is difficult because the analyst never knows the true value of the economic fundamentals. At any time, money supply and output levels are not known with certainty; they must be forecast based on the available economic data. Of course, expectations about the future of the exchange rate are even harder to assess because these expectations are unobservable. The analyst can always survey market participants about their expectations, but he can never be sure if the surveys accurately reflect the market's views. If we assume the monetary model is valid, the goal of the successful exchange-rate forecaster is to predict the values of the fundamentals better than the competition and then use the monetary model or some variant to derive forecasts of the exchange rate.

The fatal flaw in this strategy is the assumption that the monetary model can be used to successfully forecast the exchange rate once the values of the fundamentals are known. Although the monetary model had some early success, economists have established that the model fails empirically except perhaps in unusual periods such as hyperinflations.[3] For one thing, research did not establish a strong statistical relationship between exchange rates and the values of the fundamentals. Moreover, a key assumption of the model was found to be false: the model assumes that the price level can move freely. Yet the price level seems to be "sticky," meaning that it moves very slowly compared with the movement of the exchange rate.

What about other models? After the failure of the monetary model became apparent, economists went to work developing other ideas. Rudiger Dornbusch developed a variant of the monetary model called *the overshooting model,* in which the average level of prices is assumed to be fixed in the short run to reflect the real-world finding that many prices don't change frequently. The effect of this assumption is to cause the exchange rate to over-shoot its long-run value as a result of a change in the fundamentals; eventually, however, the exchange rate returns to its long-run value. Ultimately, this model was shown to fail empirically: economists couldn't find the strong statistical relationships between the fundamentals and the exchange rate that should exist if the model were true.[4]

Another extension of the simple monetary model is called *the portfolio balance model.* In this approach, the supply of and demand for foreign and domestic bonds, along with the supply of and demand for foreign and domestic money, determine the exchange rate. Early tests of the model were not very encouraging.[5] Later, economists formulated a more sophisticated version of the portfolio balance model, in which investors were assumed to choose a portfolio of domestic and foreign bonds in an optimal way. According to the more sophisticated portfolio balance theory, the degree to which investors are willing to substitute domestic for foreign bonds depends on how much investors dislike risk, how volatile the returns on the bonds are, and the extent to which the returns on the different bonds in the portfolio move together. Unfortunately, economists did not find much empirical support for the more sophisticated version of the portfolio balance model.[6]

Economic News. Thus, the three major models of the exchange rate—the monetary, the overshooting, and the portfolio balance models—do not provide a satisfactory account of the exchange rate. Nonetheless, it is possible that *news about the fundamentals* affects the exchange rate even if the fundamentals themselves don't influence the exchange rate in the manner suggested by the three major exchange rate models.

The news about the fundamentals can be defined as the difference between what market participants expect the fundamentals to be and what the fundamentals actually are once their values are announced. For example, market participants form expectations about the value of the money supply before the government announces the money supply figures, and these expectations are translated into decisions to buy or sell currency. These decisions ultimately help to determine the current level of the exchange rate. Once the government announces the value of the money supply, market participants buy or sell currencies as long as the news is different from what they expected. Thus, news about fundamentals, under this view, is an important determinant of the exchange rate.

The difficulty in testing this view is that economists don't know how to measure the news because they don't know how to measure the market's expectations. One solution is to assume that market participants form their expectations using a statistical device called linear regression. Using linear regression, an econometrician could estimate the expected level of a fundamental, such as the U.S. money supply, for each quarter during the past 20 years. He could then subtract the value of the estimated expected money supply from its actual value in each quarter to generate an estimate of the news about the quarterly U.S. money supply. The news for other fundamentals can be estimated in a similar way.

Once the econometrician has estimated each fundamental's news for each quarter during the last 20 years, he can check to see if it explains the level of the exchange rate. Studies by economists who have carried out this procedure generally indicate that news about the fundamentals explains the exchange rate better than the three major exchange-rate models.[7] However, two factors make this result hard to interpret. First, we have no direct evidence suggesting that market participants form their expectations using linear regression models or that they form their expectations as if they were using these models. Second, these studies use the final values of the fundamentals, values released by governments months, if not years, after the forecasts were made. Yet, forecasters must use the government's preliminary estimates of the fundamentals when they make their predictions. In other words, the econometrician is assuming that market participants are making forecasts using information they don't have. Hence, the result that news about the fundamentals seems to explain the level of the exchange rate better than the models is hard to interpret.

One way to avoid the problem of using final values of fundamentals is to collect the initial estimates from newspapers, government announcements, and wire services and examine their ability to affect the level of the exchange rate. Studies that have done this have found that announcements about fundamentals affect the exchange rate only in the very short run: the effects of announcements generally disappear after a day or two.

When we look at the evidence from the three major exchange-rate models, from the news analysis, and from the effects of announcements, it is hard not to be pessimistic about the fundamentals' ability to explain the exchange rate. But the evidence we have examined so far is backward-looking: the fundamentals don't seem to explain exchange-rate behavior over the past couple of decades. However, we can also do a forward-looking analysis: do the fundamentals help us forecast the level of the exchange rate?

The surprising answer to this question, given by economists Richard Meese and Kenneth Rogoff in the early 1980s, is no. Meese and Rogoff examined the ability of the fundamentals to predict the level of the exchange rate for horizons up to one year. They considered fundamentals-based economic models as well as statistical models of the relationship between the fundamentals and the exchange rate that did not incorporate economic assumptions. They found that a naive strategy of using today's exchange rate as a forecast works at least as well as any of the economic or statistical models. Worse, they found that when they endowed the economic or statistical models with final values of

the fundamentals—giving the models an advantage that forecasters could not possibly match—the naive strategy still won the forecasting contest. Despite many attempts since the publication of Meese and Rogoff's results, economists have not convincingly overturned their findings.

Thus, if we look backward or forward over periods of up to a year, the fundamentals don't seem to explain the exchange rate, contrary to what standard models in international finance textbooks imply. But this result might be dismissed by claiming that only the models tested have failed to explain the exchange rate. Perhaps economists will discover a model that works in the future.

Although a fundamentals-based model that works is a possibility, evidence from other countries suggests otherwise. In the European Exchange Rate Mechanism (ERM), exchange rates between major European currencies are kept relatively stable by the countries' central banks. If fundamentals are closely associated with the currencies, they should be stabilized as well. However, when we examine European fundamentals, we find that they fluctuate about as much as do the fundamentals of nonstabilized currencies, such as the U.S. dollar. Hence, the evidence from the European experience does not suggest a close connection between the fundamentals and the exchange rate, leading one to suspect that no fundamentals-based model will predict the short-run exchange rate.[8]

It's possible that the fundamentals really do explain the exchange rate, but we can't see the relationship because we can't observe the true fundamentals. Perhaps if economists discovered different economic models that use fundamentals other than money supplies and real output levels, the exchange rate could still be explained in terms of basic economic quantities. For example, some economic models imply that the true fundamentals are business technologies and tastes and preferences of consumers. However, the evidence from European countries renders this potential solution implausible. According to such a model, stabilization of European currencies in the ERM corresponds to stabilization of the true fundamentals. But why should business technologies and tastes and preferences of consumers change less in Europe than they do in the United States? At present, economists have found no evidence to suggest they do and, indeed, have little reason to suppose that they will ever find such evidence.

The Alternative View: Market Sentiment Matters

The alternative view is that exchange rates are determined, at least in the short run (i.e., periods less than two years), by market sentiment. Under this view, the level of the exchange rate is the result of a self-fulfilling prophecy: participants in the foreign exchange market expect a currency to be at a certain level in the future; when they act on their expectations and buy or sell the currency, it ends up at the predicted level, confirming their expectations.

Even if exchange rates are determined by market sentiment in the short run, the fundamentals are still important, but not in the commonly supposed way. From reading the newspapers, we know that market participants take the fundamentals very seriously when forming exchange-rate expectations. Thus, if we wish to understand the level of the exchange rate, we need to know the values of the fundamentals and, more important, how market participants interpret those levels. However, the evidence we reviewed shows no pattern or necessary connection between the fundamentals and the level of the exchange rate. When market participants use the fundamentals to form expectations about the exchange rate, they don't use them in any consistent way that could be picked up by an economic or statistical model. As we have seen, we can do as well forecasting the exchange rate by quoting today's rate.

Although the naive forecast is at least as accurate as statistical or model-based forecasts, it's still not very good. It's just that statistical or model-based forecasts are so bad that even the naive forecast can do at least as well. How can we improve our forecast? Unfortunately, economists are just starting to

build models of market sentiment, so we can't get much guidance from economic theory just yet. Nonetheless, we know that exchange rates are likely determined by market sentiment, so it seems reasonable to try to understand the psychology of the foreign exchange market to improve forecasts of the short-run exchange rate.

To understand the psychology of the foreign exchange market, we need to know about the various economic theories. Even if they aren't very accurate, their implications may still influence expectations in the market, although we would not expect any particular model to have any consistent influence. We also need to find out what the market is thinking. Probably the best way to do so is to be an active participant in the foreign exchange market and to talk to other participants to learn which events they think are important for a particular currency's outlook. These events might be announcements of fundamentals, political events, or some other factors. The analyst could then concentrate on forecasting those events. Of course, there will probably be no pattern to which events are important. For example, the U.S. budget deficit may well be important for the dollar one year and unimportant the next.

Speculative Attacks. In some cases, the forecaster might be able to make a reasonable guess about the direction of the exchange rate's movement, even if he can't be precise about the timing. As an example, let's review what happened to the exchange rate between the Swedish krona and the German deutsche mark in the early 1990s.

Sweden applied to enter the ERM in May 1991 in a bid to stabilize its currency. To stabilize the krona-deutsche mark exchange rate, interest rates in Sweden and Germany had to be the same. Therefore, the Swedish and German central banks couldn't independently use monetary policy—that is, change short-term interest rates—if they wanted to keep the exchange rate stable.[9] If Sweden wanted to act independently, it had to use fiscal policy (tax and government spending policies) to stimulate the country's growth rate. However, a weak Swedish economy provoked

Daily Percent Dollar Return on Deutsche Mark
Figure 1

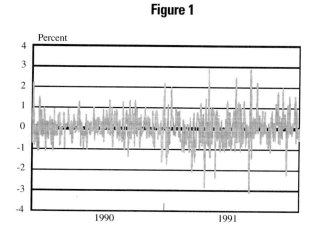

speculators, who mounted an attack on the krona in September 1992. Speculators knew that the weak economy would tempt Sweden to abandon its fixed exchange rate and use monetary policy to cut short-term interest rates, especially since the new Swedish government was adopting restrictive fiscal policy. Speculators believed that if the Swedish central bank cut the short-term interest rate, the krona wouldn't be as attractive to investors. Thus, the speculators thought that after interest rates were cut, the currency would depreciate with respect to other ERM currencies. But since speculators expected the depreciation to happen, they decided to sell the currency immediately, i.e., mount a speculative attack on the currency.

This attack put the Swedish central bank in an uncomfortable position. To combat the currency's depreciation, the central bank raised short-term interest rates temporarily to repel the speculative attack—exactly the policy it didn't want in the face of sluggish economic growth. In fact, the Swedish central bank raised the short-term interest rate to an astonishing 500 percent and held it there for four days.[10]

The speculators were deterred, but not for long. The speculators understood that the Swedish central bank had to raise short-term interest rates temporarily to support the cur-

rency. But they were betting that the central bank wouldn't fight off the attack for long, especially in the face of disquiet in the country resulting from weak economic growth and the higher interest rates needed to fight the speculative attack. The high short-term interest rates had made the economic situation in Sweden even more precarious, so, in November, the speculators attacked again, selling the krona in favor of other ERM currencies. This time the Swedish central bank did not aggressively raise interest rates and the krona depreciated.

Profit opportunities such as this one can sometimes be exploited by speculators who recognize that a country's exchange-rate policy is inconsistent with the monetary policy needed, given a country's domestic situation. By paying careful attention to a country's economic and political developments, a speculator can sometimes forecast the direction of a currency's move when it breaks out of a stabilized exchange rate system. But the timing is not easily forecast; it is probably determined by market sentiment.[11]

What About Technical Rules?

Many market participants don't rely on the fundamentals. Instead, they use technical rules, which are procedures for identifying patterns in exchange rates. A simple technical rule involves looking at interest rates in two countries. Suppose the first country is the United States and the second is Canada. If the one-month U.S. interest rate is higher than the one-month rate in Canada, the U.S. dollar will tend to appreciate with respect to the Canadian dollar. But if the one-month Canadian interest rate is higher, the U.S. dollar will tend to depreciate with respect to the Canadian dollar. Economists and foreign exchange participants have often noted this fact.[12]

Indeed, it is possible to make money, on average, by using this rule. The problem is that implementing this rule carries risk. There is an ongoing debate about how big this risk is, and whether the average profits are explained by the level of risk. After all, it would not be surprising that the market pays a premium to those willing to assume substantial risk. Furthermore, the profits may have occurred only by chance and may not recur. Sometimes, economists report other technical rules that seem to make money in the foreign exchange market.[13] However, the considerations noted in the interest-rate differential rule apply to any technical rule. Even if the rule makes profits on average, the profits might be explained by the level of risk assumed in applying the rule. Moreover, the profits may well disappear when we account for technical statistical problems. Since economists are undecided at present about whether technical rules really do make money, it seems prudent to be cautious when evaluating the merits of any such rule.

What About Long-Run Forecasting?

Even though economic models or the fundamentals don't help us understand the exchange rate in the short run (except to the extent that they influence market psychology), there is evidence that models do better in the long run. For example, economists Martin Eichenbaum and Charles Evans report that currencies react as theory would suggest to unanticipated movements in the money supply, but only in the long run, after a period of about two years. Standard monetary theories

would imply that an unanticipated decline in the U.S. money supply would lead to an appreciation of the dollar with respect to other currencies. Eichenbaum and Evans found that the dollar does, in fact, appreciate in response to an unanticipated monetary contraction; however, the full effects on the dollar are not registered until two years after the contraction, suggesting that models may well work in explaining the exchange rate in the long run.[14]

Is Any Aspect of the Exchange Rate Predictable in the Short Run?

Although the level of the exchange rate in the short run is not very predictable, volatilities and correlations of currencies are much more predictable. The daily volatility of a currency measures the extent to which the currency's value in terms of another currency fluctuates each day. The value of high-volatility currencies fluctuates more each day than that of low-volatility currencies. Correlations measure the extent to which currencies move together. In general, volatilities and correlations vary with time, rising or falling each day in a somewhat predictable way.

The time-varying nature of the daily volatility of the dollar in terms of the deutsche mark can be seen in the figure. Notice that, in 1991, days on which the volatility of the dollar is high tend to cluster together, and in 1990, days with lower volatility follow one another. Since daily volatility clusters together, it is predictable. If we want to predict tomorrow's volatility, we need only look at the recent past. If daily volatility has been high over the recent past, we can be reasonably sure that it will be high tomorrow.

This idea forms the basis for statistical models of a currency's volatility. The GARCH model, developed by economist Tim Bollerslev, who built on work by economist Robert Engle, uses the volatility-clustering phenomenon to predict future volatility. In essence, a GARCH model measures the strength of the relationship between recent volatility and current volatility. Once this strength is known, it can be used to forecast volatility.

GARCH models have good empirical support for exchange rates and are being used in practical applications in the foreign exchange market.[15]

GARCH models can be extended to handle two or more currencies, and they can measure the strength of recent correlations in predicting current ones. Once this strength is understood, it can be used to forecast correlations.

Uses of Volatility and Correlation Forecasts

Volatility and correlation forecasts have important uses in finance. First, currency derivatives, securities whose value depends on the value of currencies, require measures of volatility and sometimes correlations to price them. GARCH models can supply estimates of these volatilities and correlations. Second, volatilities of individual currencies coupled with correlations between currencies can be combined to determine the volatility of a portfolio of currencies. Since the volatility of a portfolio measures the extent to which the portfolio's value fluctuates, the volatility can be used to assess a portfolio's risk. Portfolios with higher volatilities are riskier because they have a tendency to lose more per day—or gain more per day—than do portfolios with lower volatilities (see Using GARCH to Measure Portfolio Risk). Finally, knowledge of volatilities and correlations can help an investor choose the proportions of each currency to hold in a portfolio. For example, knowing a portfolio's volatilities and correlations may show an investor how to rearrange the proportions of currencies in a portfolio so that he has the same return, on average, but a lower risk of loss.

Using GARCH to Measure Portfolio Risk

Here, we illustrate the use of a GARCH model to manage risk in a simple portfolio of two currencies, the yen and the deutsche mark. Using daily data on the yen and the deutsche mark from January 2, 1981, to June 30, 1996, the time-varying volatilities and correlations were estimated using Engle and Lee's (1993a,b) GARCH model. Suppose we have a portfolio with $1 million invested in yen and $1 million invested in deutsche marks. Then we can calculate the value at risk (VaR) of the portfolio. The VaR is the maximum loss the portfolio will experience a certain fraction of the time during a specific period. For example, we can see from the table that daily VaR at the 95 percent confidence level is $12,000. That means that 95 percent of the time, the largest daily loss on the portfolio will be $12,000. But 5 percent of the time, the loss will be bigger, sometimes by a substantial amount. The daily loss measures the difference between the value of the portfolio at the end of one trading day and its value at the end of the next trading day.

As another example, consider weekly VaR at the 98 percent confidence interval. The numbers indicate that 98 percent of the time, the loss over five trading days will not exceed $35,000. But 2 percent of the time, the losses will be bigger. See Hopper (1996) for more discussion.

**Value at Risk of a Currency Portfolio
with $1 Million Invested in Both Yen and Deutsche marks**

	One-Day Horizon	Five-Day Horizon
95 percent	$12,000	$27,000
98 percent	$15,000	$35,000
99 percent	$18,000	$41,000

These numbers for the value at risk apply to the risk in the portfolio on July 1, 1996, the day after the end of the data period. However, the reason for using a GARCH model is that volatility varies over time. The value at risk would be higher in times of greater volatility and lower when the market is less volatile.

Conclusion

The evidence discussed in this article suggests that economic models and indeed fundamental economic quantities are not very useful in explaining the history of the exchange rate or in forecasting its value over the next year or so. This fact has important implications for market participants. It is all too common to encounter private-sector foreign exchange economists who tell very cogent stories designed to buttress their short-term forecasts for the values of currencies. These stories are often based on plausible economic assumptions or models. These economists hope that market participants will act on their forecasts and trade currencies. However, if these forecasts are justified by a belief that economic models or fundamentals influence the exchange rate in the short run, it's likely they are not very good. Indeed, we have seen that these forecasts will probably be outperformed by the naive forecast: tomorrow's exchange rate will be what it is today.

On the other hand, to the extent that these forecasts reflect market sentiment or a self-fulfilling prophecy, they may be useful. Unfortunately, it is difficult to judge when this is the case. The difficulty is accentuated by the unobservability of market expectations. A forecaster might be using a model he believes in, and his forecast might turn out to be correct if the market also temporarily believes the implications of the model. But it is hard, if not impossible, to know what the market expects; hence, it is hard to judge the merits of a forecast.

Fortunately, the situation is better regarding volatilities and correlations, which follow predictable patterns. The GARCH model and its more sophisticated variants can be used to price derivatives, assess currency portfolio risk, and set allocations of currencies in portfolios. Economists are continually discovering new empirical facts about volatility and correlations. No doubt the GARCH model will eventually be supplanted by an alternative, but for now, economists will use the GARCH model, or some variation of it, to forecast volatilities and correlations of currencies.

When this article was written, Greg Hopper was a senior economist in the Research Department of the Philadelphia Fed. He is now in the Credit Analytics Group at Morgan Stanley, Co., Inc., New York.

Endnotes

[1] When purchasing power parity holds, particular goods and services cost the same amount in the domestic country as they do in the foreign country. There is an extensive literature that documents that purchasing power parity doesn't hold except perhaps in the very long run.

[2] In the monetary model, the price level must fall in this situation to ensure that money demanded by consumers is the same as money supplied by the central bank.

[3] See the papers by Frenkel (1976, 1980), Bilson (1978), and Hodrick (1978) for empirical analysis of the monetary model.

[4] For an empirical treatment of the overshooting model, see the paper by Backus (1984).

[5] See, for example, the paper by Branson, Halttunen, and Masson (1977).

[6] See the papers by Frankel (1982) and Lewis (1988) for empirical analysis of the more sophisticated portfolio balance model. The fundamental problem with the model is that investors must have an implausibly high aversion to risk to explain the exchange rate.

[7] For empirical analysis of news models, see the papers by Branson (1983), Edwards (1982, 1983), and MacDonald (1983).

[8] See Rose (1994) for a detailed discussion of this point.

[9] If a central bank can't change the short-term interest rate independently, it can't use monetary policy independently to stimulate the economy. Hence, countries with stabilized exchange rates must give up the independent use of monetary policy.

[10] If speculators expect the value of the currency to fall, and they are right, speculators can profit by selling the currency short. As an example, suppose a speculator anticipates that the value of the Swedish krona with respect to the deutsche mark will fall in one week. The speculator could borrow krona and sell them for deutsche marks at the current exchange rate. If the speculator is correct and the krona does depreciate, at the end of the week the speculator can buy back the krona for fewer deutsche marks than he sold them for. Provided the krona fell enough over the week, the speculator can repay the loan with interest and make a profit in deutsche marks. However, if the central bank makes short-term interest rates

high enough, it can make this transaction unprofitable. Thus, one defense against a speculative attack is to dramatically raise short-term interest rates.

[11] For further discussion of the myriad problems that can arise when countries attempt to fix their exchange rates, see the article by Obstfeld and Rogoff (1995).

[12] See my 1994 *Business Review* article for a nontechnical discussion.

[13] For an example, see Sweeney (1986).

[14] For further evidence on the effects of unanticipated monetary contractions on the exchange rate, see Schlagenhauf and Wrase (1995).

[15] GARCH stands for Generalized Autoregressive Conditional Heteroskedasticity. For the technical details of how GARCH models work, see Bollerslev (1986). Examples of technical applications of GARCH models of exchange rates include Bollerslev (1990) and Kroner and Sultan (1993). Heynen and Kat (1994) use GARCH to forecast volatility.

References

Backus, David. "Empirical Models of the Exchange Rate: Separating the Wheat from the Chaff," *Canadian Journal of Economics* (1984), pp. 824-46.

Bilson, John. "The Monetary Approach to the Exchange Rate—Some Empirical Evidence," IMF *Staff Papers*, 25 (1978), pp. 48-75.

Bollerslev, Tim. "Generalized Autoregressive Conditional Heteroskedasticity," *Journal of Econometrics*, 31 (1986), pp. 307-27.

Bollerslev, Tim. "Modelling the Coherence in Short-Run Nominal Exchange Rates: A Multivariate Generalized ARCH Model," *Review of Economics and Statistics*, 72 (1990), pp. 498-505.

Branson, William. "Macroeconomic Determinants of Real Exchange Rate Risks," in R.J. Herring, ed., *Managing Foreign Exchange Risk*. Cambridge, U.K.: Cambridge University Press, 1983.

Branson, William, Hannu Halttunen, and Paul Masson. "Exchange Rates in the Short Run: The Dollar-Deutschemark Rate," *European Economic Review*, 10 (1977), pp. 303-24.

Dornbusch, Rudiger. "Expectations and Exchange Rate Dynamics," *Journal of Political Economy*, 84 (1976), pp. 1161-76.

Edwards, Sebastian. "Exchange Rates and News: A Multi-Currency Approach," *Journal of International Money and Finance*, 1 (1982), pp. 211-24.

Edwards, Sebastian. "Floating Exchange Rates, Expectations, and New Information," *Journal of Monetary Economics*, 11, (1983), pp. 321-36.

Eichenbaum, Martin, and Charles Evans. "Some Empirical Evidence on the Effects of Monetary Policy Shocks on Exchange Rates," NBER Working Paper 4271 (1993).

Engle, Robert F. "Autoregressive Conditional Heteroskedasticity with Estimates of the Variance of U.K. Inflation," *Econometrica*, 50 (1982), pp. 987-1008.

Engle R., and G. Lee. "A Permanent and Transitory Component Model of Stock Return Volatility," Discussion Paper 92-44R, Department of Economics, University of California, San Diego (1993a).

Engle R., and G. Lee. "Long Run Volatility Forecasting for Individual Stocks in a One Factor Model," Discussion Paper 93-30, Department of Economics, University of California, San Diego (1993b).

Frankel, Jeffrey. "In Search of the Exchange Rate Risk Premium: A Six Currency Test Assuming Mean-Variance Optimization," *Journal of International Money and Finance*, 1 (1982), pp. 255-74.

Frenkel, Jacob. "A Monetary Approach to the Exchange Rate: Doctrinal Aspects and Empirical Evidence," *Scandinavian Journal of Economics*, 78 (1976), pp. 200-24.

Frenkel, Jacob. "Exchange Rates, Prices, and Money: Lessons From the 1920s," *American Economic Review*, 70 (1980), pp. 235-42.

Heynen, Ronald C., and Harry M. Kat. "Volatility Prediction: A Comparison of the Stochastic Volatility, GARCH (1,1), and eGARCH (1,1) Models," *The Journal of Derivatives*, 2 (1994), pp. 50-65.

Hodrick, Robert. "An Empirical Analysis of the Monetary Approach to the Exchange Rate," in J. Frenkel and H.G. Johnson, eds., *The Economics of Exchange Rates*. Reading, Mass.: Addison Wesley, 1978, pp. 97-116.

Hopper, Greg. "Is the Foreign Exchange Market Inefficient?" Federal Reserve Bank of Philadelphia *Business Review* (May/June 1994).

Hopper, Greg. "Value at Risk: A New Methodology For Measuring Portfolio Risk," Federal Reserve Bank of Philadelphia *Business Review* (July/August 1996).

Kroner, Kenneth F., and Jahangir Sultan, "Time-Varying Distributions and Dynamic Hedging with Foreign Currency Futures," *Journal of Financial and Quantitative Analysis,* 28 (1993), pp. 535-51.

Lewis, Karen. "Testing the Portfolio Balance Model: A Multilateral Approach," *Journal of International Economics,* 7 (1988), pp. 273-88.

MacDonald, Ronald. "Some Tests of the Rational Expectations Hypothesis in the Foreign Exchange Markets," *Scottish Journal of Political Economy,* 30 (1983), pp. 235-50.

Meese, Richard, and Kenneth Rogoff. "Empirical Exchange Rate Models of the 1970s: Do They Fit Out of Sample?" *Journal of International Economics,* 14 (1983), pp. 3-24.

Obstfeld, Maurice, and Kenneth Rogoff. "The Mirage of Fixed Exchange Rates," *Journal of Economic Perspectives,* 9 (1995), pp. 73-96.

Rose, Andrew. "Are Exchange Rates Macroeconomic Phenomena?" Federal Reserve Bank of San Francisco *Economic Review,* 1 (1994), pp. 19-30.

Schlagenhauf, Don, and Jeffrey Wrase. "Liquidity and Real Activity in a Simple Open Economy Model," *Journal of Monetary Economics,* 35 (1995), pp. 431-61.

Sweeney, Richard J. "Beating the Foreign Exchange Market," *Journal of Finance* (1986), pp. 163-82.

Fixed versus Floating Exchange Rates

P E T E R   B .   **K E N E N**

In the 1990s, a new consensus emerged regarding exchange rate regimes. Governments must choose between flexible exchange rates and firmly fixed exchange rates. Pegged rates of the adjustable sort, like those of the Bretton Woods system and European Monetary System (EMS) before 1993, are no longer viable because of their vulnerability to speculative attacks. Note that I have substituted "flexible" for "floating" rates, because many of those who subscribe to the new consensus are not fully convinced that markets know more than governments and do not rule out official intervention to influence market-determined rates. Some, indeed, continue to believe that wide-band target zones or crawling bands are still viable. I subscribe to the new consensus insofar as it warns against adopting adjustable pegs, whether they be formal as in the case of the EMS or informal as in the case of Asian countries that maintained de facto dollar pegs for their currencies before the recent crisis. The consensus seems also to suggest, however, that firmly fixed rates are both viable and sensible, but I have reservations. For all but the smallest countries, which are economic appendages of larger countries and might as well adopt those large countries' currencies, flexible rates are more appropriate.

Several arguments have been adduced for fixing exchange rates firmly. All of them have limited validity, but they are not compelling, individually or collectively.

The Real Costs of Exchange Rate Changes

The first argument is often posed as an objection to flexible rates but applies to adjustable rates as well. The uncertainty produced by exchange rate changes acts as a tax on trade and, more importantly, a tax on investment in traded-goods industries. Although it is possible to hedge against exchange rate risk by using derivative instruments, you cannot hedge risk perfectly unless you know the size of your foreign currency exposure. An exchange rate change, however, affects not only the domestic currency values of your future foreign currency receipts and payments but also affects their foreign currency values by affecting the volume and value of future trade flows. Empirical work on exchange rate uncertainty has not found strong adverse effects on trade flows or investment, although studies concerned with developing countries have found stronger effects than studies concerned with industrial countries. In most of this work, however, including my own, exchange rate uncertainty is measured by the short-term variability of the nominal or real exchange rate, because it is hard to devise an appropriate measure of the more relevant phenomenon, uncertainty about the real rate over a long horizon. Hence, the issue remains unresolved.

A second, related argument for fixed rates asserts that exchange rate changes give rise to protectionist pressures and can thus prevent the realization of the gains from trade.

This argument has surfaced periodically in widely different contexts. The decision of the United States to sponsor the Plaza Accord of 1985 is often ascribed to the build-up of protectionist pressures produced by the previous appreciation of the dollar. A decade later, in Europe, protectionist pressures produced by the exchange rate changes of the early 1990s were cited frequently by advocates of monetary union, who said that an irrevocable fixing of exchange rates was the only way to insulate the Single European Market from such pressures in the future. Finally, the depreciation of the Brazilian currency in 1999 caused Argentina to erect trade barriers that stalled and threatened to reverse trade liberalization in MERCOSUR. This argument, like the first, cannot be dismissed out of hand. It must nevertheless be noted that fixing the exchange rate deprives a government of two very valuable policy instruments, the nominal exchange rate and monetary policy, and it may therefore be tempted to adopt beggar-thy-neighbor trade policies to cope with output-reducing shocks.

Fixed Exchange Rates and Monetary Discipline

The final argument for fixed rates is concerned with the impact of the exchange rate regime on the quality of monetary policy. It has several versions.

The first version says that a fixed exchange rate will neutralize monetary shocks, including those produced by an incompetent central bank. A country with a fixed exchange rate will "import" or "export" money automatically whenever there is a shift in demand or supply and thus keep a monetary shock from affecting the real economy. The argument holds fully, however, only with perfect capital mobility. An excess supply of money will then cause a capital outflow and loss of reserves, which will reduce the money supply by just enough to remove the excess supply of money. Similarly, an excess demand for money will produce a capital inflow, and the resulting increase in reserves will raises the money supply by just enough to satisfy the excess demand for money. There

are no other effects whatsoever on the domestic economy. The argument holds symmetrically, however, and thus has a dark side. If your central bank is less competent than my central bank, you should fix your currency to mine and thus export the mistakes of your central bank. If your central bank is more competent than mine, however, fixing your currency to my currency will cause you to import mistakes made by my central bank. This, of course, exposes the flaw in the argument. It cannot hold universally, as a reason for worldwide pegging, unless all central banks are equally incompetent and their mistakes are uncorrelated. Each country will then share the consequences of the others' errors and be rewarded by the right to share its own errors with them.

The second version of the argument is similarly based on the supposition that some central banks are less competent than others and have less credibility. They can, it is said, import credibility from their more competent counterparts by fixing the exchange rate and thus commit themselves explicitly to emulate the monetary policy of the more competent central banks. This strategy was followed by several European countries, which pegged their countries' currencies to the deutsche mark to import credibility from the Bundesbank. Were they successful? It is hard to say. Inflation rates fell sharply in Europe during the 1980s and reached low German levels in the late 1990s. But inflation rates fell sharply in other countries too, including the United Kingdom and United States, and it has been impossible to show econometrically that there was a significant EMS effect. Furthermore, the logical foundations of the argument are weak. Why should exchange rate targeting be more credible than straightforward inflation targeting? An exchange rate target may be more transparent and less readily manipulated than an inflation target. It is also more fragile, however, because an attack on a fixed exchange rate can force the abandonment of the fixed rate by stripping away a country's reserves. An inflationary surprise, by contrast, cannot force the abandonment of an inflation target.

This where the case for a currency board comes in. Think of a central bank as having two hands—one for operating in the foreign exchange market, the other for operating in the domestic money market. The fixed exchange rate ties one hand. The central bank must intervene to keep the exchange rate from changing. By itself, however, the fixed rate does not tie the other hand. The central bank can still conduct money market operations to influence interest rates, bail banks out from liquidity crises, or bail the government out of a fiscal policy mess. A currency board, however, ties the other hand. The central bank cannot buy or sell domestic currency assets; it cannot conduct open market operations, make loans to domestic banks, or make loans to the government. Therefore it cannot sterilize the monetary effects of its operations on the foreign exchange market or even cushion the effects of those operations on the liquidity of the banking system. Accordingly, the attack on the Argentine peso during the Mexican crisis of 1994–95 caused a full-fledged banking crisis. The fixed exchange rate survived. The banks did not. Furthermore, Argentina's success in keeping its exchange rate fixed did not protect it four years later, when the Brazilian crisis of 1998–99 triggered another attack on the Argentine peso.

Fixed Exchange Rates and Disinflation

The third version of the argument is linked closely to the second. It says that exchange rate pegging can be used to achieve a large, quick fall in inflation when a country has suffered chronically from very high inflation—even hyperinflation. The argument combines two elements. On the one hand, an exchange rate peg combined with goods-market arbitrage stabilizes the prices of traded goods. Put differently, it exploits the fact that chronically high inflation leads to the widespread indexation of domestic prices based on the exchange rate. But inflation leads to the depreciation of the domestic currency, which then leads to the further increase of domestic prices. Fixing the exchange rate

helps to halt this process quickly. On the other hand, the commitment to a pegged exchange rate is implicitly a commitment to monetary and fiscal stability, without which a fixed rate cannot survive. In other words, exchange rate pegging is, as before, a way to buy credibility. This sort of "shock therapy" has worked well in several countries, including Bolivia, Poland, Argentina, and Brazil. In most of them, however, inflation did not stop immediately. The prices of traded goods were stabilized quickly, but the prices of nontraded goods went on rising, along with wage rates. They rose more slowly than before, but by enough to cause a large appreciation of the real exchange rate and a deterioration of the current-account balance. It was therefore necessary to devalue the domestic currency. Hence, those who continue to recommend this sort of shock therapy are also quick to warn that governments adopting it should also devise an exit strategy—a way to introduce exchange rate flexibility before the real rate appreciates substantially.

Conclusion

Let me recapitulate by making four strong statements:

•Pegged but adjustable exchange rates are not viable, but the constraints imposed by rigidly fixed rates may be extremely expensive. They impose very tight constraints on monetary policy.

•A single country cannot fix its exchange rate comprehensively unless all other countries fix their rates too. That is what the Asian countries learned in the 1990s, when the dollar appreciated against the yen and what Argentina learned later, when the Brazilian real depreciated in terms of the dollar.

•Long ago, however, Robert Mundell warned us that the world is not an optimum currency area. National economies are vulnerable to what we now describe as asymmetric shocks, and many cannot cope with them without changing their exchange rates. It is neither wise nor realistic to advocate worldwide pegging.

•When price stability is the principal objective of monetary policy, using a symmetrical inflation-rate target may be the least expensive and most sensible way to confer credibility on monetary policy.

With more time for me to write and more time for you to read, I would set out the principal arguments for flexible exchange rates. If I did that, however, I would have to attach counter-arguments to each argument, as I have just done for the fixed rate arguments. Flexible rates can be very volatile, because they are driven chiefly by volatile capital flows. They do not necessarily move in line with purchasing power parity, nor do their movements always foster current account adjustment. In fact, they sometimes move in ways that produce current account imbalances. Furthermore, they transmit asset market shocks directly to goods markets.

In 1987, right after the Louvre Accord, I urged the major industrial countries to adopt a wide-band target-zone regime much like the one adopted by the EMS in 1993. I should have recalled what I wrote much earlier, in 1973, during the deliberations of the Committee of the Twenty, which was trying to design what it described as a system of stable but adjustable exchange rates. That was, I said, an oxymoron. Stability is incompatible with adjustability.

Cato Journal, Vol. 20, No. 1 (Spring/Summer 2000).
Copyright © Cato Institute. All rights reserved.

Peter B. Kenen is the Walker Professor of Economics and International Finance at Princeton University.

Exchange Rate Choices

24

RICHARD N. COOPER

By late 1998 101 countries had declared that their currencies were allowed to float against other currencies, meaning that the currency was not formally pegged to some other currency or basket of currencies. This was up from 38 ten years earlier, suggesting a significant move toward greater flexibility of exchange rates. Yet during the 1990s half a dozen countries installed currency boards, a particular strong form of exchange rate fixity; ten European currencies were eliminated in favor of a common currency, the euro; other countries were actively considering installing currency boards, or even adopting the US dollar for domestic use.

After a quarter century of floating among the major currencies, exchange rate policy is still a source of vexation, and the appropriate choice is by no means clear. Should a country allow its currency to float, subject perhaps to exchange market intervention from time to time? Or should it fix its currency to some other currency or currencies, and if so to which one(s)? Economists do not offer clearly persuasive answers to these questions. Yet for most countries, all but the largest, with the most developed domestic capital markets, the choice of exchange rate policy is probably their single most important macro-economic policy decision, strongly influencing their freedom of action and effectiveness of other macro-economic policies, the evolution of their financial systems, and even the evolution of their economies.

A Brief History of Exchange Rate Policy

The choice of exchange rate regime was not always so vexing; during much of the modern era it was in practice dictated by convention, by internationally agreed rules, or by uncontrollable external circumstances. If we date the modern era from 1867, when a trans-Atlantic cable first linked Europe and North America electronically -- connections were established within Europe from 1851, and across the Pacific in the 1870s -- international monetary experience among the major countries can be divided into four distinct periods, each with some fuzzy edges. The first covers the period roughly 1870-1914, during which most countries adopted a gold standard for their domestic money, implying fixed exchange rates among currencies beyond the modest flexibility allowed by the mint gold points and transport costs.

This relatively uniform regime -- although some countries remained on (generally depreciating) silver, and others had gold-inconvertible currencies from time to time -- was interrupted by the First World War. The period 1914-1946 saw great variation, both among countries and over time, with the widespread and episodic use of exchange controls, periods of floating exchange rates, an aborted attempt in the late 1920s to restore a variant of the gold standard, and an effort in the late 1930s to stabilize exchange rates among some major currencies by coordinating monetary policy and market intervention.

From 1946 to 1973 exchange rate policy was dominated by the Bretton Woods
Agreement of 1944, with its commitment to
currencies convertible for current account
transactions and fixed exchange rates
(beyond a narrow band of permissible flexibility) but adjustable if necessary. It was initially embraced by 44 countries, a list that
grew over time. The collective decision to
eschew exchange controls and fix exchange
rates was strongly influenced by the mainly
negative "lessons" from the experience of the
inter-war period.

The Bretton Woods arrangement came
under increasing strain in the late 1960s and
in March 1973 (earlier for Britain and
Canada) the practice of fixing exchanges was
generally abandoned by the major countries
of Europe and Japan, and we entered the
fourth period, 1973 to the present, of floating
exchange rates. Many countries, however,
elected to fix their currencies to some major
currency -- the US dollar, the French franc, the
British pound. And most members of the
European Community found intra-European
exchange rate flexibility intolerable (among
other things, it interfered with the Common
Agricultural Policy) so in 1979 they re-created
a mini-Bretton Woods system in the exchange
rate mechanism of the European Monetary
System (EMS), which in 1999 evolved into
Europe's Economic and Monetary Union
(EMU) with its common currency.

A Brief History of Thought about Exchange Rate Policy

The adoption of flexible exchange
rates by many countries in the aftermath of
the First World War did not reflect the preferences of policy-makers, but rather their
inability, in the immediate post-war circumstances, to re-establish convertibility of the
national currency into gold. Restoration of
gold convertibility, implying fixed exchange
rates among such currencies, was the desired
aim, preferably at pre-1914 conversion rates,
if necessary with some depreciation to allow
for the inflation that had occurred during
and immediately after the war.

Already in the 1920s however, some
economists, most notably John Maynard
Keynes (1923, 1930), saw the advantage for
national well-being of "managed money";
and managed money at the national level was
understood to be inconsistent with rigorous
adherence to gold standard conventions.
Keynes' proposed solution to this dilemma
was to widen the gap between the official gold
purchase price and the gold selling price. Any
country that did this would introduce a band
of floating exchange rates which would give
some scope for independent national monetary policy.

Keynes' proposal was not formally
adopted, but the breakdown of the gold
(exchange) standard from 1931 created more
scope for independent national action than
Keynes had urged or desired. The experience
with floating exchange rates, under admittedly extremely difficult circumstances, did not
leave contemporaries with a good feeling
about them. Ragnar Nurkse, in an influential
study for the League of Nations, summarized
the inter-war experience with floating
exchange rates in these terms (1944, p. 210):

A system of completely free and
flexible exchange rates is conceivable
and may have certain attractions in theory; and it might seem that in practice
nothing could be easier than to leave
international payments and receipts to
adjust themselves through uncontrolled
exchange variations in response to the
play of demand and supply. Yet nothing would be more at variance with the
lessons of the past.

He went on to elaborate three serious
disadvantages of floating rates: risk for trade
transactions that cannot be hedged at moderate cost; costly and disturbing shifts in labor
and capital among sectors in response to
exchange rate changes that might prove to be
temporary; and "self-aggravating" movements in exchange rates that intensify disequi-
libria rather than promote adjustment.

Nurkse's antipathy to flexible exchange
rates was widely shared, both among men of
affairs and within the academy. John H.
Williams of Harvard and the Federal Reserve

Bank of New York wrote in 1937, following the Tripartite Agreement to stabilize exchange rates among the US dollar, the British pound, and the French franc, that "…there is no evidence of any desire for a really flexible currency" (quoted in Nurkse, p. 211 n).

The major exception to this general sentiment was Milton Friedman (1953), who argued in a memorandum written in 1950 for the US Economic Cooperation Administration, which administered the Marshall aid to Europe, that among the alternatives available a strong case could be made for allowing the European currencies, at the time heavily burdened by direct controls on international transactions, to float against one another. The ECA was desirous of reducing the heavy restrictions on intra-European trade as well as trade with the rest of the world; but most countries resisted trade liberalization in part out of fear of unsustainable imbalances in payments, largely vis-a-vis the dollar but partly vis-a-vis one another. (Within Europe, Belgium had the strongest currency.) And against the background of the Great Depression and the Keynesian revolution in thinking about macro-economic management, all were committed to maintaining some version of full employment, i.e. to nationally managed money. Friedman saw exchange rate flexibility as a way to reconcile otherwise conflicting objectives. Friedman argued (p. 199) that a system of flexible exchange rates would eliminate the necessity for far-reaching international coordination of internal monetary and fiscal policy in order for any country separately to follow a stable internal monetary policy.

Friedman was initially nearly alone in his views. Most contemporary economists favored fixed exchange rates and feared the instabilities that flexible exchange rates might bring, or reveal (see, e.g. Triffin (1957, 1966), Kindleberger (1966), Bernstein (1945)).

But just as experience during the 1920s and 1930s cultivated a distaste for exchange rate flexibility, experience during the 1950s and 1960s cultivated increasing antipathy, especially in academic circles, to the Bretton Woods version of fixed exchange rates — that is, rates fixed beyond narrow bands of permissible variation, but adjustable if necessary to correct a "fundamental disequilibrium" in international payments. It became clear that national authorities held on to their fixed rates for too long, and that by the time a fundamental disequilibrium was evident to them, it was also evident to everyone else. This arrangement created a mechanism for periodic transfers of public wealth, held in the form of gold or foreign exchange reserves, to private parties who speculated successfully on a discrete change in exchange rates, selling before an expected devaluation and repurchasing afterward. Even with pervasive controls on capital movements, determined firms and individuals could move much capital legally through manipulating the "leads and lags" of commercial payments and other loop-holes in the control system; and of course funds also moved illegally, with bribes or misrepresentations of trade invoices or elsewhere.

This prospect in turn inhibited authorities from changing exchange rates, hoping that the payments difficulties were temporary, and led them to impose and increasingly tighten controls on all international transactions in order to reduce payments deficits -- thus thwarting the very purposes for which a well-functioning payments system is desired.

Observing this excessive rigidity, as well as the growth in both possibilities for and magnitude of international capital movements, economists increasingly came to favor greater flexibility in exchange rates. Numerous proposals for introducing greater flexibility, short of full floating, were put forward. Some concentrated, like Keynes in the 1920s, on giving greater freedom for differences in national monetary policies, by widening the band of permissible variation around central parities; others concentrated on providing for gradual secular changes in exchange rates without provoking massive speculation around prospective discrete changes (e.g. Williamson, 1965). And of course numerous combinations of the two approaches were possible. Federal Reserve Bank of Boston (1969) and Halm (1970) provide useful compendia on academic thinking in the late 1960s.

The "Bellagio Group," under the collective leadership of Fritz Machlup, William Fellner, and Robert Triffin, held a series of meetings from 1963 between academics and central bankers to review the functioning of the international monetary system in its diverse aspects, including exchange rate arrangements as well as provision for international liquidity. This group exposed key central bankers to the evolution in academic thinking, and may have played some role in persuading central bankers that flexible exchange rates were workable, or at least would not be more troublesome than the fixed exchange rate system with which they were then having to cope.

The debate was summarized tendentiously by Harry G. Johnson (1973) in his widely read "The Case for Flexible Exchange Rates, 1969," first published in the United States by the Federal Reserve Bank of St. Louis but widely reproduced thereafter.

The essay is well-balanced in its overall structure: he states the case for fixed rates; the case for flexible rates; and the case against flexible rates. But only one paragraph is devoted to stating the case for fixed rates, the remainder of the section to why it is "seriously deficient." And the section on the case against flexible rates is basically devoted to knocking it down, consisting as it does in Johnson's view "of a series of unfounded assertions and allegations." It is not a balanced account; Johnson had made up his mind and hoped to impose his conclusions on others by a devastating critique of the (unnamed) opposition.

Johnson's affirmative analysis is itself based on a series of unfounded assertions and allegations, an idealization of the world of financial markets without serious reference to their actual behavior. The key tenets were:

1) That the foreign exchange market was rather like the strawberry market or any other market small relative to the size of the economy, such that impacts of developments in this market on the overall economy could be neglected (a curious stance, since in his other writings Johnson was insistently general equilibrium in his approach);

2) That the foreign exchange market is a stable market: "a freely flexible exchange rate would tend to remain constant so long as underlying economic conditions (including government policies) remained constant; random deviations from the equilibrium level would be limited by the activities of private speculators..." (p.208);

3) That exchange rate movements would be dominated by inflation differentials between the respective countries; and that under flexible exchange rates the market would quickly develop the wide range of appropriate hedging instruments that were manifestly not present in the late 1960s permitting reductions in such uncertainties as flexible rates might occasion.

Running through the essay is the view that the major if not the sole sources of disturbance to exchange rates are government policies. And, as in Friedman, "Flexible rates would allow each country to pursue the mixture of unemployment and price trend objectives it prefers..."(p. 210); i.e. it can choose its preferred point on the Phillips curve.

It is worth noting that Johnson was making a case for floating exchange rates among the currencies of major countries, with well-diversified economies, such as Britain, Germany, or his native Canada. He explicitly excuses developing countries, indicating with approval that they would probably link their currencies to some major currency. But the choice of which currency would not be consequential provided currency movements largely tracked inflation differentials, i.e., provided real exchange rates among the major currencies remained relatively stable, as he expected they would.

The general movement to flexible exchange rates among major currencies that occurred in 1973 was short-lived. Many (continental) Europeans felt that flexible rates among their currencies would be highly disruptive of the recently completed common market (which Britain, Denmark, and Ireland joined in 1973, beginning a decade-long process of transition to full participation), especially its common agricultural policy. Under the CAP target prices were set annually for farm products before each crop season in a synthetic unit of account, the Ecu. Flexible exchange rates among participating currencies implied -- horrors! -- that farm prices might actually decline within the crop year in those currencies that appreciated. To prevent this, so-called green exchange rates, different from market rates, were applied to intra-European agricultural trade, thus necessitating internal border adjustments, i.e. disrupting free intra-European trade in agricultural products and thereby threatening the common market. Faced with this complication, and concerned about the implications of an unstable dollar for intra-European exchange rates (something that should not be a problem on Johnson's view of exchange market behavior), German Chancellor Schmidt and French President Giscard d'Estaing, both former finance ministers who prided themselves on their economic knowledge and experience, persuaded their colleagues to re-create within Europe the main features of the Bretton Woods system, albeit with a substantially wider -- nine percent versus three percent -- band of permissible exchange rate flexibility around central parities.

One factor that has inhibited serious resolution of exchange rate choices is the continuing use by the economics profession of an extraordinarily primitive theory of money in its theorizing, and its insistence on separating monetary and real factors in analyzing economies. This pedagogically useful practice prevents economists from finding any welfare costs associated with disturbing the allocative role of money prices (as opposed to relative prices), such as might occur with exchange rate fluctuations that are not associated with serious signals to reallocate resources. A recent paper by Obstfeld and Rogoff (1998) breaks with parts of this tradition, and finds in a highly stylized but promising model that the welfare cost of exchange-rate variability can be as much as one percent of GDP, a nontrivial amount.

Exchange Rate Choices for Developing Countries

The "incompatible triangle" of fixed exchange rates, independent monetary policy, and freedom of capital movements has been understood by economists for a long time. Countries have to choose which of these objectives they will drop, although most governments resist the choice and attempt to fudge in various ways, often producing financial crises in the process.

What is less obvious is that floating rates, independent monetary policy, and freedom of capital movements may also be incompatible, at least for countries with small and poorly developed domestic capital markets, i.e. for most countries. That would leave a more limited menu of choice for such countries: between floating rates with capital account restrictions and some monetary autonomy, or fixed rates free of capital restrictions but with loss of monetary autonomy. Put bluntly, two prescriptions regularly extended to developing countries by the international community, including the IMF and the US Treasury, namely to move toward greater exchange rate flexibility and to liberalize international capital movements, may be in deep tension: even deep contradiction.

Within a country, the national price level is beyond reach of anyone except its central bank; it is taken as autonomously determined by all players in financial markets. The same is not true for the price levels of small, open economies: their national price levels are strongly influenced by their exchange rates, at least in the short to medium run. Yet the exchange rate is technically not anchored by anything in the long run, being the barter price between two nominal variables (as Kareken and Wallace pointed out two decades ago) and not even in the short run if the central bank is not pegging it or does not have sufficient reserves to resist movement against large market-driven shocks. Thus a large financial player can influence the exchange rate, hence the price level, of relatively small countries by selling their currencies short. Furthermore, given the dynamics of thin financial markets, a single player does not need enough resources to move the exchange rate radically; he only has to start a run on the currency through a combination of sales and rumors. If the word goes out persuasively that a currency will depreciate, many will join the bandwagon and the currency will depreciate. If the price level adjusts and the central bank later accommodates the adjustment for macroeconomic reasons, the depreciation will have been justified ex post. This is a fundamentally unstable dynamic, with multiple equilibria, as Obstfeld (1986) has pointed out. According to Aliber (1962), the Belgian franc was dragged down by the French franc in the early 1920s. Despite very much better "fundamentals," the currency depreciation led to inflation that subsequently justified the depreciation.

On August 13, 1998, four days before the Russian government abandoned its publicly stated (but not formal) exchange rate commitment, George Soros wrote a letter to the *Financial Times* predicting the imminent demise of the ruble. It was suggested soon thereafter that the letter was a deliberate attempt to destabilize the ruble, on which Soros could be expected to make a lot of money.

In this case, on his own testimony (Soros, 1998, chapter 7) Soros actually lost money, and there is no evidence to suggest that his letter was an attempt to destabilize. But the example, and the subsequent suspicions, illustrate the point that when market expectations are already fragile, a single respected player could in fact move market prices by discrete amounts, in a manner that could become self-justifying -- something that cannot happen in an idealized competitive market.[1] In early 1999 Itamar France, governor of a Brazilian state, declared its unwillingness to continue to service its debts to Brazil's federal government, allegedly deliberately attempting to embarrass his political rival President Cardoso by precipitating a budget and foreign exchange crisis.

These examples, it is true, concerned bringing into question an exchange rate commitment; but there is no reason to believe that the target could not be any other commitment, such as a prospective budget deficit or

even a market-determined exchange rate. Domestically, at least in the United States, there are rules against market manipulation, in both commodity and securities markets, by one or a few parties. Convicted market manipulators can be sent to jail. There are no such international sanctions, and small economies are vulnerable.

The core problem is that for economies with imperfectly developed financial markets the exchange rate is the most important asset price, and it will be jerked around by changes in portfolio sentiments. But for an open economy the exchange rate is also the most important price in the market for goods and services. Jumping asset prices can badly disrupt the markets on which the economic well-being of the majority of residents depends. Hedging possibilities will be limited in a poorly developed financial market and in any case long-run investments cannot be hedged financially.

Furthermore, it is an open question whether a broad, diversified financial market based on the domestic currency can develop under floating exchange rates. With floating exchange rates and freedom of capital movement, residents face constant fluctuation in the real value of domestic assets as the exchange moves, and they have the option of investing abroad in more stable, more liquid financial instruments (albeit also with fluctuating real values in terms of home currency). Under direct competition, domestic markets are unlikely to develop to the point at which they are competitive with assets held abroad. It is noteworthy, for instance, that among Latin American countries long-term fixed interest mortgages exist only in Panama, a country that uses the US dollar domestically.

The unwelcome conclusion that flows from this discussion is that free movements of capital and floating exchange rates are basically incompatible except for large and diversified economies with well-developed and sophisticated financial markets. Of course, free movements of capital are also incompatible with fixed but adjustable exchange rates. Thus unless countries are prepared to fix permanently the values of their currencies to some leading currency, or to adopt some leading currency as their national currency, they may reasonably choose to preserve the right to control at least certain kinds of capital movements into and out of their jurisdictions, in the interests of reducing both nominal and real exchange rate variability (see Cooper (1999)).

In Johnson's view, capital movements play a highly stabilizing role. But many developing countries are only marginally creditworthy, and financially fragile, so international capital movements may aggravate rather than mitigate both real and financial economic shocks. Any general retreat from risk by asset holders will affect them adversely.

What should developing countries do? It depends very much on the details of their economic structure and their circumstances: on what kinds of real shocks they experience; on how flexible are their wages and rents; on how supple and effective is their management of fiscal and monetary policy; on their administrative capacity to enforce restrictions on capital movements, particularly surges in or out; and on a host of other factors. In any case, the choice is not easy, and countries are not obviously foolish for being reluctant to embrace floating exchange rates enthusiastically.

Exchange Rate Choices for Rich Diversified Countries

Flexible exchange rates have obtained since 1973 among the major currencies of the world: the US dollar, the Japanese yen, the British pound, the Canadian dollar, and the continental European currencies centered around the German mark. In contrast to what Nurkse might have expected, the experience has not been a disastrous one, and indeed arguably floating exchange rates helped their economies navigate more smoothly among some major world disturbances, such as the oil price shocks of 1974, 1979-80, and 1986 and the German unification of 1990. On the other hand, some have argued that because world oil prices are denominated in dollars, the three oil shocks themselves were caused by sharp movements in dollar exchange rates.

While I find this implausible, the fact that the case can be put forward suggests the complexities of cause and effect when it comes to currency arrangements and their impacts on real economies.

Nominal and real exchange rates also responded strongly to the "fiscal twist" of the early 1980s when the United States pursued an expansionist fiscal policy while Britain, Germany, and Japan, later joined by France, pursued contractionary fiscal policies. Whether one assesses the consequential sharp appreciation of the dollar in the early 1980s as benign or malign, it certainly had real and durable effects not only on foreign trade but also on the structure of output, not least because of high fixed costs sometimes associated with product entry into a national market (as emphasized by Krugman, 1989). Arguably the depth and duration of Japan's recession in the 1990s can be explained in part by excessive exchange-rate-induced industrial expansion in Japan in the mid-1980s when the cheap yen made Japanese goods highly competitive in the American market.

More recently, the dollar-yen exchange rate reached Y85 per dollar briefly in 1995 and then moved to 145 briefly in 1998, a swing of 70 percent over three years (and back to 108 by January 1999). The USA and Japan were both successfully pursuing low inflation monetary policies. What then justifies a swing of this magnitude? What disturbance does it create for trade (e.g. in stimulating anti-dumping suits by US firms) and for investment planning -- not only for exports, but for a domestic market subject to import competition? What disturbance does it create for balance sheets, especially of financial institutions? How many economically sound firms were thrown into bankruptcy? Might the prolonged recession in Japan -- including extensive overseas investment by Japanese firms -- be related in part to fear of wide swings in exchange rates? Are they hedging against future exchange rate uncertainty by diversifying their production across currency zones, especially into Europe and into North America? As noted above, exchange rate movements of this type certainly violate the expectations and contentions of advocates of floating rates thirty years ago, and they cannot signify well-functioning international monetary arrangements. But are there practical alternatives?

Before turning to various proposals, we should note another potential source of disturbance: the creation of the euro out of ten pre-existing national currencies in early 1999. A number of economists (e.g. Bergsten (1997, 1999) Masson and Turtelboom(1997), Portes and Rey(1998)) have suggested that exchange rate volatility between the dollar and the euro may well be higher than it was between the dollar and the German mark before 1999. The reasons are partly structural -- euroland is much more self-contained than the individual countries were, so exchange rate variation will cause fewer internal disturbances, hence fewer calls for action to stabilize exchange rates; and partly institutional, since the newly created European Central Bank is charged with pursuing price stability, not stabilizing currency values. Thus the ECB need pay attention to exchange rates only insofar as their movements threaten price stability, and early pronouncements by the ECB indeed indicate relative indifference to the dollar-euro exchange rate.

This greater volatility could be greatly aggravated if during the next decade foreign exchange holders around the world decide to switch their claims substantially from US dollar-denominated ones to euro-denominated ones, as some have suggested will occur (e.g. Bergsten (1997), Portes and Rey (1998)). I have argued elsewhere (Cooper, 1999) that a rapid switch from dollars to euros is not likely to occur because of the absence of sufficient suitable euro-denominated securities, and that growing internationalization of the euro will occur more gradually and smoothly in a context of world economic growth. But if a rapid switch does occur, it is likely to take place in several episodes rather than all at once, leading to episodic depreciation of the dollar, but at a rate and to an extent that is impossible to predict, since the potential for such switching will be seen to be very large.

Exchange rates are increasingly determined by financial transactions, which overwhelm trade and other current transactions in their magnitude. Financial transactions are subject to bandwagon effects, as each player seeks to be ahead of others in the market, and institutional investors seek performance that does not deviate negatively from performance of their peers. Yet the erratic exchange rates determined by such behavior also govern international trade. Particular trade transactions can be financially hedged in the short run at a cost; but investment for the purpose of engaging in trade cannot be similarly hedged. The result is likely to be both too little total investment, and too much investment in the wrong places, driven by the need of firms to hedge by locating within each major currency area, even if economic efficiency would be better served by locating elsewhere and importing. Furthermore, sustained misalignment of exchange rates is likely to increase protectionist pressures as it did in the United States during the mid-1980s and in Europe during the early 1990s.

In short, movements in exchange rates. while providing a useful shock absorber for real disturbances to the world economy, are also a substantial source of uncertainty for trade and capital formation, the wellsprings of economic progress. What can be done about it?

Broadly speaking, four types of exchange rate arrangements have been suggested for Britain, EMU, Japan, and the USA, the core of the international monetary system. The first is floating exchange rates, the arrangements that have generally prevailed during most of the past quarter century. As just noted, such arrangements have not been disastrous, but they have not lived up to earlier claims for floating rates either. In some respects they have been problematic, and they may become more troublesome in the future. What are the alternatives?

One is to establish target zones — central rates with a rather wide band of permissible variation — among the core currencies as has been advocated by Williamson (1985) Bergsten and Henning (1994) and recently espoused by Paul Volcker (1995). A second is to allow exchange rates to float, but to have monetary policy in the core areas targeted on the same price index, as advocated by McKinnon (and, in 1930, by Keynes). A third, more radical idea is to create common currency among the core countries, as suggested by Cooper (1984).

Target zones can have narrow or wide bands of permissible exchange rate variation, and they can have "soft" or "hard" edges to the bands, depending on the degree of commitment that governments publicly undertake to keep the exchange rate firmly within the band. The purpose of such an arrangement would be to prevent major misalignments in exchange rates, while allowing market forces to determine exchange rates most of the time. Its intermediate objective would be to create expectations in financial markets that exchange rates will rarely if ever move outside the permissible band.

McKinnon (1984, 1996) has proposed an alternative, but not entirely dissimilar, arrangement between Germany, Japan. and the United States (EMU could easily be substituted for Germany). Concretely, as applied to Japan and the USA (see McKinnon and Ohno, 1997): the proposal involves determining a target exchange rate based on purchasing power parity of wholesale (not retail) prices and establishing a permissible band of 10 percent around this rate, with soft edges. The width of the band would be narrowed over time as confidence in the system grew.

Wholesale prices are dominated by tradable goods, and lack domestic sales taxes and retail mark-ups. They also exclude services. Thus there should be a high correlation in the movement of British, European, Japanese, and American wholesale prices, such that monetary policy in each entity would be targeted on roughly the same price index.[2]

Cooper (1984) took the process of exchange rate coordination a strong step further, by suggesting an eventual currency union among the major industrial democracies: Europe, Japan, and the United States. A common currency would credibly eliminate exchange rate uncertainty. One currency would of course entail one monetary policy for the currency area, and a political mechanism to assure accountability. The details of such an arrangement will not be repeated here. The suggestion was not politically realistic in the mid-1980s and is not politically realistic today, but is set as a vision for a decade or two into the 21st century. The Europeans, in creating EMU, have taken a major step in the direction indicated. The idea could be taken further.

The suggestion draws its inspiration from two empirical prognostications and one empirical proposition. The first prognostication is that international financial transactions will grow relative to international trade in goods and services, and that financial factors will come to dominate exchange rate determination even more than they do today. At the same time, the exchange rate will become more important in determining the profitability of trade and investment than it is today.

The second prognostication is that real shocks among these entities will not be radically asymmetrical. Because all are large, highly diverse economies, disturbances within these economies are likely to be more important than disturbances between them, and adjustment to such shocks as occur will be no more difficult and perhaps easier than adjustments to shocks within those economies.

The empirical proposition is that financial markets will be just as fickle and as fragile (or as robust) in the future as they have been in the past.

These propositions and prognostications together suggest that as time goes on flexible exchange rates will gradually evolve from being mainly a useful shock absorber for real shocks into being mainly a disturbing transmitter of financial shocks increasingly troublesome for productive economic activity. Thus a cost-benefit calculation for flexible versus fixed exchange rates will gradually alter the balance against flexibility, even for large countries.

Endnotes

[1] While the Russian fiscal situation was anything but satisfactory, there is no evidence that the Russian ruble was overvalued in terms of foreign trade, unless the fall in oil prices was judged to be a permanent one. The fragility was created by foreign and domestic holdings of short-term ruble-denominated GKOs amidst doubts whether the government could continue to make payments on them at the relatively high interest rates required to sell them.

[2] In discussing international coordination of policies Keynes (1930) suggested that all major countries target the same index of prices of a basket of internationally traded commodities, ranging from aluminum to zinc. Concretely, writing under a gold standard, he suggested adjusting the official conversion price of gold periodically to maintain its value in terms of an index of 62 commodities -- the equivalent of targeting price stability of the index.

References

Aliber, Robert Z., "Speculation in the Foreign Exchanges: the European Experience, 1919-1926," *Yale Economic Essays*, Spring 1962.

Bacchetta, Philippe, and Eric van Wincoop, "Does Exchange Rate Stability Increase Trade and Capital Flows?" NBER Working Paper No. July 1998.

Bergsten, C. Fred, "The Dollar and the Euro," *Foreign Affairs* 76 (July/August) 1997.

Bergsten, C. Fred, and Randall Hennin, *Global Economic Leadership and the Group of Seven*, Washington: Institute for International Economics, 1996.

Bernstein, Edward M., "Monetary Stabilization: the United Nations Program," in Seymour E. Harris, ed., *Economic Reconstruction*, New York: McGraw-Hill, 1945.

Cooper, Richard N., "A Monetary System for the Future," Federal Reserve Bank of Boston, 1984; reprinted in *Essays in World Economics: The International Monetary System*, Cambridge, MA: MIT Press, 1987.

Cooper, Richard N., "Key Currencies after the Euro," *The World Economy*, 22 (January 1999), 1-23.

Cooper, Richard N., "Should Capital Controls Be Banished?" *Brookings Papers on Economic Activity*, 1999, No. 1, spring.

Fischer, Stanley, et al., *Should the IMF Pursue Capital-Account Convertibility*, Essays in International Finance, No. 207, Princeton, NJ: International Finance Section, Princeton University, May 1998.

Friedman, Milton, "The Case for Flexible Exchange Rates." *Essays in Positive Economics*, Chicago: University of Chicago Press. 1953.

Froot, Kenneth. Paul O'Connell. and Mark Seasholes, "The Portfolio Behavior of International Investors, I," forthcoming in *Journal of Finance*.

Ghosh, Atish R., Anne-Marie Gulde, Jonathan D. Ostry, and Holger C. Wolf. "Does the Nominal Exchange Rate Regime Matter?" NBER Working Paper No. 5874, January 1997.

Giavazzi, Francesco. and Alberto Giovannini. *Limirine Exchange Rate Flexibility*, Cambridge, MA: MIT Press, 1989.

Gros, Daniel, "Global Exchange Rate Stability after the Introduction of the Euro," in *The Euro and the New International Financial Order*, forthcoming 1999.

Halm, George N. ed.. *Approaches to Greater Exchange Rate Flexibility*, Princeton University Press. 1970.

Hausmann, Ricardo, Michael Gavin, Carmen Pages-Serra and Emesto Stein, "Financial Turmoil and the Choice of Exchange Rate Regime," Washington: Inter-American Development Bank, 1999.

Helliwell, John F., *How Much Do National Borders Matter?* Washington: Brookings Institution, 1998.

Johnson, Harry G., "The Case for Flexible Exchange Rates, 1969." *Further Essays in Monetary Economics*, Cambridge: Harvard University Press. 1973.

Keynes, John Maynard. *A Tract on Monetary Reform*, London: Macmillan, 1923.

Keynes, John Maynard, *A Treatise on Money*, volume 2, London: Macmillan, 1930.

Kim, Woochan, "Does Capital Account Liberalization Discipline Budget Deficits?" Harvard University Ph.D. dissertation, May 1999.

Kim, Woochan, and Shang-Jin Wei, "Foreign Portfolio Investors Before and During a Crisis," OECD Working Paper No. 210, Paris, February 1999.

Kindleberger, Charles P., *Europe and the Dollar*, Cambridge, MA: MIT Press, 1966.

Kindleberger, Charles P., "The Case for Fixed Exchange Rates, 1969," in *The International Adjustment Mechanism*, Federal Reserve Bank of Boston, 1969.

Krugman, Paul, *Exchange-Rate Instability*, Cambridge, MA: MIT Press, 1989.

League of Nations (Ragnar Nurkse), *International Currency Experience*, Geneva: League of Nations, 1944.

Maddison, Angus, *Monitoring the World Economy* 1820-1992, Paris: OECD Development Centre, 1995.

Masson, Paul, and Bart Turtelboom, "Transmission of Shocks under EMU, the Demand for Reserves and Policy Coordination," in Masson, Paul R., T.H. Krueger, and B.G. Turtelboom, eds., *EMU and the International Monetary System*, Washington: International Monetary Fund, 1997.

McKinnon, Ronald I., *An International Standard for Monetary Stabilization*, Washington: Institute for International Economics. 1984.

McKirmon: Ronald I., *The Rules of the Game: International Money and Exchange Rates*, Cambridge, MA: MIT Press, 1996.

McKinnon, Ronald I., and Kenichi Ohno., *Dollar and Yen*, Cambridge, MA: MIT Press. 1997.

Meltzer, Allan H., "Some Evidence on the Comparative Uncertainty Experienced under Different Monetary Regimes," in Colin D. Campbell and William R. Dougan, eds., *Alternative Monetary Regimes*, Baltimore, MD: Johns Hopkins University Press, 1986.

Obstfeld, Maurice, "Europe's Gamble," *Brookings Papers on Economic Activity*, 1997, no. 2.

Obstfeld, Maurice, "Rational and Self-Fulfilling Balance-of-Payments Crises," *American Economic Review* 76 (March 1986), 72-81.

Obstfeld, Maurice, and Kenneth Rogoff, "Risk and Exchange Rates," NBER Working Paper No. 6694, August 1998.

Portes. Richard, and Helene Rey, "The Emergence of the Euro as an International Currency," *Economic Policy*, April 1998. pp. 307-343.

Quirk, Peter J., "Fixed or Floating Exchange Regimes: Does It Matter for Inflation?" IMF Working Paper 94/l 34, November 1994.

Solomon, Robert, *Money on the Move: The Revolution in International Finance since 1980*, Princeton University Press, 1999.

Soros, George, *The Crisis of Global Capitalism*, New York: Public Affairs, 1998.

Stulz, Rene M. "Equity Flows. Banks. and Asia," in *NBER Reporter*, Winter 1998/1999, pp. 20-24.

Tomell, Aaron, and Andres Velasco, "Fixed versus Flexible Exchange Rates: Which Provides More Fiscal Discipline?" NBER Working Paper No. 5 108, May 1995.

Triffin, Robert, *Europe and the Money Muddle*, New Haven: Yale University Press, 1957.

Triffin, Robert, *The World Money Maze*, New Haven: Yale University Press, 1966.

Volcker, Paul, "The Quest for Exchange Rate Stability: Realistic or Quixotic?" *The Stamp 50th Anniversary Lecture*, University of London, November 1995.

Williamson, John, *The Crawling Pen, Essays in International Finance*, No. 50, Princeton International Finance Section, 1965, reprinted in Peter B. Kenen, ed., *The International Monetary System*, Boulder, CO: Westview Press, 1993.

Williamson, John, *The Exchange Rate System*, 2nd edition, Washington: Institute for International Economics, 1985.

Williamson, John, and Randall Henning, "Managing the Monetary System," in Peter B. Kenen, ed. *Managing the World Economy: Fifty Years after Bretton Woods*, Washington: Institute for International Economics, 1994.

25

Does the Exchange Rate Regime Matter for Inflation and Growth?

ATISH R. GHOSH,
JONATHAN D. OSTRY,
ANNE-MARIE GULDE,
& HOLGER C. WOLF

Although the theoretical relationships are ambiguous, evidence suggests a strong link between the choice of the exchange rate regime and macroeconomic performance. Adopting a pegged exchange rate can lead to lower inflation, but also to slower productivity growth.

Few questions in international economics have aroused more debate than the choice of exchange rate regime. Should a country fix the exchange rate or allow it to float? And if pegged, to a single "hard" currency or a basket of currencies? Economic literature pullulates with models, theories, and propositions. Yet little consensus has emerged about how exchange rate regimes affect common macroeconomic targets, such as inflation and growth. At a theoretical level, it is difficult to establish unambiguous relationships because of the many ways in which exchange rates can influence—and be influenced by—other macroeconomic variables. Likewise, empirical studies typically find no clear link between the exchange rate regime and macroeconomic performance.

This paper seeks to identify how various exchange rate regimes influence inflation and growth. It goes beyond previous studies in three important respects. First, it uses more comprehensive data—comprising all IMF members from 1960 to 1990. Second, it classifies exchange rate regimes in more detail than the traditional dichotomy between fixed and floating exchange rates. Third, it distinguishes between the central banks' declared exchange rate regimes and the behavior of the exchange rates in practice.

There is indeed a strong link between fixed exchange rates and low inflation. This results from a discipline effect (the political costs of abandoning the peg induce tighter policies) and a confidence effect (greater confidence leads to a greater willingness to hold domestic currency rather than goods or foreign currencies). In part, low inflation is associated with fixed exchange rates because countries with low inflation are better able to maintain an exchange rate peg. But there is also evidence of causality in the other direction: countries that choose fixed exchange rates achieve lower inflation.

There is also a link, albeit weaker, between the exchange rate regime and the growth of output. To the extent that fixing the exchange rate engenders greater policy confidence, it can foster higher investment. Conversely, a fixed rate, if set at the "wrong" level, can result in a misallocation of resources. In our data, countries that maintained pegged exchange rates did indeed have higher investment. But productivity grew more slowly than in countries with floating exchange rates. Overall, per capita growth was slightly lower in countries with pegged exchange rates.

This paper begins with a brief discussion of difficulties encountered in classifying exchange rate regimes. It then shows how alternative regimes affect inflation and growth. A few observations conclude the essay.

Classifying Regimes

Beyond the traditional fixed-floating dichotomy lies a spectrum of exchange rate regimes. The de facto behavior of an exchange rate, moreover, may diverge from its de jure classification.

While it is customary to speak of fixed and floating exchange rates, regimes actually span a continuum, ranging from pegs to target zones, to floats with heavy, light, or no intervention. The traditional dichotomy can mask important differences among regimes. Accordingly, this analysis uses a three-way classification: pegged, intermediate (i.e., floating rates, but within a predetermined range), and floating.

Regimes can be classified according to either the publicly stated commitment of the central bank (a de jure classification) or the observed behavior of the exchange rate (a de facto classification). Neither method is entirely satisfactory. A country that claims to have a pegged exchange rate might in fact instigate frequent changes in parity. On the other hand, a country might experience very small exchange rate movements, even though the central bank has no obligation to maintain a parity. The approach taken here is to report results according to the stated intention of the central bank, but to supplement these results by categorizing the non-floating regimes according to whether or not changes in parity were frequent. The de jure classification uses the IMF's Annual Report on Exchange Arrangements and Exchange Restrictions, while the de facto classification is based on a survey of IMF desk officers for each country. The data are taken from the World Economic Outlook database. In all, observations of GDP growth and consumer price inflation cover 145 countries and 30 years.

Inflation

Pegging the exchange rate can lower inflation by inducing greater policy discipline and instilling greater confidence in the currency. Empirically, both effects are important.

Policymakers have long maintained that a pegged exchange rate can be an anti-inflationary tool. Two reasons are typically cited. A pegged exchange rate provides a highly visible commitment and thus raises the political costs of loose monetary and fiscal policies. To the extent that the peg is credible, there is a stronger readiness to hold domestic currency, which reduces the inflationary consequences of a given expansion in the money supply.

Inflation Performance

Inflation over our sample averaged 10 percent a year, with pronounced differences in various exchange rate regimes (Chart 1). Countries with pegged exchange rates had an average annual inflation rate of 8 percent, compared with 14 percent for intermediate regimes, and 16 percent for floating regimes.

The differences among regimes are starker for the lower-income countries, where the differential between pegged and floating rates was almost 10 percentage points. As might be expected, countries without capital controls tended to have lower inflation in general. Even for these countries, however, inflation was lower under pegged regimes compared with either intermediate or floating exchange rates.

Although inflation performance is generally better under pegged exchange rates, the last panel in Chart 1 illustrates an important caveat: mere declaration of a pegged exchange rate is insufficient to reap the full anti-inflationary benefits. Countries that changed their parity frequently—though notionally maintaining a pegged exchange rate—on average experienced 13 percent inflation. While this is still better than the performance under non-pegged exchange rates (17 percent), it is significantly worse than countries that maintained a stable parity (7 percent).

Since there was a preponderance of pegged exchange rate regimes in the 1960s—when inflation rates were low—the association between low inflation and pegged rates might be more an artifact of the general macroeconomic climate than a property of the regime itself. One way to purge the data of such effects is to measure inflation rates for each regime relative to the average inflation rate (across all regimes) in that year. Doing so,

Inflation Performance (in percent per year)
Chart 1

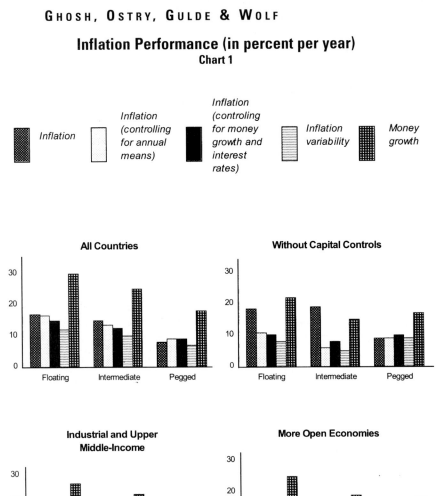

however, leaves the story largely unchanged: as Chart 1 shows, under pegged rates, inflation was 3 percentage points lower than under intermediate and 6 percentage points less than under floating regimes. Again, countries with only occasional changes in parity fared significantly better than those with frequent changes.

Explaining the Differences

What accounts for these results? They derive, in fact, from two separate effects. The first is discipline. Countries with pegged exchange rates have lower rates of growth in money supply, presumably because of the political costs of abandoning a peg. The growth of broad money (currency and deposits) averaged 17 percent a year under pegged exchange rates compared with almost 30 percent under floating regimes. This difference holds regardless of the income level of the country.

In addition, for a given growth rate of the money supply, higher money demand (the desire to hold money rather than spend it) will imply lower inflation. Pegged exchange rates, by enhancing confidence, can engender a greater demand for the domestic currency. This will be reflected in a lower velocity of circulation and a faster decline of domestic interest rates. In the extreme case of perfect credibility, domestic interest rates—even in countries with a history of high inflation—should fall immediately to the world level. Over the sample period, nominal interest rates have tended to rise, but the rate of increase for countries with floating rates was almost 6 percent, as against 2 percent for countries with pegged rates. It was actually highest for countries with intermediate regimes, where the growth rate of interest rates was almost 9 percent. A change in nominal interest rates is of importance because a fall in these rates will lead to a stronger demand for money. But the level of real interest rates (i.e., the nominal rates adjusted for inflation) also gives a direct measure of confidence. On average, the real interest rates were 0.2 percent a year under pegged regimes, 1.8

percent under intermediate regimes, and 2.3 percent under floating regimes.

For a variety of reasons—including interest rates that are set by the authorities rather than being determined by the market—the greater confidence that pegged exchanges can bring may not be fully reflected in the observed domestic interest rate. Nonetheless, it is possible to identify the "confidence effect" of various regimes by considering the residual inflation once the effects of money expansion, real growth, and domestic interest rates have been removed. A higher residual inflation implies lower confidence.

Do pegged rates lead to greater confidence? They do. Chart 1 shows the residual inflation rates. Countries with pegged exchange rates had inflation 2 percentage points lower than those with intermediate regimes, and 4 percentage points lower than those with floating regimes. This differential in favor of pegged rates is as large as 6 percentage points in the lower-income countries, but only 3 percentage points for countries without capital controls—perhaps because abjuring capital controls itself inspires confidence in the domestic currency.

Not only do countries with pegged exchange rates have lower inflation on average, they are also associated with lower inflation variability.

The Dog or the Tail?

Does pegging the exchange rate cause lower inflation? Or is it merely that countries with low inflation are better able to maintain a pegged exchange rate regime? Quite obviously, a country with reckless monetary policy will not be able to keep its exchange rate fixed for long. Part of the argument for pegged rates is precisely that they result in greater monetary discipline. But that still leaves the question of whether other variables—such as the degree of central bank independence—determine both a country's disposition toward low inflation and its ability to adopt a pegged exchange rate.

Econometric studies of this simultaneity between the choice of the exchange rate regime and inflation (using the same data) suggest that countries with low inflation do indeed have a greater proclivity toward pegged exchange rates. But they also show that, even allowing for this, pegged exchange rates lead to lower inflation.

Simpler, if less compelling, evidence comes from a comparison of countries that switched to a pegged exchange rate (from a floating regime) or vice versa. Relative to the year preceding the regime change, inflation was 0.6 percentage points lower one year after a switch to a fixed exchange rate regime, 0.5 percentage points lower after two years, and 0.5 percentage points lower after three years. Conversely, inflation was higher by 3 percentage points one year after a switch to a floating regime, 1.8 percentage points higher after two years, and 2.3 percentage points higher after three years.

A second piece of evidence comes from a comparison of countries with similar volatility in nominal effective exchange rates but different exchange rate regimes. Countries with pegged exchanges rates, of course, tend to exhibit lower effective exchange rate variability. But if the exchange rate regime matters for inflation, there should still be a difference between countries with pegged and floating exchange rates even after controlling for nominal exchange rate variability. It turns out that this is indeed the case. Controlling for nominal exchange rate variability, there remain significant differences in inflation in the various regimes. In other words, pegging the nominal exchange rate—which may instill greater confidence—has an effect on inflation beyond simply lowering nominal exchange rate variability.

Finally, it is worth checking that the results are not driven by contamination across regimes. For instance, it is possible for inflationary pressure to build up—but be held in check—during a period of pegged exchange rates and then explode into open inflation when a float is adopted. In such a case, the high inflation would be blamed on the floating regime, though it should more properly be attributed to the fixed exchange rate period. This suggests dropping the first year or two

following a regime change from the data. Conversely, if a regime is not sustained, then it is debatable whether the macroeconomic performance under that regime should be attributed to it. The last couple of years prior to a regime change ought also to be omitted. Neither modification alters the results. Dropping the first two years following a regime change lowers the differential in favor of pegged rates from 6.0 percentage points to 5.7 percentage points. Dropping the last two years of each regime lowers it to 5.8 percentage points.

Growth

The exchange rate regime can influence economic growth through investment or increased productivity. Pegged regimes have higher investment; floating regimes have faster productivity growth. On net, per capita GDP growth was slightly faster under floating regimes.

Economic theory has relatively little to say about the effects of the nominal exchange rate regime on the growth of output. Typically, arguments focus on the impact on investment and international trade. Advocates argue that pegged exchange rates foster investment by reducing policy uncertainties and lowering real interest rates. But equally, by eliminating an important adjustment mechanism, fixed exchange rates can increase protectionist pressure, distort price signals in the economy, and prevent the efficient allocation of resources across sectors.

Growth Performance

Annual GDP growth per capita averaged 1.6 percent over our sample. Although differences exist across exchange rate regimes, these are generally less marked than the differences in inflation rates (Chart 2). Different samples, moreover, lead to varied conclusions about growth under fixed and floating exchange rates. Growth was actually fastest under the intermediate regimes, averaging more than 2 percent a year. It was 1.4 percent a year under pegged exchange rates and 1.7 percent under floating rates. This pattern emerges mainly

Per Capita GDP Growth (in percent per year)
Chart 2

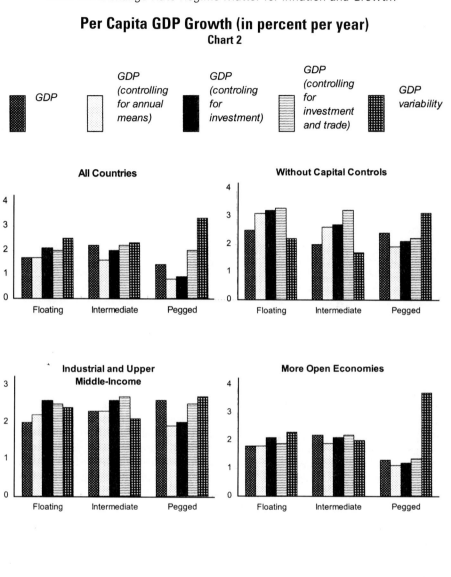
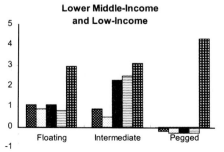
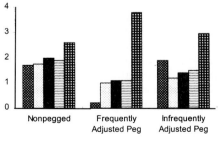

because of the lower middle-income and low-income countries; growth was somewhat higher under pegged rates for the industrial and upper middle-income countries.

Just as inflation was generally lower in the 1960s, growth rates tended to be higher. Controlling for this widens the differential in favor of floating exchange rates to 0.8 percent over all countries, and as much as 1.5 percent for the lower-income countries.

Explaining the Differences

By definition, economic growth can be explained by the use of more capital and labor (the factors of production) or by residual productivity growth. This productivity growth reflects both technological progress and—perhaps more important—changes in the economic efficiency with which capital and labor are used.

Investment rates were highest under pegged exchange rates—by as much as 2 percentage points of GDP—with the largest difference for the industrial and upper middle-income countries and almost none for the lower-income countries. With higher investment rates and lower output growth, productivity increases must have been smaller under fixed exchange rates.

Part of the higher productivity growth under floating rates is reflected in faster growth of external trade. Trade growth (measured as the sum of export growth and import growth) is almost 3 percentage points higher under floating rates. The lower-income countries—where real exchange rate misalignments under fixed rates have been more common—show an even larger difference in trade growth between pegged and floating exchange rates.

While not overwhelming, the evidence suggests that fixing the nominal exchange rate can prevent relative prices (including, perhaps, real wages) from adjusting. This lowers economic efficiency. Part, though not all, of this lower productivity growth is offset by higher investment under pegged exchange rates. A comparison of countries that switched regimes shows that a move to floating exchange rates results in an increase of GDP growth of 0.3 per-

centage points one year after the switch and of more than 1 percentage point three years after the switch. One manifestation of the rigidities that pegged exchange rates can engender is the higher volatility of GDP growth and of employment. As the last rows of Chart 2 indicate, GDP growth was more volatile under pegged exchange rates, as was employment.

Conclusions

Does the exchange rate regime matter for macroeconomic performance? The experience of IMF member countries since the 1960s suggests that it does.

The strongest results concern inflation. Pegged exchange rates are associated with significantly better inflation performance (lower inflation and less variability), and there is at least some evidence of a causal relationship. There is, however, an important caveat. Countries that have frequent parity changes—while notionally maintaining a peg—are unlikely to reap the full anti-inflationary benefits of a fixed exchange rate regime.

The choice of exchange rate regime also has implications for economic growth. Pegged rates are associated with higher investment. But they are also correlated with slower productivity growth. On net, output growth is slightly lower under pegged exchange rates. The inability to use the nominal exchange rate as an adjustment mechanism, moreover, results in greater variability of growth and employment.

Ultimately, the exchange rate regime is but one facet of a country's overall macroeconomic policy. No regime is likely to serve all countries at all times. Countries facing disinflation may find pegging the exchange rate an important tool. But where growth has been sluggish, and real exchange rate misalignments common, a more flexible regime might be called for. The choice, like the trade-off, is the country's own.

Anne-Marie Gulde is an Economist in the IMF's Monetary and Exchange Affairs Department.

Atish R. Ghosh is an Economist in the IMF's European II Department. He holds degrees from Harvard and Oxford Universities.

Jonathan D. Ostry is a Senior Economist in the IMF's Southeast Asia and Pacific Department and holds a doctorate from the University of Chicago.

Holger C. Wolf is a faculty member of the Stern Business School of New York University and holds a doctorate from Massachusetts Institute of Technology.

Bibliography

There is a vast literature on the link between the exchange rate regime and macroeconomic performance. The following provide useful surveys.

Argy, Victor, "The Choice of Exchange Rate Regime for a Smaller Economy: A Survey of Some Key Issues," in *Choosing an Exchange Rate Regime*, ed. by Victor Argy and Paul De Grauwe (Washington: International Monetary Fund, 1990).

Barth, Richard, and Chorng-Huey Wong (eds.), *Approaches to Exchange Rate Policy* (Washington: International Monetary Fund, 1994).

Baxter, Marianne, and Alan C. Stockman, *Business Cycles and the Exchange Rate System: Some Internal Evidence* (Cambridge, Massachusetts: National Bureau of Economic Research, 1988).

Crockett, Andrew, and Morris Goldstein, "Inflation Under Fixed and Flexible Exchange Rates," International Monetary Fund, *Staff Papers*, Vol. 23 (November 1976), pp. 509–44.

Frenkel, Jacob, Morris Goldstein, and Paul Masson, *Characteristics of a Successful Exchange Rate System*, Occasional Paper 82 (Washington: International Monetary Fund, 1991).

Friedman, Milton, "The Case For Flexible Exchange Rates," in *Essays in Positive Economics* (Chicago: University of Chicago Press, 1953).

Ghosh, Atish, Anne-Marie Gulde, Jonathan Ostry, and Holger Wolf, "Does the Nominal Exchange Rate Regime Matter?" IMF Working Paper 95/121 (December 1995).

Guitián, Manuel, "The Choice of an Exchange Rate Regime," in *Approaches to Exchange Rate Policy*, ed. by Richard Barth and Chorng-Huey Wong (Washington: International Monetary Fund, 1994).

Krugman, Paul, *Exchange Rate Instability* (Cambridge, Massachusetts: MIT Press, 1989).

Mussa, Michael, "Nominal Exchange Rate Regimes and the Behavior of Real Exchange Rates, Evidence and Implications," in *Real Business Cycles, Real Exchange Rates, and Actual Policies*, ed. by Karl Brunner and Alan Meltzer (Amsterdam: North-Holland, 1986).

Nurkse, Ragnar, *International Currency Experience* (Geneva: League of Nations, 1944).

Obstfeld, Maurice, "Floating Exchange Rates: Experience and Prospects," *Brookings Papers on Economic Activity: 2* (1985), pp. 369–450.

Quirk, Peter, "Fixed or Floating Exchange Regimes: Does It Matter for Inflation?" IMF Working Paper 94/134 (December 1994).

Williamson, John, "A Survey of the Literature on the Optimal Peg," *Journal of Development Economics*, Vol. 2 (August 1982), pp. 39–61.

Currency Boards

26

Sharmila King

A currency board is a stricter version of a fixed exchange rate system. Like any fixed exchange rate system, a currency board provides a stable exchange rate, which can promote trade and investment. Currency boards were popular in the first half of the 20th century, particularly in former British colonies. During the 1990s, currency boards were regarded as a good solution for economies plagued with high inflation, financial instability, and preventing currency crises. As such, the popularity of currency boards grew in the 1990s.

What is a Currency Board?

A currency board is a government organization, similar to a central bank that is responsible for maintaining the fixed exchange rate. Currency boards involve three elements. First, a country fixes its exchange rate to an "anchor currency." The anchor currency is usually that of a major country and large trading partner. For example, the Hong Kong dollar is officially fixed at HK$7.80 per US dollar. Second, the country commits itself to full convertibility of its own currency into the anchor currency. In order for convertibility to be credible, the currency board must hold sufficient reserves to back 100% of its monetary base in the economy. Furthermore, the board is prohibited from acquiring any domestic assets such as government bonds, or performing central bank functions, such as lender of last resort. The currency board must hold only

foreign reserves assets. Third, the country must commit its self to maintaining the currency board indefinitely.

The difference between a currency board and central bank can be distinguished using a balance sheet. Figure 1 shows that the primary difference between a currency board and a central bank lies on the asset side of the balance sheet, where currency boards do not hold domestic government debt. While this difference is small, it has significant implications for monetary and exchange rate policy.

The Case for Currency Boards

Currency Boards Reduce Speculative Attacks: Proponents of currency boards argue that currency boards prevent the type of attack which Mexico experienced in 1994-95 and which many East Asian economies experienced in 1997-98. Argentina was able to survive the "Tequila attack" and prevent a collapse of its own currency after the devaluation of the Mexican peso. The Hong Kong dollar maintained its peg to the US dollar despite a wave of currency devaluations throughout East Asia.

Currency Boards Lower Inflation: Currency boards reduce inflation because they limit the growth of the money supply to the growth rate of foreign reserves. A currency board issues domestic currency only when there are foreign exchange reserves to back the issue. Thus, unlike a traditional central bank, that can print money at will, currency

The Balance Sheets of a Typical Currency Board and a Central Bank
Figure 1

A Currency Board

Assets
Foreign Currency
(typically anchor currency)
Gold Reserves
Foreign Government Debt
(typically anchor currency)

Liabilities
Cash

Commercial Bank Deposits
Government & non-Government
Deposits

A Central Bank

Assets
Foreign Currency
& Bond Reserves
Gold Reserves
Domestic Government Debt

Liabilities
Cash
Commercial Bank Deposits
Government & non-Government
Deposits

---

boards leave no room for excessive monetary expansion. Further, currency boards typically peg the value of its currency to the currency of a country with a low inflation rate. Effectively the currency board imports the low inflation reputation of the anchor currency.

Ghosh, Glude, and Wolf (2000) find that the average inflation rate under a currency board is 4 percentage points lower than inflation rates under other pegged exchange rate regimes. The authors argue that roughly 3.5% of this reduction in average inflation can be attributed to increased confidence conferred by the currency board. Surprisingly, only 0.5% of the reduction in average inflation can be attributed to a lower money supply growth rate. Ghosh et al.'s study lends credence to the argument that monetary discipline under a currency board increases the credibility of a country wishing to reduce inflation.

Currency Boards Impose Fiscal Discipline: Since currency boards prevent the monetary authority from holding government debt and limit the growth rate of the money supply to the growth rate of foreign reserves, they also limit the ability of governments to monetize their debt. Proponents of currency boards argue that fiscal discipline is necessary for developing countries where political pressures to monetize the debt are enormous. Ghosh et al. find that the adoption of a strict monetary regime, a currency board, induces better fiscal performance. They find an average fiscal deficit of 2.8% of

GDP for countries operating currency boards compared to 4.2% under other pegged exchange rate regimes and 4.4% for countries with a floating exchange rate.

The Case against Currency Boards

Currency Boards Weaken the Country's Banking System: Since a currency board arrangement prevents the monetary authority from increasing the money supply in a time of crisis, it effectively limits the ability of the monetary authority to provide liquidity. A currency board, unlike a central bank, cannot act as a lender of last resort to stem a banking panic. Further, a currency board can also put pressure on banks if interest rates rise sharply as investors dump local currency. If interest rates remain high, small undercapitalized banks may find it difficult to maintain liquidity and become insolvent (Santiparbhob 1997). This monetary contraction would only fuel the banking panic.

Currency Boards May Lead to Overvaluation of a Currency, Reducing Competitiveness: Opponents of currency boards argue that currency boards limit the ability of a country to adjust to macroeconomic shocks by altering its exchange rate. For example, Zaire exports an enormous amount of copper. In 1999, the price of copper collapsed. To offset this macroeconomic shock, Zaire could lower its exchange rate in order to boost the exports of other goods. However, a currency board would prevent

Zaire from adjusting its exchange rate. To make matter worse, if Zaire's foreign reserves were reduced as a result of declining copper exports, the country would be forced into a monetary contraction. While some of these criticisms can be leveled against any fixed exchange rate system, under a pegged exchange rate regime it is much easier for a country to devalue its currency. Under a currency board arrangement, financial markets may view devaluation as a failure of the currency board, and hence eliminating the credibility and confidence that the currency board created. Critics also point to Hong Kong's experience of the 1990's when the Hong Kong dollar appreciated 30% in comparison to its competitor currencies.

While Currency Boards May Prevent a Collapse of a Country's Currency, They Do Not Prevent Speculative Attacks: The experience of Argentina during the peso crisis and Hong Kong during the Asian crisis indicates that speculators can and do attack countries with currency board arrangements. Speculators may believe that the authorities would rather devalue its currency than suffer a sharp increase in interest rates or devalue its currency to maintain competitiveness if its competitors devalue. Argentina lost more than 50% of its foreign reserves during the speculative attack on its currency in the wake of the Mexican peso crisis.

Empirical Studies Do Not Imply Causality: While there is evidence that currency boards have had success in reducing inflation and reducing fiscal deficits, opponents argue that it is possible that countries adopting currency board arrangements are already predisposed to reduce inflation and fiscal deficits and could have done so without a currency board.

Currency Boards Are Costly: Since currency boards require a country to hold a large amount of foreign reserves, they redirect funds that could have been spent elsewhere, such as investment in physical or human capital. Many economists otherwise predisposed to the idea of currency boards, oppose these arrangements for this reason.

Hong Kong's Experience with a Currency Board Arrangement

Hong Kong's currency board is twenty years old. Since the currency board was adopted on 17th October 1983, the Hong Kong dollar has been officially fixed at HK$7.80 per US dollar. Since 1863, Hong Kong has had some form of a fixed exchange rate system. From 1863 to 1935, Hong Kong adopted the silver standard and from 1935 to 1972, the Hong Kong dollar was pegged to the British pound. The Hong Kong dollar was pegged to the US dollar in some form (either fixed or a band of 2.25% around a central rate) during 1972-1974. The Hong Kong dollar floated from 1974 to 1983. During this period, real GDP growth and inflation were volatile. For example, the inflation rate in 1975 was 2.7% and in 1980 inflation climbed to 15.5%.[1] Unsatisfactory economic performance under a floating exchange rate stimulated enthusiasm for Hong Kong's current currency board. The credibility of the peg is maintained by the 100% backing of Hong Kong's monetary base with US dollars kept in Hong Kong's Exchange Fund. At the end of 2000, foreign reserves in the Exchange Fund equaled US$100.4bn.

Since the establishment of the currency board, a number of external macroeconomic shocks have hit Hong Kong. Figure 2 (next page) illustrates the response of the peg under numerous external shocks. Figure 2 clearly shows that the peg has survived political and economic crises including the speculative attack during Asia's financial crisis. One could argue that the success of Hong Kong's currency board is precisely that the government has resisted changes to the value of the peg.

However, the currency board arrangement has macroeconomic implications for Hong Kong's economy. As with all fixed exchange rate regimes, interest rates are effectively determined by the anchor currency's central bank, in the case of Hong Kong, the US Federal Reserve. Since on average Hong Kong has had a higher inflation rate than the US, real interest rates have been low or sometimes negative in Hong Kong.[2] Some argue that this easy monetary policy fueled the stock

Resilience Against External Shocks

Figure 2

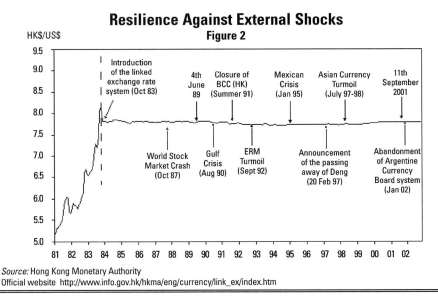

Source: Hong Kong Monetary Authority
Official website http://www.info.gov.hk/hkma/eng/currency/link_ex/index.htm

and property price bubble in the 1990's. Furthermore, following the depreciation of Asian currencies during the financial crisis of 1997-1998, the Hong Kong dollar was relatively overvalued eroding Hong Kong's competitiveness. An additional problem preventing Hong Kong's economic recovery is China's rising competitiveness. Labor and property in neighboring China is a fraction of the cost in Hong Kong. Further, the quality of labor in China is increasing. Without a depreciating exchange rate to absorb these shocks, prices and wages must adjust downwards. If the economy could not get any worse for Hong Kong the disease, Severe Acute Respiratory Syndrome (SARS) in 2003 has caused further economic damage as tourism and demand decline. Consequently, Hong Kong is experiencing a sluggish economy, a yawning budget deficit, deflation, and record high unemployment. Opponents of the currency board blame the peg for Hong Kong's economic doldrums. Proponents of the peg argue that devaluation could cause instability and is unlikely to boost exports since 10% of Hong Kong's trade is denominated in Hong Kong dollars.[3] Despite these problems, Hong Kong has no plans to abandon its currency peg with the US dollar.

Who Should Adopt a Currency Board Arrangement?

Hong Kong's experience would seem to endorse the currency board arrangement. Hong Kong appears well suited for a currency board arrangement: it has ample foreign reserves; its banking system is well capitalized and regulated; and Hong Kong has flexible wages and prices. Countries considering adopting a currency board should be aware of the disadvantages of these arrangements. The majority of countries that have adopted currency boards are small, with the exception of Argentina. Most of these countries do not rely on commodities for exports, which have unstable prices. Further, many of these countries had substantial foreign reserves before adopting a currency board arrangement and limited public sector debt. Historical evidence suggests that the rule-based nature of a currency board appears to successfully and quickly lower inflation and stabilize a formerly unstable currency.

Opponents of currency boards argue that countries ready to credibly commit to sound fiscal and monetary policies would do better without a currency board arrangement. They are particular concerned with the limitations that currency board arrangements impose on the central bank. Further, the stability that currency boards provide encourages contracts denominated in local and hard currency, inviting potential currency mismatches; this was Argentina's experience. Argentina's recent exit from a currency board arrangement suggests that when currency boards collapse, the effects are devastating.

Endnotes

[1] http://www.info.gov.hk/hkma/eng/public/hkma-lin/hkmalin_eng.pdf

[2] The ABC of a currency board, *The Economist,* Oct 30th, 1997.

[3] What's in a peg? *The Economist,* Oct 31st, 2002.

References

"The ABC of a Currency Board" *The Economist,* Oct 30th, 1997.

"What's in a Peg?" *The Economist,* Oct 31st, 2002.

Ghosh, Atish, Gulde Anne-Marie, and Wolf, Holger, "Currency Boards: The Ultimate Fix?" International Monetary Fund Working Paper WP/98/8, 1998.

Santiparbhob V. "Bank Soundness and Currency Board Arrangements: Issues and Experiences," International Monetary Fund Working Paper WP/97/11, 1997.

The Hong Kong Monetary Authority's Official Website: http://www.info.gov.hk/hkma /eng/public/hkmalin/hkmalin_eng.pdf

27

Dollarization as a Monetary Arrangement for Emerging Market Economies

GAETANO **ANTINOLFI**
& TODD **KEISTER**

Ecuador and El Salvador have recently adopted the U.S. dollar as legal tender, replacing their own national currencies.[1] This same move has received serious attention in policy debates in both Argentina and Mexico. Abandoning the national currency is a decision with far-reaching economic and political implications that are not well understood. In response to this phenomenon, a growing literature has aimed at evaluating the economic costs and benefits of "dollarizing." In this article, we provide an overview of the emerging literature and point out some issues that we feel warrant further research.[2]

Throughout, we focus on official dollarization, where the U.S. dollar (or some other currency) replaces the national currency as legal tender. Unofficial dollarization, where private agents use a foreign currency as a substitute for the domestic currency, is already widespread in Latin America and elsewhere. We focus on Latin America and the U.S. dollar because of the recent events and policy debates mentioned above. Most of the issues we discuss, however, would apply to any country considering the official adoption of a foreign currency.

Discussions of the optimal monetary and exchange rate arrangements for an emerging market economy have traditionally centered on fixed or flexible exchange rates or (most often) some hybrid of the two, perhaps combined with capital controls or other regulatory measures. We begin our discussion by examining the causes of the current surge of interest in official dollarization. We then turn to the details of the issues that we feel are most important in analyzing the potential costs and benefits of dollarizing.

Why Consider Dollarization?

Financial Crises

The current interest in official dollarization is largely a reaction to the recent string of currency crises. In the past decade, these crises have affected numerous countries, both industrialized (Italy and the United Kingdom in 1992) and emerging markets (Mexico in 1994, and East Asia and Brazil in 1997). Comparing the crises in industrialized countries with those in emerging markets reveals an important difference: although these crises are not costly in terms of lost output for industrialized economies, they are extremely costly for emerging market economies.[3] For example, in 1995 Mexican gross domestic product (GDP) declined by 7 percent in real per capita terms. (In the years before the crisis, for comparison, real per capita growth ranged between 3 percent and 10 percent.) Moreover, when one emerging economy suffers a crisis, others are often hit by interest rate increases and a recession, as happened in Argentina following the Mexican crisis. This phenomenon is known as contagion.

The events in emerging market economies share certain characteristics that allow us to identify a typical "anatomy" of a crisis.[4] Beforehand, there is an incipient capital inflow and a corresponding current account deficit. The onset of the crisis is marked by a sudden capital outflow and a large devaluation of the exchange rate. There is often a crisis in the banking system at about the same time.[5] The result is a sharp and painful fall in output. Much of the current interest in dollarization stems from a strong desire to avoid such crises in the future. Before discussing the potential costs and benefits of dollarizing, we look at some of the more traditional approaches to these problems and why they seem to be falling out of favor.

The Fear of Floating

One approach that naturally comes to mind (to an economist, at least) is to allow prices and quantities to be determined by supply and demand in markets. The definition of a flexible exchange rate system is exactly this: the price of one currency relative to another is determined by the market without any intervention by central banks. That is to say, any current account deficit has to be financed entirely by capital inflows (a financial account surplus) and vice versa, without any change in official reserves.

In reality, however, we do not observe many countries with truly flexible exchange rate systems. Rapid growth in world capital markets has led to a substantial increase in the size of international capital flows. At times, these flows become very volatile; indeed, as we mentioned above, a sudden reversal in capital flows is the typical "spark" of a crisis. Under a pure flexible exchange rate system, such volatility in capital flows causes corresponding volatility in the exchange rate. A volatile exchange rate, in turn, means that relative prices in the economy are volatile, which can be very disruptive to real economic activity.

Calvo and Reinhart (2000) have termed the unwillingness to let exchange rates be completely determined in markets "the fear of floating." They also point out several additional reasons why emerging market economies seem to be averse to floating exchange rates. These include high levels of dollar-denominated debt, high-exchange-rate pass through (reflected in domestic inflation), and in general an adverse effect of currency instability on credit market access. In support of their argument, they conduct an empirical analysis comparing the announced exchange rate regime of countries to the actual exchange rate behavior. Their findings indicate that countries classified as letting their exchange rate float, in general, do not. Hence it seems that very few, if any, countries are willing to take this approach.

The Costs of Capital Controls

Sudden reversals in the flow of capital have been an important and particularly damaging aspect of currency crises. If capital market volatility is the problem, one way of avoiding it is to introduce capital controls. Clearly the aim of such a policy would not be to stop capital inflows, because emerging market economies rely on them for investment, but to diminish their volatility. There is evidence indicating that capital controls involving taxes and reserve requirements can change the composition of capital inflows in favor of long-term investment, and thereby decrease the likelihood of large, sudden outflows. Calvo and Reinhart (1999), however, caution that these results may depend on the accounting classifications of capital flows. In addition, Edwards (1999) argues that, when analyzing the maturity of a country's foreign debt, the relevant concept is residual maturity[6] rather than contractual maturity. Using data from Chile, Edwards shows that short-term capital controls had a limited effect on Chile's residual maturity of foreign debt and that Chile had higher residual maturity than Mexico (a country without capital controls) at the end of 1996.

More generally, capital controls are typically not considered sound economic policy because they limit the ability of a country to borrow and invest, they hinder international risk sharing and technology transfer, and they prolong the survival of unsustainable domestic policies. The main practical objection to capital controls, however, is that they create a strong incentive for tax evasion and require a costly enforcement apparatus. These problems make them poor candidates for permanent solutions.[7]

The Vanishing Intermediate Regime

The unwillingness to let exchange rates float and to use direct capital controls has pushed countries toward "intermediate" exchange rate regimes in which official intervention is used to keep the exchange rate within predetermined bounds. This move, however, has been accompanied by the recent crises mentioned previously. This association has led many observers to claim that intermediate exchange rate regimes are no longer viable for emerging market economies. These observers claim that only extreme (totally fixed or totally flexible) exchange rate regimes are viable for emerging market economies. Eichengreen (forthcoming) colorfully likens adopting an intermediate regime to "painting a bull's eye on the forehead of the central bank governor and telling speculators to 'shoot here.'"[8] There are, of course, situations for which some authors are willing to defend intermediate regimes as appropriate, but they are generally viewed as temporary remedies.[9] Fischer (2001) presents empirical evidence that the proportion of emerging market economies using intermediate regimes has indeed declined over the past decade.

An important question is how extreme a policy must be in order to avoid the problems associated with the middle ground. Even a currency board has proven not to be extreme enough in some ways. Under this arrangement, the central bank commits to back its monetary base entirely with foreign reserves at all times; thus, a unit of domestic currency can be introduced into the economy only if an equivalent amount of foreign reserves is obtained. In principle, this system is equivalent to dollarization. However, even though Argentina has been operating under a currency board since 1991, the interest rate differentials between peso-denominated and dollar-denominated debt remain and have widened during periods of financial turmoil, as with the Brazilian and Mexican crises (see

Figure 1). This indicates that financial markets believe there to be a significant probability that the currency board will be abandoned under such circumstances, and the Argentine economy has suffered as a result.

The Key Issues

We now turn to what we see as the key issues in evaluating the costs and benefits of dollarization. Two of the primary benefits of dollarization are straightforward: exchange rate volatility (against the dollar) and exchange rate crises would be eliminated, and in most cases the inflation rate would be lowered substantially. One of the costs is also fairly straightforward, although occasionally misunderstood: the loss of seignorage revenue. We begin our discussion with this issue.

There are other costs and benefits that are more subtle and difficult to measure. Dollarization implies the loss of monetary policy, but, if it enhances the credibility of economic policy, dollarization could lower interest rates and substantially decrease the likelihood of future financial crises. If it increases economic integration with the United States, dollarization could yield substantial benefits in both product and financial markets. An important concern, however, is that dollarization would limit the ability of the central bank to act as a lender of last resort. We discuss these issues in turn below. Finally, a discussion of dollarization would not be complete without looking at the "initial conditions" in which many emerging market economies currently find themselves and approaching the issue from the perspective of the United States.

Seignorage Revenue

An obvious cost of dollarization is the loss of the seignorage revenue that comes with the power to print fiat currency. The size of the flow of seignorage revenue depends on both the rate of growth of output and the rate of inflation. For some emerging market economies, it constitutes a substantial fraction of government revenues. With any other fixed exchange rate arrangement, seignorage revenues are present in some form. In particular,

Figure 1

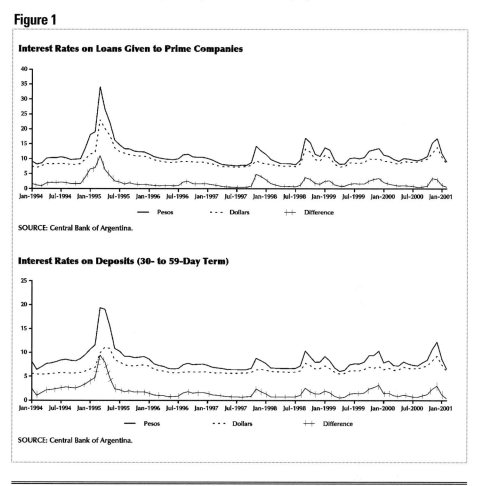

Interest Rates on Loans Given to Prime Companies

SOURCE: Central Bank of Argentina.

Interest Rates on Deposits (30- to 59-Day Term)

SOURCE: Central Bank of Argentina.

under a currency board, newly printed domestic money is used to buy interest-bearing foreign reserves. Dollarization entails losing this interest. It also entails buying back the domestic monetary base using foreign reserves and, therefore, losing the interest on this stock of reserves as well. Velde and Veracierto (1999) calculate this latter number for Argentina to be $658 million, or 0.2 percent of GDP, per year.

Note that computing the present level of seignorage revenue and calling that a "cost" of dollarization is clearly a mistake in most cases. Chang and Velasco (2000b) make this point: If a country dollarizes in order to lower its inflation rate, this reflects a decision that the benefits of lower inflation outweigh the value of the revenue that higher inflation brings. Instead, one should focus on the seignorage revenue that would have been earned at the new, lower inflation rate. This is the "loss" in seignorage revenue relative to the (ideal) case where the inflation rate is (somehow) lowered without dollarizing.

There are two reasons to believe that this amount may still overestimate the true revenue loss from dollarizing. First, a dollarizing country may be able to negotiate a deal with the United States under which it receives some of the increased U.S. seignorage revenue (which could equal the "loss" calculated above).[10] Second, a large part of the reason for dollarizing is to create a more stable economic environment that will encourage investment and growth. While it is extremely difficult to make quantitative predictions about the size of this effect, it is clear that the increase in tax revenue from increased economic activity should at least partially offset the loss of seignorage revenue.

Regarding this last point, however, it is important to note that the increase in tax revenue would take time to develop. In the meantime, a government with lower revenues would have to decrease expenditures, increase taxes, or increase the public debt. To the extent that the loss of seignorage revenue is compensated by an increase in government borrowing, it may not be the case that a stable currency necessarily provides more macroeconomic stability. This is an indication that the fiscal plan accompanying a dollarization would be critical to its success.

Fiscal Consequences

Because dollarization entails a loss of both seignorage revenue and independent monetary policy, it is likely to have important consequences for the conduct of fiscal policy. Sims (2001) argues against dollarization for precisely this reason. He argues that the option value of issuing fiat debt (which can be defaulted on through inflation) is too high to surrender because inflation is part of an optimal taxation scheme. In support of his argument, Sims computes the unexpected component of U.S. government debt yields and shows that it is substantial. His calculations show that fiat debt worked to relax the government budget constraint in times of high economic turmoil (such as the oil crisis of 1973). One possible interpretation of this fact is that, without fluctuations in the unexpected component of government bond yields, more variability would have been observed in taxation and government expenditure, which may have been very costly. More research (as Sims acknowledges) is needed to evaluate (i) how much of the variability in the unexpected component of government bond yields actually reflects inefficient variation in monetary and fiscal policy that is better avoided and (ii) how much of it reflects an "optimal" response to

real shocks.

Similarly, Chang and Velasco (2000b) argue that an optimal taxation plan would always entail surprise inflation (or devaluation) because this acts as a lump-sum tax and therefore is non-distortionary. Dollarization removes the ability of the government to use this tax. The contributions of Sims (2000) and Chang and Velasco (2000b) in this way stress the potentially high costs of losing flexibility in economic policy. Surprise inflations, however, cannot be repeatedly engineered, and anticipated inflation is typically not part of an optimal taxation plan. Hence the government has a time-consistency problem; it wants to convince people that it will not engineer an inflation increase, but once people are convinced, it wants to surprise them. Because people know this, the economy can end up in a situation of anticipated inflation. If this problem is very costly to the economy, then the benefit of using dollarization to solve it may easily outweigh the cost of the lost flexibility.[11]

Chang and Velasco (2000b) go on to point out that dollarization might decrease the incentives for fiscal discipline. Lack of fiscal discipline, in turn, may mean that crises due to high sovereign default risk would persist and the economy would not benefit from lower interest rates. Would the adoption of the dollar imply more or less fiscal discipline? Chang (2000) argues that, under alternative arrangements, changes in exchange rates or interest rates make the costs of a lack of fiscal discipline immediate. Dollarization would take those incentives away by allowing the costs of present fiscal looseness to be shifted to the future (in terms of higher future taxes, for example). Hence the incentives for fiscal discipline would decrease.

Although these incentive problems are real, it is important to recognize that there are other factors working in the opposite direction. First, as noted above, emerging markets depend heavily on foreign capital, and capital outflows could serve to make the cost of a lack of fiscal discipline immediate. Second, the incentive for domestic investors to monitor and put political pressure on the government for fiscal discipline would be higher. Heavy government borrowing would be perceived to induce macroeconomic instability and would cause interest rates for all domestic borrowers to increase. Through these channels, market discipline would be present for a dollarized government.

If dollarization does undermine the incentives for fiscal responsibility, does that mean it should be accompanied by legal restrictions on the government budget deficit? In part, this was the route taken by the European Monetary Union (EMU) in tying the Stability Pact to the launch of the euro. It is important to notice, however, that a unilateral dollarization is very different from the EMU's in this regard. In the latter case, members relinquished control to a common central bank for the conduct of monetary policy. The decision to dollarize, in contrast, entails total loss of monetary authority. As such, legal restrictions on the government budget would constrain an already shrunken set of policy alternatives, which could prove very costly in an economic downturn.[12]

Economic Integration

A potential benefit of dollarization is that it could increase the level of integration of the dollarizing economy with the U.S. economy. This may come about for several reasons, including reduced transactions costs and the elimination of uncertainty about exchange rates. Frankel and Rose (2000) present evidence that currency unions lead to large increases in trade flows between member countries.[13] Furthermore, Frankel and Rose argue that these increases do not come from the diversion of trade away from non-member countries; rather, currency union membership leads to a higher ratio of total foreign trade to GDP. In fact, they interpret their results as indicating that increased trade is the primary benefit of joining a currency union (or dollarizing).

In addition to increased trade, dollarization could increase the level of financial integration between the dollarizing country and the United States. Stockman (2001) focuses on the "central bank area" that would result from dollarization. He argues that this would be the most important effect of dollarization in Mexico—the Federal Reserve

System would become Mexico's central bank.

This scenario would lead to changes in monetary policy (which Stockman defines broadly to include supervisory and regulatory policies) that would affect the incentives of financial intermediaries and thereby affect the levels of investment and financial integration. This change is important because the level of financial development is strongly related to economic growth and is shown in some studies to cause growth;[14] thus, the potential benefits are indeed large.

Other studies, however, indicate that integration should come before dollarization. For example, Bencivenga, Huybens, and Smith (2001) show that dollarization has a different impact depending on the extent of the integration between the two economies' financial markets. They show that dollarization is beneficial when capital markets are well integrated; otherwise, dollarization may be a source of volatility and indeterminacy in the economy. Hence in their model, it is the *ex ante* level of integration of capital markets that determines the benefits of dollarization.

Bencivenga, Huybens, and Smith (2001) complement and extend the traditional optimal currency literature, where it is the integration of real markets that determines the boundaries of the optimal currency area. This theory is based on the work of Mundell (1961) and specifically addresses the issue of when two economies should use the same currency. According to the theory, the key issue in determining whether two economies fall in the same optimal currency area is whether or not there is a substantial benefit of having independent monetary policy to accommodate asymmetric shocks to the economies. An optimal currency area in general is one where: (i) asymmetric shocks are not substantial, (ii) there is high mobility of factors of production, and (iii) prices are flexible. It is important to keep in mind, however, that these considerations have not been the motivation behind the current interest in dollarization.

Using the criteria of the literature on the traditional optimal currency area, it is hard to imagine Argentina being in the same optimal currency area as the United States. Even neighboring Mexico is far from perfectly integrated with the U.S. economy. The interest in dollarization fundamentally stems from the desire to bring about financial stability. The involvement of the banking sector in the recent crises underlined the importance of this issue, which is beyond the scope of the traditional optimal-currency-area model.

The Lender of Last Resort Function

A common argument against dollarization is that it would severely limit the ability of the central bank to act as a lender of last resort when the banking sector is in distress. One of the crucial roles that banks perform is maturity transformation: taking in short-term deposits and making long-term loans. This naturally puts a bank at risk if, for whatever reason, depositors have a sudden increase in their demand for liquidity and want to withdraw their money. When there is a domestic currency that can be printed freely, the central bank always has the ability to meet this liquidity demand by lending cash to the banking sector. Banks can then repay the loans when the crisis passes. In a dollarized economy, the central bank would not have unlimited resources to lend. The fear, therefore, is that giving up the ability to print currency will make these types of crises more frequent and/or more severe.

The emerging literature has shown that this concern is likely overstated for several reasons. First, the ability of the central bank to act as a lender of last resort is equally limited under fixed exchange rates and currency boards. Nevertheless, Argentina has developed several other mechanisms to deal with liquidity crises. These include holding excess foreign reserves (above those required to back the currency in circulation), having banks contribute to a deposit insurance fund, and contracting a type of contingent credit line with foreign banks. Velde and Veracierto (1999) calculate that, together, these mechanisms cover 40 percent of total deposits. Second, as Calvo (2001) points out, central banks in industrialized countries do not generally perform their lender-of-last-resort function by printing currency; they borrow

instead. This was the case, for example, in the banking crises in Sweden and Finland in 1992. Third, as proposed by Calvo (2001) and others, a "special fund" or a credit line guarantee from an international lender of last resort could be set up to guard against a large crisis that would overwhelm domestic resources. One potential source of revenue for the fund is the increase in seignorage revenue that the United States would receive when a country dollarizes. Since the fund would likely increase the stability of dollarized-country financial markets, this could be a productive (and politically acceptable) use of the funds from the U.S. point of view.[15]

Finally, several studies have identified the domestic lender of last resort as a cause of both excess volatility in emerging economies' financial markets and currency crises.[16] This is largely related to the moral hazard problem that such a lender can create when the supervisory and regulatory aspects of the banking system are underdeveloped. This problem was particularly severe in East Asia and is now thought to be one of the primary causes of that crisis.[17] A related problem is that the lender of last resort might not be able to take the "right" action in times of crisis because of heavy political pressure. Ennis (2000), for example, shows how such pressure may prevent the lender of last resort from implementing the optimal policy and, instead, force the use of a suboptimal inflation tax to bail out a banking sector in distress. In this context, dollarization works as an ex ante commitment not to surrender to political pressure in the event of a liquidity crisis. Antinolfi and Keister (2000) show how dollarization can be seen as a way of committing to charge a (perhaps unpopular) "penalty rate" on discount window loans during a crisis—exactly the policy advocated by Bagehot (1873). These studies indicate that dollarization can actually be seen as fixing some of the problems created by a lender of last resort.[18] Such political-economy issues have received relatively little emphasis in the literature on dollarization, and in our opinion they deserve further research.

Existing Liability Dollarization

The set of initial conditions on which dollarization would be implemented is also crucial for understanding dollarization proposals. Our analysis would be incomplete without a discussion of the current state of an economy considering dollarizing, particularly with respect to existing liability dollarization. Liability dollarization refers to domestic borrowing denominated in or indexed to a foreign currency. Both sovereign debt and private debt in emerging-market economies are often dollarized.

Our main concern in this section is private sector dollar-denominated debt, which has been growing rapidly in emerging-market economies. This includes both direct borrowing by individual firms and borrowing by the domestic banking sector. Is widespread liability dollarization an indication that an economy should officially dollarize? The answer to this question must depend on what is causing the liability dollarization to occur. Why are firms willing to borrow in a foreign currency when this creates a balance-sheet mismatch that greatly increases their vulnerability to unexpected devaluations?

Two types of explanations have been offered in the literature. The first (see, for example, Burnside, Eichenbaum, and Rebelo, 2001) is based on (implicit or explicit) government guarantees of the liabilities, especially those of the banking system. Under a fixed exchange rate regime, the interest rate on dollar loans will be lower than the domestic interest rate, the difference reflecting the possibility of devaluation. This condition leads banks to borrow in dollars. In addition, because the government guarantee implies that it will act as a residual claimant on bank assets in bad states of the world (in which banks go bankrupt), banks face no ex ante incentives to purchase insurance against bad states of the world. Hence, they do not hedge (sufficiently) against foreign exchange risk. In other words, the guarantee creates a moral hazard problem that leads to a fragile banking system that is overexposed to currency risk. The reason the government would provide this guarantee is that it reduces the interest rate that domestic firms pay when financing working capital from domestic banks and, therefore, has positive effects on economic growth. This benefit the government obtains is sufficient to overcome the cost of increasing the probability of a banking crisis when the exchange rate is devalued. This is an indication that official dollarization may be warranted, as it would bring this benefit without the cost.

The second type of explanation claims that liability dollarization is a result of underdeveloped domestic financial markets (see Caballero and Krishnamurthy, 2000). The underdevelopment means that firms cannot pledge their entire return to foreign investors. As a result, assets that can be used as international collateral become essential. In such an environment, individual firms choose between borrowing in local currency (which is immune to changes in the exchange rate) and borrowing in dollars (which is cheaper). Caballero and Krishnamurthy (2000) interpret borrowing in domestic currency as purchasing insurance against exchange rate fluctuations. They go on to show how competitive markets misprice this insurance. This problem happens because, at the firm level, there are two types of collateral—internationally accepted and domestically accepted assets. At the economy-wide level, however, only internationally accepted assets are net collateral. Because firms "overestimate" the amount of collateral that they have available, they tend to purchase less insurance than would otherwise be optimal. If this is the reason for the observed liability dollarization, it is less clear that officially dollarizing would help matters. The problem of scarce internationally accepted collateral may still arise. In this case, the benefit of official dollarization is likely to be indirect—through the development of domestic financial markets and their integration with international markets.

The Effects from the Perspective of the United States

Our discussion so far has focused on the potential costs and benefits of dollarization from the viewpoint of the economy considering dollarizing. The view of dollarization from the perspective of the United States is also important. When Ecuador and El Salvador adopted the dollar, the impact on the United States was clearly minimal. It is doubtful that the same could be said about Argentina or, especially, Mexico. Two areas where a large dollarization could have an important impact on the United States are seignorage revenue and the conduct of monetary policy. We have discussed above how dollarization entails a transfer of seignorage revenue from the dollarizing government to the United States.

We have also discussed how the dollarizing country might like to either receive a share of this money or have it set aside in a fund for lender-of-last-resort functions. The second plan might receive more support in the United States, since otherwise the United States would possibly be directly involved in trying to alleviate banking crises. This possibility introduces interesting questions about the relationship between the United States and the dollarized economies that the literature has yet to explore. To the extent that the United States perceives there to be costs to having the dollar used widely, it may be reluctant to give up the benefit of the extra revenue.

The financial integration with the United States that could follow a dollarization is commonly considered to be a major benefit of dollarizing. Arguably, financial integration can prove to be a major benefit also for the U.S. economy. In addition, however, U.S. monetary policy will have stronger effects abroad, and the United States might have to take these effects into account. As an example, suppose there is a recession in a dollarized Mexico that calls for a looser policy while events in the United States call for a tighter policy. Although the United States would have the option of ignoring events in Mexico, doing so would likely cause a significant increase in the flow of illegal immigrants into the United States. Hence the optimal policy (from a selfish point of view) would likely be looser than it would have been had Mexico kept the peso.[19] In this way, it is not only the dollarizing economy that is losing monetary independence; the United States might lose some as well.

As a final (and highly speculative) note, we observe that, if the United States benefits from the increase in seignorage revenue, widespread dollarization would give an incentive to generate a higher steady-state level of inflation. Although it seems unlikely that this incentive would influence U.S. policy, it is interesting to report how Fischer (1982) concludes his paper:

Use of a foreign money also implies that the domestic government is relying on the foreign government to maintain better control over the inflation rate than it does itself—an admission that most governments would be reluctant to make. And besides, Who is to guard the guardians?

Further Reading

We have discussed some of the key issues that are important for a country considering official dollarization, including some of the likely costs and benefits. A crucial issue that we have not discussed, however, is how large these costs and benefits would be. There is little historical evidence that can be used as guidance on this question. There are many inherent difficulties in quantifying the effects of dollarization, and these are reflected in a wide range of predictions that are obtained from different models that focus on different aspects of the problem. An example of this disparity can be found in the results of Cooley and Quadrini (2001), Del Negro and Obiols-Homs (2001), Mendoza (2001), and Schmitt-Grohé and Uribe (2001), all of which are quantitative studies related to dollarization in Mexico. Some of these papers conclude that the overall benefits would be very large, while others conclude they would be small or even negative.

All four of these papers, along with some others we have referenced and some we have not, are gathered together in a special issue of the *Journal of Money, Credit, and Banking* (May 2001). We encourage the interested reader to consult this source directly for a more extensive discussion of the issues related to dollarization than is possible here. In addition, Spanish-speaking readers are encouraged to consult *La Dolarización como Alternativa Monetaria para México* (Del Negro et al., forthcoming). This volume consists largely of papers presented at a conference on dollarization sponsored by the Instituto Technológico Autónomo de México (ITAM) in December 2000.

Gaetano Antinolfi is an assistant professor of economics in the Department of Economics, Washington University, and a visiting scholar at the Federal Reserve Bank of St. Louis. Todd Keister is an assistant professor of economics in the Departamento de Economía and Centro de Investigación Económica, Instituto Technológico Autónomo de México (ITAM), and a visiting assistant professor in the Department of Economics, University of Texas at Austin. The authors would like to thank James Morley, Patricia Pollard, Bob Rasche, Mika Saito, and Frank Schmid for helpful comments. William Bock provided research assistance.

Endnotes

[1] Guatemala has also recently adopted the U.S. dollar as legal tender, but it has decided to maintain its own currency in circulation, without fixing a parity with the dollar.

[2] The interested reader can find a good, basic introduction to the topic of dollarization in Chang (2000).

[3] This reflects the general finding that an exchange rate devaluation is usually contractionary for emerging markets, whereas it is typically expansionary for industrialized countries. See, for example, Edwards (1989).

[4] For a detailed discussion, see Calvo (2000).

[5] Kaminsky and Reinhart (1999) empirically show that banking crises tend to precede exchange rate crises.

[6] Residual maturity is measured by the value of a country's liabilities that are held by foreigners and mature within a year.

[7] See De Grauwe (1996, Chapter 11) and Neely (1999) for an extensive assessment of capital controls. Calvo and Reinhart (1999) provide a discussion related to the context of dollarization.

[8] See also Obstfeld and Rogoff (1995) and Summers (1999; 2000, p.8). For a classification of different exchange rate regimes, see Frankel (1999).

[9] See Mussa et al. (2000), who argue that an unsustainable policy need not be undesirable in the short run, and Frankel (1999), from whom we borrowed the title of this section.

[10] Such a plan was actually proposed as part of the International Monetary Stability Act, introduced by then Senator Connie Mack of Florida. Details can be found in Mack (2000).

[11] On the optimal-tax property of inflation, see Calvo and Guidotti (1993). For the analysis of time-consistency problems, see Kidland and Precott (1977) and Calvo (1978).

[12] Also, see Ghiglino and Shell (2000) for a discussion of when deficit restrictions do not really constrain the government and hence have no real effects.

[13] For a critique of their result and a review of the literature in contrast with it, see Pakko and Wall (2001).

[14] King and Levine (1993) show that financial development predicts subsequent growth, and Rajan and Zingales (1998) provide evidence of causation. See also Levine (1997). Levine and Carkovic (2001) argue that the positive effects of dollarization would be indirect, working through financial development.

[15] Clearly, any such contribution of seignorage would be a matter for the Congress and executive branch to decide.

[16] See, for example, Chang and Velasco (2000a), Mishkin (1999), and Fischer (1999). See also Antinolfi, Huybens, and Keister (2001), which shows how a lender of last resort having the ability to print money can allow inflationary beliefs to become self-fulfilling.

[17] See Corsetti, Pesenti, and Roubini (1999) and Mishkin (1999) on this topic.

[18] But would dollarization itself find the necessary political support to be implemented? Ennis (2000) goes on to show that this is possible if the economy has a large population of international banks (i.e., banks that operate in several countries). It is interesting to note that this is, in essence, a form of financial-market integration, which we saw above (in a different context) to be a factor that is likely to increase the probability of success with dollarization.

[19] For an analysis of the potential relation between dollarization and Mexican migration to the United States see Borjas and O'N. Fisher (2001). Their results indicate that the flow of illegal immigrants is more volatile when Mexican authorities adopt a fixed exchange rate, whereas the flow of legal immigrants remains unaffected.

References

Antinolfi, Gaetano; Huybens, Elisabeth and Keister, Todd. "Monetary Stability and Liquidity Crises: The Role of the Lender of Last Resort." *Journal of Economic Theory*, 2001, 99(1-2), pp. 187-219.

Antinolfi, Gaetano and Keister, Todd. "Liquidity Crises and Discount Window Lending: Theory and Implications for the Dollarization Debate." Working Paper 00-02, Centro de Investigación Económica, September 2000.

Bagehot, Walter. *Lombard Street*. London: William Clowes and Sons, 1873.

Bencivenga, Valerie; Huybens, Elisabeth and Smith, Bruce D. "Dollarization and the Integration of International Capital Markets: A Contribution to the Theory of Optimal Currency Areas." *Journal of Money, Credit, and Banking*, May 2001, 33(2, Part 2), pp. 548-89.

Borjas, George J. and O'N. Fisher, Eric. "Dollarization and the Mexican Labor Market." *Journal of Money, Credit, and Banking*, May 2001, 33(2, Part 2), pp. 626-47.

Burnside, Craig; Eichenbaum, Martin and Rebelo, Sergio. "Hedging and Financial Fragility in Fixed Exchange Rate Regimes." *European Economic Review*, 2001, 45(7), pp. 1151-93.

Caballero, Ricardo J. and Krishnamurthy, Arvind. "Dollarization of Liabilities: Underinsurance and Domestic Financial Underdevelopment." Working Paper No. 7792, National Bureau of Economic Research, July 2000.

Calvo, Guillermo A. "On the Time Consistency of Optimal Policy in a Monetary Economy." *Econometrica*, 1978, 46(6), pp. 1411-28.

_____. "Balance of Payments Crises in Emerging Markets: Large Capital Inflows and Sovereign Governments," in Paul Krugman, ed., *Currency Crises*. Chicago: University of Chicago Press, 2000.

_____. "Capital Markets and the Exchange Rate, with Special Reference to the Dollarization Debate in Latin America." *Journal of Money, Credit, and Banking*, May 2001, 33(2, Part 2), pp. 312-34.

Calvo, Guillermo A., and Guidotti, Pablo E. "On the Flexibility of Monetary Policy: The Case of the Optimal Inflation Tax." *Review of Economic Studies*, 1993, 60, pp. 667-87.

Calvo, Guillermo A., and Reinhart, Carmen M. "When Capital Inflows Come to a Sudden Stop: Consequences and Policy Options." Unpublished manuscript, June 1999.

Calvo, Guillermo A., and Reinhart, Carmen A. "Fear of Floating." Unpublished manuscript, September 2000.

Chang, Roberto. "Dollarization: A Scorecard." Federal Reserve Bank of Atlanta *Economic Review*, Third Quarter 2000, 85(3), pp. 1-11.

Chang, Roberto and Velasco, Andres. "Financial Fragility and the Exchange Rate Regime." *Journal of Economic Theory*, 2000a, 92(1), pp. 1-34.

Chang, Roberto and Velasco, Andres. "Dollarization: Analytical Issues." Unpublished manuscript, August 2000b.

Cooley, Thomas F. and Quadrini, Vincenzo. "The Costs of Losing Monetary Independence: The Case of Mexico." *Journal of Money, Credit, and Banking*, 2001, 33(2, Part 2), pp. 370-97.

Corsetti, Giancarlo; Pesenti, Paolo and Roubini, Nouriel. "What Caused the Asian Currency and Financial Crisis?" *Japan and the World Economy*, 1999, 11, pp. 305-73.

De Grauwe, Paul. *International Money*. 2nd Ed. Oxford: Oxford University Press, 1996.

Del Negro, Marco; Huybens, Elisabeth and Hernández-Delgado, Alejandro, eds., *La Dolarización como Alternativa Monetaria para México*. Mexico City: Fondo de Cultura Económica, forthcoming.

Del Negro, Marco and Obiols-Homs, Francesc. "Has Monetary Policy Been So Bad That It Is Better to Get Rid of It?" *Journal of Money, Credit, and Banking*, May 2001, 33(2, Part 2), pp. 404-33.

Edwards, Sebastian. *Real Exchange Rates, Devaluation, and Adjustment*. Cambridge, MA: MIT Press, 1989.

_____. "International Capital Flows and the Emerging Markets: Amending the Rules of the Game?" Federal Reserve Bank of Boston *Conference Series 43*, June 1999, pp. 137-57.

Eichengreen, Barry. "What Problems Can Dollarization Solve?" *Journal of Policy Modeling,* forthcoming.

Ennis, Huberto M. "Banking and the Political Support for Dollarization." Working Paper 00-12, Federal Reserve Bank of Richmond, December 2000.

Fischer, Stanley. "Exchange Rate Regimes: Is the Bipolar View Correct?" Distinguished Lecture on Economics in Government, American Economic Association Meetings, January 2001. <http://www.imf.org/external/np/speeches/2001/010601a.htm>.

_____. "On the Need for an International Lender of Last Resort." *Journal of Economic Perspective,* Fall 1999, 13, pp. 85-104.

_____. "Seignorage and the Case for a National Money." *Journal of Political Economy,* 1982, 90(2), pp. 295-313.

Frankel, Jeffrey A. "No Single Currency Regime Is Right for All Countries at All Times." Working Paper No. 7338, National Bureau for Economic Research, September 1999.

Frankel, Jeffrey A. and Rose, Andrew K. "Estimating the Effects of Currency Unions on Trade and Output." Working Paper No. 7857, National Bureau for Economic Research, August 2000.

Ghiglino, Christian and Shell, Karl. "The Economic Effects of Restrictions on Government Budget Deficits." *Journal of Economic Theory,* 2000, 94(1), pp. 106-37.

Kaminsky, Graciela L. and Reinhart, Carmen M. "The Twin Crises: The Causes of Banking and Balance of Payments Problems." *American Economic Review,* 1999, 89, pp. 473-500.

King, Robert G. and Levine, Ross. "Finance, Entrepreneurship, and Growth." *Journal of Monetary Economics,* 1993, 33(3), pp. 513-42.

Kydland, Finn E. and Prescott, Edward C. "Rules Rather Than Discretion: The Inconsistency of Optimal Plans." *Journal of Political Economy,* 1977, 85(3), pp. 473-92.

Levine, Ross. "Financial Development and Economic Growth: Views and Agenda." *Journal of Economic Literature,* 1997, 35(2), pp. 688-726.

Levine, Ross and Carkovic, Maria. "How Much Bang for the Buck? Mexico and Dollarization." *Journal of Money, Credit, and Banking,* May 2001, 33(2, Part 2), pp. 339-63.

Mack, Connie. "Dollarization and Cooperation to Achieve Sound Money." Speech given at the Federal Reserve Bank of Dallas, 6 March 2000. <http://www.dallasfed.org/htm/dallas/events/mack.html>.

Mendoza, Enrique G. "The Benefits of Dollarization When Stabilization Policy Lacks Credibility and Financial Markets Are Imperfect." *Journal of Money, Credit, and Banking,* 2001, 33(2, Part 2), pp. 440-74.

Mishkin, Frederic S. "Lessons from the Asian Crisis." *Journal of International Money and Finance,* 1999, 18, pp. 709-23.

Mundell, Robert. "A Theory of Optimum Currency Areas." *American Economic Review,* 1961, 51, pp. 657-65.

Mussa, Michael; Masson, Paul; Swoboda, Alesander; Jadresic, Esteban; Mauro, Paolo; Berg, Paolo and Berg, Andy. "Exchange Rate Regimes in an Increasingly Integrated World Economy." Occasional Paper No. 193, International Monetary Fund, August 2000.

Neely, Christopher J. "An Introduction to Capital Controls." Federal Reserve Bank of St. Louis *Review,* November/December 1999, 81(6), pp. 13-30.

Obstfeld, Maurice and Rogoff, Kenneth. "The Mirage of Fixed Exchange Rates." *Journal of Economic Perspectives,* Fall 1995, 9(4), pp. 73-96.

Pakko, Michael R. and Wall, Howard J. "Reconsidering the Trade-Creating Effects of a Currency Union." Federal Reserve Bank of St. Louis *Review,* September/October 2001, 83(5), pp. 37-46.

Rajan, Raghuram G. and Zingales, Luigi. "Financial Dependence and Growth." *American Economic Review,* 1998, 88, pp. 559-86.

Schmitt-Grohé, Stephanie and Uribe, Martín. "Stabilization Policy and the Cost of Dollarization." *Journal of Money, Credit, and Banking,* 2001, 33(2, Part 2), pp. 482-509.

Sims, Christopher A. "Fiscal Consequences for Mexico Adopting the Dollar." *Journal of Money, Credit, and Banking,* 2001, 33(2, Part 2), pp. 597-616.

Stockman, Alan C. "Optimal Central Bank Areas, Financial Intermediation, and Mexican Dollarization." *Journal of Money, Credit, and Banking,* May 2001, 33(2, Part 2), pp. 648-66.

Summers, Lawrence H. "International Financial Crises: Causes, Prevention, and Cures." *American Economic Review,* 2000, 90(2), pp. 1-16.

_____. Testimony before the Senate Foreign Relations Subcommittee in International Economic Policy and Export/Trade Promotion, 27 January 1999.

Velde, François R. and Veracierto, Marcelo. "Dollarization in Argentina." *Chicago Fed Letter No. 142,* June 1999

Discussion Questions

VI

1. Why is the US dollar the most widely traded currency?

2. In figure 2 of the "Structure of the Foreign Exchange Market" the majority of trading activity takes place between 7 AM and 4 PM Greenwich Mean Time. Why?

3. Summarize the three leading models of exchange rate determination.

4. Why does Hopper believe market "sentiment" determines the exchange rate?

5. Explain why antipathy towards fixed exchange rates grew during the 1950's and 1960's in "Exchange Rate Choices."

6. According to Richard Cooper, which exchange rate regimes are best for developing and developed countries? Explain.

7. Summarize the case for and against fixed exchange rates.

8. Does the exchange rate regime matter for inflation and growth?

9. Why is credibility so important for a fixed exchange rate regime?

10. Why are currency boards considered more credible than a simple pegged exchange rate?

11. Do you think Hong Kong should abandon its currency board.
    Why or why not?

12. What are the arguments for and against dollarization?
    What types of countries are good candidates for dollarization?

The Euro

On January 1999, the European Union (EU) took the unprecedented step of adopting a new currency, the euro, without political union. Notes and coins were not circulated until January 2002. On January 4th 1999, the euro was trading at a value of $1.18; however, during the euro's first year, it steadily depreciated against the US dollar. Four years on, the euro has appreciated against the dollar to $1.13, renewing the debate that the euro could rival the US dollar as the international currency. The European Central Bank (ECB) controls the supply of euros and sets the interest rate for all counties participating in the euro. Critics of the European Monetary Union (EMU) argue that the EU is not an optimal currency area: labor mobility within Europe is low; financial structure across European nations varies significantly; and business cycles across European nations are often not synchronized. Given these differences, a one size fits all monetary policy may not be optimal. Other critics suggest that the target inflation rate of less than 2% is set too low for Germany, the largest country in the EMU, dampening its economic growth. Proponents of the EMU argue that as countries become more integrated, the differences across euro-area countries will diminish. Further, the reduction in transactions costs, increases in price transparency, and increases in competition associated with the euro will boost economic growth. This section examines the current issues in the EMU.

In "European Labor Markets and EMU Challenges Ahead" Soltwedel, Dohse and Krieger-Boden examine whether EMU will affect labor markets across the EU. They argue that since euro-area countries no longer have the exchange rate to absorb shocks that affect one country or region (asymmetric shocks), output must adjust. Economies that are best prepared to deal with an output adjustment are economies with flexible labor markets. The authors point out that labor markets in Belgium, Denmark, France, Germany, Italy, Finland, and Spain are inflexible and these countries are likely to experience rising unemployment when an adverse asymmetric shock strikes. Whether EMU will encourage labor market flexibility remains to be seen. The authors indicate that many EU countries have been slow to adopt labor market reforms.

"EMU at 1" by Mark Wynne discusses the primary developments of the euro during its first year. His study outlines some of the operational challenges facing the ECB, the emergence of the euro as an international currency, and whether the EU countries (UK, Denmark, and Sweden) that decided not to adopt the euro will eventually do so. One of the operational challenges facing the ECB is that it does not have enough historical data on euro-area prices (HICP) to base its monetary policy decisions, and inflation rates across the euro-area have begun to diverge, making monetary policy decisions difficult. For example, Ireland, Spain, and Portugal are experiencing rapid economic growth and higher inflation while the German economy is sluggish with low inflation. Wynne also highlights some of the criticisms leveled against the ECB.

EMU at 1

M A R K A . **W Y N N E**

On January 1, 1999, the European Union (EU) launched what will surely be one of the most ambitious political and economic undertakings of the twenty-first century: economic and monetary union (EMU), incorporating eleven of the fifteen current members of the EU. A new currency, the euro, replaced the national currencies of the eleven countries,[1] and a new institution, the European Central Bank (ECB), took over responsibility for monetary policy for the euro area. Many commentators in the United States thought EMU would never take place or, if it did, that it would not last very long. The successful launch of EMU was thus a surprise in some quarters, and some of the skeptics have been forced to reevaluate their positions. EMU is now one year old, and it seems appropriate to review what has happened during the first year and assess the prospects for the future.

Over the course of 1999, the euro depreciated steadily against the dollar. The ECB made its first rate moves, lowering interest rates in April in response to deflation risk in the euro area and raising them in November as the recovery took hold and the inflation outlook deteriorated. The ECB successfully defended its independence against challenges from the finance minister of one of the larger member states and has worked to establish credibility for its commitment to price stability. The TARGET payments system, key to the integration of euro area money markets, came online and has operated with-

out any major problems. The euro has emerged as an important international currency, second only to the dollar. The volume of international bonds denominated in euros exceeded dollar-denominated issuance during 1999. The four EU countries that currently do not participate in EMU all moved closer to eventual membership. However, there were few moves toward the fiscal, labor, and product market reforms that may ultimately determine the fate of EMU.

Main Developments During 1999

The euro officially became the currency of the eleven participating nations on January 1, 1999. The rates to be used for converting national currency units into euros were announced on December 31, 1998. During the changeover weekend, January 1 through January 3, the financial community had to reconfigure computer and accounting systems to handle the new currency. Furthermore, all government debt of the euro-area countries was redenominated in euros, as were the share prices of all companies listed in the euro area, along with millions of bank accounts.

The most striking and often analyzed development during 1999 was the steady depreciation of the euro against the dollar. The euro also declined against the yen and the pound sterling. When the euro made its debut on world financial markets on January 4, 1999, it was trading at $1.18. It immediately began to depreciate against the dollar, coming close to parity (and briefly below in intraday trading) by December 1999 (Figure 1).[2] The depreciation took many commentators by surprise and was contrary to the confident predictions of many that the euro would rapidly appreciate against the dollar, given the relative current account positions of the United States and the euro area.

However, if we take a longer-term perspective, the decline of the euro against the dollar over the past year is less remarkable. Figure 2 shows the exchange rate of the euro's predecessor, the European Currency Unit (ECU), against the dollar from 1996 through 1998, along with the exchange rate of the euro against the dollar during 1999.[3] Under the terms of the transition to EMU, one ECU was required to equal one euro at midnight December 31, 1998. As Figure 2 shows, in late 1998, the ECU, or rather the legacy currencies of the euro, experienced a strong appreciation against the dollar in the wake of Russia's default and the failure of the hedge fund Long Term Capital Management in the United States. Some of this appreciation may also have been driven by the "europhoria" in the period between the Brussels summit in May 1998—at which the EU heads of government decided which countries would participate in EMU—and the actual launch of EMU.

Perhaps more important for the evolution of the dollar–euro exchange rate was the fact that over the course of 1999 the U.S. economy continued to grow at a robust pace, while the euro area experienced a growth recession. Through the third quarter, GDP increased only 2.3 percent in the euro area, and in autumn 1999 the European Commission forecast an increase of only 2.1 percent for the year as a whole. Unemployment in the euro area remained stubbornly high, declining from 10.6 percent of the labor force in December 1998 to 9.6 percent at the end of 1999. Evidence strengthened that trend productivity growth was accelerating in the United States, but there were few signs that much-needed structural reforms were being undertaken in Europe.

It is too early to take the decline as symptomatic of fundamental problems with the new currency. Over the long run, the nominal exchange rate of the euro against the dollar will reflect the relative success of the ECB in maintaining the euro's purchasing power, but over the short run, cyclical and other factors will be more important.

The ECB made its first rate moves in 1999, lowering its repo rate from 3 percent to 2.5 percent in April and then raising it back to 3 percent in November.[4] It is significant that in neither case was there much political opposition from the countries most likely to have opposed these moves. The rate cut in April was probably the last thing the rapidly growing economies on the fringe of the euro area (Ireland, Finland, Spain and Portugal) needed. Indeed, Ireland, which has come to be known as the "Celtic Tiger," seems to be exhibiting the symptoms of a classic asset price bubble, with house prices rising by as much as 20 percent to 30 percent a year. Likewise, when it came time to raise rates in November, the sluggish German economy probably could have benefited from a longer period of lower interest rates. However, the ECB's mandate is to maintain price stability in the euro area as a whole. Thus, it has explained its decisions to raise or lower interest rates on the basis of developments at the euro-area level rather than in terms of what has happened in individual member states.[5]

The Challenge of Conducting Monetary Policy for the Euro Area

One of the most important tasks prior to EMU was to ensure that the ECB would have at its disposal adequate statistical information to make monetary policy decisions for the euro area. This required some degree of harmonization of statistical practices across the EU, in particular for inflation and monetary statistics. Primary responsibility for the production of official statistics in the EU rests with Eurostat, which is one of the Directorates General of the European Commission. Eurostat produces statistics for the euro area and the member states in con-

Figure 1
Dollar–Euro Exchange Rate

Dollars per euro

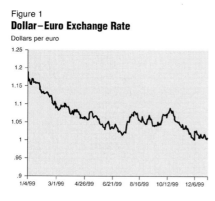

Source: Policy Analysis Computing & Information Facility in Commerce (PACIFIC) Exchange Rate Service <http://pacific.commerce.ubc.ca/xr/>. Copyrigh 1998 by Prof. Werner Antweiler, University of British Columbia, Vancouver, Canada. Reprinted by permission.

Figure 2
Dollar–ECU, Dollar–Euro Exchange Rates, 1996–99

Dollars per ECU, dollars per euro

Source: Policy Analysis Computing & Information Facility in Commerce (PACIFIC) Exchange Rate Service <http://pacific.commerce.ubc.ca/xr/>. Copyrigh 1998 by Prof. Werner Antweiler, University of British Columbia, Vancouver, Canada. Reprinted by permission.

junction with national statistical institutes and plays a key role in ensuring that statistics are harmonized. GDP estimates for the euro area are constructed on a consistent basis using the ESA95 version of the European System of Accounts (ESA). Unemployment rates for the euro area are calculated using a definition put forward by the International Labour Office in 1982.[6]

The ECB defined price stability in terms of the rate of increase in the Harmonised Index of Consumer Prices (HICP) for the euro area. The HICP program originated in the need for a common measure of inflation to assess EMU membership candidates' compliance with the convergence criteria stipulated in the treaty. The various national consumer price indexes (CPIs) differ significantly in their concept and coverage. According to the European Commission (1998), as much as 13 percent of expenditures covered by the HICP are excluded from some national CPIs, while as much as 17 percent of expenditures covered by some national CPIs are excluded from the HICP. The HICP differs from the U.S. CPI, for example, beginning with the pricing concept. While the U.S. Bureau of Labor Statistics uses the theory of the cost of living index as the framework for constructing the U.S. CPI (U.S. Bureau of Labor Statistics 1997), the HICP uses "household final monetary con-

sumption," which means that only the prices paid in monetary transactions are included. The HICP does not, therefore, include the imputed costs of agricultural products grown for personal consumption or the services of owner-occupied dwellings. The latter is included in the U.S. CPI and accounts for approximately one-fifth of the basket.[7]

A more serious problem from the ECB's perspective is that the HICP program only began in 1997. Aggregate HICP data are available for a slightly longer period, but the fact remains that the ECB must work with price statistics for which there are a limited number of observations. Even if a long time series on prices were available, it is not clear how useful it would be to the ECB. Since Lucas (1976), economists have been sensitive to the instability of estimated empirical relationships in the face of policy regime changes. While there is some debate in macroeconomics as to what exactly constitutes a regime change, few would deny that EMU is a major change in the monetary policy regime for all the participating countries.

Price Stability

Article 105 (1) of the Maastricht Treaty states that the primary objective of the ECB shall be to maintain price stability but leaves it

Figure 3
Euro-Area HICP Inflation

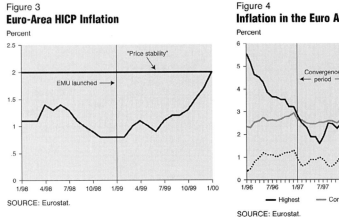

SOURCE: Eurostat.

Figure 4
Inflation in the Euro Area

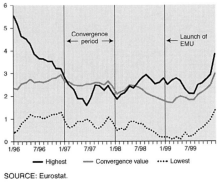

SOURCE: Eurostat.

to the ECB to define what exactly, in terms of measured inflation, constitutes price stability. Prior to EMU, the ECB announced that it would define price stability as a "year-on-year increase in the Harmonised Index of Consumer Prices (HICP) for the euro area of below 2%." Furthermore, price stability is to be maintained "over the medium term."[8] At the launch of EMU, HICP inflation in the euro area was running at an annual rate of about 1 percent, having slowed from rates in excess of 2 percent in early 1996. An energy price deceleration in 1997 and decline in 1998 contributed significantly to the favorable inflation situation at the launch of EMU. However, as Figure 3 shows, during 1999 the inflation rate accelerated as energy prices started to increase and the euro declined against the dollar and other major currencies.

Furthermore, there has been some divergence of inflation rates across the euro area over the past year. Figure 4 shows highest and lowest inflation rates across the eleven euro area countries, along with the limit set down in the Maastricht Treaty.[9] Since mid-1998, inflation in Portugal, Spain, and Ireland has exceeded the limit set down in the treaty, although as of December 1999 only Ireland's inflation rate was more than 1.5 percentage points above the average of the three lowest. The ECB does not yet include a measure of core inflation for the euro area in the statisti-

cal appendix to its Monthly Bulletin, although Eurostat, the EU's statistical agency, does include a core measure ("All items excluding energy, food, alcohol, and tobacco") on its web site.[10]

The Reference Value for M3

The twin pillars of the ECB's monetary policy strategy are a reference value for the growth rate of the broad money aggregate M3 and a broadly based assessment of the outlook for future price developments and the risks to price stability in the euro area. The choice of M3 rather than a narrower aggregate was based on research indicating the M3 aggregate has desirable characteristics in terms of stability and information about future inflation.[11]

The reference value for M3 is derived from three assumptions:

1. Price stability is defined as a rate of increase in the HICP of 2 percent or less.
2. The trend rate of growth of real GDP in the euro area is 2 percent to 2.5 percent.
3. The trend rate of decline in M3 velocity is about 0.5 percent to 1 percent a year.

These three assumptions, together with a standard quantity theory view of the determination of the price level, led the Governing Council to choose a reference value of 4.5 percent for M3 growth during 1999.[12] The

Figure 5
Euro-Area M3 Growth

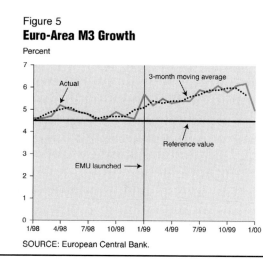

SOURCE: European Central Bank.

monthly statistics on M3 growth are assessed in relation to this reference value using a centered three-month moving average of monthly growth rates. It should be noted that the ECB's derivation of the reference value for the euro area's M3 aggregate is similar to the Bundesbank's procedure to derive its annual M3 target (see Deutsche Bundesbank 1995).

As Figure 5 shows, M3 growth drifted steadily away from its reference over the course of the year. As of December 1999, M3 growth was almost 2 percentage points above the reference value. The ECB discounted some of the deviation as due to temporary factors associated with the euro's introduction. The ECB's failure to raise interest rates aggressively in response to the deviation suggests that it may take a pragmatic view of the reference value for M3, much as the Bundesbank did of its M3 target. From the time the Bundesbank set its first monetary target (in 1974) until the start of EMU, it succeeded in hitting its target only about half the time.

Communication: Transparency and Accountability

One criticism levied against the ECB during its first year is that it is not sufficiently transparent in making monetary policy decisions and is not held adequately accountable for those decisions (see, for example, Buiter

1999 and Begg et al. 1998). The critics argue that the ECB should publish the minutes of Governing Council meetings, the votes of individual council members, and the reasoning and forecasts that underlie council decisions. The ECB has resisted publication of minutes and votes, arguing that making such information public would increase pressure on council members to vote along national lines rather than in the interests of the euro area as a whole (see Issing 1999).

Transparency in monetary policymaking has many dimensions, and much of the criticism of the ECB seems unwarranted. Table 1 compares practices of the ECB, the Federal Reserve System, and the Bank of England as they relate to transparency and accountability. The policy-making committee of the ECB—the Governing Council—meets much more frequently than the Federal Reserve System's Federal Open Market Committee (FOMC) or the Bank of England's Monetary Policy Committee (MPC). Through 1999 the ECB's Governing Council met every two weeks (except during August) at the ECB's headquarters in Frankfurt, although the Maastricht Treaty requires only that it meet at least ten times a year (Protocol No. 3 on the Statute of the European System of Central Banks and the European Central Bank, Article 10.5). A press conference was held after the first of the two meetings in each month, and the tradition

Monetary Aggregates for the Euro Area

Before EMU, each of the EU member states constructed monetary aggregates using national definitions that differed across countries. It was not possible to arrive at a consistent aggregate for the euro area by simply adding together these differing national aggregates. Thus, a key challenge prior to EMU's launch was to harmonize definitions to allow consistent measures to be constructed for the single currency area. As part of this harmonization process, the European Monetary Institute and the national central banks developed the concept of a Monetary Financial Institution (MFI), consisting of three types. The first is central banks. The second is resident credit institutions as defined by EU law, and the third is "all other resident financial institutions whose business is to receive deposits and/or close substitutes for deposits from entities other than MFIs and, for their own account…to grant credits and/or to make investments in securities." This third category consists primarily of money market funds.

The main broad monetary aggregates for the euro area are defined below. The M1 aggregate consists of currency in circulation and overnight deposits and differs little from the old national definitions of M1. The category overnight deposits includes balances on prepaid cards in those countries where prepaid card schemes exist. M2 adds to M1 deposits with agreed maturity up to two years and deposits redeemable at notice up to three months. The M3 aggregate adds to M2 repurchase agreements, liabilities of money market funds and debt securities up to two years. Note that prior to EMU, repurchase agreements were excluded from the national definitions of monetary aggregates in France and Italy, while money market fund shares/units were included only in the national monetary aggregates of France. For further information on the new euro-area aggregates and how they relate to old national definitions, see European Central Bank (1999b).

Definitions of Euro-Area Monetary Aggregates

	M1	M2	M3
Currency in circulation	✔	✔	✔
Overnight deposits	✔	✔	✔
Deposits with agreed maturity up to two years		✔	✔
Deposits redeemable at notice up to three months		✔	✔
Repurchase agreements			✔
Money market fund shares/units and money market paper			✔
Debt securities up to two years			✔

SOURCE: European Central Bank.

seems to be evolving that rate moves are only made at the meetings that are followed by a press conference. At the press conference the president of the ECB summarizes recent economic developments, then he and the vice president hold a question-and-answer session with journalists. The opening statement and the Q&A are posted on the ECB's web site (http://www.ecb.int) within hours. The ECB views the press conference, along with the editorial that appears in each issue of its Monthly Bulletin, as a substitute for the publication of minutes. (Neither the FOMC nor the MPC holds a press conference after its meetings.) Transparency is a slippery concept, and there is no meaningful way to evaluate whether a press conference following a policy decision constitutes more or less transparency than the publication of votes and minutes.[13]

The second issue concerns the publication of forecasts. The Bank of England has been an innovator in this regard, publishing on a regular basis its inflation forecast and not just a point forecast. The FOMC does not publish forecasts (although the chairman does report the range of forecasts of committee members in his twice-yearly Humphrey–Hawkins testimony).

Article 109b.3 of the Maastricht Treaty requires that

The ECB shall address an annual report on the activities of the ESCB [European System of Central Banks] and on the monetary policy of both the previous and current year to the European Parliament, the Council and the Commission, and also to the European Council. The President of the ECB shall pre-

Table 1

Transparency in Monetary Policymaking at the Federal Reserve, the ECB, and the Bank of England

	ECB	Federal Reserve System	Bank of England
Policymaking committee	Governing Council	Federal Open Market Committee	Monetary Policy Committee
Frequency of meeting	Every two weeks	Every six or seven weeks	Every month
Announced strategy	Yes	No	Yes
Quantitative definition of price stability	Yes	No	Yes
Publication of forecasts	Not yet	No	Yes
Publication of minutes	No	Yes	Yes
Publication of votes	No	Yes	Yes
Press conference	Yes	No	No
Accountable to elected body	Yes	Yes	Yes

SOURCES: European Central Bank, Federal Reserve System, Bank of England.

sent this report to the Council and to the European Parliament, which may hold a general debate on that basis.

The ECB submitted its first annual report in April 1999, and the European Parliament's Committee on Economic and Monetary Affairs reviewed it. In its response, the committee called for greater transparency from the ECB (see European Parliament 1999). Specifically, the committee noted that it

7. Regrets that the ECB has fallen short of the transparency practiced by other leading central banks; notes that the U.S. Federal Reserve Board [sic], Bank of Japan, Bank of England and Swedish Riksbank now report both sides of arguments about monetary actions; and calls for summary minutes taken at meetings of the ECB Governing Council to be published shortly after the following meeting reporting explicitly the arguments for and against the decisions taken, as well as the reasoning used in reaching these decisions;

8. Calls on the ECB to publish macro-economic forecasts on a six-monthly basis which

set out the prospects and the risks attached to those prospects for: domestic demand and its principal components, net exports, nominal and real gross domestic product, consumer price inflation, unemployment and the current account balance, together with such relevant data and research on which such forecasts are based, in order to permit a reliable assessment of monetary decisions, avoid market misinformation, ensure market transparency and hence counter speculation;

9. Calls on the ECB to publish a regular overall report of economic developments in each of the participating euro-area countries together with a summary of the national data which will facilitate comparisons of best practice; enable early warnings of potential problems within the euro-area which might require policy action by respective governments; and inform national wage bargainers of sustainable earnings developments given their own productivity, price and competitiveness trends...

At the subsequent hearings the ECB president acceded to the request to publish forecasts and promised they would be published during 2000, along with the economic models used to produce these forecasts. However, he rejected the request that the ECB publish summary minutes, arguing as before that the information the ECB provided at its press conferences and in its Monthly Bulletin came "very close in substance to the publication of summary minutes." He also rejected calls for reports on each euro-area country, arguing that the production of such reports would impede the development of a euro-area perspective. The Committee on Economic and Monetary Affairs called for publication of votes on monetary policy actions after a two-year delay, but this proposal was rejected when put to a vote of the full European Parliament.

Concerns about the ECB's accountability to the European electorate have two dimensions. The first is whether the provisions of the Maastricht Treaty that require the ECB to report to the European Parliament satisfy the need of accountability in a democratic society. The second is whether the European Parliament has the stature to represent the European electorate's concerns. Regarding the latter, two significant developments took place during 1999. In March, the Parliament for the first time forced the resignation of the European Commission over allegations of financial misconduct, thereby enhancing the Parliament's standing among EU institutions and its authority as the representative body of the EU electorate. And on May 1, the Amsterdam Treaty entered into force, substantially extending the right of co-decision of the European Parliament, making it the council's legislative equal in many areas.[14]

Emergence of the Euro as an International Currency

Prior to the euro's launch, there was much discussion about the extent to which it would compete with or even displace the dollar as the world's most important international currency. Some argued it would take a long time for the euro to replace the dollar in international transactions because of network effects. (I find it more useful to conduct transactions in dollars when more of my trading and investment partners also conduct transactions in dollars). Others argued that EMU itself was a shock of sufficient magnitude to trigger rapid adoption of the euro (see, in particular, Portes and Rey 1998).

The ECB has stated repeatedly that "internationalisation of the euro…is not a policy objective…[and] will be neither fostered nor hindered by the Eurosystem." Table 2 lists the main functions of international currencies, using the traditional classification of the functions of money (see Cohen 1971 and Hartmann 1998). The U.S. dollar is used to quote prices for industrial commodities, and many countries maintain some type of currency peg to the dollar. There are significant holdings of U.S. dollars in countries that have experienced high inflation, while foreign central banks typically use dollars to intervene in foreign exchange markets to support their local currency. Until last year the dollar was the currency of choice for international bond issuance, and most central banks continue to hold the bulk of their foreign exchange reserves in dollar-denominated assets.

Since the introduction of the euro, most commodity prices continue to be quoted in dollars, but large European firms now use the euro for quotation purposes. For instance, Airbus no longer uses the dollar to quote aircraft prices. As of the end of 1999, three countries (Estonia, Bulgaria, and Bosnia–Herzegovina) were pegging their currencies to the euro through currency board arrangements. A larger group of countries (Cyprus, Macedonia, Cape Verde, Comoros, and the fourteen countries of the West African Colonies Françaises d'Afrique [CFA] zone) had more traditional fixed exchange rate pegs to the euro. Denmark and Greece are also pegged to the euro, albeit under a cooperative arrangement under the terms of ERM II, the successor to the Exchange Rate Mechanism (ERM) of the European Monetary System.[15] A third group (Croatia, the Czech Republic, the Slovak Republic, and Slovenia) has man-

Table 2
Functions of International Currencies

	Private use	**Official use**
Unit of account	Pricing/quotation currency	Pegging currency
Medium of exchange	Payment/vehicle currency In exchanges of goods and services In currency exchange	Intervention currency
Store of value	Investment/financing currency	Reserve currency

SOURCES: Cohen (1971), Hartmann (1998).

aged floats vis-à-vis the euro. A fourth group (Hungary, Iceland, Malta, Poland, Turkey, Bangladesh, Botswana, Burundi, Chile, Israel, and the Seychelles) has either fixed or crawling pegs to baskets of currencies that include the euro. Finally, a fifth group of countries pegs to the Special Drawing Right (SDR) issued by the International Monetary Fund in which the euro has a weight of about one quarter. (The other currencies in the SDR basket are the U.S. dollar, the Japanese yen, and the pound sterling).

Perhaps the most significant benefit to the EU from internationalization of the euro would be the seigniorage revenue it would earn from foreign demand for euros. Although euro notes and coins will not be introduced until 2002, it is worth considering the revenue this may generate. At the end of 1999, approximately $600 billion of U.S. currency was in circulation. According to Porter and Judson (1996), more than half the stock of U.S. currency—and possibly as much as 70 percent—was held outside the United States at the end of 1995. If we choose a conservative estimate of 50 percent and assume that absent these foreign holdings the federal government would have to issue an equivalent amount of short-term debt at the then-prevailing interest rate of 5.3 percent, the flow of seigniorage to the U.S. Treasury from the foreign holdings was about $15.6 billion (= $600 billion x 50 percent x 5.3 percent). As of November 1999, there was approximately € 330 billion of currency outstanding in the euro area. Since euro notes and coins have not yet been introduced,

this total consists of the notes and coins of the ten legacy currencies (Luxembourg was in a monetary union with Belgium prior to EMU). It is unlikely that many of the legacy currencies circulated to a significant extent beyond their national borders, with the exception of the Deutsche mark. Seitz (1995) estimates that approximately 40 percent of the stock of Deutsche marks circulates outside Germany. In November 1999, Deutsche mark notes and coins in circulation amounted to € 126 billion, or about 38 percent of the euro-area total. Thus, the estimated seigniorage revenue currently accruing to the euro area (specifically, to Germany) from non-euro-area holdings of Deutsche marks amounts to about € 2 billion a year (= € 126 billion x 40 percent x 4 percent, using the interest rate on two-year euro-area government bonds as of November 1999 as an estimate of what the government would have to pay to raise the funds by borrowing).[16] This probably constitutes a lower bound on the amount of seigniorage the EU will earn from non-EU holdings of the euro once the notes and coins are introduced. The euro's domestic habitat is significantly larger in economic terms than that of the Deutsche mark, making the euro more attractive to non-EU residents than the Deutsche mark was. The estimated foreign seigniorage revenue currently earned by the United States is probably an upper bound on what the EU can expect to earn.

Euro notes will include € 100, € 200, and € 500 denominations.[17] Currently, the highest denomination note issued by the

Federal Reserve is the $100 bill. Higher denomination notes may make the euro an attractive alternative to the dollar as a store of value in countries undergoing high inflation. It may also make the euro more attractive for transactions in the underground economy. The existence of high-denomination euro notes in and of itself will not cause individuals who currently hold dollars as a secure store of value in high-inflation countries or for illicit purposes to immediately switch to euros. These individuals will also have to be convinced that the euro will retain its value as well as, or better than, the dollar. This, in turn, will depend on the ECB's track record in maintaining price stability in the euro area.

Target

The architects of EMU faced a key challenge in the creation of a payments system that integrated money markets in all EU countries. The TARGET system (TARGET stands for Trans-european Automated Real-time Gross settlement Express Transfer) consists of fifteen national real-time gross settlement systems and the ECB payment mechanism. It provides a uniform platform for processing cross-border payments. Prior to EMU, payments between EU countries relied almost exclusively on correspondent banking arrangements. Since the beginning of 1999, these relationships have declined dramatically, although most banks seem to be maintaining one or two correspondent accounts for each euro-area country until the euro notes and coins are introduced in 2002.

The TARGET system was created, first, to provide a pan-European payments system that would integrate national money markets and support the monetary policy of the ECB, and second, to safeguard financial markets and institutions from systemic events. The former was accomplished by linking the existing national payments systems. The latter was accomplished by moving to a real-time gross-settlement standard for national payments systems prior to EMU and away from end-of-day settlement, or netting systems, in which participants accu-

mulate large open positions against their counter-parties.

On January 4, 1999, its first day of operation, the TARGET system processed about 156,000 payments, with a total value of about € 1.18 trillion. Of these, about 5,000 were cross-border payments, totaling about € 245 billion. The volume of cross-border payments rapidly increased to 20,000 to 30,000 a day, with a total value between € 300 billion and € 400 billion, after only a week of operation. The successful launch of TARGET—and the consolidation of national money markets—was reflected in the rapid reduction in interest rate spreads in overnight money markets in January 1999.

Of the other systems available for processing payments in euros, the three largest are Euro 1, Euro Access Frankfurt (EAF), and the Système Net Protégé (SNP) (known since April 1999 as Paris Net Settlement, PNS). There are also two smaller local systems: Servicio Español de Pagos Interbancarios (SEPI) in Spain and Pankkien väliset On-line Pikasiirot ja Sekit (POPS) in Finland. Together these systems settle a daily average volume of € 400 billion, and the Euro 1 system (a cooperative undertaking between EU-based commercial banks and the EU branches of foreign banks) is by far the most extensively used alternative to TARGET. The existence of competitively priced alternative payments systems caused some concern (see, for example, Prati and Schinasi 1999) that TARGET might not attract the volume of high-value payments needed to significantly contribute to a lowering of payments-system systemic risk. That concern appears to have been unfounded: through September 1999, the average value of TARGET payments was € 5.8 million. The average value of cross-border payments was € 12.9 million, while the average value of domestic payments was € 4.4 million. The average values of the payments settled by the three biggest other systems (Euro 1, EAF, and PNS) were € 2.8 million, € 3.3 million, and € 4.5 million, respectively.

What About the Outs?

Not all fifteen members of the EU chose to participate in EMU from the outset. Greece failed to meet the convergence criteria laid down in the Maastricht Treaty, while the UK, Sweden, and Denmark chose to stay out for domestic political reasons. Greece formally applied for membership in March and hopes to become a member at the beginning of next year. As part of the convergence process, the Greek drachma was revalued on January 17, 2000. The situation in the UK, Sweden, and Denmark as to eventual membership in EMU is less clear.

When the Maastricht Treaty was first put to a referendum in Denmark, it was decisively rejected by the electorate. The treaty was ratified in a subsequent referendum, but only after it had been amended to provide an opt-out from the single currency for Denmark (Protocol No. 12 of the Maastricht Treaty). However, since the start of EMU the Danish krone has been pegged to the euro with a ±2.25 percent fluctuation band under the terms of ERM II, meaning that, in effect, Danish monetary policy is dictated by the ECB. The Danish prime minister has already launched a political campaign to bring Denmark into EMU, and in September the ruling Social Democrats will hold a referendum on Denmark's entry into EMU.

Although Sweden satisfied all the convergence criteria for participation in EMU, it did not join at the outset because of domestic "Euroscepticism." Some of this skepticism waned in the closing months of 1998, when Denmark and Sweden were more adversely impacted by fallout from the Russian default than was Finland, which had elected to join EMU. Over the past year, attitudes in Sweden have wavered between joining and not joining. However, in January the ruling Social Democratic Party announced for the first time that it formally supports Swedish membership in EMU.

Which leaves only the UK. The government secured an opt-out from EMU when the Maastricht Treaty was negotiated (Protocol No. 11 of the Maastricht Treaty). With the change of government in the UK in 1997, official attitudes toward the EU changed significantly, and the new Labor government declared its intention to take the UK into EMU when the time is right. In late 1997 the UK Treasury announced five economic tests that would be used to determine when the UK should join (see HM Treasury 1997):

1. Are business cycles and economic structures compatible so that the UK and other members of EMU could live comfortably with a common interest rate on a permanent basis?
2. If problems emerge, is there sufficient flexibility to deal with them?
3. Would EMU membership enhance the attractiveness of the UK to overseas investors?
4. How would EMU membership affect the competitive position of the UK's financial services industry?
5. Will EMU membership promote higher growth, stability, and a lasting increase in jobs?

These tests are sufficiently vague that the government could easily announce that the tests are satisfied at any time. The UK took a further step forward in February 1999 with the publication of a National Changeover Plan (HM Treasury 1999) that details how UK membership in EMU might come about and presents a timetable for replacing sterling with the euro.

A more binding constraint on UK membership is the Labor government's commitment to put the issue to a referendum. As Figure 6 shows, the UK public remains skeptical about the single currency, and in the June 1999 elections to the European Parliament, the anti-euro Conservative Party won 36 seats, compared with the Labor Party's 29 seats. However, while public opinion in the UK remains decidedly against membership in EMU, a significant segment of British industry believes it is in the UK's interest to join. A June 1999 survey of members of the Institute of Directors revealed that 67 percent were in favor of the UK joining the single currency (in principle). In July the Confederation of British Industry (CBI) announced that it was in favor of the UK joining EMU. The CBI adopted a pro-EMU stance after a poll of its members showed that some 52 percent backed eventual membership.[18] However, the CBI has subsequently announced that it will no longer actively campaign for UK membership until the government takes a more active role in promoting the issue.

Opponents of UK membership in EMU often argue that the UK business cycle is more closely aligned with the U.S. business cycle than with the cycle in continental European countries and that the criterion of cyclical convergence will never be satisfied. This fact is documented by Wynne and Koo (forthcoming), among many others. They show that the correlation between the cyclical component of output in the UK and the United States is 0.67, which exceeds the correlation of UK output with that in France (0.58) or Germany (0.45). The relative magnitudes are similar if we look at employment instead of output. However, the relevance of this fact to the debate about UK membership in EMU is not obvious. To begin with, we do not fully understand why the UK business cycle is more closely correlated with the U.S. cycle than with the cycle in the rest of Europe. The correlation may reflect the significant volume of trade and investment flows between the UK and the United States (most U.S. foreign direct investment in Europe goes to the UK), or it may be due to other factors.

These flows, in turn, may be influenced over time by the UK's attitude toward EMU. If the UK were to remain outside EMU permanently, some of these investment flows might shift to the euro area. Already a number of Asian investors in the UK have indicated they will rethink their location choices should the UK delay for long its decision on EMU membership. Rose (1999) presents evidence suggesting the real effects of a monetary union may be substantial. Specifically, he shows that two countries that share a common currency tend to trade three times as much as they would if they had different currencies. Furthermore, Frankel and Rose (1998) demonstrate that the closer the trade links between countries, the more highly correlated their business cycles are.

Outlook

I noted at the beginning of this article that many commentators in the United States doubted EMU would ever happen or thought that, if it did, it would be a source of conflict within the EU and between the EU and the United States (see Feldstein 1997a,b). The common thread in the skeptics' arguments was that the EU does not constitute an optimum currency area in the sense of Mundell (1961).[19] While there were some differences in economic performance across the euro area over the past year, we did not see the kind of dramatic asymmetries the skeptics believe will cause EMU to collapse. Despite sluggish growth in two of the larger economies (Germany and Italy), unemployment continued to decline across the euro area, although it does remain at unacceptably high levels. Germany, which accounts for about one-third of euro-area economic activity, only experienced one quarter of negative growth (at the end of 1998) rather than a full-blown recession. How well the institutions of EMU will deal with more severely asymmetric cycles if and when they occur is an open question.[20]

In the near term it is also essential that the EU address the issue of lender of last resort for the euro area. The ECB has a very limited role in bank supervision and regulation, and the Maastricht Treaty does not spell out what exactly the responsibilities of the ECB are in the event of a major financial crisis. Article 105 of the Maastricht Treaty mandates that the European System of Central Banks (ESCB) shall "promote the smooth operation of the payments system." The same article also states that "the ESCB shall contribute to the smooth conduct of policies pursued by the competent authorities relating to the prudential supervision of credit institutions and the stability of the financial system" and that the European Council may confer upon the ECB specific tasks related to supervsion. Begg et al. (1998) argue that the current arrangements are unsafe and that there is no secure mechanism for creating liquidity in the event of a crisis. Banking supervision remains a national responsibility, and there are questions about whether the ECB would have access to the rel-

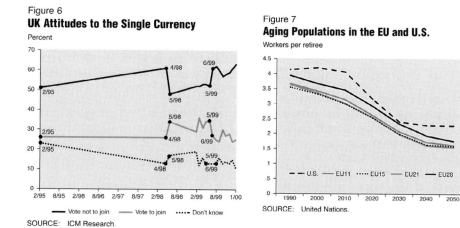

Figure 6
UK Attitudes to the Single Currency
Percent

— Vote not to join   — Vote to join   ••••• Don't know
SOURCE: ICM Research.

Figure 7
Aging Populations in the EU and U.S.
Workers per retiree

--- U.S. — EU11 ••••• EU15 — EU21 — EU28
SOURCE: United Nations.

evant information to allow it to make quick decisions if a crisis occurs.[21] The European Parliament's Committee on Economic and Monetary Affairs (EPCEMA) recently noted that "...the ESCB's arrangements for the emergency provision of liquidity to financial institutions in distress have been called into question by the International Monetary Fund and by private sector observers, and EPCEMA urges the ESCB to make clear that the necessary procedures for approval and disbursement of such 'lender of last resort' facilities are in place and have been rehearsed."

In its convergence report prepared as part of the transition to EMU, the European Monetary Institute (the forerunner of the ECB) drew attention to the long-term problems posed by pay-as-you-go pension systems in the EU.[22] The ECB reiterated this point in its January 2000 Monthly Bulletin, noting that "the ageing of populations represents a serious challenge to the sustainability of the pay-as-you-go financed public pension schemes" in the euro area. To give some sense of the scale of the problem faced by the euro-area economy, Figure 7 presents projections of the number of potential workers per retired person over the next fifty years for the United States and the EU.[23]

The decline in the ratio in the United States reflects the aging of the baby-boom generation and is the primary demographic factor fueling the debate over the long-term sustain-

ability of the Social Security program here. However, as Figure 7 shows, the aging problem is more severe in the EU than in the United States. The figure presents four variants for the EU. The first two are for the euro area (EU11) and the current fifteen members of the EU (EU15). Variant 3 (EU21) shows the projections if the EU expands to include the six current applicants considered the most likely candidates for early membership (Estonia, Poland, the Czech Republic, Hungary, Slovenia, and Cyprus). The final variant (EU28) shows what happens if the EU expands to include all thirteen of the current applicants (in addition to the six just mentioned, Latvia, Lithuania, the Slovak Republic, Bulgaria, Romania, Malta, and Turkey).

The rapid rise in the dependency ratio (decline in the number of workers per retiree) in the EU reflects declining birth rates and increased longevity. The decline in the birth rate in three of the largest euro-area economies (Germany, Italy, and Spain) has been so dramatic in recent years that, were it not for immigration, the populations of these countries would have fallen.[24] The aging of the population might not be so problematic were it not for the extensive reliance on publicly funded pensions in these countries and the relatively generous nature of these pensions. In Germany, for example, workers are entitled to a public pension equal to 72 percent of their average net lifetime earnings.

Additionally, public expenditure on health care for the elderly is high and has risen with recent costly advances in medical technology. In short, demographic developments over the next decades could prove a serious threat to the fiscal positions of many of the euro-area governments that will necessitate painful reforms at some point. Some changes have recently been made (France now indexes pensions to prices rather than wages; Germany switched from indexing to gross wages to indexing to net wages), but more remains to be done.

Obviously the aging of the EU population is independent of whether the countries share a common currency. Rather, its significance stems from the institutional framework of EMU and, in particular, the restrictions on national fiscal policies as set out in the Maastricht Treaty and elaborated upon in the Growth and Stability Pact.

Article 104 of the Maastricht Treaty states that

1. Member States shall avoid excessive government deficits.
2. The Commission shall monitor the development of the budgetary situation and of the stock of government debt in the Member States with a view to identifying gross errors. In particular it shall examine compliance with budgetary discipline on the basis of the following two criteria: (a) whether the ratio of the planned or actual government deficit to gross domestic product exceeds a reference value…(b) whether the ratio of government debt to gross domestic product exceeds a reference value….
5. If the Commission considers that an excessive deficit in a Member State exists or may occur, the Commission shall address an opinion to the Council.
6. The Council shall, acting by a qualified majority on a recommendation from the Commission…decide after an overall assessment whether an excessive deficit exists.
7. Where the existence of an excessive deficit is decided…the Council shall make a recommendation to the Member State concerned with a view to bringing that situation to an end within a given period…

8. If a Member State persists in failing to put into practice the recommendations of the Council, the Council may decide to give notice to the Member State to take, within a specified time-limit, measures for the deficit reduction which is judged necessary by the Council in order to remedy the situation…
11. As long as a Member State fails to comply with a decision taken in accordance with paragraph 9, the Council may decide to apply or, as the case may be, intensify one or more of the following measures: – to require the Member State concerned to publish additional information, to be specified by the Council, before issuing bonds and securities; – to invite the European Investment bank to reconsider its lending policy towards the Member State concerned; – to require the Member State concerned to make a non-interest-bearing deposit of an appropriate size with the Community until the excessive deficit has, in the view of the Council, been corrected; – to impose fines of an appropriate size.

The Growth and Stability Pact adopted at the Dublin Summit in December 1996 is intended to clarify and strengthen the provisions of the treaty in regard to excessive deficits by strengthening fiscal discipline under EMU.[25] The existence of large, unfunded public pension liabilities will certainly complicate EMU participants' ability to abide by the terms of the treaty and the Growth and Stability Pact.[26]

Conclusions

By any reasonable standards, the first year of EMU must be judged a success. The changeover weekend went by without incident, the TARGET payments system was launched without any major problems, and the ECB has successfully taken over monetary policy for the euro area. The ECB faced the first serious challenge to its independence and effectively defended its status. It also conducted its first policy moves, easing monetary policy in April in the face of a growing threat of deflation and weak real activity in the euro area. In November it reversed course, tightening policy as the balance of risks shifted to higher inflation, and the euro-area recovery took hold.

The success of the first year does not mean that it will be all plain sailing from here on. Many challenges remain, and how the EU and the ECB tackle these will determine the ultimate fate of EMU. One issue highlighted in this article is the rapidly aging population of the EU. The aging of the population over the coming decades in conjunction with generous pension provisions will put a severe strain on the public finances of the euro-area economies. One solution might be to admit large numbers of immigrants, but Europe does not have a tradition of encouraging large-scale immigration. The only alternative is drastic reform of the public pension programs in all the countries, something no government has yet been willing to tackle. More generally, structural reforms of labor and product markets are crucial if the EU is to address the high unemployment rates and sluggish growth that have plagued it for the past decade. Small moves have been made in this direction, but a lot more needs to be done.

I thank Bill Gruben, Evan Koenig and Carlos Zarazaga for comments on an earlier draft and Eric Millis for research assistance. Martin Boon at ICM Research in London kindly supplied the results of the ICM Research/Guardian polls of UK attitudes to the single currency. Responsibility for remaining errors rests with the author.

Endnotes

1   The eleven countries participating in EMU are Austria, Belgium, Finland, France, Germany, Ireland, Italy, Luxembourg, the Netherlands, Portugal, and Spain.

2   On January 27 the euro closed at below parity for the first time ($0.9883 in New York).

3   The European Currency Unit (ECU) was a synthetic currency defined on the basis of a basket of the currencies of the EU member states. Specifically, on December 31, 1998, one ECU consisted of 3.301 Belgian francs, 0.6242 German marks, 0.1976 Danish krones, 6.885 Spanish pesetas, 1.332 French francs, 0.08784 British pounds, 1.44 Greek drachmas, 0.008552 Irish punts, 151.8 Italian lira, 0.13 Luxembourg francs, 0.2198 Dutch guilders

and 1.393 Portuguese escudos (see European Central Bank 1999a, 72).

4   Arguably the first policy action of the ECB was taken in December 1998, when the eleven euro-area central banks (the so-called Eurosystem) coordinated a reduction in their short-term interest rates to a common 3 percent level before the formal launch of EMU.

5   To this end, in its Monthly Bulletin the ECB publishes statistics only for the euro area as a whole and not for individual member states. Statistical information is provided on developments in the four EU countries that do not participate in EMU (Denmark, Greece, Sweden, and the UK) and also on developments in the United States and Japan.

6   Formally, people are counted as unemployed if they are without work, are available to start work in the next two weeks, and have actively sought employment at some point during the previous four weeks.

7   The relative importance of owner's equivalent rent in the U.S. CPI as of December 1997 was just over 20 percent.

8   Interestingly, the ECB does not define how long the "medium term" is.

9   The Maastricht Treaty stipulates that, as one of the convergence criteria for assessing suitability for EMU membership, a country's inflation rate should not exceed the average rate of the three best performers by more than 1.5 percentage points.

10 See http://europa.eu.int/comm/eurostat/.

11 See, for example, the recent working paper by Coenen and Vega (1999), which builds on other research conducted by the ECB's predecessor, the European Monetary Institute.

12 In December 1999, the Governing Council announced that this value will also be used for 2000.

13 Note also that the president of the ECB has indicated that none of the decisions to change interest rates were made by a formal vote.

14 One of the objectives of the Intergovernment Conference that drew up the Amsterdam Treaty, which was signed in October 1997, was to enhance the democratic accountability of EU institutions.

15 The main components of the European Monetary System, which existed prior to EMU, were the Exchange Rate Mechanism, which was essentially a system of fixed exchange rates between the currencies of the participating countries, and the European Currency Unit, which has now been replaced by the euro.

[16] Note that the seigniorage revenue will be distributed among participating countries using a formula prescribed in the Maastricht Treaty Protocol No. 3 on the Statute of the European System of Central Banks and the European Central Bank, Articles 29 and 31.

[17] The denominational structure of the euro will consist of coins at the 1, 2, 5, 10, and 20 euro cent denominations, coins at the €1 and €2 denominations, and notes at the €5, €10, €20, €50, €100, €200, and €500 denominations.

[18] The *Economist* newspaper surveyed British economists in early 1999 and found that about 65 percent favored UK membership in EMU.

[19] Ironically, the critics seem to overlook the later papers by Mundell (1973a,b) in which he proposes additional criteria for evaluating the suitability of a single currency for a group of countries. As a result of these works, he has been referred to in some circles as the father of the euro. See also Mundell (1998a,b).

[20] The studies of Frankel and Rose (1998) and Rose (1999) just cited are also relevant to this question. Insofar as sharing a common currency enhances trade flows within the euro area and these trade flows lead to more synchronous business cycles, the concern about asymmetric shocks may prove unfounded. However, within a monetary union as long-standing and fully credible as the United States, asymmetric cycles may occasionally emerge. Through the 1980s and 1990s different regions of the United States experienced shocks that caused localized recessions of varying degrees of severity; the term "rolling recessions" entered policy debates to describe this phenomenon.

[21] Prati and Schinasi (1999) articulate similar concerns.

[22] See also the recent report by the G-10 (Group of Ten 1998).

[23] Specifically, the figure shows the ratio of the population aged 25 to 64 to the population aged 65 and older and is taken from the "medium variant" projections in United Nations (1998).

[24] In its most recent forecasts the United Nations (1998) projects that the population of Italy will fall from 57.3 million in 2000 to 41.2 million in 2050, that of Germany from 82.2 million to 73.3 million, and that of Spain from 39.6 million to 30.2 million.

[25] For further details see the May 1999 issue of the ECB's Monthly Bulletin.

[26] The need for fiscal rules under a monetary union is a contentious issue. Artis and Winkler (1997) argue that the excessive deficit provisions of the treaty can be justified on the grounds that under monetary union the costs of an overly expansionary fiscal policy will be borne by all members of the monetary union and not just by the country pursuing the policy, creating an incentive for countries to be more lax with their fiscal policy. Bergin (2000), arguing from the perspective of the fiscal theory of the price level, makes a similar point.

References

Artis, Michael J., and Bernhard Winkler (1997), "The Stability Pact: Safeguarding the Credibility of the European Central Bank," European University Institute Working Paper RSC no. 97/54 (Florence, Italy: European University Institute).

Begg, David, Paul De Grauwe, Francesco Giavazzi, Harald Uhlig, and Charles Wyplosz (1998), "The ECB: Safe at Any Speed?" Monitoring the European Central Bank, no. 1 (London: Center for Economic Policy Research).

Bergin, Paul R. (2000), "Fiscal Solvency and Price Level Determination in a Monetary Union," *Journal of Monetary Economics* 45 (February): 37–53.

Buiter, Willem H. (1999), "Alice in Euroland," Center for Economic Policy Research Policy Paper no. 1.

Buiter, Willem H., Giancarlo Corsetti, and Nouriel Roubini (1993), "Excessive Deficits: Sense and Nonsense in the Treaty of Maastricht," *Economic Policy* 16 (April): 57–100.

Coenen, Günter, and Juan-Luis Vega (1999), "The Demand for M3 in the Euro Area," European Central Bank Working Paper no. 6.

Cohen, Benjamin J. (1971), *The Future of Sterling as an International Currency* (London: Macmillan).

Deutsche Bundesbank (1995), *The Monetary Policy of the Bundesbank* (Frankfurt am Main: Deutsche Bundesbank).

European Central Bank (1999a), *Annual Report 1998* (Frankfurt am Main: European Central Bank).

——— (1999b), *Euro Area Monetary Aggregates: Conceptual Reconciliation Exercise* (Frankfurt am Main: European Central Bank).

European Commission (1998), *Report from the Commission to the Council: On the Harmonisation of Consumer Price Indices in the European Union* (Brussels: Commission of the European Communities).

European Parliament (1999), *Report on the Annual Report for 1998 of the European Central Bank,* European Parliament Session Document, October 15, 1999.

Feldstein, Martin (1997a), "EMU and International Conflict," *Foreign Affairs* 76 (November/December): 60–73.

—— (1997b), "The Political Economy of the European Economic and Monetary Union: Political Sources of an Economic Liability," *Journal of Economic Perspectives* 11 (Fall): 23–42.

Frankel, Jeffrey A., and Andrew K. Rose (1998), "The Endogeneity of the Optimum Currency Area Criteria," *Economic Journal* 108 (July): 1009–25.

Group of Ten (1998), *The Macroeconomic and Financial Implications of Ageing Populations* (Basle: Bank for International Settlements).

Hartmann, Philipp (1998), *Currency Competition and Foreign Exchange Markets: The Dollar, the Yen and the Euro* (Cambridge: Cambridge University Press).

HM Treasury (1997), *UK Membership of the Single Currency: An Assessment of the Five Economic Tests* (London: HM Treasury).

—— (1999), *Outline National Changeover Plan* (London: HM Treasury).

Issing, Otmar (1999), "The Eurosystem: Transparent and Accountable or 'Willem in Euroland,' " Center for Economic Policy Research Policy Paper no. 2.

Lucas, Robert E., Jr. (1976), "Econometric Policy Evaluation: A Critique," *Carnegie – Rochester Conference Series on Public Policy* 1: 19–46.

Mundell, Robert A. (1961), "A Theory of Optimum Currency Areas," *American Economic Review* 51 (September): 657–65.

—— (1973a), "A Plan for a European Currency," in *The Economics of Common Currencies,* ed. Harry G. Johnson and Alexander K. Swoboda (London: George Allen and Unwin), 143–72.

—— (1973b), "Uncommon Arguments for Common Currencies," in *The Economics of Common Currencies,* ed. Harry G. Johnson and Alexander K. Swoboda (London: George Allen and Unwin), 114–32.

—— (1998a), "The Case for the Euro–I," *Wall Street Journal,* March 24, A22.

—— (1998b), "The Case for the Euro–II," *Wall Street Journal,* March 25, A22.

Porter, Richard D., and Ruth A. Judson (1996), "The Location of U.S. Currency: How Much Is Abroad?" *Federal Reserve Bulletin* 82 (October): 883–903.

Porter, Richard D., and Ruth A. Judson (1996), "The Location of U.S. Currency: How Much Is Abroad?" *Federal Reserve Bulletin* 82 (October): 883-903.

Portes, Richard, and Hélène Rey (1998), "The Emergence of the Euro as an International Currency," *Economic Policy* 26 (April): 307–43.

Prati, Alessandro, and Garry J. Schinasi (1999), "Financial Stability in European Economic and Monetary Union," Princeton Studies in International Finance no. 86 (Princeton, N.J.: Princeton University Printing Services).

Rose, Andrew K. (1999), "One Money, One Market: Estimating the Effect of Common Currencies on Trade," NBER Working Paper Series, no. 7432 (Cambridge, Mass.: National Bureau of Economic Research, December).

Seitz, Franz (1995), "The Circulation of Deutsche Mark Abroad," Discussion Papers of the Economic Research Group of the Deutsche Bundesbank, no. 1/95.

United Nations (1998), *World Population Prospects: The 1998 Revision,* vol. I, Comprehensive Tables (New York: United Nations).

U.S. Bureau of Labor Statistics (1997), *BLS Handbook of Methods* (Washington, D.C.: U.S. Government Printing Office).

Wynne, Mark A., and Jahyeong Koo (forthcoming), "Business Cycles Under Monetary Union: A Comparison of the EU and U.S.," *Economica.*

The Creation of the Euro and the Role of the Dollar in International Markets

PATRICIA S. POLLARD

During the nineteenth and the first half of the twentieth centuries, the British pound was the preeminent international currency. It was used in both international trade and financial transactions and circulated throughout the British empire. With the decline of British economic power in the 20th century, the U.S. dollar replaced the pound as the leading international currency. For over 50 years the U.S. dollar has been the leading currency used in international trade and debt contracts. Primary commodities are generally priced in dollars on world exchanges. Central banks and governments hold the bulk of their foreign exchange reserves in dollars. In addition, in some countries dollars are accepted for making transactions as readily as (if not more so than) the domestic currency.

On January 1, 1999, a new currency—the euro—was created, culminating the progress toward economic and monetary union in Europe. The euro replaced the currencies of 11 European countries: Austria, Belgium, Finland, France, Germany, Ireland, Italy, Luxembourg, the Netherlands, Portugal, and Spain.[1] Two years later Greece became the 12th member of the euro area. Although the Japanese yen and particularly the German mark have been used internationally in the past several decades, neither currency approached the international use of the dollar. With the creation of the euro, for the first time the dollar has a potential rival for the status as the primary international currency. What

changes in the international use of the dollar have occurred in the first two years of the euro's existence? What changes are likely over the next decade? Moreover, what are the implications for the United States and the euro area as a result of these changes? To answer these questions, this article begins with an overview of the functions of an international currency and the major factors that determine whether a currency will be used outside its borders. It then examines the use of currencies in international markets prior to the establishment of the euro and the changes brought about by the creation of the euro.[2]

Functions of an International Currency

Economists define money as anything that serves the following three functions: a unit of account, a store of value, and a medium of exchange. To operate as a unit of account, prices must be set in terms of the money. To function as a store of value, the purchasing power of money must be maintained over time.[3] To function as a medium of exchange, the money must be used for purchasing goods and services. For an international currency, one used as money outside its country of issue, these functions are generally divided by sector of use—private and official, as listed in Table 1.[4]

A currency serves as a unit of account for private international transactions if it is used as an invoice currency in international

Functions of an International Currency
Table 1

Function	Sector Private	Official
Unit of account	Invoice	Exchange rate peg
Store of value	Financial assets	Reserves
Medium of exchange	Vehicle/substitution	Intervention

trade contracts. It serves as a store of value if international financial assets are denominated in this currency. It serves as a medium of exchange internationally if it is used as a vehicle currency through which two other currencies are traded, and as a substitute for a domestic currency.

A currency serves as a unit of account for official international purposes if it is used as an exchange rate peg. It serves (i) as a store of value if governments and/or central banks hold foreign exchange reserves in this currency and (ii) as a medium of exchange if it is used for intervening in currency markets.

The three functions of an international currency reinforce each other. For example, the use of a currency for invoicing trade and holding financial assets increases the likelihood that the currency will be used as a vehicle currency. In the official sector, if a country pegs its exchange rate to another currency, it is likely to hold reserves in that currency and conduct its interventions in exchange markets in that currency. In addition, the use of an international currency by one sector reinforces its use by the other sector. For example, using a currency as an exchange rate peg facilitates the use of that currency in debt contracts and foreign trade.

Determinants of an International Currency

What determines the likelihood that a currency will be used in the international exchange of goods, services, and assets? Five key factors are as follows:

- Size of the economy
- Importance in international trade
- Size, depth, liquidity, and openness of domestic financial markets
- Convertibility of the currency
- Macroeconomic policies

The size of a country's economy is important because it determines the potential use of the currency in international markets. Economic size is linked with the importance of a country in international trade and the size of its financial markets. For example, exports account for a much greater share of the output of the Korean economy than for the U.S. economy. Nevertheless, because the U.S. economy is nearly 14 times larger than the Korean economy, U.S. exports comprise a much larger share of world exports.

Clearly the dominance of the U.S. economy and the decline of the U.K. economy in the twentieth century were related to the rise of the dollar and the decline of the pound as international currencies. Likewise, the growth of the German and Japanese economies in the last several decades of the twentieth century prompted the use of their currencies in international markets. As a result, the overwhelming dominance the dollar held in international markets in the 1950s and 1960s diminished.

Table 2 compares the relative size of the U.S., euro-area, and Japanese economies. The U.S. economy is the largest in the world, accounting for about 22 percent of world output. The establishment of economic and monetary union in Europe, linked through the euro, has created the world's second

Comparison of United States, Euro-Area, and Japanese Economies in 1999
Table 2

	United States	Euro area	Japan
Share of world GDP (%)	21.9	15.8	7.6
Share of world exports (%)	15.3	19.4	9.3
Financial markets ($ billions)	40,543.8	24,133.4	20,888.5
Bank assets ($ billions)	7,555.3	12,731.3	6,662.5
Domestic debt securities outstanding ($ billions)	15,426.3	5,521.9	6,444.9
Stock market capitalization ($ billions)	17,562.2	5,880.2	7,781.4

Note: GDP is based on purchasing power parity equivalents. World exports excludes intra-euro-area trade.
Source: GDP: IMF, *World Economic Outlook,* October 2000. Exports: IMF, *Direction of Trade Statistics Quarterly,*
September 2000. Bank assets: European Central Bank, *Monthly Bulletin;* Board of Governors of the Federal Reserve
System, *Flow of Funds Accounts;* IMF, *International Financial Statistics.* Debt securities: Bank for International
Settlements, *Quarterly Review of International Banking and Financial Market Developments.* Stock market: Eurostat.

largest economy. The Japanese economy is less than half the size of the euro area.[5]

The share of a country in international trade as well as the size and openness of its financial markets are determinants of the demand for that country's currency in world markets. The United States accounts for a lower share of world exports than does the current euro area, as shown in Table 2. The size of U.S. financial markets as measured by the sum of bank assets, outstanding domestic debt securities, and stock market capitalization, however, is much larger than in the euro area. Japan is a distant third in terms of its share of world exports, but its financial markets are close in size to those in the euro area.

The convertibility of a country's currency is another important determinant of its use in international markets. Restrictions on the ability to exchange a currency for other currencies limits its global use. At the end of World War II almost every country, with the exception of the United States, restricted convertibility of its currency. This inconvertibility persisted for the first decade after the war. The convertibility of the U.S. dollar prompted its use as the currency in which international trade was conducted.

Macroeconomic policies also play an important role in determining whether a country's currency will be used internationally. These policies affect a country's economic growth and its openness to the world economy. Policies fostering a low inflation environment are especially important. Countries experiencing hyperinflation and/or political crises often see the use of their currencies collapse not only internationally but also within the domestic economy, as residents turn to a substitute currency.

Clearly the size and openness of the U.S. economy have been major factors in encouraging the international use of the dollar in the post-World War II period. Its use as an international currency in the private sector and the effect of the emergence of the euro in this sector is examined in the next section.

The Private Uses of an International Currency

As stated above, a currency operates as an international currency in the private sector (i) if international trade and debt contracts are priced in this currency; (ii) if this currency is used to facilitate the exchange of other currencies; and (iii) if this currency is used as a substitute currency.

Invoice Currency

The dollar is the main currency that functions as a unit of account for private international transactions. Although data on the currency of invoice in international trade are limited, the available data confirm the dominance of the dollar. In 1995 the U.S. dollar was used as the invoice currency for more than half of world exports, down only slightly from 1980, as shown in Table 3. The

Trade Invoiced in Major Currencies
Table 3

Currency	Percent of world exports		Internationalization ratio	
	1980	1995	1980	1995
U.S. dollar	56.4	52.0	4.5	3.9
Japanese yen	2.1	4.7	0.3	0.6
Deutsche mark	13.6	13.2	1.4	1.4
French franc	6.2	5.5	0.9	1.0
British pound	6.5	5.4	1.1	1.1
Italian lira	2.2	3.3	0.5	0.8
Netherlands guilder	2.6	2.8	0.7	0.9
Euro-4	24.6	24.8	NA	NA

Note: Euro-4 is the share of the four euro-area currencies listed in the table. No data were available for the other euro-area currencies. World exports includes intra-euro-area trade. The internationalization ratio is the ratio of the share of world exports denominated in a currency to the share of the issuing country in world exports.
Source: Bekx (1998, Table 3, p. 8).

Deutsche mark was the next most popular invoice currency, used for approximately 13 percent of world exports, followed by the French franc and the British pound. While the yen's use in world trade lagged behind these European currencies, its share had more than doubled since 1980. The combined share of the four major euro currencies was less than half that of the U.S. dollar.

More importantly, there is a clear distinction between the use of the dollar and other invoice currencies. The U.S. dollar is the only currency whose use in world trade far surpasses its country share in world trade, as shown by its internationalization ratio in Table 3. An internationalization ratio less than 1.0, as with the yen, lira, and guilder, indicates that not all of that country's exports are denominated in the local currency. An internationalization ratio greater than 1.0, as with the dollar, the mark, and the pound, indicates that other countries use that currency to invoice some (or all) of their exports.[6]

What determines the currency of invoice in world trade? A number of studies including those by Grassman (1973), Page (1981), and Black (1990) revealed the following patterns. Trade in manufactured goods among the industrial economies is most often priced in the currency of the exporter. If the exporter's currency is not used, then the importer's currency is the most frequent choice. Only rarely is a third country's currency used. Trade between industrial and developing countries is generally priced in the currency of the industrial country or that of a third country. Trade between developing countries is often priced in the currency of a third country. When a third country's currency is used for invoicing trade, the U.S. dollar is the most likely choice. Trade in primary commodities is almost always invoiced in U.S. dollars because these products are predominantly priced in dollars on international exchanges.

According to Hartmann (1996), two factors that explain these patterns are transaction costs and acceptability. The lower the cost of buying and selling a currency in the foreign exchange market, the more likely is its use for invoicing trade. In addition, the more accepted a currency is for other transactions, the more likely it is to be used as an invoice currency. Clearly these two factors are mutually supportive. The more accepted a currency is, the lower its transaction costs; the lower its transaction costs, the more likely it is to be accepted.

Related factors that explain these patterns are convertibility and the expected stability of the currency. As noted above, the use of the dollar as an invoice currency was prompted by the lack of convertibility of most other currencies in the 1950s. The limited use of developing countries' currencies in world trade arose in part because many of these countries restricted (and some continue to restrict) the convertibility of their currencies. Black (1990) showed that the share of a country's exports denominated in its domestic currency declines the greater is the expected depreciation of its currency. Thus, the currencies of countries with high inflation are seldom used in international trade.

The mere creation of the euro as a currency should provide ample incentive for its use as an invoice currency. Replacing the currencies of 12 countries with a single currency reduces the transaction costs involved in currency exchanges. Although only a small number of firms within the euro area have already switched to invoicing in euros, the advent of euro notes and coins, along with the withdrawal from circulation of the notes and coins of the legacy currencies in 2002, will prompt several changes. According to Page (1981), the use of the dollar is negligible in intra European Union trade, so the creation of the euro should not have had a noticeable effect on invoicing in the region. Where its effect is likely to be largest is in extra-euro-area trade, where most exports are likely to be invoiced in euros. It is unlikely, however, that trade currently invoiced in dollars and involving neither the euro area nor the United States will shift in the near term to euros. This argument is supported by the European Central Bank (ECB), which estimates that the percent of world exports denominated in euros "is likely not to differ significantly from that of euro area exports" (ECB, 1999, p. 36). Thus, the internationalization ratio for the euro area will be close to 1.

What effects will the use of the euro as an invoice currency have on the euro area and the United States? For firms in the euro area, gains will arise from a reduction in transactions costs and exchange rate risk. In intra-euro-area trade, exchange rate risk has already been eliminated and the transactions costs will be eliminated by 2002. Turning to the external trade of the euro area, the small-

er euro-area countries will gain the most from the reduction in transactions costs because, prior to the establishment of the euro, the limited demand for their currencies resulted in higher costs for exchanging their currencies for other currencies. A rise in the share of euro-area external trade invoiced in euros may also reduce the exposure of its businesses to short-term exchange rate variability. To the extent that there is an increase in the use of the euro in trade between the euro area and the United States, the exposure of U.S. businesses to exchange rate risk will rise. The importance of such a change is unclear. There exists a wide range of options to hedge exchange rate risk, but these options are not costless. Magee and Rao (1980), however, argue that the currency of denomination in trade contracts is irrelevant if both the exporter and importer have the same risk preferences; this is so because the contract price should incorporate an exchange rate risk premium.

The dollar is also the main currency used for pricing internationally traded commodities, with the British pound being the only other currency used. As Tavlas (1997) notes, the commodity exchanges on which these products are traded are located in countries "that have a comparative advantage as financial centers," thus explaining the dominance of the United States and the United Kingdom and hence the currency choice.

The creation of the euro is unlikely to lead to any change in the pricing of these commodities. The location of major commodity exchanges in the United States, while not a necessary requirement for dollar pricing, does increase the likelihood that these commodities will continue to be priced in dollars. Although it is possible that an integrated Europe will develop commodity exchanges to rival those of the United States, such a shift is likely to be gradual. Any shift in pricing of these commodities is unlikely to occur until the stability of Europe's new monetary system is well established.[7]

Suppose, however, that there is eventually a shift in the pricing of commodities from dollars to euros. Would such a change increase the volatility of these prices for U.S.

Volatility of Real Oil Prices in the United States and Germany* (Percent)
Table 4

Year	Volatility of real U.S. $ price	Volatility of real DM price	F-test probability[†]
1985	4.5	5.7	48.8
1986	17.8	17.3	93.6
1987	5.7	5.8	96.6
1988	8.2	8.1	96.3
1989	6.3	6.9	79.0
1990	18.9	17.8	84.0
1991	8.6	9.5	74.8
1992	4.4	4.5	95.9
1993	4.6	4.9	85.6
1994	5.4	5.2	91.3
1995	5.3	6.2	61.4
1996	6.1	6.6	80.5
1997	6.8	6.3	79.4
1998	8.2	6.7	50.4
1999	9.4	10.0	84.3
2000	11.6	13.4	64.2

NOTE: Shaded rows indicate no statistical difference in the volatility of real dollar vs. real mark crude oil prices.
* Volatility is measured by the standard deviation of monthly changes in the real price of oil.
† The last column shows the probability that the standard deviations of the two series are statistically equal.
SOURCE: IMF, *International Financial Statistics,* and Wall Street Journal.

consumers while lowering the volatility for euro-area consumers? For this to occur, exchange rate fluctuations must not only introduce another source of volatility into the price of these commodities but must be positively correlated with the price volatility. There is no reason to expect this to hold. An examination of data on the real price of crude oil in U.S. dollars and in Deutsche marks illustrates this point. The real price of oil in the U.S. depends on the dollar price of oil in international markets and the U.S. inflation rate, whereas the real price of oil in Germany depends on the dollar price of oil in international markets, the mark/dollar (now euro/dollar) exchange rate, and the German inflation rate. Table 4 indicates the yearly volatility of each of these measures from 1985 to 2000. In 3 of the 16 years there was no statistical difference in the volatility of the real dollar price and the real mark price of crude oil.[8] In 8 of the 16 years the volatility

of the real mark price was greater than the volatility of the real dollar price. In the remaining 5 years the volatility of the real dollar price was greater than the volatility of the real mark price. These data do not provide clear support for the idea that having commodities priced in a country's domestic currency on world exchanges results in lower variability in the real domestic-currency price of the commodity.

Financial Assets

In international bond markets the U.S. dollar was the currency of choice for nearly all issues in the 1950s. By the 1970s, however, the currency denomination of bond issues had become more diversified, as shown in Table 5. Nevertheless, the U.S. dollar has remained the most popular currency choice for issuing bonds in international markets, as shown in Table 6.[9] By the 1960s the euro legacy currencies, taken together as a group, had become

Funds Raised in International Bond Markets by Currency of Issue (Percent)
Table 5

Currency	1950-59	1960-69	1970-79	1980-89
U.S. dollar	78.2	69.9	49.2	50.7
Japanese yen	0.0	0.0	5.2	8.9
Swiss franc	7.1	5.4	17.5	1.4
Euro area[*]	3.2	20.3	24.1	15.8
Deutsche mark	2.0	16.3	17.9	8.0
Other E.U.[†]	8.7	3.1	0.7	6.8
Pound sterling	8.3	2.9	0.6	6.4

[*]Euro area includes the currencies of all current members of the euro area and currency composites, such as the ecu.
[†] Other E.U. includes the currencies of Denmark, Greece, Sweden, and the United Kingdom.
Source: OECD, *International Capital Market Statistics,* 1996, and *Financial Statistics Monthly,* June 1997.

the second most widely used currency in international bond markets, a status that continues today. The Japanese yen was not used at all until the 1970s, and its share of new issues lags far below that of the dollar or euro. The use of the Swiss franc in international bond markets, which rivaled the Deutsche mark in the 1970s, declined precipitously in the 1990s.[10]

In international money markets as well, the dollar is the currency of choice, but again its dominance has declined, as noted in Table 6. The increased use of the euro legacy currencies in these markets during the 1990s is particularly noteworthy. In 1993 these currencies accounted for 8.5 percent of the outstanding debt in international money markets. By 1998 this share had increased to 19.2 percent.

The creation of the euro led to a sharp rise in its use in international debt markets relative to its legacy currencies. The share of new issues of international securities denominated in the euro legacy currencies was 24.6 percent in 1998. In the following year, the share denominated in euros was 36.8 percent. Although the use of the euro relative to its legacy currencies rose strongly in both the bond and money market, the increase was highest in the money market. In international debt markets, there is now a clear alternative to the use of the dollar.[11]

In international banking there is also evidence of currency diversification over the last two decades. Table 7 shows the assets and liabilities of banks accounted for by transactions with foreign residents (either in the domestic or foreign currencies). During the 1980s, 60 percent of the cross-border assets of banks were in dollars and 19 percent in euro legacy currencies. In the 1990s, the dollar's share fell to 47 percent and the euro legacy currencies' share rose to 27 percent. A similar pattern is noted for cross-border liabilities. The advent of the euro, however, has had little initial effect on international banking. The dollar's share of cross-border assets remained nearly constant while its share of cross-border liabilities increased slightly. The opposite pattern held for euros. There was a slight increase in the share of cross-border assets denominated in euros, relative to the euro legacy currencies, and virtually no change in liabilities.[12]

The use of a country's currency in international capital markets is determined by the size, openness, and liquidity of that country's financial markets and the stability of its currency. The decline in the dollar's dominance in world capital markets, prior to the creation of the euro, is a result of the emergence of other strong economies that, in conjunction with the liberalization and deregulation of financial systems worldwide, increased the attractiveness of assets denominated in other currencies.

International Debt Securities by Currency of Issue (Percent)
Table 6

Currency	Amounts outstanding			Share of new issues		
	1993	1998	2000	1998	1999	2000
Total securities						
U.S. dollar	41.1	45.9	48.7	54.1	45.2	44.0
Japanese yen	13.2	11.3	8.2	5.6	5.3	8.3
Swiss franc	7.3	3.8	2.2	3.3	2.0	1.7
Euro area*	24.8	27.2	30.1	24.6	36.8	33.9
Other E.U. †	7.9	8.5	8.2	8.9	8.0	9.2
Pound sterling	7.6	7.9	7.8	8.3	7.7	9.1
Bonds and notes						
U.S. dollar	38.9	45.3	48.7	51.1	43.8	42.3
Japanese yen	14.0	11.7	8.6	6.3	6.7	11.4
Swiss franc	7.7	3.8	2.2	2.7	1.6	1.4
Euro area*	25.7	27.6	30.0	28.0	38.3	34.2
Other E.U.†	8.1	8.5	8.1	9.0	7.3	8.4
Pound sterling	7.8	7.9	7.7	8.2	7.0	8.2
Money Market						
U.S. dollar	79.4	59.9	49.1	61.0	48.8	47.5
Japanese yen	0.2	2.5	2.3	4.0	1.4	1.9
Swiss franc	1.8	4.5	2.3	4.7	2.9	2.3
Euro area*	8.5	19.2	32.4	17.2	32.9	33.2
Other E.U.†	4.1	8.4	9.5	8.8	9.8	11.0
Pound sterling	4.0	8.3	9.3	8.7	9.7	11.0

*Euro area includes the currencies of the 11 original members of the euro area and currency composites, such as the ecu.
† Other E.U. includes the currencies of Denmark, Sweden, and the United Kingdom.
SOURCE: Bank for International Settlements, Quarterly Review of International Banking and Financial Market Developments, March 2001.

This is particularly evident in the bond markets where there has been a rapid increase in the number of currencies used.

The creation of the euro has spurred changes within euro-area financial markets. Integration has been most evident in the money market. Overnight interbank interest rates have become nearly harmonized throughout the euro area, aided in part by the creation of the TARGET payments system and also by the common monetary policy.[13] Although the unsecured deposit market has become highly integrated, other aspects of the money market (for example the repo market and short-term securities market) remain more segregated.[14]

There also has been some progress in the bond market as both the size and integration of the market have increased accompanied by an increase in liquidity in the secondary market.[15] Although there has been an increase in euro bonds issued by residents outside the euro area, most of the international issues were placed by euro-area residents.[16] One reason for the sharp increase in the latter issues is that the establishment of the euro reduced barriers to cross-border investment within the euro area. For example, insurance companies and some pension funds within the euro area are restricted in their ability to issue international debt. Liabilities in a foreign currency must be 80

Bank's Cross-Border Positions: Amounts Outstanding* (Percent)
Table 7

Currency	1983-89	1990-99	1998	1999	2000:Q3
Assets					
U.S. dollar	59.7	47.0	45.2	45.4	47.0
Japanese yen	10.0	12.0	11.6	10.3	9.9
Euro area [†]	18.6	27.4	28.1	31.8	30.7
Pound sterling	3.4	4.3	4.9	4.9	5.1
Liabilities					
U.S. dollar	62.4	49.3	47.6	49.9	51.9
Japanese yen	7.9	8.0	8.4	7.8	7.4
Euro area[†]	17.2	26.8	26.3	26.9	25.4
Pound sterling	4.3	5.6	6.5	6.7	6.9

*Includes both domestic and foreign currency assets and liabilities.
[†] Euro area includes the banks of the 11 original members of the euro area.
SOURCE: Bank for International Settlements, Quarterly Review of International Banking and Financial Market Developments, March 2001.

Government Bond Yields
Monthly data, various euro-area countries
Figure 1

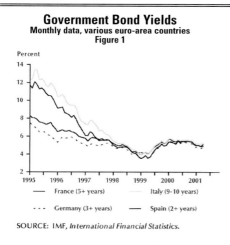

— France (5+ years)   —— Italy (9-10 years)

- - - Germany (3+ years)   —— Spain (2+ years)

SOURCE: IMF, *International Financial Statistics.*

percent matched by assets in that same currency. With the creation of the euro this matching rule becomes less restrictive.

Despite this progress, Santillán et al. (2000) note that the euro-area corporate bond market lags that of the United States with regard to liquidity, size, and market completeness. Indeed the ability of European capital markets to rival those of the United States, at least in the short-term, is not certain. Cecchetti (1999) cautions that differences in legal structures across Europe will limit the degree of integration of financial structures.

Kregel (2000) argues that the European monetary union is based on "an internal contradiction which attempts to combine the preservation of the institutional characteristics of national markets with convergence of macroeconomic performance." Thus he states it is not clear that the introduction of the euro will eliminate national segmentation.

This segmentation also exists in the euro-area government bond market. Although differences in yields on government bonds issued by the member states of the euro area have declined in the last several years, complete convergence has not occurred. According to a report by the Bank for International Settlements (BIS) (2000b), these differences are caused not so much by differences in risk but by "technical and liquidity considerations." The report further notes that this lack of integration implies that no euro-area government bond market can serve as a benchmark for the whole euro area and as such there is no "well defined reference government yield curve" that would aid the pricing of euro-area corporate bond issues, among other things.

Figure 1 illustrates these points using long-term government bond yields for four euro-area countries. There was a noticeable

Foreign Exchange Market Transactions
Involving Select Currencies (Percent of Total) April 1998
Table 8

Category	U.S. dollar	Japanese yen	Deutsche mark	French franc	Euro area*	Pound sterling
Spot	78.8	24.7	42.7	3.3	56.8	11.6
Forwards	81.4	26.7	28.0	5.1	50.7	12.3
Swaps	95.2	16.7	20.0	6.5	48.8	10.2
Total	87.4	20.8	29.8	5.1	52.2	11.0

*Euro area includes the currencies of the current member countries plus the Danish krone and the ecu.
Source: Bank for International Settlements, *Central Bank Survey of Foreign Exchange and Derivatives Market Activity 1998.* Basle: BIS, May 1999.

convergence in yields as monetary union approached. Although differences remain, these are likely related to the lack of a common benchmark. As Figure 1 shows, there is no standard maturity structure for bonds in the euro area.

The euro-area government bond market thus does not present itself as a challenger to the U.S. market, which benefits from having a single issuer— the U.S. Treasury. In addition, in the United States, the Federal Reserve plays a role in the liquidity of the government bond market.[17] Prati and Schinasi (1997) argue that the use of open market operations as the primary tool of monetary policy by the Federal Reserve "has fostered the development of efficient money and securities markets in the United States." Daily Federal Reserve activity in the securities market, they state, occurs not simply from a monetary policy objective but the desire to promote "the smooth functioning and stability of financial markets." Whereas, the infrequent interventions by individual European central banks in securities markets "tended to discourage the development of private securities markets and foster the predominance of bank-intermediated finance." The ECB has continued this practice of infrequent interventions. In general, it is active in securities markets only once per week.

For now U.S. financial markets continue to lead the world in both size and liquidity. As a result, the U.S. dollar remains the major currency in international bond markets. The euro, however, has already become a major player in these markets, and its use will likely expand as euro-area financial market integration proceeds. The development of a euro-area capital market similar to the U.S. market should provide benefits to both economies by increasing the options available to borrowers and lenders on both sides of the Atlantic.

Vehicle Currency

There are no direct data available on vehicle currencies, but this information can be gleaned from the shares of currencies in foreign exchange transactions, as shown in Table 8.[18] In 1998 the dollar was involved in 87 percent of all currency exchanges.[19] The euro legacy currencies were involved in 52 percent of all exchanges, with the Deutsche mark the most often traded of these currencies. The yen was used in 21 percent of all currency trades. The dollar's dominance was especially clear in forward and swap transactions. The dollar was involved in 81 percent of all forward trades compared with the mark's and yen's shares of 28 and 27 percent, respectively. In swaps the contrast was even greater. The dollar was involved in 95 percent of all swaps, with the mark and yen taking part in 20 and 17 percent, respectively, of all trades.

The use of the dollar in foreign exchange transactions was well above its use in international trade and debt contracts, indicating its role as a vehicle currency. The BIS (1999) notes that evidence of the dollar's role as a vehicle currency is provided by its use in seven of the ten most heavily traded currency pairs. The report also notes that it is standard practice for the dollar to be used as a vehicle currency in swaps, which explains the high percentage of swaps involving the U.S. dollar and the low use of the yen and mark in these trades.

The use of a currency as a vehicle currency is determined primarily by transactions costs. Transactions costs are inversely related to volume in each bilateral currency market.[20] This volume is in turn determined by a currency's share in international trade and capital flows. Thus, the use of a currency in invoicing international trade, in international capital markets, and as a reserve currency lowers the transactions costs associated with the use of that currency.

A vehicle currency emerges whenever the indirect exchange costs through the vehicle are less than direct exchange costs between two non-vehicle currencies. For example, given the depth of the exchange market for dollars, it may be less costly to exchange Mexican pesos for U.S. dollars and then exchange U.S. dollars for Korean won rather than to exchange pesos directly for won. Indeed, the existence of transaction costs may reinforce the use of the dollar as an invoice currency.

The extent of liquidity in asset markets also affects the development of a vehicle currency. Banks prefer to hold most of their foreign currencies in the form of interest-earning assets rather than cash. The liquidity of these assets is a key determinant of the transactions costs involved in switching from one currency to another. Liquidity is determined not simply by the size of a country's capital markets but also by the extent to which secondary markets operate.

The prospects of the euro becoming an important vehicle currency thus depend primarily on the transactions costs associated with euro exchanges. Clearly the size of the euro currency market relative to the markets for individual euro currencies will result in lower relative transactions costs for the euro. These transactions costs will also depend on the extent to which the euro is adopted as (1) an invoice currency, (2) a reserve currency, and (3) a prevalent currency in international capital markets.

Preliminary data indicate that the euro has not increased its role as a vehicle currency to a level beyond that of the mark. According to the BIS (2000a), the market share of the euro in currency markets during 1999 was close to the share of the Deutsche mark in 1998. Indeed, because a vehicle currency is no longer needed to facilitate exchanges among the euro currencies, the use of the euro as a vehicle currency has probably declined relative to that of the mark. Evidence on the limited use of the euro as a vehicle currency is also provided by data from foreign exchange markets in emerging market countries. The use of the euro in these markets during 1999 was concentrated in Eastern Europe, again similar to that of the mark in 1998. In Thailand and Korea for example, the euro was involved in less than 1 percent of local currency trades (BIS 2000a).

Substitute Currency

Another role that an international currency may play is as a substitute for domestic-currency transactions. Uncertainty surrounding the purchasing power of a domestic currency can lead to the use of a foreign currency as a unit of account, store of value, and medium of exchange in the domestic economy. This generally occurs as a result of hyperinflation and/or political instability.

In the decades prior to the creation of the euro, the dollar and the mark were the only currencies used extensively outside their respective borders, with the dollar being the predominate substitute currency. In part, this predominance of the dollar was a result of the links between the United States and countries using a substitute currency. Nevertheless, the ease of availability of the dollar, which both determines and encourages its other uses as an international currency, continues to facilitate the use of the dollar as a substitute currency.

Measures of the extent to which currencies are used as substitute currencies are not easily obtained. However, the best estimates indicate that about 55 percent of the total U.S. currency held by the non-bank public was held abroad at the end of 1995.[21]

Seignorage Revenues from Foreign Holdings of U.S. Dollars
Figure 2

Billions of 1996 $ **Percent of federal government expenditures**

Source: Department of Commerce, Bureau of Economic Analysis, and Board of Governors of the Federal Reserve System.

About 35 percent of Deutsche mark holdings were abroad (Seitz, 1995).

The use of the U.S. dollar as a substitute currency began in earnest in the 1920s as a result of hyperinflations in several European countries.[22] Its use in Latin America expanded in the 1980s also as a result of hyperinflation. Most recently, the collapse of the Soviet Union expanded the use of the dollar in that region.[23] Although the dollar is the preferred substitute currency in the former Soviet Union, the German mark is more prevalent in some Eastern European countries as well as in the former Yugoslav republics.

The use of the dollar as a substitute currency provides a direct benefit to the United States through seigniorage earnings. These earnings are generally estimated by calculating the amount the U.S. government would have to pay if, rather than holding cash, individuals in these countries held U.S. Treasury securities. The top panel of Figure 2 provides a rough estimate of the real seigniorage earned by the United States as a result of foreign holdings of U.S. currency during the period 1973-99.[24] In real terms, seigniorage revenues have averaged $8.7 billion on a yearly basis over this period. One method of estimating the importance of these seigniorage revenues is to calculate the share of government expenditures accounted for by these revenues. This is shown in the right panel of Figure 2. On average less than 1 percent of the expenditures of the U.S. federal government have been financed by seigniorage revenues on currency held abroad.[25]

The euro is not likely to rapidly replace the dollar as the substitute currency of choice. In fact, the use of the euro as a substitute currency is likely to lag behind its use as an international currency. Foreign holders of a substitute currency want a stable, secure currency. Uncertainty surrounding the value of the euro, particularly given its decline against the dollar during the first two years of its existence, will limit the near-term attractiveness of the euro as a substitute currency.

If the euro does become increasingly used as a substitute currency, the seigniorage earnings of the ECB will rise. It is difficult to predict how large these revenues might be, as they depend on the world demand for substitute currencies, the shares of the euro and the dollar, and interest rate conditions. Emerson et al. (1992) estimated that these seigniorage revenues would, at most, amount to $2.5 billion a year for the ECB.

Currency Pegs
Table 9

Year	U.S. dollar Number	Percent	Euro currencies Number	Percent	Other E.U. Number	Percent
1975	52	40.6	14	10.9	8	6.3
1980	39	27.7	15	10.6	1	0.7
1985	31	20.8	14	9.4	1	0.7
1990	25	16.2	15	9.7	0	0.0
1995	22	12.2	17	9.4	0	0.0
2000	23	12.6	24	13.2	0	0.0

Source: IMF, *Annual Report on Exchange Arrangements and Exchange Restrictions*, various issues.

The Official Uses of an International Currency

Exchange Rate Peg

Under the Bretton Woods system that existed from 1946 to 1973, most currencies in the world were tied to the U.S. dollar. With the demise of the Bretton Woods system, many countries chose to let their currencies float while others set the value of their currency against that of another country. Of those countries choosing the latter option, most continued to peg their currency to the U.S. dollar. In 1975, 52 members countries (about 41 percent) of the International Monetary Fund (IMF) pegged their currency to the dollar, as shown in Table 9. The euro legacy currencies were the second most popular choice. The French franc was the peg for the African Financial Community (CFA) franc, the currency used by the then 13 members of the CFA; and the Spanish peseta was the exchange rate peg for the currency of Equatorial Guinea. The pound was the only other European Union currency to be used as an exchange rate peg.

Over time the popularity of currency pegs has declined. However, both the number and percentage of member countries pegging their currencies to the euro have risen. In 2000, 24 IMF member countries tied their currencies to the euro.[26] The 14 CFA members continue to constitute the majority of countries whose currencies are tied to the euro. Most of the remaining 10 countries whose currencies are pegged to the euro hope to be in the first or second wave of enlargements of the European Union. In addition, Denmark, which is one of the three members of the European Union who are not currently members of the euro area, ties its currency to the euro through the Exchange Rate Mechanism (ERM) II.[27]

According to these data, the U.S. dollar is now the second most popular choice for a currency peg, with 23 countries officially tying their currencies to the dollar.[28] In practice, however, the dollar remains the currency against which most countries limit movements in their domestic currencies. For example, 20 countries in addition to those listed in Table 9 strictly limit the movement of their domestic currencies against the dollar. Some of these currencies are officially tied to another currency. Jordan, for example, officially pegs its currency to the SDR but in practice pegs to the U.S. dollar.

The primary reason countries choose to peg their currency to another currency is to reduce exchange rate risk and/or to control inflation. Keeping the currency stable against the peg, or setting limits on exchange rate changes, minimizes the risk to those borrowing or lending in foreign currencies or engaged in international trade. The unexpected failure

Currency Competition of Foreign Exchange Reserves
Figure 3

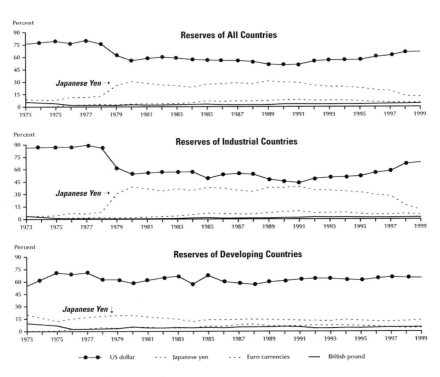

Source: IMF, Annual Report (various years).

of a currency peg, however, can produce sharp changes in the exchange value of the local currency and lead to losses on contracts priced in foreign currencies. Partly as a result, pegs have become less popular over the last 30 years. For those countries who do peg, the currency choice is usually determined by trade and financial links. This explains why, among countries with currency pegs, Latin American and Caribbean countries are pegged to the dollar while most European and African countries peg to the euro. Likewise, because oil is priced in dollars on world markets, many oil exporting countries either officially or in practice limit the fluctuations of their currency against the dollar.

The introduction of the euro has not resulted in any countries shifting their peg from the dollar to the euro. Nonetheless, it is likely that the share of currencies pegged to the euro will rise as more of the countries hoping to be admitted to the European Union may peg their currencies to the euro. In addition, any European Union country wanting to enter the euro area will have to first peg to the euro.

Any effect on the euro area and the United States caused by an increase in the number of countries pegging their currencies to the euro relative to those pegging to the dollar will occur through the effects of these pegs on foreign currency reserves.

Reserve Currency

In 1973 the dollar accounted for 76.1 percent of the official foreign currency reserves held by the member countries of the IMF, as shown in the top panel of Figure 3. The euro legacy currencies had an 8.7 percent share of foreign currency reserves, and the pound sterling had a 5.6 percent share. Holdings of yen were only 0.1 percent of total reserves.

Currency Composition of Long-Term Debt in Developing Countries (Percent)
Table 10

Currency	1970	1980	1990	1999
U.S. dollar	47.1	49.8	41.2	56.0
Japanese yen	2.3	6.9	10.5	12.6
Euro-area currencies	13.8	12.1	14.3	9.3
Pound sterling	11.2	3.4	2.3	1.2
Multiple currencies	11.6	10.9	14.7	8.2
Other currencies	14.0	16.9	17.0	12.7

Source: World Bank, *Global Development Finance*, 2001.

The dollar's share in foreign currency reserves declined in the late 1970s as some countries diversified their holdings, shifting primarily into euro legacy currencies, particularly Deutsche marks. Although the dollar's share fell again in the late 1980s, it has increased somewhat since 1991 to stand at 66.2 percent in 1999. [29] The share of the euro currencies peaked in 1989 at 31.1 percent and has fallen steadily since then, standing at 12.5 percent in 1999. The share of the yen rose slowly through most of the 1970s and 1980s, reaching a peak of 8.5 percent in 1991. Since then the yen's share has fallen, reaching 5.1 percent in 1999.

In the 1970s the developing countries, as a group, had more diversified holdings of foreign currencies than did the industrial countries, as shown in the middle and lower panels of Figure 3. Throughout most of the 1980s and 1990s, however, the developing countries held a greater share of their reserves in dollars than did the industrial countries. Currently there is little difference in the currency composition of reserves across developing and industrial countries. These changes can be explained by examining why countries hold reserves. Governments and central banks hold reserves for three main purposes: (i) to finance imports; (ii) to finance foreign debt; and (iii) to intervene in currency markets to manage the exchange rate. [30] In advanced economies, private markets generally fulfill the role of financing trade and debt. Hence, reserves are held primarily for intervention purposes.

In developing countries all three purposes are important. The currencies in which imports are invoiced in developing countries is a key determinant of the composition of reserves. Similarly, because reserves also are important for financing foreign debt, the currency composition of this debt will affect the currency composition of reserves. As shown in Table 10, the long-term debt of developing countries is most commonly denominated in U.S. dollars.

Euro-area currencies are the next preferred choice, but this share has declined slightly over the past 30 years. Most noticeable has been the decline in the use of the pound in debt contracts of developing countries. This decline is partly reflected in the relative fall in pound reserves held by developing countries. In contrast, the rise in use of the yen in debt contracts between 1970 and 1990 is reflected in the rise in yen foreign exchange reserves.

The currency choice of reserves for intervention purposes depends in part on a country's exchange rate regime. Heller and Knight (1978) showed that, if a country pegged its exchange rate to a particular currency, that currency's share in its reserves rose. Dooley et al. (1989) showed that industrial economies with flexible exchange rates had a high share of dollar reserves and a low share of Deutsche mark reserves. Among industrial economies, the main fixed exchange rate regime was the ERM. The establishment of the ERM in 1979 coincides with the sharp rise in the share of euro legacy currencies (particularly marks) in the foreign currency reserves of industrial economies.[31] The importance of the exchange rate arrangement in determining the currency composition of a country's reserves is linked to the use of these reserves for intervening in the currency markets.

The risk and return on currencies is also a factor in determining the currency composition of reserves. Most reserves are held in the form of government securities. Thus, changes in the relative return on these securities in conjunction with the depreciation risk, particularly if sustained over a long period, may cause shifts in a country's composition of reserves. In addition, the liquidity of government securities markets is a factor in determining the choice of reserve currency because reserves may need to be sold quickly for intervention purposes.

What has been the initial effect of the creation of the euro on the currency composition of reserves? As Figure 3 indicates, the dollar's share has risen and the euro's share has fallen. This occurred for two reasons: the elimination of ecu reserves and the reclassification of intra-euro-area holdings of euro currency reserves.[32] At the end of 1997, ecu reserves accounted for 10.7 percent of the foreign currency reserves of industrial countries and 5.0 percent of the reserves of all countries. Most of these ecu reserves were claims on the European Monetary Institute, the precursor to the European Central Bank. They had been issued to the central banks of the European Union countries in exchange for gold and dollar deposits. In late 1998 the deposits were returned to these central banks and the ecu reserves were eliminated. This explains the sharp drop in euro legacy currency reserves in the industrial countries in 1998. With the advent of the euro in 1999, holdings by euro-area countries of the euro legacy currencies ceased to be foreign currency reserves. This led to a further decline in the share of the euro in the foreign currency reserves of industrial countries.

The importance of the transition to the euro in driving movements in the currency composition of worldwide reserves over the last two years is further indicated by looking at the developing countries. As the bottom panel of Figure 3 indicates, the euro share of reserves held by developing countries rose slightly in the last few years. In 1997 the euro legacy currencies accounted for 12 percent of the reserves of developing countries. At the end of 1999, the euro accounted for 13.6 percent of their reserves. Thus, while there is no evidence that the creation of the euro has led to a drop in the relative holdings of euros outside the euro area, neither is there evidence of a marked rise in these holdings.

The lack of a noticeable shift in the composition of world reserves is not surprising. The trade and debt financing needs of the developing countries remain primarily in dollars. Certainly, as the euro's use as an international medium of exchange rises, countries are likely to increase their holdings of euro reserves. It is also unlikely that the creation of the euro has had a noticeable effect on the demand for reserves for intervention purposes.[33] Central banks are unlikely to sell much of their dollar holdings to buy euros without good cause. The ECB notes "central banks traditionally refrain from abrupt and large changes in the level and composition of their foreign reserves" (ECB, 1999, p. 41). Johnson (1994) argues that as long as the Federal Reserve achieves an acceptable degree of price stability in the United States, changes in reserve holdings should occur gradually.

The implications of a shift in international reserves away from the U.S. dollar and toward the euro depend on the speed at which such a change would occur. A massive sale of dollars by central banks and the purchase of euros would cause a sharp drop in the value of the dollar relative to the euro. This shift would also raise interest rates on U.S. government securities since, as noted above, most reserves are held in government securities. In contrast, the euro would rise in value and interest rates in the euro area would drop. As discussed above, this scenario is improbable. The ECB (1999) asserts that portfolio shifts are "expected to take place at a slower pace in the central bank community than in the private sector." Indeed, despite concerns with the euro area over the decline in the foreign exchange value of the euro, the national central banks have not sold noticeable amounts of their substantial holdings of dollar reserves.[34]

A gradual shift in international reserves toward the euro is unlikely to have much effect on the United States or the euro area. Because nearly all international reserves are invested in government securities, the reserve currency country does not gain any seigniorage benefits. The most important benefit is the possibility that reserve currency status lowers the interest rate at which the government can borrow. Thus, it is argued that the euro area will benefit through a reduction in the interest rate at which governments can borrow while the U.S. government will see its borrowing costs rise.

A negative interest rate effect on the United States would require not simply a rise in the share of reserves held in euros, but an absolute decline in holdings of dollar reserves. Given the trends in the growth of worldwide reserves, the latter change will take longer (if ever) to occur than the former. In addition, the extent of the interest rate benefit to a reserve currency is not well established. Blinder (1996) is skeptical of the importance of such a link. He argues that if such a benefit were significant then there should be a larger difference between interest rates on government and corporate bonds in the United States than in other major countries; yet he finds no evidence to support this argument. The euro area is more likely to see a fall in government borrowing costs from measures to standardize government bond markets than through an increase in the use of the euro as a reserve currency (BIS, 2000b).

Intervention Currency

A corollary to the dollar's role as the primary international reserve currency is its use as the main currency for intervening in foreign exchange markets. This latter role is also aided by the use of the dollar as a vehicle currency and by the liquidity of the U.S. bond market, as discussed earlier in this article. Although data on interventions are limited, it is believed that nearly all intervention in the currencies markets, with the exception of those undertaken by the United States, takes place in dollars.[35]

The most important determinants of the choice of intervention currency are liquidity and acceptability. In countries that peg their exchange rate, the currency peg will determine the intervention currency. Since countries prefer to hold their reserves in the form of interest-earning assets, the liquidity of these assets is extremely important. The relative illiquidity of the euro-area and Japanese bond markets gives the dollar an advantage over the use of these two currencies.[36]

The acceptability of an international currency is related to its role as a medium of exchange for private transactions. The more frequently a currency is used for private transactions the larger is the exchange market for that currency, which increases the ease with which a country can use the currency for intervention purposes.

Conclusion

Factors determining whether a country's currency will be used readily outside its border include the size and openness of its economy and financial markets as well as its macroeconomic policy environment. In the postwar period, these factors have favored the use of the U.S. dollar as the predominant international currency. In the early postwar period, there were few alternatives to the dollar in international markets as a result of restrictions on convertibility and limits on capital mobility. In the last several decades, as other major economic powers emerged (notably Germany and Japan) and markets opened, the dollar's dominance has been reduced. Nonetheless, the dollar has remained the most important international currency.

On January 1, 1999, the euro was created, linking an economic area nearly the size of the U.S. economy. The euro's impact will be felt in markets throughout the world economy. For the first time the dollar faces a potential challenge to its role as the world's major international currency.

In the first two years of its existence, the euro's presence has been felt most in international securities markets. Issues of euro-denominated foreign bonds surged in 1999. The euro legacy currencies accounted for 28.0 percent of new bond issues in 1998. The share of new issues denominated in euros was 38.3 percent in 1999. In international money markets, the euro's presence was even more obvious. International money market instruments denominated in euros in 1999 accounted for 32.9 percent of the market, well above the 17.2 percent share of the legacy currencies in 1998. Although the euro's share of international debt securities declined in 2000, the euro continues to be a widely used alternative to the dollar in these markets. Little change, however, has occurred in the use of the euro relative to the dollar in the other functions of an international currency.

In the short term there is unlikely to be much change in this pattern. Over time, however, the use of the euro relative to the dollar will likely increase, particularly as euro-area financial markets become more integrated and more liquid. Nevertheless, the decline in the dollar's share and the rise in the euro's share in international transactions is likely to occur gradually. In part, this is because the more often a currency is used in international transactions, the lower are the costs associated with using that currency and hence the more attractive is the currency for conducting international exchanges. Thus, there is much inertia in the choice of an international currency. The British pound, for example, continued to play a major role as an international currency long after its dominance of the global economy waned.

Policies on the part of the governments and central banks in the euro area and the United States will play a crucial role in the use of their currencies in international markets. The ability of the euro-area governments to foster sustained economic growth in the region is important. Equally important is the credibility of the ECB. The ability of the ECB to maintain a low inflationary environment in the euro area is a key factor in determining the use of the euro outside the region. In addition, concerns about the attachment of European governments and the public to a monetary union will undermine the use of the euro in international markets.

The ultimate determinants of the continued use of the dollar as an international currency are the economic policies and conditions in the United States. As Lawrence Summers noted when he was Deputy Secretary of the U.S. Treasury, "Ultimately, the dollar's relative standing in the international financial system will always depend more on developments here than on events elsewhere" (Summers, 1997). In the absence of an economic crisis in the United States, the dollar is not likely to lose its standing as the most popular international currency.

Any shifts in the roles of the dollar and euro will affect both the United States and the European Union. The extent to which a country benefits from having its currency used internationally is not clear. The use of a currency for invoicing may reduce the costs borne by that country's importers, but these costs may be small at best. The use of a currency as a reserve currency may reduce the borrowing costs of that country's government, but again the extent of this benefit is not known. The use of a currency as a substitute currency does provide seigniorage benefits but also complicates monetary policy. Moreover, if these seigniorage revenues arise as a result of an economic and/or political instability, the benefit to the country earning the seigniorage may be more than offset by the costs of the instability.

The creation of the euro has the potential to produce benefits to both the United States and the euro area that could far outweigh the effects of any shifts in international currency holdings. Developments in European financial markets alone should increase the investment options available to consumers as well as reduce the costs of borrowing for businesses. These developments will benefit those on both sides of the Atlantic.

Patricia S. Pollard is a research officer and economist at the Federal Reserve Bank of St. Louis. Heidi L. Beyer provided research assistance.

Endnotes

1 Although the national currencies will continue to exist until 2002, they are merely subunits of the euro.

2 Between the time that the Treaty on European Union established the process for the completion of economic and monetary union and the creation of the euro, many economists studied the likely international role of the euro. Among these are Bekx (1998), Bénassy-Quéré, Mojon, and Schor (1998), Bergsten (1997), Hartmann (1996), Johnson (1994), Kenen (1993), Pollard (1998), and Portes and Ray (1998). Most of these studies concluded that the euro would be a major international currency but that the process would be gradual. Bergsten and Portes and Ray, however, expected a quick ascent for the euro.

3 This is the most difficult role for currency to achieve. Inflation reduces the purchasing power of money. As long as inflation is moderate, the ability of money to operate as a unit of account and medium of exchange ensure its continued use. Hyperinflation causes money to lose its store of value function and is associated with an increase in the use of barter and substitute currencies.

4 This sectoral division of the three functions of international money was first adopted by Cohen (1971).

5 In 1994 the Chinese economy surpassed the size of the Japanese economy. Based on purchasing power parity valuations of GDP, China accounted for 11.2 percent of the world's output in 1999. Nevertheless, Japan remains the world's third major economic power.

6 An internationalization ratio greater than or equal to 1.0 does not imply that all of the home country's exports are priced in its currency. According to data provided in Bekx (1998) in 1995, 92 percent of U.S. exports, 75 percent of German exports, 62 percent of British exports, and 52 percent of French exports were invoiced in their domestic currencies.

7 In October 2000, Iraq began requiring payment for its oil exports in euros. There is no indication that this move will be followed by other major oil producers. A general shift to requiring payment in euros would probably hasten a switch to pricing oil in euros, but such a dual system is not without precedent. Bénassy and Deusy-Fournier (1994) state that until 1974 oil was priced in dollars, but payment was made in pounds sterling.

8 Measured by a 95 percent or higher probability.

9 The data in Tables 5 and 6 rely on different sources and hence may not be directly comparable.

10 Some policymakers in Switzerland were concerned that the creation of the euro might result in a sharp rise in demand for assets denominated in Swiss francs. See Laxton and Prasad (1997) for an analysis of this argument.

11 Kool (2000) addresses the use of the euro in international bond markets.

12 The data in Table 7 do not exclude bank transactions between members of the euro area.

13 TARGET is an acronym for Trans-European Automated Real-time Gross settlement Express Transfer system.

14 For a discussion of developments in these markets, see European Central Bank (2000) and International Monetary Fund (1999).

15 See Santillán et al. (2000) for an analysis of the effects of the euro on the money and bond markets in Europe.

16 Unlike the trade data, international bond market data currently do not exclude cross-border transactions within the euro area.

17 The recent reduction in the federal debt has raised concerns about the future liquidity of the U.S. Treasury market. See Fleming (2000) and Bennet et al. (2000) for a discussion of the effects of the decline in public debt and ways to maintain liquidity in the Treasury market.

18 These data are gathered from a triennial survey of foreign exchange markets conducted by the BIS.

19 Since there are two currencies involved in an exchange, the total share of all currencies traded on international exchanges will equal 200 percent. However, a single currency can, at most, be involved in 100 percent of all exchanges.

20 The use of transactions cost theory to explain the rise of a vehicle currency was developed by Krugman (1980) and Chrystal (1984).

21 See Anderson and Rasche (2000) and Porter and Judson (1996). According to Anderson and Rasche, the share of U.S. currency held abroad increased throughout the 1970s and 1980s but fell slightly in the 1990s.

22 The dollar was preferred to the British pound as the latter had yet to return to the gold standard after World War I.

23 According to the U.S. Treasury (2000), Argentina and Russia are believed to have the largest holdings of U.S. currency outside the United States.

24 These seigniorage revenues are estimated by using the interest rate on one-year Treasury bills and adjusting nominal revenues using the GDP deflator.

[25] The seigniorage benefits must be weighed against the problems the foreign holdings of currency create for monetary policy. As Porter and Judson (1996) note, if foreign demand for a country's currency is unrelated to domestic demand, then the interpretation of movements in monetary aggregates becomes more difficult.

[26] These 24 include San Marino, which uses the Italian lira as its currency, and Greece, which is now a member of the euro area.

[27] Established in 1979, ERM was the fixed exchange rate system of the European Monetary System. With the creation of the euro, ERM was replaced by ERM II, linking the currencies of Denmark and Greece (until January 2001) to the euro.

[28] These 23 include five countries (Ecuador, Marshall Island, Micronesia, Palau, and Panama) that use the U.S. dollar as the local currency. In January 2001, El Salvador (which is not included in the 23) also adopted the U.S. dollar.

[29] These shifts in holdings of reserves are affected both by changes in the physical holdings of currency and changes in exchange rates. Since the IMF measures reserve holdings in U.S. dollars, a rise in the exchange value of the dollar ceteris paribus will raise the dollar share of foreign exchange reserves.

[30] See Ben-Bassat (1980, 1984) and Dooley et al. (1989).

[31] Data in Masson and Turtelboom (1997) indicate that the European Union countries held 69 percent of the Deutsche mark reserves held by industrial countries in 1995.

[32] The ECU, or more formally, European currency unit, was a weighted average of the European Union currencies. Although it never existed as a paper currency, it was used as the unit of account for official European Union activities and a small ecu private bond market existed. The ecu was superceded by the euro.

[33] Hong Kong, however, announced in late 1999 that it was increasing the share of the euro in its foreign currency reserves.

[34] The national central banks transferred a small portion of their reserves to the ECB upon its creation but kept most of the remaining reserves. As of September 2000, the foreign exchange reserves of the ECB were $43.7 billion while the reserves of the national central banks were $212.2 billion. In contrast, the United States held $31.2 billion in foreign exchange reserves. Although the national central banks may have wanted to hold on to their reserves to handle any possible crisis in the early years of the euro, the available pool of reserves is more than sufficient to handle any problems.

[35] Under the rules of the ERM, mandatory interventions (when the exchange rate reached its upper or lower limit) had to take place in one of the member currencies. Non-mandatory (intra-band) interventions could take place in any currency, and generally dollars were used. See Giavazzi (1989) for details.

[36] The existence of swap arrangements between central banks can offset some of these liquidity problems.

References

Anderson, Richard G. and Rasche, Robert H. "The Domestic Adjusted Monetary Base." Working Paper 2000-002A, Federal Reserve Bank of St. Louis, January 2000.

Bank for International Settlements. *BIS Quarterly Review.* Basle: BIS, February 2000a.

_____. 70th Annual Report. Basle: BIS, June 2000b.

_____. *Central Bank Survey of Foreign Exchange and Derivatives Market Activity 1998.* Basle: BIS, May 1999.

Bekx, Peter. "The Implications of the Introduction of the Euro for Non-EU Countries." Euro Papers Number 26, European Commission, Directorate General Economic and Financial Affairs, July 1998.

Ben-Bassat, Avraham. "The Optimal Composition of Foreign Exchange Reserves." *Journal of International Economics,* May 1980, 10(2), pp. 285-95.

_____. "Reserve-Currency Diversification and the Substitution Account." *Princeton Studies in International Finance,* 1984 (53).

Bénassy, Agnès and Deusy-Fournier, Pierre. "Competition Among the World's Dominant Currencies Since Bretton Woods Collapsed." Unpublished manuscript, Centre for International Economics (CEPII), Paris, April 1994.

Bénassy-Quéré, Agnès; Mojon, Benoît and Schor, Armand-Denis. "The International Role of the Euro." Working Paper 98/03, CEPII, July 1998.

Bennett, Paul; Garbade, Kenneth and Kambhu, John. "Enhancing the Liquidity of U.S. Treasury Securities in an Era of Surplus." *Federal Reserve Bank of New York Economic Policy Review,* April 2000, 6(1), pp. 89-119.

Bergsten, C. Fred. "The Dollar and the Euro." *Foreign Affairs,* July/August 1997, 76(4), pp. 83-95.

Black, Stanley W. "The International Use of Currencies," in Yoshi Suzuki, Junichi Miyake, and Mitsuaki Okabe, eds., The *Evolution of the International Monetary System: How Can Efficiency and Stability Be Achieved?* Tokyo: University of Tokyo Press, 1990.

Blinder, Alan S. "The Role of the Dollar as an International Currency." *Eastern Economic Journal,* Spring 1996, 22(2), pp. 127-36.

Cecchetti, Stephen G. "Legal Structure, Financial Structure, and the Monetary Policy Transmission Mechanism." Working Paper No. 7151, National Bureau of Economic Research, June 1999.

Chrystal, K. Alec. "On the Theory of International Money," in John Black and Graeme S. Dorrance, eds., *Problems of International Finance.* New York: St. Martin's Press, 1984.

Cohen, Benjamin J. *The Future of Sterling as an International Currency.* London: Macmillian Press, 1971.

Dooley, Michael P.; Lizondo, J. Saul and Mathieson, Donald J. "The Currency Composition of Foreign Exchange Reserves." *IMF Staff Papers,* June 1989, 36(2), pp. 385-434.

Emerson, Michael; Gros, Daniel; Italianer, Alexander; Pisani-Ferry, Jean and Reichenbach, Horst. *One Market, One Money: An Evaluation of the Potential Benefits and Costs of Forming an Economic and Monetary Union.* Oxford: Oxford University Press, 1992.

European Central Bank. "The Euro Area One Year After the Introduction of the Euro: Key Characteristics and Changes in the Financial Structure." *ECB Monthly Bulletin,* January 2000, pp. 35-49.

_____. "The International Role of the Euro." *ECB Monthly Bulletin,* August 1999, pp. 31-53.

Fleming, Michael J. "The Benchmark U.S. Treasury Market: Recent Performance and Possible Alternatives." Federal Reserve Board of New York *Economic Policy Review,* April 2000, pp. 129-45.

Giavazzi, Francesco. "The European Monetary System: Lessons from Europe and Perspectives in Europe." *Economic and Social Review,* January 1989, 20(2), pp. 73-90.

Grassman, Sven. "A Fundamental Symmetry in International Payments Patterns." *Journal of International Economics,* May 1973, 3(2), pp. 105-16.

Hartmann, Philipp. "The Future of the Euro as an International Currency: A Transactions Perspective." London School of Economics *Financial Markets Group Special Papers,* November 1996.

Heller, H. Robert and Knight, Malcom. "Reserve-Currency Preferences of Central Banks." *Princeton Essays in International Finance,* December 1978, (131).

International Monetary Fund. "Progress with European Monetary." *International Capital Markets: Developments, Prospects, and Key Policy Issues,* September 1999.

Johnson, Karen H. "International Dimension of European Monetary Union: Implications for the Dollar." *International Financial Discussion Paper* No. 469, Board of Governors of the Federal Reserve System, May 1994.

Kenen, Peter B. "EMU, Exchange Rates and the International Monetary System." *Recherches Economiques de Louvain,* 1993, 59(1/2), pp. 257-81.

Kool, Clemens J.M. "International Bond Markets and the Introduction of the Euro," Federal Reserve Bank of St. Louis *Review,* September/October 2000, 82(5), pp. 41-56.

Kregel, Jan A. "Can European Banks Survive a Unified Currency in a Nationally Segmented Capital Market?" Working Paper No. 305, Jerome Levy Economics Institute, July 2000.

Krugman, Paul. "Vehicle Currencies and the Structure of International Exchange." *Journal of Money, Credit and Banking,* August 1980, 12(3), pp. 513-26.

Laxton, Douglas and Prasad, Eswar. "Possible Effects of European Monetary Union on Switzerland: A Case Study of Policy Dilemmas Caused by Low Inflation and the Nominal Interest Rate Floor." Working Paper WP/97/23, International Monetary Fund, March 1997.

Magee, Stephen, P. and Rao, Ramish K.S. "Vehicle and Nonvehicle Currencies in International Trade." *American Economic Review,* May 1980, 70(2), pp. 368-73.

Masson, Paul R. and Turtelboom, Bart G. "Characteristics of the Euro, the Demand for Reserves, and Policy Coordination Under EMU." Working Paper No. 97/58, International Monetary Fund, May 1997.

Page, S. "The Choice of Invoicing Currency in Merchandise Trade." *National Institute Economic Review,* November 1981, 85, pp. 60-72.

Pollard, Patricia S. "The Role of the Euro as an International Currency." *The Columbia Journal of European Law,* Spring 1998, pp. 395-420.

Porter, Richard D. and Judson, Ruth A. "The Location of U.S. Currency: How Much Is Abroad?" *Federal Reserve Bulletin,* October 1996, 82(10), pp. 883-903.

Portes, Richard and Rey, Hélène. "The Emergence of the Euro as an International Currency," in *EMU: Prospects and Challenges for the Euro.* Oxford: Blackwell Publishers, 1998.

Prati, Alessandro and Schinasi, Garry J. "European Monetary Union and International Capital Markets: Structural Implications and Risks." Working Paper No. 97/62, International Monetary Fund, May 1997.

Santillán, Javier; Bayle, Marc and Thygesen, Christian. "The Impact of the Euro on Money and Bond Markets." Occasional Paper No. 1, European Central Bank, July 2000.

Seitz, Franz. "The Circulation of Deutsche Mark Abroad." Discussion Paper No. 1/95, Economic Research Centre of the Deutsche Bundesbank, May 1995.

Summers, Lawrence H. *Testimony Before the Senate Budget Committee,* 21 October 1997.

Tavlas, George. "The International Use of the U.S. Dollar: An Optimum Currency Area Perspective." *The World Economy,* September 1997, 20(6), pp. 709-47.

United States Treasury Department and the Board of Governors of the Federal Reserve System. *The Use and Counterfeiting of United States Currency Abroad.* Washington D.C.: February 2000.

30

European Labor Markets and EMU Challenges Ahead

RÜDIGER SOLTWEDEL,
DIRK DOHSE, &
CHRISTIANE KRIETER-BODEN

The debate about European Economic and Monetary Union (EMU) has so far been dominated by questions of fiscal convergence and macroeconomic stability. Far less attention has been given to EMU's effects on labor markets, although labor market performance will be crucial in determining the long-term success or failure of EMU.

Currency unions like EMU have certain undisputed benefits. They reduce the costs for foreign exchange and hedging transactions and heat up competition in goods and factor markets, which stimulates trade, investment, growth, and employment. However, the members of currency unions must also relinquish two important policy instruments for responding to economic shocks: an independent monetary policy and currency devaluation. When these tools are unavailable, asymmetric shocks—shocks that affect some countries or regions in a currency union but not others—put pressure on national labor markets and may boost unemployment rates in affected areas.

The exchange rates between the currencies of European Union (EU) member states played an important role as shock absorbers before the establishment of EMU on January 1, 1999. EU members hit by asymmetric shocks responded by adjusting prices (particularly the nominal exchange rate) rather than by adjusting output. The incidence of asymmetric shocks has been higher for Finland, Greece, Ireland, Italy, Portugal, Spain, Sweden, and the United

Kingdom than for Austria, Denmark, France, Germany, and the Benelux countries.

Among the EU members prone to asymmetric shocks, Finland, Italy, and Spain also have inflexible labor markets and are therefore the countries most likely to experience rising unemployment as they adjust to shocks (see table). From a labor market point of view, Austria and the Netherlands appear to be the EU members best prepared for EMU. Although Ireland, Portugal, and the United Kingdom have high exposure to asymmetric shocks, their labor markets are flexible enough to absorb shocks without huge increases in unemployment. In contrast, Belgium, Denmark, France, and Germany would probably see greater structural unemployment in response to shocks, however rare such shocks might be.

Historic patterns of susceptibility to shocks may not persist in the euro area, one reason being that EMU has eliminated some of the major sources of asymmetric shocks—namely, inconsistent national monetary policies and speculative attacks on national currencies; moreover, EMU members have less scope for implementing destabilizing national fiscal policies. However, even a common monetary policy can be a source of asymmetric shocks. U.S. monetary policy, for example, has generated asymmetric shocks to regions in the United States because of structural differences in regional economies.

Labor market risks in EU members, 1998

Probability of asymmetric shocks[1]	Labor market flexibility[1]	
	High	Low
Low	Austria, Netherlands	Belgium, France, Germany (Denmark)[2]
High	Ireland, Portugal (United Kingdom)[2]	France, Italy, Spain (Greece, Sweden)[2]

Source: Dohse and Krieger-Boden (1998)
[1] Compared with EU average.
[2] Countries in parentheses were not members of EMU as of May 2000.

Hence, the probability of asymmetric shocks depends upon the economic structures—and their development over time—of countries participating in a currency union. The critical question is how EMU will affect these structures and whether business cycles will be synchronized across EMU members. There are two opposing views on this question. One line of reasoning suggests that tighter forward and backward trade linkages between countries in a currency union will make their economic structures and business cycles more similar and shocks more symmetric, particularly if demand or other common shocks predominate, or if trade is concentrated within a given industry (see, for example, Frankel and Rose, 1998). The opposite line of reasoning emphasizes that, in a common currency area, there are better opportunities for the exploitation of economies of scale (for example, via localized knowledge spillovers), encouraging the geographic concentration of industries and making it more likely that a given shock will have asymmetric effects on different regions because of differences in their production structures (see, for example, Krugman, 1993).

On theoretical grounds, both hypotheses are equally plausible, and the empirical evidence is inconclusive. Our estimates suggest that, in most EU countries, regional specialization increased in the early 1980s but decreased in the early 1990s. Hence, policy should take a cautious stance and prepare for potential shocks.

A Regional Perspective

In addition to the structural differences between national economies that make some of the EU countries more susceptible to shocks than others, there are marked differences between regions within a number of EU countries. EMU is likely to affect these regions differently. For example, western Germany's Rhineland region, with its geographic proximity to Belgium, France, and the Netherlands, will most probably benefit more from the currency union than eastern Germany's Oberlausitz region, which is adjacent to Poland. Furthermore, the sectoral structure of western Germany's economy is closer to the EU norm than is that of eastern Germany's economy, which suggests that the latter may be more susceptible to asymmetric shocks than the former. The same distinction can be made between the economy of Italy's Mezzogiorno and the more advanced economies of its northern and central regions.

In fact, asymmetric shocks in the EU are much more pronounced on a regional than on a national level. Differences between the GDP growth rates of regions in the same country are almost double those between the GDP growth rates of the countries themselves.

Europe's unemployment problem also has a marked regional dimension, with unemployment rates in economically troubled regions more than 10 times higher than in the best-performing regions.

These regional unemployment disparities have not only been far more persistent in Europe than in the United States but have also become more acute over time: the dispersion of regional unemployment rates across the EU was three times higher in 1995 than in the late 1970s.

Unemployment problems are concentrated in countries and regions at the periphery of the EU: Finland, eastern Germany, Ireland, southern Italy, and southern Spain. Labor market stickiness is very pronounced (that is, labor market conditions do not change quickly in response to changes in supply and demand) in these regions, and EMU will probably have a less beneficial impact on them than on other countries or regions, because they engage in relatively little trade with the rest of EMU, profit less from the elimination of exchange rates, and are more prone to asymmetric shocks.

The major reason why EMU poses a threat to European labor markets is the high probability of region-specific (asymmetric) shocks, in combination with the lack of functioning adjustment mechanisms at the regional level. Well-functioning regional labor markets are crucial to weathering adverse region-specific shocks. Whereas labor migration plays a substantial role in allowing regions in the United States to adjust to shocks, interregional labor mobility is limited in Europe, leaving regional wage flexibility as the main adjustment mechanism. Empirical studies show, however, that wage policy in Europe is not region-specific: wage setting in prosperous regions spills over to problem regions where productivity growth is slower than in the rest of the economy. Furthermore, labor market institutions such as unemployment benefits, minimum wages, job-protection laws, and regulations governing work hours are shaped, for the most part, at the national level and offer few possibilities for region-specific adjustments to shocks.

If there is neither labor mobility nor wage flexibility, there will be either increased interregional transfers or an increase in unemployment (open or disguised) in regions hit by adverse shocks. However, long-run transfers are, in fact, not an adjustment mechanism but a practice that prevents adjustment and structural change. In addition—and not to be underestimated—massive regional transfers have substantial moral hazard effects.

Will EMU Spur Labor Market Reform?

In preparing for monetary union and responding to increasing adjustment pressures, EU members have taken steps in opposite directions. On the one hand, some countries have attempted to stifle competition, a move that might easily lead to a vicious circle. On the other hand, there are indications of a potentially virtuous circle, as several EU member states have implemented, at different speeds and to different degrees, measures to decentralize and deregulate their economies and to increase the flexibility of their labor markets (the Netherlands and the United Kingdom have gone the farthest down this road).

The vicious-circle scenario relates to the efforts of politicians, unions, and special interest groups to fend off the adjustment pressures generated by the completion of the single market, the globalization of markets, and the introduction of EMU, and to protect European workers against what they consider to be "unfair" competition and "wage dumping" by imposing minimum standards for working conditions on the basis of the EU's social charter, which was agreed upon by EU member governments in 1989, and its ensuing action program. Because differences in productivity will not disappear overnight, however, adopting uniform minimum standards may lead to rising unemployment in low-productivity countries and regions and increase demand for EU development assistance. Financing these subsidies, though, is likely to restrain the economic dynamics of the prosperous areas.

The virtuous-circle scenario builds on the fact that, by joining EMU, countries have subjected themselves to external pressures that are forcing them to adjust and that there is no turning back. Member governments might use the implementation of EMU to cut back on the welfare state and bring incentive structures into line with economic sustainability to foster market dynamics. Burda (1999) even argues that EMU is a "Trojan horse for decentralization." However, there is no room for complacency. The circle will not be virtuous unless countries adopt policies capable of fostering and harnessing the forces of structural reform.

As a matter of fact, all EU member countries committed themselves to the comprehensive and consistent labor market reforms that constitute the "job strategy" of the Organization for Economic Cooperation and Development (OECD, 1995), although they have been slow to take action. Because the various elements of labor market flexibility, such as wage flexibility, flexible work hours, and geographic mobility, are—up to a point—substitutes for broader reform, there is no need for all countries to follow the same reform model to attain higher overall labor market flexibility. Country-specific preferences may lead to different approaches to achieving flexibility with broadly similar impacts on labor market efficiency. What is crucial, though, is to take into account the inherent complementarities among broad policy areas affecting the labor market.

Institutional and Regional Diversity

The institutional homogeneity prevailing in most EMU countries may lead to a mismatch between institutions and economic conditions in problem regions and jeopardize the efficiency gains expected from the implementation of the monetary union. Given the widely divergent economic and social conditions from country to country as well as within countries, it seems appropriate not only that reform packages be country-specific but also that they take the regional dimension into account. Because of the lack of institutional variety within national employment systems, there is hardly scope for appropriate dynamic reactions to idiosyncratic shocks. To achieve broader regional diversity, opt-out clauses from nationwide regulations may be helpful.

More institutional diversity could be brought about by allowing what we call "institutional competition" among the various subnational layers of government. We see institutional competition as a means of shaping such factors as the physical and institutional infrastructure of a region, local taxes, and the responsiveness and flexibility of the local administration in order to attract mobile factors of production. Institutional competition—to borrow a concept central to the free-market theories of Austrian economist Friedrich August von Hayek—may work as a discovery procedure for superior policies and institutional arrangements that spur regional economic growth and increase regional employment.

This article draws on a paper prepared by the authors while Rüdiger Soltwedel was a visiting scholar at the IMF: "EMU Challenges European Labor Markets," IMF Working Paper 99/131 (Washington: International Monetary Fund, 1999).

Rüdiger Soltwedel is head of the Regional Economics research department at the Kiel Institute of World Economics, Kiel, Germany.

Dirk Dohse is head of the Regional Growth and Spatial Structure research group at the Kiel Institute of World Economics, Kiel, Germany.

Christiane Krieger-Boden is a staff member at the Kiel Institute of World Economics, Kiel, Germany.

References and Suggestions for Further Reading:

Michael C. Burda, 1999, "European Labor Markets and the Euro: How Much Flexibility Do We Really Need?" http://www.bundesbank.de/en/monats-bericht/7.2beitraege.htm.

Marco Buti, Daniele Franco, and Hedwige Ongena, 1998, "Fiscal Discipline and Flexibility in EMU: The Implementation of the Stability and Growth Pact," *Oxford Review of Economic Policy,* Vol. 14, No. 3, pp. 81-97.

Dirk Dohse and Christiane Krieger-Boden, 1998, "Währungsunion und Arbeitsmarkt. Auftakt zu unabdingbaren Reformen," Kieler Studien, No. 290 (Tübingen: J.C.B. Mohr).

Jeffrey A. Frankel and Andrew K. Rose, 1998, "The Endogeneity of the Optimum Currency Area Criteria," *Economic Journal,* Vol. 108, No. 449, pp. 1009-1025.

Paul Krugman, 1993, "Lessons of Massachusetts for EMU," in *Adjustment and Growth in the European Monetary Union,* ed. by Francisco Torres and Francesco Giavazzi (Cambridge University Press).

Paolo Mauro, Eswar Prasad, and Antonio Spilimbergo, 1999, Perspectives on Regional Unemployment in Europe, IMF Occasional Paper No. 177 (Washington: International Monetary Fund).

Organization for Economic Cooperation and Development, 1995, *The OECD Jobs Study: Implementing the Strategy* (Paris: OECD).

Discussion Questions

VII

1. What are asymmetric shocks? Why are they a problem for EMU countries?

2. Explain why flexible labor markets are important for the success of EMU.

3. What are some of the criticisms aimed at the ECB? Are they valid? Explain why or why not.

4. Do you think the euro will replace the US dollar as an international currency? Why or why not?

5. Do you think the EMU will be successful? Why or why not?

Financial Crises

VIII

During the 1990's, East Asian countries were experiencing double-digit growth rates and an influx of capital fueling the ever-higher expectations of future economic growth. Asian countries were considered the fastest growing, most dynamic economies in the world. When the Thai baht collapsed in 1997, few economists predicted the financial crisis that ensued. It became apparent that the Thai financial problems dubbed by some as "Baht-ulism" would spread. South Korea, Malaysia, Philippines, and Indonesia experienced currency runs, banking crises, and general financial panic.

Following the Asian crisis, Russia in August 1998 and Argentina in December 2001 experienced a currency crisis and financial collapse. Russia and Argentina's source of economic collapse differed from East Asia; both countries were forced to default on their sovereign debt. This section presents a number of articles examining the Russian crisis, Argentina's crisis, and the Asian crisis. The first article, "A Case Study of a Currency Crisis: The Russian Default of 1998" by Chiodo and Owyang, examines the events leading to Russia's currency crisis and Russia's default. The authors believe that the Asian financial crisis and government budget deficits contributed to Russia's default. They also present three currency crisis models and examine whether these models can be used to explain the Russian crisis.

During the 1990's Argentina's economy was the model economy in Latin America. Argentina had successfully eliminated hyperinflation, strengthened its banking system, and attracted foreign investment. Towards the end of 2001 and early 2002, Argentina's government defaulted on its external debt, restricted bank deposit withdrawals, and abandoned its currency board arrangement which pegged 1 peso to $1. Ramon Moreno in "Learning from Argentina's Crisis" outlines the factors causing the crisis and argues that the crisis was not unpredictable.

"The Onset of the East Asian Crisis" by Radelet and Sachs presents a systematic diagnosis of the crisis and analyzes a number of popular explanations, arguing that many of these explanations do not stand up to close scrutiny. Radelet and Sachs claim that the crisis was not predicted and they present evidence such as bond ratings and financial commentary to support their position. The chief cause of the crisis, they believe, was the dramatic swing in capital flows that occurred soon after the Thai crisis. The ensuing financial panic and poor policies by the IMF led what might have been a moderate financial crisis into a huge financial crisis. Following the crisis, many Asian countries began to look at more formal currency arrangements that might stave off a repeat of such a crisis. Mark Spiegel's paper, "Argentina's Currency Crisis: Lessons for Asia," examines this proposal in light of Argentina's currency collapse. Spiegel presents a number of currency arrangements that Asian countries have debated, ranging from an Asian Monetary Fund to an intra-Asian currency arrangement similar to the EMU. He argues that Asian countries are diverse in their degree of development and that exchange rate arrangements should not be a cure to fundamental macroeconomic problems. Spiegel concludes, "...no fixed exchange rate regime, even one as institutionally strong as Argentina's, is completely sound".

One common theme among the crises is that these countries experienced huge capital inflows, prior to the currency collapse, and huge capital outflow exacerbating the financial collapse. The final article in this section, "Capital Controls and Emerging Markets" by Moreno, examines the costs and benefits of capital controls. He presents two case studies, Chile and Malaysia, to illustrate some of the difficulties implementing capital controls and the trade-offs associated with the controls.

A Case Study of a Currency Crisis: The Russian Default of 1998

31

A B B I G A I L   J .   **C H I O D O**   &
M I C H A E L   T .   **O W Y A N G**

A currency crisis can be defined as a speculative attack on a country's currency that can result in a forced devaluation and possible debt default. One example of a currency crisis occurred in Russia in 1998 and led to the devaluation of the ruble and the default on public and private debt.[1] Currency crises such as Russia's are often thought to emerge from a variety of economic conditions, such as large deficits and low foreign reserves. They sometimes appear to be triggered by similar crises nearby, although the spillover from these contagious crises does not infect all neighboring economies—only those vulnerable to a crisis themselves. In this paper, we examine the conditions under which an economy can become vulnerable to a currency crisis. We review three models of currency crises, paying particular attention to the events leading up to a speculative attack, including expectations of possible fiscal and monetary responses to impending crises. Specifically, we discuss the symptoms exhibited by Russia prior to the devaluation of the ruble. In addition, we review the measures that were undertaken to avoid the crisis and explain why those steps may have, in fact, hastened the devaluation.

The following section reviews the three generations of currency crisis models and summarizes the conditions under which a country becomes vulnerable to speculative attack. The third section examines the events preceding the Russian default of 1998 in the context of a currency crisis. The fourth section applies the aforementioned models to the Russian crisis.

Currency Crises: What Does Macroeconomic Theory Suggest?

A currency crisis is defined as a speculative attack on country A's currency, brought about by agents attempting to alter their portfolio by buying another currency with the currency of country A.[2] This might occur because investors fear that the government will finance its high prospective deficit through seigniorage (printing money) or attempt to reduce its nonindexed debt (debt indexed to neither another currency nor inflation) through devaluation. A devaluation occurs when there is market pressure to increase the exchange rate (as measured by domestic currency over foreign currency) because the country either cannot or will not bear the cost of supporting its currency. In order to maintain a lower exchange rate peg, the central bank must buy up its currency with foreign reserves. If the central bank's foreign reserves are depleted, the government must allow the exchange rate to float up—a devaluation of the currency. This causes domestic goods and services to become cheaper relative to foreign goods and services. The devaluation associated with a successful speculative attack can cause a decrease in output, possible inflation, and a disruption in both domestic and foreign financial markets.[3]

The standard macroeconomic framework applied by Fleming (1962) and Mundell (1963) to international issues is unable to explain currency crises. In this framework with perfect capital mobility, a fixed exchange rate regime results in capital flight when the central bank lowers interest rates and results in capital inflows when the central bank raises interest rates. Consequently, the efforts of the monetary authority to change the interest rate are undone by the private sector. In a flexible exchange rate regime, the central bank does not intervene in the foreign exchange market and all balance of payment surpluses or deficits must be financed by private capital outflows or inflows, respectively.

The need to explain the symptoms and remedies of a currency crisis has spawned a number of models designed to incorporate fiscal deficits, expectations, and financial markets into models with purchasing power parity. These models can be grouped into three generations, each of which is intended to explain specific aspects that lead to a currency crisis.

First-Generation Models

The first-generation models of a currency crisis developed by Krugman (1979) and Flood and Garber (1984) rely on government debt and the perceived inability of the government to control the budget as the key causes of the currency crisis. These models argue that a speculative attack on the domestic currency can result from an increasing current account deficit (indicating an increase in the trade deficit) or an expected monetization of the fiscal deficit. The speculative attack can result in a sudden devaluation when the central bank's store of foreign reserves is depleted and it can no longer defend the domestic currency. Agents believe that the government's need to finance the debt becomes its over-riding concern and eventually leads to a collapse of the fixed exchange rate regime and to speculative attacks on the domestic currency.

Krugman presents a model in which a fixed exchange rate regime is the inevitable target of a speculative attack. An important assumption in the model is that a speculative attack is inevitable. The government defends the exchange rate peg with its store of foreign currency. As agents change the composition of their portfolios from domestic to foreign currency (because rising fiscal deficits increase the likelihood of devaluation, for example), the central bank must continue to deplete its reserves to stave off speculative attacks. The crisis is triggered when agents expect the government to abandon the peg. Anticipating the devaluation, agents convert their portfolios from domestic to foreign currency by buying foreign currency from the central bank's reserves. The central bank's reserves fall until they reach the critical point when a peg is no longer sustainable and the exchange rate regime collapses. The key contribution of the first-generation model is its identification of the tension between domestic fiscal policy and the fixed exchange rate regime.[4]

While the first-generation models help explain some of the fundamentals that cause currency crises, they are lacking in two key aspects. First, the standard first-generation model requires agents to suddenly increase their estimates of the likelihood of a devaluation (perhaps through an increase in expected inflation). Second, they do not explain why the currency crises spread to other countries.

Second-Generation Models

The second-generation models suggested by Obstfeld (1994), Eichengreen, Rose, and Wyplosz (1997), and others are particularly useful in explaining self-fulfilling contagious currency crises. One possible scenario suggested by these models involves a devaluation in one country affecting the price level (and therefore the demand for money) or the current account by a reduction of exports in a neighboring country. In either case, devaluation in a neighboring country becomes increasingly likely.

Eichengreen, Rose, and Wyplosz (1997) find that a correlation exists between the likelihood of default across countries. That is, the probability of a speculative attack in country A increases when its trading partner, country B, experiences an attack of its own. They estimate that a speculative attack somewhere in the world increases the probability of a domestic currency crisis by about 8 percent. The spillover from one currency crisis into neighboring countries can be attributed to a number of different scenarios. First, an economic event, such as a war or an oil price shock, that is common to a geographical area or a group of trading partners can affect those economies simultaneously; in addition, an individual shock can be transmitted from one country to another via trade. Second, a devaluation or default in one country can raise expectations of the likelihood of a devaluation in other countries. Expectations can rise either because countries are neighboring trade partners or because they have similar macroeconomic policies or conditions (e.g., high unemployment or high government debt). Since the crises are self-fulfilling, these expectations make the likelihood of devaluation increase as well. Lastly, a devaluation can be transmitted via world financial markets to other susceptible countries. Any combination of scenarios can serve as an explanation of the apparent international linkages that are responsible for the spread of speculative attacks from one country to another.

Third-Generation Models

The literature on contagious currency crises has helped clarify the spread of devaluations and their magnitudes. However, the first two generations of models have not provided a policy recommendation for the central bank in the face of a crisis. Indeed, Krugman's first-generation model suggests that a crisis cannot be thwarted—that once a devaluation is expected, it is inevitable. Thus, third-generation currency crisis models suggested by Krugman (1999) and Aghion, Bacchetta, and Banarjee (2000, 2001) examine the effects of monetary policy in a currency crisis.

These models argue that fragility in the banking and financial sector reduces the amount of credit available to firms and increases the likelihood of a crisis. They suggest that a currency crisis is brought on by a combination of high debt, low foreign reserves, falling government revenue, increasing expectations of devaluation, and domestic borrowing constraints. Firms' access to domestic loans is constrained by assuming they can borrow only a portion of their wealth (somewhat similar to requiring the firm to collateralize all domestic loans). In these lending-constrained economies, the credit market does not clear: interest rates rise, but not enough to compensate investors for the increase in perceived default risk. Increasing the domestic interest rate, then, does not raise the supply of domestic lending in the normal fashion. Moral hazard, a firm's ability to take its output and default on its loan, forces banks to restrict lending. Therefore, increasing the interest rate reduces the amount of loans as it increases firms' incentive to default.

These third-generation models offer a role for monetary policy (aside from the decision to abandon the exchange rate peg) through a binding credit constraint in an imperfect financial market. If firms' leverage in the domestic market is substantially reduced, they may be forced to accumulate a large amount of foreign-denominated debt. When, in domestic markets, the amount of available lending depends on the nominal interest rate, the central bank can deepen a crisis by further reducing firms' ability to invest. The typical prescription for a currency crisis is to raise interest rates and raise the demand for domestic currency.[5] However, in the third-generation models, an interest rate increase can greatly affect the amount of lending and further restrict firms' access to financial capital. In cases where lending is highly sensitive to the interest rate, an increase in the nominal interest rate can be detrimental, altering the productive capacity of the economy by stifling investment. The perceived drop in output puts additional pressure on the exchange rate, perhaps through actual or expected tax revenue, exacerbating the crisis. In this situation, an alternative strategy for the central bank is warranted: it is actually beneficial to lower the interest rate to spur investment.[6] These three generations of models suggest four factors that can influence the onset and magnitude of a currency crisis. Domestic public and private debt, expectations, and the state of financial markets can, in combination with a pegged exchange rate, determine whether a country is susceptible to a currency crisis and also determine the magnitude and success of a speculative attack. In the next section, we provide an example of a recent currency crisis, keeping these four factors in mind.

The Russian Default: A Brief History

After six years of economic reform in Russia, privatization and macroeconomic stabilization had experienced some limited success. Yet in August 1998, after recording its first year of positive economic growth since the fall of the Soviet Union, Russia was forced to default on its sovereign debt, devalue the ruble, and declare a suspension of payments by commercial banks to foreign creditors. What caused the Russian economy to face a

Table 1

Timeline of Russian Events

April 1996	Negotiations with the Paris and London Clubs for repayment of Soviet debt by 1997. Trade surplus moving toward balance.
	Inflation around 11 percent.
	Oil selling at $23/barrel.
	Analysts predict better credit ratings for Russia.
	Russian banks increase foreign liabilities.
	Real wages sagging.
	Only 40 percent of workforce being paid fully and on time.
	Public-sector deficit high.
September/October 1997	Negotiations with Paris and London Clubs completed.
November 11, 1997	Asian crisis causes a speculative attack on the ruble.
	CBR defends the ruble, losing $6 billion.
December 1997	Year ends with 0.8 percent growth.
	Prices of oil and nonferrous metal begin to drop.
February 1998	New tax code submitted to the Duma.
	IMF funds requested.
March 23, 1998	Yelstin fires entire government and appoints Kiriyenko.
	Continued requests for IMF funds.
April 1998	Another speculative attack on the ruble.
April 24, 1998	Duma finally confirms Kiriyenko's appointment.
Early May 1998	Dubinin warns government ministers of impending debt crisis, with reporters in audience.
	Kiriyenko calls the Russian government "quite poor."
May 19, 1998	CBR increases lending rate from 30 percent to 50 percent and defends the policy with $1 billion.
Mid May 1998	Lawrence Summers not granted audience with Kiriyenko.
	Oil prices continue to decrease.
	Oil and gas oligarchs advocate devaluation of ruble to increase value.
May 23, 1998	IMF leaves Russia without agreement on austerity plan.
May 27, 1998	CBR increases the lending rate again to 150 percent.
Summer 1998	Russian government formulates and advertises anti-crisis plan.
July 20, 1998	IMF approves an emergency aid package (first disbursement to be $4.8 billion).
August 13, 1998	Russian stock, bond, and currency markets weaken as a result of investor fears devaluation; prices diminish.
August 17, 1998	Russian government devalues the ruble, defaults on domestic debt, and declares moratorium on payment to foreign creditors.
August 23-24, 1998	Kiriyenko is fired.
September 2, 1998	The ruble is floated.
December 1998	Year ends with a decrease in real output of 4.9 percent.

NOTE: CBR, Central Bank of Russia

financial crisis after so much had been accomplished? This section examines the sequence of events that took place in Russia from 1996 to 1998 and the aftermath of the crisis. (For a timeline, see Table 1.)

1996 and 1997

Optimism and Reform. In April 1996, Russian officials began negotiations to reschedule the payment of foreign debt inherited from the former Soviet Union. The negotiations to repay its sovereign debt were a major step toward restoring investor confidence. On the surface, 1997 seemed poised to be a turning point toward economic stability.

- The trade surplus was moving toward a balance between exports and imports (see Figure 1).
- Relations with the West were promising: the World Bank was prepared to provide expanded assistance of $2 to $3 billion per year and the International Monetary Fund (IMF) continued to meet with Russian officials and provide aid.
- Inflation had fallen from 131 percent in 1995 to 22 percent in 1996 and 11 percent in 1997 (see Figure 2).
- Output was recovering slightly.
- A narrow exchange rate band was in place keeping the exchange rate between 5 and 6 rubles to the dollar (see Figure 3).
- And oil, one of Russia's largest exports, was selling at $23 per barrel—a high price by recent standards. (Fuels made up more than 45 percent of Russia's main export commodities in 1997.)

In September 1997, Russia was allowed to join the Paris Club of creditor nations after rescheduling the payment of over $60 billion in old Soviet debt to other governments. Another agreement for a 23-year debt repayment of $33 billion was signed a month later with the London Club. Analysts predicted that Russia's credit ratings would improve,

allowing the country to borrow less expensively. Limitations on the purchase of government securities by nonresident investors were removed, promoting foreign investment in Russia. By late 1997, roughly 30 percent of the GKO (a short-term government bill) market was accounted for by nonresidents. The economic outlook appeared optimistic as Russia ended 1997 with reported economic growth of 0.8 percent.

Revenue, Investment, and Debt. Despite the prospects for optimism, problems remained. On average, real wages were less than half of what they were in 1991, and only about 40 percent of the work force was being paid in full and on time. Per capita direct foreign investment was low, and regulation of the natural monopolies was still difficult due to unrest in the Duma, Russia's lower house of Parliament. Another weakness in the Russian economy was low tax collection, which caused the public sector deficit to remain high. The majority of tax revenues came from taxes that were shared between the regional and federal governments, which fostered competition among the different levels of government over the distribution. According to Shleifer and Treisman (2000), this kind of tax sharing can result in conflicting incentives for regional governments and lead them to help firms conceal part of their taxable profit from the federal government in order to reduce the firms' total tax payments. In return, the firm would then make transfers to the accommodating regional government. This, Shleifer and Treisman suggest, may explain why federal revenues dropped more rapidly than regional revenues.

Also, the Paris Club's recognition of Russia as a creditor nation was based upon questionable qualifications. One-fourth of the assets considered to belong to Russia were in the form of debt owed to the former Soviet Union by countries such as Cuba, Mongolia, and Vietnam. Recognition by the Paris Club was also based on the old, completely arbitrary official Soviet exchange rate of approximately 0.6 rubles to the dollar (the market exchange rate at the time was between 5 and

Figure 1

Russian Merchandise Trade Balance

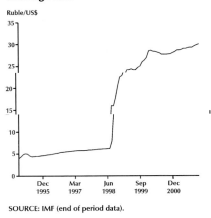

SOURCE: CBR.

Figure 2

CPI Inflation
Percent Change over Previous Year

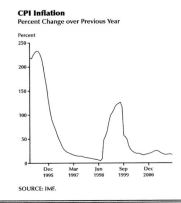

SOURCE: IMF.

Figure 3

Exchange Rate

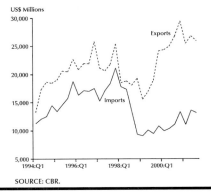

SOURCE: IMF (end of period data).

6 rubles to the dollar). The improved credit ratings Russia received from its Paris Club recognition were not based on an improved balance sheet. Despite this, restrictions were eased and lifted and Russian banks began borrowing more from foreign markets, increasing their foreign liabilities from 7 percent of their assets in 1994 to 17 percent in 1997.

Meanwhile, Russia anticipated growing debt payments in the coming years when early credits from the IMF would come due. Policymakers faced decisions to decrease domestic borrowing and increase tax collection because interest payments were such a large percentage of the federal budget. In

October 1997, the Russian government was counting on 2 percent economic growth in 1998 to compensate for the debt growth. Unfortunately, events began to unfold that would further strain Russia's economy; instead of growth in 1998, real GDP declined 4.9 percent.

The Asian Crisis. A few months earlier, in the summer of 1997, countries in the Pacific Rim experienced currency crises similar to the one that eventually affected Russia. In November 1997, after the onset of this East Asian crisis, the ruble came under speculative attack. The Central Bank of Russia (CBR) defended the currency, losing nearly $6 billion (U.S. dollars) in foreign-exchange reserves. At the same time, non-resident holders of short-term government bills (GKOs) signed forward contracts with the CBR to exchange rubles for foreign currency, which enabled them to hedge exchange rate risk in the interim period.[7] According to Desai (2000), they did this in anticipation of the ruble losing value, as Asian currencies had. Also, a substantial amount of the liabilities of large Russian commercial banks were off-balance-sheet, consisting mostly of forward contracts signed with foreign investors. Net obligations of Russian banks for such contracts were estimated to be at least $6 billion by the first half of 1998. Then another blow was dealt to the Russian economy: in December 1997, the prices of oil and nonferrous metal, up to two-thirds of Russia's hard-currency earnings, began to drop.

1998

Government, Risk, and Expectations. With so many uncertainties in the Russian economy, investors turned their attention toward Russian default risk. To promote a stable investment environment, in February 1998, the Russian government submitted a new tax code to the Duma, with fewer and more efficient taxes. The new tax code was approved in 1998, yet some crucial parts that were intended to increase federal revenue were ignored. Russian officials sought IMF funds but agreements could not be reached. By late March the political and economic situation had become more dire, and, on March 23, President Yeltsin abruptly fired his entire government, including Prime Minister Viktor Chernomyrdin. In a move that would challenge investor confidence even further, Yeltsin appointed 35-year-old Sergei Kiriyenko, a former banking and oil company executive who had been in government less than a year, to take his place.

While fears of higher interest rates in the United States and Germany made many investors cautious, tensions rose in the Russian government. The executive branch, the Duma, and the CBR were in conflict. Prompted by threats from Yeltsin to dissolve Parliament, the Duma confirmed Kiriyenko's appointment on April 24 after a month of stalling. In early May, during a routine update, CBR chair Sergei Dubinin warned government ministers of a debt crisis within the next three years. Unfortunately, reporters were in the audience. Since the Asian crisis had heightened investors' sensitivity to currency stability, Dubinin's restatement of bank policy was misinterpreted to mean that the Bank was considering a devaluation of the ruble. In another public relations misunderstanding, Kiriyenko stated in an interview that tax revenue was 26 percent below target and claimed that the government was "quite poor now." In actuality, the government was planning to cut government spending and accelerate revenue, but these plans were never communicated clearly to the public. Instead, people began to expect a devaluation of the ruble.

Investors' perceptions of Russia's economic stability continued to decline when Lawrence Summers, one of America's top international-finance officials, was denied a meeting with Kiriyenko while in Russia. An inexperienced aide determined that Summers's title, Deputy Secretary of the Treasury, was unworthy of Kiriyenko's audience and the two never met. At the same time, the IMF left Russia, unable to reach an agreement with policymakers on a 1998 austerity plan. Word spread of these incidents, and big investors began to sell their government bond portfolios and Russian securities, concerned that relations between the United States and Russia were strained.

Liquidity, Monetary Policy, and Fiscal Policy. By May 18, government bond yields had swelled to 47 percent. With inflation at about 10 percent, Russian banks would normally have taken the government paper at such high rates. Lack of confidence in the government's ability to repay the bonds and restricted liquidity, however, did not permit this. As depositors and investors became increasingly cautious of risk, these commercial banks and firms had less cash to keep them afloat. The federal government's initiative to collect more taxes in cash lowered banks' and firms' liquidity.[8] Also, in 1997, Russia had created a U.S.-style treasury system with branches, which saved money and decreased corruption, yet also decreased the amount of cash that moved through banks. The banks had previously used these funds to buy bonds. Also, household ruble deposits increased by only 1.3 billion in 1998, compared with an increase of 29.8 billion in 1997.

The CBR responded by increasing the lending rate to banks from 30 to 50 percent, and in two days used $1 billion of Russia's low reserves to defend the ruble. (Figure 4 shows the lending rate.) However, by May 27, demand for bonds had plummeted so much that yields were more than 50 percent and the government failed to sell enough bonds at its weekly auction to refinance the debt coming due.

Meanwhile, oil prices had dropped to $11 per barrel, less than half their level a year

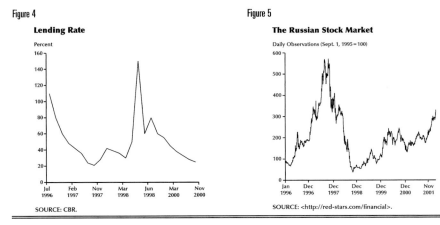

Figure 4

Lending Rate

Percent

SOURCE: CBR.

Figure 5

The Russian Stock Market

Daily Observations (Sept. 1, 1995 = 100)

SOURCE: <http://red-stars.com/financial>.

earlier. Oil and gas oligarchs were advocating a devaluation of the ruble, which would increase the ruble value of their exports. In light of this, the CBR increased the lending rate again, this time to 150 percent. CBR chairman Sergei Dubinin responded by stating "When you hear talk of devaluation, spit in the eye of whoever is talking about it" (quoted in Shleifer and Treisman, 2000, p. 149). The government formed and advertised an anti-crisis plan, requested assistance from the West, and began bankruptcy processes against three companies with large debts from back taxes. Kiriyenko met with foreign investors to reassure them. Yeltsin made nightly appearances on Russian television, calling the nation's financial elite to a meeting at the Kremlin where he urged them to invest in Russia. In June the CBR defended the ruble, losing $5 billion in reserves. Despite all of the government efforts being made, there was widespread knowledge of $2.5 to $3 billion in loans from foreign investors to Russian corporations and banks that were to come due by the end of September. In addition, billions of dollars in ruble futures were to mature in the fall. In July the IMF approved additional assistance of $11.2 billion, of which $4.8 billion was to be disbursed immediately. Yet between May and August, approximately $4 billion had left Russia in capital flight, and in 1998 Russia lost around $4 billion in revenue due to sagging oil prices. After losing so much liquidity, the IMF assistance did not provide much relief. The Duma, in an effort to protect

natural monopolies from stricter regulations, eliminated crucial parts of the IMF-endorsed anti-crisis program before adjourning for vacation. The government had hoped that the anti-crisis plan would bring in an additional 71 billion rubles in revenue. The parts that the Duma actually passed would have increased it by only 3 billion rubles. In vain, lawmakers requested that the Duma reconvene, lowering investors' confidence even further.

Default and Devaluation. On August 13, 1998, the Russian stock, bond, and currency markets collapsed as a result of investor fears that the government would devalue the ruble, default on domestic debt, or both. Annual yields on ruble-denominated bonds were more than 200 percent. The stock market had to be closed for 35 minutes as prices plummeted. When the market closed, it was down 65 percent with a small number of shares actually traded. From January to August the stock market had lost more than 75 percent of its value, 39 percent in the month of May alone. (Figure 5 shows the Russian stock market's boom and bust.) Russian officials were left with little choice. On August 17 the government floated the exchange rate, devalued the ruble, defaulted on its domestic debt, halted payment on ruble-denominated debt (primarily GKOs), and declared a 90-day moratorium on payment by commercial banks to foreign creditors.

The Aftermath

Russia ended 1998 with a decrease in real out-put of 4.9 percent for the year instead of the small growth that was expected. The collapse of the ruble created an increase in Russia's exports while imports remained low (see Figure 1). Since then, direct investments into Russia have been inconsistent at best. Summarized best by Shleifer and Treisman (2000), "the crisis of August 1998 did not only undermine Russia's currency and force the last reformers from office…it also seemed to erase any remaining Western hope that Russia could successfully reform its economy."

Some optimism, however, still persists. Figure 6 shows Russian real GDP growth, which grew 8.3 percent in 2000 and roughly 5 percent in 2001—lower but still positive. Imports trended up in the first half of 2001, helping to create a trade balance. At the same time, consumer prices grew 20.9 percent and 21.6 percent in 2000 and 2001, respectively, compared with a 92.6 percent increase in 1999. Most of the recovery so far can be attributed to the import substitution effect after the devaluation; the increase in world prices for Russia's oil, gas, and commodity exports; monetary policies; and fiscal policies that have led to the first federal budget surplus (in 2000) since the formation of the Russian Federation.

How Do the Theories Explain the Russian Crisis?

As discussed earlier, four major factors influence the onset and success of a speculative attack. These key ingredients are (i) an exchange rate peg and a central bank willing or obligated to defend it with a reserve of foreign currency, (ii) rising fiscal deficits that the government cannot control and therefore is likely to monetize (print money to cover the deficit), (iii) central bank control of the interest rate in a fragile credit market, and (iv) expectations of devaluation and/or rising inflation. In this section we discuss these aspects in the context of the Russian devaluation. We argue that an understanding of all three generations of models is necessary to

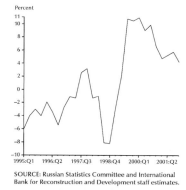

Figure 6 **Real GDP Growth**
Quarterly Change from Previous Year

SOURCE: Russian Statistics Committee and International Bank for Reconstruction and Development staff estimates.

evaluate the Russian devaluation. Krugman's (1979) first-generation model explains the factors that made Russia susceptible to a crisis. The second-generation models show how contagion and other factors can change expectations to trigger the crisis. The third-generation models show how the central bank can act to prevent or mitigate the crisis.

The Exchange Rate and the Peg

When the ruble came under attack in November 1997 and June 1998, policymakers defended the ruble instead of letting it float. The real exchange rate did not vary much during 1997. Clearly a primary component of a currency crisis in the models described here is the central bank's willingness to defend an exchange rate peg. Prior to August 1998, the Russian ruble was subject to two speculative attacks. The CBR made efforts both times to defend the ruble. The defense was successful in November 1997 but fell short in the summer of 1998. Defending the ruble depleted Russia's foreign reserves. Once depleted, the Russian government had no choice but to devalue on August 17, 1998.

Revenue, Deficits, and Fiscal Policy

Russia's high government debt and falling revenue contributed significantly to its susceptibility to a speculative attack. Russia's federal tax revenues were low because of both low output and the opportunistic practice of local governments helping firms conceal profits. The decrease in the price of oil also lowered output, further reducing Russia's ability to generate tax revenue. Consequently, Russia's revenue was lower than expected, making the ruble ripe for a speculative attack. In addition, a large amount of short-term foreign debt was coming due in 1998, making Russia's deficit problem even more serious. Krugman's first-generation model suggests that a government finances its deficit by printing money (seigniorage) or depleting its reserves of foreign currency. Under the exchange rate peg, however, Russia was unable to finance through seigniorage. Russia's deficit, low revenue, and mounting interest payments put pressure on the exchange rate. Printing rubles would only have increased this pressure because the private sector would still have been able to trade rubles for foreign currency at the fixed rate. Thus, whether directly through intervention in the foreign currency market or indirectly by printing rubles, Russia's only alternative under the fixed exchange rate regime was to deplete its stock of foreign reserves.

Monetary Policy, Financial Markets, and Interest Rates

During the summer of 1998, the Russian economy was primed for the onset of a currency crisis. In an attempt to avert the crisis, the CBR intervened by decreasing the growth of the money supply and twice increasing the lending rate to banks, raising it from 30 to 150 percent. Both rate hikes occurred in May 1998, the same month in which the Russian stock market lost 39 percent of its value. The rise in interest rates had two effects. First, it exacerbated Russia's revenue problems. Its debt grew rapidly as interest payments mounted. This put pressure on the exchange rate because investors feared that Russia would devalue to finance its nondenominated debt. Second, high government debt prevented firms from obtaining loans for new capital and increasing the interest rate did not increase the supply of lending capital available to firms. At the same time, foreign reserves held by the CBR were so low that the government could no longer defend the currency by buying rubles.

Expectations

Three components fueled the expectations of Russia's impending devaluation and default. First, the Asian crisis made investors more conscious of the possibility of a Russian default. Second, public relations errors, such as the publicized statement to government ministers by the CBR and Kiriyenko's refusal to grant Lawrence Summers an audience, perpetuated agents' perceptions of a political crisis within the Russian government. Third, the revenue shortfall signaled the possible reduction of the public debt burden via an increase in the money supply. This monetization of the debt can be associated with a depreciation either indirectly through an increase in expected inflation or directly in order to reduce the burden of ruble-denominated debt. Each of these three components acted to push the Russian economy from a stable equilibrium to one vulnerable to speculative attack.

Conclusion

In this paper we investigate the events that lead up to a currency crisis and debt default and the policies intended to avert it. Three types of models exist to explain currency crises. Each model explains some factor that has been hypothesized to cause a crisis. After reviewing the three generations of currency crisis models, we conclude that four key ingredients can trigger a crisis: a fixed exchange rate, fiscal deficits and debt, the conduct of monetary policy, and expectations of impending default. Using the example of the Russian default of 1998, we show that the prescription of contractionary monetary policy in the face of a currency crisis can, under certain conditions, accelerate devaluation. While we believe that deficits and the Asian financial crisis contributed to Russia's default, the first-generation model proposed by Krugman (1979) and Flood and Garber (1984) and the second-generation models proposed by Obstfeld (1984) and Eichengreen, Rose, and Wyplosz (1997) do not capture every aspect of the crisis. Specifically, these models do not address the conduct of monetary policy. It is therefore necessary to incorporate both the first-generation model's phenomenon of increasing fiscal deficits and the third-generation model's financial sector fragility. We conclude that the modern currency crisis is a symptom of an ailing domestic economy. In that light, it is inappropriate to attribute a single prescription as the prophylactic or cure for a currency crisis.

Abbigail J. Chiodo is a senior research associate and Michael T. Owyang is an economist at the Federal Reserve Bank of St. Louis. The authors thank Steven Holland, Eric Blankmeyer, John Lewis, and Rebecca Beard for comments and suggestions and Victor Gabor at the World Bank for providing real GDP data.

Endnotes

[1] Kharas, Pinto, and Ulatov (2001) provide a history from a fundamentals-based perspective, focusing on taxes and public debt issues. We endeavor to incorporate a role for monetary policy.

[2] The speculative attack need not be successful to be dubbed a currency crisis.

[3] Burnside, Eichenbaum, and Rebelo (2001) show that the government has at its disposal a number of mechanisms to finance the fiscal costs of the devaluation. Which policy is chosen determines the inflationary effect of the currency crisis.

[4] Obstfeld (1986) outlines a multiple equilibrium model in which a currency crisis is brought about when government policy (financing a deficit through seignorage, for example) causes agents to expect a crisis and push the economy to a bad equilibrium.

[5] Flood and Jeanne (2000) argue that increasing domestic currency interest rates can act only to speed devaluation.

[6] The expansionary monetary policy in this case is assumed not to be inflationary since it only alleviates liquidity constraints.

[7] The requirement of forward contracts was the CBR's way of preventing runs on its foreign currency reserves.

[8] As a result of a 1998 elimination of tax-offsets paper issued by government agencies to pay for goods and services, the receipts of which could be used to decrease their tax duties, banks and companies were forced to provide more cash to pay their taxes, thus lowering their liquidity.

References

Aghion, Philippe; Bacchetta, Philippe and Banerjee, Abhijit. "A Simple Model of Monetary Policy and Currency Crises." *European Economic Review*, May 2000, 44(4-6), pp. 728-38.

Aghion, Philippe; Bacchetta, Philippe and Banerjee, Abhijit. "Currency Crises and Monetary Policy in an Economy with Credit Constraints." *European Economic Review*, June 2001, 45(7), pp. 1121-50.

Ahrend, Rudiger. "Foreign Direct Investment Into Russia—Pain Without Gain? A Survey of Foreign Direct Investors." *Russian Economic Trends*, June 2000, 9(2), pp. 26-33.

Burnside, Craig; Eichenbaum, Martin, and Rebelo, Sergio. "On The Fiscal Implications of Twin Crises." Working Paper No. 8277, National Bureau of Economic Research, May 2001.

Desai, Padma. "Why Did the Ruble Collapse in August 1998?" *American Economic Review: Papers and Proceedings*, May 2000, 90(2), pp. 48-52.

Economist. "Surplus to Requirements." 8 July 2000, p. 79.

Eichengreen, Barry; Rose, Andrew and Wyplosz, Charles. "Contagious Currency Crisis." March 1997. http://www.haas.berkeley.edu/~arose/

Fischer, Stanley. "The Russian Economy at the Start of 1998." U.S.-Russian Investment Symposium, Harvard University, Cambridge, MA, 9 January 1998.

Flemming, Marcus. "Domestic Financial Policies Under Fixed and Under Floating Exchange Rates." *IMF Staff Papers*, 9 November 1962.

Flood, Robert P. and Garber, Peter M. "Collapsing Exchange Rate Regimes: Some Linear Examples." *Journal of International Economics*, August 1984, 17(1-2), pp 1-13.

Flood, Robert P. and Jeanne, Olivier. "An Interest Rate Defense of a Fixed Exchange Rate?" Working Paper WP/00/159, International Monetary Fund, October 2000.

Kharas, Homi; Pinto, Brian and Ulatov, Sergei. "An Analysis of Russia's 1998 Meltdown: Fundamentals and Market Signals." *Brookings Papers on Economic Activity*, 2001, 0(1), pp. 1-67.

Krugman, Paul. "A Model of Balance-of-Payment Crises." *Journal of Money, Credit, and Banking,* August 1979, 11(3), pp. 311-25.

_____. "Balance Sheets, the Transfer Problem, and Financial Crises." *International Tax and Public Finance,* November 1999, 6(4), pp. 459-72.

Malleret, Thierry; Orlova, Natalia and Romanov, Vladimir. "What Loaded and Triggered the Russian Crisis?" *Post-Soviet Affairs,* April-June 1999, 15(2), pp. 107-29.

Mudell, R.A. "Capital Mobility and Stabilization Policy Under Fixed and Flexible Exchange Rates." *Canadian Journal of Economics,* November 1963.

Obstfeld, Maurice. "Rational and Self-Fulfilling Balance-of-Payments Crises." *American Economic Review,* March 1986, 76(1), pp. 72-81.

_____. "The Logic of Currency Crises." *Cahiers Economiques et Monetaires,* Banque de France, 1994, 43, pp. 189-213.

Popov, A. "Lessons of the Currency Crisis in Russia and in Other Countries." *Problems of Economic Transition,* May 2000, 43(1), pp. 45-73.

Russian Economic Trends. Various months.

Shleifer, Andre and Treisman, Daniel. *Without A Map: Political Tactics and Economic Reform in Russia.* Cambridge, MA: MIT Press, 2000.

Velasco, Andrés. "Financial Crises in Emerging Markets." *National Bureau of Economic Research Reporter,* Fall 1999, pp.17-19.

Learning from Argentina's Crisis

RAMON MORENO

Since December 2001, Argentina has suspended payments on its external debt, restricted bank deposit withdrawals, and abandoned a currency board arrangement that had pegged the peso to the U.S. dollar since 1991. Argentina faces inflation of over 70% this year and an economic contraction that rivals the U.S.'s Great Depression. These developments have surprised many observers because for most of the 1990s Argentina was considered a model of successful economic policy. Indeed, many thought that the instability that had characterized the Argentine economy for much of its history was a thing of the past.

Could Argentina's crisis have been anticipated and avoided? This *Economic Letter* observes that the recent events in Argentina were not entirely unpredictable, as they were associated with rapid increases in public and external debt that cast doubt on the sustainability of borrowing. Conditions that accentuated vulnerability to crises are also highlighted.

Prelude

For most of the 1990s, Argentina was seen as a model of successful policymaking. By pegging its exchange rate to the dollar under a currency board type arrangement in 1991, Argentina ended hyper-inflation, reducing inflation rates to single-digit levels. The banking sector in Argentina, traditionally weak, was strengthened considerably, in

part because of an increase in foreign bank entry. A 1998 World Bank financial sector review rated Argentina second only to Singapore among emerging markets in the quality of its bank supervision (Perry and Serven 2002). Greater economic stability attracted foreign investment inflows, contributing to an acceleration in economic growth; indeed, even as lenders withdrew their financing in East Asia in 1997, capital inflows continued to Argentina.

Things began to turn sour in 1999.The collapse of the Brazilian currency led to sharp declines in export revenues, and economic growth was negative for three years in a row. Nevertheless, with some brief exceptions, financial markets remained relatively undisturbed until 2001, when uncertainty about the growing public debt and the persistent economic contraction led to very sharp increases in the yields investors demanded to hold Argentine government bonds. Uncertainty extended to the durability of the currency peg and the ability of the financial system to make good on dollar liabilities that were backed to a significant extent by peso assets, including government debt. The result was massive deposit withdrawals from the banking system.

In response to these developments, in December 2001, Argentina suspended payments on its external debt and restricted deposit withdrawals (the "corralito"). In January 2002, it abandoned its peg to the U.S. dollar. Reflecting continuing uncertain-

Figure 1
Argentina: Public debt to GDP

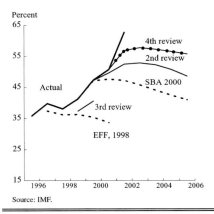

Source: IMF.

ty about financial conditions, interest rates have continued to rise and the currency has depreciated 356% against the U.S. dollar in the year to September 20. The impact of the Argentine crisis has been severe. Output is forecast to decline 15% and inflation to rise to 72% in 2002 (*Latin America Consensus Forecasts*, September 16, 2002).

What Caused Argentina's Crisis?

Many observers have explained the crisis in terms of the deficiencies of Argentina's peg to the U.S. dollar under a type of currency board arrangement. While the currency board did play a role, it also can be argued that the main cause of the crisis was Argentina's persistent inability to reduce its high public and external debts. These made the economy vulnerable to adverse economic shocks and shifts in market sentiment.

Figure 1 illustrates the trend in the public debt/GDP ratio in Argentina since 1995, as reported by the International Monetary Fund (IMF) (2002a, p. 19). This ratio measures the total amount of public debt relative to the ability of the economy to produce (taxable) income to service it. In the figures, the thick solid line shows the actual path while the thinner solid lines and dashed lines represent alternative scenarios anticipated by the IMF first under a 1998

Extended Fund Facility (EFF) program and then under a 2000 Stand-by Arrangement (SBA). (For descriptions of these financing arrangements, see IMF 2002b.) The figure reveals that Argentina's public debt/GDP ratio rose rapidly, from 35% in 1995 to nearly 65% in 2001. It is also apparent that under IMF consultations, it was consistently anticipated that Argentina's public debt/GDP ratio would stabilize or fall, but this did not happen. The actual path of the public debt/GDP ratio far exceeded the IMF projections in five different reviews between 1998 and 2000.

Argentina's experience stands in contrast to South Korea's, where a financial crisis in 1997–1998 forced the government to intervene to rescue failing banks and led to a rescheduling of its external debt. In South Korea, the public debt/GDP ratio rose sharply, from over 10% in 1997 to over 30% in 2000, but then declined (IMF 2002a, p. 18). However, even at its peak, South Korea's public debt/GDP ratio was less than half Argentina's, and the path of the debt remained below that projected by the IMF in three separate reviews.

There is no unambiguous threshold at which public debt becomes unsustainable, and Argentina's public debt/GDP ratio of 65% in 2001 was still lower than that observed in some European countries. However, given the history of defaults and macroeconomic instability in emerging markets like Argentina, their threshold sustainable public debt may be much lower than in advanced economies. Furthermore, limitations on tax collection capability imply that a higher public debt/GDP ratio makes emerging markets more vulnerable to adverse shifts in market sentiment that raise the cost of funds. In line with this, large spikes in the yield on public debt occur in emerging markets that are rarely seen in advanced economies.

For example, between January and November 2001, investor uncertainty raised the yield on an Argentine 10-year government bond (denominated in U.S. dollars) about 20 percentage points, to around

35%, signaling the growing unwillingness of investors to hold Argentine debt. (There were also brief spikes in yields on Argentine debt in 1996 and in late 1998 to early 1999. See Mussa 2002, Figure 3.1, which uses a different but related measure.) Such a sharp rise in the interest rate, as well as a default and (self-fulfilling) crisis, is more likely if the public debt/GDP ratio is 65% (as in Argentina) than if it is around 30% (as in South Korea).

Argentina also was vulnerable because its capital account was open and there was a large amount of borrowing in foreign currency from abroad. A large external debt made Argentina vulnerable to default not only in the event that interest rates rose, but also in the event that the currency depreciated sharply, as this increased the repayment burden in domestic currency.

Argentina's external debt profile in 1990 and 2000 may be assessed using two alternative measures, the external debt/GDP and the external debt/export ratios. As external debt typically has to be serviced in foreign currency, the external debt/GDP ratio is a more informative measure of the size of the debt relative to payment capacity if output can easily be shifted to earn more exports. Otherwise, the debt/export ratio provides a better indicator. By either measure, Argentina's debt rose significantly between 1990 and 2000: the external debt/GDP ratio rose from 44% to 51%, and the external debt/exports rose from 421% to 471%.

To put some perspective on the vulnerability implied by these numbers, consider the IMF's report (2002a), which finds that the probability of a debt crisis (involving payment arrears or debt rescheduling) rises to about 15%–20% for countries with external debt/GDP ratios above 40% (from around 2%–5% when debt is below the threshold). The likelihood of a crisis also rises when the external debt/export ratio is high. Argentina's exports of goods and services are quite low, about 10% of GDP, implying very high external debt/export ratios that accentuate its vulnerability to

external debt crises. Once again, the contrast with South Korea is informative. From 1990 to 2000, South Korea's external debt/export ratio rose from 48% to 78%, but it still remained orders of magnitudes below Argentina's ratio.

Why Did Argentina's Debt Ratios Rise?

Argentina's debt ratios rose for at least two reasons. First, primary fiscal surpluses (government revenues minus expenditures exclusive of interest payments on the debt) were not large enough to cover interest payments and also retire some of the outstanding public debt. Between 1991 and 2000, Argentina's primary surpluses averaged 0.14% of GDP. These surpluses were remarkable achievements, given Argentina's past history, but they were still well below interest payments, which averaged 2.4% of GDP over this period. There were significant obstacles to reducing expenditures and raising revenues. On the expenditure side, the government was a large employer (Krueger 2002) and, for political reasons, found it hard to cut its wage bill. The central government also found it hard to control spending by provincial governments, whose liabilities it was eventually forced to assume. At the same time, revenues were adversely affected by difficulties in tax collection and, after 1999, by falling output and rising unemployment.

Second, export growth (and therefore economic growth) was not sufficiently robust to improve the country's ability to meet its debt obligations and lower debt/GDP ratios. In the 1990s, the dollar value of Argentina's exports of goods and services grew at 7.7% a year, less than the nearly 9% growth in its external debt and well below the rate of growth of exports in Asian economies such as South Korea or Malaysia (10%–11%). Export growth has been dampened by Argentina's trade barriers, which remain relatively high outside the Southern Cone common market area of Mercosur, of which Argentina is a member.

These trade barriers have increased since the crisis broke out. Exports also suffered following the 1999 collapse of the Brazilian real because Argentina's rigid currency board arrangement produced an overvalued currency. Indeed, the focus on maintaining a rigid peg at all costs appears to have diverted attention away from the risks of not paying attention to real sector fundamentals.

Conclusions

In the view of some observers, Argentina's debt position would have been sustainable if only market uncertainty had not triggered a crisis. While there is some truth to this view, it does not take into account the fact that Argentina could have reduced its vulnerability to potentially destabilizing shifts in market sentiment by aggressively reducing its public and external debts. This is illustrated by the contrasting experiences of Argentina and Asian economies like South Korea. With much lower debt levels, the latter is less likely to experience adverse shifts in market sentiment and is less vulnerable to them should they occur.

Cutting Argentina's public debt requires reductions in government spending, tax reforms designed to increase government revenues, and policies to stimulate export growth over the medium to long run. The successful adoption of such policies is the key challenge facing Argentina and a number of other emerging economies, and it is an important prerequisite for achieving stability in a globalized economy.

Ramon Moreno Research Advisor

References

[URLs accessed October 2002.]

International Monetary Fund. 2002a. "Assessing Sustainability." Manuscript (May 28). http://www.imf.org/external/np/pdr/sus/2002/eng/052802.htm

International Monetary Fund. 2002b. "How Does the IMF Lend? A Factsheet." (August 20.) http://www.imf.org/external/np/exr/facts/howlend.htm

Krueger, Anne. 2002. "Crisis Prevention and Resolution: Lessons from Argentina." Speech to National Bureau of Economic Research Conference on "The Argentina Crisis." Cambridge, MA (July 17). http://www.imf.org/external/np/speeches/2002/071702.htm

Mussa, Michael. 2002. *Argentina and the Fund: From Triumph to Tragedy.* Policy Analyses in International Economics, No. 67 (July). Washington, DC: Institute for International Economics.

Perry, Guillermo, and Luis Serven. 2002. "The Anatomy of a Multiple Crisis: Why Was Argentina Special and What Can We Learn from It?" Background paper for the NBER Project on Exchange Rate Crises in Emerging Markets: The Argentina Crisis. Manuscript (May 10).

33

The Onset of the East Asian Financial Crisis

S T E V E **R A D E L E T**
& J E F F R E Y **S A C H S**

Yet it is also true that small events at times have large consequences, that there are such things as chain reactions and cumulative forces. It happens that a liquidity crisis in a unit fractional reserve banking system is precisely the kind of event that can trigger – and often has triggered – a chain reaction. And economic collapse often has the character of a cumulative process. Let it go beyond a certain point, and it will tend for a time to gain strength from its own development as its effects spread and return to intensify the process of collapse. Because no great strength would be required to hold back the rock that starts a landslide, it does not follow that the landslide will not be of major proportions.

Milton Friedman and Anna Schwartz
A Monetary History of the United States, 1867-1960

I. Introduction

The East Asian financial crisis is remarkable in several ways. The crisis hit the most rapidly growing economies in the world, and prompted the largest financial bailouts in history. It is the sharpest financial crisis to hit the developing world since the 1982 debt crisis. It is the least anticipated financial crisis in years. Few observers gave much chance a year ago that East Asian growth would suddenly collapse.[1] The search is on for culprits within Asia – corrupt and mismanaged banking systems, lack of transparency in corporate governance, the shortcoming of state-managed capitalism. At least as much attention, if not more, should be focused on the international financial system. The crisis is a testament to the shortcomings of the international capital markets and their vulnerability to sudden reversals of market confidence. The crisis has also raised serious doubts about the IMF's approach to managing financial disturbances originating in private financial markets. Perhaps most importantly, the turmoil demonstrates how policy missteps and hasty reactions by governments, the international community, and market participants can turn a moderate adjustment into a financial panic and a deep crisis.

One ironic similarity between the Mexican (1995) and Korean (1997) crises is that both countries joined the OECD on the eve of their respective financial catastrophes. There is a hint of explanation in that bizarre fact. Both countries collapsed after a prolonged period of market euphoria. In the case of Mexico, a high-quality technocratic team had led the country through stabilization, privatization, liberalization, and even free trade with the United States. Indeed, the supposed cornerstone of Mexico's coming boom was admission to NAFTA, which occurred in November 1993, just months before the collapse. In Korea, a generation-long success story of industrial policy and export-led growth had culminated in Korea's admission to the exclusive club of advanced economies.

Korea had even succeeded in democratization without jeopardy to its enviable growth record. In both countries, collapse came not mainly because of a prolonged darkening economic horizon, but because of a euphoric inflow of capital that could not be sustained.[2]

In this sense, the Asian crisis can be understood as a "crisis of success," caused by a boom of international lending followed by a sudden withdrawal of funds. At the core of the Asian crisis were large-scale foreign capital inflows into financial systems that became vulnerable to panic. However, this is more than the bursting of an unwanted bubble (cf. Krugman, 1998). Much of the economic activity supported by the capital inflows was highly productive, and the loss of economic activity resulting from the sudden and enormous reversal in capital flows has been enormous. There were few, if any, expectations of a sudden break in capital flows. By early 1997, markets expected a slowdown – even a devaluation crisis – in Thailand, but not in the rest of Asia. Indicators as late as the third quarter of 1997 did not suggest a financial meltdown of the sort that subsequently occurred. A combination of panic on the part of the international investment community, policy mistakes at the onset of the crisis by Asian governments, and poorly designed international rescue programs have led to a much deeper fall in (otherwise viable) output than was either necessary or inevitable.

This paper provides an early diagnosis of the financial crisis in Asia. It builds on existing theories, and focuses on the empirical record in the lead-up to the crisis. The main goal is to emphasize the role of financial panic as an essential element of the Asian crisis. To be sure, there were significant underlying problems besetting the Asian economies, at both a macroeconomic and microeconomic level (especially within the financial sector). But these imbalances were not severe enough to warrant a financial crisis of the magnitude that took place in the latter half of 1997. In our view, certain policy choices and events along the way exacerbated the panic and unnecessarily deepened the crisis. We explore this possibility by examining the initial imbal-ances and weaknesses, the buildup to the crisis, and the events that led to the financial panic in the latter part of the year. The paper covers the period only till the end of 1997, and it does not aim to provide policy recommendations for the future, either regarding the Asian crisis or the reorganization of the international financial system to reduce the likelihood of such crises in the future. These goals are left for a companion study (Radelet and Sachs, 1998).

The argument proceeds in VII sections. In Section II we provide a general overview of financial crises and their diagnosis. Section III gives a description of recent macroeconomic and financial events in the crisis countries. In Section IV we show that the crisis was not anticipated by key market participants, at least till the end of 1996, and in general not till mid-1997, following the devaluation of the Thai Baht. Section V describes the triggering events of the crisis. Section VI discusses, and critiques, the early IMF role in policy management in the Asian crisis (up to December 1997). Section VII offers some observations about future directions of research.

II. Diagnosing Financial Crises

Not all financial crises are alike, even though superficial appearances may deceive. Only a close historical analysis, guided by theory, can disentangle the key features of any particular financial crisis, including the Asian crisis. We identify five main types of financial crises, which may in fact be intertwined in any particular historical episode:

1) Macroeconomic policy-induced crisis: Following the canonical Krugman (1979) model, a balance of payments crisis (currency depreciation; loss of foreign exchange reserves; collapse of a pegged exchange rate) arises when domestic credit expansion by the central bank is inconsistent with the pegged exchange rate. Often, as in the Krugman model, the credit expansion results from the monetization of budget deficits. Foreign exchange reserves fall gradually until the Central Bank is vulnerable to a sudden run, which exhausts the remaining reserves, and pushes the economy to a floating rate.

2) Financial panic: Following the Dybvig-Diamond (1983) model of a bank run, a financial panic is a case of multiple equilibria in the financial markets. A panic is an adverse equilibrium outcome in which short-term creditors suddenly withdraw their loans from a solvent borrower. In general terms, a panic can occur when three conditions hold: short-term debts exceed short-term assets; no single private-market creditor is large enough to supply all of the credits necessary to pay off existing short-term debts; and there is no lender of last resort. In this case, it becomes rational for each creditor to withdraw its credits if the other creditors are also fleeing from the borrower, even though each creditor would also be prepared to lend if the other creditors were to do the same. The panic may result in large economic losses (e.g. premature suspension of investment projects, liquidation of the borrower, creditor grab race, etc.).

3) Bubble collapse: Following Blanchard and Watson (1982) and others, a stochastic financial bubble occurs when speculators purchase a financial asset at a price above its fundamental value in the expectation of a subsequent capital gain. In each period, the bubble (measured as the deviation of the asset price from its fundamental price) may continue to grow, or may collapse with a positive probability. The collapse, when it occurs, is unexpected but not completely unforeseen, since market participants are aware of the bubble and the probability distribution regarding its collapse. A considerable amount of modeling has examined the conditions in which a speculative bubble can be a rational equilibrium.

4) Moral-hazard crisis: Following Akerlof and Romer (1996), a moral-hazard crisis arises because banks are able to borrow funds on the basis of implicit or explicit public guarantees of bank liabilities. If banks are undercapitalized or under-regulated, they may use these funds in overly risky or even criminal ventures. Akerlof and Romer argue that the "economics of looting," in which banks use their state backing to purloin deposits is more common than generally perceived, and played

a large role in the U.S. Savings and Loan crisis. Krugman (1998) similarly argues that the Asian crisis is a reflection of excessive gambling and indeed stealing by banks that gained access to domestic and foreign deposits by virtue of state guarantees on these deposits.

5) Disorderly workout: Following Sachs (1995), a disorderly workout occurs when an illiquid or insolvent borrower provokes a creditor grab race and a forced liquidation even though the borrower is worth more as an ongoing enterprise. A disorderly workout occurs especially when markets operate without the benefit of creditor coordination via bankruptcy law. The problem is sometimes known as a "debt overhang." In essence, coordination problems among creditors prevent the efficient provision of worker capital to the financially distressed borrower, and delay or prevent the eventual discharge of bad debts (e.g. via debt-equity conversions or debt reduction).

The theoretical differences among these five types of crises are significant at several levels: diagnosis, underlying mechanisms, prediction, prevention, and remediation. For example, to the extent that panic is important, policy makers face a condition in which viable economic activities are destroyed by a sudden and essentially unnecessary withdrawal of credits. The appropriate policy response, then, is to protect the economy through lender-of-last-resort activities. Alternatively, if the crisis results from the end of a bubble or the end of moral-hazard-based lending, it may be most efficient to avoid lender-of-last-resort operations, which simply keep the inefficient investments alive. Unfortunately, in real-life conditions, these various types of financial crisis can become intertwined, and therefore are difficult to diagnose. The end of a bubble, for example, may trigger a panic, or a panic may trigger insolvency and a disorderly workout. Attentiveness to these kinds of possibilities is extremely important for policy design.

Table 1 outlines four major considerations in the differential diagnosis and treatment of financial crises. Key distinguishing features are: (1) whether the crisis is anticipated at least in probabilistic terms (e.g. in cases

Distinguishing Among Financial Crises
Table 1

	Policy-induced crisis	Financial Panic	Bubble Collapse	Moral-hazard induced crisis	Disorderly workout
Anticipation of crisis by market participants & analysts	High	Low	Market participants and analysts understand probability of collapse	High. Creditors are lending based on state guarantees rather than fundamental values	High. Market participants understand the lack of coordination among creditors
Destruction of real economic activity	Not necessarily	High	Low. The end of the bubble may improve resource allocation	Low. The end of the moral-hazard based lending improves resource allocation	High. Creditor grab race; liquitity crisis of the borrower; premature liquidation of the borrower
Lending induced by moral hazards	Not necessarily	Not necessarily	Possibly	Yes. Most or all creditors are protected by explicit or implicit guarantees	Not necessarily
Case for offical intervention	Macroeconomic adjustment, especially budgetary reduction	Lender of last resort	No. Delaying the bursting of the bubble can lead to a deeper crisis later	No. State guarantees prolong the misallocation of resources	Yes. Public institutions may provide framework for an orderly workout

Five Asian* Economies: External Financing
(billions of dollars)
Table 2

	1994	1995	1996	1997e	1998f
Current account balance	-24.6	-41.3	-54.9	-26.0	-17.6
External financing, net	47.4	80.9	92.8	15.2	15.2
Private flows, net	40.5	77.4	93.0	-12.1	-9.4
Equity investment	12.2	15.5	19.1	-4.5	7.9
Direct equity	4.7	4.9	7.0	7.2	9.8
Portfolio equity	7.6	10.6	12.1	-11.6	-1.9
Private Creditors	28.2	61.8	74.0	-7.6	-17.3
Commercial banks	24.0	49.5	55.5	-21.3	-14.1
Non-bank private creditors	4.2	12.4	18.4	13.7	-3.2
"Official flows, net"	7.0	3.6	-0.2	27.2	24.6
Int'l financial institutions	-0.4	-0.6	-1.0	23.0	18.5
Bilateral creditors	7.4	4.2	0.7	4.3	6.1
Resident lending/other, net**	-17.5	-25.9	-19.6	-11.9	-5.7
Reserves excl. gold (- = increase)	-5.4	-13.7	-18.3	22.7	-27.1

e = estimate, f = IIF Forecast
* South Korea, Indonesia, Malaysia, Thailand and the Philippines.
** Including resident net lending, monetary gold, and errors & omissions.
Source: Institute of International Finance, Inc. (IIF), "Capital Flows to Emerging Market Economies,"
January 29, 1998.

of policy inconsistency, bubble collapse, disorderly workout), or whether the crisis is essentially unanticipated (financial panic); (2) whether the crisis destroys real economic value (e.g. a financial panic or disorderly workout) or instead brings to a close a period of resource mis-allocation (e.g. a collapse of a bubble); (3) whether the crisis mostly involves debtors backed by official resources (e.g. as in moral-hazard-induced banking crises), or debtors that lack state guarantees (e.g. panics which undermine non-bank corporate borrowers); and (4) whether there is a case for official intervention (e.g. as lender of last resort).

Financial panic is rarely the favored interpretation of a financial crisis. The essence of a panic is that a "bad" equilibrium occurs that did not have to happen. Market analysts and participants are much more prone to look for weightier explanations than simply a bad accident. Once in a while, though, a relatively clean test of the panic interpretation occurs. Perhaps the best recent case is the Mexican crisis in 1995. After the Mexican devaluation in December 1994, the Mexican Government was unable to roll over its short-term dollar-denominated debts (tesobonos). The Government was thrown to the brink of default. An emergency lender-of-last-resort operation led by the U.S. Government and the IMF provided the Mexican Government with up to $50 billion to repay the short term debts. The Mexican Government avoided default, repaid the emergency loans early, and resumed economic growth in 1996. Ex post, it is difficult to understand the market's failure to roll over $28 billion in tesobonos due in 1995 as anything other than panic in the face of a currency devaluation.

In the following sections, we will point out several reasons to suppose that the Asian financial crisis also has substantial elements of panic and disorderly workout. First, the crisis was largely unanticipated. Although a small number of market participants were concerned ex ante, the vast majority of players did not view the Southeast Asian economies as bubbles waiting to burst. Second, the crisis involved considerable lending to debtors that were not protected by state guarantees, and those loans are now going bad in large numbers. To be sure, many borrowers did have explicit or implicit guarantees (or thought they did), but a substantial number of purely private banks and firms without such insurance are now facing bankruptcy. Third, the crisis has led to a seizing up of bank credits to viable enterprises, especially through the lack of working capital for exporters. Fourth, the market has reacted most positively to initiatives that bring creditors and debtors together for orderly workouts, such as in Korea. Fifth, the triggering events of the crisis involved the sudden withdrawal of investor funds to the region, rather than simply a deflation of asset values (although falling land and stock prices contributed to the crisis, especially in Thailand).

III. Macroeconomic and Financial Processes in the Asian Crisis

The Asian financial crisis has involved several interlinked phenomena. The single most dramatic element – perhaps the defining element – of the crisis has been the rapid rever-

sal of private capital inflows into Asia. Table 2, reproduced from a recent report by the Institute for International Finance, gives an estimated breakdown of the reversal of flows for the five East Asian countries hit hardest by the crisis (Indonesia, Korea, Malaysia, Philippines, and Thailand, hereafter referred to as the Asian-5). According to these estimates, net private inflows dropped from $93 billion to -$12.1 billion, a swing of $105 billion on a combined pre-shock GDP of approximately $935 billion, or a swing of 11 percent of GDP. $77 billion of the $105 billion decline in inflows came from commercial bank lending. Direct investment remained constant at around $7 billion. The rest of the decline has come from a $24 billion fall of portfolio equity and a $5 billion decline in non-bank lending.

The sudden drop in bank lending followed a sustained period of large increases in cross-border bank loans, as shown in Tables 3 and 4. Again taking the Asian-5 countries as our point of reference, total foreign bank lending to these countries expanded from $210 billion at end-1995, to $261 billion at the end of 1996, an increase of 24 percent in a single year. Between the end of 1996 and mid-1997, bank lending expanded further to $274 billion, or an increase of 10 percent at an annual rate. The growth in bank loans clearly slowed during the first half of 1997, and actually declined slightly in the case of Thailand. Nonetheless, the continued increase in bank lending till mid-1997 is an important piece of evidence: outside of Thailand, the foreign banks were not running until the last moment, though the pace of bank lending was abating somewhat. Since net outflows of bank loans reached $21 billion for 1997 as a whole according to the IIF, and since inflows during the first half of the year were $13 billion according to the Bank of International Settlement (BIS), we can surmise that outflows during the second half of the year were approximately $34 billion (note that BIS data for the second half of 1997 have not yet been released). With a combined pre-shock GDP of around $935 billion, net inflows of bank loans amounted to around 5.9 percent of GDP

International Claims Held by Foreign Banks - Maturity and Sector *(billions of dollars)*
Table 3

	Total Outstanding	Obligations by Sector			Short Term	Reserves	Short Term / Reserves
		Banks	Public Sector	Non-bank Private			
A. End of 1995							
Indonesia	44.5	8.9	6.7	28.8	27.6	14.7	1.9
Malaysia	16.8	4.4	2.1	10.1	7.9	23.9	0.3
Philippines	8.3	2.2	2.7	3.4	4.1	7.8	0.5
Thailand	62.8	25.8	2.3	34.7	43.6	37.0	1.2
Korea	77.5	50.0	6.2	21.4	54.3	32.7	1.7
Total	209.9	91.3	20.0	98.4	137.5		
B. End of 1996							
Indonesia	55.5	11.7	6.9	36.8	34.2	19.3	1.8
Malaysia	22.2	6.5	2.0	13.7	11.2	27.1	0.4
Philippines	13.3	5.2	2.7	5.3	7.7	11.7	0.7
Thailand	70.2	25.9	2.3	41.9	45.7	38.7	1.2
Korea	100.0	65.9	5.7	28.3	67.5	34.1	2.0
Total	261.2	115.2	19.6	126.0	166.3		
C. Mid-1997							
Indonesia	58.7	12.4	6.5	39.7	34.7	20.3	1.7
Malaysia	28.8	10.5	1.9	16.5	16.3	26.6	0.6
Philippines	14.1	5.5	1.9	6.8	8.3	9.8	0.8
Thailand	69.4	26.1	2.0	41.3	45.6	31.4	1.5
Korea	103.4	67.3	4.4	31.7	70.2	34.1	2.1
Total	274.4	121.8	16.7	136.0	175.1		
Memo Item: Mexico							
end-1994	64.6	16.7	24.9	22.8	33.2	6.4	5.2
end-1995	57.3	11.5	23.5	22.3	26.0	17.1	1.5

in 1996, 2.8 percent of GDP in the first half of 1997, and -3.6 percent of GDP in the second half of 1997. Thus, the swing in bank loans between 1996 and the second half of 1997 is a remarkable 9.5 percent of GDP. It is very difficult to attribute a reversal of this magnitude in such a short period of time to changes in underlying economic fundamentals.

The bank lending went to both domestic banks and domestic non-bank borrowers during this period, as shown in Table 3. In Korea, lending was heavily to banks; in Indonesia, lending was heavily to non-bank corporate borrowers. In all countries except Korea, bank lending to non-banks exceeded lending to banks. We might suppose that international banks assumed that lending to banks was at least partly protected by lender-of-last-resort facilities, both domestic (e.g. from the central bank) and international (e.g. from the IMF). The same might be true for a portion of private sector firms with particularly strong political connections. There is no reason to suppose, however, that foreign banks expected such guarantees on lending to the majority of non-bank private corpora-

International Claims Held by Foreign Banks
Distribution by Country of Origin *(billions of dollars)*
Table 4

	Total Outstanding	Japan	Claims held by banks from: USA	Germany	All others
A. End of 1995					
Indonesia	44.5	21.0	2.8	3.9	16.8
Malaysia	16.8	7.3	1.5	2.2	5.8
Philippines	8.3	1.0	2.9	0.7	3.7
Thailand	62.8	36.9	4.1	5.0	16.8
Korea	77.5	21.5	7.6	7.3	41.1
Sub-Total	209.9	87.7	18.9	19.1	84.2
Total, all reporting countries *	429.3	132.6	264.0		
B. End of 1996					
Indonesia	55.5	22.0	5.3	5.5	22.7
Malaysia	22.2	8.2	2.3	3.9	7.8
Philippines	13.3	1.6	3.9	1.8	6.0
Thailand	70.2	37.5	5.0	6.9	20.8
Korea	100.0	24.3	9.4	10.0	56.3
Sub-Total	261.2	93.6	25.9	28.1	113.6
Total, all reporting countries *		389.4	165.7	292.3	
C. Mid-1997					
Indonesia	58.7	23.2	4.6	5.6	25.3
Malaysia	28.8	10.5	2.4	5.7	10.2
Philippines	14.1	2.1	2.8	2.0	7.2
Thailand	69.4	37.7	4.0	7.6	20.1
Korea	103.4	23.7	10.0	10.8	58.9
Sub-Total	274.4	97.2	23.8	31.7	121.7
Total, all reporting countries *		404.4	166.3	301.2	

* Reporting countries include G-10 plus Austria, Denmark, Finland, Ireland, Luxembourg, Norway, Spain, plus 15 financial centers
Source: Bank for International Settlements

tions. Notably, lending to non-banks as well as to banks continued to increase strongly until mid-1997.

The withdrawal of foreign capital has had several interlocking macroeconomic and microeconomic effects. Most immediately and dramatically, exchange rates depreciated, after a defense of a pegged exchange rate (as in Thailand and the Philippines)[3] or a crawling peg (as in Indonesia, Malaysia, and Korea). Domestic interest rates soared upon the withdrawal of foreign credits, leading directly to a tightening of domestic credit

conditions even before central banks reacted to the crisis.[4] Since the withdrawal of credits immediately led to a sharp reduction of absorption (which had been financed by foreign capital inflows), not only the nominal exchange rate, but also the real exchange rate (defined as the ratio of tradeable to non-tradeable goods prices) depreciated.

The combination of real exchange rate depreciation and sharply higher interest rates led to a rapid rise in non-performing loans (NPLS) in the banking sectors of the Asian economies, especially as real estate projects went into bankruptcy. In many cases, real estate developers had borrowed in unhedged dollar-denominated loans from domestic banks to finance real estate projects. These projects failed under the weight of currency depreciation. Moreover, to the extent that banks had open short positions in dollars (i.e. net dollar borrowers), the exchange rate depreciation led to a sudden loss of bank capital. The combination of sharply rising NPLS and direct balance sheet losses due to currency depreciation has wiped out a substantial portion of the market value of bank capital in Indonesia, Thailand, and Korea.

The sudden withdrawal of foreign financing was itself an enormous contractionary shock. The resulting collapse of domestic bank capital added sharply to the contraction by severely restricting bank lending. Banks cut back their own lending both because the banks themselves were illiquid (as a result of the withdrawal of foreign credits, and in some cases, deposits) and because they were de-capitalized. The de-capitalized banks restricted their lending in order to move towards capital-adequacy ratios required by bank supervisors and reinforced by the IMF. The rush to improve bank capital adequacy took on urgent proportions in Indonesia, Korea, and Thailand, after the IMF threatened to require the closure of undercapitalized banks. This threat was credible in view of the moves to suspend or close financial companies and banks throughout the region at the start of each of the IMF adjustment programs.

As described below, the IMF programs up till the end of 1997 apparently added both to the panic and to the contractionary force of the financial crisis. The IMF programs generally called for six key actions: immediate bank closures; quick restoration of minimum capital-adequacy standards (especially in the first Thai and Indonesian programs); tight domestic credit; high interest rates on central bank discount facilities; fiscal contraction; and non-financial sector structural changes. Of all of these measures, the bank closures, capital adequacy enforcement, and tight credit were probably the most consequential, in that they probably added to the virulence of the banking panics that were already underway in these economies. Domestic bank lending stopped abruptly in the three countries with Fund programs (Indonesia, Korea, and Thailand). There were widespread anecdotes of firms unable to obtain working capital, even in support of confirmed export orders from abroad.

On December 22, 1997, Moody's downgraded the sovereign debt of all three of these countries, putting them below investment grade. The "junk bond" status of these countries immediately applied to the banking and non-bank corporate sectors as well, by virtue of the "sovereign ceiling" doctrine, according to which all domestic enterprises must have a credit rating no higher than the sovereign. There were two major immediate implications of the downgrade. First, most of the commercial banks in these countries could no longer issue internationally recognized letters of credit for domestic exporters and importers, since the banks were all rated as sub-investment grade. Second, the downgrading immediately prompted a further round of debt liquidations, since many portfolio managers are required by law to maintain investments only in investment-grade securities. Moreover, the downgrade triggered various put options linked to credit ratings, enabling borrowers to call in loans immediately upon the downgrade.

As a result of the creditor panic, the bank runs, and the sovereign downgrades, Korea, Indonesia and Thailand were thrown into partial debt defaults. In the case of Korea, these defaults were initially handled by an emergency standstill of debt repayments, followed by a concerted rollover of the short-term debt into longer term instruments backed by Korean Government guarantees. This rollover applies to around one-third of the Korean external debt falling due in 1998. In the case of Indonesia, the defaults were unilateral, and have not been followed to this point by any negotiated arrangements. In Thailand, the extent of outright default remains unclear, though certain payments by non-bank borrowers are clearly in effective default.

IV. Why the Asian Crisis Was Not Predicted

Capital Flows into Southeast Asia

We have stressed that at the core of the Asian financial crisis were the massive capital inflows that were attracted into the region during the 1990s. Capital inflows increased from an average of 1.4 percent of GDP between 1986-90 to 6.7 percent between 1990-96. In Thailand, capital inflows averaged a remarkably high 10.3 percent of GDP between 1990-96. The bulk of Thailand's inflows came in the form of offshore borrowing by banks and private corporations, which together averaged 7.6 percent of GDP in the 1990s. Portfolio capital inflows (1.6 percent of GDP) and Foreign Direct Investment (FDI) (1.1 percent of GDP) were substantially smaller. Although Thailand was the most extreme case, across the region the bulk of the capital inflows were from offshore borrowing by banks and the private sector. Malaysia is the only exception, where extraordinarily large FDI inflows (6.6 percent of GDP) were larger than bank and private sector borrowing (3.6 percent of GDP). In each country, net portfolio capital inflows averaged less than 2 percent of GDP. In Malaysia, where short-term foreign investors have been harshly criticized, net portfolio inflows were either very small or actually negative in each year of the 1990s. Importantly, net government borrowing was less than half a percent of GDP in each country, except in the Philippines, where it averaged 1.3 percent of GDP. Banks (in Thailand and Korea) and private corporations (in Indonesia) were the main forces behind the capital inflows, not the government.

The surge in capital inflows had its roots in changes in both internal economic policies and world markets. Internationally, capital market liberalization in the industrialized countries facilitated a greater flow of funds to emerging markets around the globe, including the Philippines. New bond and equity mutual funds, new bank syndicates, increased Eurobond lending and other innovations allowed capital to flow across borders quickly and easily. In addition, low interest rates in the U.S. and Japan favored increased outward investment from these countries to Southeast Asia and other emerging markets. Domestically, five broad factors contributed to the capital flows:

- Continuing, and in some cases increasing, high economic growth gave confidence to foreign investors;
- Wide-ranging financial deregulation made it much easier for banks and domestic corporations to tap into foreign capital to finance domestic investments;
- Financial sector deregulation was not accompanied by adequate supervision, especially in Thailand. Lax supervision created an environment conducive to high rates of foreign borrowing, since it allowed banks to take on substantial foreign currency and maturity risks;
- Nominal exchange rates were effectively pegged to the U.S. dollar, with either limited variation (Thailand, Malaysia, Korea, and the Philippines) or very predictable change (Indonesia). Predictable exchange rates reduced perceived risks for investors, furthering encouraging capital inflows;
- Governments gave special incentives that encouraged foreign borrowing, even after concern arose about "hot money" flows in the early 1990s. Banks operating in the Bangkok International Banking Facility (BIBF), which operated exclusively in borrowing and lending foreign currencies, received special tax breaks. In the Philippines, banks are subject to a tax rate of 10 percent for onshore income from foreign exchange loans, whereas other income is subject to the regular corporate income tax rate of 35 percent. Philippine banks also face no reserve requirements for foreign currency deposits, while for peso deposits the reserve requirement currently is 13 percent, down from 15 percent in 1996 (IMF, 1997a).

Capital flows from abroad can be an important engine for growth, if they are channeled to productive investment activities. However, foreign capital flows can make macroeconomic management much more complex when they are large, volatile, unsustainable, and/or poorly utilized.

Macroeconomic pressures tend to manifest themselves through two channels:

- Capital inflows lead to a real appreciation of the exchange rate, and to an expansion of non-tradeables sectors at the expense of tradeables sectors. Even though this real appreciation tends to be temporary (since it is reversed when the net foreign borrowing is serviced in future years), new investments tend to be drawn towards nontradeables, partly as a result of myopic expectations regarding real exchange rate trends.

- High levels of capital inflows place new pressures on underdeveloped financial systems. In both commercial banks (which are intermediating rapidly growing levels of foreign financing), and central banks (which are trying to regulate and supervise rapidly growing activities), institutional change generally cannot keep pace with the high levels of international capital flows. There are ample conditions for excessive risk taking, poor banking judgment, and even outright fraud.

Both of these kinds of pressures, over time, contribute to increasing financial risk.

Following a liberalization and a rapid inflow of capital, some slowdown of foreign borrowing is to be expected. The most profitable investment opportunities are seized early on; overinvestment in nontradeables (e.g. real estate) becomes evident; and a slowdown in export growth gives pause to both foreign and domestic investors. There is no reason, however, to expect a sudden and sharp reversal of capital flows. The preceding inflow of foreign funds into Asia was a precondition for the subsequent crisis, but the capital inflows do not, by themselves, provide an explanation of the crisis that followed.

Signs that the Crisis Was Unpredicted

One of the most unusual aspects of the Asian crisis is the extent to which it was unpredicted by market participants and market analysts. Although some observers did anticipate the possibility of a crisis (see, for example, Park, 1996), such warnings were rare. This actually tells us a lot. Just as the silence of the hound alerted Sherlock Holmes to the real culprit in The Silver Blaze, the fact that the financial markets did not signal alarm helps us to understand the real nature of the current crisis. All signs point to a very recent and dramatic shift in expectations. For example, capital inflows remained strong through 1996, and in most cases till mid-1997. The only exception to this is found in the equity markets in Thailand and Korea, where foreign investors became uneasy in 1996. In Malaysia, both bank and equity investors showed optimism until 1997. Equity markets began a rather steep decline in March 1997, while bank inflows continued to be very strong at least till mid-year. In Indonesia, both the stock market and bank lending remained strong till mid-1997.

Another indicator of market sentiment is the risk premia attached to loans to the emerging market economies. To the extent that markets anticipated the growing risks of capital inflows, lending terms and conditions would have tightened in advance of the onset of the crisis. In fact, the evidence suggests just the opposite. A recent study by William Cline and Kevin Barnes (1998) at the Institute for International Economics found that bond spreads (i.e., the interest rate premium over U.S. Treasury securities) fell in emerging markets, including Southeast Asia, between mid-1995 (as the Mexico crisis came to a close) and mid-1997 to levels well below what could be justified by economic fundamentals in these countries. Similarly, syndicated loan spreads were also low and falling before the crisis. In Indonesia, Malaysia, the Philippines, and Korea, syndicated loan spreads were lower in early 1997 than they had been in 1996. Only in Thailand did spreads begin to rise somewhat in early 1997, but from a very low base. The spread on Thai sovereign bonds stood at an extremely low 39 basis points in the second quarter of 1996, and was just 43 basis points at the end of 1996. The spread began to rise in early 1997, but was still just 79 basis points in August, a month after the crisis had begun.

The credit rating agencies such as Standard & Poor's and Moody's provide an

Market Creditworthiness
Moody's and Standard & Poor's Long-Term Debt Ratings, 1996-97

Table 5

	Jan. 15, 1996		December 2, 1996		June 25, 1997		December 13, 1997	
	Rating	Outlook	Rating	Outlook	Rating	Outlook	Rating	Outlook
Moody's (Foreign currency debt)								
Indonesia	Baa3		Baa3		Baa3		Baa3	
Malaysia	A1		A1		A1		A1	
Mexico	Ba2		Ba2		Ba2		Ba2	
Philippines	Ba2		Ba2		Ba1		Ba1	
South Korea	A1		A1	Stable	A2		Baa2	Negative
Thailand	A2		A2		A2		Baa1	Negative
Standard & Poor's					Oct. 97		Oct. 97	Oct. 97
Indonesia: Foreign currency debt	BBB	Stable	BBB	Stable	BBB	Stable	BBB-	Negative
Domestic currency debt			A+		A+		A-	Negative
Malaysia: Foreign currency debt	A+	Stable	A+	Stable	A+	Positive	A+	Negative
Domestic currency debt	AA+		AA+		AA+		AA+	Negative
Philippines: Foreign currency debt	BB	Positive	BB	Positive	BB+	Positive	BB+	Stable
Domestic currency debt	BBB+		BBB+		A-		A-	Stable
South Korea: Foreign currency debt	AA-	Stable	AA-	Stable	A+		A-	Stable
Thailand: Foreign currency debt	A	Stable	A	Stable	A	Stable	BBB-	Negative
Domestic currency debt			AA		AA+		A	Negative
Mexico: Foreign currency debt	BB		BB		BB		BB	
Domestic currency debt	BBB+	Negative	BBB+	Stable	BBB+	Positive	BBB+	Positive

Rating Systems, from highest to lowest:
Moody's: Aaa, Aa1, Aa2, A1, A2, A3, Baa1, Baa2, Baa3, Ba1, Ba2, Ba3
S&P's: AAA, AA+, AA, AA-, A+, A, A-, BBB+, BBB-, BBB+, BB+, BB-, BB

Euromoney Country Risk Ratings
(country rank out of approximately 180)
Table 6

	March '93	March '95	March '97	Sept. '97	Dec. '97
Indonesia	.41	.40	.43	.43	.49
Malaysia	.33	.28	.28	.28	.35
Philippines	.71	.60	.54	.49	.57
Thailand	.34	.30	.34	.46	.51
South Korea	.32	.26	.22	.27	.30
Singapore	.14	.8	.3	.11	.16
Japan	.1	.2	.13	.13	.18
Hong Kong	.25	.24	.27	.25	.25

Expectations of Export Growth
Table 7a

	Expected '96	Outcome '96	Expected '97	Revised '97
Indonesia	14.3	4.9	15.0	10.0
Malaysia	18.0	7.3	15.0	7.4
Philippines	25.0	17.7	23.0	22.8
Thailand	22.0	-1.7	7.7	-0.1

Note: Expected 1996 from December 1995 forecast; Expected '97 from December 1996 forecast; Revised 1997 from August 1997 forecast

Exchange Rate Expectations
Table 7b

	August Forecast: 3-month Horizon	October 29 Rate
Indonesia	2500	3610 (44.4)
Malaysia	2.75	3.40 (23.6)
Philippines	28.00	35.1 (25.3)
Thailand	32.00	39.1 (22.2)

Note: Expectation error as percent of August forecast in parentheses
Source: August Forecast, Goldman Sachs, *Asian Economic Quarterly,* August, p. 12. October rate, *Economist* magazine, Nov. 1, 1997.

ongoing assessment of credit risk in the emerging markets. We may therefore examine, directly, whether there was a recognition of increasing risk in these markets. If the markets expected a financial crisis and public sector bailouts, the ratings of sovereign bonds should have fallen in the run-up to the crisis. Instead, upon examining data such as those in Table 5, we find that the rating agencies did not signal increased risk until after the onset of the crisis itself. Long-term sovereign debt ratings remained unchanged throughout 1996 and the first half of 1997 for each of the Asian countries except the Philippines, where debt was actually upgraded in early 1997. In each country, the outlook was described as "positive" or "stable" through June 1997. Only many weeks after the crisis had begun did these ratings agencies downgrade the regions' debt. At that point, rather than helping creditors assess future risk, the downgrades simply pushed interest rates higher and added to the panic.

Aside from credit rating agencies, a number of independent firms provide ongoing risk analysis. One widely circulated assessment is the Euromoney Country Risk Assessments, shown in Table 6. We can trace the changes in risk attached to the key Asian economies according to the Euromoney rankings. In most cases, Asia's country rankings changed little or even improved (in the cases of the Philippines and South Korea) between March 1993 and March 1997, providing little warning of the growing risks to investors. Even in September 1997, after the crisis had begun, the Philippines' ranking continued to improve, and Indonesia's and Malaysia's remained steady. Only Thailand's and South Korea's rankings fell sharply. Rankings for the other countries did not tumble until December, five months after the onset of the crisis. Note that the country rankings for Singapore (from 3rd in March 1997 to 16th in December 1997) and Japan (from 1st in March 1993 to 18th in December 1997) have both fallen sharply.

The leading investment banks also provide ongoing forecasts of overall economic performance and market returns. Therefore,

we can look at the major forecasts to see whether there were growing indications of risk in the lead-up to the crisis. Table 7 shows the export and exchange rate forecasts as produced by Goldman Sachs, perhaps the most capable of all the investment banks in the region. These forecasts show the extent to which the dramatic slowdown in export growth in 1996 and 1997 was unanticipated. Even after the poor 1996 performance, analysts expected a rebound in 1997 (except in Thailand), which was not forthcoming (except in the Philippines). With regard to exchange rates, no one in the markets anticipated the extent to which currencies would depreciate, even once the crisis began. The August 1997 forecasts shown in Table 7b – produced one month after the crisis had begun in Thailand – show little expectation of the slide which took place in the following months.

Another measure of expectations for the region may be found in IMF reports on the Asian economies. The IMF makes two kinds of public assessments: overall market forecasts, as presented in the its periodic World Economic Outlooks, and country assessments, generally contained in the reports of Executive Board discussions of Article IV consultations with member countries. With regard to the market forecasts, the IMF gave very little indication of a sense of macroeconomic risk to the Asian region. As late as the October 1997 World Economic Outlook (IMF, 1997b), the IMF predicted 6.0 percent growth for Korea in 1998, and 7.4 percent for developing Asia (or 5.4 percent for developing Asia excluding China and India). These marked a predicted slowdown of about 1.5 percentage points relative to 1995.

With regard to the Article IV consultations, the 1997 IMF Annual Report (IMF, 1997c) contains summaries of IMF Executive Board discussions on Indonesia, Korea, and Thailand that took place during the second half of 1996. Since the Annual Report is not completed until much later (transmitted in July 1997), the IMF staff may update the summary with an additional paragraph in the event of dramatic changes in policies or

Overall Central Government Budget Balance
(% of GDP)
Table 8

Year	Indonesia	Malaysia	Philippines	Thailand	Korea	Mexico
1990	0.4	-3.0	-3.5	4.5	-0.7	-2.8
1991	0.4	-2.0	-2.1	4.7	-1.6	-0.2
1992	-0.4	-0.8	-1.2	2.8	-0.5	1.5
1993	0.6	0.2	-1.5	2.1	0.6	0.3
1994	0.9	2.3	1.1	1.9	0.3	-0.7
1995	2.2	0.9	0.5	2.9	0.3	-0.6
1996	1.2	0.7	0.3	2.3	-0.1	n.a.

economic circumstances. Thus, we may interpret the summaries as conveying the basic attitude of the IMF up to the date of the Annual Report, i.e. until mid-1997. In general, the IMF Executive Board expressed concerns about the Asian economies, but in the context of overall optimism. There are several common features in the analysis of the three countries. The IMF recommends: (1) more flexible exchange rates; (2) improved banking sector supervision; (3) tightened fiscal policy; and (4) increased openness to capital flows. The most explicit concerns were raised in the case of Indonesia; the least, in the case of Korea. But in no case did the Board express major concerns. Some excerpts of the Board discussions are included in the Appendix.

Stock prices provide the only indication of growing concern among market participants in the months preceding the crisis. The Thai stock market fell continuously after January 1996, a full 18 months before the crisis began. The main index fell 40 percent in 1996 alone, and dropped an additional 20 percent in the first six months of 1997 as concern grew over the health of property companies and financial institutions. The Seoul bourse also fell sharply during 1996 and early 1997. In the case of Thailand, the stock market decline was matched by a slight decline in foreign bank lending in the first half of 1997. In the case of Korea, foreign bank lending continued to rise in the first half of 1997, albeit at a slower rate than in 1996. In Indonesia, by contrast, both the stock market and bank lending show continued confidence until mid-1997. In Malaysia, the stock market began to turn down in March, while foreign bank lending rose very strongly in the first half of 1997 (increasing by a remarkable 29.7 percent in the six-month period).

Why Didn't the Alarm Bells Ring?

One reason that the crisis was largely unanticipated by international lenders and most market observers was that many of the signals that analysts normally associate with impending problems showed little sign of deterioration. Most fundamental aspects of macroeconomic management remained sound throughout the early 1990s. Government budgets, which were at the center of economic crises in Latin America in the 1980s, registered regular surpluses in each country. This will be an important fact to remember when we turn to appropriate solutions for addressing the crisis. While governments may have been too enthusiastic in promoting large-scale infrastructure investment financed by foreign inflows, and while there are no doubt important fiscal liabilities outside of the formal budget, all five countries maintained a fairly responsible budgetary position between 1990 and 1996, as shown in Table 8. Thailand's budget reportedly deteriorated markedly in late 1996 and early 1997, partly in response to the crisis itself, rather than as an independent cause. Partly as a result of budgetary prudence, inflation rates have been below 10 percent across the region during the 1990s. Sovereign debt remained at prudent levels, and had been steadily falling in the Philippines and Indonesia, the two countries in the region with historically high levels of sovereign foreign debt.

Similarly, domestic savings and investment rates were very high throughout the region, suggesting that even if foreign capital flows slowed, robust growth could continue. Moreover, while current account deficits were large, capital inflows were even larger, so foreign exchange reserves were actually growing across the region (except in Malaysia were they leveled off after 1993). Foreign exchange reserves at the end of 1996 were well over four months of imports in each country except South Korea, where they were equivalent to 2.8 months of imports. In Thailand, official figures suggest that reserves reached a seemingly very healthy $38.6 billion at the end of 1996, equivalent to over 7 months of imports (although it is apparently around this time that Thailand began to take forward positions in the foreign exchange market, so the official figures may overstate the actual level of net reserves).

At the same time, world market conditions did not portend a crisis, as they had in Latin America when world interest rates rose, commodity prices were highly volatile, and industrial country growth rates were slow. Indeed, world interest rates have been unusually low in recent years, so that the burden of repaying foreign obligations did not seem onerous. Although some important prices (e.g., semiconductors) slumped, key commodity prices have been relatively stable, so external terms of trade changed little. Of course, the Japanese economy has been very sluggish throughout the 1990s, but the U.S. economy, which is the major market for most of Asia's exports, has been very robust. In sum, the macroeconomic fundamentals across Asia seemed sound, and the usual alarm bells were not ringing. As a result, the crisis was not easily predictable.

Some Signs of Growing Risk

There were, however, several signs of growing financial vulnerability during 1996 and early 1997. In some cases (e.g., growing current account deficits, overvalued exchange rates, and slowing export growth), these signs seemed merely to suggest growing imbalances and the need for a modest adjustment, but not an impending major crisis. In other cases, important indicators appear to have been missed by the market (e.g., rapid expansion of commercial bank credit and growing short-term foreign debt).

In line with the high levels of capital inflow, current account deficits were growing increasingly large across the region in the early 1990s, and were far higher than they had been in the late 1980s. Between 1985 and 1989, current account deficits averaged just 0.3 percent of GDP in the five countries (Table 9). In fact, South Korea and Malaysia had current account surpluses of 4.3 percent and 2.4 percent of GDP, respectively. The largest deficit was Indonesia's 2.5 percent of GDP, which resulted primarily from the fall in world petroleum prices in the mid-1980s. By contrast, between 1990-96, current account deficits averaged 4.0 percent of GDP, and in most countries were rising. Only Indonesia's deficit remained basically unchanged relative to the earlier period, although it rose slightly to 3.5 percent of GDP in 1995 and 1996. Korea's current account position shifted by 6 percentage points of GDP, which is a very large change, but the deficit still averaged less than 2 percent of GDP, which appeared prudent. However, in 1996 the deficit abruptly grew to 4.8 percent of GDP. Malaysia's deficit increased by 8 percentage points of GDP, Thailand's by nearly 5 percentage points, and the Philippines' by about 3 percentage points (though in this case, the actual increase was probably larger, since certain Philippines inflows are probably mis-classified as current

Balance of Payments 1985-96
(% of GDP)
Table 9

	Korea 1985-89	Korea 1990-96	Indonesia 1985-89	Indonesia 1990-96	Malaysia 1985-89	Malaysia 1990-96	Philippines 1985-89	Philippines 1990-96	Thailand 1985-89	Thailand 1990-96
Current Account	4.3	-1.7	-2.5	-2.5	2.4	-5.6	-0.5	-3.3	-2.0	-6.8
Balance of Trade	3.6	-1.2	5.9	1.5	13.7	3.2	-2.9	-8.7	-2.2	-4.7
Exports	30.7	25.0	21.9	24.2	56.1	73.2	17.1	17.4	22.9	29.6
Import	-27.2	-26.2	-15.9	-19.7	-42.5	-70.0	-20.0	-26.1	-25.1	-34.3
Capital & Financial Account	-2.5	2.5	3.5	4.1	0.5	9.6	1.4	5.5	4.2	10.2
Direct Investment (net)	-0.1	-0.3	0.5	1.2	2.4	6.9	1.0	1.1	1.1	1.5
Portfolio Investment (net)	0.2	1.9	0.0	0.9	1.0	-1.0	0.2	0.3	1.2	1.5
Equity Securities	0.0	0.8	0.0	0.5	0.0	0.0	0.0	0.0	0.8	0.7
Debt Securities	0.1	1.1	0.0	0.4	1.0	-1.0	0.2	0.3	0.4	0.9
Other Investment (net)	-2.4	1.0	3.0	2.0	-2.8	3.8	0.2	4.0	2.0	7.1
Monetary Authorities	0.0	0.0	0.0	0.0	0.0	0.0	-0.6	0.0	0.0	0.0
General Government	-1.2	-0.3	2.6	0.5	-1.7	-0.3	2.3	1.1	0.2	-0.4
Banks	-0.8	1.2	0.4	1.2	0.0	2.4	-1.2	1.6	1.5	4.0
Other Sectors	-0.4	1.2	0.4	1.2	0.0	2.4	-1.2	1.6	1.5	4.0
Financing	-1.7	-0.6	-0.1	-1.1	-2.9	-5.0	-1.8	-1.8	-3.0	-3.6
Reserve Assets	-1.4	-0.6	-0.2	-1.0	-2.7	-5.0	-1.0	-1.7	-2.7	-3.5

account receipts). But the current account deficit is not always a good predictor: Indonesia and South Korea, with the smallest deficits, have arguably been the hardest hit countries, while Malaysia's deficit was much larger in 1995 (8.6 percent of GDP) than it was in 1996 (5.3 percent) or early 1997.

In line with the current account deficits and large capital inflows, exchange rates appreciated significantly in real terms between 1990 and the first quarter of 1997. It is difficult to precisely measure real exchange rates in these countries, since there are no accurate, direct data on the prices of tradable and non-tradable goods, or on labor productivity or labor costs. In Table 10, we show a common approximation in which the real exchange rate is calculated as the ratio $(EP)^*/P$, where P is the home-country consumer price index, $(EP)^*$ is the foreign country wholesale price index expressed in the local currency, by converting the foreign WPI to the domestic currency using the contemporaneous nominal exchange rate.[5] $(EP)^*$ is calculated using a geometric average of prices for the major developed-country trading partners.[6] (We calculated alternative measures of the Real Exchange Rate (RER) using foreign consumer and import prices indices in the numerator, as well as a simple ratio of domestic wholesale to consumer prices indices, with similar results).

In Table 10, we observe a significant real appreciation between 1990 and 1997 Q1 in all five countries. The real appreciation exceeds 25 percent in each of the four Southeast Asian nations, and was especially rapid after 1994, when the US dollar began to appreciate against other major world currencies. Indeed, in many ways the appreciation of the dollar against the yen marked a turning point for Southeast Asia and the beginning of the stage of overvaluation. The appreciation in Korea was a more modest 12 percent (but amounted to over 30 percent between 1987 and 1997). In fact, the actual real appreciations may have been even larger than these indices indicate, since our proxy for non-tradeables prices (the domestic CPI) does not include property, real estate, and other non-tradables sectors that were booming in the early 1990s.

Despite their simplicity, these indices are informative. Such large appreciations in a relatively short period of time have often been associated with a subsequent balance-of-payments crisis. Nevertheless, we should be careful not to overstate the magnitude of the appreciations. While they signaled the need for some kind of correction, the appreciations were not nearly as large as those in Latin America. Mexico's exchange rate appreciated in real terms by 40 percent between 1988 and 1993, just before its most recent crisis. In Argentina, Brazil, and Chile, exchange rates have appreciated by 45 percent or more since 1990, without the kind of crisis seen in either Mexico or Southeast Asia.

As expected with the real appreciation, export growth rates fell sharply in 1996 and 1997. Export growth, as measured in nominal dollar terms, fell from an average of 24.8 percent in the five countries in 1995 to just 7.2 percent in 1996, and fell further in early 1997. In Thailand, exports were actually lower (by 2 percent) in nominal dollar terms in 1996 than they had been in 1995. (In fact, the slowdown in Thailand's exports was ultimately a critical factor in the reversal of expectations in mid-1997 that launched the crisis). Broadly speaking, the export slowdown should have provided some indication that investment quality was weakening, and that firms would be less able to repay foreign exchange obligations. Nevertheless, the slowdown was thought to be very short term and accounted for by specific commodities (e.g., semiconductors), rather than a sign of an impending crisis.

Probably the biggest signs of growing risk were in the financial sector. Financial institutions were becoming increasingly fragile throughout the 1990s. Banks strained to keep up with both rapidly growing incomes (and the concurrent demand for more sophisticated financial services) and the huge amounts of capital flowing in from abroad. Credit to the private sector expanded very rapidly, with much of it financed by offshore borrowing by the banking sector. Financial sector claims on the private sector jumped from around 100 percent of GDP in 1990 to over 140 percent in Malaysia, Thailand, and Korea (Table 11). In

Real Exchange Rate Index (Based on WPI; Trade-Weighted, 1990 = 100)
Table 10

Year	Indonesia	Malaysia	Philippines	Thailand	China	Korea	Argentina	Brazil	Chile	Mexico
December 1988	98	98	90	102	80	102	156	159	94	106
" 1989	93	94	85	98	85	95	692	175	99	107
" 1990	100	100	100	100	100	100	100	100	100	100
" 1991	99	99	82	97	103	99	66	112	91	85
" 1992	92	87	69	90	98	94	49	119	74	74
" 1993	88	88	71	88	86	93	42	148	71	67
" 1994	92	86	62	89	109	91	44	53	66	111
" 1995	89	84	63	87	95	88	46	39	65	123
" 1996	80	78	56	80	84	88	44	35	61	95
March 1997	75	72	53	75	79	89	42	33	55	81
June 1997	78	75	54	76	80	89	42	33	55	79
September 1997	99	92	66	104	77	88	42	33	53	75
December 1997	150	180	75	124	74	157	41	33	53	75

Notes:
1. An increase means depreciation.
2. End-of Period Exchange Rates
3. Estimates are based on trade weights of OECD countries excluding Mexico and Korea.

the Philippines, the stock of credit was much smaller (reaching just 49 percent of GDP in 1996), but credit grew by an average of over 40 percent per year from 1993 to 1996. Only in Indonesia did credit growth remain comparatively modest. Both the commercial banks and their supervisors at the central banks had difficulty adapting to these changes.[7]

Apparently much of this credit headed for speculative investments in real estate markets, rather than into increasing productive capacity for manufactured exports as in earlier periods. Although official data show only a small share of private bank credit for real estate, these figures probably understate the true amount, as firms apparently diverted their own working capital and other loans towards real estate. The weaknesses of these financial systems were widely recognized and discussed, both in and out of official circles. We note, for example, the cover story of an April 1993 edition of the *Far East Economic Review* – published more than four years before the crisis – which wondered aloud whether Indonesia's new Cabinet would "fix the banks." But little action was taken to strengthen the banks, and some policy changes (e.g., the establishment of the Bangkok International Banking Facility) actually weakened the system further.

At least part of the expansion in private credit was ultimately financed by commercial bank offshore borrowing. Partial financial liberalization in the late 1980s and early 1990s gave banks much more latitude to act as financial intermediaries and channel foreign money into domestic enterprises. In the Philippines, foreign liabilities of commercial banks skyrocketed from 5.5 percent to 17.2 percent of GDP between 1993 and 1996, and continued to grow rapidly through the middle of 1997 (Table 13). In Thailand, these liabilities jumped even more sharply, from 5.9 percent of GDP in 1992 to 28.4 percent of GDP in 1995. Indeed, the net foreign assets of the Thai banking system fell from 14 percent in 1993 to zero in 1995. In Malaysia, foreign liabilities of the banking sector grew rapidly to peak at 19.5 percent of GDP in 1993, before

falling off sharply by 1996. These liabilities did not grow as rapidly in Indonesia, where much of the offshore borrowing was undertaken directly by private firms, without using domestic banks as intermediaries (hence the somewhat smaller buildup in commercial bank credit to the private sector in Indonesia). Nonetheless, the risks to the Indonesian economy were similar: rupiah revenue streams were expected to repay dollar liabilities, leaving these firms exposed to significant exchange rate risks.

The sharp increase in foreign borrowing by domestic banks and private corporations is evident from data from the Bank for International Settlements (BIS), as we saw earlier in Table 3. Total obligations to foreign banks of the five countries grew from $210 billion to $260 billion in 1996 alone. Obligations by the banking sector jumped from $91 billion to $115 billion, even after foreign bank lending to Thai banks had leveled off because of growing concerns about the Thai financial system. Particularly significant is the sharp increase in short-term debt, especially in Indonesia, Thailand, and Korea. The short-term debts owed to banks by these three countries reached $147 billion in 1996. Of course, the actual amounts of short-term liabilities were even larger, since these data do not include offshore issues of commercial paper and other non-bank liabilities. The use of short-term foreign currency borrowing to finance domestic investments in real estate and other non-tradeable activities was particularly dangerous. Banks became increasingly vulnerable for at least two reasons. First, by borrowing in foreign exchange and lending in local currencies, the banks were exposed to the risk of foreign exchange losses from a depreciation. Even if the domestic loans were denominated in dollars, borrowers that were not earning foreign exchange (e.g. real estate) faced bankruptcy in the event of depreciation. Second, to the extent that banks borrowed offshore in short-term maturities and lent onshore with longer payback periods, they were exposed to the risk of a run.

A particularly telling indicator of these risks is the ratio of short-term debt to foreign

Money and Credit
Table 11

	1990	1991	1992	1993	1994	1995	1996
Indonesia							
M2 (share of GDP)	43.3	43.7	45.8	43.4	44.9	48.3	52.5
M2 (annual growth rate)		17.5	19.8	20.2	20.0	27.2	27.2
Claims on Private Sector (share of GDP)	50.6	50.7	49.5	48.9	51.9	53.7	55.8
Claims on Private Sector (share of GDP)		16.7	11.4	25.5	23.0	22.6	21.4
Malaysia							
M2 (share of GDP)	66.2	69.3	78.9	90.6	88.9	92.7	97.8
M2 (annual growth rate)		16.9	29.2	26.6	12.7	20.0	21.8
Claims on Private Sector (share of GDP)			111.4	113.3	115.0	129.6	144.6
Claims on Private Sector (share of GDP)				12.1	16.5	29.7	28.9
Philippines							
M2 (share of GDP)	34.1	34.5	36.2	42.1	45.7	50.4	54.0
M2 (annual growth rate)		17.3	13.6	27.1	24.4	24.2	23.2
Claims on Private Sector (share of GDP)	19.3	17.8	20.6	26.4	29.1	37.5	48.6
Claims on Private Sector (share of GDP)		7.3	25.4	39.6	26.5	45.2	48.7
Thailand							
M2 (share of GDP)	69.8	72.7	74.8	78.9	78.5	80.8	79.9
M2 (annual growth rate)		19.8	15.6	18.4	12.9	17.0	12.6
Claims on Private Sector (share of GDP)	83.1	88.6	98.4	110.8	128.1	142.0	141.9
Claims on Private Sector (share of GDP)		22.7	24.8	26.3	31.2	26.0	13.7
Korea							
M2 (share of GDP)	38.3	38.8	40.0	42.0	43.5	43.7	45.7
M2 (annual growth rate)		21.9	14.9	16.6	18.7	15.6	15.8
Claims on Private Sector (share of GDP)	102.5	103.1	110.7	121.3	128.8	133.5	140.9
Claims on Private Sector (share of GDP)		20.9	19.6	21.8	21.6	19.2	17.0

Selected Crisis Indicators
Table 12

Country	Current Account/ GDP (%) 1996	Capital Account/ GDP (%) 1996	Real Exch. Rate (1990=100) 1996	Financial Inst. Claims on Private Sector/GDP (%) 1990	Financial Inst. Claims on Private Sector/GDP (%) 1996	Short Term Jun-94	Debt/ Reserves Jun-97
Argentina	-1.4	2.5	44.0	15.6	18.4	1.3	1.2
Chile	-4.1	8.8	61.0	47.0	57.0	0.5	0.4
Indonesia	-3.5	4.9	80.0	50.6	55.4	1.7	1.7
Jordan	-3.1	5.4	...	64.4	65.3	0.5	0.4
Korea	-4.8	4.8	88.0	56.8	65.7	1.6	2.1
Malaysia	-5.3	9.4	78.0	71.4	144.6	0.3	0.6
Mexico	-0.6	1.2	95.0	22.7	21.6	1.7	1.2
Peru	-5.9	5.1	...	10.1	19.6	0.4	0.5
Philippines	-4.3	11.0	56.0	19.3	48.4	0.4	0.8
South Africa	-1.6	2.1	...	85.0	137.7	15.0	3.1
Sri Lanka	-4.7	4.2	...	19.6	25.2	0.3	0.2
Taiwan	4.4	-4.0	...	97.0	165.0	0.2	0.2
Thailand	-8.0	10.6	80.0	83.1	141.9	1.0	1.5
Turkey	-0.8	5.0	...	16.7	23.5	2.1	0.8
Venezuela	13.1	-2.6	...	25.4	9.6	0.8	0.3

Sources: Bank for International Settlements, IMF, authors' calculations

exchange reserves. Essentially, this measure compares a country's short-term foreign liabilities to its liquid foreign assets available to service those liabilities in the event of a creditor run. Table 14 shows this ratio for a large number of countries in mid-1994 (on the eve of the Mexican crisis) and mid-1997 (the outset of the Asian crisis). Mexico and Argentina each had short-term debt in excess of foreign exchange reserves in 1994, indicating their vulnerability to a crisis. In mid-1997 in Indonesia, Thailand, and Korea – the three countries most severely afflicted by the crisis – short-term debt also exceeded available foreign exchange reserves. It is also instructive to note that the ratio exceeded 1.0 in several other countries that were not affected by the crisis (including the Asian countries in 1994). This suggests that short-term debt in excess of reserves does not necessarily cause a crisis, but that it renders a country vulnerable to a financial panic. Once a crisis starts, each creditor knows that there are not enough liquid foreign exchange reserves for each short-term creditor to be fully paid, so each rushes to be the first in line to demand full repayment. Under normal circumstances, short-term debts can be easily rolled over. However, once creditors begin to believe that the other creditors are no longer willing to roll over the debt, each of them will try to call in their loans ahead of other investors, so as not to be the one left without repayment out of the limited supply of foreign exchange reserves. Even sound corporations may be unable to roll over their debts. Countries with relatively large foreign exchange reserves relative to short-term debt (e.g., Taiwan) are much less vulnerable to a panic, since each creditor can rest assured that sufficient funds are available to meet his claims.

Predictability and Explanation of the Crisis

Summarizing the findings of this section, we note the following. First, the crisis was not predicted by most market participants and analysts. This fact is supported by data on capital flows, risk premia, credit ratings, IMF reports, and other indicators. The biggest warnings came in Thailand, where the expectations of currency depreciation grew markedly in 1996 and early 1997. Korea also gave off increasing warnings. There were few

Net Foreign Assets of the Banking System (share of GDP)
Table 13

	1990	1991	1992	1993	1994	1995	1996
Indonesia							
Foreign Assets of the Banking System (net)	5.4	7.6	11.4	8.6	6.4	6.7	9.6
Monetary Authorities (net)	5.9	8.0	12.6	11.4	9.5	8.9	11.3
Deposit Money Banks (net)	-0.5	-0.4	-1.2	-2.8	-3.1	-2.2	-1.7
Foreign Assets	6.0	4.9	5.0	3.4	3.4	3.8	3.9
Foreign Liabilities	6.5	5.2	6.2	6.2	6.5	6.0	5.6
Malaysia							
Foreign Assets of the Banking System (net)	22.1	18.7	23.0	34.3	33.2	27.2	23.7
Monetary Authorities (net)	23.3	23.5	32.2	47.3	36.7	29.8	28.2
Deposit Money Banks (net)	-1.3	-4.8	-9.2	-13.0	-3.5	-2.6	-4.9
Foreign Assets	5.8	4.3	3.6	6.5	5.7	4.8	4.4
Foreign Liabilities	7.0	9.1	12.7	19.5	9.2	7.4	9.2
Philippines							
Foreign Assets of the Banking System (net)	-9.1	-1.5	2.6	7.4	7.4	6.2	3.2
Monetary Authorities (net)	-13.0	-5.5	-0.6	3.8	5.4	6.2	10.6
Deposit Money Banks (net)	4.0	4.0	3.1	3.5	2.0	0.0	-7.4
Foreign Assets	10.2	8.4	8.7	9.0	8.7	8.8	9.8
Foreign Liabilities	6.2	4.4	5.6	5.5	6.7	8.8	17.2
Thailand							
Foreign Assets of the Banking System (net)	14.0	16.4	15.9	14.3	4.1	0.0	-1.7
Monetary Authorities (net)	16.5	18.5	19.0	20.4	21.0	22.7	21.2
Deposit Money Banks (net)	-2.4	-2.0	-3.2	-6.1	-16.9	-22.6	-22.9
Foreign Assets	2.6	2.9	2.7	5.0	4.7	5.8	3.9
Foreign Liabilities	5.0	4.9	5.9	11.1	21.6	28.4	26.8
Korea							
Foreign Assets of the Banking System (net)	5.7	3.8	5.1	6.6	6.7	6.4	5.2
Monetary Authorities (net)	6.0	4.9	5.7	6.2	6.8	7.2	7.2
Deposit Money Banks (net)	-0.3	-1.1	-0.6	0.4	-0.1	-0.8	-0.2
Foreign Assets	3.8	3.8	4.2	4.9	5.4	6.1	7.3
Foreign Liabilities	4.1	4.9	4.8	4.5	5.5	6.9	9.3

Source: Bank for International Settlements, IMF

if any alarm bells in Indonesia, Malaysia, or the Philippines. Second, traditional warning signs (current account deficits, overvalued exchange rates, export growth) gave some reasons for concern, but the signals were muted and generally ignored. While East Asian currencies had appreciated in real terms in the 1990s, the real appreciation was considerably less than in most of Latin America. Current account deficits were very high in Thailand and Malaysia in 1996, but considerably lower in Indonesia and Korea. Malaysia's current account deficit had declined markedly in 1996 compared with the preceding year.

The biggest indicators of risk were financial, but were generally ignored. Short-term debts to international banks had risen to high levels relative to foreign exchange reserves in Indonesia, Korea, and Thailand.

Domestic claims on the private sector (measured as a percent of GDP) had also risen significantly, suggesting growing strains in the banking sector. This was especially the case in Malaysia, the Philippines, and Thailand, and much less so in Indonesia and Korea. These indicators show some growing weaknesses, and point to the need for moderate adjustments in the Asian economies. These imbalances, however, were not large enough to warrant a crisis of the magnitude that has been seen in Asia.

Perhaps the most notable fact, however, is that these financial indicators show the vulnerability to crisis, but do not guarantee the onset of crisis. They seem to be, in short, necessary but not sufficient conditions. In 1994, Indonesia, Korea, and Thailand already had ratios of short-term debt to foreign exchange

Short-Term Debt Reserves, 1994 and 1997 (Millions of U.S. $)
Table 14

Country	June 94 Short-Term Debt	Reserves	Short-Term Debt/Reserves	June 97 Short-Term Debt	Reserves	Short-Term Debt/Reserves
Argentina	17,557	13,247	1.325	23,891	19,740	1.210
Chile	5,447	10,766	0.506	7,615	17,017	0.447
Indonesia	18,822	10,915	1.724	34,661	20,336	1.704
Jordan	647	1,291	0.501	582	1,624	0.358
Korea	35,204	21,685	1.623	70,182	34,070	2.060
Malaysia	8,203	32,608	0.252	16,268	26,588	0.612
Mexico	28,404	16,509	1.721	28,226	23,775	1.187
Peru	2,157	5,611	0.384	5,368	10,665	0.503
Philippines	2,646	6,527	0.405	8,293	9,781	0.848
South Africa	7,108	475	14.964	13,247	4,241	3.124
Sri Lanka	511	1,983	0.258	414	1,770	0.234
Taiwan	17,023	90,143	0.189	21,966	90,025	0.244
Thailand	27,151	27,375	0.992	45,567	31,361	1.453
Turkey	8,821	4,279	2.061	13,067	16,055	0.814
Venezuela	4,382	5,422	0.808	3,629	13,215	0.275

Sources: Bank for International Settlements, IMF

reserves well in excess of 1.0, but they were not hit by the Tequila shock. In 1997, South Africa evinces major vulnerabilities to panic, but fortunately, without an episode of panic. These patterns may indeed be the best confirmation of the multiple-equilibrium character of financial panics: we can identify conditions of vulnerability, and the need for modest adjustments, but we can not predict the actual onset of crisis, since the crisis requires a triggering event that leads short-term creditors to expect the flight of other short-term creditors.

V. Triggering Events

The cracks began to appear at almost the same time in Korea and Thailand in early 1997. In January, Hanbo Steel collapsed under $6 billion in debts. Hanbo was the first bankruptcy of a Korean chaebol in a decade. In the months that followed, Sammi Steel and Kia Motors suffered a similar fate. These bankruptcies, in turn, put several merchant banks under significant pressure, since much of the foreign borrowing of these companies had been, in effect, channeled through (and in some cases guaranteed by) the merchant banks. In Thailand, Samprasong Land missed payments due on its foreign debt in early February, signaling the fall in the property markets and the beginning of the end for the financial companies which had lent heavily to property companies. During the ensuing six months, the Bank of Thailand lent over Bt 200 billion ($8 billion) to distressed financial institutions through its Financial Institutions Development Fund (FIDF). As concerns began to mount, the BOT also committed almost all of its liquid foreign exchange reserves in forward contracts, much of it to speculators that correctly guessed that the combination of slow export growth and financial distress would ultimately require a devaluation. By late June, net forward sales of reserves approximately equaled gross reserves. This does not mean that the central bank had run out of usable reserves (since the open forward positions could be closed at a partial, not complete, loss), but usable reserve levels had fallen sharply. In late June 1997, the Thai Government removed support from a major finance company, Finance One, announcing that creditors (including foreign creditors) would incur losses, contrary to previous announcements and market expectations. This shock accelerated the withdrawal of foreign funds, and prompted the currency depreciation on July 2, 1997. In turn, the Thai baht devaluation triggered the capital outflows from the rest of East Asia.

The proximate causes of the withdrawal differed somewhat across the region.

- **Bank failure.** In Thailand, the failures of finance companies helped set off the exodus.
- **Corporate failure.** In Korea, the withdrawal of funds was based on concerns over the health of the corporate sector.
- **Political uncertainty.** In Korea, Thailand, the Philippines, and Indonesia, political uncertainty hastened the credit withdrawals, since each country faced the potential for a change in government. (Korea and Thailand have both changed governments since the onset of the crisis. A new President will be elected in the Philippines in May 1998. Elections are scheduled for mid-March in Indonesia, though with no chance of a change through the ballot box. Suharto's weakening health, along with the absence of a clear successor, and growing discomfort with economic role played by the President's family – rather than the president's electoral vulnerability – are the notable features of the Indonesia political uncertainty).
- **Contagion.** Many creditors appeared to treat the region as a whole, and assumed that if Thailand was in trouble, the other countries in the region probably had similar difficulties. Part of the contagion effect was the sudden loss of government credibility throughout the region. After all, the Thai government had pledged for months that Finance One was in good shape, that plenty of foreign exchange reserves were available, and that the baht would not be devalued. Malaysia, the Philippines, and Indonesia were all hit hard by contagion effects.
- **International interventions.** Although at times the IMF can help restore confidence in battered economies, it can also send a signal to creditors of impending crisis, leading to an accelerated outflow of foreign funds. This depends especially on the specific measures

that the IMF recommends. In the case of the Asian programs, the IMF recommended immediate suspensions or closures of financial institutions, measures which actually helped to incite panic.

The withdrawal of foreign funds triggered a chain reaction which quickly developed into a financial panic. The exchange rate depreciation associated with the withdrawal itself sparked new withdrawals of foreign exchange, as domestic borrowers with unhedged currency positions rushed to buy dollars. Throughout Southeast Asia, few firms had hedged their exposure, since they believed that government would retain a stable exchange rate. In addition, most central banks required that firms seek prior approval before undertaking any hedging, making it somewhat more burdensome for firms to cover their risks (this was not the case, however, in Indonesia). At the same time, as the currency depreciated, foreign lenders became more concerned that their customers would be unable to repay their debts, and began to call in their loans, reinforcing the depreciation.

The withdrawal of funds also set off a liquidity squeeze and a sharp rise in interest rates. As a result, firms that were profitable before the crisis found it difficult to obtain working capital or to remain profitable with significantly higher interest rates. Offshore creditors become concerned about the profitability of their customers and grew increasingly reluctant to roll over short-term loans. The lack of clear bankruptcy laws and workout mechanisms added to the withdrawal of credit, since foreign lenders feared they would have little recourse to collect on bad loans. The banking system quickly came under intense pressure. Non-performing loans rose quickly, and depositors withdrew their funds either out of concern over the safety of the banking system or in order to meet pressing foreign exchange obligations. The losses on foreign exchange exposure and the rise in non-performing loans eroded the capital base of the banks, adding to their stress. In Korea, the fall in the stock market exacerbated the erosion of the capital base, since banks were allowed to hold some of the capital as equity in other companies. As a result, even liquid banks were constrained in their ability to make loans, as they struggled to stay ahead of the minimum capital adequacy standards.

The rapid evolution into panic was aided by policy misjudgments and mistakes across the region. Had Thailand responded to the fall in property prices in early 1997 by floating the baht and moderately tightening monetary and fiscal policies, the Asian financial crisis could have been largely avoided. Thailand and Korea, of course, made the paramount mistake of trying to defend their exchange rate peg until they had effectively exhausted a substantial proportion of their foreign exchange reserves. In Indonesia, the state enterprises were instructed to withdraw a sizeable portion of their deposits from the banking systems and purchase central bank notes, adding to the intense liquidity squeeze and driving up interest rates. Large investment projects of dubious economic value were postponed, then given the go-ahead, the postponed again in both Indonesia and Malaysia, adding to the confusion. Malaysia and Thailand introduced mild controls on foreign exchange transactions. Malaysia announced the formation of a large fund to be used to prop up stock prices, then abandoned the plan a few days later. Thailand and Korea injected large sums into failing financial institutions, opening a large hole into what had previously been prudent fiscal positions. Inflammatory statements by government officials and market participants alike (especially the well-known interchanges between the Malaysian Prime Minister and George Soros) further frayed nerves and added to the panicked withdrawal of funds.

Once the trigger was pulled, several powerful feedback mechanisms amplified the withdrawal into a panic. Undercapitalized Japanese banks with heavy exposure in the rest of Asia felt further downward pressure on their balance sheets as a result of the emerging crisis, and therefore began to call in loans. Similarly, Korean banks with extensive exposure in South East Asia began to call in loans as a result of the Korean crisis. Downgrades by the major ratings agencies led to new rounds of withdrawals.

The regional crisis intensified and threatened to spread when the Hong Kong dollar came under attack in November as a result of currency depreciations in the rest of Asia and the consequent loss of trade competitiveness in Hong Kong itself. Hong Kong banks faced steeply rising interest rates on liabilities, and it is likely that they reacted in part by calling in loans from the rest of Asia (data on Hong Kong bank loans to the rest of Asia are not publicly available). Moreover, the attack in Hong Kong strongly indicated the potential for the crisis to cross international borders, and fears rose that the problems would spread throughout the rest of Asia and beyond. Indeed, the New Taiwan dollar also came under pressure and fell sharply, despite Tawain's huge stock of reserves. These events almost certainly accelerated withdrawals from Southeast Asia, and especially Korea.

Contagion, Panic, and Crisis in Indonesia

The extent of the crisis in Indonesia calls for special comment, since at this writing it is the country that has been hardest hit in the region. This outcome is in many ways ironic, since at the outset many observers thought it would be the least affected country, and in the early stages Indonesia was praised for taking quick and conserted action.[8] Indonesia appears to be the clearest case of contagion in the region. Of course, there were many problems and weaknesses in the Indonesian economy before the crisis, including under-supervised banks, extensive crony capitalism, corruption, monopoly power, and growing short-term debt, some of which at least one of us has discussed previously.[9] Yet by most measures, Indonesia's imbalances were among the least severe in the region, and clearly much less dramatic than in Thailand. Consider the following:

•   the current account deficit, at 3.5 percent of GDP, was the lowest of the Asian-5 countries;

•   export growth in 1996 of 10.4 percent, while down from the 1995 level of 13 percent, was the second highest in the region;

Figure 1.   Exchange Rate: Indonesia

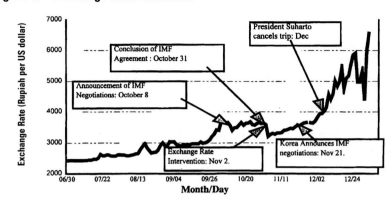

Figure 2.   Exchange Rate: Thailand

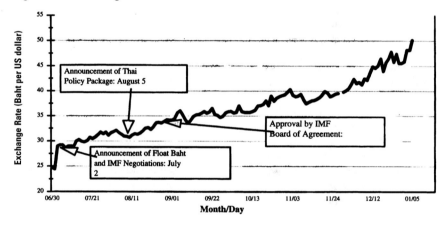

Figure 3.   Exchange Rate: Korea

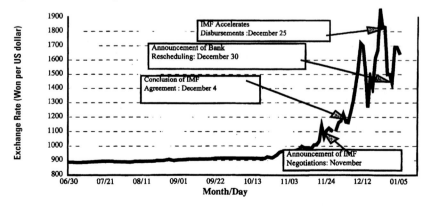

- the budget had been in surplus by an average of over 1 percent of GDP for 4 years;
  - credit growth had remained at more modest levels than elsewhere in the region;
- foreign liabilities of the commercial banks, at 5.6 percent of GDP, were substantially below those of the other affected economies (although corporate foreign debts were high);
  - there had been no major corporate bankruptcies, and the stock market continued to rise strongly through early 1997 until the onset of the crisis in Thailand.

Indonesia was applauded early on for first widening the rupiah's trading band to 12 percent, and then moving to a float without spending its foreign exchange reserves in a futile defense of the currency. When the rupiah did come under severe attack in August, problems arose when the government abruptly raised interest rates, which had the effect of intensifying short-run pressure. The governments' decision to cancel 150 investment projects was designed to be a bold attempt to restore international confidence, but the reversal of the decision just a few days later for 15 of the largest projects undermined the strategy and simply added to the confusion. By early September Indonesia had joined Thailand, Malaysia, and the Philippines in the crisis.

Nonetheless, since reserve levels remained strong at well over $20 billion, Indonesia did not seem an obvious candidate for an IMF program. When Indonesia signed its first IMF[10] program on October 31st, the rupiah immediately strengthened as a result of large concerted interventions by Japan and Singapore. Yet, the boost in the rupiah was very short lived. As the impact of abrupt bank closures and the ensuing bank runs (discussed in the next section), higher interest rates, and decapitalization of the banks set in, the rupiah depreciated by 23 percent and the stock market fell by 19 percent (in rupiah terms) between November 3rd and December 4th. The slide was augmented by confusion over the bank closures, since two of the President's relatives publicly balked (and threatened legal action) when their banks were ordered closed.

(This event illustrates one of the dangers of hasty bank closures – such abrupt institutional changes are almost always poorly thought through and badly implemented, thereby creating a sense of confusion and panic rather than building confidence.) Quite suddenly, within a couple of weeks of the start of the IMF program, Indonesia began to look even weaker than its neighbors.

In December, the effects of the severest drought in many years set in, with food prices rising and food shortages emerging in some parts of the archipelago. The drought complicated the task of crisis management enormously (both economically and politically), since food prices jumped sharply, the foreign exchange costs of food imports rose, and displaced urban day laborers could not easily return to rural areas to find work. At the same time, world petroleum prices fell, sharply reducing Indonesia's export receipts, adding to pressure on the exchange rate.

On December 4th, Korea signed its IMF program, adding a new round of uncertainty to the entire region. Then, on December 5th, it was announced that President Suharto was ill and had to cancel a foreign trip. The markets fell precipitously, accelerating a fall that had been underway for a month. The prospect of a severe illness or death of Suharto, with no clear Presidential successor in sight, added to the ongoing panic. By early January, Indonesia had become the pariah of the region, with the IMF and US Treasury publicly blasting a proposed budget (which, upon later inspection, turned out to be far less onerous than initially described).[11] Indonesia's waffling on promised structural reforms and its flirtation with the ill-advised notion of introducing a currency board only added to negative perceptions about the country. At this point, the crisis in Indonesia has become as much political as it is economic. (Note that both Thailand and Korea each received a boost from a change in government, whereas there seemed little prospect of political change in Indonesia). The economic and political issues have fed off of each other, adding a whole new dimension to the dynamics of the panic.

Figure 4.
Stock Market Indices
January 1995 to February 1998
(Jan 1995 = 100)

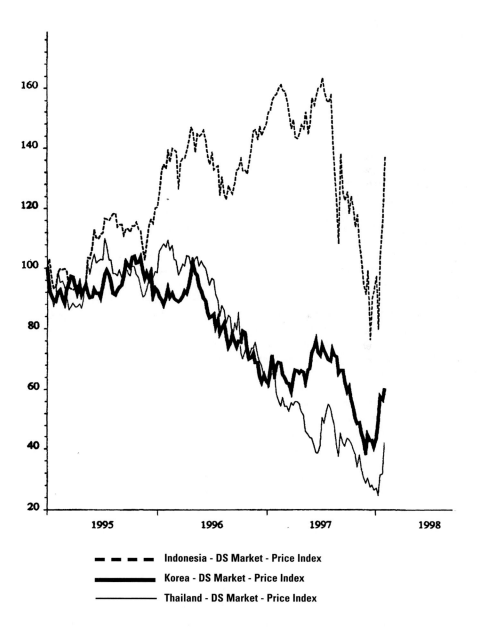

- – – – Indonesia - DS Market - Price Index
- —— Korea - DS Market - Price Index
- —— Thailand - DS Market - Price Index

Indonesia's extensive meltdown is far more severe than can be accounted for by flaws in economic fundamentals, since those were not especially poor. The "moral hazard cum bubble" model seems to be even less appropriate for Indonesia than for Thailand and Korea (where it is also an exaggeration of fundamental weaknesses). To reiterate in the case of Indonesia, most foreign lending was to private firms, and not to banks. While many of these companies may have been assumed to have implicit government backing, much of the lending to corporations was surely unprotected by government guarantees and was seen in that light. There was also no sign of market concern of a growing crisis, since the stock market and other indices performed very strongly right up until early July. International credit ratings remained high and positive, and international banks continued to lend, well after they had cut back on loans to Thailand and Korea. In short, Indonesia seems to be a clear case of contagion leading to panic, and ultimately to a severe, unnecessary economic contraction.

VI. The IMF Programs

One month after Thailand floated the baht, it announced on August 5th a policy reform package that had been formulated in cooperation with the IMF. The 34-month, $17.2 billion standby arrangement was approved by the Fund Board on August 20th. The IMF contributed $4 billion, the World Bank and Asian Development Bank $2.7 billion, and individual governments the balance of $10.5 billion (including $3.5 billion from neighboring Southeast Asian countries). Japan contributed $4 billion; the United States did not contribute to the package. Indonesia followed suit by signing a 36-month, $40 billion package on October 31st. The IMF contributed $10 billion, and the World Bank and the ADB added $8 billion, and other governments the balance (including $5 billion and $3 billion in "second line of defense" from Japan and the U.S., respectively). Somehow, the official figure of $40 billion includes $5 billion of "assistance" from Indonesia's own reserves!

Korea signed its $57 billion three-year standby on December 4, with $21 billion from the IMF, $14 billion from the World Bank and the ADB, and $22 from a group of industrial countries. With the Philippines continuing its previously-signed standby program, four of the five afflicted economies came under the tutelage of the IMF.

The IMF programs have had nine main declared goals:

- prevent outright default on foreign obligations;
- limit the extent of currency depreciation;
- preserve a fiscal balance;
- limit the rise in inflation;
- rebuild foreign exchange reserves;
- restructure and reform the banking sector;
- remove monopolies and otherwise reform the domestic non-financial economy;
- preserve confidence and creditworthiness;
- limit the decline of output.

To achieve these objectives, the programs have been based on six key policy components:

• *Fiscal policy.* The IMF placed fiscal contraction at the very heart of the programs. For example, the official press release on the Thai program states that "Fiscal policy is the key to the overall credibility of the program." The press release on Indonesia similarly put fiscal policy at the forefront: "First, the authorities will maintain tight fiscal and monetary policies..." The objectives of fiscal contraction were to (i) support the monetary contraction and defend the exchange rate, and (ii) provide for funds necessary to inject into the financial system.

• *Bank closures.* In Thailand, 58 out of 91 finance companies were immediately suspended, and 56 of these were eventually liquidated. In Indonesia, 16 commercial banks were closed. In Korea, 14 (of 30) merchant banks were suspended. The goals of these actions were to limit the losses being accumulated by these institutions, and to send a strong signal that governments were serious about implementing reforms in order to restore confidence in the banking system.

• *Enforcement of capital adequacy standards.* While banks were facing rapid decapitalization because of losses on foreign exchange exposure and an increase in nonperforming loans, the initial Fund programs pushed for a rapid recapitalization. The goal was to return the banking system to solid footing as quickly as possible.

• **Tight domestic credit.** Through contractionary base money targets, the IMF programs raised interest rates and reduced domestic credit availability. The purpose was to defend the exchange rate.

• **Debt repayment.** Foreign exchange targets in each program provided for full payment of foreign debt obligations, backed by "bailout funds" mobilized by the IMF.

• **Non-financial structural changes.** In each program, structural reforms were included that were aimed at reducing tariffs, opening sectors for foreign investment, and reducing monopoly powers.

The three original programs failed to meet their objectives, and none of the programs lasted in its original form for more than a few weeks. New letters of intent were signed with Thailand, Korea, and Indonesia on November 25, December 24, and January 15, respectively. Currency depreciation and stock market collapse continued long after the programs were signed, and there was no sign of an immediate restoration of confidence. Bank closures in Thailand and Indonesia added to the sense of financial panic, rather than stemming the outflow. Output is now projected to fall much more sharply than originally targeted, and the original targets for inflation and exchange rates have been revised. Credit ratings collapsed in each country after the agreements were in place.

The Fund has attributed this continuing decline mainly to unexpected contagion effects, political uncertainty, and poor implementation of the programs by the governments in the region. There is clearly some truth in these observations. Korea's collapse made matters worse in Indonesia and Thailand, Suharto's health and the elections in Korea created market jitters, and each government has stopped short of full implementation of agreed reforms. But there are several reasons to believe that the underlying design of the programs added to, rather than ameliorated, the panic. Four areas, in particular, are open to question.

1. Bank Closures. There is no question that many financial institutions in the region were unviable, and needed to be merged or liquidated. The appropriate question is how to do so, and over what time frame, in the midst of a financial panic. Abruptly shutting down financial institutions without a more comprehensive program for financial sector reform, as was done in Thailand and Indonesia, only served to deepen the panic. With no deposit insurance in place, the hastily-arranged closures predictably ignited a bank run, with depositors in other institutions fearing that their bank would be next in line.[12] The closures added to the ongoing liquidity squeeze, making it more difficult for banks to continue their normal lending operations. Since it was not immediately clear how the foreign liabilities of these banks would be handled, foreign creditors of other banks became more reluctant to roll over their loans, adding to the squeeze.

Kindleberger (1978) offers some close historical analogies:

> "Apart from lags and mistakes of discount policy, the authorities may precipitate panic by brusque action in early stages of distress. In the summer of 1836, with credit extended in acceptances drawn by American houses on British joint-stock banks, the Bank of England refused to discount any bills bearing the name of a joint-stock bank, and specifically instructed its Liverpool agent not to rediscount any paper of the so-called "W banks" (Wiggins, Wildes, and Wilson) among the seven American banks in Britain, an action that "seemed vindictive" and led immediately to panic. As it

turned out, the Bank of England had to reverse its policies. It had long conferences with the "W banks" in October, extended them lines of discount in the first quarter of 1837, but failed to prevent their failure in June of that year. The Bank's instinct was right: to frustrate the extension of dangerous credit. But credit is a dangerous thing. Expectations can quickly be altered. Something, sometimes almost nothing, causes a shadow to fall on credit, reverses expectations, and the rush for liquidity is on." (pp. 112-3)

The vulnerability of expectations to such sharp shifts from "almost nothing" results from the condition of multiple equilibrium that we have stressed throughout this essay. Creditor runs are self-fulfilling.

A far better approach would have been to implement a longer-term, more comprehensive strategy for bank restructuring, rather than a quick show of force designed simply to demonstrate resolve. Problem banks could have been put under some form of receivership, which would have protected depositors and allowed good borrowers continued access to credit.

The IMF appears to have recognized the error in its bank closure strategy. According to press reports, a confidential IMF document reviewing the first standby arrangement with Indonesia concluded that "(t)hese closures, however, far from improving public confidence in the banking system, have instead set off a renewed 'flight to safety.'" The report found that Indonesians had withdrawn $2 billion from the banking system and shifted funds from private to state-owned banks, which depositors felt offered stronger guarantees. The report concluded that by the end of November, two-thirds of Indonesia's banks "had experienced runs on their deposits."[13] The text of Indonesia's second agreement with the Fund reinforced the point:

"Following the closure of 16 insolvent banks in November last year, customers concerned about the safety of private banks have been shifting sizeable amounts of deposits to state and foreign banks, while some have been withdrawing funds from the banking system entirely. These movements in deposits have greatly complicated the task of monetary policy, because they have led to a bifurcation of the banking system. By mid-November, a large number of banks were facing growing liquidity shortages, and were unable to obtain sufficient funds in the interbank market to cover this gap, even after paying interest rates ranging up to 75 percent."

The memorandum continues at a later stage by observing that

"...the continued depreciation of the rupiah, the slowdown in growth, and high interest rates since then have led to a marked deterioration of the financial condition of the remaining banks. This deterioration has been exacerbated by deposit runs and capital flight, forcing many banks to increasingly resort to central bank liquidity support."[14]

The Fund program in Korea focused on merchant banks (which do not take household deposits) rather than commercial banks. Nonetheless, the sudden closure of 14 merchant banks and the IMF's insistence on a rapid tightening of bank capital-adequacy ratios added to the sense of panic over the financial system. As in Indonesia, depositors and foreign lenders accelerated their withdrawals from the banking system, while the banks cut back on their loans in order to enhance their balance sheets. The second round of programs in Thailand and Indonesia included more comprehensive financial restructuring plans, although even here the plans were not complete.

2. Bank Recapitalization. There is no question that after the crisis, many banks needed to be recapitalized. As mentioned previously, the combination of a sharp increase in non-performing loans at the onset of the crisis and the effect of exchange rate movements on the banks' foreign liability positions quickly eroded the capital bases of even the strongest banks. The question is: how quickly should banks be pushed to recapitalize, especially during times of widespread economic distress? Pushing banks to recapitalize within an unrealistic time frame can cause them to sharply curtail lending, including by otherwise strong banks. This, in turn, can lead to a more severe credit crunch, increased distress for private firms, and a further rise in non-performing loans. This seems to be exactly what took place in the last few months of 1997. The first two IMF programs, in particular, pushed hard for quick recapitalization of the banks. For example, the first Indonesian program required that "(t)he instruction issued by the central bank to raise capital adequacy to 9 percent by end-1997, and 12 percent by end-2001, will be strictly enforced." Thus, banks were initially expected not only to return to their previous capital adequacy level of 8 percent, but to actually add to their capital. The first Thai program stated that "(c)ommercial banks and remaining finance companies will be required to raise capital in anticipation of possible further deterioration in their asset quality.... Severely under-capitalized institutions that cannot raise their capital to the legally required level will be taken over by the FIDF (performance criterion as of November 15, 1997)." The second programs in these countries eased the requirements somewhat, but were still quite strict. The second Thai program required the government to establish "timetables for the recapitalization of all undercapitalized financial institutions during 1998," while the second Indonesian program stated that "(c)apital adequacy rules are being

enforced within the context of the bank restructuring strategy."[15] Only the Korean program initially provided for a longer time frame for full enforcement of the capital adequacy standards. Private discussions with several bankers in the region revealed uncertainty as to how fully and over what time frame these standards would be applied, with the result that banks substantially curtailed lending. Had more forbearance been given on the capital adequacy ratios early in the crisis, with a clear and longer term schedule for otherwise strong banks to return to full compliance, the extent of the credit squeeze would have been much less severe.

3. Monetary Policy. There are really two aspects to the IMF's monetary policy which have not been carefully disentangled. The first is quantitative domestic credit targets. In most programs, there are limits to high-powered money or central bank credit. The second is interest rate targets, or floors on interest rates, which are usually added as prior actions to an IMF program. Both types of policies are highly problematical. The problem with quantitative credit targets is that they may directly interfere with the Central Bank's lender-of-last-resort function. If the central bank is instructed not to provide domestic credit, market participants will know that the lender-of-last resort mechanism has been switched off. Thus, a tightening of quantitative credit limits may actually trigger a panic by short-term creditors who come to doubt the ability or willingness of the central bank to provide liquidity. As H.S. Foxwell put it in 1908 (cited in Kindleberger, p. 111), "To refuse accommodation altogether is always held to be dangerous . . . the Bank [of England] was responsible for the solvency of this crowd of small, ill-managed institutions [country banks], but dared not call them to account, on peril of provoking a general collapse of credit."

A closely related but distinct issue is interest rate policy. There is no question that following the withdrawal of foreign capital, interest rates had to rise. After all, capital flows equivalent to 9 percent were reversed in a matter of weeks, leading to an immediate elimination of current account deficits across the region. As a result, interest rates rose sharply at the outset of the crisis. A sharp economic contraction was inevitable. The problem was the IMF's insistence on raising interest rates even higher and demanding a fiscal surplus (see below) on top of the huge withdrawal of funds (and shrinking current account deficit) that was already underway. These steps led to an unnecessarily harsh economic contraction.

The IMF instructed the Central Banks of Indonesia, Korea, and Thailand, to drain reserves from the system in order to maintain interest rates above certain floors. There is little question that higher interest rates have undermined the profitability of banks and private firms in the short run, and added to the economic downturn. (Indeed, the passage from the second Indonesia program cited above states that high interest rates contributed to a marked deterioration of the financial condition of the banks.) The policy question is the effect that higher interest rates might have on the exchange rate, and whether any benefits with respect to the exchange rate would outweigh the negative effects on short-run production. The Fund assumes that higher interest rates will lead to stability or appreciation of the currency, and that the benefits of currency stabilization outweigh the short-run output costs. For example, Deputy Managing Director Shigemitsu Sugisaki stated recently that:

> "We know that higher interest rates are likely to hurt the corporate sector, but an appreciation of the currency that follows a tightening of monetary conditions would greatly benefit those corporations indebted in foreign currency. There is no alternative in the short term. A relaxation of monetary policy would only lead to further depreciations of the currencies."

Despite sharply higher interest rates, currencies have not appreciated, so the supposed benefits of this policy are in question. It is entirely possible that in the unique conditions of the midst of a financial panic, raising interest rates could have the perverse effect in the very short run of weakening the currency. Kindleberger (1978) has made this point clearly, based on the historical experience:

> "Tight money in a given financial center can serve either to attract funds or to repel them, depending on the expectations that a rise in interest rates generates. With inelastic expectations – no fear of crisis or of currency depreciation – an increase in the discount rate attracts funds from abroad, and helps to provide the cash needed to ensure liquidity; with elastic expectations of change – of falling prices, bankruptcies, or exchange depreciation – raising the discount rate may suggest to foreigners the need to take more funds out rather than bring new funds in."

There is little evidence indeed that higher interest rates have succeeded in supporting Southeast Asian currencies during the panic phase of the crisis. As the accompanying figures show, exchange rates continued to plummet after the signing of IMF programs. The exchange rate targets in these programs were breached in a matter of days in all three countries. Part of the problem was not in the interest rate policy, but in accompanying measures: the bank closures almost surely helped to induce a panic that simply overwhelmed short-term interest rates. It is possible, though, that the interest rate policy itself had the adverse effects that Kindleberger noted. Creditors understood that highly leveraged borrowers (whether Indonesian conglomerates, Korean chaebol, or banks in all countries) could quickly be pushed to insolvency as a result of several months of high interest rates. Moreover, many kinds of interest-sensitive market participants, such as bond traders, are simply not active in Asia's limited financial markets. The key participants were the existing holders of short-term debts, and the important question was whether they would or would not roll over their claims. Higher interest rates did not feed directly into these existing claims (which were generally floating interest rate notes based on a fixed premium over LIBOR). It is possible, however, that by undermining the profitability of their corporate customers, higher interest rates discouraged foreign creditors from rolling over their loans.

4. *Fiscal Policy.* The Fund initially demanded a fiscal surplus of 1 percent of GDP in each country. It is not clear why government budgets were made so central to the programs, since fiscal policy had been fairly prudent across the region, and budget profligacy was clearly not the source of the crisis. Moreover, while the Fund argued that fiscal contraction was necessary to reduce the current account deficit, there was no clear rationale provided for why additional contraction was necessary on top of the massive contraction that was already automatically taking place in the region. The fiscal targets simply added to the contractionary force of the crisis. Nor was there any clear analytic basis for the precise figure of 1 percent of GDP (indeed, the figure appears to have been largely arbitrary). Under the circumstances, a small deficit would seem to have been more appropriate, funded entirely by foreign exchange inflows in support of the program. The Fund also appears to have recognized the inappropriateness of the fiscal surplus demanded in the first round of programs. The second programs in Indonesia and Korea target a 1 percent deficit and a balanced budget, respectively, and recent reports suggest the IMF has re-thought its position in Thailand and will allow the government to run a small deficit.[16]

VII. Conclusions and Extensions

In our interpretation, the East Asian crisis resulted from vulnerability to financial panic that arose from certain emerging weaknesses in these economies (especially growing short-term debt), combined with a series of policy missteps and accidents that triggered the panic. Since we view the crisis as a case of multiple equilibrium, our hypothesis is that the worst of the crisis could have been largely avoided with relatively moderate adjustments and appropriate policy changes. Explanations that attribute the entire massive contraction to the inevitable consequences of deep flaws in the Asian economies – such as Asian "crony capitalism" – seem to us to be strongly overstated. Without question, there were macroeconomic imbalances, weak financial institutions, widespread corruption, and inadequate legal foundations in each of the affected countries. These problems needed attention and correction, and they clearly contributed to the vulnerability of the Asian economies. However, most of these problems had been well-known for years, and the Asian-5 countries were able to attract $211 billion of capital inflows between 1994 and 1996, under widely known conditions of Asian capitalism. To attribute the crisis fully to fundamental flaws in the pre-crisis system is to judge that the global financial system is prone to sheer folly, or somehow expected to avoid losses despite the fundamental flaws. Paul Krugman's explanation of the crisis – that investors knew that their investments were to weak borrowers, but felt protected by explicit and implicit guarantees – also seems to us to be only a partial explanation. One obvious reason is that much of the lending was directed to private firms that did not enjoy these guarantees. Approximately half of the loans by international banks and almost all of the portfolio and direct equity investments went to non-bank enterprises for which state guarantees were far from assured. This comes to around three-fifths of the total capital flows to the region.

Moreover, the actual market participants, by their statements and actions (e.g., decisions on credit ratings), while recognizing the flaws in these economies, simply didn't foresee a crisis, with or without bailouts. It is difficult, therefore, to make the case that a crisis of this depth and magnitude was simply an accident waiting to happen. We do not believe that such a vicious crisis was necessary, nor that its depth should be interpreted as an indication of the extent of the underlying economic problems in the region. Instead, we believe that a much more moderate adjustment would have been possible had appropriate steps been taken in the early stages of the crisis.

We have stressed the role of financial panic to make several points of significance for policy analysis. First, capital markets are subject to multiple equilibria. Second, credit collapses such as those in Asia are not simply the end of socially destructive bubbles, but also (or even mainly) result in the destruction of socially productive output. Third, because of the vulnerability to panic in international markets, there may be a role for an international lender of last resort. Fourth, because of the possibility of panic, small events can have large consequences (as in the epigram at the start of the paper). In particular, abrupt actions by domestic and international policy makers can gravely worsen an incipient crisis, by helping to trigger the capital outflow.

This paper has not addressed several highly pertinent issues in the Asian crisis, which are left for a companion paper and future work. First, can we say more about the balance between socially productive and unproductive investments in Asian in the run-up to the crisis? This involves a detailed look at the sectoral allocation of credit and investment. Second, do the moral hazards that result from IMF-led bailouts undermine the broad social value of such operations? In particular, did the Mexican bailout help to prepare the base for the subsequent Asian crisis? Third, how should an incipient financial crisis, centered on weak banks, be managed in order to avoid inciting a financial panic? When and how should bad banks be closed? Fourth, can orderly workout mechanisms (e.g. the rollover negotiations directly between creditors and debtors, as in the case of Korea) substitute for IMF loans, or are loans and orderly workouts in fact complementary actions? Fifth, what should be done now in Asia, especially in view of the de-capitalization of banks throughout the region, which is hindering production and trade finance throughout the region? Sixth, what institutional steps could be taken in the future to reduce the likelihood of future financial crises of this sort? Is there a case for controls on short-term capital movements, and if

so, should these be applied country by country, or also through international mechanisms?

Appendix:

Summaries of IMF Executive Board discussions on Indonesia, Korea, and Thailand:

Indonesia (Board discussion, July 1996):

> The Board strongly endorsed the authorities' aim to reduce broad money growth in 1996. Directors agreed with the authorities' emphasis on maintaining an open capital account and welcomed the steps already taken to widen the exchange-rate band and give greater flexibility to exchange rate policy. . .
>
> In the Board's view, further substantial reforms, including financial sector reforms and the development of a strong capital market, were essential for maintaining rapid, sustained growth. Directors urged the authorities to address weaknesses in the banking sector, and in particular to act decisively to resolve the problem of insolvent banks and recover non-performing loans. They considered these actions as critical to reduce the vulnerability of the economy to shocks and to lessen moral hazard.

Korea (Board discussion, November 1996):

> In their discussion, Directors welcomed Korea's continued impressive macroeconomic performance: growth had decelerated from the unsustainably rapid pace of the previous two years, inflation had remained subdued notwithstanding some modest pickup in the months prior to the consultation, and the widening of

the current account deficit largely resulted from a temporary weakening of the terms of trade.

Directors praised the authorities for their enviable fiscal record and suggested that fiscal policy could best contribute to strengthening medium-term macroeconomic performance by maintaining a strong budgetary position as much-needed spending on social overhead capital was undertaken. They also welcomed the recent acceleration of capital account liberalization; although some Directors agreed with the authorities' gradual approach to capital market liberalization, a number of Directors considered that rapid and complete liberalization offered many benefits at Korea's stage of development.

Thailand (Board discussion, July 1996):

Directors strongly praised Thailand's remarkable economic performance and the authorities' consistent record of sound macroeconomic fundamentals. They noted that financial policies had been tightened in 1995 in response to the widening of the external current account deficit and the pickup of inflation, and this had begun to bear results, but they cautioned that there was no room for complacency.

The recent increase in the current account deficit had increased Thailand's vulnerability to economic shocks and adverse shifts in market sentiment. On the one hand, Directors noted, economic fundamentals remained generally very strong, characterized by high saving and investment, a public sector surplus, strong export growth in recent years, and manageable debt and debt-service returns. On the other hand, the level of short-term capital inflows and short-term debt were somewhat high. Also, the limitations of present policy instruments constrained the authorities' ability to manage shocks. Caution in the use of foreign saving was warranted, Directors observed, and early action was required to reduce the current account deficit. While fiscal policy could play a role in the short term, over the medium term the emphasis should be on measures to increase private saving.

We are grateful for excellent research assistance from Mumtaz Hussain, Dilip Parajuli, and Amar Hamoudi, and for comments from Malcolm McPherson and Jay Rosengard of HIID; Juan Belt, Juan Buttari, and James Fox of USAID; Joseph Ramos of the UN Economic Commission; and David Cole and Betty Slade.

Partially sponsored by the Office of Emerging Markets, Center for Economic Growth and Agricultural Development, Bureau for Global Programs, Field Support and Research, U.S. Agency for International Development under the Consulting Assistance on Economic Reform (CAER) II Project (Contract PCE-0405-C-00-5015-00). The views and interpretations in this paper are those of the authors and should not be attributed to USAID.

Notes

[1] Yung-Chul Park (1996) is a notable exception, but voices such as his were rare and generally went unheeded. Paul Krugman's (1994) provocative critique of East Asian growth suggested a slowdown in growth, not a collapse, a point that Krugman himself made clear in the Fall of 1997, at the start of the financial crisis.

[2] A member of the Bundesbank Board has reported to us his own discussions with 2 German banks. He asked these banks why they extended such large loans to Korea in 1997, just on the verge of the financial collapse. Several banks replied that Korea's new membership in the OECD had given them confidence that Korean economic performance would continue to be strong (private communication, February 1997).

[3] Technically, the Philippine peso operated under a floating regime, but there was so little variation in the exchange rate that it was perceived to be effectively pegged to the dollar by market participants.

[4] As we note later, central banks augmented the rise in interest rates by a further tightening of domestic credit in the context of IMF-supported adjustment programs.

[5] The idea of using the CPI in the denominator and the WPI in the numerator is that the CPI is heavily weighted towards nontradeable goods, while the WPI is heavily weighted towards tradeables.

[6] Specifically, we use all trading partners that are members of the OECD, except Mexico and Korea.

[7] Earlier studies (e.g., Sachs, Tornell, and Velasco, 1996) have stressed the role of rapid increases in bank lending as a predictor of subsequent financial crisis.

[8] See, for example, "In Battle for Investors, This Is No Contest: Amid a Crisis, Indonesia Opens Up and Thrives as Malaysia Stumbles." Asian Wall Street Journal, September 5-6, 1997.

[9] Radelet (1995) raises concerns about "quasi-public sector" foreign liabilities of well-connected Indonesian firms and rising short-term debt, while Radelet (1996) documents the overvaluation of the rupiah.

[10] McLeod (1997) argues that an IMF program was not necessary, a conclusion with which we agree.

[11] The IMF and the US Treasury severely criticized the proposed 32 percent increase in spending as indicating that Indonesia was not serious about reform, which sent markets reeling. However, all of the increase was simply due to exchange rate movements. Within three weeks the Fund had quietly approved a new budget with a 46 percent increase in spending, but the damage to market perceptions had been done.

[12] Two aspects of the bank closures added to the panic. First, regarding deposits at the 16 banks closed in early November, the Indonesian government announced that accounts would be protected in the closed banks only up to 20 million rupiah (or around $7,000 at the time). This protection was not extended to deposits in banks that remained open. Second, the very fact that the President's son's bank was one that was closed quickly gave rise to the view in Indonesia that no bank was safe. The attempt to show "toughness" and political resolve backfired, by dramatically undermining confidence in the entire banking system.

[13] "IMF Now Admits Tactics in Indonesia Deepened the Crisis," New York Times, January 14, 1998.

[14] "Indonesia - Memorandum of Economic and Financial Policies," Jakarta Post, January 17, 1998.

[15] Bank of Thailand website; Jakarta Post, January 17, 1998.

[16] "IMF Concedes Its Conditions for Thailand Were Too Austere," New York Times, February 11, 1998.

References

Akerlof and Romer. 1994. "Looting: The Economic Underworld of Bankruptcy for Profit." NBER Working Paper no. 1869 (April).

Bank for International Settlements. 1998. "The Maturity, Sectoral, and Nationality Distribution of International Bank Lending." Basle, Bank for International Settlements (January).

Blanchard, Olivier, and Mark Watson. 1982. "Bubbles, Rational Expectations, and Financial Markets." In Paul Wachtel (ed.), Crises in the Economic and Financial Structure (Lexington Books).

Cline, William R. and Kevin J.S. Barnes. 1997. "Spreads and Risks in Emerging Markets Lending," Institute of International Finance Research Paper No. 97-1 (November).

Diamond, Douglas and Phillip Dybvig. 1983. "Bank Runs, Liquidity, and Deposit Insurance." Journal of Political Economy, vol. 91, pp. 401-419.

Friedman, Milton and Anna Schwartz. 1963. *A Monetary History of the United States 1867-1960*, National Bureau of Economic Research (Princeton: Princeton University Press).

International Monetary Fund. 1997a. "Philippine —Recent Economic Developments," Staff Country Report No. 97/28 (April).

International Monetary Fund. 1997b. *World Economic Outlook* (October).

International Monetary Fund. 1997c. *Annual Report.*

Institute of International Finance. 1998. "Capital Flows to Emerging Market Economies," January 29, 1998.

Jakarta Post. January 17, 1998.

Kindleberger. 1996. Manias, Panics, and Crashes: *A History of Financial Crises*, Third Edition, (New York: John Wiley and Sons).

Kline, William R., and Kevin J.S. Barnes. 1997. "Spreads and Risks in Emerging Markets Lending." Institute for International Finance Research Paper No. 97-1, (November).

Krugman, Paul. 1998. "What Happened to Asia?" Unpublished manuscript (January).

Krugman, Paul. 1994. "The Myth of Asia's Miracle." *Foreign Affairs* 73(6), November/December, pp 62-78.

Krugman, Paul. 1979. "A Model of Balance of Payments Crises." *Journal of Money, Credit, and Banking*, vol 11, pp. 311-325.

McLeod. 1997. "On Causes and Cures for the Rupiah Crisis." *Bulletin of Indonesian Economic Studies*, vol. 33-3 (December), pp. 35-52.

New York Times. January 14, 1998.

New York Times. February 11, 1998.

Park, Yung Chul. 1996. "East Asian Liberalization, Bubbles, and the Challenges form China." Brookings Papers on Economic Activity (2).

Radelet, Steven. 1995. "Indonesian Foreign Debt: Headed for a Crisis or Financing Sustainable Growth?" *Bulletin of Indonesian Economic Studies*, vol. 31-3 (December), pp. 39-72.

Radelet, Steven. 1996. "Measuring the Real Exchange Rate and Its Relationship to Exports: An Application to Indonesia." HIID Development Discussion Paper No. 529 (May).

Radelet, Steven and Jeffrey Sachs. 1998. "The East Asian Financial Crisis: Diagnosis, Remedies, Prospects." *Brookings Papers on Economic Activity*, forthcoming.

Sachs, Jeffrey. 1995. "Do We Need an International Lender of Last Resort?" Unpublished manuscript presented as Frank D. Graham Lecture at Princeton (April).

Sachs, Jeffrey, Aaron Tornell and Andres Velasco. 1996. "Financial Crises in Emerging Markets: The Lessons from 1995," Brookings Papers on Economic Activity (August).

Argentina's Currency Crisis: Lessons for Asia

34

MARK SPIEGEL

Before Argentina's currency crisis erupted this year, renewed interest in pegged exchange rate regimes had been gaining momentum, especially in Asia. That region's 1997 financial crisis led many of its nations to explore whether formal currency arrangements might forestall a repeat of such crises. The initial efforts concentrated on developing institutions to raise liquidity regionally, and since then the feasibility of greater monetary policy coordination also has been considered. Asian countries found particular inspiration from the successful launch of the European Monetary Union (EMU). The EMU consists of 11 European nations that adopted a single currency, the euro, and ceded monetary policy to a single central bank authority; at the same time, however, these countries retain a large amount of other policy independence, particularly concerning domestic public finance. As such, the EMU provides a model of a viable currency union that closely matches a potential ASEAN arrangement (the ASEAN nations are Brunei, Cambodia, Indonesia, Laos, Malaysia, Myanmar, the Philippines, Singapore, Thailand, and Vietnam). The launch of the EMU was followed by the Chiang Mai Initiative in June 2000, in which the ASEAN nations plus Japan, China, and Korea agreed to adopt a system of swap arrangements. There was some speculation that the successful launch of these swap arrangements would lay the foundation for more intensive regional monetary policy coordination.

However, the difficulties experienced by Argentina this year have slowed much of the momentum for the adoption of formal fixed currency arrangements. The shock of seeing Argentina's currency board regime, which had been perceived as strong and credible despite some misgivings about the appropriateness of its currency peg, appears to have renewed doubts about the sustainability of any formal exchange rate arrangements.

In this *Economic Letter*, I review the circumstances surrounding the collapse of Argentina's monetary regime and describe some lessons these circumstances may provide for proposed Asian currency arrangements.

Argentina's Currency Board Regime

Argentina maintained a currency board regime from April 1, 1991, through January 6, 2002, under which the Argentine peso was pegged one for one to the U.S. dollar. In several respects, the regime did not meet the criteria of an "orthodox" currency board, as defined by Hanke and Schuler (2002). These criteria include three key features: first, the board must maintain a fixed exchange rate with its anchor currency; second, it must allow for full convertibility, that is, it must allow holders of the currency to move into or out of the anchor currency without restriction; third, the monetary liabilities of the currency board must be fully backed in hard—that is, foreign currency—assets.

In addition, an orthodox currency board should not participate in activities such as purchasing government securities, regulating commercial banks, or acting as a lender of last resort. It is easy to see how any of these activities could undermine a currency board's primary goal of maintaining the peg with the anchor currency.

Argentina's currency board violated all of these rules at some point in its existence (Hanke and Schuler 2002). The charter governing Argentina's currency board allowed it to be partially backed by domestic—rather than hard foreign currency—assets. The currency board initially was allowed to hold as little as 66.6% of its assets in true foreign reserves. The remainder could be backed by Argentine government bonds. As such, the currency board could pursue discretionary monetary policy. In 2001 alone, the foreign reserve backing for Argentina's currency board ranged from a high of 193% to a low of 82%. In addition, the Argentine central bank set reserve ratios and, therefore, retained some financial regulatory power. The currency board also acted as lender of last resort, for example, during the Mexican peso crisis of 1995, when it extended funds to illiquid commercial banks (Spiegel 1999). Therefore, it would be more accurate to characterize Argentina's exchange rate regime not as an orthodox currency board but as a fixed exchange rate regime with a hard dollar peg. Nevertheless, it must be granted that the rules faced by Argentina's currency board exceeded those commonly found in pegged regimes.

With the appreciation of the dollar in the late 1990s, the Argentine currency board experienced overvaluation. Argentina's exports became less competitive on the world market. These effects spilled over to the real side of the economy. Argentina has been in recession now for four years.

In addition, Argentina had been running massive fiscal budget deficits for some years. In 2000, the government raised income taxes in an effort to balance its budget, and in 2001 it levied a tax on financial transactions. But these efforts failed as Argentina's economic recession worsened. The climbing deficit led to an increase in devaluation concerns. Roughly $20 billion in capital fled the country in 2001. Peso interest rates climbed to between 40% and 60%, which further weakened the government's budget position.

At the end of 2001, Argentina moved to a dual exchange rate system, adopting a preferential exchange rate peg for exports. This move eliminated the characteristic of full convertibility—and with it any semblance of a currency board. However, this failed to reassure the public. The government then froze bank deposits, formally initiating a financial crisis, and in January 2002 it abandoned the exchange rate regime for a floating regime.

Asian Currency Arrangements

The currency arrangements proposed for Asian nations vary widely in intensity, ranging from regional insurance schemes aimed at forestalling future financial crises to agreements that could culminate in an Asian version of the EMU with a single currency for the region.

Japan first proposed creation of an "Asian Monetary Fund" in 1997 in the wake of Asia's financial crisis. The proposal was for an institution that would provide a framework for financial cooperation and policy coordination. Opposed by both the United States and the IMF, the proposal was shelved. However, policy coordination in the region was reborn with the Chiang Mai Initiative in 2000. This initiative would expand existing swap arrangements to the ASEAN nations as well as to China, Japan, and Korea. The swap arrangements are designed to provide liquidity support for member countries in distress in an effort to prevent regional contagion and systemic risk.

A full-fledged intra-Asian currency arrangement analogous to the European Monetary Union also has been considered (see, for example, Bayoumi and Mauro 1999). The argument in favor of such a regime is that it would stabilize exchange rates within the region, while allowing for flexibility against the three major global currencies, the dollar, the euro, and the yen.

However, Ogawa and Ito (2000) have argued simply for a greater weighting of other currencies in Asian monetary arrangements. They argue that the excessive targeting of the dollar fueled the Asian crisis of 1997. If Asian countries had instead adopted a currency basket with a yen weight commensurate with Japan's share in trade, the nations would not have experienced as significant a boom over the 1993–1995 period, as their currencies would have appreciated with the yen. More importantly, the depreciation of their currencies along with the yen in 1996 and 1997 would have mitigated their recessions.

Lessons from the Argentine Experience

One obvious and important lesson for the Asian countries from Argentina's failed currency board is that an improper exchange rate peg is doomed to failure, no matter how rigorously one imposes conditions to engender credibility. A basket peg is likely to serve the ASEAN nations best, because their trade volumes with the United States, Europe, and Japan are of similar magnitudes. For example, Rajan (2002) notes that during the 1997 Asian crises, Singapore, which pursued a flexible basket peg, outperformed Hong Kong, which pursued a dollar peg. Another lesson is that exchange rate arrangements are no cure for problems in the area of macroeconomic policy. Despite the relatively strong set of rules governing the conduct of Argentina's currency board, the regime collapsed in relatively short order when domestic and foreign investors determined that the Argentine government's fiscal policies were unsustainable.

One important implication for prospective Asian currency arrangements is that the degree of disparity in development levels across these countries is likely to prove difficult. The Asian nations as a group, particularly if Japan is included, represent a more heterogeneous set of nations than the EMU, making it more likely that the nations differ in their desired macroeconomic policies.

A third lesson is that rules can go only so far in enhancing the credibility of an exchange rate regime. It is generally understood that a nation can buy credibility by increasing the cost of abandoning the announced peg. In the case

of Argentina, this cost was clearly very high. Nevertheless, the collapse of the Argentine regime demonstrates the ease of circumventing the rules of an exchange rate regime. The introduction of a dual exchange rate system and the freezing of bank accounts were readily adopted policies in Argentina, despite currency board rules to the contrary.

This lesson raises the question of whether dollarization would have done much better, and the answer is, not necessarily. Under dollarization, Argentina would have experienced the same exchange rate appreciation and therefore the same loss of competitiveness vis-à-vis its primary trading partners who were not tied to the dollar. Therefore, the government probably would have ended up in a similar unsustainable fiscal situation. Moreover, there is little reason to believe that dollarization would have precluded the government from abandoning the peg. For example, one proposal to deal with the current crisis that is now being circulated is the forced conversion of asset claims into bonds, presumably at depreciated peso prices. There is no reason that the same reduction in liabilities could not be achieved under a dollarized regime. The government could simply freeze all deposits and convert them to bonds with a financial haircut in place. Once the legal protection of property claims is open to abrogation, no exchange rate regime can ensure asset values.

Finally, many would argue that the ultimate lesson from Argentina's currency crisis is that no fixed exchange rate regime, even one as institutionally strong as Argentina's, is completely sound. As a result, it will sooner or later lose its credibility. Moreover, since financial contracts will have been written in the domestic currency, this loss of credibility will have real effects and likely will precipitate a financial crisis, or at least a severe disruption to the real side of the economy. As such, floating may be a superior policy over the long run.

At the same time, floating exchange rate regimes pose important difficulties for developing countries. First, because many of these countries are relatively open, external shocks can do more damage to them than to most developed nations. Second, because developing countries lack the ability to issue debt in their own currency, depreciations immediately correspond to increases in indebtedness in domestic currency. As a result, floating regimes may exacerbate the potential for financial crises stemming from widespread bankruptcies.

Finally, floating regimes place responsibility for maintaining price stability back squarely in the hands of the national central bank. Because developing country institutions are often less well-established, it may be difficult for a developing nation's central bank to resist, for example, monetizing the deficit of its treasury. As a result, price stability may be unattainable domestically. Instead, nations may look to exchange rate pegs as mechanisms to import developed nations' monetary policies that are otherwise unattainable given their own level of institutional development.

Conclusion

The collapse of Argentina's currency board has had a devastating impact on that nation. Perhaps the most important lesson from Argentina's experience is that an exchange rate regime is only as good as its peg. No set of rules surrounding the regime, regardless of their strength, can force a nation to remain attached to a peg that has outlived its usefulness. As a result, even "good" pegs are likely to be less than perfectly credible. Despite the drawbacks outlined here, the alternative of pure floating must be seriously considered.

Mark Spiegel
Research Advisor

This Economic Letter is based on a presentation Mark Spiegel prepared for a panel on "Optimal Currency Arrangements for Emerging Market Economies: The Experience of Latin America and Asia" organized by the Latin American and Asian Economics and Business Association on July 15, 2002, in Tokyo, Japan.

References

Bayoumi, Tamim, and Paolo Mauro. 1999. "The Suitability of ASEAN for a Regional Currency Basket." International Monetary Fund Working Paper WP/99/162.

Hanke, Steve, and Kurt Schuler. 2002. "What Went Wrong in Argentina?" *Central Banking* 12(3), pp. 43–48.

Ogawa, Eiji, and Takatoshi Ito. 2000. "On the Desirability of a Regional Basket Currency Arrangement." NBER Working Paper 8002 (November).

Rajan, Ramkishen S. 2002. "Argentina and East Asia: The Peg Does It Again." Mimeo, University of Adelaide.

Spiegel, Mark M. 1999. "Dollarization in Argentina." *FRBSF Economic Letter* 99-29 (September 24).

Capital Controls and Emerging Markets

35

RAMON **MORENO**

The financial crises in the 1990s resurrected the debate on whether emerging markets should stay open to foreign capital or impose capital controls. The stakes are high. Emerging markets that have been open to foreign capital have seen it contribute to sharply improved living standards; at the same time, the volatility of capital flows has made these markets vulnerable to economic boom and bust cycles. Under these circumstances, one may dispute whether the benefits of liberalizing capital controls outweigh the costs. To shed light on this question, this Economic Letter discusses the benefits and costs of liberalizing capital controls, cites some empirical evidence, and briefly reviews the recent experiences Chile and Malaysia have had with capital controls.

Why Lift Capital Controls?

Capital controls are regulations or taxes that make cross-border financial transactions or investments costly or difficult, typically by restricting the access of a country's residents to foreign currency. Toward the end of the 1980s, many countries lifted such restrictions. Their reasons for liberalizing capital flows were partly pragmatic, as technological innovations, such as new financial instruments, made it easier to circumvent capital controls, and as, in a number of cases, economic instability provided large incentives for doing so. Their reasons also reflected a general shift in thinking among policy-makers toward favor-

ing greater reliance on market forces and less government intervention.

At least two benefits of a more open capital account have been cited. First, more openness can stimulate growth by reducing distortions and enhancing access to foreign financing. The wealthiest countries have open capital accounts, suggesting a relationship between openness and higher levels of prosperity. And it is apparent that foreign financing is very important for those emerging markets fortunate enough to attract it, accounting for a large share of their economic activity. According to Lopez-Mejia (1999), in 1996 (before the Asian crisis) capital flows were equivalent to about 4.5% of GDP in Asia and Latin America, or 20% and 30% of exports, respectively. The importance of these flows was probably even larger for the top 12 emerging market recipients, who received 75% of total capital flows.

Second, an open capital account may improve economic performance over the business cycle by encouraging more prudent domestic macroeconomic and financial policies, as well as improved short-term access to financing. Policymakers in countries with open capital accounts must adopt prudent policies because investors are free to put their money elsewhere, whereas policymakers in countries with capital controls can pursue less prudent policies because investors cannot easily move their funds, at least in the short run. This may explain why, between the 1980s and the 1990s, a number of countries that opened their capital accounts simultaneously reduced budget deficits and dramatically reduced money growth and inflation. There is also evidence that over the business cycle, economies with more open capital accounts have more access to credit, implying that consumption or investment can be boosted more easily during a recession.

Costs of Lifting Capital Controls

The potential long-run benefits of lifting capital controls must be weighed against two short-run costs. First, greater openness increases a country's vulnerability to global shocks or to sudden changes in investor sentiment. Moreno and Trehan (2000) find evidence indicating that shocks to global interest rates, inflation, and capital flows can explain a large proportion of the global incidence of currency crises. Capital flows are subject to pronounced cycles that may induce boom and bust cycles in production and investment among recipient countries and trigger financial or currency crises when financing is withdrawn. One source of vulnerability is mismatching of maturities or currencies, which makes recipient countries illiquid. As is well known, this illiquidity makes a system vulnerable to panics. For example, foreign financing may be in U.S. dollars, while the local borrowers' earnings are in local currency. A sudden withdrawal of funds could lead to a collapse in the currency, bankrupting local borrowers of foreign currency by raising their debt burdens in their own currency. The impact of cycles in capital flows may be more extreme in countries with weak financial systems, where government guarantees may encourage excessive risk-taking with foreign funds.

Second, greater openness also restricts policymakers' options. A country cannot simultaneously maintain an open capital account, peg the exchange rate, and adopt an independent monetary policy (that is, a money or interest rate target). This constraint, sometimes known as the "impossible trinity," complicates efforts to implement stabilization policy. For example, if, as a result of attractive returns, capital is flowing into a country and the central bank keeps the domestic interest rate high, the currency will tend to appreciate, which may hurt exporters and dampen economic activity. If the central bank chooses to stabilize the exchange rate instead, it must print money in order to buy up the foreign currency that is flowing in (allowing domestic interest rates to fall), which may lead to excessive domestic money creation, an unsustainable boom in economic activity, and inflation (and a crash if the capital inflow suddenly reverses). With capital controls, a central bank can set both the interest rate and the exchange rate simultaneously, at the cost of limiting capital inflows that could finance productive activity.

The constraints facing policymakers in countries with open capital accounts became painfully apparent during the East Asian financial crises of the late 1990s. According to the Institute for International Finance, the inflow of private capital to the region peaked at $118 billion in 1996 and then fell to an outflow of nearly $38 billion in 1998. The withdrawal of capital caused currencies to collapse and led to steep reductions in investment and growth. Some countries initially raised interest rates in order to stabilize the currency and reassure investors. However, in the uncertain environment, interest rates in some cases had to be raised very high, further weakening economic activity and the financial sector. In an open economy, aggressively lowering interest rates to stimulate economic activity also had disadvantages, as the prospect of further depreciation could keep investors away. Also, many firms had borrowed in foreign currencies without hedging their currency exposure, and the resulting depreciations could (and eventually did) cause widespread bankruptcies. Countries with capital controls in place, like China or Vietnam, were largely insulated from these pressures.

Do the Benefits of Liberalizing Outweigh the Costs?

There are few systematic studies on the growth effects of liberalizing capital controls, and the available evidence suggests that the impact is not the same for all countries. Edwards (2001) studied the experience of advanced and developing countries in the 1980s (but not the 1990s, due to the time span of the capital controls index he uses) and found that, on average, countries with lower capital controls have faster real GDP or total factor productivity growth than countries with more stringent controls. (These results appear to be robust to outlying observations, but are sensitive to measurement error.) However, only countries, including some emerging markets, whose income exceeds a certain threshold benefit from lower capital controls (among these countries are Israel, Venezuela, Hong Kong, Singapore, and Mexico). Poorer countries with less stringent capital controls grow more slowly.

Evidence suggesting that capital controls are associated with less prudent macroeconomic policies is mixed. Grilli and Milesi-Ferretti (1995) found that such controls are associated with higher inflation, while Rodrik (1998) found no evidence of such a relationship. Glick and Hutchison (2001) report evidence that capital controls are associated with a higher, rather than lower, likelihood of currency crises. Their results suggest that economic policies are indeed less prudent in economies with capital controls and contribute more to crises than does the greater vulnerability to shocks that result from openness.

Case Studies

Two case studies illuminate the benefits and costs of liberalizing capital controls: Chile's controls on capital inflows in the 1990s, and Malaysia's controls on capital outflows in September 1998.

In an effort to limit surging capital inflows, in June 1991 Chilean policymakers imposed an unremunerated reserve requirement (URR), first on foreign borrowing (except trade credit) and later on short-term portfolio inflows (foreign currency deposits in commercial banks and potentially speculative foreign direct investment). The reserve requirement rose from 20%, to 30%, but

then fell to 0% when capital flows to Chile (and other emerging markets) dried up in 1998. A minimum stay requirement for direct and portfolio investment from abroad also was imposed (eliminated in May 2000), as were minimum regulatory requirements for corporate borrowing abroad. Banks also were required to report capital transactions. The controls do not appear to have been very effective. According to Ariyoshi et al. (2000), capital inflows rose, despite the controls, from 7.3% of GDP in 1990–1995 to 11.3% in 1996–1997, before falling in 1998; investors found ways to circumvent the controls, leading policymakers to expand the program. It is also unclear whether the controls succeeded in shifting the composition of foreign capital towards longer maturities. Finally, the program did not seem to give Chile increased monetary autonomy. The real exchange rate continued to appreciate, at an average rate of 4% a year from 1991 to mid-1997. While the differential between domestic and foreign real interest rates rose (from 3.1% in 1985–91 to 5.2% in 1992–97), this may have been due to continued sterilized intervention in foreign currency markets, not the capital controls.

In 1998, as capital flowed out of East Asia, uncertainty about the stability of the Malaysian currency (the ringgit) and the economic outlook generated speculation against the ringgit. As noted earlier, the openness of the capital account limited Malaysia's (and other East Asian economies') options to boost growth. The government eventually decided to stimulate the economy by easing monetary policy aggressively. To prevent the capital outflows such a measure might trigger, on September 1, 1998, capital controls were imposed, focusing on two broad areas. First, to prevent speculation against the ringgit, access to local currency by non-residents was restricted, and rules requiring all ringgit to be repatriated effectively closed the offshore market in ringgit. Second, the repatriation of portfolio capital held by non-residents was blocked for 12 months (this was subsequently replaced by an exit tax on short-term investments), and capital outflows by residents were restricted. Restrictions focused on short-term maturities and did not apply to international trade or long-term foreign investment transactions. The exchange rate was then pegged, interest rates were lowered, and commercial banks were encouraged to lend.

While Malaysia's capital controls successfully curbed capital flows, there is no agreement on whether they were needed to restore growth. The Malaysian economy recovered soon after controls were imposed, but strong demand for the region's exports brought about comparable recoveries in other East Asian economies that did not impose controls. For example, Malaysia's growth switched from -7.4% in 1998 to 5.8% in 1999. In Korea, which imposed no controls, the comparable figures are -6.7% and 10.9%. Some argue that Malaysia was more vulnerable than the other Asian economies in 1998, so that its performance would have been poorer without capital controls, but there is disagreement on this point.

Conclusions

Two broad conclusions emerge from the research and experiences surveyed here. First, recent research suggests that poorer countries face a trade-off, as capital controls appear to be associated with faster growth (the reverse is true for wealthier countries), but less macroeconomic stability and a greater incidence of crises. Second, studies of the experiences of Chile and Malaysia highlight some of the difficulties in the design and application of capital controls. Chilean policymakers attempted to minimize the costs of capital controls by designing restrictions that were not too onerous or distortionary. As a result, however, the effectiveness of these controls was apparently limited. Changes in conditions may also make controls unnecessary. For example, the pattern of recovery in East Asia after recent crises suggests that Malaysia might have done as well without imposing capital controls.

Ramon Moreno - Research Advisor

References

Ariyoshi, A., K. Habermeier, B. Laurens, I. Otker-Robe, J. Canales-Kriljenko, and A. Kirilenko. 2000. *Capital Controls: Country Experiences with Their Use and Liberalization.* IMF Occasional Paper No. 190 (May).

Edwards, S. 2001. "Capital Mobility and Economic Performance: Are Emerging Markets Different?" NBER Working Paper No. W8076.

Glick, R., and M. Hutchison. 2001. "Capital Controls and Exchange Rate Stability in Developing Countries." FRBSF *Economic Letter* No. 2001–21 (July 20). http://www.sf.frb.org/publications/economics/letter/2001/el2001-21.html

Grilli, Vittorio, and Gian Maria Milesi-Ferretti. 1995. "Economic Effects and Structural Determinants of Capital Controls." Staff Papers, International Monetary Fund. 42(September): 517–51.

Lopez-Mejia, Alejandro. 1999. "Large Capital Flows: A Survey of Causes, Consequences and Policy Responses." IMF Working Paper WP/99/7.

Moreno, Ramon, and Bharat Trehan. 2000. "Common Shocks and Currency Crises." FRBSF Working Paper No. 2000–05. http://www.sf.frb.org/econrsrch/workingp/2000/wp00–05.pdf.

Rodrik, Dani. 1998. "Who Needs Capital Account Convertibility?" In Peter B. Kenen (ed.) *Should the IMF Pursue Current Account Convertibility?* Essays in International Finance, No. 207 (May). International Finance Section, Department of Economics, Princeton University.

Discussion Questions

1. According to Radelet and Sachs, what are the major explanations for the Asian crisis? Which explanation do they prefer?

2. What do Radelet and Sachs propose to prevent future financial crises?

3. Are their any similarities between Argentina's crisis and the Asian financial crisis?

4. What was the cause of the Russian crisis described by Chiodo and Owyang?

5. How would Sachs and Radelet classify Argentina's crisis? How about the Russian Crisis?

6. What are the arguments for and against capital controls? On what side do you think Moreno comes out on?

7. For each of these crises, describe what role of the IMF played. Did they help or hinder? Were their policies consistent?

Restructuring the New World

This section examines several current topics in international finance that are particularly pertinent for the future of the world's international financial architecture. The section begins by looking at policies coping with financial crises such as countries defaulting on debt or requiring a bail-out. The last ten years have witnessed several financial crises; the crises in South America and Russia involved debt default and all the crises, including the Asian crisis, required some form of bail-out. The first three articles examine the policy options available for countries in financial distress. This section concludes with money laundering, which is not only a domestic issue but increasingly an international issue. Economies are more integrated and the increase in international capital flows is making it easier to disguise illegal monies.

The first article in this section is the second by Richard Cooper that we have selected for the reader. In "Chapter 11 for Countries?" Cooper examines debt solutions for foreign creditors of governments in financial distress.

Creditors are concerned that their holdings of government debt will not be repaid when the country develops economic difficulties. Often creditors will decline to roll over the debt or sell the debt before the maturity date, exacerbating economic crisis. Cooper summarizes US bankruptcy proceedings for firms and analyzes whether similar bankruptcy proceedings can be applied to government debt.

Jeffrey Sachs, formerly at Harvard and now at Columbia, proposes that the international system needs a provision for unloading unpayable debt in "The International Lender of Last Resort: What are the Alternatives?" He argues that over the past decade the international system has had an international lender of first resort rather than an international lender of last resort as there has been too much lending by the IMF.

The final article in this section, "Dirty Money" by Miriam Wasserman, discusses the history, cost, and consequences of money laundering and anti-money laundering laws. Money or property gained from illegal activities is "laundered" into money that appears to have been legally earned. It is difficult to determine how much money is laundered but it is estimated at 2-5% of global GDP. The economic cost of money laundering, Wasserman writes, is that money is not used where it is most productive but rather allocated on the basis of ease of avoiding national controls. Wasserman also points out that as criminals find methods of laundering large amounts of money, government officials are often corrupted in the process.

Chapter 11 for Countries?

RICHARD N. COOPER

Late in 2001 the new Deputy Managing Director of the International Monetary Fund (IMF), Anne Krueger, boldly suggested that under certain conditions international debt repayments by a sovereign borrower (= government) should be temporarily suspended while negotiations take place on restructuring its debt. Thus the IMF officially endorsed one of the more radical suggestions for improvements in the international financial architecture that have been made since the Mexican financial crisis of 1995 and the several Asian crises of 1997. This article provides analytical and historical background to evaluate this and other proposals for reform.

The problem addressed by the proposal is straightforward. When any debtor develops economic difficulties, creditors worry about being repaid, and they move as quickly as they can to protect their positions, for example by declining to renew credits or roll over claims that have matured. They may even sell the claims before maturity, although for that of course they must find buyers. The difficulty several governments faced in rolling over maturing debt played an important role in several recent debt crises -- Mexico (1995), Russia (1998), Brazil (1998-99), and Argentina (2001-02). Even creditors that would be willing to roll over their claims at a satisfactory interest rate may hesitate to do so on grounds they will be alone, and thus caught in a payments crisis. When the ability of the borrower to continue to service the debt is doubtful, lenders become eager to exit quickly, to protect their principal.

This problem can arise for any debtor and its diverse creditors. We deal with it domestically through bankruptcy proceedings. A debtor in trouble can "file chapter 11" of the bankruptcy law, which legally suspends payments to all creditors (except the tax authorities). That suspension gives a breathing space for one of several things to happen. The debtor can re-organize its financial affairs to make resumption of debt service more likely. As part of re-organization it can borrow anew, e.g. for working capital, with legal preference given to the new creditors. It can negotiate with its old creditors for an extension of maturity and even an easing of terms, interest or principal. All this is done within the United States under the protection and with the guidance of a court of law. Only if a business firm cannot restore value as a going concern are the debtor's assets liquidated with proceeds distributed to the creditors, again under the guidance of a court. Analogous processes exist in most countries, although Europe tends to be tougher on debtors than the United States.

One of the key features of domestic bankruptcy proceedings is that not every creditor needs to agree to the negotiated deal to be bound by it. If creditors carrying two-thirds of the claims agree to a settlement, all creditors are covered -- the so-called "cram down" provision. Concretely, a single small creditor cannot hold up a deal in an attempt to get better treatment.

No such procedure covers international claims on sovereign borrowers. So if a government runs into payments difficulty, each creditor may move to protect its interests, risking a rush to the door in times of difficulty, or even possible difficulty. The IMF proposal is designed to fill this gap, to provide the international analogue to national bankruptcy proceedings, as applied to governments. (International lending to corporations is of course covered by bankruptcy law in some country, usually the country where the securities were issued.)

Although this need has been recognized for some time, at least since the debt crises of the early 1980s, it was given a strong push by the case of Elliott Associates versus Peru. In early 1996 Elliott purchased, at a heavy market discount, loans to Peruvian banks guaranteed by the Peruvian government in 1983. The purchase was made while negotiation between Peru and its creditors was proceeding. In November 1996, by agreement with 180 creditors, Peru exchanged cash and Brady bonds (collateralized as to principal by US Treasury securities) for their claims. Elliott sued for full payment of principal and accrued interest. The claim was dismissed by a Federal court, but reinstated on appeal. To assure payment, Elliott in fall 2000 obtained restraining orders both in New York and in Brussels against coupon payments to Brady bond holders, i.e. to the creditors who had agreed to the debt restructuring. To avoid a formal default, Peru settled with Elliott out of court by paying $56 million, against Elliott's purchase price of $11 million less than five years earlier.

This episode rewarded a holdout at the expense of creditors who reached a negotiated settlement, and cast a legal fog around the whole issue of debt restructuring, at least with respect to private creditors. (Where only public creditors are involved, official debt restructuring is negotiated among governments in the "Paris Club." The same governments have needed to meet repeatedly over the past two decades, and each can expect an unduly tough stand in one negotiation to be reciprocated at subsequent negotiations in which it may have a greater stake in reaching a settlement.)

The analogical application of bankruptcy proceedings to governments is attractive. Like all analogies, it can be carried only so far. In bankruptcy, two business judgments must be made: what would be the value of the firm's physical assets on liquidation must be compared with the firm's prospects of ultimately paying more than that if, relieved of some debt, it is allowed to continue to operate.

Governments do not service debt out of operating earnings, but out of tax revenues, which face competing social claims. Thus political and ultimately ethical judgments must be made about the desirability of continuing to service the outstanding debt, not just the technical feasibility of doing so. That is a much more complicated and controversial judgment than those that must be made in normal bankruptcy proceedings.

The IMF probably has the best capacity to judge the near future fiscal and balance-of-payments prospects of a debtor country; and even, although it does not advertise the fact, to judge the technical competence and integrity of the sitting government to carry out its promises. But it is not especially well suited to make the ethical trade-offs between violating a contractual promise to pay creditors versus the social costs in terms of education, health care, or security of carrying out that promise. That judgment needs to be made by politically responsible officials. Here, the IMF could provide a forum for such discussion, although ministries of finance should receive inputs from other parts of government, as it does in the United States.

So there is a rationale in principle for a legally sanctioned pause in debt servicing in the case of sovereign debt held by private parties, discouraging holdouts, and providing preferred new credits where appropriate. Several questions need to be asked about putting it into effect and making it really work: 1) What should be its coverage, in terms of a country's indebtedness? 2) To which countries should it apply? 3) Would the possibility of an enforced pause in servicing reduce international flows of capital, particularly to developing countries? 4) What steps need to be taken to put such an arrangement into place?

The obvious candidates for coverage are overseas holdings of a government's bonds and overseas bank credit to the government. These are the claims on which sovereign immunity from legal action is typically waived in the debt contract. But if a pause were limited to overseas creditors, foreign holders could arrange to sell maturing debt to residents and be repaid through correspondents. This is of course more difficult to control when the bonds in question are of domestic issue, rather than an international issue, but where foreign holdings of domestic bonds are extensive -- as was the case in Mexico, Russia, Brazil, and most recently Argentina. Foreign creditors moreover will not appreciate being held up while domestic creditors are repaid. Thus for both practical reasons and for reasons of parity in treatment domestic holdings of government bonds must also be subject to the pause. And if domestic banks rely heavily on government bonds as a source of their liquidity, suspending repayments of government securities may also require introducing restrictions on bank deposit withdrawals, unless suitable arrangements are made with the central bank to liquify them when necessary.

What about other domestic claims on the government, or a situation where foreign holdings of domestic issues are negligible but international credits are covered? Again, foreign creditors are not likely to agree to overt discrimination, except possibly in cases where the crisis is clearly external rather than budgetary in origin -- and even then only if residents are subject to effective controls on their ability to convert domestic into foreign currency. It would not be acceptable, in terms either of efficacy or of equity, to halt payments to foreigners in the name of providing temporary relief and a pause for debt re-negotiation while allowing residents to be repaid and freely export the proceeds.

The point seems obvious, yet implementing it in today's world is highly problematic. Many countries have dismantled their controls on foreign exchange or greatly reduced them to cover only financial institutions. And those that remain are highly pervious to a public determined to export capital — including purchases of foreign currency (e.g., greenbacks). Again, in recent crises none of the countries had really effective exchange controls, and Malaysia was widely criticized for tightening them in 1998.

What about country coverage? Everyone has in mind "emerging markets," which have acquired access to the international capital market through various channels. But this is a constantly changing category. Moreover, should it include the low-income members of the OECD, such as Mexico, or even of the EMU, such as Portugal? Should it include Italy, whose future fiscal outlook is by no means rosy? Or Germany, which recently threatened to break through the EMU's dreaded three percent budget deficit barrier? Or the United States, whose outstanding debt and foreign holdings of domestic debt exceed that of any other country? What would be the grounds for extending the provision to some members of the IMF but not to others?

The question naturally arises whether inclusion of an automatic rollover provision in all or most government debt would deter the flow of capital to developing countries. It is worth noting that corporate debt has long been subject to bankruptcy proceedings in the United States and many other countries, and the both corporate bond market within the United States and the international market are robust; there may be some deterrence, but whatever its magnitude, it has not kept the corporate bond market from thriving.

Moreover, some deterrence to the flow of private capital to emerging markets would not necessarily be a bad thing. Research on the domestic benefits of foreign capital is surprisingly ambiguous, and in a world ridden with import protection and with taxes and hence incentives for tax evasion the benefits are not even unambiguous on theoretical grounds. On balance, the evidence suggests a net contribution to per capita income in debtor countries, although the evidence is much stronger for foreign direct investment (involving importation of management skills, marketing know-how, and technology as well as funds) than it is for portfolio equity or interest-bearing debt. Indeed, if the economic losses associated with financial crises in the 1990s are attributed in large part to heavy foreign indebtedness, and to the withdrawal of foreign funds, the net effect of interest-bearing debt during the 1990s has probably been negative rather than positive. At least after the fact, it is clear that too much international borrowing and lending took place, and any device that introduced greater caution into such lending would be beneficial. But for reasons to be discussed below, it is a major error to attribute these financial crises primarily or even substantially to foreign capital, although the actual or feared withdrawal of foreign funds certainly deepened the crises after they had begun.

Assuming then that a rollover provision would represent a net improvement in current institutional arrangements, how could it be brought about? One suggestion, which seems to be favored by the US Treasury, is that such temporary standstill or rollover clauses should be adopted voluntarily in debt contracts involving cross-border transactions, or at least those involving currencies other than those of the borrower. Debt contracts, whether bonds or loans, contain many conditions today, including, when the borrower is a national government, the waiver of sovereign immunity; it would be simple in principle to add a clause permitting temporary extension of the maturity of the debt, either at the initiative of the debtor or by the debtor with approval of some third party, such as the IMF. Any potential debtor eager to get access the capital market, however, would be reluctant to start the process, particularly since it could be done only for new debt, and would in this respect subordinate new creditors to outstanding creditors. It would take many years before all outstanding debt contained such clauses, even if adoption on new debt were universal. But sufficient publicity on the advantages of such provisions, plus pressure by international financial institutions, might gradually bring it about; and the process

could be accelerated if the major rich countries adopted the practice in their external debt, or even in all their public debt.

A second possible route would be through legislation in the major creditor countries, plus in those countries where debtors had significant assets, such as aircraft or ships, that might be legally seized by a creditor -- a list that would of course vary from debtor to debtor. Such legislation would be designed to immunize debtors in distress from successful lawsuits, provided the agreed conditions were satisfied. Sales of claims on debtors in distress to residents of countries without such legislation would undoubtedly occur, but the courts in such countries would be rendered impotent to do anything effective.

A third possible route would be through by treaty, which to be effective would have to cover at least the countries in the preceding paragraph. One form of such treaty would be formal amendment of the Articles of Agreement of the International Monetary Fund, which would be an especially desirable route if the IMF were asked to play a key role in the process, for example by certifying the need for a standstill and that the debtor country had met the conditions for a settlement. This third route is the cleanest and most coherent, although the ratification process would necessarily take substantial time.

A government can run into serious debt problems because of exceptionally bad luck -- for example, an unforeseen sharp and durable drop in world demand for its principal export product, which may also be a major source of government revenue; or because of exceptionally short-sighted behavior in undertaking the borrowing. And of course the lenders are also taking a gamble, especially when the country is being short-sighted -- and they are usually paid for taking this gamble in the higher interest rates they receive. The possibility of default should in such cases not be a surprise, nor should they pretend that it is a surprise. The losers will be the people of the debtor country if the economy needs to be severely squeezed to enlarge the trade surplus to service the outstanding debt. Yet squeezing the economy often worsens the government's budget deficit, so it is caught in a double bind.

Other Financing Problems

A country may need some relief from debt servicing -- or at least the possibility of relief -- even when the debt burden is not unbearable in the long run. If a lot of debt is coming due in the near future, creditors may worry about the ability of the country to re-finance in the short run, and in the process make the refinancing impossible -- an example of a self-fulfilling prophesy, which is a common problem in the world of finance. Of course, borrowers would be well-advised not to get themselves into this situation in the first place, for example by borrowing at longer term. But sometimes bunched borrowing may be unavoidable, due to external events beyond the country's control. To avoid the often harsh consequences of a creditor panic, requiring a reduction in economic activity, the international community should be able, just as a central bank is within a national economy, to liquify the economy with foreign exchange in the short-run in order to persuade foreign creditors and potential creditors that they individually will not be left holding an unserviceable claim.

This issue arose in Mexico in January 1995, and in South Korea in January 1998. Large currency depreciations had occurred in the preceding month in both cases, making exports much more competitive and prospectively reducing the substantial trade deficits. But a large amount of short-term debt matured in the coming months -- government tesobonos in the case of Mexico, interbank loans in the case of Korea -- and creditors were individually reluctant to extend their credits, even though by that time the economic fundamentals of each country seemed to be satisfactory, or on the way to becoming satisfactory. The international community assembled a large official support package in each case, centered on an IMF program and loan but augmented by funds from other institutions and governments; and in the case of Korea pressed creditor banks into extending their maturing credits. In the end the efforts succeeded, but the economic costs were excessively high and in each case the effort was ad hoc and full of suspense over whether the req-uisite support could be assembled and whether it would work. And in both cases, large amounts of the assembled official funds had to be used to cover the privately held maturing debt, so creditor panic was partially neutralized rather than averted.

[It is noteworthy in both these cases that resident funds began to leave in volume before the currency devaluations; withdrawals of foreign funds occurred mainly afterward, when there was still doubt whether the government or banks would be able to repay their obligations.]

As a result of these and other experiences, the IMF has taken two important steps to improve its ability to deal with such crises in future: it has streamlined its procedure, so that when necessary it can act much more quickly than was true heretofore, although its processes still take more time than may be available in an emerging financial crisis; and it has augmented the resources available to it for emergency lending through the New Arrangements to Borrow, which with the earlier General Arrangements enables the IMF to call on 25 countries for up to $46 billion under appropriate conditions. The IMF was originally set up to lend into temporary imbalances in current account transactions. In the mid-1990s the IMF extended its purview to cover international capital transactions as well. Some recent problems, however, have been primarily or wholly budgetary rather than external in origin. This was especially true of Russia in 1998, but also of Brazil (1998) and Argentina (2001), although all three developed an international dimension. The governments could finance their deficits only on increasingly onerous terms. Rolling over the debt at ever higher interest rates aggravated the budgetary problem, and of course also enlarged the imbalance in external payments insofar as foreigners held government debt and declined to renew it.

The IMF lends to governments, so IMF loans provide temporary budgetary as well as balance of payments relief. But it is doubtful that the IMF should provide budgetary relief when there is no strong external dimension to the problem. To create the presumption that it will is likely to invite strategic behavior by governments to get relatively cheap sources of funds at medium-run maturity -- longer than they can usually get on their public debt under stressful conditions.

Thus there are three quite different circumstances calling for IMF support:
1) to help finance a temporary deficit in international payments arising, for example, from a cyclical fall in foreign demand for a country's exports, or to cover the period before a currency devaluation can improve the trade balance. This was the traditional purpose of the IMF.
2) to help avert a creditor panic, when much external debt matures in a short period of time, even when there is no long-term payments problem, to assure creditors that the country has enough liquidity to repay the debts -- in which case the ready availability of IMF support may make it unnecessary to use it, as bankers are always willing to lend to those whose credit is high.
3) to participate in the consolidation and perhaps reduction of external debt that has become too heavy for the government or country to carry indefinitely. Here the IMF provides funds to help persuade private creditors to accept some debt reduction in exchange for some cash up front, under conditions when the alternative of default is even less attractive.

The Krueger proposal, while not addressing IMF financing, concerns only the third of these circumstances. Normal IMF action and resources have been able to deal with the first, except when extensive capital flight by foreigners and residents alike imposes requirements beyond the current account deficit. The IMF may or may not have enough resources, quickly enough, to deal with the second case; it has not yet been fairly tested.

Of course, the world of affairs rarely falls cleanly into each of these three categories. Elements of each may be present at the outset; and of course the first case may easily provoke the second, or even the prospect of the third.

The IMF's ability to deal with financial crises, and to forestall creditor panic, would be immeasurably increased if it had the capacity to provide sufficient resources to cover even the worst contingency; if it had such resources, the probability of the worst contingency would be greatly reduced. Such capacity could be provided by empowering the IMF to issue its own "currency," Special Drawing Rights (SDRs) in such emergencies. At present, the IMF can issue SDRs (by 85 percent vote of its Board) for the purpose of meeting the long-run needs of the world economy for additional international liquidity. SDRs have been issued only twice, in 1970-72 and 1979-81, in amounts worth about $27 billion today, making up a paltry 1.4 percent of the world's international reserves. (A third, special allocation doubling the total was agreed in 1997, and awaits US ratification.)

The proposal here would add a different purpose, more pressing these days, for issuance of SDRs. The conditions for temporary issuance would have to be tightly drawn, and any SDRs actually issued would subsequently be withdrawn when the emergency had passed, just as the Federal Reserve first injected and then withdrew extensive credit following the collapse of LTCM in 1998. The classical conditions for action by a lender-of-last-resort to banks, laid down by Walter Bagehot in 1873, is that in emergency it should stand ready to lend without limit, at a penalty interest rate, against good collateral (as priced in normal times), and make this readiness known ahead of time. These actions are to assure adequate liquidity in a financial system, not to bail out insolvent banks, which requires a different course. But dealing with insolvent institutions is much easier in a favorable financial environment than in one seized up for lack of liquidity.

With the ability to use SDRs, the IMF could play a surrogate role of lender of last resort for international financial crises, something it cannot assure today because of potential shortage of funds. It could then concentrate on the conditions instead of having to worry also about creating a coalition of willing new lenders in each case. IMF conditionality provides a functional substitute for collateral, although the pledging of collateral by states, as was done by Mexico against the US Treasury loan of early 1995, should not be excluded.

Moral hazard can be reduced not only by stringent conditions, but also by a number of other measures, such as conditioning the terms of IMF lending on prior acceptance of internationally-agreed standards, the presence of standstill clauses in international loan covenants, and a rate of interest that is above normal rates.

Empowering the IMF in this way would require an amendment to the IMF's Articles, but that would be a natural addition if the Articles are to be amended to provide for a standstill in debt repayment with IMF involvement, as under the Krueger proposal.

On the Inevitability of Financial Crises

Financial crises seem to be an inevitable concomitant of economic development, a kind of adolescent growing pain. As countries evolve from low-income, agricultural economies to modern high-income economies a severe tension develops sooner or later between the real economy and the financial superstructure that is necessary to sustain it. A key feature of development is to socialize private savings, drawing them away from jewelry and other private stores of value into financial institutions so that the saving can be mobilized for productive investment. This is the social role of banks. A key problem with this desirable process is that bankers (or their backers) now have more money at their disposal than they ever dreamed of. All kinds of attractive projects become financially possible. Some bankers do not seem troubled by the fact that they are dealing with other people's money. They start to invest on a large scale, which may create a real boom, and an associated euphoria. Production, profits, employment, and capital gains all rise. Things are going so well that any initial caution is soon forgotten. But unless productivity is rising synchronously, such booms have an element of a Ponzi scheme, unsustainable in the long run. Former Federal Reserve Chairman William McChesney Martin once famously said that the role of the central bank is to take away the punch bowl just as the party really gets going. But that requires a prudent, independent, non-partisan central bank with its eye on the long run -- something most developing countries quite deliberately do not have, at least until they have been through a few serious financial crises.

Every country experiencing a financial crisis in the 1990s had an unsustainable domestic situation, a mismatch between financial claims and the performance of the real economy. The details differed significantly. Sometimes private banks were involved, sometimes governments, often both. Several governments discovered the wonders of the financial market, domestic as well as international, wherein bonds can be floated to finance government expenditures without the need, in the short run, to impose unpopular taxes. Thus did Russia, Brazil, and Argentina all avoid difficult choices, for awhile.

Americans have no reason to be smug. The United States had almost one serious financial crisis a decade during its formative developmental period from the 1810s, culminating in the catastrophic Great Depression of the 1930s. Even the lessons learned then and reflected in a host of regulatory legislation did not save the United States from the savings and loan crisis of the 1980s, brought on through legislation aimed to help important constituents of key congressmen. It was sometimes fashionable to blame these crisis on foreigners, and indeed there were occasionally international aspects; but they were overwhelmingly domestic in origin. Britain, France, and other European countries had similar experiences during the 19th century.

Could these crises, US or foreign, have been avoided? In logic, probably. But it would have required Platonic monetary guardians, detached, disinterested, far-sighted -- the antithesis of the modern politician -- to achieve it. In practice the capitalist system works by harnessing greed, not charitable inclination, to achieve economic progress. It has been smashingly successful during the past 200 years, especially the past 50 years, and its success is now spreading from Europe and America around the world. But the progress was not smooth, being punctuated by financial and economic crises which provoked improvements in institutional structure and legal incentives to channel the greed in socially constructive directions. It has been a process of trial and error, one that is on-going, for each new generation of financial wizards will try to find lucrative loopholes in the rules and structures put in place by the previous generation -- usually in response not to their foresight but to their own acknowledged mistakes and omissions.

The bottom line is that financial crises seem, empirically, to be an inevitable companion to the economic development of any country. Specifically, they are not the fault of the international economic system, nor does their presence signify serious defects in the international system, contrary to what has often been claimed in recent years. To be sure, the internationalization of financial markets enlarges the possible availability of funds, and increases the number of people who can be taken in by the current euphoria, to which supposedly hard-nosed western bankers and money managers are not immune. Thus foreign capital can affect the magnitude and detailed dynamic of financial crises. But history suggests the prime mover is domestic in origin, and in all recent crises resident funds were implicated in precipitating the crisis.

As country after country has discovered, usually the hard way, a high level of disclosure of information is required for well-regulated and well-functioning financial markets. Yet full disclosure is anathema to commercial and financial practice in many societies. There must also be a clear hierarchy of financial responsibility and risk, ranging (in the United States) from shareholders with the most, through bond holders and other creditors, to depositors with the least. If something goes badly wrong, it must be clear who bears the costs. Yet governments in developing countries are often complicit in apparently private economic decisions, and politically-influential shareholders are reluctant to accept their losses -- indeed will struggle vigorously to avoid

them. A financial system cannot function well so long as this is the case. Such struggles will not be eliminated simply by changing laws and regulations.

Deposit banks play a vital role in development. They are trusted institutions where financially unsophisticated citizens are willing to place their savings. This is a big social improvement over private savings held in the form of commodities such as gold bracelets, for they permit savings to be mobilized for development. To work, people must be confident that they can retrieve their savings when needed. That in turn requires either that the banks invest the savings carefully, on average, or that the state directly or indirectly guarantee the savings.

Banks in many developing countries have engaged in a massive violation of the trust that has been placed in them, by directing the savings into operating expenses of loss-making corporations, dubious "national champion" investments (some of which succeed, many of which do not), and real estate speculation or loans to politically well-connected individuals. Bank shareholders resist the implication that they should lose their stakes, and the struggle continues over who shall bear the losses that have already been incurred in financial crises. Until a clear and generally accepted hierarchy of responsibility is established, national financial systems will remain unreformed and will fail to achieve their social potential.

While the international system may not be responsible for financial crises, the foreign dimension, having contributed to the preceding euphoria, may aggravate the crisis and increase its economic costs. Moreover, crises can spread from one country to another through a variety of channels, trade as well as financial. So maybe the international community can help to mitigate the damage. Every proposal for reform needs to be assessed with this possibility in mind, but also taking into account the possible harm it can do, either by significantly retarding the international flow of beneficial capital, or on the contrary by encouraging incautious lending on the assumption that any trouble will be covered by official international action.

The proposal for an internationally sanctioned standstill on sovereign debt, if it could be cleanly and comprehensively implemented, would represent a modest improvement on existing arrangements. The proposal to empower the IMF to issue SDRs in a financial emergency, under stringent conditions, would represent a complementary modest improvement. Both would require amending the IMF Articles, no easy task. Neither proposal will banish financial crises.

The International Lender of Last Resort: What Are the Alternatives?

JEFFREY D. SACHS

I will offer some observations on the question of whether we need an international lender of last resort. And my answer will be yes, as long as we start putting the emphasis on last. We have had too much of an international lender of first resort in recent years, with too much lending from our international lender of last resort, the International Monetary Fund. Probably a package of measures and redesign could be undertaken to reduce the need for a real international lender of last resort, but in the final analysis we are still going to require one. Circumstances will arise where it will be important, even after we have taken better steps to take the burden off the IMF concerning the number of cases that it has to handle.

Analytically, a number of arguments can be distinguished for a lender of last resort in general, although they all come to the same basic theme, which is, of course, the concept of a true liquidity crisis. Among theorists, this concept is regarded with some skepticism, although I think that the case for it is quite strong. A liquidity crisis, in the most general sense, I would take to be a circumstance where a borrower cannot obtain short-term funds despite the fact that the rate of return on the short-term borrowing would exceed the market cost of capital. For some reason the market mechanism has broken down, and the borrower cannot obtain funds, even though there is, depending on the model framework or the conceptual framework, an equilibrium in which that flow of funds ought to take

place. Such a liquidity crisis can be identified in at least three distinguishable cases, and it is important to keep them separate.

Identifying Liquidity Crises

The first, I would say, is financial panic. Financial panic is a circumstance where the level of short-term indebtedness is very high relative to short-term liquidity and, for whatever reason, a market equilibrium unfolds in which the short-term debt is called. And the borrower has no recourse to refinance the short-term debt. From a theoretical point of view, this is the kind of framework that we use to analyze bank runs in a domestic economy. It has also become one of the favorite vehicles for trying to understand a range of international crises, from Mexico to East Asia, in the last few years.

What has distinguished all of the international emerging market crises, in my view, is that they have hit countries where the level of short-term indebtedness to international banks is high and, in particular, where this short-term debt is a multiple of the value of foreign exchange reserves. For whatever reason, something triggers a massive withdrawal of the short-term capital. The trigger occurs in part because of the very observation that short-term liquid assets are not sufficient to cover the short-term debts, and you get a self-fulfilling liquidity crisis as a result. Now that interpretation is much debated, but it is the one that I would strongly favor for understanding these crises.

A second kind of liquidity crisis, which I would suggest is different from a financial panic, is a debt overhang liquidity crisis. By that I mean a case where you have a bankrupt debtor that still needs working capital. This concept is well-understood in bankruptcy law; just because you are bankrupt does not mean you do not need funds. In Chapter 11, we have Section 364 of the U.S. Bankruptcy Code, which is the debtor-in-possession finance vehicle. It provides a mechanism for the bankruptcy court to get short-term working capital to the bankrupt, understanding that markets cannot do it because any new creditor knows that without a special legal regime to cover the new lending, any new loans just get piled onto the massive mountain of bad debt.

This is a liquidity crisis according to the definition that I gave beforehand, but it is quite different from a panic because nobody is panicked, necessarily; you just have a bankrupt debtor that cannot get normal market access. This situation can be a case for a lender of last resort, as well. But as the bankruptcy law shows, you do not necessarily need a lender of last resort, you need a legal regime, in order to get working capital in such a circumstance. To apply that idea to the current context, of course, I am thinking about sovereign bankruptcy, about governments that are financially insolvent but still need working capital. And, of course, the IMF does lend to such governments, and there may be a very legitimate role for such lending.

The third kind of liquidity crisis that I would distinguish is a class of problems that are very real but somewhat different from the other two. For want of a better title, I call this public sector collapse. The idea is that basic public order, the state's monopoly on the legitimate use of force, its ability to collect taxes and to provide basic public goods like law and order, collapses at various points in many countries around the world. It could be the result of a revolution, civil strife, a struggle for independence. In this very messy world that we live in, lots of states cannot perform as

states, even to collect the minimal amount of tax revenues needed to run themselves. The collapse may not reflect an overhang of bad debt, and it certainly need not reflect a financial panic. But it still can create a condition that I would define as a liquidity crisis, where the return to working capital is very high, in that such funds would allow the state to consolidate its basic power, a step that may be vital to the survival of people in the midst of civil strife. And in that case also, the markets probably will not provide liquidity, and you may need a lender of last resort that is able to tie the loans to a consolidation of state power within the international system.

Roles of the International Lender of Last Resort

When we think about what the IMF actually does as our international lender of last resort, and how it does it, I find it helpful to distinguish these three types of cases and then to try to think through whether we have a reasonable regime for them. So, again, we have financial panic, debt overhang, and public sector collapse. Clearly, in response, an international lender of last resort will have multiple potential roles, at least analytically. Four come to mind from this three-way classification I just gave, because financial panic has two parts to it.

First, an international lender of last resort is supposed to forestall panic, simply by being there. One of the major functions of a lender of last resort is that you stop the panic from ever happening, in principle, because everybody says "No reason to panic, there is a lender of last resort standing in the background." So that is potential function number one. Potential function number two is to lend into a financial panic that is already occurring; thus, we see the Thai or the Indonesian or the Korean loans of the second half of 1997.

The third potential role of a lender of last resort is to lend into a debt overhang. By analogy, in the bankruptcy context, under American law, for example, we usually allow the bankrupt to gain access to working capital by prioritizing the new lending, the post-bankruptcy debt, under Section 364 of the Bankruptcy Code. Instead, we have the IMF lending into a bankruptcy situation, where the IMF is already assigned a privileged position in repayment. So we use the privilege as a way to get working capital into a bankruptcy situation. And the fourth potential role, of course, is to lend into a situation of public sector collapse, to help a state to consolidate power in a way that private markets will not be able to finance.

Alternatives to a Lender of Last Resort

Now having noted these multiple roles, it is also immediately evident that many functional alternatives to a lender of last resort exist. In every one of these categories, other ways can be found to handle the very same problem. And if we are going to analyze properly what the IMF, for example, should do, we should understand these different ways to handle the problems. So let me just run through them very briefly.

In Forestalling Financial Panics

First, forestalling a financial panic. Let us recognize that a number of ways exist to prevent a financial panic from happening in the first place. If you believe, as I do, that the essence of the recent crises was a very high level of short-term debt relative to liquid assets, which ended up triggering a panic because of a devaluation or bad political news or contagion, then the alternative to a lender of last resort is direct mechanisms to prevent the debt-to-reserve ratios from getting out of whack, reaching levels of two to one, for example, as in Asia in 1997 or in Latin America in 1994. Now for that reason, I believe that controls on short-term capital inflows to banking sectors of emerging markets, for example, make eminent sense. Direct limits, as a prudential measure, not as global macro capital controls but as a prudential measure, seem to me to be eminently sensible.

I also happen to believe that flexible exchange rates are the appropriate response,

because if you actually look at the histories of these crises, in virtually every case a period of exchange rate pegging led to a drain of reserves, which caused the ratio of short-term debt to liquid assets to skyrocket. I do not see any compelling case for any of this pegging to begin with. And I also think that for many, many reasons, almost none of these countries qualify as part of an optimal currency area with any of the major industrial countries.

So my view is that prudential limits on capital inflows plus flexible exchange rates would have prevented a great many of these crises from ever having come to pass. With these two changes, the burden on the international lender of last resort could have been relieved. I should add that here, as in many other areas, we probably had a massive unintended consequence of our own regulatory environment. The BIS capital adequacy standards that give a risk-weighting of only 20 percent to interbank short-term lending probably contributed to the explosion of cross-border, short-term claims, which fueled the emerging market boom and afterward caused the emerging market bust.

So, as a contribution to the crisis, I would put a not inconsiderable weight on the BIS regulations, which are too asset-oriented and not adequately liability-focused in the first place. They do not focus on the risk of liquidity crises. And second, they cause a sharp bias toward short-term lending, because of the way that we do the risk weighting in the capital adequacy standards, giving such low risk to interbank short-term loans. These standards have made the whole system more vulnerable to financial panic.

In Handling a Financial Panic

Now in terms of handling a financial panic, beyond preventing panic, functional alternatives to IMF lending also exist. The first one is suspension of payments. Instead of just lending large amounts of money to a country in the midst of a panic, one alternative is that the country stop paying on the short-term debt. While that idea may sound horrifying, that is of course how most of these crises actually end. The Korean crisis did not end on

December 4, 1997, when a $57 billion IMF package came into shape, but on December 29, 1997, when the Fed engineered a rollover of short-term debts and everybody breathed a sigh of relief that we were no longer playing on a day-to-day basis in Korea. So the normal way that these panics end is not necessarily through infusion of new capital, but rather suspension of repayment of short-term debt. This outcome has a hallowed history in finance, both domestic and international. It is not the horrifying element that it seems to be, but often a natural way that short-term panics get resolved.

Even in the 1999 Brazil crisis, I think one of the best parts of the rescue package was the informal agreement that the commercial banks would keep their lines of credit in place. In other words, we saw not a big lending package but rather an agreement not to take out funds. This is how, I think, normal banking ought to work in these contexts. The idea that big bailout packages are needed would be much less persuasive if the banks would agree to stand pat as a normal part of their behavior (which I think they would do, by the way, if the IMF were not in there telling them that they can get everything out). All in all, it seems to me normal that banking should proceed through suspension or orderly rollover of outstanding debt.

In Debt Overhang Crises

If I turn to the third category requiring lender of last resort loans, the debt overhang case, here again we find functional alternatives to IMF loans, although the IMF can readily play a role because it has this privileged position in lending when a mountain of debt is already present. What are the functional alternatives? First is the option of a standstill on debt repayments. Of course, the normal first thing in a bankruptcy workout is to stop the outflow of debt repayments. At this moment we still do not have an international regime that can handle standstills appropriately. I think it is a terrible, terrible loss in the current

system that obviously bankrupt debtors can be absolutely pursued, without any recourse to a standstill.

Second, instead of an IMF loan, we could arrange debtor-in-possession financing, a` la Section 364. A key point is that you do not need an official creditor to lend. The bankruptcy judge does not make an IMF-style loan; what the bankruptcy judge does is to say that the next $100 million tranche is going to have priority over the pre-bankruptcy debt. And we could have an international system that set these priorities. I think such arrangements would have an advantage over the current regime, where we only put in official money in such bankruptcies, because it would keep the action closer to the market. And you would still have a market test on lending. We do not have an official mechanism for giving priority to new loans, but it is at least conceivable that we could authorize an international regime to make such arrangements.

The third point about a debt overhang is that in domestic bankruptcy law you end up by canceling debt. We do this in the international system through the Brady plan or through Heavily Indebted Poor Country (HIPC) programs, or through other devices, but we do it just dreadfully. And I say, as one who has been watching the process for 15 years, one can name 25 countries where it was obvious for more than a decade that they were bankrupt before the debt was actually canceled. Yet the process drags on for 10 or 15 years before we acknowledge the fact, because we still do not face up to sovereign bankruptcy.

We have no concept for sovereign bankruptcy, we have no regime for it, we fake it, until the political pressures become intolerable or until the Ponzi scheme finally reaches the point where you simply cannot find anyone to lend more money to pay off the old debt. That is the situation we are in with 42 HIPC countries right now, but we are still playing the Ponzi game with them. One way to relieve the burden on an international lender of last resort would be to actually get rid of bad debt. And we do not have a clean system for doing that yet.

In Public Sector Collapse

Then finally, we get to the fourth category, public sector collapse. It is conceivable, of course, that you could have J.P. Morgan syndicates that could lead the recovery of societies undergoing civil strife, but I do believe, from my own experience in a lot of crisis countries and from what I can gather from the public evidence, that here is a role where the IMF or some other public agency is absolutely needed. When you have desperate humanitarian conditions and you have states that do not function as states, you cannot rely on private markets to sort out the consolidation of public power. So it seems to me that this is a clear case where the IMF or something like it has a vital role to play, and where the IMF has often played it decisively.

Evaluating Our Current System

Let me conclude by asking, given the foregoing, how we are actually doing currently. In terms of preventing financial panic, I think we do very, very poorly. First, we have too many pegged exchange rate regimes. The IMF has championed many of them, as in Russia in 1997 or Brazil at the end of 1998. These were situations where it was clear the currencies were on the verge of collapse and yet we lent money, even to sustain collapsing currencies. This action just invited a financial crisis, by allowing countries to run out of reserves.

Second, I think we have handled short-term debt very badly. Both the BIS regulations and the way that liberalization has been done have exposed vulnerable countries to massive amounts of short-term debt. Third, I think that the way that the IMF has intervened, in situations where the panic is just starting, has often inflamed the panic or exacerbated it rather than calmed it. In a lender of last resort circumstance, subtlety and art are of the

essence, and so maybe bailing out Long-Term Capital Management makes sense if you are worried about a rapidly growing liquidity crisis and want to stop the panic. I happen to believe that was a good call. Closing 16 commercial banks on November 1, 1997, in Indonesia, when there was no deposit insurance, is what I would call a bad call. It set off one of the most virulent banking panics in modern history in Indonesia, and it is one of the reasons the country ended up in flames. So in terms of preventing financial panic, I would give very low marks to the current system. It is just not geared toward addressing the real issues that cause these panics to take place.

In terms of handling financial panics, here again the evidence shows, if you look at it dispassionately, that the big bailout loans have generally not functioned very well. Some have said they have not functioned because they have been too small, even though they were very big in dollar terms, but in any event they certainly have not stopped the outflow of capital. That was true, interestingly, even in the Mexican bailout, which was probably the cleanest of all of these rescues and the one where the U.S. Treasury put in the most money. It was not that the money that was put up stopped the panic through a return of confidence. No, the money was drawn down to repay the outflow in short-term capital, pure and simple. After it was gone, then confidence started to return.

But the evidence is that the bailout plans, the $57 billion for Korea, the $41 billion for Brazil, the $22 billion July 1998 program for Russia, the Mexican bailout, in no case actually stopped the outflow of financial capital. What I think has been more successful, actually, is rollovers of debt. When the situation gets bad enough, the Fed calls in the parties and says, "Everybody smile, we're rolling over the debt." And when this happens, it seems to me it has had a wonderful effect. All of a sudden, in a weird kind of way, the press says, "Ah, we avoided default." Of course, that is default. But since we put such a pleasant smile on it, confidence gets restored. So the magic of managing crises is exactly that—you call them something else, and then the myth becomes that we avoided default in Korea. Fabulous, if that is what you want to say, do it. And it works, it works a lot better than the first $57 billion worked, because that did not stop the panic; that led to a miserable Christmas weekend for Rubin and Summers in 1997, precisely because Korea ran out of money and therefore forced the Fed to act.

So in terms of handling panic, I do not think we have done a good job. The tactics are inflammatory, the big bailouts do not work, and now we are going toward what are called private sector bail-ins, as if this idea is anything more than a normal market response, which is a much better way in general.

In terms of debt overhang problems, there are many. Probably 40 or more countries around the world have governments that are really insolvent right now. We play a very complicated institutional international game, but it does not work very well because we have no international regime for insolvency of sovereign governments, comparable to Chapter 9 for U.S. municipalities. I will not elaborate, except to say that this problem has been going on for about 150 years, and it remains true today. We are playing games, at very, very high costs.

Finally, let me stress that in circumstances of public collapse, as I mentioned before, the stakes are usually extremely high. The IMF recently inaugurated new contingency lending mechanisms for countries in conflict or in immediate post-conflict circumstances, and I want to applaud that initiative because these are often the most delicate humanitarian circumstances in the world. It is extremely important to get money into those countries, to consolidate state power as fast as possible.

Bottom line, do we need an international lender of last resort? The answer is yes, because we are always going to have liquidity crises. But do we need an IMF that is managing 70 countries around the world? The answer is no. The reason we have such an institution is that we have made no provision for discharge of unpayable debt. That keeps an endless routine of IMF programs going. We have also allowed the highly volatile short-term capital to rule the system in recent years, through dangerous exchange rate and capital account policies. The combination has made these financial panics much more prevalent than they need to be.

Jeffrey D. Sachs is Director of the Harvard Center for International Development and a Galen L. Stone Professor of International Trade at Harvard University. Remarks delivered at the conference.

Dirty Money

MIRIAM WASSERMAN

The first strike against terrorism after the September 11 attacks on the World Trade Center and the Pentagon was a financial one. Not two weeks had passed since the attacks when President Bush signed an executive order freezing the U.S. assets of 27 entities that included terrorist organizations, individual terrorist leaders, a corporation alleged to be a front for terrorism, and several nonprofit organizations. In the days and weeks that followed, policies to impede the covert flow of illicit funds through the global financial system were among the measures at the heart of Congressional debates on how to fight terrorism.

This response should come as no surprise. Measures against money laundering have increasingly become an important front in the fight against crime. Such measures can facilitate detection of financial trails that provide important sources of evidence, potentially linking the members of a criminal organization and leading to convictions of the ring leaders—who are hard to connect to the day-to-day criminal operations. Moreover, finding and seizing money or assets that result from criminal activity can also serve to take the motive out of crime. And, in the case of terrorist financing, it can make it more difficult to commit future acts.

Even before September 11, banks and other financial and nonfinancial institutions in the United States had been required to keep increasingly detailed records of financial transactions and report suspicious dealings. International organizations have worked on designing common standards to fight money laundering and have begun to pressure countries with lax regulations to adopt stricter laws.

Anti-money laundering policies promise to become even more stringent in the aftermath of September 11. The U.S. Congress passed the USA PATRIOT Act, which expanded antimoney laundering provisions. It will affect a broad range of companies, such as securities brokers and dealers, commodity firms, and investment companies. It also imposes more exacting requirements for U.S. financial institutions dealing with foreign customers and institutions, and provides for greater scrutiny to open new accounts at U.S. financial institutions. Many foreign countries are following suit.

But, fighting money laundering is no easy task. With increasing globalization and advances in banking technologies, moving money around the world has become easier and, with the growth in international capital flows, it has also become easier to mask illegitimate monies in the stream of legitimate transfers. Even as nations such as Switzerland and the Cayman Islands have begun to restrict their coveted bank secrecy regimes, nations with underregulated financial systems, such as the Pacific island nation of Nauru, have emerged as centers of importance in the realm of global finance.

Similarly, as new domestic laws have made money laundering more difficult in particular areas of the financial system, criminals have sought new ways to disguise their loot. And, when it comes to terrorism finance, authorities have to think very differently about the issue. Instead of looking for dirty money in the process of being cleansed, they now also have to detect funds that may have legitimate origins but are destined for criminal ends.

Money Laundering 101

Criminals have always tried to hide their money. The greater the amount illegally earned, the more difficult it becomes to camouflage its origins and enjoy the proceeds of crime. Sudden, inexplicable wealth can draw the attention of authorities. And, ever since Al Capone was put behind bars for tax evasion, criminals have known that handling and using the spoils of their endeavors can be one of their weakest links.

The practice of disguising wealth, whether legitimate or illegitimate, from government attention has a long history. More than 3,000 years ago, merchants in China protected their wealth from government confiscation using some of the same schemes in use today: converting money to movable assets; moving cash outside a jurisdiction to invest in a business; and trading at inflated prices to expatriate funds, according to a study cited by money laundering expert Nigel Morris-Cotterrill.

Today, nobody knows for sure how much money is laundered globally. It is difficult to know if money is being counted more than once as it cycles through the system and harder still to know how much goes undetected. Nonetheless, experts believe the amounts are large. The most cited figure is between 2 and 5 percent of global GDP—or between $600 billion to $1.5 trillion per year. Still, this is an admittedly rough estimate based on extrapolations of the global sales of illegal drugs on the lower bound, and estimates of the size of underground economies on the upper bound.

To disguise the unlawful nature of funds, criminals must go through a process that varies from crime to crime but that generally involves three separate stages. First, cash must be converted into a more portable and less suspicious form—sometimes achieved by using cashier's checks or money orders—and then it is entered into the financial system. Once there, it goes through a series of transactions that resemble legitimate activity and often involve crossing several national borders, making it more difficult for law enforcement agencies to follow the trail. Finally, the funds must be integrated into the legitimate financial system.

Of course, not every criminal act calls for the profits to be laundered. Petty criminals can get away with working in cash. But bigger criminals have to resort to increasingly elaborate methods to create the illusion of legitimate wealth.

Take, for example, the drug trade. Illegal drug trafficking is believed to be the largest source for laundering in the United States and accounts for 60 to 80 percent of all federal money laundering prosecutions, according to James Richards, author of *Transnational Criminal Organizations, Cybercrime, and Money Laundering.* Just the bulkiness of drug money creates logistical problems. Justice Department officials have estimated that the weight of cash generated by drug sales is about ten times that of the drug itself for heroin and six times for cocaine. While traffickers only need to smuggle and distribute about 22 pounds of heroin to net $1 million, they then have to contend with 220 pounds of street cash.

Not surprisingly, the assets of drug traffickers and other criminals who produce vast volumes of cash are believed to be most vulnerable to detection at the stage of placing cash into the financial system. Thus, they often try to avoid triggering the mandatory reporting requirements of large cash transactions by U.S. banks, or steer clear of U.S. financial institutions altogether. Bulk cash smuggling across international borders is perhaps the most widespread way of doing this. Smuggling is done in a variety of ways, from employing an army of couriers who physically transport loads of concealed cash to using trucks and containers.

Once the dollars leave the United States, they can be placed in banks in countries that have weaker controls. Or, cash can simply be brought back into the United States, points out Richards. In this scheme, cash smuggled out of the country is brought back in, this time declared at the border supported by false invoices and receipts. As the funds are recognized by U.S. Customs, they can be deposited at any U.S. bank without raising red flags. There is some evidence this technique is widespread: Brownsville, Texas, and Nogales, Arizona, had the most funds declared upon entry into the United States from the Mexican border—$8 billion and $5 billion, respectively, between 1988 and 1990—amounts much higher than would be justified by their population or flow of commerce, according to the Financial Crimes Enforcement Network of the U.S. Treasury Department (FinCEN), as cited by Richards.

Launderers have also sought ways to use the U.S. financial system without raising suspicion. Some criminals break down the cash earned into many smaller wads for deposit. This technique came to be called "smurfing" by law enforcement officials in Florida after the little blue cartoon characters. In this method, many people—the smurfs—make large numbers of deposits, always below $10,000, at several different institutions on a daily basis, thus avoiding triggering U.S. bank reporting regulations. (See section on the Colombian Black Market Peso Exchange.)

Front companies are another common way of placing cash in the system. By running cash-intensive businesses, such as restaurants or liquor stores, launderers can blend legal and illegal profits and make large cash deposits into banks without eliciting questions. In addition, criminals may look beyond banks to businesses such as foreign exchange bureaus, money remittance businesses, and check cashers to convert cash into easier-to-handle instruments or to send the funds abroad.

And, there is also the option of using underground banking structures such as Hawala. Hawala is an old system that originated in South Asia but now operates in many countries. Such informal financial networks are very attractive to those seeking to transfer money without government notice because the transactions leave no paper trail. A person who wants to send money abroad takes the cash to an underground banker who gives him a marker or some form of receipt. The broker in turn, informs his contacts in the transfer's destination so that the designated receiver can claim the money at the other end, minus a commission. The money does not physically need to be transported abroad, as two-way flows support the exchange: Cash for the payment is provided by customers wanting to send money in the opposite direction.

A World of Opportunities

Once the money is placed in the financial system somewhere in the world, technology and globalization facilitate the process of disguising the origin of the funds and reintegrating them into the realm of legitimate finance. Wire transfers, for instance, offer launderers the possibility of quickly moving money through different accounts and different countries until it becomes impossible to trace the origin of the funds. One of the most recent trends, according to the U.S. Treasury, involves funds wired to or through a U.S. financial institution—primarily from Switzerland, Italy, Germany, and England—and then withdrawn in any one of about 57 nations through an automated teller machine (ATM). The largest number of this type of ATM withdrawals is made in Colombia.

Another way in which funds deposited abroad can be repatriated and given a semblance of respectability is through loans. Illicit funds deposited in foreign banks can be used as collateral for loans drawn for legitimate investments elsewhere.

Furthermore, criminals have increasingly resorted to products and services in so-called offshore banking havens such as Nauru. These jurisdictions tend to offer a certain level of banking or commercial secrecy, low or no tax rates, and relatively simple requirements for licensing and regulating banks and other businesses. Money launderers often take advantage of laws that favor easy incorporation and the use of nominee owners or bearer shares—which allow anonymous ownership of companies. Such laws allow them to create "shell" companies that do not conduct any commercial or manufacturing business and whose sole purpose is to serve as conduits for fund flows.

Whatever the "cleansing" method, the transactions involved are usually extremely complicated—and deliberately so. In the investigation of alleged money laundering by Raul Salinas (the brother of the former Mexican president), for instance, the U.S. Government Accounting Office (GAO) found that Mr. Salinas (Regional Review Q1 2002: 19) was able to transfer between $90 million and $100 million between 1992 and 1994 from Mexico to London and Switzerland through a private banking account with Citibank in New York. Key in enabling him to do this was a private investment company in the Cayman Islands named Trocca, which was formed by Cititrust (Cayman), then an affiliate of Citicorp—now known as Citigroup—to hold Mr. Salinas's assets. The laws in the Cayman Islands protected the confidentiality of the documentation linking Mr. Salinas to Trocca. To further insulate Mr. Salinas's connection to Trocca, "Cititrust (Cayman) used three additional shell companies to function as Trocca's board of directors—Madeleine Investments SA, Donat Investments SA, and Hitchcock Investments SA," states the GAO report. In addition, many of the fund transfers from Mexico to New York were made by Mr. Salinas's wife using her maiden name. The whole affair was only discovered after Mr. Salinas was arrested and charged with murder in 1995. (In 1999, Raul Salinas was sentenced to 50 years in prison in Mexico on charges of planning the 1994 murder of Jose Francisco Ruiz Massieu, his former brother-in-law and a leader of the Institutional Revolutionary Party.)

The Cat-and-Mouse Game

In spite of money laundering's long history and broad impact, laws against the practice are relatively recent in the United States—and even more so in other countries. Money laundering was not considered a federal crime in the United States until the mid 1980s. The term itself first appeared in print in the early 1970s in the context of the Watergate scandal, when it was used to describe a process to circumvent a law prohibiting anonymous campaign contributions, according to Jeffrey Robinson, author of *The Laundrymen: Inside Money Laundering, the World's Third-Largest Business*. Members of Nixon's Committee to Reelect the President used a contact who received donations in Mexico and then forwarded them to Bernard L. Barker, a real estate salesman in Miami, to protect the identity of the private citizens that made the donations. When Barker was arrested for breaking into the Democratic National Committee headquarters in the Watergate building, the money trail helped link the Watergate break-in back to Nixon.

The growth of the illegal drug trade—with the vast illicit fortunes it generated—was the main factor motivating the evolution of anti-money laundering legislation in the United States and Europe. Reports of people depositing bags of currency of doubtful origin into banks led Congress to pass the Bank Secrecy Act (BSA) in 1970—the backbone of domestic money laundering legislation. Though it did not make laundering a criminal activity, the Act required financial institutions to create and preserve a paper trail for various financial transactions in order to facilitate criminal, tax, or regulatory investigations. As a result, financial institutions have to file reports for most cash transactions over $10,000 and keep such records for five years; and individuals have to report whenever they physically carry more than $10,000 in monetary instruments (coins, currency, travelers' checks, bearer bonds, securities, and negotiable instruments) into or out of the United States.

But criminals would not be deterred and money laundering methods evolved to circumvent these new restrictions. As launderers developed new methods, new laws and more stringent punishments were crafted to cover the regulatory gaps. As it became more difficult to make large cash deposits in banks, for instance, criminals found other businesses that served their needs such as check cashers or money remitters. In response, the currency reporting requirement of the Act was expanded to cover check cashers, currency exchange businesses, casinos, the U.S. Postal Service, and businesses that issue, sell, or redeem traveler's checks, among others. Nonetheless, the reporting requirement was "widely disregarded until 1985," writes Robinson. That year, Bank of Boston was fined $500,000 for not reporting 1,163 transactions valued at $1.2 billion.

In order to further strengthen the fight against dirty money, Congress made money laundering a crime in its own right with the passage of the 1986 Money Laundering Control Act (MLCA). The legislation made money laundering punishable by up to 20 years in prison, provided for both civil and criminal forfeitures of funds, and made it illegal to break down financial transactions to avoid triggering currency transaction reports.

The MLCA defined money laundering fairly broadly. Financial transactions that ordinarily would not be considered illegal became criminal if they knowingly involved the proceeds of a "specified unlawful activity." These activities comprise a long, and expanding, list of over 200 criminal offenses including such diverse items as health care fraud, counterfeiting, drug trafficking, espionage, extortion, murder, and—since 1996—terrorism. (Interestingly, tax evasion is not currently part of the list. So, for instance, a doctor not reporting all his income and sending what he doesn't report to an offshore bank would not be considered to be laundering money unless the money was illegally earned. The Internal Revenue Service recently estimated that as many as one to two million Americans may be evading taxes by secretly depositing money in tax havens like the Cayman Islands and with

drawing it using American Express, MasterCard, and Visa cards.)

Specifically, the MLCA made it a crime to knowingly conduct transactions above $10,000 with property derived from a specified crime. For lower amounts, transactions are illegal if they are intended to conceal the origin of the funds, avoid reporting requirements, or conceal illegal proceeds from tax authorities. For any amount, it is also considered money laundering when a monetary transaction into or out of the United States is being carried out with the intent to facilitate a future crime from the specified list. So, in the case of terrorism, even if the funds originated in a "legitimate" donation, their transportation, transfer, or transmission is considered money laundering if they are used to support a criminal cause.

In addition to the passage of the MLCA, the reporting requirements imposed by the Banking Secrecy Act have been expanded. The Annunzio-Wylie Anti-Money Laundering Act of 1992 made it mandatory for financial institutions to report any suspicious transactions relevant to possible violations of the law by their clients. As of January 2002, this also included money service businesses, such as issuers of money orders and traveler checks. The law explicitly prohibited banks from informing their customers when they have filed a suspicious activity report. And, it protected banks from civil liability for doing so, by furnishing them with certain "safe harbor" provisions.

Though domestic laws have become increasingly strict, their effectiveness has been limited to the extent that other countries' laws are lax. Just as money laundering techniques spread from banks to other firms in the attempt to circumvent regulation, money laundering activity spread to other countries where the laws were weaker. In fact, some nations developed a large industry based on laws that benefited financial secrecy and discouraged international law enforcement cooperation. The tiny Pacific island of Nauru, which sits halfway between Hawaii and Australia with a population of merely 12,000, for instance, allowed people to set up banks for as little as $25,000 without even setting foot on the island. The nation has been accused of facilitating the laundering of $70 billion in Russian Mafia money through almost 450 banks based there (all registered to the same government post office box).

At issue are not just small nations looking to make quick wealth. There are also international differences in how countries define money laundering and the crimes they accept as underlying unlawful activities. Countries tended to consider only those crimes that had the most pernicious effects on their own soil. The United States, for example, included foreign drug trafficking as an underlying offense, but foreign corruption was not on the list until the USA PATRIOT Act was passed.

Resolving these differences requires international cooperation. From the IMF to the United Nations, several international organizations have taken initiatives against money laundering. Chief among them, the Financial Action Task Force (FATF), created in 1989 by the G-7 (the group of the world's largest industrialized nations, including the United States), which has worked to establish international standards against money laundering. Most recently, the strategy of the FATF members shifted towards a more active role. The organization has named 19 "noncooperative" jurisdictions hoping that increased international scrutiny would pressure them to make their anti-money laundering laws and enforcement practices stronger. In December of 2001, FATF imposed countermeasures on Nauru, deeming that it had not adequately addressed the legal deficiencies in its offshore banking sector.

Costs and Consequences

The fight against money laundering has not been uncontroversial. Like all legislation, money laundering laws have to play a delicate balance between the costs to businesses and individual citizens with the benefits of legislation. To some critics, the reporting requirements impose high costs on banks and other financial institutions. Though numbers are unreliable, as procedures vary somewhat by institution, the U.S. Treasury's Financial Crimes Enforcement Network estimated in 1999 that it costs financial institutions $109 million a year to comply with the reporting and record-keeping requirements of the Banking Secrecy Act. But whether these costs are high depends on our estimate of the costs crime and laundering impose on society, and on the law's effectiveness in combating them.

The legal definition of money laundering and the penalties imposed by the law have also raised some questions. For instance, the MLCA can make the defense of some alleged criminals, such as drug traffickers, a difficult issue for lawyers. An attorney who receives over $10,000 in fees can be accused of money laundering, given that it would be difficult to prove ignorance of the potentially tainted origin of the funds. Precisely because of their problematic nature, prosecutions of this type are rare and have to be approved by the Justice Department.

In addition, the criminal penalties for money laundering drew fire because they were often higher than for other white-collar crimes such that defendants received higher sentences than if charged only with the underlying criminal offense. In response to the criticisms, the sentencing guidelines for money laundering were revised this past November to make punishments more sensitive to the seriousness of the underlying crimes.

But perhaps the most controversial aspect has been the effect that money laundering laws have on privacy and how they affect business-client relationships. The fact that financial institutions and other businesses are obligated to report suspicious transactions to the government changes the nature of their relationship with their clients. It places some businesses that traditionally served clients in confidence partly on the side of enforcement. Moreover, in some cases, it requires that businesses ask more questions of their clients. In order to be able to report suspicious transactions, financial institutions have to make sure they know their customers well. They are expected to conduct a risk assessment and determine the appropriate level of due diligence. In some instances, this might include verifying a customer's identity, determining their sources of wealth, reviewing their credit and character, and understanding the type of transactions the customer would typically conduct.

For banks, which were subject to these regulations well before September 11, the key issue is to make sure they tell customers about what they do and why they do it, says John Byrne, Senior Federal Counsel and Compliance Manager at the American Bankers Association. "You want to be able to explain to your consumer: We don't share or sell your information or, we do, if you allow it," says Byrne. Banks also have to make clear that, if they ask clients for information, they do so to "protect the institution, to protect the country, and to protect the client."

Some European countries and Canada have imposed suspicious activity reporting that goes well beyond the financial sector—requiring attorneys to report on suspicious transactions by clients. This February, the American Bar Association issued a statement urging the government to protect the principle of lawyer-client confidentiality in its fight against money laundering. Other countries have adopted laws or policies that make lawyers "the eyes and ears of the government," Washington, D.C., lawyer Stephen Saltzburg told the media. "This is the single most alarming threat to the attorney-client privilege that anyone has seen in a long time," Saltzburg said. In the future, balancing our concerns for privacy with the need to prevent crime and terrorism will continue to be one of the most difficult issues in dealing with money laundering. As the evolution of money laundering legislation shows, increased efforts and widened scope are certain to make money laundering more difficult. But, they are not likely to end it. So long as crime exists, the fight against money laundering is likely to continue to be a cat-and-mouse game with new methods and loopholes being discovered as soon as prior regulatory gaps are closed. In this context, money laundering laws and awareness of the issue help prevent innocent citizens and organizations from being corrupted by easy money or from becoming unwitting accomplices to crime. The alternative is to turn a blind eye and let corruption flourish.

The Black Market Peso Exchange

Perhaps the largest money laundering system in the United States is the Colombian Black Market Peso Exchange, estimated to launder at least $5 billion a year in drug proceeds. The network has existed for decades as a way to avoid Colombian currency controls and tax laws. Drug traffickers turned to it in order to convert the dollars earned from drug sales in the United States into pesos back home. They sell their dollar proceeds for pesos to brokers who take on the task and the risk of cleaning the money.

The brokers take the dollars at exchange rates usually between 20 and 40 percent below the official Colombian exchange rate. They place the cash in U.S. banks by smurfing or other schemes. Then, they sell the dollars in Colombia to importers or businessmen and use the pesos to pay the traffickers in their home turf. The dollars deposited in U.S. banks are wired to personal accounts or used to pay legitimate companies for goods, as Colombian importers often buy American appliances, electronics, car parts, and cigarettes to be smuggled into and sold in Colombia. In an attempt to disrupt this arrangement, Colombian and U.S. authorities have begun to work with the firms that take the end payments. In summer of 2000, at the request of the U.S. government, Panamanian authorities seized a Bell model 407 helicopter purchased by a Colombian individual from Bell Helicopter Textron, of Fort Worth, Texas. The government also froze payments in the company's bank account, alleging the money was linked to laundering of drug proceeds. The evidence: Bell had received as payment 31 separate wire transfers from individuals and companies with no known relationship to the purchaser of the $1.5 million helicopter. For its part, Bell contended that it did not know that drugs were the source of the funds and that, in its view, it had complied with U.S. laws.

The U.S. government has campaigned to educate U.S. manufacturers and distributors about the forfeiture and indictment they can face if they are caught knowingly participating in the black market scheme. The Colombian government has also been pressuring U.S. companies to look more closely at customers. In 2000, Colombian states went so far as to sue Philip Morris, alleging that its products are frequently smuggled into Columbia as part of the black market exchange, costing the government dearly in lost tax revenues—Colombian police estimate that only 4 percent of Marlboros consumed in the country got there legally, according to Newsweek. But companies seeking to comply may face additional costs. General Electric told Frontline that, as a result of stricter controls, including not allowing distributors to export out of the country, sales to South Florida decreased by about 25 percent between 1995 and 1999.

Corrupting Power

Law enforcement and financial authorities have focused on money laundering, in part, as a way of combating crimes ranging from drug and arms trafficking to terrorism, fraud, and embezzlement. But, beyond serving as an enforcement tool to combat other crimes, large-scale money laundering poses problems in and of itself. As criminals try to find ways to legitimize large amounts of money, this creates the potential for corrupting government officials and financial institutions. And, even if money laundering does not corrupt the whole institution, banks can see their reputations tarnished and the public's trust in them eroded if they are embroiled in a money laundering scandal.

There can also be macroeconomic consequences. "Money laundering allocates dirty money around the world not so much on the basis of expected rates of return but on the basis of ease of avoiding national controls," says International Monetary Fund economist Vito Tanzi. Thus, money is not used where it is most productive. Moreover, though there are no clear examples of this so far, large and sudden movements of dirty money—say, responding to changes in legislation or law enforcement—could lead to instability in particular countries or banking systems.

In addition, money laundering can end up undermining the legitimate private sector; front companies used to hiding ill-gotten gains may offer their services at discounted prices, crowding out legitimate businesses. Hotels and restaurants built to serve as cover for illicit cash may be created in tourist markets that are already saturated. In Colombia, large-scale smuggling of electronic appliances, cigarettes, and other goods is one way in which drug proceeds are introduced into the country. These items are sold at very discounted prices, weakening the domestic manufacturing industry.

Discussion Questions

1. What is the Chapter 11 for countries that Cooper describes? How does his approach differ from the status quo?

2. Describe Sach's plan. Do you think it would work?

3. Moral hazard is described as a situation where agents are encouraged to take risks because they will be sheltered from the consequences of their actions. Some have argued that bankruptcy or a lender of last resort can create moral hazard. How would Cooper and Sachs respond to this criticism?

4. Compare and contrast Sachs's and Cooper's plans. Which do you agree with?

5. What is money laundering? Why is money laundering such a serious problem?

6. How can the US reduce money laundering?

Sources

Section I: *Issues in Trade and Protectionism*

1. "How Costly Is Protectionism?" Robert C. Feenstra, *Journal of Economic Perspectives*, Summer 1992, pp. 159-178.

2. "Toughest on the Poor: America's Flawed Tariff System," Edward Gresser, *Foreign Affairs*, November/December 2002.

3. "Steel Policy: The Good, the Bad, and the Ugly," Gary Clyde Hufbauer and Ben Goodrich, IIE *International Economic Policy Briefs*, Number PB03-1, 2003, pp. 1-27.

4. "America's Bittersweet Sugar Policy," Mark A. Groombridge, *Trade Briefing Paper*, Center for Trade Policy Studies, Number 13, December 4th, 2001, pp. 1-12.

5. "Using Sanctions to Fight Terrorism," Gary Clyde Hufbauer, Jeffery J. Schott, and Barbara Oegg, *IIE Policy Brief* 01-11, November 2001.

Section II: *WTO, Trade Labor, and the Environment*

6. "The Doha Development Agenda," Anne McGuirk.

7. "Bridging the Trade-Environment Divide," Daniel Esty, *Journal of Economic Perspectives*, Volume 15, No. 3, 2001, pp. 113-130.

8. "Labor Standards: Where Do They belong on the International Trade Agenda?" Drusilla Brown, *Journal of Economic Perspectives*, Volume 15, No. 3, Summer 2001, pp.89-112

9. "Borders beyond Control," Jagdish Bhagwati, *Foreign Affairs*, January/February 2003.

10. "Intellectual Property Rights and the WTO," Philip G. King, unpublished manuscript, 2003.

11. "Reducing America's Dependence on Foreign Oil," Martin Feldstein, presented at the AEA meetings, January 2003.

Section III: *Trade and Development; NAFTA*

12. "The Global Governance of Trade as if Development Really Mattered," Dani Rodrik, UNDP, New York, 2001.

13. "Farm Fallacies That Hurt the Poor," Kevin Watkins.

14. "Economic Developments during NAFTA's First Decade," Joanna Moss, unpublished manuscript, 2003.

Section IV: *Globalization*

15. "Trading in Illusions," Dani Rodrik, *Harvard Magazine*, July-August 2002: Volume 104, Number 6, Page 29.

16. "Five Wars of Globalization," Moises Naim, *Foreign Policy*, January/ February 2003, pp. 29-36.

17. "Spreading the Wealth," David Dollar and Aart Kraay, *Foreign Affairs*, January/February 2002.

18. "The New Wave of Globalization and Its Economic Effects," Chapter 1 of *Globalization, Growth and Poverty: Building an Inclusive World Economy*, The World Bank, 2002.

Section V: *The Balance of Payments*

19. "What Drives Large Current Accounts Deficits?" Cletus Coughlin and Patricia Pollard, *International Economic Trends*, Federal Reserve Bank of St. Louis, May 2001.

20. "Does the US Have a Current Account Deficit Disorder?" William Poole, Federal Reserve Bank of St. Louis Speeches, April 10th, 2001.

Section VI: *Exchange Rates and Macroeconomic Policy*

21. "The Structure of Foreign Exchange Markets," Sam Cross, *The Foreign Exchange Market in the United States*, Chapter 3, Federal Reserve Bank of New York, 1998.

22. "What Determines the Exchange Rate: Market Factors or Market Sentiment?" Gregory P. Hopper, *Business Review*, Federal Reserve Bank of Philadelphia, September/October 1997, pp. 17-29.

23. "Fixed versus Floating Exchange Rates," Peter Kenen, *The Cato Journal*, Volume 20, No. 1, Spring/Summer 2000.

24. "Exchange Rate Choices," Richard Cooper, Federal Reserve Bank of Boston Conference Series 43, June 1999, pp. 93-136.

25. "Does the Exchange Rate Regime Matter for Inflation and Growth?" Atish R. Ghosh, Jonathan Ostry, Anne-Marie Gulde, and Holger C. Wolf, *IMF Economic Issues*, Number 2.

26. "Currency Boards," Sharmila K. King, unpublished manuscript, 2003.

27. "Dollarization as a Monetary Arrangement for Emerging Market Economies," Gaetano Antinolfi and Todd Keister, *Review*, Federal Reserve Bank of St. Louis, November 2001, Volume 83, Number 6, pp. 29-40.

Section VII: *The Euro*

28. "EMU at 1," Mark A. Wynne, *Economic and Financial Review,* First Quarter, 2000, Federal Reserve Bank of Dallas, pp. 14-28.

29. "The Creation of the Euro and the Role of the Dollar in International Markets," Patricia Pollard, *Review,* Federal Reserve Bank of St. Louis, May 2001, Volume 83, Number 5, pp. 17-36

30. "European Labor Markets and EMU Challenges Ahead," Rudiger Soltwedel, Dirk Dohse, and Christiane Krieger-Boden, *Finance and Development,* June 2000, Volume 37, Number 2, pp. 1-5.

Section VIII: *Financial Crises*

31. "A Case Study of Currency Crisis: The Russian Default of 1998," Abbigail J. Chiodo and Michael T. Owyang, *Review,* Federal Reserve Bank of St. Louis, November 2002, Volume 84, Number 6, pp. 7-18.

32. "Learning from Argentina's Crisis," Ramon Moreno, Federal Reserve Bank of San Francisco *Economic Letter,* Number 2002-31, October 18th, 2002, pp. 1-3.

33. "The Onset of the East Asian Financial Crisis," Steven Radelet and Jeffrey Sachs, NBER Working Paper #6680, August 1998.

34. "Argentina's Currency Crisis: Lessons for Asia," Mark Spiegel, Federal Reserve Bank of San Francisco *Economic Letter,* Number 2002-25, August 23, 2002, pp. 1-3.

35. "Capital Controls and Emerging Market," Ramon Moreno, Federal Reserve Bank of San Francisco *Economic Letter*, Number 2001-25, August 31, 2001.

Section IX: *Restructuring the New World*

36. "Chapter 11 for Countries?" Richard Cooper, *Foreign Affairs,* July/August 2002, pp. 90-103.

37. "The International Lender of Last Resort: What Are the Alternatives?" Jeffrey Sachs, Federal Reserve Bank of Boston Conference Proceedings 43, June 1999, pp. 181-203.

38. "Dirty Money," Miriam Wasserman, *Regional Review,* Federal Reserve Bank of Boston, Q1, 2002, pp. 14-21.